D1570350

STALIN'S GUERRILLAS

STALIN'S GUERRILLAS
Soviet Partisans in World War II

KENNETH SLEPYAN

UNIVERSITY PRESS OF KANSAS

Chapters One and Five contain some material previously published in "The Soviet Partisan
Movement and the Holocaust," *Holocaust and Genocide Studies* 14, 1 (Spring 2000): 1–27.
Reprinted with permission of Oxford University Press.

Published by the University Press of Kansas (Lawrence, Kansas 66045),
which was organized by the Kansas Board of Regents and
is operated and funded by Emporia State University,
Fort Hays State University, Kansas State University,
Pittsburg State University, the University of Kansas,
and Wichita State University

Slepyan, Kenneth.
  Stalin's guerrillas : Soviet partisans in World War II / Kenneth Slepyan.
    p. cm. — (Modern war studies)
  Includes bibliographical references and index.
  ISBN 0-7006-1480-X (cloth : alk. paper)
  1. World War, 1939–1945—Underground movements—Soviet Union.
  2. Soviet Union—History—German occupation, 1941–1944. I. Title.
  II. Title: Soviet partisans in World War II. III. Series.
  D802.S75S59 2006
  940.54'8647—dc22   2006016898

Library of Congress Cataloging-in-Publication Data

British Library Cataloguing-in-Publication Data is available.

Printed in the United States of America

10 9 8 7 6 5 4 3 2 1

To my mother, Mary Efron,
and to the memory of my father, Norbert Slepyan

CONTENTS

ACKNOWLEDGMENTS

This book has a long history, having started as a dissertation at the University of Michigan in 1991, when I went to the Soviet Union for my first research trip (the return flight the next year left from the Russian Federation). Given this length of time, I owe a great many thanks to the numerous people and institutions that have generously provided their assistance.

Early support for this work at the University of Michigan was provided through the History Department, the Center for Russian and East European Studies, the Rackham Graduate School, and the university's exchange program with the Russian State Humanities University. Help was also provided by a Social Science Research Council Dissertation Fellowship and by the International Research and Exchanges Board. Later assistance for research and writing was provided by the Charles Revson Foundation for the support of research using archival materials from the former Soviet Union at the U.S. Holocaust Memorial Museum and by the National Council on Eurasian and East European Research. I would especially like to thank President Charles Shearer and Deans James Moseley and William Pollard for their support through Transylvania University's David and Betty Jones Faculty Development Fund and Kenan Sabbatical Grant programs.

At the University of Michigan, I was fortunate to have wonderful mentors. My adviser, William Rosenberg, gave invaluable guidance not only by offering insightful critiques on the dissertation but also by generously continuing to provide assistance and critical support after that project was completed. Jane Burbank forced me to clarify key issues surrounding identity and agency. Michael Kennedy helped me think through the relationship of legitimacy and the partisan war. John Shy would not let me forget that the partisans were, after all, fighting a war. Ron Suny's work on nationality and Soviet politics has been an inspiration throughout the years, and I thank him too for his good cheer and support. I also owe special thanks to my undergraduate mentor, William Wagner, whose encouragement and advice were so important guiding my first steps in Russian and Soviet history.

As this project made its way from dissertation to book, it had the benefit of several sets of readers. Daniel Rowland and Karen Petrone read early versions of the entire manuscript, and their comments both challenged and encouraged me to push the work further. Jeffrey Burds and David Stone, the once-anonymous readers for the University Press of Kansas, helped me clarify and refine significant points and arguments. Others who have read and commented on various sections include Michael Gelb, Alexander Hill, Hiroaki Kuromiya, Keri Manning, Melissa McEuen, Catherine Nolan-Ferrell, and Frank Russell. Chapters and sections have also been presented at the Midwest Russian Historians' Workshop, the Center for Advanced Holocaust Studies at the U.S. Holocaust Museum, the Conference on Russian Masculinity at the Russian and East European Center at the University of Illinois at Urbana-Champaign (UIUC), the History Department at UIUC, and numerous conferences around the country. To the readers and participants at these venues, I offer my thanks as well. I have also received helpful suggestions and support from friends and colleagues, including Joseph Binford, Gregg Bocketti, Richard Brody, Choi Chatterjee, Don Dugi, Tom Ewing, Deborah Field, Jeffrey Freyman, Craig Koslofsky, Francois Le Roy, Sakah Mahmud, Jeremy Popkin, Dana Rabin, Daniel Ringrose, Gretchen Starr-Lebeau, and Mark Steinberg. I would also like to thank the historians, archivists, and staff at the Center for Advanced Holocaust Studies (CAHS), including Peter Black, Martin Dean, Michael Gelb, Severin Hochberg, and Paul Shapiro, for the very productive and stimulating summer I spent at CAHS in 1998. I am indebted to my colleagues in the Social Sciences Division at Transylvania University for their support in both research and pedagogical matters. Also at Transylvania, Katie Banks and Holly Barnhill cheerfully supplied critical and much-appreciated secretarial help. I salute the library staff at Transylvania for their ability and speed in obtaining hard-to-find materials and books. Dick Gilbreath of the University of Kentucky composed the maps that grace the book. Jeffrey Burds provided invaluable bibliographic assistance. Many thanks also to the archivists and staff at the State Archive of the Russian Federation, the Institute of History at the Academy of Sciences, the Russian State Archive of Social-Political History, the Central Repository of Documents on Youth Organizations, and the Central Museum of the Armed Forces. The Hoover Institution and the U.S. Holocaust Memorial Museum helped with locating and securing visual materials. In addition, I would especially like to thank Michael Briggs, Susan McRory, Susan Schott, and Joan Sherman of the University Press of

Kansas for their assistance, patience, and support in guiding me through the publication process.

My family has been a source of encouragement throughout this long process. Unfortunately, my uncle Stanley Efron passed away shortly before this book was published. I will always be grateful to him for his support of and interest in this project. I wish to thank my mother, Mary Efron, and my uncle Marshall Efron for their patience and unflagging optimism that one day this book would actually be finished. My daughters, Mara and Anya, have reminded me that there is more to life than pecking at a computer, such as soccer, Harry Potter, and guinea pigs (not necessarily in that order). They also have earned special mention for having gone through infancy, toddlerhood, and a significant portion of childhood without destroying or drawing on a single book or manuscript page. And, of course, I have a unique debt of gratitude to Karen Petrone, who has managed to combine the roles of wife and partner, friend and colleague, and fellow traveler on the parenting road with unequaled grace and aplomb. The partisans were a part of our lives even before our marriage, and over the years, I have increasingly felt that they have been like the proverbial houseguests who have stayed perhaps a bit too long. Karen, however, has put up with them most graciously. Without her steadfast support in seeing this project through, her insightful and honest critiques, and her efforts in thousands of other ways, this work would never have come to fruition. To her, of the many people who have contributed to making this book possible, I owe the most thanks of all.

Kenneth Slepyan
Lexington, Kentucky

A NOTE ON TRANSLITERATION AND NAMES

This work follows the Library of Congress transliteration system without diacritical marks to transliterate Russian personal names, place-names, and other words. For reasons of familiarity and historical context, I have also used Russian spellings for names and places (with the exception of Ukrainian geographic terms)—hence, *Belorussia* instead of *Belarus* and *Vershigora* rather than *Vershyhora*. Although the use of a particular language often connotes political or national sympathies, I ask that readers not infer any such meanings in this text.

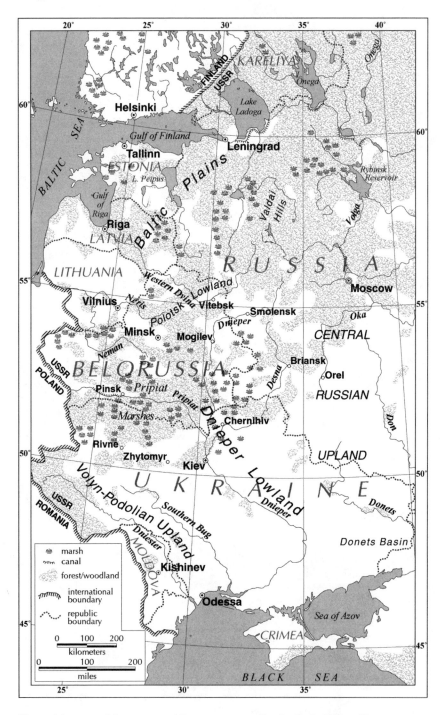

Physical features of Axis-occupied Soviet territory. (Credit: Dick Gilbreath)

INTRODUCTION

In Vasilii Grossman's monumental novel about the battle of Stalingrad, *Life and Fate*, at a crucial point in the fighting Krymov, an Old Bolshevik and commissar, is ordered to House 6/I, an isolated Soviet outpost in the city. It is rumored that its commander, the charismatic Captain Grekov, has been "corrupting the minds of his soldiers with the most appalling heresies." Krymov, whose instructions are to "establish Bolshevik order," assures his superiors that he has dealt with this "partisan nonsense" (*partizanshchina*) before.[1] Once in House 6/I, he is incensed by the irregularity of Grekov's command: no combat logs, no personnel rosters, no sense of subordination to higher authority. But far worse for Krymov is the profound alienation of Grekov's soldiers from the Party and the Soviet system. One mocks the formula "to each according to his needs" by asking how it applies to the distribution of alcohol, and another asks hopefully about the liquidation of the collective farms after the war. Krymov tells them that he is there to "sort out unacceptable partisan attitudes that have taken root in this building." Later, Krymov asks Grekov what he wants. "Freedom. That's what I'm fighting for," Grekov replies. When Krymov responds, "We all want freedom," Grekov retorts, "Tell us another! You just want to sort out the Germans." Krymov angrily replies that this "evil, anti-Soviet spirit" must be stamped out and offers Grekov a chance for redemption if he helps out, assuring him, "You'll still get your glory." Although Grekov asserts that he is a loyal Soviet citizen, it is clear that he and Krymov are ideological enemies. That night, Krymov is wounded by a stray bullet, which he suspects was fired deliberately by one of Grekov's men. He is carried back to Soviet lines. A few days later, almost all the inhabitants of House 6/I, including Grekov, are killed when the Germans overrun the position, and Krymov himself is later sent to the gulag.[2]

The story of House 6/I reveals some of the complexities surrounding the notion of the "partisan spirit" and the various perceptions of and responses to it, as well as indicating the multiple ways Soviet citizens interpreted the meaning of the war. To Communists such as Krymov and to some partisans, it was a test of the Soviet system and of the soundness of the Party's ideology. It was about continuing to live a model Soviet life as defined by Bolshevik order and discipline. The war was also about freedom, which in this case meant freedom from domination by outside powers. To Grekov and his men and to other partisans, the war was also about another kind of freedom—living outside the boundaries of both Nazi and Soviet totalitarianism. They hoped, too, that victory in the war would bring real changes in Soviet society, the same society that Krymov was fighting to uphold. Grekov's soldiers found their version of freedom in the autonomy, chaos, and isolation that predominated at Stalingrad and were exemplified in House 6/I. However, as Grossman shows, that freedom was precarious at best: House 6/I, caught between the hammer of Nazism and the anvil of Stalinism, was inevitably doomed.

In many ways, the issues that both the Soviet partisans and the regime in World War II faced were similar to those confronted by Grekov's band and Krymov. The partisans, too, were cut off from other Soviet institutions and thus not under the immediate, overt political control of outside authorities. Like the members of House 6/I, they had the opportunity to redefine their identities as Soviet citizens and their ideas about what Soviet society should be and what it should stand for. Likewise, just as Grossman's Party officials in Stalingrad worried about ideological unorthodoxy among the soldiers in House 6/I, the Soviet leadership fretted over the possibility of losing physical and ideological control over the tens (and later hundreds) of thousands of armed men and women operating behind enemy lines. And prevailing over all was the reality of a most brutal war against the cruelest of enemies.

This study is a political and social history of the organized Soviet armed resistance to German occupation—the Soviet partisan movement. It asks: what did it mean to be a partisan in Stalin's Soviet Union? For both the regime and the Soviet citizens, this question posed a set of difficult issues. Confronted with a war for national survival, the Soviet state had little choice but to use all the weapons at its disposal, including guerrilla warfare. But the employment of partisans also threatened the stability of the regime. The memory of the Civil War, in which Red partisans had flouted military and political discipline even to the point of defecting to the Whites, haunted Bolshevik leaders. Moreover, since the partisans operated behind enemy lines and outside the usual means of overt state control, the Soviet leadership was deeply concerned that they would be "contaminated" by Nazi or "nationalist" ideologies. The experiences of the previous decade of Soviet power alone, which

included collectivization and the ensuing famine, the hardships of forced industrialization, and the terrors of the purges, were enough to make Soviet
leaders wonder whether the armed partisans would remain loyal to the Soviet
state and whether they might resist the reestablishment of Communist rule.
Moreover, in the recently annexed westernmost territories of the Union—
formerly eastern Poland and the Baltic states—the population's loyalty to its
new masters was even more uncertain. Once the decision to engage in a full-
scale partisan war was made, the regime had to find a way to facilitate, support, and direct the partisans without promoting what John Erickson has
called "the organized dissidence which was implicit in the organization for
guerrilla warfare."[3] For this to happen, a partisan administrative apparatus
would have to be established, but the process was complicated by the rivalries
of competing corporate and regional institutions.

The partisans had their own problems. First and foremost was their fight
against a vicious enemy and the difficulties of surviving amid an impoverished and often hostile population. Physically and sometimes emotionally
and psychologically isolated from the Soviet "mainland" (bol'shaia zemlia),
the partisans had to reexamine what it meant to be Soviet. In the popular
imagination, they were customarily associated with autonomy from the state,
wildness, spontaneity, and the freedom to pursue the "good life"—to enjoy
wine, women, and song. Could these notions of partisan life, embodied in the
pejorative term partizanshchina, be reconciled with the Stalinist values of
discipline, order, vigilance, and obedience to the state? This concern was exacerbated by social differences within the movement, which threatened to
fragment the partisans along ethnonational, regional, corporate, and gender
lines. At the same time, the partisans had to convince deeply suspicious state
authorities that they were indeed loyal to the Stalinist regime. In this study I
will explore how a particular group of Soviet citizens—comprising a variety
of corporate and political affiliations, from numerous ethnonational backgrounds, and in close contact with the enemy while separated from the rest
of Soviet society—fought a war, created communities, and appraised their relationship to Stalinism and the Soviet regime.

Previous histories of the Soviet partisan movement have focused more on
the partisans' military contributions to the Soviet war effort. To Soviet historians, the partisan movement was an essential part of the mythology of the
Great Patriotic War, as World War II was known in the Soviet Union. Every
Soviet history of the war argued that the partisan movement was a genuine,
patriotic mass movement organized and led by the Communist Party and
thus was a concrete manifestation of the organic link between Party and

People. Although this movement in itself could not win the war, its growing numerical strength and military prowess greatly weakened the German hold on the occupied territories, significantly reduced the flow of supplies to the front, and forced the diversion of powerful forces to combat the partisans, thus transforming the occupied territories into a second front. Moreover, by their very existence, the partisans reminded Soviet citizens under occupation that resistance to the Germans was not only possible but necessary. These achievements helped pave the way for the Red Army's liberation of the occupied territories and at the same time revealed the true patriotic spirit and enthusiasm of the people for the Soviet project.[4] This line of argument, of course, was closely controlled by the state, which carefully guarded the themes Soviet historians could cover.[5] Since the advent of glasnost and the subsequent fall of the Soviet Union in 1991, there have been some efforts to discuss the movement in more nuanced terms, yet even recent post-Soviet treatments tend to repeat these themes, substituting the ideology of patriotism for the *rodina* (motherland) for Communism.[6]

Ironically, most Western historiography on the partisan forces, based primarily on German archival materials and Soviet memoirs and secondary sources, in some ways endorses much of the traditional Soviet line. Western studies, written mostly during the 1950s and 1960s, emphasize that the partisans were under the complete control of the Party and that the Soviet leadership developed a highly sophisticated command-and-control system to ensure that the partisans would remain under Moscow's thumb. Consequently, the partisans possessed little independence and initiative and essentially became tools of the government in its efforts to reestablish Soviet power in the occupied territories. The most comprehensive Western work on the partisan movement, *The Soviet Partisans in World War II*, argues that though the partisans were militarily insignificant, they played a crucial political role as the state's representatives in the occupied territories. The partisans were instrumental in spreading Soviet propaganda and reestablishing collective farms, soviets, and other institutions.[7] Indeed, as John Armstrong, the book's principal author, has noted, they were "the long arm of the totalitarian state."[8]

The opening of Soviet archives in the 1990s enabled a new generation of scholars to investigate the partisan movement. Their studies, to date, have also tended to concentrate on the military aspects of the struggle and the military-political relationship among the partisans, the Axis security forces, and the civilian population. The integration of both Soviet and German archival materials found in these works provides us with a much deeper understanding of the operational elements of the partisan war and the terrible dynamics that contributed to the seemingly endless cycle of violence on the Eastern Front.[9] Other works have investigated the "war within the war"— that is, the ethnic conflicts involving Poles, Ukrainians, Jews, Russians, Germans, and others in the Eastern European borderlands, struggles that continued well into the postwar period—and thus have uncovered another dimension of the fighting in the East.[10]

In this study, I take a different approach to the Soviet partisan war. It is not my purpose to provide a narrative military history of the movement. Rather, my goal is to investigate the partisan movement as a social phenomenon produced by the intersection of Stalinist society and the wartime environment and to understand what the war experience meant to the partisans. The term *partisan* in this volume refers to civilians, members of the security services, and Red Army soldiers who lived behind enemy lines and fought as irregulars. Most of their units were organized in enemy-held territory, although some were established in Soviet territory and dispatched across the lines.[11]

A central premise of this work is that the Soviet partisans cannot be separated from the society from which they emerged. Recent studies on interwar Soviet government and society have demonstrated that the regime was unable to exert anything approximating total control (regardless of its own claims or intentions), nor was the population a passive and pliable mass. Indeed, the war came at a critical juncture in the transformation of Soviet society. The Soviet leadership was determined to create a thoroughly modern state and society based on an urban, industrial, and scientifically minded culture. In the cities, newly arrived peasant workers, however, retained their customary work habits and social relationships, thwarting official efforts to inculcate "modern" industrial labor processes and often interpreting Bolshevik values in ways that differed significantly from official meanings. Collectivization subdued the peasantry but did not obliterate peasant society and culture. Instead of transforming the Soviet citizenry into a modern, urbanized, and industrialized proletariat in the factory and on the collective farm, a hybrid society emerged, combining both pre-Revolutionary and Soviet elements. In many ways, the population was cynical and even hostile to the regime and some of its goals, yet it was becoming increasingly urbanized and Sovietized in much of its attitudes and values.[12]

The Soviet writer Konstantin Simonov remarked on the importance of the formative experiences of the 1930s to the "front generation." As the hero of his wartime novel about Stalingrad, *Days and Nights*, recalled in thinking about the prewar days:

The war . . . Recently, whenever he recalled his former life, he
unconsciously reduced it all to this common denominator, and divided
everything that had happened to him before the war into good and
bad—not in the abstract, but in relation to the war. Some civilian
habits and inclinations hampered him now that he was fighting, others
helped him. There were more of the latter, as there should have been.
People who had begun their independent lives in the years of the first
Five-Year-Plan, as he had, had gone through such a rough school for
living, had learned such discipline and self-control, that war itself,
except for its constant possibility of death, could hardly break them
with its daily hardships.[13]

Along with the physical hardships of the 1930s and the ostensible internaliz-
ing of self-discipline, the development of Stalinism during that decade accustomed Soviet citizens to war. The core notions of Stalinism itself were based
on a rhetorical and ideological foundation of confrontation and conflict with
ever-present internal and external enemies. Stalinist socialism called for political discipline, obedience, order, social hierarchy, and material stratification, all values that found a natural home in a wartime environment. Moreover, the war brought to life the dangers the regime had warned about for so
long. In the 1930s, the enemy was either abstracted (for example, backwardness, nature), fictional, or hidden (kulaks, spies, saboteurs, and so on), but
nothing was as immediate as the real enemy that appeared in 1941. The German invasion finally put an end to conflict as metaphor, and it also seemed to
justify the sacrifices of the 1930s.

     But the partisans were also heirs to a long history of irregular warriors,
especially the Cossacks, Emelian Pugachev and other peasant rebels, and
the famed Red and anarchist partisans from the Civil War, whose historical
legacy was defined partly by a rough egalitarianism and freedom antithetical
to Stalinist hierarchy and discipline. How, then, did partisans reconcile these
competing values and beliefs? To what extent did these values make sense in
wartime? How would the partisans, living in isolation from the rest of the
country and surrounded by a brutal foe in a world of material shortages, now
view Stalinism? In short, did the war bring the Stalinist social vision and the
demands of actual social reality closer together?

     To explore these questions, I concentrate on three broad but closely re-
lated issues in this work: first, the tension between partisan autonomy and
state control; second, the importance of identity as a vehicle for group and

individual autonomy as well as for the reestablishment of state power; and third, the question of who "belonged" in the partisan movement.

A primary theme in this book is the investigation of the way in which partisan initiative and self-reliance intersected with the demands of state control, a situation in some ways reminiscent of the relationship between factory directors and central state planners in the 1930s. Like the five-year plans, directing the partisan movement challenged Soviet administrative capabilities. In order to survive and to attain their combat objectives, partisans had to be largely self-sufficient. The separation from state agencies and prolonged isolation, accompanied by the realization that they could expect very little outside help, reinforced the partisans' notions of self-reliance. For their part, state authorities, accustomed to directing all forms of public activity, were especially determined to impose their will on the partisans for both military and political reasons. Soviet leaders realized that if the movement was to achieve its maximum effect, partisan missions would have to be coordinated with other partisan and conventional operations to ensure that they hit the most vital and necessary targets. Equally important, the regime justifiably feared that the partisans could become a destabilizing and even potentially anti-Soviet force, as had often occurred during the Civil War. These concerns were heightened by the very real possibility that the partisans might be "affected" by enemy or separatist ideologies. Stalinist authorities thus had to develop administrative structures and other measures to coordinate and control hundreds of thousands of people beyond their physical reach. Meanwhile, the partisans sought to maintain their autonomy even as they professed loyalty to the Soviet state and depended on that state for critical supplies and for regulating relations among the competing bands. Out of this dynamic came a new perception of the Soviet Union and its institutions.

The importance of social identities and the ways they influenced relations among partisans and between the partisans and Soviet authorities is a second major theme. As in the 1930s' Stakhanovite movement, in which officials and workers contested the meaning of Stakhanovism, both state authorities and the partisans had their own definitions of what it meant to be a partisan. Authorities hoped that official identities would enhance partisan loyalty and inhibit anti-Soviet actions. Partisan identities were both reflections of war experiences and mediators of them. Although partisans were relatively free from the most overt forms of state control, they were still subject to the influence of Soviet institutions, propaganda, and discourse. Soviet leaders and partisans employed many of the same themes and representations in their definitions, yet ambiguities in the meaning of these terms created differences in how they interpreted the fundamental attributes defining the proper "Soviet partisan." Moreover, social and demographic characteristics of gender, age, nationality, and corporate affiliation all influenced how the partisans defined themselves in relation to the state and to other partisans. The conditions of partisan warfare offer a unique opportunity to examine the multidirectional processes of identity formation in a turbulent and war-torn Soviet society.

A third theme that emerges from this study focuses on the question of belonging, that is, who was to be included in—and excluded from—the partisan movement and thus, by extension, the Soviet body politic. This element was crucial in Soviet life well before the war, culminating in the 1930s with the drafting of the 1936 "Stalin Constitution" and even more dramatically in the evolving definition of "enemy of the people." By the beginning of World War II, three criteria had emerged by which Soviet officials defined belonging: first, the well-established notion of class origin; second, the related (in Bolshevik eyes) element of political activism and overtly expressed political loyalty; and third, ethnicity and nationality. Officials and partisans alike were obsessed with the question of belonging. For officials, defining who belonged in the movement was essential for controlling the partisans and, as the nature of the war and the partisans' mission changed later on, for affirming the legitimacy of the Soviet state. For partisans, belonging also had pragmatic and political dimensions. The composition and structure of their units had a direct impact on their ability to function and survive as military and social communities. Partisans had their own ideas regarding what groups and individuals were loyal and productive citizens, and therefore, they believed that the inclusion of so-called questionable elements would impair their operational effectiveness and complicate their relations with Moscow. In defining who belonged to the movement, partisans and state officials determined just how inclusive the "all-people's" (*vsenarodnaia*) war mobilization actually was and how the relative worth of particular social groups was measured by the state and other citizens in this time of national crisis.

I do not attempt to make a systematic comparison with other resistance movements, but it is worth noting some important similarities and differences between these groups. Like resisters in many of the other armed resistance movements in Nazi-occupied Europe, the Soviet partisans had to deal with relations between civilians and partisans over supply procurements and allegations of banditry, the repercussions of partisan attacks leading to reprisals against civilians, and the tendency for bands to form unique identities and cultures. And certainly, in both the Soviet Union and throughout Western and

Central Europe, the organizational strength and discipline of the Communist Party (relative to other groups) played a key role in leading resistance.[14]

Yet at the same time, several significant differences separated the Soviet partisans from other armed resistance groups. First, unlike those in other movements, Soviet partisans fought in the name of a state that was never defeated and remained a powerful political and military presence. The continuation of the Soviet government and its oversight of the organized armed resistance thus had a powerful effect on the partisans' self-representations, their political and military objectives, and their overall relations with civilians. For example, in the case of Yugoslavia, whose Partisans under Marshal Tito formed the most significant armed Communist opposition outside the Soviet Union, there was no real government to which to answer, leaving the Partisans free to pursue their own policies. Although other European resistance movements theoretically were subordinated to governments-in-exile and to Allied intelligence agencies such as the British Special Operations Executive and the U.S. Office of Strategic Services, the ties that connected the resisters on the ground with their overseers in London and Washington were much looser than those that held the Soviet partisans to Moscow. Even leaders in the European Communist resistance commonly prioritized local concerns over Moscow's interests.[15] Consequently, European resisters had much more freedom to develop their own policies, methods, and identities than their Soviet counterparts.

A second critical difference involved the varied bases of the European national resistance movements. European resistance movements often embodied both conservative and radical reformist elements in their ranks, some of whose groups espoused dramatic changes in their respective national political and social orders. Though some groups might be ideologically or politically closer to the defeated regimes or their governments-in-exile, none had the power to impose its will on other groups or to make a credible claim that it was the sole voice representing the nation. Such was not the case in the Soviet Union, where there was only one official resistance—that sponsored by the regime itself. The Communist Party, the Soviet institutions, and the country itself were all inextricably linked together. And even though individual partisans or even groups and units might have supported other ideologies and policies, they could not publicly state these positions if they wanted to remain a part of the Soviet resistance. Indeed, to do so would be enough to become labeled as anti-Soviet and marked for destruction by the regime. Multiple voices did exist in the Soviet resistance, but unlike in other movements, they had to be whispered. Like their counterparts elsewhere, Soviets resisted for multiple personal and political reasons, but publicly, they had to display that resistance in terms that demonstrated their loyalty to the Communist state and its institutions. Resisting solely on ethnonational or religious grounds would make the resister an enemy not only of the Germans but also of the Soviet state. Indeed, ethnonational separatists in the border regions of the USSR hoped that the German-Soviet conflict would end in their own independence. In the case of Ukraine, for example, the members of the Organization of Ukrainian Nationalists (OUN) and its Ukrainian Insurgent Army (known by its Ukrainian initials as the UPA) ultimately found themselves engaged in a three-way war with both the Soviets and the Germans.

Another important point concerns the political goals of the resistance movements. With the possible exception of the Polish Armia Krajowa, the Serbian Chetniks, and some conservative groups within the Western European resistance movements, many European resisters fought to defeat wartime fascism but also to usher in a new postwar world, one that redefined the economic, political, and social order. By contrast, the stated purpose of the Soviet partisan movement—regardless of what the wishes of many of its participants may have been—was not to effect a change in the regime or its system but to reassert and strengthen the status quo antebellum or, to be more precise in the case of the Soviet partisans, the antebellum following the Soviet annexation of eastern Poland and the Baltic states between 1939 and 1940. Although some have argued that the war was the culmination of the Bolshevik Revolution and Communist efforts to transform the countryside, the goals of the partisan movement were to be achieved within the already existing political order. Indeed, in the postwar period, part of the romance associated with European resistance was the aura of having fought in a lost cause for a more just and equitable world; in the postwar Soviet Union, there was no hint in public portrayals of the movement, even in Nikita Khrushchev's time, that the partisans ever represented a pro-Soviet but anti-Stalinist alternative to the existing Soviet state.

Finally and perhaps most critically in understanding the differences between the Soviet and European resistance movements, one must consider the baggage of the preceding decades of Soviet power. The experiences of collectivization, industrialization, the purges, nation building, and almost every other aspect of Soviet life from 1917 on marked the Soviet population in very different ways from its Western and Central European counterparts. Moreover, the regime continued to exist, and it exerted its presence through the partisans. To take just one example, when Soviet partisans, acting in the name of the state, requisitioned supplies from peasants, the latter might see them not only as bandits but also as continuing the state's practice of coercive grain procurements from the Civil War and later collectivization—a very different rural experience from that of the rest of Europe.

Thus, as I have indicated, there are significant comparisons to be made regarding the Soviet and European resistance efforts, and these shall be noted when applicable. At the same time, it is also important to note the substantial differences that distinguished the experiences of Soviet partisans and occupied civilians from their counterparts elsewhere in Nazi-occupied Europe.

Chapter One focuses on the tension involved in the state's attempt to define and limit participation in the partisan forces in the context of a national war for survival. From the days of the Civil War, Soviet authorities were deeply suspicious about partisans and partisan warfare. In Bolshevik eyes, partisans were associated with a host of negative traits, including lack of discipline, political and military unreliability, love of spontaneity, and lack of political consciousness. Though it was clear from the outset of Operation Barbarossa, the German invasion of the Soviet Union in 1941, that the Soviet Union had to organize a partisan force to harass the enemy's rear area, state leaders were concerned (with good reason, given the history of the previous two decades) that such a force might turn against them. Consequently, the government attempted to limit who could organize and join partisan groups, all the while publicly defining the state-sponsored insurgency as a people's movement and a manifestation of "all-people's war" (*vsenarodnaia voina*). As the resistance expanded numerically and broadened its demographic base in 1942 and, simultaneously, as the country underwent a deepening military crisis, the regime sought a new formula for participation to respond to the realities and threats on the ground, thereby helping to turn the resistance into a more genuine popular movement. This transformation expanded the partisans' potential military strength and enabled the government to use the movement to meet critical political goals.

Chapter Two examines the partisans' world, including the German occupation regime and its antipartisan operations, relations with the civilian population, material life in the detachments, and the nature of partisan combat. The precariousness of the partisans' physical existence, their often tense and ambiguous interactions with civilians, and the combination of vulnerability, amateurism, and romance that marked their combat operations powerfully shaped their understanding of the war and their role in it as well as their relations with the regime.

In the hypercentralized Soviet state, administration was always a major concern, and that of the partisan movement was no exception, as Chapter Three demonstrates. The Soviet leadership faced the challenge of how to direct tens of thousands of armed men and women behind enemy lines to inflict maximum damage on the enemy while ensuring their loyalty without the customary overt means of control. The absence of any clear institutional leadership in the first year of the war exacerbated this problem and reduced the partisans' military effectiveness. Eventually, a multiagency organization was created, the Central Staff of the Partisan Movement. However, it was plagued by many of the same problems that permeated Soviet bureaucracies. Moreover, the partisans themselves had their own needs and concerns, and they sought to manipulate the Central Staff for their own ends. The question of partisan administration was more than a contest between state control and partisan autonomy, however, for the partisans realized that they were dependent on state intervention in order to maintain their own security, especially from other partisans.

While the state was evolving its administrative structures, partisans and officials alike struggled to define what it meant to be a partisan and what the partisan mission was. Like efforts in the interwar period to define and ascribe class and nationality categories, this effort, too, involved an issue of control. If authorities successfully imposed a set of values and beliefs on the partisans, the partisans would be more likely to do Moscow's bidding. Chapter Four investigates the interaction of officials and partisans in the construction of Soviet partisan identities in 1941 and 1942. A significant tension emerged between the partisans' desire for autonomy and the need to demonstrate their loyalty to the suspicious government. Corporate, ethnic, and regional loyalties further shaped the partisans' ideas of how to fight the guerrilla war, as well as their relations with other partisans. These representations reflected the ways in which the partisans conceptualized themselves, their mission, and their relations with each other and outside authorities. Partisan identities reflected the commonalities and divisions that existed in broader Soviet society, and they illustrated the ways in which the war both brought the country together and created or exacerbated national and social tensions.

Chapter Five details the ensuing multisided struggle for dominance within the partisan bands among state authorities and veteran partisans as new recruits swarmed the movement in 1943. The official inclusion of groups previously marginalized by the partisans, such as women, national minorities, former collaborators, politically unaffiliated individuals, and those who had until then attempted to sit out the war, gave these citizens a new opportunity to prove their loyalty to the greater Soviet community, thereby demonstrating the legitimacy of the Soviet state. However, veteran partisans, who had defined themselves as an exclusive and patriotic elite, were threatened by this broadened popular participation, which they believed cast doubts on the movement's political loyalty and military effectiveness. The conflict ended in an informal compromise between the authorities and the veteran partisans: the newcomers were allowed to join the units, but they remained marginalized, thus continuing the hegemony of the veterans, while presenting the facade of an all-inclusive, national, and popular movement. In working out this compromise, the state and partisans continued to formulate the ways in which ethnonationality, gender, and political affiliation marked individuals and groups in the Soviet body politic.

How did partisan units incorporate all these divisive elements into functioning and cohesive military communities amid the dangers of living in enemy-occupied territory? Chapter Six analyzes the relationship between prewar social values and practices, political and cultural beliefs, and the experiences of partisan daily life in the detachments. The reestablishment of Soviet institutions and cultural norms in the units not only deflected official suspicions about partisan loyalty but also helped the partisans alleviate the psychological and social stresses caused by constant enemy encirclement, material shortages, and physical isolation. Institutions such as the Party and the NKVD (the People's Commissariat for Internal Affairs, the regime's primary agency for state security), though often disparaged and feared by the partisans, nonetheless were seen by many as essential to maintaining unit discipline and security. The continued application of 1930s' cultural norms, such as Stalin's cult of personality (now conferred on the unit commander), the emergence of unit elites and social stratification, and the celebration of Soviet holidays, gave these practices new significance and meaning. Moreover, by continuing to live in a recognizable Soviet manner, partisans implicitly enhanced their identification with the broader Soviet community even as they prized their individual and group autonomy. The continuation of Soviet norms in the partisan environment had substantial implications for the validation of Soviet legitimacy.

The conclusion of this study looks at the tension between the dual partisan concerns of identification with and alienation from the Soviet state in the postwar period. Even though they were publicly celebrated as heroes on their return, partisans were still not trusted by state officials. The partisan "elite" played important roles in peacetime reconstruction, but the state's continuing concern about their reliability meant that most partisans were consigned to the Red Army, and some were even sent directly to the gulag. And in the postwar mythologizing of the war experience, state censors suppressed the veterans' public memories of their war and changed history to comply with official narrative. For veterans who wanted the autonomy to tell their own story, this treatment was profoundly alienating, despite their celebration in the war's master narrative as the paradigmatic Soviet heroes. Yet they continued to identify with and support a regime that sought to control their memories. Only when it was impossible to keep suppressed the contradictions of the state's claims and the veterans' own lived reality, as occurred in the 1980s, did the war experience lose its power to give the Soviet Union political legitimacy.

In his classic history of the Soviet-German war, Alexander Werth commented that the partisan movement not only was the least thoroughly explored topic of the war but also "will remain . . . *unexplorable* for the simple reason that all the participants of the many partisan operations died, and there is nobody left to tell the story."[16] It is my hope that this study, in its way, will contribute to the telling of that story and expand our understanding of its participants and the country in whose name they fought, in what was simultaneously a heroic, tragic, and often terrible tale.

1

PUTTING THE PEOPLE INTO "ALL-PEOPLE'S WAR," 1941–1942

On 3 July 1941, as part of a critical address to the Soviet people detailing the government's response to the German invasion, Joseph Stalin called on citizens to engage in a full-scale partisan war:

> In areas occupied by the enemy, guerrilla units, mounted and on foot, must be formed, diversionist groups must be organized to combat the enemy troops, to foment guerrilla warfare everywhere, to blow up bridges and roads, damage telephone and telegraph wires, set fire to forests, stores, transports. In the occupied regions conditions must be made unbearable for the enemy and his accomplices. They must be hounded and annihilated at every step and their measures frustrated.[1]

It appeared that Stalin sought to involve all citizens in partisan warfare; indeed, this interpretation is quite consistent with the tone of the rest of his radio address, in which he termed the conflict a "patriotic war of liberation against the fascist enslavers."[2] The appeal was entirely in keeping with the military emergency caused by Operation Barbarossa, which threatened the very survival of the Soviet state. It also built on the notion of the Soviet Union as a mass participatory state, in which citizens were expected to demonstrate their loyalty to the Soviet system through participation in public events.

Despite these powerful reasons to implement a partisan war, government leaders feared doing so. The Bolsheviks' experience with partisan warfare during the Civil War had demonstrated that partisans were impossible to control and that their political reliability could not be guaranteed. Indeed, a powerful element within Bolshevism itself was an innate suspicion of the masses' political consciousness, a strand of thought quite visible in one of the founding documents of Bolshevism, V. I. Lenin's *What Is to Be Done*. Even more to the point, could Stalin and the Soviet leadership realistically trust a population that had undergone the brutality of collectivization and the horrors of mass famine and that was now outside their authority? A truly popular and spontaneous partisan movement, embodying powerful, uncontrolled, and uncontrollable forces, contradicted the very core of Stalinist values emphasizing order, control, obedience, discipline, and hierarchy. Only those deemed politically reliable, such as Communists, Komsomols (members of the Communist Youth League), and non-Party activists, could be trusted to adhere to these Stalinist principles and remain loyal to the Soviet Union. Hence, despite the call for a widespread partisan movement, implying a spontaneous, popular mass uprising, Soviet officials sought to create a partisan force that was organized and directed by the state, comprising primarily local elites and notables, to ensure the partisans' political reliability.

This attempt to control the resistance through recruitment ultimately failed as new partisans from "questionable" backgrounds joined the insurgency beginning in the spring of 1942. Moreover, the worsening military situation that summer made it clear that larger partisan forces were desperately needed. In September 1942, a new policy was implemented that called on the partisan effort to become a genuine "all-people's" struggle, embracing and encouraging *all* Soviet citizens to participate in organized resistance against the German occupiers. This new policy acknowledged the changes that were already occurring in the movement and would lead to a further broadening of its social base. It also meant that even though the partisans remained controlled by Moscow—indeed, that control had become even stronger due to the creation of a specialized partisan administration—the guerrilla resistance was in fact becoming more of an actual people's movement.

The question of whether the partisan forces were to be exclusive or inclusive thus touched on a significant tension within Soviet political culture, particularly within the context of the wartime national emergency. Soviet political values had both exclusive and inclusive tendencies, encouraging mass participation while restricting real action to a very limited few. The national emergency required mass mobilization and participation, yet government authorities felt—with good reason—that they could not trust the bulk of the population to follow their orders without the usual forms of coercive control. The effort to resolve these tensions ultimately led the Soviet leadership to define the partisan movement in new ways and, in so doing, to redefine the wartime Soviet body politic even though it was still based on political foundations established in the 1930s.

THE POLITICS OF PARTISAN WARFARE
BEFORE WORLD WAR II

In October 1946, participants at a conference of former partisan commanders bemoaned the fact that despite recent experience, guerrilla warfare was still not taken seriously by military leaders. In particular, they recalled the Soviet Union's lack of preparation for waging a guerrilla war in 1941, despite experiments conducted in the 1920s and the first half of the 1930s. Former commander S. A. Vaupshasov recalled, "In 1936 the work was liquidated, I will not speak about the reason."[3]

Vaupshasov's reluctance to speak openly was understandable, given the political dynamics of Stalin's Soviet Union. Irregular warfare had a long history in the Muscovite, tsarist, and more immediate Soviet past. But even before the Soviet period, a tension existed in the Russian conceptualization of partisan warfare between state order and popular spontaneity, between control and freedom.

That the partisan training program and its participants fell victim to the contradictions of maintaining external and internal security in Stalin's Soviet Union reflects the tension embedded in the long political and social legacy of irregular warfare in Russian and Soviet history. Partisan war implied decentralization and independence from state authority. In the context of Russian and Soviet history, it could also mean opposition to the state. There were certainly "patriotic" examples of people's or guerrilla war to point to, such as the exploits of Kuzma Minin and Prince Dmitrii Pozharskii and Ivan Susanin during the Time of Troubles or those of Denis Davydov during the Patriotic War of 1812. In the nineteenth century, Russian military theorists elaborated principles of partisan warfare based on independent army detachments operating behind enemy lines, thus maintaining state control over irregular warfare.[4] However, the spontaneity of irregular warfare was also associated with the mass rebellions against the tsarist state led by Stenka Razin and Emelian Pugachev (among others) in the seventeenth and eighteenth centuries. Songs, tales, poems, and, in the twentieth century, movies contributed to this enduring popular mythology, which, at its heart, celebrated freedom and the have-nots living well at the expense of the haves.[5] Some of the same attributes were applied to the partisans of the more recent Civil War. Hence, Soviet leaders, who innately distrusted any popular actions they could not control, could only tolerate with difficulty what John Erickson has termed the "organized dissidence" that constituted partisan warfare.[6]

The experience of the Civil War, perhaps the heyday of the irregular fighter, brought this point home to most Bolshevik officials. Partisan warfare was an important component of the Soviet military effort; in fact, it was often quite difficult to distinguish regular Red Army formations from their irregular counterparts. Partisan "armies," some consisting of up to 30,000 men, harassed and attacked the White forces. However, most partisans were not formally attached to the regime, nor did they necessarily see themselves as Reds. Many had ties to Socialist Revolutionary or anarchist groups; others adopted positions close to the so-called Greens.[7] Consequently, the Bolsheviks could not rely on the partisans' political loyalty and reliability. The anarchist Nestor Makhno was just one example: though he initially sided with the Bolsheviks, he later rejected their authority and actively opposed them.

These attitudes were further manifested in partisan behavior. Partisans, be they Red, Green, or some other color or ideological stripe, were notoriously independent. They elected their own commanders, prioritized local concerns over national ones, and usually obeyed outside authority only when they believed it was in their best interests to do so.[8] Some Left Communists, such as Nikolai Bukharin and Georgii Piatakov, extolled the virtues of partisan warfare, seeing it as another manifestation of the creation of a new revolutionary order,[9] but most Bolsheviks, notably Lenin and Leon Trotsky, defined the partisans' behavior with the pejorative term *partizanshchina*, which they characterized as militarily unreliable, disobedient, and with egalitarian and anarchistic tendencies and a propensity to plunder and pillage from the local population or, at the other extreme, to defend local interests at the expense of the Bolshevik state's.[10] The hierarchical Bolshevik regime was determined to bring these forces under its control and institutionalize them. The government established the Central Headquarters of Partisan Detachments, attached to the People's Commissariat of Military and Naval Affairs in 1918. Regional Party bureaus, answering to the Central Committee, controlled—or, rather, tried to control—the partisan units. However, given the fluid and everchanging structure of Soviet power in the Civil War, the partisans actually reported to a wide range of institutions, from revolutionary military councils to local soviets—that is, when they reported at all.[11] The decision to create a regular and disciplined army, the very antithesis of partisans and partizanshchina, was an attempt to control these spontaneous and "populist" elements in the revolutionary movement, as well as to construct a more effective fighting force.[12]

The partisans' rebelliousness and autonomy that so frustrated officials also made them popular heroes in the eyes of the public. Civil War partisans exuded an earthy, crude, egalitarian, and romantic persona, which Richard Stites has likened to the American mythological counterpart, the cowboy.[13] The partisans' exploits lived on in the public imagination, heralded in popular literature and later cinematic epics.[14] The clash of values between partisan freedom and Bolshevik discipline was also evident in the literature of the Civil War era. Isaak Babel's Red Cavalry stories show the unease that the Bolshevik intelligentsia felt when confronted by anarchic Cossack populism. Less ambiguous was the classic socialist realist novel *Chapaev* by Dmitrii Furmanov, the tale of the tempering of a well-intentioned but undisciplined populist leader by his politically educated commissar.[15]

Bolshevik authorities in the Civil War found it much easier to control the irregular warriors in fiction than in real life, and for this reason, many in the Red Army hoped to do away with the partisans and peasant-based militias after the Civil War. Anxieties about the military effectiveness and reliability of the peasant population were reflected in postwar debates over the structure of the Red Army. Military theorists of the 1920s, among them Sergei Gusev, argued that a militia-based peasant army might succumb to the peasants' counterrevolutionary and local particularistic sentiments. Mikhail Frunze contended that only the proletariat could be counted on to wage a modern offensive war, whereas the unreliable peasantry had to be relegated to fighting a defensive partisan war.[16] The disorder, chaos, and often stunning ineffectiveness that marked the Red Army's performance during that conflict and in the war with Poland suggested to the army's leaders that a more disciplined and technologically advanced force was necessary to defend the country and the Revolution.

Despite the Bolsheviks' pronounced hostility toward irregular warfare, the relative weakness of the Red Army in the 1920s forced military leaders to incorporate guerrillas in their plans and to engage in some form of mass mobilization and militarization of the population. The burgeoning mass civil defense society, Osoaviakhim, sought to inculcate military values into the population and foster local activism while keeping the organization under the strict control of the state. Civil defense specialists provided rudimentary military training and instructed peasants and workers on how to guard their factories, assist the Red Army, and, in case of enemy occupation, engage in partisan warfare.[17]

The comparative weakness and technological backwardness of the Red Army in relation to its potential opponents meant that the armed forces also had to take the possibility of partisan warfare seriously. Hence, P. A. Karatygin, the deputy head of the intelligence department in the Ukrainian Military

District, postulated that a synthesis of regular forces and an armed popular uprising, directed by centralized authority, could wreak havoc in an enemy's rear area.[18] By the early 1930s, partisans had become a part of the Red Army's defense plans, and they were even included in formal maneuvers. The head of the Red Army's intelligence service, Ia. K. Berzin, and the commander of the Kiev Military District, Iona Iakir, established detachments, training schools, bases, and weapons caches in the Belorussian, Kiev, and Leningrad Military Districts.[19] The state security apparatus also actively prepared bands for engaging in partisan warfare.[20]

These partisans were not the wild, romantic types of the Civil War. Instead, they were trained professionals, reflecting both the growing sophistication of the Red Army and Moscow's determination to control popular activity. In this sense, the Soviet vision of partisan warfare remained remarkably consistent with that of the tsarist generals from the previous century, who were also quite ambivalent, at best, about spontaneous popular participation and preferred that the partisan cadres be tied institutionally to the regime through the regular Red Army, the NKVD, the Party, and the Komsomol. They also included trusted foreign refugees and Communists, as well as members of Osoaviakhim who had demonstrated a special aptitude for partisan warfare. These guerrilla specialists were trained in the art of sabotage and small-unit raids and ambushes.[21] This selection of personnel is revealing: partisan warfare was to be conducted by trained cadres who were institutionally bound to the Soviet state through the political, military, and security organs, thus eliminating the need to base an insurgency on a potentially disloyal population that had recently suffered from collectivization and borderland ethnic tensions.

The "modernization" of the Red Army's doctrine and equipment in the mid-1930s helped to spell the end of this impressive, if limited, partisan program. The new doctrine called for an invasion to be stopped at the border, followed by an immediate offensive, thus eliminating the need for partisans. Moreover, to the advocates of military modernization, including Chief of Staff Mikhail Tukhachevskii, partisans were an anachronism now that the Red Army was being equipped with armor and parachutists.[22] In the meantime, Stalin's political cronies, such as Defense Commissar Kliment Voroshilov, insisted that Soviet territory was inviolable and that the Red Army could handle any foe. Partisan instructor Vaupshasov recalls Voroshilov saying in 1935 that any enemy who dared invade the USSR would be repulsed with little cost in blood and matériel. A year later, Voroshilov boasted, "We not only will not let the enemy go beyond the borders of our motherland, but we will beat him on the territory from which he came."[23] These sentiments precluded the implementation of a partisan war.

The trained cadres were not just simply reassigned to other duties, however. The internal Manichean logic of Stalinist politics meant that the military decision to halt the partisan program almost inevitably led to a literal bloodletting against its supporters and participants, feeding as it did into the leadership's intense distrust of irregular warfare. The declaration that the Soviet Union's borders were inviolable and protected by the invincible Red Army instantly placed all who championed the value of partisan warfare under suspicion of being defeatists and traitors. According to I. G. Starinov, a partisan training instructor who had served in Spain advising Republican guerrillas, partisan instructors and specialists were accused of having "a lack of faith in the power of the Soviet socialist state" and preparing for "enemy activity in the rear of the Soviet armies."[24] Voroshilov—who, ironically, would later briefly command the partisan forces in World War II—claimed that the instructors were "training bandits and storing arms for them," although his own personal intervention saved Starinov from arrest.[25] It is difficult to say how real the leadership perceived these threats to be, as other branches of the security services claimed that foreign groups had indeed established secret weapons bases and armed groups.[26] In any case, all the upper-level commanders who had sponsored the partisan program, including Berzin, Iakir, V. K. Bliukher, and I. P. Uborevich, fell in the purges that devastated the Red Army's officer corps in the late 1930s. The corps of partisan instructors was also swept away. The few survivors included some of the most famous future partisan leaders in World War II.[27]

Not only were the advocates of partisan warfare repressed; so, too, were veteran partisans from the Civil War. As early as 1935, partisans who could not demonstrate that their detachments were connected to Party or soviet organizations lost social privileges and suffered reduced pensions.[28] Red partisans were also targeted in the purges, and, like the Old Bolsheviks, they suffered disproportionately.[29] The repression of the late 1930s thus greatly hindered Moscow's later attempts to facilitate a partisan war. Officials and partisans alike had to relearn the hard-earned lessons of the past. Few of the thousands of purged instructors and veterans who would have been able to teach them could be brought back from the NKVD's prisons and camps. So extensive were the purges that even the elaborate plans and theories developed during the interwar years were buried with their proponents: in the fall of 1941, the only field manuals that anyone could obtain were outdated guides from the Civil War.[30]

The suppression of partisan war planning and of the Civil War partisans was part of a physical and symbolic transformation taking place in the Soviet Union in the 1930s. It was one element of the regime's self-conscious drive to represent itself as the very model of a modern, industrial, and disciplined nation. Seen in this light, the freedom and spontaneity represented by the Civil War partisan symbolized national weakness, anarchy, unreliability, and technological backwardness. Such traits had no place in the Stalinist definition of the Soviet Union, which emphasized state control over society and individuals through the use of technology, social hierarchy, and conformity, all in the context of an entirely regimented, mass-participatory politics.[31]

The 1934 cinematic depiction of *Chapaev* signaled the transformation of the partisan image and foreshadowed the end of the partisan program. With its exciting plot and action scenes, the film apparently was genuinely popular, even without official support.[32] In fact, it had such resonance that during World War II, both partisans and officials (including the head of the partisan movement) referred to incidents in the film, rather than Chapaev's actual life, when discussing what the Civil War hero would have done in a particular situation.[33]

In the film, Chapaev's partisans were ordinary men and women of the people who nonetheless accomplished great feats—a propaganda trope that resonated throughout the Soviet Union. According to film scholar John Haynes, the cinematic Chapaev synthesized the form of the old Cossacks of legend with the content of the modern Soviet hero, "implicitly dedicated to the cowboy ideal of forging a new life in the land of the free."[34] Tension was generated by the relationship between the well-meaning but politically uneducated and wild Chapaev and his politically conscious and disciplined commissar. Out of his relationship with the urbane and modern commissar-mentor, Chapaev became the embodiment of the New Soviet Man, who brought together both action and ideology in his being. Hence, "reason prevails over impulses, consciousness over spontaneity," which, in turn, as Marc Ferro noted, "legitimize[s] the party's leadership."[35] But the film did more than that. Ferro further concluded that "the film implicitly defines itself rather coherently with the Whites' system of values since it stresses redemption by blood, the myth of sacrifice, military discipline, the display of rank, the legitimacy of institutionalized knowledge, the glorification of the patriarchal and legitimate family, and submission to centralized power."[36] This list actually describes Stalinist values as they emerged in the 1930s. By portraying these values in the romantic context of the Civil War partisan, the Stalinist state simultaneously and deceptively recalled the Revolution's heroic legacy while sanitizing the partisan image and transforming it into a supporter of Stalinism. Needless to say, this depiction was completely antithetical to the culture of partizanshchina of the Civil War. It did, however, create the impression that the regime supported the partisans' populist aspirations and was fulfilling their revolutionary and egalitarian promise.

ALL-PEOPLE'S WAR WITHOUT THE PEOPLE

Operation Barbarossa, the German invasion of the Soviet Union, made a mockery of all Soviet prewar planning to repel the enemy at the border. Taken totally by surprise by the German blitzkrieg, Red Army units were either destroyed or encircled by the swift-moving mechanized forces of Germany. Hundreds of thousands of soldiers were caught in the encirclements, and German armored spearheads advanced rapidly eastward. By the middle of July 1941, Smolensk, on the road to Moscow, was taken. September saw the capture of Kiev, with the surrender of over 600,000 Red Army troops. By the beginning of October, Leningrad was already besieged and the Germans had begun their campaign to seize Moscow, a drive that would take them to the outskirts of the city by early December.

The Red Army's failure to halt the Wehrmacht came as a devastating and traumatic surprise not only to the Soviet people but also to the country's leadership and especially to Stalin.[37] Among other things, it forced the government to reappraise the necessity for partisan warfare. As noted earlier, the Bolsheviks had very real anxieties about engaging in partisan warfare, heightened by the fear that Soviet citizens, especially in the newly acquired Baltic and former Polish territories, might regard the Germans as liberators. At the same time, in the midst of this national crisis, how could the government fail to call on its citizens under occupation to resist the enemy?

The government's answer to this question reflected the contradictions found in a mass participatory regime that distrusted its own population. Soviet propaganda, following Stalin's cue from the 3 July 1941 radio address, deemed that all citizens were taking up arms as partisans. Indeed, even before Stalin's speech, Soviet media described the war as "a great patriotic war" and "a patriotic war of liberation" involving the entire nation. Partisans were a vital manifestation of this national patriotism. Central newspaper accounts of the partisan resistance from the summer of 1941 constantly stressed that the partisan ranks were filled with ordinary people. Thus, E. M. Iaroslavskii, a high-ranking Party official, wrote as early as 15 July 1941 in *Pravda* that the partisans, responding immediately to Stalin's call, formed a "mighty people's movement" and that "the fascists will soon be convinced—if they are not already convinced—that the partisan movement is an all-people's movement."[38] Collective farmers, who surely had not forgotten the horrors of collectivization and famine, were cited as eagerly defending the Soviet order. Aleksandr Fadeev, who would later write the postwar partisan classic *The Young Guard*, stated in *Pravda*, "The partisan war is the answer of the Soviet peasants to the unheard-of atrocities and robberies by the . . . fascist cannibals."[39] Numerous stories and articles described the partisans as a cross section of Soviet society. On 1 November 1941, *Krasnaia zvezda*, the Red Army's newspaper, stated that the partisans were "the true sons of the Soviet people—workers, peasants, intelligentsia—the partisans are prepared to fight until the last drop of blood for the great cause of freedom, for the Soviet motherland."[40] Another 1941 article noted that the "great strength of the partisans is in their kinship with the local population."[41] The partisans were also portrayed as "a people's army, operating in the rear of the enemy," who fought just like Red Army soldiers.[42] In addition, the media made it clear that this popular uprising was led by Communists and local notables such as collective farm chairmen, schoolteachers, and non-Party activists. In August 1941, *Pravda* told the story of the "Ded" (Grandfather) partisan detachment, led by the chair of the local village council, whose life experiences, wisdom, courage, and resourcefulness carried tremendous authority with his partisans.[43] *Krasnaia zvezda* reported in February 1942 that when the districts of the Moscow region were occupied, partisan bands were "led by Soviet and party organizations . . . the best people in Moscow Oblast."[44] Thus, Soviet propagandists confirmed the continuation of prewar hierarchies and Party control even as they celebrated initiative and participation.

Propaganda was one thing; state policy was quite another. In 1941 and the first nine months of 1942, actual Soviet policy discounted and even discouraged popular initiative and participation. On 29 June and 18 July 1941, the first national directives calling for partisan warfare envisioned a much more limited struggle, to be based on the Party and state security apparatus. The leadership trusted only the personnel in these organizations to defend the Soviet regime in the absence of any overt, formal state controls. In so doing, however, the Soviet leadership ignored peacetime experiences and planning, which called for a partisan war to be waged by trained specialists.[45] The partisans of 1941, including those from the NKVD-NKGB (the People's Commissariat for State Security, which was separated from the NKVD in February 1941), were rank amateurs by comparison.

On 29 June 1941, as the Belorussian capital of Minsk was being surrounded, the Party's Central Committee and the Council of People's Commissars (Sovnarkom) issued a joint decree to Party and government organizations in frontline regions to form partisan units in the enemy's rear area.[46]
These instructions were followed by more detailed guidelines sent to Party
organizations on 18 July 1941. Oblast and raion (district) Party secretaries in
every area threatened with occupation were ordered to form underground
Party cells and partisan units and to provide the detachments with food,
weapons, radios, and other necessary supplies, which were to be stored and
hidden before enemy occupation.[47] However, the directive gave local officials
few practical instructions for fulfilling these orders. Officials were not told
from where or from whom to obtain supplies or how to organize units. No
consideration was given to the suitability of available resources, local terrain,
or the willingness of the surrounding population to support a guerrilla war.
Perhaps most important, no attempt was made to coordinate partisan activities at the national or republican levels, nor was the Party or any other institution given responsibility for providing centralized leadership. Local Party
leaders were only instructed to send the names of partisan commanders to the
Central Committee; they were told that "the leaders of the party organizations [must] personally direct the struggle in the German Army's rear."[48] As
time passed, regional Party organizations, military political organs at the
army and front levels, and local NKVD organs all played supervisory roles,
but their efforts were poorly realized and they often worked at cross-purposes
with one another. The government's failure to establish a clear administrative framework for coordinating the activities of the Party, NKVD, and Red
Army meant that the partisans were left without leadership, which resulted
in paralyzing conflicts among the political, military, and security establish-
ments. Consequently, the partisans existed in a supervisory vacuum, with no
real guidance—or control—emanating from Moscow.

Instead of relying on institutional control, the Soviet leadership depended
on the recruitment of regime loyalists to ensure partisan reliability. According
to the 18 July instructions, Party officials were to select leaders from only the
"staunchest" members of the Party, Komsomol, and other state organs, as
well as non-Party citizens who had already proven their dedication to the Soviet cause. Although the directive stated that in "every city and village hundreds and thousands of our friends and brothers" wanted to fight the enemy,
rank-and-file recruits were to include only "participants in the Civil War and
those comrades who *have already showed their worth* in the destruction battalions, the people's militia, and also workers from the NKVD."[49] Orders from

the NKVD echoed these requirements.[50] Thus, popular loyalty to the regime was not assumed; rather, individuals had to have demonstrated it in their past public actions. Ordinary citizens who had led a nonpolitical public life yet internally accepted the Soviet state or who simply wanted to defend their homeland were not wanted. From the regime's perspective, the risk of their succumbing to partizanshchina was just too great.

One is struck by the leadership's ambivalence toward popular participation in the insurgency. Despite Stalin's call for a partisan war and the already deployed slogans "Great Patriotic War" and "all-people's war," all of which generated images of a mass, spontaneous, national uprising,[51] officials envisioned that the partisans were to be organized and led by the state, especially the Party. Their units were to conform to the Party's administrative boundaries and hierarchies, and their members were limited to Party cadres and recognized non-Party activists. Public claims that ordinary citizens desired to resist the enemy were contradicted by official instructions to recruit only those who had already actively displayed their loyalty to the Soviet state. These restrictions reflected official fears of partizanshchina rearing its ugly head, and they also served as a means to control the movement, as there were no administrative or coercive mechanisms to guarantee the partisans' loyalty. This tension between the public discourse of mass popular participation forming a spontaneous movement and the leadership's desire and need for political reliability was not to be addressed for over a year, and in some ways, it was never fully settled. It further revealed the confusion and desperation of a supposedly mass-based regime that remained inherently suspicious of its citizenry even in the midst of the national emergency brought about by the German invasion.

THE PARTISANS OF 1941:
PERSONNEL AND EXPERIENCES

Partly because of Soviet policy and partly because of actual conditions behind the lines, the partisans of 1941 tended to conform to Moscow's ideal of the partisans as being politically affiliated and stakeholders in the regime. Organizers tried to follow the 18 July guidelines, but they also followed their own instincts, including in their detachments only those people known to them, which, more often than not, meant other Communists or members of the local elite. Moreover, few other citizens, especially in the countryside, were willing at that point in time to risk their lives for a regime that had brutalized so many and whose destruction seemed so imminent.

Certainly, Party members and fellow travelers dominated the underground armed resistance at its inception.[52] In Moscow, to cite one example, approximately 78 percent of the partisans were either Party or Komsomol members.[53] This figure might be on the extreme end of Communist participation, but archival evidence indicates overwhelmingly that Party members took the lead in organizing and forming the first partisan units. In all, Soviet sources estimate that over 65,000 Communists and tens of thousands more Komsomols participated in partisan detachments and underground Party organizations in 1941, although given the uncertainty of Soviet records, these— and all other figures—must be regarded as estimates.[54]

The NKVD also contributed heavily to the guerrilla resistance in 1941 through its so-called destruction battalions (*istrebitel'nye batal'ony*) and specially organized sabotage groups. With each unit composed of between 100 and 200 Red Army reservists, NKVD workers, and civilian volunteers, most of whom were Communists or Komsomols, the destruction battalions were organized under the jurisdiction of the NKVD border guards to protect army rear areas, important local institutions, and infrastructure against German saboteurs and parachutists.[55] Often, however, they were placed in the front lines in the vain hope of stopping the advancing Germans, where they suffered heavily. Surviving battalions were transformed into partisan bands when their home regions were occupied.[56] As their status changed, there was some confusion over their exact mission. One newly recruited participant recalled his thoughts after the war: "A destruction battalion, there was something hazy, unclear. What is it we ought to destroy? Why 'destruction'? All are destroyed, all destroy. Why are we a destruction battalion? We will fight against parachutists, against saboteurs."[57] These battalions, like almost all the other partisan formations in 1941, were distinguished by their lack of training and military experience.

The NKVD's Administration for Special Tasks also organized special partisan units in the Soviet rear area and sent them across the lines to attack German communication lines and supply depots. According to NKVD head Lavrenti Beria, by August 1941, the NKVD had deployed 14 detachments with 1,162 men and 15 diversionary groups with 400 men into Belorussia. The NKVD also created the Independent Motor Rifle Brigade of Special Appointment, known by its Russian acronym, OMSBON. The OMSBON, some 25,000 strong, included NKVD cadres, Party and Komsomol members, athletes, and approximately 2,000 foreign émigrés; it was better trained than partisan units and came the closest to the standards of the 1920s and 1930s. Frequently operating in small groups, OMSBON detachments conducted sabotage operations, organized new units, and established Moscow's presence in the occupied territories.[58]

True to the intent of the 18 July instructions, the first partisan detachments were marked by their exclusivity. This exclusivity was just as much a product of the partisans' own fears and anxieties as of official orders. Orel NKVD head K. F. Firsanov observed that the first civilian partisans "formed the detachment, [they] all know each other . . . [they're] all Communists, workers and are united. If they accepted a large number of new people, then spies will penetrate the unit. This caution had some foundation, but it also created a certain exclusivity."[59] These concerns were not groundless, as a single spy could give a band's location to the enemy. In any case, local Soviet notables mirrored the same distrust of the surrounding population as their superiors.

By September 1941, there were, on paper, some 87,000 partisans enlisted in detachments throughout the Soviet Union, but by January 1942, this number had fallen to 30,000.[60] This catastrophic decrease indicates how very close the partisan forces came to collapsing by the end of the 1941–1942 winter, as the Germans wiped out most units or forced them to disband or retreat to Soviet territory. In heavily forested regions, some bands held out, but they were effectively neutralized. In more open areas, such as the Ukrainian steppes, the guerrilla resistance essentially ceased to be, with one historian estimating that only 7 percent of all detachments formed in 1941 survived to the next spring.[61] Why did the first partisans fare so badly? The conditions of partisan operations and life will be explored in much more detail in later chapters, but suffice it to say for now that they suffered from the combined effects of inadequate planning and preparation, isolation, lack of popular support, and poor leadership. Many also attempted to operate in unsuitable terrain, further reducing their chances of survival.

More immediately, however, the mostly civilian partisans generally lacked the military experience necessary to fight what was arguably the world's finest—and most brutal—army. And though Soviet propagandists cited the partisans' natural military abilities, the reality was very different.[62] Most of the initial recruits had little idea of what it really meant to be a partisan, as one Civil War veteran related: "I must say that we did not represent how difficult it would be to be a partisan, how it would be in reality. I knew partisan war in the years of the Civil War. Then I was in the Komsomol . . . I must say

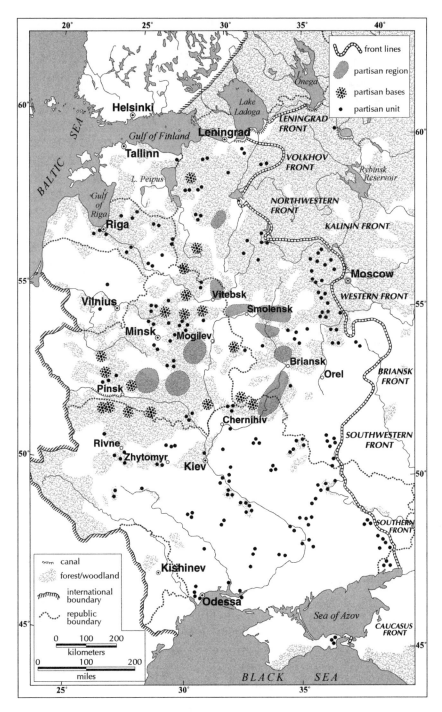

Disposition of partisan operations and bases, winter 1941–1942. (Credit: Dick Gilbreath)

that if we had represented [partisan war] as it was, then many would have wondered, can we hold up?"[63] Combat "training" before the occupation generally failed to prepare the cadres for the realities of guerrilla warfare, especially in units organized by Party members, who themselves had little or no practical experience. A. F. Fedorov, an oblast first secretary turned partisan commander, described his unit's training area as "a typical Osoaviakhim camp" where they "trained regularly in target practice and cleaning of the rifle, and studied drill regulations and service regulations." Food was plentiful, and there was little sense of danger, "just as if there wasn't a war."[64] Skills such as how to plant explosives, set up an ambush, conduct reconnaissance, and even read a map were strikingly absent. Moreover, the theoretical works and field manuals from the prewar period, like their authors, were also suppressed.[65] Apparently, there were no current field manuals to help the recruits, not even any surviving from the experiments of the 1920s and 1930s. As late as October 1941, the Red Army's Main Political Administration reissued an outdated Civil War–era manual, leaving a regional NKVD official to quip, "I attentively read this manual as advised and then I put it in my files where it remains as an historical document."[66] This inexperience was telling: one district Party official instructed a newly formed band to "hide in the bushes. The Germans will not look at every bush." He then allegedly advised the partisans to arm themselves with axes, since "the axe is a dreaded weapon."[67]

As noted, the burden of leading the partisans fell primarily on the local Party leadership. Yet these cadres were not physically or psychologically capable of leading a guerrilla war. The most able-bodied male Communists were usually the first to respond to mobilization calls to join the Red Army, as happened in Ukraine, where 42.9 percent of all Party members joined the Red Army; consequently, it was the less physically fit who joined the partisan bands.[68] In the first six months of the war alone, over 1 million Party members and 2 million Komsomols, or almost half the total Party membership, were mobilized to serve in the Red Army.[69] The manpower problem was exacerbated by the urban-rural imbalance in Party membership,[70] which meant that the bulk of cadres were located in the cities, not in the countryside where the partisan war was to be fought. Finally, in the newly annexed western Belorussian and Ukrainian regions, where Party control had not yet been fully consolidated, Communists disappeared, severely hindering the subsequent development of a Soviet partisan resistance in these areas.[71]

Perhaps even more critical was the lack of psychological preparation. As

80 percent of Communists had joined the Party since the mid-1920s, few had any experience with underground political work or partisan warfare.[72] After twenty years of Soviet power, the idea of becoming a partisan seemed highly improbable to many, especially because most had joined the Party after the Revolution and Civil War. Fedorov, a Party member since 1927, recalled his incredulity when he was instructed to form a unit: "Create an underground! Even the words seemed bookish, dead. 'A Bolshevik underground'—after all this is from the history of the Party. And here we were, not so very young people but of Soviet formation, who had to prepare themselves for the transfer to an illegal position."[73] The possibility of living in a hostile environment evidently unnerved supposedly reliable cadres, who refused to join the underground resistance even before the Germans arrived. Some feared the retribution the Germans would unleash against their families.[74] Others who had joined bands in preparation for occupation came down with alleged sudden illnesses, causing them to leave their posts for healthier environs.[75] To Fedorov, it was "very distressing when it turned out that a good man and worker was infected with this terrible bacillus of cowardice."[76] In his eyes, these Communists failed this most fundamental test of their mettle.

Isolation exacerbated these problems, especially the lack of contact with Soviet authorities on the other side of the front. Few radios were available to the partisans, a situation worsened by the government's confiscation of all private radio sets in the first weeks of the war.[77] Thus, the head of the Political Administration of the Northwestern Front in September 1941 reported that none of the thirty-four partisan detachments operating in his area had radios.[78] Those few units that did found that the very forests that protected them sometimes blocked transmissions or that their sets could not communicate with other models.[79]

These problems and others also afflicted partisan groups organized in Soviet-held territory by the Party, the Komsomol, and even the "professional" Red Army and security services. V. N. Merkulov, then head of the NKGB, complained in July 1941 that groups were "knocked together hurriedly" and sent out across the lines after their members knew each other for only a few hours. Moreover, they lacked proper weapons, such as grenades and explosives. Once on the ground, they knew little about local conditions and did not even have maps and compasses to guide them.[80] That these bands were ineffective is not surprising. Historian V. I. Boiarskii estimates that of the 287 groups (11,733 partisans) organized by the NKVD-NKGB in Leningrad between 22 June 1941 and 7 February 1942, only 60 bands with 1,965 parti-

sans remained in occupied territory by the latter date, a *survival* rate of 17
percent. Sixty-four bands with 2,186 partisans eventually reunited with the
Red Army, but 163 groups with 7,582 partisans were either destroyed or un-
accounted for.[81]

The first bands were generally quite small, usually numbering fewer than
50 persons. Typically, they were poorly equipped, and many were fortunate if
they had enough rifles for each partisan. Machine guns, submachine guns,
and other automatic weapons, so important for the hit-and-run tactics of
guerrilla warfare, were rare, and many units relied on Molotov cocktails to attack German armored vehicles, since they had no antitank guns. For example,
in Orel Oblast, one of the better-equipped regions, the 10,000 men in the
NKVD destruction battalions had only 8,000 rifles, 60 machine guns, 12,000
grenades, and approximately 20,000 Molotov cocktails.[82] Weapons often came
from reserve stocks or were found on the battlefield, and it was common for
a unit to be equipped with a mixture of Soviet, French, British, Finnish, Polish, and captured German arms.[83] Even under the best of circumstances, the
ability of these groups to hurt the enemy would be minimal.

Perhaps most important, the partisans initially found little support from
the surrounding Soviet population, not only in the newly annexed regions but
even within the pre-1939 borders. Early on, many Soviets viewed the Germans favorably as a civilized people who would treat them fairly. This attitude was fostered by memories of the relatively benign German occupation
during World War I; by positive Soviet propaganda about Germany following
the signing of the Molotov-Ribbentrop Pact; by the Germans' own propaganda, which played on anti-Communist and anti-Semitic sentiments, pro-
claiming liberation from the Communists and the Jews; and by the initial
"tactful" behavior of many of the occupying troops.[84] In the newly annexed
regions, the experience of mass deportations was still a raw and open wound,
and inside the pre-1939 borders, the scars of collectivization still lingered.
Peasants generally hoped that the "liberators" would dismantle the hated collective farms. Thus, one woman reported that the inhabitants in her village
in western Belorussia's Brest region "smiled and said, 'well, good'" when the
Germans arrived and gave them eggs and meat, a scene that was replicated
throughout the occupied territories.[85] Others were less demonstrative—or
perhaps more wary—and took a wait-and-see position, which itself was quite
common in all of occupied Europe but which in the Soviet case was particularly exacerbated by the discontent of so many with their native government.[86]

In areas where the Germans were not so popular, intimidation inhibited support for the partisans. The seemingly overwhelming success of the blitz-krieg created the impression of German invincibility and inevitable victory, buttressed by rumors that the Soviet government had fled or collapsed and that key cities, such as Leningrad and Moscow, had been captured, thus making any resistance futile.[87] These rumors were given credence by the rapid disintegration of local Soviet power. Soviet counterpropaganda, by contrast, was sparse and abstract and failed to speak to local situations.[88] And although frontline units generally behaved decently as they sped through the countryside, the murderous activities of the Einsatzgruppen, the mobile killing squads composed of Schutzstaffel (SS) troops and police, and other formations, which targeted primarily Jews and Communists, sent a warning to gentile non-Communists about what they could expect if they opposed the new occupiers.[89] In fact, the early "antipartisan" missions conducted by SS and Wehrmacht units were little more than facades for the murder of Jews and the general subjugation of the rest of the population.[90] For example, in an August sweep of the Pripiat Marshes for partisans, the SS Cavalry Brigade reported that it had killed 13,788 "looters" at the cost of 2 killed and 15 wounded, an astounding disparity that speaks for itself. In another operation, a police general reported that only 480 rifles had been found among 6,000 dead "partisans."[91] Similarly, Einsatzgruppe formations, working closely with the army, used antipartisan reprisal expeditions to murder tens of thousands of Jews, whom the Germans blamed for instigating the partisan movement in the first place.[92] In such circumstances, the best hope for civilians was to keep their heads down, avoid both partisans and occupiers, and hope that the storm would pass them by.

The partisans of 1941 caused relatively little damage to the enemy. An underground Party instructor informed the Belorussian Central Committee in August 1941 about the activities—or, rather, inactivity—of one detachment located in the Pinsk region:

> The leadership of the detachment was, until recently, wrongly oriented
> in its relations to the tasks of the partisan detachment. The commander
> and the political officer considered that since the detachment had neither
> machine-guns nor automatic weapons, and because of the high technical
> equipment of the German troops, [the detachment] could not inflict
> significant damage on them, so that the main task of the partisan
> detachment then consisted of preserving [the detachment's] strength
> and preparing it for decisive action, possibly only at the moment of the
> Germans' retreat.[93]

When actions did take place, they were generally ineffectual. Often, an attack or ambush resulted in a few enemy casualties but exposed the partisans to counterattacks, leading to their destruction or forcing them to seek safety elsewhere.[94] The case of a partisan group operating in Sebezh Raion, Kalinin Oblast, provides a typical example. Consisting of fourteen men armed with rifles, pistols, grenades, and some explosives, the group spent most of its short life on the run. On 11 September, the partisans ambushed a truck convoy and killed a motorcyclist. On 27 September, they blew up some railroad tracks, but a lack of explosives and the German pursuit forced the partisans to leave the district in the beginning of October. They met with another group, but German forces again compelled the partisans to look for a safe haven. Continually chased and harassed, the detachment eventually had no choice but to cross into Soviet-held territory. However, as the partisans tried to cross the lines, they encountered heavy fire, which scattered them. Six were killed before the survivors made it to safety.[95] Many of the units that survived until winter disbanded because the lack of food, shelter, appropriate clothing, and cover made them vulnerable to starvation, disease, exposure, and the enemy.

By late in the 1941–1942 winter, the Soviet partisan movement had reached its nadir. The reliance on regime stakeholders satisfied the government's concerns about partisan loyalty and political reliability but failed to generate a guerrilla force that had popular legitimacy and military viability. However, in the first months of the invasion, it is hard to see what other loyal and dedicated elements could have been found in the occupied territories to fight the partisan war. Lack of enthusiasm for the regime (not to mention outright hostility toward it in some regions), the hope for a better life under new masters, as well as fear, intimidation, and the seeming hopelessness of a Soviet victory all contributed to an apathetic populace. Yet a combination of events would breathe new life into the resistance—indeed, transform it into a genuine popular movement. This development would then force the leadership to take a new approach to the question of balancing popular participation and political reliability.

DEMOGRAPHIC EXPANSION AND
MILITARY CRISIS: 1942

Although the partisan bands had been severely diminished by early 1942, they were not totally defeated, as small groups managed to hold together. Some even gained control of relatively large and secure base areas from which to operate, especially in eastern Belorussia and the forested regions of Leningrad, Smolensk, Briansk, and Orel, more because rear-area German security was undermanned than due to the partisans' strength. In the spring, as the weather became more hospitable, new recruits began to join their ranks in ever-increasing numbers. It is perhaps at this point that we can speak of the insurgency becoming a popular and spontaneous "movement," even while recognizing that the Soviet regime continued to control the partisans' actions and subject them to intense scrutiny. This development was propelled by three critical factors: new faith in the survivability of the Soviet state after the successful counteroffensive before Moscow, the addition of Red Army stragglers to the partisan ranks, and the effects of German occupation policies on popular attitudes. According to official wartime figures, there were almost 70,000 accounted partisans as of June 1942. By August, that number had grown to 93,000, and by the beginning of February 1943, it had risen to over 120,000.[96] This growth gave the movement enormous military and political potential even as it subverted the regime's attempts to keep the resistance limited to those deemed to be politically reliable.

The success of the Soviet winter counteroffensive launched in December 1941 played a vital role in the rebirth of the partisan resistance. For the first time in the war, the Wehrmacht suffered a striking defeat and lost its aura of invincibility. In some areas, German troops were thrown back over a hundred miles. The turning back of the German blitzkrieg at the gates of Moscow inspired many citizens to fight, seeing that the enemy could be defeated. Even Stalin's defiant speeches of 6 and 7 November, distributed via leaflet, appear to have struck a popular chord. Partisans noted that the number of peasants joining or providing support for their units increased as news of the Red Army's success spread.[97] In Smolensk, the number of partisans tripled in January and February after the Red Army's victory, and Belorussia and the Briansk region also had substantial gains.[98] Of course, it is impossible to know the extent to which this new willingness to resist was due to opportunism and hoping to be on the winning side and how much was due to patriotism or hatred for the invaders. Many of the new enlistees were no doubt motivated by a mix of emotions and reasons. As Christian Streit has pointed out, few citizens wished to engage in resistance until the Red Army had demonstrated by its own victories that fighting as a partisan was not "a useless act of suicide."[99] Yet the ultimate victory of the Soviet Union was hardly a foregone conclusion, with the Germans remaining hundreds of miles inside the country's borders. Indeed, the Red Army's counteroffensive continued into March 1942 at Stalin's insistence, wearing down Soviet forces and leaving them ill prepared for campaigning in 1942. And, of course, some joined the partisan effort simply out of a spirit of adventure and for a chance to live the good life in the forest, as will be discussed in the following chapters. In any case, the success of the Red Army provided new faith in the regime's viability and was essential to the expansion of resistance behind enemy lines.

A critical part of this expansion came from Red Army *okruzhentsy* (stragglers cut off behind enemy lines in the great encirclement battles of 1941) and escaped prisoners of war (POWs), who joined already existing formations or organized their own bands. These soldiers provided the numbers, discipline, and military experience needed to hold the partisan ranks together and to transform the movement into a more effective military force. By the summer of 1942, okruzhentsy and former POWs comprised between one-third and two-thirds of all partisans in the most active regions.[100]

What compelled these men to continue fighting as partisans, especially when millions had capitulated and when the magnitude of the initial defeats seemed so overwhelming? Sheer survival was perhaps the most important motivation. The Wehrmacht treated its Soviet prisoners of war brutally. Only the most minimal effort was made to provide POWs with food, shelter, and medical care, and they were subjected to indiscriminate beatings and shootings. Of the 5.7 million Soviet prisoners of war, it is estimated that between 2.8 and 3.7 million died while in German captivity.[101] Information about conditions in the camps soon spread to the masses of cut-off soldiers hiding in the villages and woods through the testimony of civilian witnesses and escapees. They also soon learned that the Germans often shot armed and unarmed okruzhentsy wandering around the countryside as suspected or even *potential* partisans.[102] Consequently, Red Army soldiers sought refuge in the forests, where they banded together in small groups.[103] Still others fought to avenge the deaths of comrades, because of ethnonational or even Soviet patriotism, or because they felt duty-bound to support their comrades at the front.[104] In some cases, whole units transformed themselves into partisans when their positions were overrun. But whatever the reason, the taking up of arms by an okruzhenets, especially in 1941 and early 1942, was a tremendous act of faith, since without communications, he had no idea where the front was or whether the Red Army was still fighting, while German propaganda trumpeted, quite plausibly, that Moscow had already fallen.[105]

These okruzhentsy brought a new skill and determination to the resistance. Although they may not have been trained in partisan tactics, they at least knew how to handle a rifle and conduct basic military operations. Partisan memoirist Petr Vershigora contended that escaped POWs were the

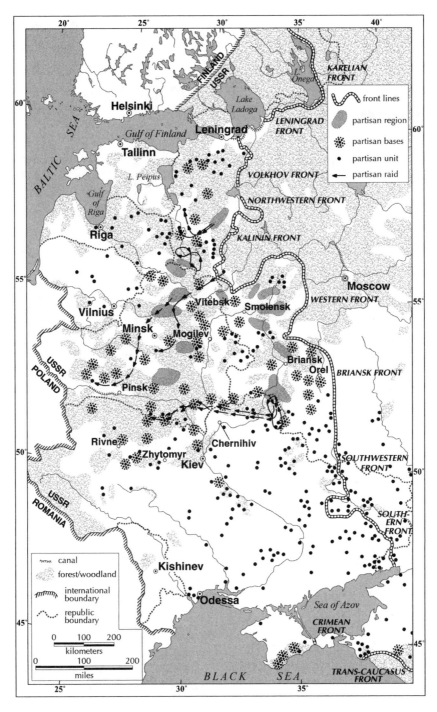

Disposition of partisan operations and bases, summer–fall 1942. (Credit: Dick Gilbreath)

"backbone" of many detachments precisely because they knew from personal experience what the German occupiers were all about.[106] Another partisan related to Soviet officials that former prisoners of war "will fight like lions. They fight not from fear, but for the Soviets."[107]

The most important factor for the subsequent transformation and growth of the partisan movement was the change in popular perceptions of the Germans. Most peasants, adhering to the belief that the war had little to do with them (*moia khata s kraiu*), hoped that the fighting would pass them by.[108] Attitudes toward the Germans varied throughout the occupied territories, but many certainly hoped that Germans would free them from one of the most hated aspects of the Soviet regime, the collective farms. Other initial actions taken by the Germans, such as the opening of churches, also had the potential to win them popular support. However, the basic ideological and economic premise of Barbarossa, rooted in notions of racial supremacy and ruthless exploitation, meant that the occupation regime was inevitably cruel. The Wehrmacht had planned to live off of the conquered lands, thereby consciously condemning hundreds of thousands of civilians to starvation.[109] Far from dismantling the collective farms, as most Soviets had hoped, the occupiers transformed them, according to Karel Berkhoff, into institutions of "full-blown serfdom," and corporal punishment and even arbitrary executions were used to enforce a rigid and cruel discipline.[110] Thus, one underground Party organizer in Mogilev later reported that after the Germans arrived, the peasants spoke of their dissatisfaction with the collective farms, making it very difficult for the partisans to defend the collective farm system. However, "after several months of management by the Germans, the fundamental mass of peasants became convinced and turned against them."[111]

Civilian dissatisfaction was further exacerbated by the harsh occupation regime. Strict curfews, restricted travel, tough labor discipline, and eventually compulsory mobilization for work in Germany alienated the population still more. The barbaric treatment of Red Army POWs in public horrified civilians, especially since many witnesses' own loved ones were also Red Army soldiers. Some civilians were even shot for feeding wandering okruzhentsy.[112] The genocide of the Jews also shocked their Slavic neighbors, who, even if they sometimes were complicit in these murders, nevertheless realized that any regime that could openly commit such atrocities would have little regard for other groups in the conquered population; this was indicated in a Ukrainian ditty: "The Germans have come-*gut* / For the Jews-*kaput* / For the Gypsies-*tozhe* [also] / For the Ukrainians-*pozhe* [later]."[113] Even the opening of churches failed to win over the public, for a shortage of priests, cold, hunger, travel restrictions, popular indifference, and estrangement from the clergy combined to limit attendance.[114]

German counterinsurgency tactics, which emphasized brute force over winning hearts and minds, increased the alienation of the occupied population. To cite just one example, when partisans engaged German troops in the Ukrainian village of Baranivka in the fall of 1941, the Germans shot more than ten hostages and burned almost the entire village in what historian Truman Anderson has described as a "very restrained reprisal" when compared to standard Ostheer (Eastern Army) practices.[115] As early as December 1941, a German intelligence officer with the 16th Panzer Division recognized that although Soviet citizens had been willing to support the Germans, the unit's occupation policies—including the troops' contempt for the local population, the cruel and indiscriminate measures employed to fight the partisans and their supposed supporters, and, worst of all, the murder of Ukrainian victims along with Jews—were leading to an increasing anti-German sentiment.[116]

The more vicious German reprisals became, the more the peasantry turned to the partisans as their only viable alternative. An underground district Party secretary in Smolensk Oblast described the way in which German policies were a political boon to the Soviet regime:

> The same thing happened in Siberia during the Civil War years. The peasants only understood Kolchak [a leader of the White forces during the Civil War] when they had been through it themselves, when they had experience of this Kolchak. Here it is the same thing. And now when the fascists reveal themselves and what they represent to the peasants, when the peasants now have before them the ways of the Bolsheviks or the ways of the fascists, Stalin and Hitler, they say "No, Stalin is right." With whom could they compare Stalin and the Bolsheviks? With no one, because they did not know anyone else. And now everywhere this became known . . . Thus the peasants can, even if primitively, unmask the face of the fascists and immediately turn from them, and go over reliably and firmly to the side of Soviet power.[117]

Or as a joke circulating Ukraine in 1942 put it, "What was Stalin unable to achieve in twenty years [that] Hitler achieved within one year? That we started to like Soviet rule."[118]

For those not swayed by German atrocities to support the Soviet cause, the partisans employed pressure and intimidation. Native officials working with the Germans, such as village elders, faced assassination if they refused to help the partisans.[119] Other forms of intimidation were also used. One partisan, for instance, told a village that it must form a self-defense group; otherwise, it would be designated counterrevolutionary. "If we do not atone for our guilt," she told the assembled villagers, "then we will swim in our own blood."[120] Even as late as 1943, partisans burned down villages that allegedly opposed them, as occurred in the villages of Make and Akhrome in Kalinin Oblast, although such acts were far less common than those perpetrated by the Germans.[121] Partisan demands on the peasants "criminalized passivity" and placed even supporters of the regime in a terrible bind. As one Soviet citizen caught in this twilight world despairingly put it:

> We live between the hammer and the anvil. Today we are forced to obey the partisans or they will kill us, tomorrow we will be killed by the Germans for obeying them. The nights belong to the partisans, but during the days we are in no-man's land. Oh, I know the partisans can protect us now, but for how long?[122]

Such sentiments suggested increased support, if not sympathy, for the partisans, but it was a support determined more often by necessity than by love for the regime in whose name the partisans fought.

THE CONVERGENCE OF PUBLIC IMAGE
AND OFFICIAL POLICY

It is important to remember that whether they joined the partisans out of patriotism, hatred of the Germans, direct or indirect Soviet pressure, or simply a desire to live, these new civilian and Red Army partisans did not match the regime's narrow demographic profile for the proper partisan. The expansion in the winter of 1941 and spring of 1942 rendered moot the 18 July instructions to limit participation to the politically reliable. The partisans now constituted a veritable movement with a growing popular base, which would only increase as the war went on. Over the course of 1942, the Soviet leaders, most importantly Stalin, addressed how the regime was going to accommodate itself to this new fact on the ground even while they remained deeply suspicious about the partisans' reliability and susceptibility to partizanshchina. This reappraisal of the regime's position toward partisans and partisan warfare was given added urgency by the growing crisis of 1942 as the Germans advanced to the banks of the Volga and the Caucasus Mountains. Of course, the regime had very little control over who would take up arms against the occupiers, but its policies regarding mass participation were critical to the way in which it now defined the movement and what the partisans' mission was in the overall Soviet military and political strategy. Nor was it by any means inevitable, given its legitimate fears over partizanshchina, that the government would embrace or even accept the partisan movement as a genuine, all-people's force. For that to happen, changes in state control and doctrine would have to occur.

The tension between the exclusionary policy and the growing popularity of the movement was evident by the war's first winter. An NKVD report on the partisan movement in Moscow Oblast, issued in late November 1941, criticized local commanders for rejecting collective farmers who attempted to enlist in the partisan bands. According to the report, these commanders did not want to take into consideration this profound political moment, and instead of leading and supporting the popular movement, they continued to remain on the sidelines. Yet official ambivalence toward mass participation was also expressed in this same document, as the commanders were still instructed to inspect all who wished to join and accept only the "best parts of the local population, [those] dedicated to our Rodina to the end."[123]

By January 1942, there were signs that the government was reevaluating its position about giving support to a mass partisan movement. At that time, a serialized story appeared in *Krasnaia zvezda*, alluding to the deficiencies of the exclusionary policy. Entitled "A Russian Story" (*Russkaia povest'*), it told the tale of a partisan detachment whose commander, Sukhov, was portrayed as a coward and a do-nothing. Sukhov's main concern seems to be keeping people out of the detachment. As he tells another partisan, "We had such a rule. We only took those in the detachment whom we personally knew. We were afraid of treason." Sukhov is opposed by Ovcharanko, a wounded okruzhenets who argues that all who want to resist should be allowed to join the partisans. After realizing that his partisans are against him, Sukhov runs away to the Germans after wounding Ovcharanko a second time. However, he gets his just deserts when the Red Army man craftily informs the Germans that the cowardly—and now treacherous—commander is really a partisan spy, and Sukhov is ignominiously executed by his own masters.[124]

If *Russkaia povest'* indeed reflected changing official thinking about the partisan war, then it is interesting for several reasons. First, it revealed that Party-recruited detachments had enforced restrictions limiting membership in their units, implying that Communists really did not trust the ordinary people. Second, it showed that not all partisans fought heroically and that

many did nothing at all to hinder the Germans. Third, it portrayed an okruzhenets as a heroic resister at a time when most partisans recruited by the
Party believed that okruzhentsy were spies and defeatists and when okruzhentsy were almost never publicly identified as partisans. Finally, in the death
of Sukhov and the triumph of Ovcharanko, it indicated that the resistance
had to become a mass movement, opened to all who wanted to fight the occupiers. Thus, the story gave new emphasis to the importance of mass participation and possibly suggested to those aware of the regime's actual exclusionary policy that a change might be needed.

A serialized story in a newspaper was one thing, but actually changing
policy was another. The publication of *Russkaia povest'* hinted at the future
direction of the guerrilla resistance. However, no evidence of policy changes
became apparent until later that summer. More effective ways of controlling
the partisans would have to be instituted first, since without the institutional
controls, state authorities relied only on Party affiliation to ensure political
loyalty.

Because of competition and confusion among the Party, the NKVD, and
the Red Army, all of whom had some jurisdiction over segments of the partisan movement, Stalin had concluded by December 1941 that a special agency
was needed to provide centralized control.[125] In late May 1942, the Central
Staff of the Partisan Movement, under the leadership of Belorussian First Secretary Panteleimon Kondrat'evich Ponomarenko, was established to oversee
the partisans' military and political activities. The Central Staff gave Moscow
a far more powerful instrument to both direct and control the partisans than
did the earlier reliance on Party affiliation and past service to the regime.

The appointment of Ponomarenko to head the Central Staff significantly
shaped the expansion of the movement. In many ways, he was typical of the
Soviet bureaucrats who rose to power in the interwar period. The son of
Ukrainian peasants, a participant in the Civil War, and a Party member since
1925, Ponomarenko was trained as a transport engineer in the 1930s and had
risen rapidly in the Party apparatus as a protégé of G. M. Malenkov's, becoming Belorussian first secretary in 1938.[126] Quite similar to his rival Nikita
Khrushchev in temperament (he was apparently jovial and personable but
could be ruthless as well),[127] he was sensitized by his Party background to the
potential political significance of the partisan movement. Supporters such as
his deputy at the Central Staff, NKVD-NKGB General S. S. Bel'chenko, were
impressed by his "thorough education, brilliant memory, inexhaustible capacity for work, wide range of interests, ability to listen to others, and to get
quickly to the heart of a question."[128] His detractors, including former par-

P. K. Ponomarenko (seated center), chief of staff of the Central Staff of the Partisan Movement, in conversation with Belorussian partisans in Moscow, 1942. (Credit: RGAKFD)

tisan instructor and NKVD official Colonel I. G. Starinov, contended that Ponomarenko was a dilettante who understood little of the practicalities and intricacies of partisan military operations.[129] It is true that Ponomarenko lacked a real understanding of the military and logistical aspects of partisan warfare, which at times significantly affected operations. However, he grasped, perhaps better than anyone in the Stalinist leadership, that the partisan war was not only a military struggle but also a political one. It was his vision more than anyone else's that would transform the official objectives and priorities of the partisan movement.

At the beginning of the war, Ponomarenko had already initiated plans for a partisan insurgency in Belorussia, preempting the directive of 29 June, and he soon established a training center in Gomel'.[130] In contrast to the 18 July directives, he firmly believed that the partisan war should be transformed into a genuine mass struggle.[131] This position was expressed not only in a July 1941 essay he wrote in *Pravda* but, more revealingly, in his reports to Stalin. Throughout 1941, he claimed that the state-sponsored insurgency was actually becoming a true mass movement, and he reported to Stalin instances of peasants spontaneously taking up arms against the Germans, stressing their loyalty to and identification with the regime and its institutions, including the collective farms. He observed that German atrocities were helping the partisans win support and recruits from the local population, and he urged Stalin to make use of this potential by establishing more training centers to teach prospective partisans the art of sabotage.[132] In keeping with his populist sentiments, his military naïveté, and perhaps a desire to churn out as many "trained" partisans as possible, Ponomarenko believed that only ten days were needed to train a partisan. This position horrified experienced instructors, who contended that the experiences of the 1930s demonstrated that three to six months of intensive training was required.[133]

With Ponomarenko's ascent to the leadership of the Central Staff, Stalin seemed to support his vision implicitly. Ponomarenko's new position also gave him authority to argue for an expanded partisan war, which he did in a memorandum he sent to Stalin, Beria, and Malenkov in July 1942. He observed that over the spring and summer, the partisan movement had enjoyed a "stormy growth," especially in Belorussia and Ukraine. Many peasants, including whole families, had gone to the partisans, and he repeated his contention, first asserted the previous summer, that the resistance was increasingly becoming a mass movement, capable of effectively disrupting the German rear area. Now, however, there was more credibility to Ponomarenko's claims. Although the newly established partisan chief, like other Soviet leaders, remained concerned about manifestations of partizanshchina, he nevertheless argued that with the proper safeguards, a mass partisan movement could be controlled.[134] Ponomarenko then prepared a draft order for Stalin's signature, sanctioning mass participation for and greater state support of the partisan movement. Stalin evidently still distrusted the idea of a mass participatory movement, for the draft order remained unsigned.

The steadily worsening military situation as the summer of 1942 rolled on certainly provided incentive to broaden the partisan war as the country fell into greater peril. After decisively defeating a Soviet spring offensive near Kharkiv, Army Group South launched its summer blitzkrieg in late June. Finally capturing the Crimean naval city of Sevastopol and sweeping through Ukraine and southern Russia, elements of the army group reached Stalingrad by late August and pushed into the northern Caucasus. The nation was seized with a sense of desperation and emergency. It was in this period that Stalin issued his infamous Order 227 (Not a Step Back!), forbidding unauthorized retreats and allowing the use of deadly force by officers and NKVD "blocking battalions" to prevent soldiers from fleeing the battlefield. To many citizens following the news reports, it seemed as if the war might indeed be lost.[135]

Even state agencies were seized with panic. Beginning in mid-July, state radio broadcasts to the partisan units and the occupied territories took on an increasingly urgent tone, switching from declaring imminent liberation by the Red Army (a holdover from the optimistic mood initiated by the Moscow counteroffensive) to appealing to the partisans to "help the warriors of the Red Army as only you can." These calls were followed on 1 August by an even more desperate appeal: "The brutal enemy is breaking into the vital, important center of the country . . . Your holy duty is to help the Red Army even more in its heroic struggle."[136]

A second impetus came from the partisans themselves. At the end of August, the government convened a conference that was chaired by Ponomarenko and attended by fifteen commanders, commissars, and underground Party officials.[137] Out of this conference, which was marked by relatively free and candid discussions, came a new state directive that indicated the extent to which Moscow's views toward partisan warfare had changed.

The conference touched on a variety of issues concerning the insurgency, including questions of supply and institutional jurisdictions—as well as the matter of mass participation. Ponomarenko's opening remarks revealed the tension that persisted in Moscow's views toward the partisans. According to Ponomarenko, the partisans were clearly loved by all Soviet citizens and had formed a true popular movement that arose "from the people, from the very deepest masses." But because of its mass character, he said, the movement required "complete leadership" from the Party to guarantee its reliability and effectiveness.[138] Thus, Ponomarenko simultaneously affirmed the movement's popular foundations and the need for the Soviet state—and, more precisely, the Party—to control it. This construction indicates the contradictory concerns of even supporters such as Ponomarenko to capitalize on the movement's mass enthusiasm while continuing to suspect the masses' capacity for reliable independent action. Now, however, conditions forced the regime to call on the people's initiative for its own strategic and political ends.

The partisans agreed with Ponomarenko's assessment of their growing popular base. S. A. Kovpak, a leading Ukrainian commander, claimed that he had such good relationships with the peasants in his area that "there have been many instances when the peasants themselves gave their livestock to us. They come at night and say, 'Take my cow, please; the Germans will take it all the same, and I would like to know that you will be able to eat.' There have been mass manifestations of this, tens of examples." Another commander reported that the local population joined his detachment in droves: by August 1942, his unit numbered 650 partisans.[139]

The partisans also recognized the interrelationship between popular support and military success in guerrilla warfare. The commander of the 1st Voroshilov Partisan Detachment, G. F. Pokrovskii, stated: "[When] the population is certain that the Red Army exists, that the German rear burns, that we are the bosses there and not the Germans, we will use our sympathy with the population, and we will add to our knowledge of where the [enemy] staffs are located and attack them where they do not expect to be attacked. And an unexpected action always gives positive results."[140] This and similar comments indicated the partisan leaders' awareness that the war in the rear area was both a military and a political conflict, which necessitated the total involvement of the Soviet population.[141]

After the conference, on the night of 1 September, Stalin hosted a reception for the partisans at the Kremlin. As Voroshilov told the assembled partisans, "[although] Comrade Stalin has a lot of work," he "does not neglect [the partisan war] and would like to talk with you."[142] The conversation lasted for several hours, possibly because, as one partisan commander later complained, some "said in a half an hour what could have been said in ten minutes."[143] According to witnesses, the *vozhd* (leader) was interested in all aspects of the movement, including how the partisans lived, what they ate, what equipment they needed, and especially the nature of the relationship between the civilian population and the Germans.[144] One partisan said he told the gathering: "You must have stronger ties with the people. This guarantees your success. It is necessary to include as many Soviet people in the struggle with the occupiers as possible. The partisan movement will become one of the decisive conditions of victory over the enemy."[145] This linking of mass popular participation with victory essentially constituted a reversal of the 18 July 1941 directive. The call for mass participation was no longer to be merely a propaganda ploy; it would be a key element in Soviet military and political strategy behind enemy lines. Stalin made clear what his expectations were for this mass movement. M. F. Shmyrev, the commander of a large and well-known Belorussian partisan brigade, reported to a Soviet historical commission a few days after the meeting that "[Stalin] viewed partisan work as exceptionally serious. He believed that if the partisan movement could be directed in strength, then it was possible to explode the German front, that it was possible to help the Red Army by destroying German communications, upon which the Germans depended for the movement of their military and food supplies."[146] When another partisan asked him about the possibility of the Allies opening a second front in the near future, Stalin—who had only weeks earlier been informed by Winston Churchill that the promised "second front" would not be opened by the Allies in 1942—replied, "The second front is a regular joke . . . You must open the second front, the partisans, the people, and we will help."[147] This statement, uttered at a time when the country was fighting for its very existence, revealed just how desperate the Soviet situation was.

The August conference and Stalin's Kremlin reception were the culmination of the center's reevaluation of partisan doctrine. Any analysis of Stalin's thoughts on this matter must, of course, be speculative, but it seems apparent that by September 1942, he had changed his mind about the nature and purpose of the partisan war, although the reasons for this change are not entirely understood. It is probable that Ponomarenko's influence on this point was crucial. The military professionals in the Central Staff disagreed with Ponomarenko's approach to partisan warfare, but they also supported the broadening of the insurgency and the clarification of the partisans' mission to concentrate on communications lines and critical infrastructure.[148] The creation of the Central Staff, with its relatively rigorous command-and-control mechanisms, must have eased his fears regarding the state's ability to oversee the partisans. Anything that could hinder the German advance or divert forces from the main battle theaters would be helpful, even at the risk of promoting the arming of tens and hundreds of thousands of citizens beyond his immediate control. Perhaps he could accept these measures only after meeting some of the principal partisan leaders to get their measure and appraise their trustworthiness for himself. In addition, although it may be coincidental, it was precisely at this time, in the midst of the unfolding of the Stalingrad battle, that Stalin began to heed the advice of military professionals rather than relying on his own intuition or the amateurish opinions of cronies such as L. Z. Mekhlis and V. M. Molotov.[149] Ponomarenko's understanding of partisan operations may have been tinged with amateurism, as Starinov contended, but nevertheless, his call to expand the insurgency and emphasize its political importance recognized the critical ways in which the movement could contribute to the war effort.

NKO ORDER 189:
"ON THE TASKS OF THE PARTISAN MOVEMENT"

In the middle of these discussions, Stalin directed Ponomarenko to draft an order detailing the partisan movement's new objectives and modes of operation.[150] The high-level discussions over the summer, reinforced by those at the Kremlin reception, fundamentally reoriented the partisan war and the mechanics of its administration. The actual order, People's Commissariat of Defense (NKO) Order 189, "On the Tasks of the Partisan Movement," directed the resistance in a much more explicitly political direction than had previously been the case. In fact, this order, for the first time, really put "the people" into the regime's formula all-people's war and gave state sanction and support to a mass-based movement.[151]

Following Stalin's expressed sentiments at the Kremlin reception, the order stated that the destruction of the Germans could only be carried out by simultaneous blows by the Red Army at the front and the partisans in the rear. As the order pointed out, this combination of strikes from both directions had its precedents in Russian history, first against Napoleon in 1812 and later against the Whites in the Civil War. However, the partisan insurgency had, to that point, not lived up to this potential: "The partisan movement still has not developed completely, it still has not become the cause of each and everyone who finds himself in the clutches of the German predators. All the conditions are at hand for the general, rapid development of an all-people's partisan struggle against the German occupiers."[152] Left unsaid in this declaration was that up to that time, official policy had been to exclude the common people from the partisans' ranks and, in fact, to discourage the formation of an all-people's movement. Nor was it mentioned, of course, that the regime's unpopularity may have contributed to the earlier apathy.

To fulfill their military potential, the partisans were still to attack German infrastructure (communications lines, railroads, highways, bridges, warehouses, depots, airfields, and so forth), disrupt German administrative organs, prevent the seizure of grain either by distributing it to the local population or by destroying it, assassinate German officials and Soviet collaborators in German service, and provide intelligence for the Red Army. They were also ordered to conduct political and agitation work with the local population to "unmask" German lies about the war and the Soviet Union and to publicize Soviet victories. To meet these political objectives, partisan units were to publish and distribute newspapers, leaflets, and other printed material.[153] These general activities were quite similar to those listed in 1941, although the 1942 instructions were much more detailed, indicating the center's growing appreciation and knowledge of partisan warfare, especially regarding the interdiction of German supply lines.[154]

What was perhaps most significant was the call to expand the movement itself, which had both military and political implications. Stalin ordered: "It is essential, first of all, for the partisan movement to become an all-people's [movement] so that the partisan movement develops still more broadly and deeply, and so that the partisan struggle embraces the broadest masses of the Soviet people on the occupied territory."[155] This all-people's movement was "to draw into the partisan struggle increasingly the broad elements of the population" to reinforce existing detachments, create new units, and provide for partisan reserves. Every city, town, village, and population point was to participate in the struggle, and the "hidden partisan reserves should not be limited, but should include in them all honorable male and female citizens, desiring to be liberated from the German yoke."[156]

Although Soviet historians have claimed that NKO Order 189 was essentially an extension of the 18 July instructions, made more concrete for the changed situation, the difference between the two directives was quite substantial.[157] First, the expansion of the movement's size meant a greater Soviet presence throughout the occupied territories and hence a broader threat to the enemy. It also meant the creation of more-powerful units, capable of conducting larger attacks and operations. Though not necessarily constituting a second front, the expanded partisan forces would require the Germans to draw more strength from the front to combat the insurgency, and it would increase the threat to their supply lines and their ability to pacify their rear areas.

Second, in contrast to the 18 July instructions, the explicit sanctioning of a mass partisan movement in NKO Order 189 meant that the success of the resistance would be defined, in part, by its inclusion of all elements of the Soviet population in its ranks. All Soviets would now be encouraged to participate in this national struggle and thereby align themselves with the Soviet state. More than ever, Soviet authorities defined the war in the occupied territories as a war of national liberation, and they hoped to use the size and vitality of the partisan movement as a measure of the state's popular legitimacy, regardless of the reason why citizens actually joined the effort.

These sentiments were articulated in the central press in the weeks and months following the order's promulgation. On 29 September, *Krasnaia zvezda* claimed in a page one editorial, using language strikingly similar to the order itself, that the emergence of an "all-people's movement" was inevitable considering "the very character of the war we are conducting: a patriotic, just, liberating war." This struggle against foreign occupiers was

the cause of each and all who found himself in the clutches of the brutal fascist predators. Wherever there is now a Soviet person—at the front, in the rear, or in occupied territory—he has only one goal in life, before him stands only one task: to defend his *rodina*, to destroy the hated German invaders. All honorable Soviet men and women, desiring to be liberated from the German yoke, these are the partisans' reserves. Constantly drawing on the new strength from the broadest elements of the population, the partisan movement will grow all the more, will even more quickly erode the German military machine.[158]

An editorial on 14 November in *Pravda* also called on the partisans to fulfill the demands of NKO Order 189:

Fan the flames of the all-people's movement! This order of the great Stalin signifies the transfer of the partisan movement to a new, higher level. This means that the detachments must draw all the more broad elements of the population into the partisan struggle.[159]

Although these editorials repeated themes present from the first days of the war, the underlying message indicated Moscow's changed policies and goals. Their strident tone acknowledged the partisans' earlier isolation from the people and the need to correct that problem. The ostensible goal seemed to be the expansion of military activities, but the urgency placed on incorporating the "broad masses" revealed additional priorities. By joining the partisans, citizens would publicly demonstrate their unity in hatred of the Germans and their love for the rodina. In so doing, they would prove the Soviet Union and its system had mass support. It was now the partisans' main task to facilitate this popular participation. Propaganda and policy, on one side, and image and reality, on the other, were finally converging.

THE PEOPLE AND THE ALL-PEOPLE'S WAR:
A DEMOGRAPHIC ANALYSIS

An analysis of the sociological composition of the partisan war indicates the extent to which the regime's goals of expanding popular participation were achieved. Of course, it is impossible to evaluate what direct effect, if any, NKO Order 189 had on the demographics of the partisan movement. Nonetheless, it is evident that the movement became more representative of the broader population in the occupied territories as the war continued.

Much of the data examined below is derived from personnel lists composed by the partisans, as well as additional records gathered by officials at the Central Staff of the Partisan Movement. These records are far from perfect, often lacking uniformity and clarity and portraying the unit at only one moment in its history, yet they contain a remarkable amount of information and provide some of the most reliable and detailed records to date on the social composition of individual partisan detachments.[160]

The composition of the Soviet partisan forces changed dramatically over time. Numerical shifts in the movement were affected significantly by citizens' perceptions about the course of the war, particularly the victories at Moscow in December 1941, at Stalingrad in early 1943, and at Kursk in the summer of that year, all of which led to dramatic expansions of the movement over the course of several months. In June 1942, the number of partisans registered by the Central Staff was 69,705. Six months later, 102,562 partisans were registered, and by June 1943, the number had jumped to 138,889. By the beginning of 1944, the Central Staff accounted for over 181,000 partisans, despite the liberation of almost all of the Russian Republic and substantial portions of Ukraine and eastern Belorussia.[161] Indeed, partisans noted that military victories often led to new recruits joining the detachments.[162] Local events were also decisive in persuading Soviet citizens that resistance was not only a realistic alternative but also the only possible course of action. German occupation policies—including the massive food requisitions, the forced recruitment of labor to Germany (the Ostarbeiter program, which conscripted Soviets to work in Germany), and atrocities against the civilian population—convinced many that resistance offered the only chance for survival.[163] The ability of local detachments to endure and inflict losses on the Germans also served to motivate others to join the partisans.[164] In addition, the onset of warmer weather seems to have facilitated growth in the movement, as living in the open air became feasible.

Geography played a crucial role in the distribution of partisan forces. The heaviest concentration was located in the densely forested and swampy regions of Belorussia, particularly in the eastern sections of the republic, which had greater popular support for the partisans. The forested areas of the Russian Republic, notably Leningrad, Smolensk, and Kalinin Oblasts, as well as the Briansk forest region of Orel Oblast, were also key locations of partisan activity. The predominantly open-steppe terrain of Ukraine partially inhibited the development of the movement in that republic. Thus, in December 1942, 49.1 percent of all partisans were in Belorussia, 39.4 percent in Russia, and 8.7 percent in Ukraine, with the other republics constituting the remaining 2.8 percent.[165] These percentages give only a snapshot of what was a dynamic phenomenon, but they do illustrate the general distribution of the insurgents in the occupied territories.

As noted earlier, politically affiliated citizens initially comprised a high proportion of the partisans in 1941 and 1942. The expansion of the movement, combined with losses suffered by Communists due to combat, disease, and desertion, significantly reduced their percentage in the movement.[166] Stricter admissions requirements in the occupied territories largely prevented the Party from expanding its ranks during the war.[167] For the whole wartime period, full and candidate Party members made up 13.6 percent of the partisans in Ukraine, between 6 percent and 8.9 percent in Belorussia, and approximately 12 percent in Russia.[168] More partisans were affiliated with the Communist Youth League, the Komsomol, which was less exclusive and reflected the significant numbers of partisans in their midtwenties or younger. In Leningrad, from November 1942 to April 1943, Komsomols accounted for between 13 percent and 33 percent all partisans, whereas in Ukraine and Belorussia, they amounted to approximately 20 percent.[169] In general, the percentage of politically affiliated partisans in a given unit, including those in either the Party (full and candidate members) or the Komsomol combined, ranged between 25 percent and 40 percent.[170]

Red Army personnel maintained a significant presence in the partisan movement, although, like their Party counterparts, their numerical and proportional status in the movement changed over time. Overall, Soviet figures indicate that for the entire war, Red Army partisans comprised over 18 percent of the forces in Leningrad, 10 percent in Orel, 22 percent in Lithuania, and 11 percent in Belorussia.[171] Former Red Army soldiers predominated in the leadership ranks of the movement. In Leningrad Oblast, 62 percent of detachment and brigade commanders were former servicemen; in Belorussia, they made up 42 percent of unit commanders, 27.5 percent of commissars, and almost 45 percent of the chiefs of staff, thus providing needed military experience to the predominantly civilian forces.[172]

These statistics present only a static and therefore misleading picture of the politically and militarily affiliated partisans, however, since actual percentages declined from their highs of 1941 and 1942 due to attrition and the massive influx of civilian recruits in 1943.[173] For example, in March 1942, in the 1st and 2nd Battalions of the "Batia" Complex combined, Red Army okruzhentsy accounted for 66.8 percent of the partisans.[174] Just six months later, the percentage of former soldiers in the complex dropped to 22.9 percent.[175] By the summer of 1943, commanders reported that the growth of their detachments depended on Soviet redefectors from German auxiliary units rather than on Red Army servicemen, as had previously been the case.[176]

Politically affiliated and Red Army personnel continued to dominate the movement politically and socially. Numerically, however, politically unaffiliated civilians comprised the majority of the movement, especially in 1943 and 1944 as the fortunes of war swung decisively in the Soviets' favor after the victories at Stalingrad and Kursk and as authorities pressured the partisans to expand the movement.[177] Because of poor record-keeping practices and the idiosyncrasies of Soviet class and social origin classifications, it is difficult to get a precise picture of the civilian social composition of the partisans. According to Soviet secondary sources, peasants generally comprised roughly between 40 percent and 60 percent of all civilian partisans, whereas manual and office workers accounted for one-third each.[178] But these categories tell us little, for a manual worker might be a mechanic on a collective farm whereas an office worker might be the farm's accountant, with little in his or her social or educational background to distinguish this recruit from other peasant comrades. What is clear, however, is that as the war continued, civilians increasingly filled the partisans' ranks. Figures from two Leningrad brigades in the 1943–1944 winter give some indication of the nature of these demographic changes. In the 3rd Leningrad Partisan Brigade, of 2,760 partisans indicated in November 1943, fully two-thirds were civilians from the local population, and only 41 (1.5 percent) were Red Army okruzhentsy, although only seven months earlier, 388 (26.8 percent) of the brigade's partisans hailed from the Red Army.[179] Also revealing are the figures recorded by the 5th Leningrad Partisan Brigade for the period from August 1943 to January 1944. Of 400 partisans who joined the brigade during this time, 267 (66.8 percent) were from the local population, including 178 peasants, 42 students, 33 workers, and 14 white-collar workers. Of the remaining 133 partisans, 120 were escaped prisoners of war and 13 were former collaborators in German service.[180] The expansion of the partisan movement during the later stages of the war thus stemmed from a mass influx of ordinary Soviet citizens, fulfilling the demands set out in NKO Order 189.

Not surprisingly, most partisans also tended to be young and male. A sample of ten detachments taken from units operating in northern Ukraine, eastern Belorussia, and the Orel, Smolensk, and Leningrad regions between March 1942 and September 1943 indicates that the percentage of partisans thirty years old or younger hovered between 69 percent and 80 percent.[181] In Russia and Belorussia overall, fully 94.5 percent were under forty-five years of age, with 49 percent being twenty-five or younger.[182] These numbers help explain the relatively large percentage of partisans who were Komsomols. The younger demographic also gave the movement a certain spirit, especially when appeals were made to the daredevilry of saboteurs and scouts. More negatively, the youth of the partisans no doubt contributed to the disciplinary problems and propensity for marauding that plagued the movement, giving credence to the government's concerns about partizanshchina infecting the detachments.

Men composed the overwhelming majority of partisans. Initially, there were relatively few women in the movement; in fact, women probably accounted for no more than 5 percent of all partisans and in some areas even less.[183] Women were usually not actively recruited in the beginning of the war, as both men and women believed that family responsibilities and customary notions that women should not take up arms prohibited them from fighting. Commanders often forbade women from joining detachments, especially if they were unarmed, arguing that they lacked military training and that the units did not have enough supplies to waste on them.[184]

As the war continued, however, the percentage of women partisans increased. The greater female participation was due, in large part, to pressure exerted by Soviet authorities, determined to fulfill the expectations of NKO Order 189. Soviet archival sources indicate that by the beginning of 1944, women comprised 9.3 percent of the partisan forces.[185] This figure, however, hides important regional and unit differences: in Ukraine, where mobility was a defining feature of partisan operations, women accounted for 6.1 percent of the partisans, whereas in Belorussia, where more units operated out of fixed bases, they made up 16 percent of the movement.[186]

Within units, gender composition also varied widely. In some, women might account for only 2 percent of all partisans,[187] especially in Red Army–dominated bands where the prevailing military culture frowned on women combatants. In other units, the percentage of women might be over 10 percent.[188] Most women were younger than twenty-five years old, which was not surprising given that older women were more likely burdened by family responsibilities and thus less free to go to the forest. They might also have been generally less attractive to the sexually driven male partisans who had the power to admit them into the unit.[189] Although women shared many of the same motivations as men for becoming partisans, they typically were more likely to be affiliated with the Party or Komsomol, thus suggesting that they were more politically motivated to fight than most of their male counterparts.[190]

As the Soviet Union was a multinational state, NKO Order 189 had significant implications for Soviet nationality policy toward the partisan movement and the occupied territories. As in other demographic categories, levels of participation by nationality varied by time and place. Nationalities in their home republics usually predominated in the units located there. Thus, for example, in the 1st Voroshilov Partisan Detachment, a Red Army unit fighting in the Briansk forest, 83 percent of the detachment identified themselves as Russian, 8 percent as Ukrainian, 2 percent as Belorussian, and the remaining 7 percent as members of other groups including Georgians, Uzbeks, and Tadzhiks, all of whom were former Red Army personnel.[191] Similarly, in the 3rd and 7th Leningrad Partisan Brigades in January 1944, 92.2 percent and 93 percent, respectively, of the partisans were Russian.[192]

National composition was more varied in Ukraine and Belorussia, where the presence of a significant number of Russian civilians and large numbers of Russian okruzhentsy meant that a larger percentage of "foreigners" participated in these national partisan movements. In Belorussia, Belorussians accounted for 72 percent of the partisans, with Russians making up 19 percent, Ukrainians 5 percent, and "others" 4 percent.[193] Partisan units in eastern Belorussia seem to have followed a similar pattern.[194] In the recently annexed regions of Belorussia, more Ukrainians, Jews, and Poles were present, reflecting these borderlands' diverse ethnic mix.[195] For example, in the Pinsk Partisan Complex, Belorussians comprised only 58 percent of the total, compared to 20 percent Russians, 9 percent Ukrainians, and 13 percent "others," most of whom were Jews and Poles.[196]

Ukrainian units were similarly diverse. Most Ukrainian bands were destroyed or disbanded in 1941, and Ukrainians in the recently annexed western regions of Galicia and Volhynia showed little enthusiasm for fighting for their new Soviet brethren.[197] Thus, in 1942 and 1943, the "Ukrainian" partisan movement depended on a large immigration of units located in Russia. For example, S. A. Kovpak's and A. N. Saburov's detachments were identified as Ukrainian by state officials, despite the fact that in 1942 they recruited most of their partisans in Russia's Briansk forest.[198] Often regarded as the quintessential Ukrainian partisan unit, Kovpak's complex (officially designated the 1st Ukrainian Partisan Division in January 1944)) was composed of 40 percent Russian, 35.5 percent Ukrainian, 16.5 percent Belorussian, 4 percent Jewish, and 4 percent other nationalities when it disbanded in October 1944.[199] Saburov's complex contained even fewer Ukrainians.[200] By contrast, in some units, such as I. F. Fedorov's detachment, Ukrainians comprised over 80 percent of the unit's strength even as early as June 1942.[201] Overall, according to Ponomarenko, Ukrainians totaled only 59 percent of the partisans in the re-

public. Russians comprised the next largest group with 22.2 percent, followed
by Belorussians with 6.6 percent. Other unnamed nationalities accounted for
the remaining 12.2 percent.[202] But again, this is a static picture. As John Armstrong has noted, though the partisans remained to some degree an ethnically
as well as a "socially alien element" in Ukraine, the movement in that republic became Ukrainian as more civilians joined in 1943.[203] And Soviet authorities attempted to strengthen the supposedly Ukrainian identity of the partisan
movement, regardless of the actual partisans' ethnonational origins.

For much of the war, the bulk of the Belorussian and Ukrainian partisan forces were located in the eastern regions, in the areas within the Soviet
Union's 1939 borders. The Polish and Ukrainian populations of the formerly
Polish regions were generally hostile to the Soviet annexation, and the Belorussians in these lands did not exhibit much more enthusiasm for their new
masters. Thus, as late as January 1944, the Central Staff reported that in
Belorussia's eastern oblasts, there were approximately 80,000 Soviet partisans and less than half that number in the recently annexed districts.[204] As for
the Volhynian and Galician districts, only the importation of bands from the
eastern Ukrainian regions in daring "partisan raids" enabled the Soviets to
acquire a foothold there.[205]

Although the partisan movement was overwhelmingly Slavic in its national composition, almost every nationality in the Soviet Union was represented in its ranks. For some groups, their inclusion was a conscious effort
on the part of Soviet authorities to implement NKO Order 189, but for others, it was simply the result of chance and circumstance. The 1st Voroshilov
Partisan Detachment, for example, included twenty-eight nationalities, including Georgians, Ossetians, Uzbeks, and Kazakhs.[206] These partisans were
almost always male okruzhentsy who, unable to blend in with the local population, had little choice but to join a partisan band. They were usually isolated
in the movement, but some rose to positions of prominence in individual units
due to their military rank or experience.[207]

Jews composed the largest of the non-Slavic national groups. Relatively
few Jews joined the partisans when the window of opportunity was the wid-
est, in the summer and fall of 1941. The speed of the German advance, their
ignorance of German plans for them, and the reluctance of Jewish youth to
abandon families inhibited Jews from fleeing to the woods for protection.
Moreover, Jews saw the forest, with its large numbers of anti-Semitic armed
bands, as just as dangerous a place for them as the cities. By the time they
realized their special fate at German hands, it was too late: the ghettos had
been established, and hundreds of thousands of Jews had already been mur-

dered.[208] Those few who reached the partisan camps were often turned away if they lacked weapons or were accompanied by women, children, and the elderly, a fate that plagued other civilians regardless of ethnicity. But even though Slavic civilians faced extraordinary brutality, they were not targeted for outright murder like the Jews, who thus were compelled to seek immediate safety anywhere they could. Some managed to form family camps and combat groups. A number of these Jewish partisans, though poorly armed, survived and even inflicted revenge on Nazi and indigenous tormentors alike.[209] However, most Jews who sought survival in the woods eventually perished.[210]

But NKO Order 189 brought a change in the Jews' status. The order's broad-based inclusion of all Soviet peoples applied by default to Jews as well.[211] In some "Slavic" formations, Jews came to comprise as much as 10 percent of a unit's overall strength.[212] The Ukrainian Staff estimated that Jews made up the fifth-largest ethnic group in the Ukrainian movement, following the Russians, Ukrainians, Belorussians, and Poles.[213] Ultimately, perhaps between 20,000 and 30,000 Jews joined the partisans, although these figures are crude estimates only because many Jews continued to hide their ethnoreligious identity or were included as "others" in the "nationality" category in unit rosters.[214]

Hence, despite the fact that partisans from all nationalities of the Soviet Union could be found in the movement, thereby lending some credence to the official claim that it was indeed an all-people's movement, it was nonetheless overwhelmingly Slavic in terms of its numbers and orientation. At the same time, though the partisan movements in the occupied republics were supposedly manifestations of republican national uprisings, only in Russia and Belorussia could such a case be made according to national composition. In Ukraine, Ukrainians barely formed a majority of the partisans, and the partisan movements in the Baltic states were so tiny as to make any claims of a national uprising completely ludicrous. According to Central Staff statistics compiled in February 1944, there were 1,633 partisans in Lithuania, 812 in Latvia, and 178 in Estonia.[215] Moreover, in Latvia and Estonia, partisan forces were imported from other regions, notably Leningrad.[216]

To most Soviet leaders at the beginning of World War II, partisan warfare had several contradictory meanings. They remembered quite well their own experiences with irregulars in the Civil War, and they were certainly well aware of how Cossacks and peasants had at times used such methods to resist state authority. They even suppressed their own trained partisan force, selected from the ranks of the Party, army, and security services, in the interwar period because of fears that these partisans were really plotting against the state. Given these suspicions, Soviet authorities worried that a spontaneous mass uprising against the Germans could evolve into a mass uprising against the Soviet state as well. Yet the country was fighting for its very survival, and Stalin and other leaders claimed that the war involved and was supported by the entire nation and that all citizens had to fulfill their patriotic duty. Partisan warfare truly was one important weapon against an overwhelming yet more and more overstretched opponent.

The government's initial, instinctive response was to walk a fine line between the contradictions embodied by a state that promoted society's mass participation while deeply distrusting that very society. In other words, at the onset of the war, the regime continued its peacetime practices despite the growing national emergency. Stalin's and the Soviet media's calls for partisan warfare evoked images of a populace rising up against hated foreign invaders. In 1941 and the beginning of 1942, most ordinary citizens were unwilling or unable to resist the occupation. For the most part, this reluctance mattered little, for the state sought to keep the insurgency limited to those it deemed politically reliable, which, in the absence of effective governmental controls, was considered necessary to keep the guerrillas loyal to the Soviet cause. By following this dual approach, the state would gain propaganda points by referring to a mass movement that did not exist while facilitating the development of a loyal and obedient force that would harass the enemy. In any case, considering both the sentiments of the population at that time and the seeming omnipotence of the Germans, it is doubtful that a more genuinely inclusive promotion of partisan forces by the government would have had much effect.

The exclusionary partisan policy failed, however, to establish an effective Soviet presence in the occupied territories. The suppression of the interwar training programs and personnel meant that neither the partisans of 1941 nor the leaders of the regime were prepared to wage an insurgency. Predictably, the partisans' situation deteriorated throughout 1941 and early 1942, threatening the very existence of the resistance. Yet factors quite outside the government's control led to the growth of the insurgency on an increasingly popular basis and in ways that violated the instructions of 18 July. This growth gave Soviet authorities a potentially stronger partisan force to oppose the enemy just as the military crisis deepened in the summer of 1942. Stalin's decision to accept and encourage a genuine mass resistance movement was facilitated by the establishment of the Central Staff and by the ongoing efforts of officials such as Ponomarenko to promote it. By making the all-people's war the actual basis for Soviet policy rather than just a propaganda theme, Stalin and others in the Soviet leadership now gave more emphasis to the mass participatory element of Soviet political culture. The deep suspicion toward the population remained, of course, but the exigencies of national defense and the creation of more powerful state controls enabled the leadership to overcome its anxieties, at least for the time being. The challenge for Soviet authorities now was to control this larger but even more potentially unruly force. As for the partisans, not only did they have to deal with the suspicions of their own government, they also had to fight a ruthless and powerful enemy in a hostile environment.

2

BREAD AND BULLETS:
THE CONDITIONS OF PARTISAN
SURVIVAL

The Soviet partisans lived in a twilight world, subject to both the cruelties of Nazi occupation and the pressures from the Soviet state, whose presence was felt even across the battle lines. The partisans also remained intimately connected with the civilian population, from whom they gained food, recruits, and information. In this chapter, I will describe and analyze the material conditions that defined the partisans' physical and psychological existence. The enemy was an omnipresent threat, and the bands were always vulnerable to the occupiers' antipartisan operations. Procuring enough food, obtaining necessary clothing and shelter, and coping with the threats of wounds and disease posed daily challenges to the partisans' survival.

To overcome these difficulties, the partisans had to win the hearts and minds of the surrounding population. Yet surviving and gaining civilian support were not always complementary objectives: at times, the partisans' immediate survival, especially in terms of procuring supplies, depended on exploiting or even endangering the civilian population. Relations between partisans and local civilians therefore were critical to the success or failure of resistance in the occupied territories.

As the partisans' main purpose was to fight the enemy, their military operations also warrant discussion. On the one hand, the inexperienced partisans at first concentrated on attacking soft targets, that is, indigenous administrators and often unguarded (and insignificant) infrastructure. As the movement developed, their operations became more sophisticated and ambitious, including reconnaissance, ambushes, sabotage, and long-distance raids. At the same time, the ever-increasing numbers of civilians joining the detachments meant that the partisan forces always retained a strong element of amateurism in their ranks. How they approached combat and the particular missions they conducted shaped not only the nature and impact of the guerrilla war on the Eastern Front but also the way in which the partisans understood the war and their relation to it.

THE OCCUPATION REGIME AND
ANTIPARTISAN OPERATIONS

Despite their own propaganda—and the hopes of some Soviets that the Eastern Army (Ostheer) was an army of liberation—the Nazis intended nothing less than the wholesale subjugation of the indigenous population in the East. The occupied lands were to be exploited to the fullest under German colonization, and their inhabitants were to be subjected to exploitation, slave labor, and extermination.[1] At the beginning of the campaign, German soldiers were given a set of orders, now known collectively as the criminal orders, that empowered them to execute Communists, Red Army political officers, Jews, and other perceived enemies of the Third Reich and gave them immunity from prosecution for a host of actions that would otherwise constitute war crimes. Indigenous social and cultural institutions, with the noted exception of Christian religious institutions, were either abolished or significantly reduced. A strict internal passport system regulated movement, and individuals could be arrested as partisans or spies based on the slightest suspicion. Despite proclamations to the contrary, the collective farm system was generally maintained, and since the Ostheer was expected to live off the land, crops and livestock were confiscated even more thoroughly than under the Soviets. Most dreaded of all were the forced-labor drafts of the Ostarbeiter program, which sent workers to Germany. These drafts increased substantially in 1943 and 1944, and as in France and elsewhere, they eventually impelled many to join the partisans. These policies, together with the genocide of the Jews and the murderous treatment of POWs, reveal the unprecedented brutality of the German occupation of the Soviet lands.[2]

For all of their ambitions of establishing an Aryan lebensraum and their vaunted military might, the German armed forces were spread very thinly on the Eastern Front, even in 1941. Nowhere was this truer than in the rear areas. Initially, nine security divisions, consisting primarily of older reservists and poorly trained replacements, along with four SS Einsatzgruppen (totaling no more than 3,000 men, whose primary objective was the extermination of Communists and Jews), were assigned to the "pacification" of the conquered territories. By the end of 1941, some 110,000 men secured 850,000 square miles of occupied territory. In practical terms, this meant that a single security division guarded approximately 13,500 square miles; in the rear area of the German Ninth Army, one of the principal commands in Army Group Center, only 1,700 men were deployed for security. Although security units were sometimes supplemented by regular army troops, the latter were deployed only on a temporary basis.[3] In general, it is estimated that German rear-area security troop strength from 1942 ranged between 190,000 and 250,000 men, few of whom were capable of frontline service.[4] To bolster their strength, the Germans recruited extensively among the occupied population to form indigenous police units. By the end of 1942, native police formations, relying on disaffected national minorities and prisoners of war desperate to escape the horrendous conditions of the prison camps, had grown from 33,000 to over 300,000 men.[5] The Hungarian, Romanian, Italian, and Finnish allies also contributed forces of varying quality.[6]

The problem of insufficient and poor-quality manpower was not offset by superior firepower. Few armored vehicles, artillery, and aircraft were assigned to rear-area units, and what mobile elements they had were often dispatched to the front, where they were desperately needed.[7] In fact, by 1943, a number of partisan units were better supplied with machine guns, automatic weapons, and light field artillery than their opponents. Only rarely, usually during concentrated antipartisan operations, did the Germans deploy aircraft, tanks, and heavy artillery against the partisans.[8]

Even in the nineteenth century, the Prussian—and later German—army dealt harshly with irregular resistance, seeing it as a violation of the rules of war and as a threat to social stability and order.[9] Under the Nazis, however, the Wehrmacht knew no limits. Although a few security units at times tried to win Soviet hearts and minds using more carrots than sticks, German efforts to pacify suspected partisan-friendly territories generally involved the destruction of villages and the seizure or shooting of their inhabitants.[10] When not engaged in reprisals, the Germans employed a variety of antipartisan methods. The most prevalent was a "passive defense" based on occupying garrisons and strong points located in key cities, towns, and villages and across vital communications routes. This method was adopted more because of the weakness of the occupying forces than out of strategic design. Although guerrilla activity was inhibited in areas where garrisons were present, these passive measures generally were not very successful. Garrisons were often weak, with troops suffering from poor morale, weak discipline, and boredom. Some even arranged truces with local partisan units and occasionally warned them when a major action was about to begin.[11]

Active measures designed to turn the partisan hunters into the hunted were potentially more effective, but these efforts often became nothing more than vicious reprisals against civilians, for the elusive partisans often escaped.[12] As noted earlier, such operations in 1941 were essentially facades for the mass murder of Jews. By mid-1942, however, as the partisan insurgency grew stronger, antiguerrilla operations became more serious, requiring the development of more sophisticated methods necessary to destroy real threats. Sometimes, the Germans employed small patrols in hopes of catching their quarry on the move. Occasionally, they used stealth and subterfuge: in western Belorussia, an indigenous auxiliary unit, wearing Soviet uniforms, attacked a partisan camp and destroyed two detachments.[13]

For the partisans, the most feared type of attack was the massive sweep, involving thousands of men and heavy weapons (including artillery, tanks, and aircraft, often pulled from the front) in an effort to eliminate massive partisan concentrations. These operations usually occurred before major actions at the front, such as those aimed at the Briansk forest region in May and June 1943 before the Kursk offensive or in Belorussia during the spring of 1944 before the Red Army's Operation Bagration.

Sweeps usually began with a blockade to prevent the partisans from escaping and to cut them off from their supply sources. The attackers then advanced either together toward a central point or in a ring formation with one part of the ring remaining stationary while the others advanced, pushing the partisans against the blocking units and thereby, in theory, annihilating them. Simultaneously, the advancing forces destroyed the partisans' supply sources by burning down peasant villages, while German air cover and the seizure of airfields made resupply from the mainland almost impossible. Theoretically, a sweep would completely eradicate the partisans, as they could neither flee from it nor defend against it. In practice, however, these operations rarely succeeded because the areas targeted were too large for the number of troops at hand and because the defenders often escaped the closing ring through gaps in the lines. Even if an area was "cleansed," the Germans lacked the manpower to prevent the partisans from returning.[14]

Defending against sweeps severely tested the partisans. Some regions were fortified with barbed wire, strong points, and minefields, but the partisans lacked the manpower and heavy weapons to defend them adequately against determined attackers. The defensive perimeter of the Briansk forest region, for example, was about 370 miles. Although the normal frontage held by a Red Army rifle division of approximately 7,000 men was a little over seven miles, the 600 partisans of the 2nd Voroshilov Partisan Brigade were responsible for nearly seventeen miles of the perimeter; the neighboring 1st Voroshilov, with approximately 500 men, guarded seven miles.[15] Given these frontages, partisans usually defended the primary approaches of attack. As the enemy advanced, the partisans fought back by setting up ambushes, launching flanking attacks, and, if need be, deploying into smaller groups to evade the tightening net. If these tactics failed, they would attempt a break-out, which was difficult to achieve because it usually required the cooperation and coordination of many units and was complicated by such factors as un-reliable interunit (and intraunit) communication, lack of training, uncertain morale, and the fierce independence of many formations.[16]

The pressure of the sweeps could deeply strain relations between units. In September and October 1942, the Germans launched a major sweep in the Smolensk region against the "Batia," Grishin, and Sadchikov partisan units. According to the "Batia" commissar, F. N. Muromtsev, Grishin's men ran away, leaving the "Batia" Complex to bear the brunt of the assault. As the fighting continued, the Grishin and Sadchikov bands refused to help "Batia's" men. Muromtsev was so incensed by their inactivity that in a report to the Kalinin Staff of the Partisan Movement, he termed the Grishin regiment's flight "desertion" and stated that the Sadchikov detachment, "a true organi-zation of deserters, besmirched the flag of the partisans."[17] Over twenty years later, he still was arguing about these events with N. I. Moskvin, a commissar in Grishin's regiment, who took umbrage at Muromtsev's accusations of de-sertion and treachery. He countered that "Batia's" partisans fought poorly and that Muromstev himself was "nervous" and "disoriented."[18]

Even if they were generally ineffective, extended blockades and large-scale attacks demoralized and devastated the partisans and civilians caught inside. Partisan commissar E. N. Prokhorenko wrote in his diary after six days of blockade in the fall of 1942, "One's head spins, one feels a great weak-ness, and one is still further plagued by illness. In these days the eczema on my hand has spread to the other side. Young and healthy people endure the hunger more easily."[19] Another commissar, A. F. Kniazev of the 1st Voroshilov, reported that during the blockade of the Briansk forest region in May and June 1943, he and his men lived on berries and mushrooms and that "people swelled from hunger." In such conditions, partisans lived on grasses, swamp plants, nettles, and between three and five ounces of flour a day.[20]

The pressures only intensified when the sweeps commenced. Letters from partisans intercepted by state security forces recorded the numbing demoral-ization generated by these attacks. One partisan, speaking for many, wrote, "I describe our partisan fate. Now we are not very well in the Briansk forest, the Germans squeezed us. Food became difficult. How I wish to unite with the Red Army."[21] Desertions increased substantially, and many of those who survived went deep into the forest to avoid further fighting.[22] As one partisan in A. F. Fedorov's complex noted in his diary during a German assault: "On the soil of sickness, exhaustion, amongst several fighters and commanders of the detachments began an unhealthy mood. 'Little detachments are better, it's possible to hide, there always will be provisions of food. Let's go.' It cost Fedorov a great effort to overcome such unhealthy moods, but they were not completely liquidated. Subsequently, several people, weak in spirit, shrinking from difficulties, ran away."[23] These were not idle fears. After twenty days of sustained attack, a Belorussian brigade commanded by M. F. Biriulin broke into small groups, which the Germans then annihilated.[24] The 2nd Voroshilov Partisan Brigade lost well over a third of its strength, including its commander, I. S. Gudzenko, and his commissar, Oleinikov, during the May–June 1943 expedition against the Briansk forest. Overall, out of a strength of over 14,000 partisans, the Briansk forest partisans lost some 841 killed in action, 128 drowned, 697 wounded, 2,480 missing, and 30 captured—a casualty rate of 29.5 percent.[25]

Antipartisan operations were marked by exceptional brutality, intensified by the Nazi racialist ideology of conquest and subjugation. Captured partisans were often tortured during interrogation and then customarily executed. People suspected of aiding them could expect a similar fate. Villages were destroyed along with their grain stores and livestock, and their inhabitants might be driven off, taken for slave labor, or shot. Barbarous as these policies were, they were singularly ineffective in quelling the resistance. On the contrary, they fueled its growth, for no matter how vicious the partisans might be, their attacks were far more selective than the Germans' indiscriminate reprisals.[26]

Regardless of how destructive sweeps were in a given area, partisan forces almost always reemerged. Most units survived the attacks in some form, and the Germans could never keep sufficient troops in place to secure an area for any length of time. And all too often, the methods employed to reduce partisan activity had the opposite effect because surviving peasants joined the partisans to avenge their families and friends and because they increasingly saw that the Germans left them no alternative if they themselves wanted to stay alive.

German counterinsurgency efforts failed to destroy the movement; in fact, their very brutality facilitated its growth. Yet the partisans remained highly vulnerable and even under ordinary conditions lived with omnipresent

Public execution of three partisans in the village of Toropets, near Velikie Luki. (Credit: USHMM, courtesy of Ralf Rossmeissl)

threat. The constant uncertainty and fear took a psychological toll, as even the most cheerful of individuals realized how dangerous their situation was. Ina Konstantinova wrote her sister, "Ours is the usual partisan existence. Before going to sleep, you put grenades under your head and your rifle beside you; then on waking up you're not sure whether you'll retain your head on your shoulders. But I'm confident I'll keep mine. Do you agree?" She was killed in action in March 1944.[27]

The partisans never forgot that one lost battle could be their very last. After 1942, Red Army soldiers rarely faced mass encirclement; for the partisans, it defined their existence.

THEIR DAILY BREAD:
EVERYDAY CONDITIONS OF PARTISAN LIFE

In addition to combat, the problems involved in procuring sufficient food, clothing, medical equipment, weapons, and ammunition were immediate concerns. These material needs strained the partisans' resources and ingenuity and further illuminated just how isolated and precarious their lives were. Ponomarenko, following Stalin's wishes, made it clear that the partisans were not to expect to be supplied from the mainland but rather should acquire their provisions and weapons from the enemy. To be sure, it would have been difficult if not impossible for the Soviet rear area to meet and transport the required supplies to the occupied territories. However, Stalin and Ponomarenko firmly believed, on principle, that the partisans should obtain their own supplies. Ponomarenko wrote about this to all subordinate partisan staffs in August 1942: "Only inactive detachments will experience needs, but it is hardly expedient that the center should supply such detachments. It is forbidden to accustom detachments to demand and receive supplies only from the center, and to encourage this carelessness."[28] Although the center did send some arms and specialized equipment, especially radio gear, medical supplies, and materials for sabotage, Moscow's basic philosophy regarding logistics remained consistent throughout the war.

Thus, obtaining regular and sufficient provisions on a regular basis was perhaps the partisans' most mundane yet daunting task, particularly as the size of units expanded from tens of fighters into the hundreds and even thousands. Almost all food, with the exception of occasional luxury items, was procured from the surrounding countryside, which, by the summer of 1942, had been largely denuded by harsh German requisitions, the Soviets' own scorched-earth policy, a decline in the sowing of arable land, and a fall in the laboring population.[29] Malnutrition and starvation in the occupied territories were common, and necessities such as salt were frequently impossible to secure.[30] Indeed, when parts of Ukraine and central Russia were liberated in 1943, the people there were engulfed in famine.[31]

The partisans ultimately ate better than much of the civilian population, sometimes enjoying luxury goods flown in from the mainland, such as tea, vodka, sugar, and tobacco (usually consumed only on special occasions).[32] Yet they hardly lived high on the hog. Rations varied from unit to unit and depended on such factors as location, season, and the military situation, but on average, partisans received approximately one and a half pounds of bread a day, supplemented by potatoes, mushrooms, and other vegetables and sometimes meat. This was somewhat less than the standard ration for Red Army soldiers of nearly two pounds of bread and two hot meals per day.[33] In times of shortage, such as during a German blockade, the bread ration could fall to only seven ounces—or less—per day, or the partisans would have to rely on *sukhari* (rusks) and whatever edible grasses, vegetation, and berries they could scrounge. Poor nutrition contributed to the rise of scurvy and other diseases. Stomach disorders, brought on from eating grasses and nettles, were frequent.[34] The monotonous consumption of bread or sukhari lowered morale. Even important regional officials, among them A. P. Gorshkov, who commanded over 10,000 partisans in the Briansk forest, were sometimes not adequately provisioned. Gorshkov told Soviet historians, "If once a year you and I had black rusks, of course we'd eat with relish, but when every day they give you black rusks, then any appetite you had for it disappears."[35] In the most extreme situations, such as those endured in the Crimea in the 1942–1943 winter, partisans engaged in cannibalism or starved to death.[36]

Clothing, too, was a primary concern, especially in such a poverty-stricken environment as the Soviet countryside, where conditions only worsened because of the occupation. Partisans were outfitted in a hodgepodge of styles, including Soviet and enemy uniforms taken from the captured and dead and civilian dress, which both contributed to their romantic aura and revealed the scarcity of suitable clothing. Ina Konstantinova wrote home to her mother, "And how handsome our Daddy is, Mom! . . . He is now wearing German riding breeches, a field shirt with crimson collar tabs, a leather double-breasted jacket and an officer's cloak."[37] Adequate winter gear was especially lacking, often obtainable only from the mainland,[38] but given Moscow's philosophy and its limited ability to supply the partisans, such support was insufficient. In October 1942, for example, Ponomarenko requested from the State Defense Committee only 5,000 sets of winter clothing per month, for use by command personnel and for cases of extreme need, at a time when the movement numbered some 115,000 partisans.[39] Leather boots and especially *valenki* (felt boots) were prized possessions, and partisans sometimes wore *lapti*, the sandals made from birch bark.[40] Predictably, in January 1943, Smolensk officials reported that almost 70 percent of the partisans in their jurisdiction had only their summer clothes, a "situation that cannot but affect military work and the morale-political mood."[41] Women partisans particularly suffered from the lack of appropriate clothing and undergarments, for which Moscow was often the only supply source.[42]

Housing conditions were also generally rough, to put it mildly. After the disastrous 1941–1942 winter, surviving units established bases in the forests and swamps. There, the partisans slept under the stars in the summer or built *zemlianki* (dugouts) that protected them from both the elements and the enemy. They were often so well camouflaged that occupation troops sometimes did not see them until they were literally on top of them.[43] Partisans in quiet sectors even lived in villages, taking to the woods only when an attack was imminent. Larger and better-organized formations, operating from fixed bases, had special buildings or dugouts that served as workshops, cooking and bathing facilities, and clubs, but smaller and more mobile units had no such accommodations.[44]

Although propagandists and partisans represented the people's avengers as masters of their environment, whom nature itself consciously favored over the invaders, the reality was that Mother Nature showed them little regard. One partisan wrote home, "Mama, if I remain alive, then it's because I had to live in the forest until the end of the war like a forest beast."[45] Partisans living in the swamps and forests suffered in the summer from heat and dehydration caused by the lack of fresh water. They also endured incessant assaults—not from the Germans but from mosquitoes, who attacked every exposed piece of skin. Partisan commander N. Z. Koliada told newspaper correspondents, "There are very many mosquitoes, this is simply our scourge," further noting that waiting in ambush was a torture because the partisans had to remain still while the mosquitoes ravaged them.[46] One band in the Briansk forest was even forced to abandon its camp because of constant insect attacks, retreating to a village where it would be destroyed by the Germans.[47] Winter brought its own miseries. Preparation of dugouts and efforts to secure provisions for winter began in late summer and early fall, but escape from the constant cold and snow was next to impossible, particularly if the partisans were forced to move from their prepared bases and could not secure other shelter. Beyond that,

tracks in the snow and cooking fires threatened to give their camps away to
the enemy. Little relief from physical hardship could be found in spring or fall
either, when the rains and melting snows brought the *rasputitsa*, the en-
gulfing mud that covered everything and everyone, making travel and maintaining hygiene almost Herculean tasks.[48]

Movement through the forests and swamps even in ordinary conditions
was difficult enough. A correspondent for *Krasnaia zvezda* recorded his impressions of moving through the swampland of a typical partisan environment:

> Oh, the swamps, the swamps! I will not forget them for a long time.
> There were swamps with hummocks and cranberries, spongy swamps
> covered with moss, like a sponge—here it was still possible to walk. But
> there are wretched swamps, which on a map appear to be quite passable.
> When you arrive at such a swamp, it quivers and sways under you like
> a step. After two or three steps—holes. They call them "windows." A
> ten-meter pole could not reach the bottom of these "windows."[49]

Another partisan exclaimed after the war, "I swore to myself that if I survived
I would live a thousand kilometers from a swamp. I couldn't bear it any-
more."[50] Maintaining good health in such conditions was extremely difficult. Some claimed that the forest air was good for them, but partisans were
nevertheless afflicted by innumerable ailments, including stomach disorders,
skin and dental problems, and life-threatening diseases such as typhus, ma-
laria, tuberculosis, and scurvy. Because medical personnel and supplies were
so scarce, one commander recommended that "falling ill simply wasn't advised."[51] More typical was the experience of the diary writer who recorded
that he went "from disease to disease."[52] Not only individuals but also whole
units were often affected. Commander S. A. Kovpak reported in August 1942
that of his 1,300 men, over 500 had scurvy, and in the early spring of 1943, so
many members of the Diat'kovo Partisan Brigade in Orel were ill with stomach disorders due to attempts to supplement their dwindling food supply that
the commander forbade the addition of flowers, leaves, nettles, and grass to
the cutlets and bread they consumed. In the midst of this, the brigade also
suffered 168 cases of typhus out of a total complement of 1,089.[53]

Wounds, whether suffered in combat or from the numerous accidents
that occurred among people unaccustomed to handling weapons, were the
most dreaded of all. Such fears are common to all soldiers, but they took
on terrible significance behind enemy lines. One partisan told Soviet historians, "For us to be wounded was the same as being murdered: no airfield,

Partisans make their way through a typical swamp. (Credit: Minaeva Collection)

nothing . . . There were many doctors in the detachment, but there were few medical supplies."[54] A doctor in a Baranovichi partisan unit recorded that "the most terrible thing for fighters was not that they could be killed, but that they wouldn't be finished off when they were wounded."[55]

They had good reason to be afraid. In the so-called partisan regions, such as in the Briansk forest, relatively extensive medical services were established, but in other areas, the few available doctors had to conduct rounds, traveling from unit to unit. In Minsk Oblast's Molotov Brigade, medical care was supplied by a veterinarian and untrained young women who learned their nursing skills on the job.[56] Partisans in Rivne were so desperate for medical personnel that they recruited their doctor from Vinnytsia, hundreds of miles away.[57] Although some medical equipment was sent from the mainland, most supplies were acquired from local resources.[58] Surgical operations, often conducted without anesthesia or suitable disinfectants, were performed in the most unsanitary conditions, including in huts where livestock was housed. One partisan recalled having to hold down the legs of an unfortunate patient while a doctor performed an abdominal operation without anesthesia.[59] Patients who survived such procedures were exposed to infections, frequently necessitating amputations.[60] Only the will to live, one doctor believed, enabled so many wounded to survive.[61] If a unit was forced to evade the enemy, its wounded might be left behind, with only a nurse for care and a few weapons for protection.[62] As air transport was established with the mainland, some wounded were airlifted to safety, but evacuations remained few compared to the total number of wounded, and the air link was vulnerable to German interdiction, weather, the availability of aircraft, and the security of the airfields.[63]

Naturally, concerns over food, clothing, shelter, and health care directly affected partisan morale. Severely deprived partisans complained bitterly about their lot and questioned the purpose of the partisan war and even the ultimate victory of the Soviet Union. Partisans in the Molotov Brigade, depressed by the long 1942–1943 winter and the successful German counterattacks after the Soviet counteroffensive at Stalingrad petered out, "became fed up with this way of life. How could we not long to be free, to live like regular people, like human beings? Hadn't we had enough suffering, enough exhausting, sleepless nights?"[64] A fighter in the Briansk forest was overheard to say in the fall of 1942, "To the devil with this food, soup without salt, no bread, and they make us fight. To hell with such a war"; another exclaimed, "The partisans become thin from hunger in the forest, we cannot get bread, the Germans occupy all the villages. We never will know if we will get to the Rodina."[65] In the Kursk region, the onset of cold weather in October 1942 brought on this comment: "How will we live barefoot, naked? We have come to the forest to sit for such a long time, they talk about the successes of the Red Army, but there is no success, the Red Army has not come. I came to you in the detachment and stagnated. It would have been better to stay at home."[66]

These comments reflect the common hardships, frustrations, and fears of living behind enemy lines. Yet though the deprivations were extreme, such conditions were not entirely alien to a population that had endured hunger and other material shortages in the preceding decades. Indeed, difficulties in obtaining sufficient, not to say varied, food, clothes, housing, transportation, and medical attention were standard features of Soviet life in the 1930s, and familiarity with these conditions may have helped the partisans survive their current troubles, although the archival record does not note utterances to this effect.[67] These deprivations, in the context of the partisan war, also brought to the fore two critical issues. First, the scarcities added to the partisans' sense of vulnerability and danger, since they could not always be assured of meeting their most basic survival needs. If extreme circumstances continued for an extended time, unit morale could suffer significantly, even leading to the unit's dissolution. Second, because their daily necessities were procured from their immediate surroundings, the acquisition of goods fundamentally affected the partisans' relations with the local civilians.

"ORGANIZED LOOTING": PROCUREMENT OPERATIONS AND CIVILIAN-PARTISAN RELATIONS

Supplying smaller units (fewer than fifty people) in the movement's formative period posed relatively few problems. However, as the size of units grew into the hundreds and thousands, procurement became a substantial challenge. The onus of supplying the partisans thus fell on local civilians. In the best of times, the population was not wealthy. And after twenty-five years of war, revolution, civil war, famine, collectivization, more famine, and more war, it had little left to give. Consequently, the growth of the partisan forces added to the strain on local peasants. Scorched-earth policies implemented by the partisans to prevent German grain procurements further increased peasant misery, not to mention resentment against those they held responsible. Only in 1943, as the tide of war turned against the Germans and as the Red Army anticipated regaining the occupied territories, did the partisans attempt to defend the peasants' crops, as the Germans intensified *their* agricultural procurements and engaged in their own scorched-earth policies. The population, caught between the rapacious demands of the Germans and the partisans, faced starvation. The extent to which peasants gave up their food voluntarily varied from place to place. Some seemed to have willingly supplied provisions because they had close ties with the unit, especially if the latter was from their own locality, and they were aiding family and friends. Peasants were often most unwilling to give provisions to "foreigners," that is, to units that had been organized in and deployed from the mainland or that originated from other districts.[68]

Many units organized special procurement subunits, whose primary responsibility was to bring in food.[69] Some claimed that they procured their meat and bread almost exclusively from the Germans and collaborators, but most simply requisitioned whatever they needed from the surrounding population or, as one veteran termed it, engaged in "organized looting."[70] Political officers often led procurement expeditions, since negotiating with locals for food was viewed as a political task, but the partisans always went well armed because they could not be sure how they would be received.[71]

Yet behind even peaceful negotiations was the ever-present threat that the partisans might simply take what they wanted and kill anyone who stood in their way. Partisans appeared in villages and requested goods, while advising the peasants, "If you give to the Germans, it will go badly for you."[72] Sometimes, whole units entered villages firing their weapons and demanding supplies.[73] If intimidation failed to work, then they might take what they wanted by force. A typical report from Sumy Oblast in 1943 complained that partisans, led by a Party member, pillaged a loyal village and even took goods belonging to the wives of the underground Communists and Red Army soldiers.[74] In the most extreme (though by no means uncommon) cases, village elders who refused to aid the partisans were executed for collaboration with the enemy.[75] Other units tried more subtle approaches, including trickery: one unit dressed in German uniforms and demanded goods from the local population, claiming that they were needed to fight the partisans.[76] Such behaviors led some army officers and Party officials to regard the partisans as nothing more than bandits and ruffians.[77] Indeed, partisans tried to counteract these depictions and convince local civilians "that the partisans were not bandits, but the people's avengers." In an effort to apply a veneer of legality to the process, procurement squads sometimes even gave the peasants a receipt for what they took, which they hoped would lend credibility to *their* claims that they were the legal representatives of Soviet power.[78] Some desperate commanders threatened to kill partisans, including officers, who plundered from civilians.[79] Similar problems existed in other European resistance movements, as partisans often crossed the thin and not always clear line between guerrilla and bandit.[80] In the Soviet context, however, requisitions had added meaning. For many peasants and partisans alike, the overt or implied use of force to seize grain or other provisions in the name of the Soviet state surely reminded them of the Civil War and collectivization and revealed the underlying fissures still dividing the state and its agents from the rural population. For some peasants, the fact that procurement operations were often led by commissars who were former district Party officials only reinforced the idea that the partisans were also an occupying power.

The ongoing need for food and other provisions also led to conflicts among the partisans themselves. To reduce friction between detachments in areas where multiple units operated, partisan staff or local Party officials sometimes established sectors to supply each unit. Procurement squads did not always respect these boundaries, however, often seizing provisions whenever and wherever they could.[81] As one procurement officer declared, despite the existence of such rules, "in truth, every detachment took what it wanted."[82] In such an environment, violence was common. An internal memorandum from the "Batia" Complex in March 1942 reported that in one village, "a pointless exchange of shots" between its own subunits resulted in the wounding of several partisans.[83]

Supplying the needs of thousands of economically unproductive people had disastrous consequences on local resources, already strained by German procurement programs. Partisan implementation of Stalin's scorched-earth policy beginning in the summer of 1941 further worsened the peasants' situation. Partisans destroyed telegraph and telephone poles, public buildings, farm machinery, stables, and even peasant huts and villages, acts that hardly endeared the "people's avengers" to the peasants, since the latter's very existence was threatened, especially in the cruel winter months. Peasants occasionally resisted the partisans, as occurred in one village in the Krasnodar region. Partisans attempted to destroy a mill, but they were thwarted when the local peasantry rose up to defend it, for they had no other place to grind their grain.[84] Partisans were also ordered to destroy all produce and leave only a few acres of arable land unscathed for the peasants' own use.[85] Of course, it was physically impossible to fulfill this task, both because the partisans lacked the capability and because they and the peasants needed more food in order to survive. Nevertheless, in 1942 and 1943, the partisans destroyed 10 percent of all grain and 20 percent of all meat produced in the occupied territories at a time when production had fallen from the already low levels of the 1930s, further dashing German expectations that the occupied East could become the Reich's breadbasket.[86]

The consequences of these policies and the partisans' own procurement requirements on the local population were immense and terrible. In July 1943, the commander of the 208th Partisan Regiment, located in Mogilev Oblast, petitioned Soviet authorities to move his unit west because the eastern oblasts, which for two years had served as the "food and material base for many partisan detachments," had been depleted of their resources. He acknowledged that the peasants underwent "considerable suffering," for the partisans were "forced" to take their last remaining provisions and clothes.[87] In one Leningrad district, the combination of too many partisans and an impoverished population, according to a Party official, resulted in numerous partisans "dying from starvation." What happened to the local civilians was not reported.[88] In January 1943, D. M. Popov, the first secretary of the Smolensk Obkom, notified Ponomarenko that the material base of the civilians and partisans had so deteriorated that some detachments had lost up to a third of their strength because the units could not be supported.[89] Seven months later, another Smolensk partisan official reported that food supplies in the oblast were so depleted that the population was reduced to eating grasses and roots to survive.[90]

Ponomarenko was quite sensitive to the political, if not the humanitarian, consequences of procurement. Though he constantly urged partisans to rely on their own and local resources rather than the state's, he also criticized those he believed took too much from the surrounding population. When D. V. Emliutin, the commander of the United Partisan Detachments of the Briansk Forest (Ob'edinennye partizanskie otriady Brianskikh lesov, or OPO), told Ponomarenko and others at the August 1942 Moscow conference that his units had collected over 14,000 puds of grain,[91] as well as thousands of cattle to support his 10,000 partisans and additional civilians, Ponomarenko wondered how the commander had obtained so many cows. Emliutin unconvincingly replied that they had been taken from the police and from civilians who opposed Soviet power. After further questioning, he indicated that perhaps he had expropriated cattle from friendly peasants but asserted that only the "communal cattle" had been taken. Ponomarenko was still displeased that Emliutin had confiscated so many cattle beyond his immediate needs:

> Someone goes to you and he even takes a cow. This is a serious affair. This can determine the mood of the peasants. They remain and you leave and even take their cows. Then he goes to the [German] police detachment, in order somehow to regain his cow. The peasant discusses this: until the last minute he had hoped to keep his cow. He is angry with those who took it first. And this is the point. He, of course, thinks that the Germans would take it, but he hopes that somehow he might keep it, and here comes Emliutin and takes it.[92]

Emliutin's zealous requisitioning practices, Ponomarenko indicated, weakened the partisans' political support among the population. Rather than being the people's avengers, the partisans took on the guise of the people's bandits, thus giving credence to German claims that the partisans were nothing but brigands and robbers.[93]

By the summer of 1942, Ponomarenko realized that the destruction of crops was alienating the peasants. On 15 August 1942, he informed Stalin that "in our opinion, the slogan of annihilating the harvest is impossible, the peasantry don't like it . . . The partisans fall into a disadvantageous situation, since for their supplies they rely on local peasant resources."[94] Stalin's reaction to Ponomarenko's recommendation is not known, but it seems that this policy remained unchanged.

After the promulgation of the all-people's war doctrine in September 1942 and, later, with the anticipation of liberation after the victory at Stalingrad, peasant attitudes increasingly became a matter of state concern. In February 1943, Ponomarenko criticized detachments in Smolensk that had procured so many goods from civilians that the latter were completely destitute:

> During the incorrect carrying out of procurement a worsening [of relations] between the partisans and population can occur. It is the task of political officers, first of all, to see to it that the population is not offended. The population sees the partisans as its defenders, its own sons and brothers, and is prepared itself to join the detachments. Therefore, the tendency toward crime is an incorrect relationship to the population.

He then reminded officials and partisans that supplies had to be obtained from the enemy, asserting that the partisans had the military capability, weapons, and leadership necessary to provision themselves fully at the occupiers' expense.[95] Ponomarenko's concern about the political effects of partisan procurement practices indicates that he was well attuned to what issues the peasants considered when deciding to support one side or the other. His insistence that the partisans supply themselves from the enemy, however, either was a cunning attempt to displace blame from the center for failing to provide for the partisans or showed his ignorance about how the partisans were supposed to live and fight. In any case, his actual authority to prevent criminal measures was quite limited, especially since the line between official procurement and banditry was never very clear, even in peacetime when considered in the context of collectivization.[96] Certainly, the partisans had little choice but to procure goods from the civilian population, regardless of the political consequences.

After Stalingrad, as the Red Army advanced, German labor draft and food procurement efforts intensified. In a reversal of roles, now it was the Germans who attempted to stop peasants from working in the fields.[97] The Soviet press and government, too, recognized the necessity of protecting the citizens and food supplies for use after the liberation of the occupied territories. A lead article in *Pravda* in March 1943 stated that as the Germans concentrated near population points, "the sacred responsibility of the partisan is to frustrate the plans of the enemy, not to give him the chance to carry out black deeds."[98] Several weeks later, in his May Day address, Stalin ordered partisans to save "Soviet citizens from being driven into German slavery" and to avenge "the blood and tears of our wives and children, mothers and fathers, brothers and sisters."[99] Later that summer, the Central Staff ordered that every effort be made to protect civilians, as well as their harvest and livestock. The occupiers were to be denied access to grain, and German procurements were to be interrupted whenever possible by guarding the fields or by destroying German supply convoys transporting already procured grain. In areas where they were not yet firmly established, partisans were ordered to help with the harvest, take what they needed, and distribute the rest to the peasants before the Germans arrived.[100] These proclamations and measures were hardly the result of a newfound humanitarianism. Rather, they were intended to prevent the Germans from getting their hands on additional agricultural and human resources and to secure those resources for the Soviets. But lest peasants think these actions were precursors to abolishing collective farms after the war, as widespread rumors indicated, radio broadcasts to the occupied territories in 1943 assured the people that the collective farms would be reestablished on liberation.[101]

The new emphasis on saving grain and livestock gave some credence to the claims that the partisans were fighting in the people's interests, in contrast to their procurement operations, which resembled actions in the days of collectivization. Just as partisan military operations provoked German reprisals against civilians, thus undermining their claims of being the people's defenders, the partisans' procurement operations revealed deep antagonisms with local civilians. Strains in these relations were exacerbated by the preceding decades of Soviet history, especially since Communists played such a significant role in the insurgency. The maintenance of a large military force required forced provisioning from the countryside, but these requisitions in turn threatened the political mission of winning the hearts and minds of the people. Thus, many peasants believed themselves to be caught between two occupiers, the Germans and the partisans.

FIRST BLOOD: THE WAR AGAINST
THE INTERNAL ENEMY

The general military objectives of the partisan movement remained broadly consistent throughout the war and focused on one goal: to create the "unbearable conditions" for the enemy that Stalin called for in his 3 July 1941 speech. This effort included destroying the infrastructure of enemy occupation (including warehouses and supply depots), disrupting the organs of German administration, breaking communications links such as railroads and telegraph lines, and harassing hostile troops. Other missions were added or given higher priority as the partisans' capabilities strengthened and as military and political circumstances changed; they involved, among other things, providing intelligence for the Red Army, protecting Soviet human and material resources, and conducting large-scale and coordinated sabotage operations. In 1941, Soviet understanding about the nature of partisan warfare was quite limited. The lessons of the interwar period, which concentrated on how to conduct sabotage, gather intelligence, and maintain secrecy, seemed to have been forgotten or lost. The directive of 18 July placing the organization and leadership of the partisan units in the hands of local Party organs emphasized political reliability over military knowledge and experience.

Thus, in 1941, most partisan operations worked to fulfill the scorched-earth policy and to punish so-called collaborators.[102] Relations between the partisans and civilians were profoundly affected by the brutalized experiences each group had had during the preceding decades of Soviet power. At the beginning of the German invasion, the partisans believed that they operated within a hostile or at best ambivalent population. There was just cause for this perception. Many Soviet citizens, especially in the countryside, had not forgotten the hardships imposed on them by the regime in the 1930s. People in the regions annexed in 1939 and 1940 also hated the Soviet regime that had cruelly established its rule and deported hundreds of thousands of residents. Although this anger generally diminished the farther east the Germans went, the invaders still found willing helpers.[103] Partisans in Kalinin Oblast, for example, reported that inhabitants, including "a large number repressed by the organs of Soviet power," informed the Germans where their bases were located and that they were even refused aid by former Party members and Soviet activists.[104] In fact, ordinary citizens, as well as participants in local administration and the police, often gave the Germans such precise information about the names and whereabouts of the partisans (who, after all, were frequently their neighbors and relatives) that whole districts were sometimes cleansed with relatively little effort.[105] Even those who were more sympathetic to the Soviet cause or to the defense of their native land understandably and logically regarded the partisans as troublemakers whose actions would lead to German reprisals against them. One commander reported that the inhabitants of Vitebsk Oblast pleaded, "You can take our milk, you can take our bread, only please leave," and a Leningrad partisan was told by one villager, "We are German subjects—move on! We don't have any bread ourselves. Many of your sort came through here. Better that you were at the front with the Army!"[106] Another commander in the Baranovichi region reported in his unit's history that at the beginning of the war, most locals "did not believe in the victory of the Red Army and viewed the partisans as people who uselessly carried out the struggle."[107]

To state authorities and to the partisans, these views and actions were treasonous. State propagandists encouraged partisans to wipe out collaborators,[108] but given their own suspicions, hatreds, and fears, the partisans hardly needed prodding, and their campaign took on a primal urgency.[109] The partisans' interpretation of who was a collaborator could be quite broad, stemming as it did from prewar Manichean definitions of friends and enemies, which did not take into account nuances and complexities. At the beginning of the occupation, peasants working in the fields were sometimes viewed as collaborators, and some were even killed, as occurred on a state farm in Gomel' Oblast.[110] More typically, however, partisans attacked indigenous police and administrators. Although some preferred to attack only Germans and did not even "try to fight the police," as one commander claimed, this view was the exception rather than the rule. Partisans were so determined to eliminate those suspected of helping the enemy that a German report covering the period from 11 December 1941 to 23 January 1942 calculated that in the rear area of the Second Panzer Army (located in Orel Oblast), the partisans killed 33 German soldiers, 38 Russian policemen, and over 200 civil officials and civilians.[111] Partisans responsible to the Kalinin Front claimed that by July 1942, they had killed 917 traitors and 199 police.[112] Smolensk commander Koliada boasted to newspaper reporters that by July 1942, he had had shot approximately 200 people in one district alone, including "all police, village elders and burgomeisters." The executions stopped only because the partisans eventually realized that they needed to distinguish between those who were forced to serve the Germans and those who did so under their own free will.[113]

The desire to kill traitors and the traitors' kin prevailed throughout the partisans' ranks.[114] It was, in part, a continuation of the dehumanization of political opponents that had occurred with increasing ferocity since the inception of the Soviet regime itself. A partisan ditty reflected this sentiment: "Balalaika, Balalaika / No chickens, no eggs / No butter, no fat / A policeman is not a human being."[115] The war in the occupied territories was indeed a civil war in the bitterest sense of the term. Collaborators and partisans from the same family seemed to have little compunction about killing one another. Thus, in Smolensk Oblast, the sister of an émigré who had returned with the invaders told the Germans the whereabouts of her husband's detachment. The partisans shot her in retaliation.[116] In another instance, four young women who wanted to join a detachment were given a cruel but not unusual test. They were ordered to shoot three recently captured policemen, who, incidentally, were either relatives or former lovers:

Nadia and Katia Markova stood opposite [the three policemen]. One of the police, Marusia's uncle, said to Marusia, "I taught you how to hold a rifle and here you are" . . . Another policeman — the head of the police had courted Katia, also talked to her. But the girls screwed up their eyes and fired. Marusia hit her uncle in the chest, but did not kill him. He said, "give me another one, Marusia, I'm already dead." But she did not have enough spirit. Then Apretov [the detachment commander] took him and killed him.[117]

In this war of retribution, even the innocent suffered. One young partisan noted in his diary in January 1942, "We shot a traitor. Morale 'good.' In the evening I went to do the same to his wife. We are sorry that she leaves three children behind. But war is war!!! Toward traitors, any humane consideration is misplaced."[118] Those children were relatively lucky: one commissar reported that his unit annihilated not only policemen "but even their relatives up to the third generation, and even the children."[119] Another partisan wrote his wife that the NKVD should shoot the family of a traitor "because fascists have no place on our land."[120] Some even murdered the families of suspected Red Army deserters, as occurred in the village of Ivnia in Kursk Oblast in December 1941.[121]

In the murky world of the underground resistance, it was not always

clear, however, who was a collaborator. One commissar, M. T. Lukashov, recalled in his memoirs that as he was about to execute the head of a local police
unit, the latter told him that he was really a Soviet spy and provided evidence
to this effect. Lukashov was not entirely convinced, but he let the man go.[122]
Agents, too, realized how trigger-happy the partisans were. The partisan
memoirist Petr Vershigora related how a Soviet undercover agent understood
that, sooner or later, she would be killed. "I only hope that it will not be from
ours. It would be better from a German bullet," she told him.[123]

These ferocious policies added to the partisans' difficulties with civilians.
Some might have supported these killings as a sign that the Soviet people had
not been broken, as S. S. Bel'chenko, the deputy partisan chief of staff and
general in the state security services, asserted after the war.[124] Yet the friends
and relations of those killed could not be expected to support their executioners. The Germans used these killings to support their claims that the partisans
were not Russian (or Belorussian or Ukrainian) patriots but mere bandits.[125]
Soviet authorities were sensitive to the political impact of these attacks: an
article in *Krasnaia zvezda* in November 1941 accused the Germans of using
"criminal elements" as "false partisans" who attacked the civilian population. The Germans then drove these supposed false partisans away, claiming
that they were protecting the people. The newspaper proclaimed that real Soviet partisans were the "true sons of the people—workers, peasants, intelligentsia. The partisans are prepared to fight until the last drop of blood for the
great cause of freedom for the Soviet motherland."[126]

The murderous campaign against collaborators between 1941 and 1942
(which continued throughout the war but with modifications)[127] needs to be
put in the context of not only a particularly vicious war but also an ongoing
cycle of violence that had afflicted the region since World War I and continued
with the Russian Civil War and, later, collectivization. The Soviet annexation
of the eastern Polish territories and the Baltic states was also accompanied by
a wave of violent deportations that deepened the hatred of many locals and
added to their desire for revenge against the Soviets and their assumed accomplices, especially Jews. The German invasion added the Nazis' lethal
racialist ideology to this explosive mix, enabling the Germans to unleash an
unprecedented wave of mass murder that swept through the occupied territories.[128] From the war's very beginning, Germany employed the harshest
policies against suspected partisans and their families. To prevent their children from being shot and their homes burned down, wives were sometimes
forced to retrieve their husbands from partisan detachments, and the men

would then be killed. More frequently, the occupation troops simply destroyed villages suspected of aiding the partisans and slaughtered or drove away defenseless parents, children, and spouses as part of collective reprisals. Police also targeted individual family members and friends.[129] Moreover, these killings took place amid the large-scale and oft-witnessed Axis massacres of the Jews, which brutalized and terrified the inhabitants of the occupied territories even further.[130]

The partisans' killings, ruthless though they were, fulfilled important political objectives. From the partisans' perspective in 1941 and 1942, these actions were among the few "positive" measures they could undertake, since any actions against German troop formations at that time were almost pointless and potentially suicidal. The killings hindered the Germans' ability to administer and exploit the territories supposedly under their control. They also graphically demonstrated to onlookers that even though formal Soviet power was gone, the long arm of the Soviet state (to borrow John Armstrong's term) was still present.[131] This showing of the flag even in the face of enemy occupation could either stiffen Soviet resistance against the foe or demoralize and terrorize those who thought the Soviet presence had been vanquished once and for all.

Yet there was another meaning to the partisans' actions. Their desire to destroy perceived collaborators, often labeled by the prewar epithets of "spies," "kulaks," "sons of kulaks," and "enemies of the people," was especially fervent. These actions were more than just a savage response to a bleak military situation. Many partisans had clearly absorbed a Stalinist ethos, which proclaimed the existence of external and internal enemies who had to be annihilated. Unlike the enemies of the 1930s who were almost entirely falsely accused, many of the wartime enemies were undeniably real. The Stalinist claim that the Soviet Union was constantly threatened was bolstered by the appearance of collaborators, many of whom were identified as "formerly repressed people." Partisans, collaborators, apolitical opportunists, nationalist separatists, and now the Germans and their allies continued the behaviors of the Civil War and the 1930s by identifying and physically destroying their enemies or anyone else who got in their way. The partisans killed their enemies not only because they were soft targets but also because of a mentality that held all opponents had to be physically annihilated regardless of costs or consequences. This view applied to even those who were forced to serve the enemy against their will: the black-and-white Stalinist worldview was blind to the subtle shades of gray that composed the portrait of wartime reality. To the partisans, the internal and external enemies were visible and active, and the danger to the rodina was clear and present, unlike the "conspiracies" of the prewar period. The emergence of actual internal enemies and the partisans' perceived need to kill them validated the most violent aspects of Stalinism. And if nothing else, the implementation of this Stalinist mind-set further intensified the cycle of violence that helped give the Eastern Front its particular veneer of brutality and cruelty and caused so much needless suffering.

CHANGES IN MILITARY
PRIORITIES AND OPERATIONS

By the middle of 1942, more experience, greater numbers, and centralization from Moscow began to transform the partisan movement into a more effective military force.[132] Partisans gradually learned the tactics and methods of guerrilla warfare. Growing confidence on the ground and direction from the Central Staff enabled them to step up their assaults against the enemy and to hit more important targets. The development of partisan tactics and types of attacks led to a particular style of warfare that came to define the military operations of the movement. These included ambushes, attacks against enemy garrisons and installations, intelligence gathering and reconnaissance, and, as the front moved westward, combined operations with the Red Army.

Units also became more standardized and larger, enabling the partisans to undertake a variety of missions. Initially, a host of unit names and types emerged, including the detachment (*otriad*), group (*gruppa*), battalion (*batal'on*), regiment (*polk*), brigade (*brigada*), division (*divisiia*), and complex (*soedinenie*). Few units at that time numbered over 100 partisans, and most counted fewer than 50. The growth of the movement inevitably led to larger and more powerful units, often with subunits having specialized combat and support functions.

The detachment, with between 100 and 800 men and women, was the basic independent unit. Its members often came from the same locality or, in the case of okruzhentsy, from the remnants of the same military unit, thus giving each detachment its own particular culture and style. They conducted small-scale operations such as sabotage missions, ambushes, reconnaissance patrols, and attacks on administrative posts and minor garrisons, but most of these units lacked the power to hit more substantial targets on their own.

Brigades and regiments were usually composed of between four and seven detachments and numbered between 500 and 2,000 partisans.[133] The brigade became the standard unit by the fall of 1942, especially in eastern Belorussia, Leningrad, and central Russia. It was powerful enough to operate independently and attack significant targets, whereas its subunits, some based as far as ten miles away from headquarters, undertook their own independent, small-scale operations.[134]

A complex, or brigade group, usually consisted of several brigades or, more rarely, detachments. The complex emerged in late 1942 and 1943. With a few exceptions, the complex was the largest partisan formation, usually consisting of between 1,000 and 3,000 men and women. The complex was most common in Ukraine, where long-range raids, sometimes covering hundreds of miles, were the preferred method of operation. A complex's brigades were large and mobile enough to operate effectively on their own during a raid, but they could quickly concentrate or disperse, depending on the tactical situation.

Partisan command structures were based on military models and included a commander, a commissar, a chief of staff, a head of intelligence, a quartermaster, and a medical section head. Some units organized by non-Party civilians lacked commissars or intelligence chiefs and only added them when they came into contact with Soviet officials or more formally organized Soviet units. Internal organization also became more sophisticated. Subunits (platoons, groups, companies) took on specialized tasks, such as reconnaissance, sabotage, administration and supply, and medical support.[135]

Relatedly, as the war progressed, the partisans became better armed, either through procurement from the enemy or through supplies sent from the mainland (despite Ponomarenko's reluctance). Although there rarely were enough weapons to go around, weapons and ammunition supplies did become much more plentiful as enlistments steadily increased, especially in the last year of the insurgency. Partisans particularly favored grenades and automatic weapons, such as submachine guns and machine guns. These weapons best suited guerrilla-type engagements, which were based on speed and close-quarter fighting. Better-armed units had special weapons subunits equipped with heavy weapons, such as light artillery and antitank guns of various types. These developments strengthened the units considerably and enabled them to tackle a broader range of targets and missions. Indeed, by 1943, some

German security units complained that the partisans were better armed than they were.[136]

Despite the increasing size and power of the individual partisan bands, only occasionally did units operate as a single, concentrated force. Instead, one might think of the partisan camp as a base where small groups were constantly coming and going as they undertook a variety of missions and tasks, including procurement, sabotage, reconnaissance, ambushes, and other operations. Thus, in D. N. Medvedev's complex, which numbered approximately 1,500 partisans, there were rarely more than 800 or 900 people present at the camp at any one time.[137]

As the movement grew in strength, partisan regions (*partizanskii krai*) were established in areas that had been cleared of occupation forces or, more commonly, that had never been garrisoned by the occupiers. The first such region was established in September 1941 in Leningrad Oblast.[138] Other partisan zones were established in the Briansk forest; in the Kalinin, Leningrad, and Smolensk regions; and in the forested Ukrainian regions bordering the Belorussian and Russian Republics. These regions often encompassed thousands of square miles each and, in some cases, hundreds of thousands of civilians. For example, in the Briansk forest, the partisans occupied a zone roughly 105 miles wide and 43 miles deep that included over 200,000 civilians, and in Smolensk by April 1942, twenty-five administrative districts—half of the oblast's raions—were liberated in one of the four partisan regions in the area.[139] Ponomarenko and some partisans fretted that the regions encouraged passivity, thereby "emasculating the soul," as one observer put it, as their inhabitants became more concerned about defense and living a good life than about striking at the enemy.[140] The large concentrations of partisans were also a tempting target for the Germans, since a region's destruction could mean the elimination of thousands of partisans in a single operation. Consequently, the regions became the objects of numerous antipartisan blockades and sweeps.[141] Nevertheless, they proved very useful as partisans established operational bases, provided mutual support, pooled scarce resources, recovered from operations, protected civilian forest camps, and reconstituted Soviet power and institutions. The physical size and political and military importance of these regions also guaranteed that Moscow would watch them very closely.

The main tactical strengths the partisans possessed were speed, maneuverability, shock, and surprise. As both officials and partisans became more experienced, their operations almost always were defined by one of these elements. Ambushes, depending as they did on surprise and shock, were the

Two partisans await the enemy. (Credit: RGAKFD)

quintessential partisan operation, sometimes involving small groups of partisans or even an entire detachment. They were intended to interdict the German lines of communication and to unnerve the occupiers as they moved
through narrow forest, swamp, and mountain roads. Ambushes were also
used defensively to disrupt attacks against camps during antipartisan sweeps.

Partisans heralded the ambush as one of their defining modes of attack,
as depicted in a popular song from the Leningrad region:

Once in the icy winter time
Fritz left the house in a bitter frost
Looking, slowly going up the hill
Horses pulling the Germans' wagon.
We sit in ambush in a calm dignity
In time, the enemy comes closer
Suddenly a shot, grenades explode
And a "hurrah" loudly shouts out.
The fritzes scurried terror-stricken
No, snakes! You will not leave now

Partisans prepare for the enemy on a forest road. (Credit: RGAKFD)

> The frost strangles you, the grenade muffles you
> And the bullet overtakes your path.[142]

Thus, the ambush was represented as a demonstration of the partisans' skill, discipline, strength, and cunning, against which the unsuspecting and terror-struck Germans were powerless to defend.

Reconnaissance and intelligence gathering were other critical tasks. As one partisan related, "Intelligence, intelligence, and still more intelligence . . . Intelligence to the partisans was half of their success." It enabled them to pinpoint enemy movements and weaknesses and to strike unexpectedly and with great effect.[143] As the war continued, Soviet authorities, especially generals, gave intelligence gathering an increasingly high priority, not only for military purposes but also for obtaining information about political, economic, and social developments in the occupied territories and even the weather reports that were necessary for Soviet long-range aviation.[144] The partisans chosen for these missions tended to be extremely resourceful and independent, especially since they had to operate on their own or in small groups for long periods of time. Scouts possessed a certain mystique, heralded in unit songs and

A Briansk partisan questions a captured German soldier. (Credit: RGAKFD)

poems, not only because of their bravery and courage but also because their autonomy gave them wide latitude for action.[145] Units also developed networks of agents who observed and infiltrated enemy formations and administrations, bribed and coerced indigenous administrators and police into providing information, and tapped nearby telephone lines when they had the proper equipment.[146] Thus, the Kravtsov Partisan Brigade had a network of over 600 agents.

As their strength grew, partisans raided key fixed installations, such as administrative centers,[147] warehouses, depots, railroad stations, airfields, bridges, and even enemy garrisons and towns. Such assaults might involve one or several bands, depending on the size and defensive strength of the target. For example, the successful attack against the "blue bridge," a double-span railroad bridge across the Desna River, in March 1943 involved over 1,100 partisans from three units. The bridge was a critical link in the main supply route for the Germans' Army Group Center, with between fifteen and twenty trains crossing the structure each day. Its destruction significantly reduced railroad traffic along Army Group Center's main supply artery for several crucial weeks as the Germans accumulated forces and equipment for the forthcoming Kursk offensive.[148] An article in *Krasnaia zvezda* featured the attack on the bridge as an example of the partisans' mastery of planning, tactics, and courage, for they used a combination of cunning and audacity to storm the heavily defended position.[149] Such attacks added to the partisans' public mystique and elevated their self-image.

Raids on police and troop garrisons also hit the Germans hard. Gradually, occupation authorities were forced to abandon their more isolated outposts on the fringes of the forest zones, usually defended by only ten to twenty men (often indigenous police with a couple of German commanders), and move them to larger, better-fortified positions. As the garrisons retreated to larger towns and cities, the now unprotected village elders and other indigenous and foreign administrators were either killed or forced to support the partisans. As a consequence, beginning in 1942 and accelerating in 1943 and 1944, German control in and near forested zones evaporated. The partisans usually filled the vacuum, although they might sometimes have to contest the area with Ukrainian or Polish nationalist bands.[150]

Partisans located near the front directly assisted Red Army combat operations by providing intelligence, interdicting German supplies and reinforcements, and sometimes directly participating in battles by engaging in flanking attacks on enemy positions.[151] As the front moved closer to the partisan-controlled regions in 1943 and 1944, this assistance became especially vital. Joint partisan-army operations seized key strong points, population centers, bridges, and roads and made encircling attacks against frontline enemy units. In particular, partisans helped the Red Army cross major rivers, including the Dniepr, Desna, and Pripiat.[152] And on the eve of Operation Bagration, the Red Army's June 1944 offensive that drove the Wehrmacht from Belorussia, partisans attacked German railway lines. Once the offensive commenced, they attacked German units and seized population centers.[153]

With liberation looming so close, these operations were also among the most dangerous. As the Germans retreated, the partisans came into increasing contact with combat-hardened troops, who were loath to have enemy forces in their immediate rear area. Between December 1943 and July 1944, the Germans organized nineteen large-scale antipartisan operations throughout the much-reduced occupied territories.[154] The severity of German assaults on the partisan regions increased dramatically and resulted in some of the bitterest fighting of the guerrilla war. The fighting in the Polotsk lowland area near Vitebsk in the spring of 1944 was particularly fierce; it is estimated that German attacks resulted in approximately 7,000 partisans killed and an additional 7,000 taken prisoner.[155]

The growing strength and sophistication of partisan operations were balanced by the troops' decidedly uneven quality. Relatively few partisans had any proper military training, and their leaders were often chosen more for their political connections, reliability, and charisma than for their military abilities. A Belgian soldier in German service observed that the "partisans adhered to no set doctrine, used no set order of battle," making it difficult to predict what they would do in any given situation.[156] Even the Red Army okruzhentsy, who provided the bulk of the military expertise, had spent their time at the front in the midst of defeat and had no preparation in partisan warfare. And though spontaneity sometimes worked to their advantage, too often it reflected not native cunning but ignorance about the best tactics to employ in particular conditions. Some partisans even eschewed formal military planning as being antithetical to the romance and élan embodied in the persona of the partisan. One former political officer turned brigade commander complained that regular army officers criticized his methods, saying, "my activities were incorrect from the point of view of tactics and strategy, etc. I said that we don't need any strategy, the devil with it, let them curse."[157] This view was echoed by Ponomarenko himself, who told the partisan leaders at the August 1942 Moscow conference that "life itself" taught the partisans proper tactics, not abstract theory.[158]

Given these sentiments, coupled with a lack of training and hodgepodge equipment, it is not surprising that partisan military capabilities were uneven at best. Ambushes were blown due to poor concealment or bad fire discipline, assaults were often badly coordinated or planned, and the failure to deploy scouts enabled enemy forces to concentrate less than half a mile from partisan base camps.[159] One example involved the Lazo Partisan Regiment, which was operating in Smolensk Oblast and planning an attack on a small German garrison in July 1942. The commander and commissar were inexperienced civilians, although both the deputy commander and the commissar were escaped POWs. According to a plenipotentiary from the Western Front, the regiment failed to conduct sufficient reconnaissance or maintain secrecy. A scout ordered to reconnoiter the garrison defected to the Germans and allegedly told them about the upcoming attack. Yet even though the commanders knew that the Germans were informed, they continued with the operation and were themselves ambushed by the now-reinforced garrison. The Germans then counterattacked, eventually forcing the regiment to divide into two groups to evade the enemy.[160]

Partisan casualties further reflected their inexperience. Although it is impossible to cite any figures with precision, a few examples are telling. In early September 1942, the Briansk forest commander, Emliutin, reported that he

The people's avengers: partisans on the attack, Leningrad region, 1942. (Credit: RGAKFD)

had more than 4,000 men killed over the course of the year when his current strength was a little over 10,000.[161] During the same period in the Leningrad area, according to an official report, of a total of 6,662 partisans, 892 had been killed, 931 were wounded, and 98 were missing in action.[162] A Central Staff report from February 1944, based on incomplete data, stated that of 287,953 known partisans (not including those in Ukraine), 34,659 had either died, gone missing, or deserted to the enemy and been subsequently shot for treason, for an overall loss rate of about 12 percent.[163] It is important to note that these figures do not include the wounded or those who died from other causes.

The partisans' increased military capabilities, on the one hand, and their distinct amateurism, on the other, reflected the schizophrenic nature of the movement. They often fought with exceptional bravery, skill, and imagination. But they were also limited by inexperience, poor or nonexistent training, and a devil-may-care attitude that occasionally brought them success but more frequently led to pointless losses. Lack of training also meant that they were prone to panic. As the movement grew, especially in 1943, the surviving veterans with hard-won experience were diluted by the vast numbers of raw recruits who had to learn about combat through trial and error. As one partisan related, every battle became a lesson, but this knowledge all too often came at a heavy price.[164]

PARTISAN OPERATIONS I: SABOTAGE

Two types of operations in particular came to define Soviet guerrilla warfare: sabotage and the long-distance partisan raid. These missions required unique qualities that embodied certain "partisan" characteristics, which both the partisans themselves and Soviet officials used to define the movement.

Soviet authorities certainly regarded sabotage as one of the most, if not the most, important of the partisans' activities. Ponomarenko was a particularly enthusiastic advocate of the potential of mass sabotage. He noted in a September 1941 memo to Stalin that "sabotage was the most comfortable and familiar way for the peasant to participate in the partisan movement," as he mistakenly believed that sabotage was easy and could be accomplished covertly without fear of German retribution.[165] The memo also revealed the extent to which Party leaders continued to believe that peasants naturally engaged in sabotage and subterfuge of various sorts, a belief persisting from the Civil War. Ponomarenko gradually realized that saboteurs required some training, and the Central Staff established a section to develop and produce special mines, such as delayed-action and electromagnetic mines, and explosives, as well as information bulletins and manuals; it also ran training schools and sent instructors behind enemy lines.[166] These efforts eventually paid off. Between April and June 1943 alone, partisans attacked 1,700 German trains, destroying some 1,300 engines, 15,000 wagons, cisterns, railroad platforms, and 78 railroad bridges.[167]

The partisans' own misgivings about sabotage also had to be overcome. Some believed that sabotage was less prestigious than other operations, especially since it did not involve attacking enemy troops directly. The 1st Voroshilov commissar, Kniazev, observed that his partisans were "used to daring, dashing raids on Magyar [Hungarian] garrisons, and many were upset: how could they be occupied with this trifle of placing a mine under a rail?"[168] Such sentiments were common. As another commander noted, too many partisans disdained demolition operations, preferring to engage the enemy directly like "hunters" regardless of the human costs.[169] Even as late as 1943, staff officers reported that too many units did not have enough demolitions specialists.

Soviet saboteurs placing explosives on a rail line. (Credit: Minaeva Collection)

N. A. Mikhailov, the head of the Komsomol, observed in May 1943, after attending a special Komsomol conference devoted to sabotage, that detachment commanders were indifferent to the problem and that "saboteurs still have not become the central or the most respected people among the fighters in the detachments."[170]

Fear or prudence influenced still others. In August 1943, Communists in the 3rd Leningrad Partisan Brigade were criticized by the brigade's Party organization for "being frightened of the difficulties [of sabotage operations] and for not fulfilling their tasks."[171] They had good reason to be afraid. Usually working under the cover of darkness, with primitive explosives and in close proximity to German patrols, saboteurs faced numerous dangers. Most sabotage squads were small, often having no more than five to ten members, and their missions sometimes took days or even weeks to complete.[172] Just reaching the target required evading enemy patrols and guard posts. Once at the target, one or two demolitions experts set the explosives while protected by the rest of the group. However, some mines were quite sensitive and could explode at the slightest shake of the railroad track. When lacking explosives, the partisans literally dismantled a section of the line. Some groups, using antitank guns, ambushed moving trains. Most satisfying but riskiest of all was

A train destroyed by a partisan mine, Lithuania, 1944. (Credit: RGAKFD)

to destroy a moving train with a mine. To ensure the train's destruction and to prevent a German patrol from discovering a planted explosive, many saboteurs placed the mine on the track 1,000 to 1,500 feet in front of the train, leaving themselves about forty seconds to make it to safety. Unfortunately, if the train was carrying fuel or ammunition and exploded, the partisans themselves could be caught in the blast. Those who succeeded in getting away from the area before the detonation then once again had to avoid enemy patrols, which were almost inevitably sent after them. As sabotage became more widespread, the Germans increased their countermeasures. They cleared all trees and bushes for over 150 feet on each side of the main railway lines to eliminate cover, and they mined and placed barbed wire at the railbed approaches to hinder access. Mutually supporting pillboxes and other defensive installations protected rail lines and especially depots, bridges, rail junctions, stations, water towers, and other critical infrastructure; in addition, armored trains, aircraft, and infantry patrolled the tracks.[173]

Losses among saboteurs were quite high. In May and June 1943, the aforementioned 3rd Leningrad Brigade dispatched thirty diversionary groups,

of which five were destroyed after demolishing their targets, eight were destroyed before reaching their objectives, and seventeen were not heard from
over the next two months.[174] Partisan sayings such as "[The Germans] do not
kill saboteurs, they kill themselves" and "Sappers make only one mistake in
their lives" testified to the perils of working with explosives, many of which
were made in quite primitive and dangerous conditions.[175]

Some individuals were understandably frightened by these dangers, but
others were attracted to them. Staff officers referred to sabotage work as demanding "great courage" and as "the most dangerous" of partisan operations.[176] Although partisans such as those in the 1st Voroshilov were initially
nonplussed about performing demolition work, their opinion changed once
they became familiar with the intricate process of destroying rails, bridges,
and trains. Sabotage came to be seen as art that required practice and skill to
be mastered, and thus, sabotage work became a source of individual and unit
pride for those who excelled at it.[177] Because sabotage became so integral to
their mission, partisans used it to define themselves against regular soldiers.
One partisan wrote home that the slogan "If you do not kill at least one German a day, it is a day wasted" should have been changed for the partisans to
"If you do not blow up a train or bridge, then your day is wasted."[178] The
dangers posed by sabotage also may have appealed to self-styled daredevils,
particularly youth and Komsomol members, who made up the overwhelming
majority of saboteurs in some units.[179] Many believed that saboteurs received
the majority of medals and awards given to the partisans.[180] Indeed, during
the desperate days of August 1942, Ponomarenko ordered that any partisans who destroyed twenty train cars carrying equipment, fuel, or troops in a
single attack would be awarded the Hero of the Soviet Union title.[181]

With the danger, technical mastery, and raw courage involved in sabotage
work, it is not surprising that officials and other partisans heralded the saboteur as part of the movement's elite. Stories in the central press, as well as
posters, films, and radio broadcasts, celebrated the exploits of saboteurs.[182] A
poster in 1941, captioned "Glory to the hero-partisans destroying the fascist
rear," showed a partisan clipping telephone lines while in the background
bridges collapsed and flames burned on the horizon. *Izvestiia* described a
saboteur as "a highly qualified electrician" who "mastered sabotage and deserved fame as the best sapper."[183] Partisans echoed this language of heroism and industrial production. One commander referred to the "art" of diversionary work and compared the demolitions expert to a lathe turner, stating
that the "skilled diversionist was regarded as a partisan with a valuable pro-
fession, [demanding] extremely high qualifications."[184] Saboteurs were also

"Glory to the hero-partisans, destroying the fascist rear!" 1941. (Credit: Hoover
Institution Archives, Poster Collection, RU/SU1922)

called the chief controllers, an ironic reference to a key railroad supervisory function.[185]

The centerpiece of Soviet sabotage efforts was the two massive coordinated attacks against German railway traffic in the summer and fall of 1943. The first operation, code-named Rail War (*rel'sovaia voina*), was quite complex, involving 541 detachments and 96,000 partisans, which showed just how far Soviet partisan efforts had come from the dark days of 1941.[186] The plan targeted primarily the rail lines in Belorussia and central Russia supporting the Wehrmacht's Army Group Center.[187] Secondary attacks were also scheduled for Ukraine and the Leningrad area. Rather than attacking the trains themselves, partisans were to explode gaps in the rails, thus supposedly rendering the railways useless. Units were assigned to attack specific sectors and given quotas of rail to destroy just as if they were factory crews fulfilling their norms for the economic plan.[188]

The plan was approved by Stalin on 14 July 1943 and commenced on the night of 3–4 August in Belorussia, although the Briansk-Orel partisans began their operations on 22 July to assist the Red Army's counteroffensive at Kursk. It continued into September. Although the attack failed to paralyze the enemy's rear area, German reports indicated that rail movement was slowed substantially throughout the month of August; in some sectors, such as the rear area of the German Eighteenth Army (in the Leningrad region), it essentially came to a halt.[189] Insufficient explosives, however, prevented the partisans from conducting the follow-up attacks necessary to ensure success, especially since the Germans had large numbers of rails in reserve for repairs.[190] Moreover, some staff officers believed that the basic premise of attacking the rails instead of the trains themselves was faulty, for the former could be repaired relatively easily compared to repairing or replacing trains. They also contended that it made no sense to destroy rails that the Red Army itself would soon capture and need to use.[191] Indeed, the criticism that one Russian historian leveled at the operation rings true: he observed that it was "conducted, like a typical Soviet campaign (who destroys more rails, who reports it first)" and "was insufficiently thought out."[192] However, it did cost the Germans considerable expense and effort to repair the damage at a time when the front was under heavy pressure. And if nothing else, the simultaneity and scale of the Rail War operation no doubt contributed to the Germans' psychological despondency and fear that the partisans were everywhere and that no place in the occupied territories was safe, especially at night.[193]

Rail War was followed by an even larger operation, code-named Concert (*Kontsert*), which began on 20 September 1943 and lasted until December, involving 678 detachments and 120,000 partisans. The success of this attack, too, was hindered by the lack of necessary supplies, as well as by bad weather: of the 272,300 lengths of rail targeted, the partisans succeeded in demolishing only 148,557.[194] But because more attention was given to attacking actual trains during this operation, it had a greater material effect on the Germans.[195] The Rail War and Concert operations and the coordinated strikes just before the Red Army's Belorussian offensive in June 1944 demonstrated the capacity of the Central Staff apparatus both to coordinate large-scale attacks and to interfere with German military operations in their own rear areas.[196] They also indicated that sabotage had come into its own as an instrument of partisan warfare.

PARTISAN OPERATIONS II:
THE LONG-RANGE RAID

Another quintessential partisan operation was the long-range raid. Publicly, these raids were almost exclusively associated with the Ukrainian partisans, although Belorussian and Russian partisans conducted them as well. The participants became among the most famous of the movement, including such luminaries as S. A. Kovpak and his commissar, S. V. Rudnev; A. F. Fedorov; P. P. Vershigora; and A. N. Saburov. The partisan raids served both military and political goals. They reestablished a Soviet military and political presence in Ukraine, particularly in the hostile western regions, and came to embody a uniquely "Ukrainian" style of partisan warfare.

The partisan raid was eventually defined as a source of Ukrainian strength, but ironically, its origins lay in the fundamental weakness of the partisan movement in Ukraine. Lacking both forest cover and popular support throughout much of the republic, the Ukrainian partisans had been all but destroyed by the summer of 1942, with the exception of several thousand who had found refuge in the southern reaches of the Briansk forest, including Kovpak's, Saburov's, and Fedorov's bands.[197] The situation remained unchanged until September 1942, when Stalin, according to one witness, evidently annoyed that "Ukrainian" partisans were staying in Russian forests, "dropped a hint to Kovpak at the Kremlin reception that he should operate somewhere in Ukraine itself."[198] Kovpak's and Saburov's complexes departed on 26 October from their forest bases, moving along parallel routes toward Right Bank Ukraine, which they reached by November 1942.[199] A. F. Fedorov's complex also regained its position in its home oblast, Chernihiv, from which, in the following spring, it moved into the northern regions of Rivne and Lutsk. Other nominally Ukrainian complexes, under the commands of M. I. Naumov, Ia. I. Mel'nik, and M. I. Shukaevich, later embarked on their own raids, eventually spreading throughout western Ukraine. Sometimes covering up to thirty miles per night on foot, the raiders attacked communications lines and garrisons, destroyed factories, demolished telegraph and telephone lines and other infrastructure useful to the occupiers, collected intelligence, recruited new fighters, and raised new formations along their line of march.[200]

The raids had significant political ramifications. Colonel V. F. Sokolov, the head of the Ukrainian Staff of the Partisan Movement's Operations Department, credited them with increasing popular sympathy for the partisans and for the Soviet cause.[201] As Kovpak noted in his memoirs, the sudden appearance of Soviet partisans, many of them wearing Red Army uniforms, in Right Bank Ukraine after the Germans had proclaimed the destruction of the Red Army could only "make quite an impression" on the local inhabitants.[202] Raids also served to keep the occupiers on edge, as the latter could never be sure that an area would not come under attack from a roving partisan unit.[203] New partisans were recruited at a phenomenal rate: a typical example was the Zhytomyr Partisan Complex, which grew from 1,408 to 2,620 partisans during its raid from Sumy to Zhytomyr Oblasts and spawned 15 new detachments west of the Dniepr, thus sharply increasing the Soviet presence there.[204] Even more important was the reemergence of the Party. The raiders had less political effect in the areas they merely transited, but at their terminus, they established and led district and regional Party organizations. Thus, the Rivne Obkom was reborn in February 1943 under the leadership of the commander V. A. Begma, and A. F. Fedorov headed a reconstituted Volhynia Obkom after his complex was ordered to that region in June 1943.[205] And as the raiders moved west, they battled Ukrainian separatists, demonstrating that Soviet power was not absent from western Ukraine.[206]

Conducting a long-range raid carried enormous risks, in addition to the normal perils of combat. Away from their bases, the partisans had to procure supplies from villagers whose loyalty was unknown, since air supply from the Red Air Force was neither sufficient nor reliable.[207] Taking care of the wounded, already difficult in primitive partisan conditions, became even more complicated due to the unit's almost constant movement.[208] The partisans lost many of their former tactical advantages when fighting in unfamiliar terrain amid a population with whom they had few ties. They also became more exposed to German airpower. During the Kovpak complex's famous raid to the Carpathian Mountains in the summer 1943, Kovpak's commissar, S. V. Rudnev, reported in his diary that the unit's column, almost four miles long, was strafed by four German aircraft, which killed 10 men, wounded another 24, and destroyed over 100 horses. He wrote, "Here are the Carpathians! They met us bleakly. Personally, I survived a horrible day, [and my] morale was so shaken by this barbaric raid on the column that I simply cannot convey it."[209] Indeed, Kovpak's complex suffered heavily in this operation, and Rudnev himself was killed. Vershigora, the famed memoirist of the complex, estimated that over half of the Kovpaktsy, as Kovpak's partisans were known, who were with the unit in the summer of 1942 died during its numerous raids.[210] Meanwhile, Naumov's complex was so demoralized by its costly losses in its summer 1943 raid through the Ukrainian central regions (with just 300 partisans remaining out of an original complement of 1,400) that many survivors transferred to other units, deserted, or went deep into the woods, where they sat passively.[211] Some partisans, including a few commanders, resisted going on raids and may have subverted orders to launch raids on some occasions.[212]

Surviving raiders believed their toughness and exploits made them an elite among partisans. Vershigora asserted, "Movement is the mother of partisan strategy and tactics. Were we really the only ones who understood this?"[213] He later commented, "Raiding partisans will say to you that partisans operating in the partisan regions were not partisans, that they only sat."[214] Kovpak exclaimed in his memoirs that Stalin himself signified the importance of raiding units when the Soviet leader termed his complex a "'raiding' detachment. This was precisely the essence of our tactics, but with one word [Stalin] determined it."[215] The raiders' sense of superiority over other partisans was apparent when, in the spring of 1944, Kovpak's complex, now with Vershigora at the helm and known officially as the 1st Ukrainian Partisan Division, found refuge in the Belorussian forests. Belorussian officials and commanders complained that the Kovpaktsy engaged in "illegal activities," including drunkenness and terrorizing and pillaging the population. The Kovpaktsy also tried to entice local partisans into joining their unit by citing how they were rewarded by the state. According to one report, they told the locals to "throw away your rusty rifle and join us, take a new automatic, throw away your rusty grenade, you can take two from us. They give us awards, we accomplish feats, but you have been a partisan for two years and no one has given you an award."[216]

Raiders received extensive coverage in the Soviet media.[217] In the first half of 1943 alone, there were 132 Soviet Information Bureau reports about Ukrainian partisans, compared to only 94 for all of 1942.[218] Propagandists portrayed the raid as a particularly Ukrainian form of partisan warfare, just as sabotage came to be seen by the partisans and the public as a singular type of partisan activity. In a late December 1942 article in the newspaper *Sovetskaia Ukraina*, Ukrainian Staff chief Timofei Strokach cited Kovpak's and Saburov's raids as the fulfillment of Stalin's pledge to "cleanse the Soviet land" and Soviet Ukraine from the "German filth."[219]

Geographic and military factors required the partisans in Ukraine to adopt the raid as their primary military operation. The raids not only served military purposes but also helped meet political goals by reestablishing a Soviet presence in areas where it had been destroyed. Like sabotage, they elevated the partisans' role in Soviet strategic efforts and in the public perception of the war effort.

The conditions of material life and of combat exacted a heavy toll on partisans and civilians alike. Both faced a daily struggle for survival, one that pitted them against the natural elements as well as the enemy and even, at times, against their own compatriots. Relations between the partisans and civilians were often divisive, even as both periodically relied on each other for survival. Brutality and violence underscored this relationship in two ways: in the competition between the partisans and civilians for food and resources and in the fighting between partisans and Germans, which found civilians caught in the middle. Haunting these interactions were the historical memories of the participants, recalling the violence of the Civil War and collectivization, when the Soviet state and its agents had been arrayed against much of the peasant population.

Ever-present physical danger, whether in the form of everyday living or combat, also defined the partisans' existence. Obtaining sufficient supplies was always a problem, good health could never be assured, and the bands were constantly one battle away from their own destruction. The partisans were well aware of these realities. Combat, of course, was always dangerous, but the dangers for the partisans were heightened by the nature of their missions and by their own inexperience and amateurism. Although the partisans became more sophisticated combatants as the war dragged on, sabotage and raiding operations almost always involved great risks. Further, the constant and ever-growing influx of recruits meant that the units always included large numbers of inexperienced personnel, thus contributing to the potential for high casualties.

Living and fighting in the occupied territories were not the only perils the partisans faced. In addition to combating the enemy, they had to take into account the concerns and fears of the Soviet leaders, who continued to view the guerrilla resistance with suspicion.

3

BUREAUCRATS AND GUERRILLAS: THE SOVIET SEARCH FOR ORDER AND CONTROL IN THE OCCUPIED TERRITORIES

Resistance movements in the rest of Europe initially developed more or less spontaneously and without much formalized institutional or state support. In the Soviet Union, by contrast, state agencies sanctioned, organized, and led the partisan insurgency from the start. Although there were certainly spontaneous and autonomous elements in the Soviet resistance, the partisan war was, from the beginning of the German invasion, an explicit element of Soviet strategy. Yet despite the central role of the government in promoting and organizing the insurgency, the regime initially had no specialized administrative apparatus to coordinate and direct the resistance; in fact, Stalin and Beria were originally opposed to a centralized partisan administration. Gradually, though, it became clear to officials and partisans alike that centralized control was necessary if the movement was to be effective. Moreover, from the government's perspective, state control became even more essential as the insurgency expanded beyond its initially narrow demographic base.

The challenge of directing and administering a widespread partisan war was not limited to the Soviet Union. The Western Allies, governments-in-exile, and leaders on the ground throughout Europe all struggled to control and coordinate the operations of numerous resistance movements. As Jorgen Haestrup has noted, these organizers had little precedent to guide their activities, especially on such a large scale.[1] For the Soviets, as well as for others, the path to a solution was hardly clear; indeed, it would take a great deal of trial and error and much loss of life before satisfactory answers to the problems of directing partisans and resisters were found.

Because of the goals it was assigned to meet, the Soviet partisan agency would have to coordinate military, political, and intelligence operations, actions usually divided among several organizations. Of critical importance for the Soviet regime was controlling the multitudes of armed men and women exposed to multiple ideologies, beyond the direct physical control of Moscow.

In finding a solution to these challenges, the government had to balance the demands of military effectiveness with the need to ensure the partisans' political reliability.

The regime ultimately turned to familiar administrative structures to solve these problems. It was an article of faith among the Soviet leadership that centralized planning was the most superior and efficient form of organization and administration, despite evidence of its vast inefficiencies.[2] Although the exigencies of the war forced the regime to back away from trying to control all aspects of life,[3] the establishment of agencies such as the State Defense Committee to coordinate the Soviet war effort indicates that centralization remained an essential part of Soviet administrative strategy. The mantra of centralization was eventually applied to the partisans in the form of the Central Staff of the Partisan Movement. Yet, as indicated previously, in constructing a state-sponsored and state-administered partisan movement, Stalin and other leaders had to reconcile their own ideological and psychological predilections for total political conformity and centralized control with the inherent autonomy and spontaneity of partisan warfare.

Any discussion of partisan administration must also take into account the partisans themselves. Many, particularly those affiliated with state institutions, welcomed centralized control as being necessary for their security and for the success of their operations. At the same time, they were hardly a "pliable and helpless instrument in the hands of the regime," as some have argued.[4] Rather, they had their own interests and desires, shaped by local concerns and by the dangers they faced, all of which led them to circumvent, manipulate, and if necessary deceive state organs. The partisans had to be cautious, given Moscow's formidable—albeit somewhat lessened—supervisory and coercive capacities, but their opportunities for freedom of action (or willful inaction) were considerable because the regime's actual power in the occupied territories was limited, at least until the arrival of the Red Army. Moscow's authority, however, was not the only administrative problem confronting local partisan leaders.

Partisan administration involved regulating relations among the partisans themselves, in addition to state-partisan relations. Though they were capable of cooperative and friendly relations with each other, partisans often regarded their fellows as rivals for power and scarce material resources. The partisan movement resembled a Hobbesian society where the strong usually prevailed and where inhabitants did all they could to maximize their material, military, and political position at the expense of their competitors. John Armstrong has characterized this aspect of partisan life as "group autarky,"

a situation similar to that of Soviet industrial managers and regional economic directors who raided rival factories to obtain badly needed raw materials.[5]

Of course, the potential for violence was much greater between the armed
partisans than between enterprise directors. Some rivalries were caused by
personal feuds reminiscent of gang warfare in American inner cities. To cite
just one example, the commander of the Briansk forest's Chapaev Detachment, V. I. Koshelev (who, in the words of one observer, "was an incredible
drunkard, and we knew, sooner or later that he would be finished off"), killed
a battalion commander of the 2nd Voroshilov Partisan Brigade. In revenge,
the 2nd Voroshilov partisans raided the Chapaev Detachment, killing Koshelev and his adjutant.[6] In such an environment, some sort of outside control
was needed lest the movement fall into complete anarchy.

Wartime Soviet administrators depended on the models developed in
peacetime for civilian organizations. Many of the same tensions and contradictions that bureaucrats experienced in civilian settings arose in the wartime environment as well. More precisely, the old bugbears of interagency
strife and center-periphery conflict that plagued Soviet administration in the
interwar years remained endemic throughout the war. The partisans' determination to defend their own interests and their willingness to manipulate the
very institutions that were supposed to control them further complicated
the situation. It remained to be seen how effective Soviet administration of
the partisan war could be. Reports about administrative successes can be
faked—victory in war cannot.

PARTISAN ADMINISTRATION
BEFORE THE CENTRAL STAFF

The Stalinist leadership's hostility toward partisan warfare in the 1930s
continued throughout World War II. The German invasion and the catastrophic failure of the Red Army's war plans, however, tempered whatever
qualms Stalin and others had regarding the use of guerrilla forces. The critical problem was how to maximize the partisans' military effectiveness while
guaranteeing their political reliability to avoid a repetition of the Civil War
experience. The suppression of the irregular warfare specialists of the past
had been so thorough that all their knowledge and all the training gained in
the preceding twenty years seem to have been lost. To be sure, the demands
of unconventional resistance in World War II went far beyond the Soviet plans

and capabilities of the interwar years,[7] yet there is no doubt that Stalin's purging of the 1930s made the task more difficult and costly than it should have been. Moreover, without a specific administrative infrastructure to direct the partisans, the leaders relied on established institutions, including the Party, the army, and the NKVD, to secure partisan loyalty and obedience. They were not prepared, however, to conduct a partisan war when the storm of Operation Barbarossa broke on 22 June 1941.

Remarkably, given Soviet centralization, some republics and regions began to organize a guerrilla struggle on their own initiative. A few regional committees in western Ukraine had begun discussions on the creation of partisan formations by the night of 25 June, and on 27 June, the Kamenets-Podolsk Oblast Committee ordered the formation of underground Party cells and partisan detachments.[8] On 26 June, the Belorussian Central Committee, under the leadership of the future head of the partisan movement, First Secretary P. K. Ponomarenko, began preparations for partisan war.[9] Some analysts contend that these early efforts originated from the plans of the 1930s, but the confusion that followed their implementation at the national and regional levels suggests that they were knee-jerk responses rather than part of a preconceived plan.[10] Certainly, as the unfolding developments of 1941 indicated, there was no evidence of any centralized planning or administration. Instead, the Party, army, and NKVD each developed its own approach to directing the partisans. These efforts were often not even unified within these institutions but varied according to locality. The involvement of political, military, and security organs, each without jurisdiction over the others, reflected the multifaceted nature of the partisan struggle and, likewise, the regime's uncertainty regarding which part of the partisan war should be emphasized over the others. Failure to provide guidance and order led to administrative confusion and anarchy.

The instructions of 29 June and 18 July 1941, which called for partisan units to be organized by Party officials in every district, seemed to infer that the Party should supervise and direct the nascent movement, although neither document specified how this was to be done.[11] The primary organs for this role were the underground district and regional committees, supported by regional and republican committees on Soviet-held territory. However, no centralized leadership was envisioned. This plan collapsed as the occupiers destroyed or rendered ineffective the underground organizations. By the end of 1941 in Belorussia, the only remaining organizations at and above the district level were three underground oblast committees, two underground city committees, and twenty underground raion committees. In Leningrad, where twenty-six underground raion committees had been established in 1941, only eight were still functioning the following spring. In Ukraine, the Party essentially disappeared, particularly in the western regions.[12] German agents infiltrated urban underground committees, which were all but wiped out—as occurred in Briansk, Kiev, and Minsk, the latter having suffered over 400 arrests by May 1942.[13] Without formal Party organizations to lead them, individual Communists were literally and figuratively lost in the wilderness.

The army's contribution to the partisan movement centered on its front and army political administrations, which in mid-July 1941 were ordered to establish special departments to organize, direct, and assist partisan units operating in areas close to and immediately behind the front lines.[14] Operational groups were set up behind the lines to support partisans in the immediate rear area.[15] And the Red Army's military intelligence administration, the Main Intelligence Directorate (GRU), also organized special groups, beginning in July 1941, to gather intelligence and to conduct sabotage.[16] However, in most cases, the army gave very little military support to the partisans, even after its chief of political administration, L. Z. Mekhlis, criticized the front staffs for "standing on the sidelines."[17] The statement made by the commander of the Northwestern Front in late July 1941—"The partisan detachments do not wait for the assignment of tasks from above; they operate independently according to the instructions of the great leader of the peoples, Comrade Stalin"[18]—essentially summed up the view of most upper-level officers that directing partisans was not their job.

It was the NKVD-NKGB that was actually the most prevalent active organization in the first months of the partisan war. The security organs controlled a vast array of detachments, ranging from surviving border guard detachments turned partisans to the OMSBON units to the specially (and hastily) organized sabotage groups and, finally, to the even more hastily organized destruction battalions, which formed the basis for many partisan bands.[19] Indeed, some historians have estimated that the NKVD controlled over 90 percent of the detachments in 1941.[20] Although this figure probably exaggerates the NKVD's presence, there is little doubt that in the first year of the partisan war, the security organs dominated the movement.

The NKVD developed its own partisan administration to oversee its expanding operations. On 5 July 1941, it established the Department of Special Tasks under Pavel Sudoplatov to direct NKVD intelligence and sabotage operations throughout the occupied territories. In August, Beria received Stalin's permission to expand the NKVD's role, leading to the creation of the Fourth

Department to supervise the destruction battalions and sabotage groups, organize intelligence gathering, verify the operations of units, and analyze the conditions in the occupied territories. In January 1942, a superior organ, the Fourth Administration, was established, a move that challenged the creation of the Party-dominated Central Staff, as will be discussed.[21]

By late summer 1941, three institutions shared responsibility for the partisans. In theory, the Party was the dominant institution overseeing the partisans, but the NKVD could also lay claim to that title. The army, too, had legitimate supervising functions, especially in the areas near the front. The stage was therefore set for a three-way institutional conflict, a familiar occurrence in the short but turbulent history of Soviet administration. It is perhaps not surprising that the shock of the surprise attack and difficulties in organizing guerrilla warfare on an unprecedented scale led to institutional chaos, but given the regime's earlier planning for partisan warfare, a less happenstance administrative arrangement should have been expected. But the establishment of parallel responsibilities and competing jurisdictions was itself a hallmark of Soviet administrative practice.

The effects of this confusion at the center were felt at the local level. At a September 1941 conference of Southern Front political officers, some participants complained that the lack of cooperation among all three agencies was greatly hindering partisan operations. One officer grumbled that "the Oblast NKVD does not know what detachments were organized by the Oblast Party Committee, and the Oblast Party Committee does not know what detachments were organized by the NKVD."[22] Another officer was so frustrated with the void in leadership that he declared, "In general, I consider that some one from these three organizations [the Party, the NKVD, and the Red Army] should formally take on the organization of these detachments" even if this meant letting go of the army's own prerogatives.[23] Mogilevich of the Eighteenth Army, by contrast, angrily suggested that the army take control of all partisans, "in order that the leadership be concentrated in one hand" so that the partisans could fulfill their objectives. His proposal, which included stripping Party organizations of their responsibilities, was not endorsed by the other participants.[24] Other officers also accused regional Party leaders of passivity and of encouraging Communist partisans to flee to Soviet territory instead of fighting the enemy.[25] Officers on other fronts echoed these frustrations regarding the Party's deficiencies, most notably in the Crimea, where, according to one Red Army staff officer, the movement would have collapsed without the army's intervention.[26]

But the Party and NKVD also blasted the army for its alleged mishandling of the partisans. The suppression of the experiments of the 1930s meant
that army officers were unfamiliar with the principles of partisan war. Nor
were there any modern doctrines or theories regarding partisan warfare that
they could impart to the partisans.[27] Most believed that partisan warfare was,
in the words of one officer, "ungovernable anarchy." Local commanders often
integrated partisans into their front lines and sometimes even ordered them
to participate in conventional operations.[28] Thus, in the Orel region, NKVD
and Party officials complained to Beria and Malenkov that the Tenth and Six-
teenth Armies ordered poorly armed and trained partisan units to launch
frontal assaults on the large town of Zhizdra.[29] General G. K. Zhukov, then
the commander of the Western Front, stood out as an exception among general officers, realizing that partisans might better support the Red Army by
conducting reconnaissance and sabotage missions behind enemy lines.[30]

NKVD officials also interfered with partisan organization and operations,
even subverting partisans responsible to other agencies. In Briansk, the local
NKVD refused to allow Party-recruited partisans to cross into enemy territory
or to draw supplies from warehouses, forcing the partisans to steal grain from
a large bakery.[31] In Tula, they forbade the local branch of Osoaviakhim, the
civil defense organization, from setting up its own partisan formations on the
grounds that they were not "stable."[32] In Ukraine's Stalino Oblast, Red Army
political officers accused an NKVD-organized detachment of trying to remove
its Party members and preventing them from forming a unit Party organization, a move the officers evidently thwarted.[33]

Thus, representatives from the Party, NKVD, and army each accused
the others of encroaching on their jurisdictions and ordering *their* units to
perform missions for other institutions' purposes, a situation that one midlevel NKVD officer described as "anarchic."[34] Rather than trying to integrate
their efforts into a unified, organized national resistance, each institution attempted to carve out its own fiefdom at the expense of its rivals. It was the
partisans who paid the price. A. P. Matveev, the Orel Obkom first secretary,
recalled in December 1942:

> Up to February–March 1942 the leadership of the partisan movement
> was concentrated in the hands of the intelligence departments, front
> political administrations, and the organs of the NKVD and Obkom. And
> you know the old saying, when there are too many nursemaids, then
> the child is unsupervised. So it was with the leadership of the partisan

movement: all were occupied with it, but we had not organized any real leadership . . . and the partisan detachments had no sense of leadership.[35]

Only when one institution was able to dominate the others was the leadership problem resolved. Such was the case in Leningrad, where the local Party apparatus, led by the powerful A. A. Zhdanov, monopolized control over the insurgency. Zhdanov himself took an active role in facilitating the movement, holding two conferences with city and district secretaries on this subject. In July 1941, the obkom organized "troikas" in each partisan district, consisting of Party, army, and NKVD representatives. In August, a special operations center was established, headed by the obkom secretary, G. Kh. Bumagin. Coordination was enhanced further in late September when the Leningrad Obkom established the Leningrad Staff of the Partisan Movement, led by the oblast secretary, M. I. Nikitin. Red Army front operational groups and the troikas reported to the Leningrad Staff, which also had the right to supervise the partisans directly.[36] Moreover, the local NKVD apparently was willing to subordinate itself to the Party, though Beria refused to do so at the all-Union level.[37] With the establishment of a unitary command in Leningrad, much of the confusion and parallelism that marked the movement elsewhere was eliminated. Indeed, the Leningrad solution was so successful in reducing interagency conflict that Soviet historians credit it with serving as the model for the Central Staff of the Partisan Movement.[38]

Nikitin cited the importance, prestige, and continued presence of the Leningrad Party organization in its establishment of unified control over the local partisans.[39] Certainly, the power of that organization was critical to the Leningrad Staff's formation. And the experience of Leningrad indicates that a region could develop its own solution to the problems of administering the partisans if Moscow failed to provide administrative leadership and if the region was led by a sufficiently powerful official. In such cases, the Soviet system did allow for local initiative and spontaneity.

At the same time, the Leningrad solution of regional centralization was the means to an end, not an end itself. Centralization did provide more effective guidance and supervision, but the partisans still suffered heavily. By June 1942, only 5,000 partisans, at best, remained in the region.[40] Nor would centralization by itself improve the partisans' isolation, relations with the population, or combat effectiveness. Nevertheless, to Soviet officials, predisposed to believe that centralization was the panacea to almost every problem, the Leningrad solution seemed to point the way to the future.

THE FORMATION OF THE CENTRAL STAFF

Although Stalin had toyed with forming a centralized partisan command as early as July 1941, he did not take any effective steps to implement one until December 1941.[41] It is not clear why he waited so long to act; it is possible that his lack of enthusiasm was a manifestation of his dislike of partisan warfare in general. It is also possible that as the battle for Moscow was approaching its climax then, Stalin felt it was time to get serious about the partisan movement. Or perhaps other, more pressing matters diverted his attention up to that point.

In December, Stalin asked Ponomarenko to review a plan submitted by Deputy Defense Commissar E. A. Shchadenko calling for the formation of two partisan armies on Soviet territory, which would then cross the lines to attack the enemy's infrastructure.[42] Coinciding with his belief that the partisan struggle should be a genuine people's war, Ponomarenko criticized Shchadenko's recommendations, arguing that the recruitment of partisan armies in the Soviet rear area ignored the millions of potential partisans already behind German lines. He then submitted his own proposal, most likely assisted by former partisan instructor I. G. Starinov, calling for a central partisan command to wage an effective guerrilla war. Stalin was convinced and appointed the Belorussian first secretary to lead this new agency, the Central Staff of the Partisan Movement.[43]

Ponomarenko first established a school for radio operators and consulted with surviving Old Bolsheviks and Civil War partisans to familiarize himself further with the complexities and nature of underground political work and partisan warfare. He may have also drafted organizational plans for the new agency.[44] On 26 January 1942, however, Stalin unexpectedly canceled the Central Staff project. Ponomarenko later related that Stalin told him, without explanation, that "strictly speaking, the point of view has not changed, but this admittedly reasonable question [the Central Staff issue] has been put aside for the time being."[45] Beria evidently regarded the Central Staff as a threat to his role in the movement, and he convinced Stalin that the weak and vulnerable partisan forces would not benefit from a central headquarters, whereas his own highly trained saboteurs had no need of one. He also allegedly claimed that only the NKVD possessed the skills necessary to wage a successful partisan war, such as conducting sabotage and gathering intelligence, and that an amateur-led partisan movement would have no operational effect.[46] It is possible that he had help from Red Army political chief L. Z. Mekhlis, who also had an interest in preventing the establishment of a new civilian agency.[47] Stalin, too, may have been carried away in his hopes that most, if not all, Soviet territory would soon be liberated, thus making a partisan staff unnecessary.[48] Ponomarenko was able to protect the radio school by transferring its budget to the Belorussian government, but all other work was stopped.[49]

If indeed the NKVD had promised to provide general leadership of the partisans, then it failed in this task. During the spring of 1942, regional Party and military organs' calls for a central partisan agency grew more urgent.[50] The Red Army's winter counteroffensive sputtered to a halt in the spring. The disastrous attacks in May 1942 in the Crimea and at Kharkiv clearly indicated that victory was in the distant future.[51] A more effective partisan movement was needed now. On 24 May, the deputy commissar of defense, Colonel-General N. N. Voronin, complained in a memo to Stalin that the void in leadership was significantly undermining the effectiveness of the insurgency: the partisan war required centralization if it was to be an effective element of Soviet strategy.[52] This last intervention may just have done the trick, for Ponomarenko was soon recalled to Moscow from his post as a member of the military council of the Third Shock Army. There, he met an inebriated V. T. Sergienko of the Ukrainian NKVD, who told the Belorussian first secretary that he, Sergienko, would lead a revitalized Central Staff. However, according to Ponomarenko (who remains the sole source for this information), when Beria and Ukrainian First Secretary Khrushchev allegedly proposed this idea, Stalin rejected it, saying, "You have taken a narrow departmental approach to this extraordinarily significant problem. The partisan movement, the partisan struggle—this is a people's struggle. And this movement, this struggle must be led by the Party."[53] And with that, on 30 May, Stalin reinstated the Central Staff, with Ponomarenko again placed at its helm.[54]

THE CENTRAL STAFF:
ORGANIZATION AND PERSONNEL

The Central Staff encompassed an entire command-and-control system emanating from Moscow to all the occupied and frontline areas, including subordinate staffs attached to fronts and, later, oblasts and to the non-Russian republics. Modeled extensively on the Leningrad Staff of the Partisan Movement, which integrated military, state security, and Party representatives under the leadership of the Leningrad Obkom, the Central Staff was intended to cut through the overlapping jurisdictions of the army, Party, and NKVD to form a single, rationalized means of directing the movement.[55] It was not the preserve of any one organization but rather was a supraorganization, standing above competing state and Party agencies subordinated to the Supreme Command (Stavka) and the Central Committee. This approach had its precedents, as the Central Staff also resembled prewar Soviet institutions such as Glavsevmorput (the Main Administration of the Northern Sea Route), which at times brought together multiple agencies under one umbrella organization to focus on a particular area or issue.[56]

Though the Central Staff's specific organization varied throughout the war, the administrative functions and duties of its departments remained essentially the same.[57] Its most critical departments were Operations, Intelligence, and Political. Operations planned partisan missions, dispatched new detachments into the occupied territories, disbanded or merged units, disseminated technical and tactical information, and coordinated the actions of the subordinate staffs. The intelligence section not only assigned reconnaissance missions and located new or previously unknown partisan formations but also assessed political and economic conditions in the occupied territories.[58] The Political Department, established in late September 1942, concentrated on agitation and propaganda in the occupied territories, maintained ties with underground Party and soviet organizations, and publicized partisan activities in the Soviet media.[59] This same framework generally existed for subordinate partisan staffs attached to the republics, Russian regions, and Red Army fronts.

The Central Staff possessed extensive powers, at least on paper. In addition to those just listed, it could give commanders authority over other commanders and could designate disobedient units as outlaw bands marked for destruction.[60] It also dispatched supplies to the partisans, although both material shortages and Ponomarenko's philosophy that the partisans should supply themselves as much as possible limited this function.[61] In short, the Central Staff was an administrative instrument designed to bring all elements of partisan warfare firmly under Moscow's control.

The Central Staff's personnel reflected its interagency structure and mission. Although Party officials dominated the leadership cadres, the army and especially the security organs were also well represented. A troika formally composed the Central Staff leadership, with Ponomarenko from the Party at its head as chief of staff. His two lieutenants, V. T. Sergienko and T. F. Korneev, were from the NKVD and the army's General Staff, respectively.[62] Ponomarenko's deputy, S. S. Bel'chenko, was also from the NKVD.[63] Within the Central Staff and the subordinate staffs, military personnel were concentrated in Operations and other military-related departments, whereas Party and security personnel predominated in· the political and intelligence sections.[64]

Ponomarenko headed the Central Staff for almost the entirety of its existence. Although the Central Staff initially followed a collegial administration, Ponomarenko quickly dominated the other two members. On 6 September 1942, in the wake of the August Moscow conference and the issuance of NKO Order 189, however, Marshal K. E. Voroshilov was appointed supreme commander of partisan forces. Voroshilov, a member of the Politburo and, more importantly, the State Defense Committee (the real locus of institutional authority in the wartime Soviet Union), now had supposed control over *all* partisan units, including those specialized groups still under the jurisdiction of the NKVD and Red Army.[65] Up to that time, Voroshilov had not had a good war. A member of the Civil War generation, he was unable to adapt to the demands of modern warfare, a fact recognized by Stalin himself. In his previous commands of the Northwestern Direction and the Leningrad Front, he was so incompetent that he was replaced by more capable junior officers. It is possible that Stalin believed Voroshilov's publicly heralded exploits of conspiracy and underground warfare in the Civil War would be an asset to the partisans, who were fighting in similar circumstances.[66] The selection of one of the most senior Soviet military leaders to head the partisan movement, coming immediately after the issuing of NKO Order 189, indicated to some observers, especially army officers, that the regime was now serious in its efforts to militarize and professionalize the movement.[67] Certainly, some partisans were encouraged. D. V. Emliutin recalled in his memoirs that "the creation of a supreme partisan command made us much stronger, much livelier. We felt ourselves to be an integral fighting cell of the armed forces, and this caused much happiness."[68] If Emliutin or any other partisans found it ironic that their new supreme commander had participated in the purging of partisan instructors in the 1930s, they did not say so.

Voroshilov outranked Ponomarenko in both the Party and the Central Staff, but the two fought bitterly for control over the movement. Some historians have minimized Voroshilov's role in the Central Staff, but it is evident that he saw himself as its real commander.[69] He and Ponomarenko had clear differences over the direction the movement was to take: Voroshilov believed that the partisans should be militarized and become literally an army in the enemy's rear area, a vision that contrasted sharply with Ponomarenko's more politically oriented, civilian-dominated ideal. On this issue, the latter ulti-

mately had Stalin's support.[70] Voroshilov was removed from command in
mid-November 1942, and his post was abolished.[71] Command reverted to
Ponomarenko, although several observers and historians argue that Stalin essentially took charge of the movement.[72] Although Stalin intervened on some
key issues and occasionally issued direct orders, there is little documentary
evidence indicating that he was involved with the partisans on a regular or
systematic basis.

In addition to the Central Staff, an extensive network of subordinate
staffs and underground Party organizations was created to enable both greater
flexibility and more precision in directing the partisan war.[73] The initial organizational schema attached the subordinate staffs to the Red Army fronts,
but this arrangement caused much friction because front jurisdictions extended across the length of the front and in depth up to the German border;
further and most importantly, they did not conform to the civilian administrative districts to which many detachments adhered. The resulting confusion
about which Party or military organs had jurisdiction over the partisan units
was eased but not eliminated by a reorganization in September 1942 that
abolished the front staffs and established the subordinate staffs on a territorial basis. These staffs were attached to the regional Party and republican
central committees and were usually headed by regional and republican central committee secretaries.[74] The former heads of the front staffs now became
the heads of the territorial staffs, although they also remained "representatives of the Central Staff" (*predstaviteli TsShPD*) attached to the military
soviets of the front.[75] This arrangement reduced, somewhat, the "parallelism" afflicting the partisan movement, and it reinforced Party control.[76] The
last links in the partisan staff network's chain were the Party's underground
obkoms and raikoms and the Red Army's operational groups, all located behind enemy lines. These organs had immediate supervision over partisan operations, but their actual power and control over the partisans in practice
were dependent on a number of factors, including the partisans' willingness
to follow orders from "outside" authorities.[77]

The Central Staff operated from June 1942 until 13 January 1944, with a
three-week cessation in March and April 1943.[78] During these weeks, responsibility for directing partisan activities was transferred to the republican staffs
and the regional staffs in the Russian Republic.[79] The reason why this decision was made is not known, but some Soviet historians have argued that
Stalin sought to improve flexibility and to gain more-direct control over the
formations.[80] Alternatively, in the euphoria of the Soviet advance after Stalingrad, he may have hoped that enough territory had been or soon would be

liberated to make the Central Staff unnecessary. Staff officers themselves were "bewildered and alarmed" at the order, but one was told by a well-connected colleague, "Don't rack your brains over this, the Kremlin knows best."[81]

As it turned out—and not for the first time—the Kremlin did not know best. This new arrangement proved unworkable for officials and partisans alike, as the Germans halted the Soviet advance in the early spring of 1943 and subsequently recaptured Kharkiv and the Donbass, which still left significant amounts of Russian, Belorussian, Ukrainian, and Baltic territory under German occupation. Most staff officials believed that the large number of territorial and front staffs still needed coordination from the center, and they asked the Supreme Command and the Central Committee, in the words of one official, to preserve the Central Staff "in the interests of furthering the development of the mass partisan movement."[82] Orel Obkom secretary and partisan staff head A. P. Matveev told Stalin in April 1943 that a "central organ for the leadership of the partisan movement attached to Stavka" was required, since the "military soviets of the fronts do not occupy themselves [with the partisans] and regard them as a burden." Matveev continued that without a central administrative organ, it was very difficult to coordinate partisan actions with the Red Army's.[83] Rival staffs fought over property and jurisdictions, with no superior body to arbitrate these differences.[84] And without the Central Staff's authority to support them, lower staff officials lacked the clout to deal with high-ranking army officers.[85]

Realizing that centralization was still necessary, the State Defense Committee reversed itself and reestablished the Central Staff on 17 April 1943, with many of the same responsibilities it had before.[86] The most significant change was that the Ukrainian Staff remained independent under the leadership of NKVD Deputy Ukrainian Commissar T. A. Strokach. No official reasons were stated for this arrangement, but Ukraine's economic significance, its difficulties in organizing units in the Right Bank regions, and its delicate political situation exacerbated by the existence of well-organized separatist groups were probably critical factors.[87] Personal rivalry between Ponomarenko and Khrushchev may also have played a role, just as it did with Ponomarenko and Voroshilov. If so, then in this case, Stalin decided to favor Khrushchev, thereby preventing Ponomarenko from amassing too much power with his partisan fiefdom. Whatever the reasons, however, this arrangement further undermined a true centralization of the movement.[88]

The liberation of most Russian territory by January 1944 led to the permanent disbandment of the Central Staff on 13 January.[89] The republican staffs took control over the movement, since most of the units now fought on Ukrainian and Belorussian soil. They coordinated actions with the Red Army, as partisans and soldiers increasingly participated in combined operations.[90] That this disbandment again occurred with sizable amounts of territory still under enemy control suggests the leadership's eagerness to dismantle the partisan staff network as quickly as possible.

It was with this vast and complex network, dwarfing the efforts of other Allied partisan warfare agencies (notably Britain's Special Operations Executive and the U.S. Office of Strategic Services), that the Soviet regime directed the partisan war. In creating this administration, Soviet officials not only considered the particular context of the guerrilla war but also relied on administrative and organizational precedents developed in the interwar period. The Central Staff, with its representatives from multiple agencies, was the linchpin that held the apparatus together. As Alfred Rieber has pointed out, it did not end the feuding among the Party, army, and NKVD, each of which had its own agenda for the partisans, but it did preserve, in the words of one staff officer, the movement's "operational unity."[91] The establishment of the partisan staff network in such a relatively brief period was an impressive administrative and political achievement, especially when considering the leadership void that existed at the national level at the beginning of the war. Like all Soviet bureaucracies, with their clearly drawn tables of organization, it looked equal to its task on paper. Nevertheless, the ultimate proof of its success was to be found in the forests and swamps of the occupied territories, not in the corridors and offices of the Central Staff's headquarters on Moscow's Tver Boulevard.

THE PARTISAN STAFFS IN OPERATION

What looked so neat on paper in actuality was a swamp of jurisdictional confusion, for interstaff rivalries permeated the partisan administrative apparatus. The creation of an umbrella organization lessened tensions, but it could not do away with problems similar to those that had plagued other prewar administrations, especially conflicts over assets and competing regional loyalties.

Conflicts over jurisdictions were a product of the umbrella-like nature of the Central Staff. Before the advent of the Central Staff, such disputes usually occurred between independent institutions; now, these rivalries occurred within the Central Staff network itself. The Kalinin Front, for example, cut across several regions, including Russia's Kalinin and Smolensk Oblasts and Belorussia's Vitebsk Oblast. Partisan commanders in Vitebsk might receive orders from the representatives of the Kalinin Front, the Belorussian Staff, the Vitebsk Obkom, and the Central Staff itself, not to mention the operational groups of the Third and Fourth Shock Armies (both subordinated to the Kalinin Front). A Belorussian commander complained that in the resulting confusion, he could not "fulfill the orders of two bosses."[92] Safeguards to minimize the issuance of contradictory orders emanating from different bodies within the chain of command made the system cumbersome and unresponsive to immediate demands and opportunities. When the operational group of the Fourth Shock Army wanted to issue instructions to a partisan unit in Belorussia, it had to secure the approval of the Belorussian Staff, which could significantly delay the command's transmission and thus compromise a mission's success.[93] Moscow's habit of sending plenipotentiaries to oversee operations and to cut through red tape may have helped resolve immediate problems, but in the long term, it only further undermined and confused the regular administrative structure.

Still, its multiple-agency structure also enabled the Central Staff to resolve disputes more smoothly than had happened during the leadership void in 1941 and 1942. Such was the case in the Leningrad region in the fall of 1942. Three fronts (the Northwestern, Volkhov, and Leningrad) and one independent army, each entitled to have its own partisan staff representative, were located in the region. M. I. Nikitin, the head of the Leningrad Staff and the Central Staff representative at the Leningrad Front, warned Ponomarenko that the existence of one army and three front representatives in the oblast would mean that "instead of the single, directing organ of the Leningrad Staff of the Partisan Movement, conducting the leadership of the partisan movement, several directing organs are created on the oblast's territory." Multiple representatives would undermine the unity necessary to strike decisive blows against the enemy. Hence, Nikitin urged Ponomarenko to give the Leningrad Staff overall control of the area's partisans and the authority to appoint its own representatives to the Northwestern and Volkhov Fronts and to the Seventh Independent Army.[94] Ponomarenko agreed, and he acted similarly in the summer of 1942 in Ukraine, where the existence of multiple fronts threatened to disrupt the operational unity of the Ukrainian Staff.[95]

Disputes between territorial staffs were also difficult to manage, sometimes requiring intervention from the very top. Just as trusts and enterprises associated with certain regions competed with one another for control of assets and contracts in Soviet industrial policy, so, too, did territorial staffs argue over jurisdictions and partisan units.[96] Such was the case in the struggle between the Kursk and Orel Obkoms in 1942 and 1943. In late 1941 or early 1942, Orel NKVD officials "discovered" some previously unknown Kursk partisan formations. Although I. Popov, the Kursk Obkom's first secretary, wanted to direct the partisans from his oblast, he lacked the necessary staff to command them. Popov apparently agreed to their transfer to his counterparts in Orel.[97] In December 1942, Popov asked Ponomarenko to transfer the Kursk partisans back to his jurisdiction from the Voronezh and Briansk Fronts (the latter headed by Orel Obkom secretary Matveev) so that he could direct his partisans "independently." Evidently, this decision was so important that Ponomarenko forwarded the request to Stalin, who gave his assent.[98]

These regional conflicts had very real consequences for the partisans, especially since local staffs favored their "native" partisans over those from other areas. When some partisans from Orel fell under the jurisdiction of the Western Staff of the Partisan Movement (attached to the Western Front), headed by Smolensk Obkom secretary D. M. Popov, they complained that Popov had abandoned them. Although Western Staff officials apparently knew of the Orel partisans' "exceptionally serious position," they only sent a quarter of the supplies needed. One Orel official reported to Politburo member A. A. Andreev that Popov essentially told the Orel partisans, "You are not from our oblast, go to your Orel Oblast, let them show concern for you there and arrange things for you." This official accused Popov of only helping "his" Smolensk partisans. He continued:

> We are patriots of our Motherland, but we are also in no less measure
> patriots of our oblast and our districts, and we will preserve the honor
> of our oblast and districts and every day we will increase our military
> activities. But the Orel Obkom does not know about our military
> activities because the Western Staff of the Partisan Movement describes
> [our] military actions as those of Smolensk partisans . . . Realizing this,
> the political-command staff of the [Orel] detachments is outraged.
> Why does the West[ern] Staff tell lies to our higher Party-Soviet
> organization?[99]

For their part, Smolensk partisans located in the territory administered by the Kalinin Staff of the Partisan Movement complained to Smolensk's Popov that the Kalinin Staff devoted almost all of its attention to its Kalinin and Belorussian partisans, while ignoring them.[100] This regionalism, further undermining the center's efforts to construct a national partisan movement, was a natural continuation of the rivalries that had plagued centralizing efforts in industrial policy during the prewar years.

The Central Staff system itself sometimes exacerbated these local rivalries and, as will be shown later, also those between corporate agencies. Giving territorial bodies supervision over partisan detachments provided more localized supervision and, hence, potentially greater flexibility closer to the fighting. However, the lack of distinct jurisdictional boundaries, the claims of one organization that it was more effective than others, and the favoritism shown by officials to partisans from their own regions over so-called foreigners ensured that conflicts would ensue. Usually, the Central Staff or sometimes even Stalin himself intervened to resolve the dispute, but not even these efforts always succeeded in establishing administrative order and operational effectiveness.

BUREAUCRACY AND COMMUNICATIONS

Mediating disputes between competing staffs was one thing, but the efforts to establish command and control over the movement became even more difficult when the partisans themselves became involved. Although the Central Staff and its subordinate staffs exerted considerable control over the partisans and coordinated their operations to a degree previously unknown in the history of guerrilla warfare, their power was not absolute. Their limited authority was most manifest in their attempts to enforce order among the autonomously minded detachments, whose leaders, for their part, often tried to manipulate both the central and territorial administrations. From the partisans' perspective, the realities and dangers of guerrilla warfare meant that they could not always wait for instructions from the center to defend themselves against attackers. And because of their relative freedom behind enemy lines, they could attempt to disobey orders that they believed would put them in grave peril or even those that they deemed were not in their best interests.

The challenge of maintaining effective command and control over the partisans was exacerbated by the difficulties of maintaining reliable communications with units located hundreds of miles behind enemy lines. As in peacetime, the centralized apparatus required constant communication and accurate information if it was to direct the partisans effectively. Relatively secure communications between the staffs and units was eventually established, but this did not mean that the center's problems were solved. Like their peacetime political and industrial counterparts, partisans proved adept at manipulating communications *and* bureaucratic rivalries to pursue their own objectives.

To the leadership, already consumed by the fear of partisan subversion, maintaining strict control over the guerrillas was the most fundamental concern. In August 1942, Voroshilov told I. N. Artem'ev, the head of the Central Staff's communications section, that without reliable communications with the partisans, "there is no sense in creating a staff of the partisan movement. Without good communications with the partisans, they cannot do their work."[101] Authorities worried that they could lose their hold on the underground resistance organs. As late as November 1943, the director of the Central Staff's Political Department, V. N. Malin, told Lithuanian Komsomol activists that without constant and reliable communications, "all [talk of] leadership is idle."[102] Military planners also needed constant contact with the partisans, without which they could neither obtain timely and sufficient data nor send orders.[103] Moreover, as noted, the partisans feared isolation from Soviet authorities for a variety of reasons.

At the beginning of the war, communications between partisans and Soviet-held territory were hampered by the severe lack of radios. Consequently, authorities relied on couriers, but these were slow and unreliable, sometimes taking forty to fifty days to reach their destinations, thus rendering them useless for transmitting anything except the most general instructions.[104] That they would even arrive at a detachment at all was itself a dubious proposition. Movement on land was facilitated by occasional gaps in the front, such as the so-called Surazh Gates in the Vitebsk region of Belorussia,[105] but crossing the battle lines and making one's way through enemy-held territory remained extremely dangerous. By early 1942, the Orel Obkom had sent 116 couriers to 30 districts, but only 34 had established ties with partisan units and returned. The fates of the other 82 couriers were unknown.[106] One Red Army political officer noted that losses among couriers were so high "that not many comrades agree to this work."[107]

Developing reliable communications hinged on the production of hardy, mobile radio sets and training the personnel to operate them. These were priorities for the Central Staff; indeed, one of Ponomarenko's first actions was to organize a radio-training school in January 1942. Although the two-and-a-half-month training course was superficial compared to prewar standards (prewar partisan radio operators could build their own radio sets),[108] at least some 3,000 badly needed radio operators, 86 percent of whom were women, were trained and sent to the occupied territories by the end of the war.[109] Tough, portable radio sets were mass-produced: by 1943, a single factory in

Leningrad produced 2,000 radios monthly, compared to only 300 for all of 1941.[110]

These efforts bore fruit, as relatively reliable contacts between the mainland and the partisans expanded enormously after the disasters of 1941. Early in the summer of 1942, the Central Staff estimated that it had direct radio contact with only 10 percent to 15 percent of the partisan detachments. Another 15 percent were sent information via couriers from the units that did possess radios.[111] In August 1942, the Central Staff had some form of radio contact with 342 out of 813 known detachments (42 percent), serviced by 134 radio stations. By May 1943, this percentage had increased to 87 percent, and by December 1943, all 1,079 known detachments were in contact with the center via 421 radio stations.[112] Major organizations and complexes, whose subunits operated long distances away from headquarters, sometimes had multiple sets and even developed their own radio networks among their detachments, enabling greater coordination and sophisticated planning.[113]

Aircraft provided another communications link and especially enabled the transport of critical supplies, as well as the evacuation of wounded. As almost 100 percent of all radio equipment, 95 percent of sabotage devices, and 75 percent of explosives came from the mainland, aircraft were absolutely essential to the movement's survival and effectiveness.[114] In some cases, they brought the only source of food, as occurred in the Crimea when starvation had reduced some partisans to cannibalism.[115] Like radios, however, few aircraft were available to the partisans in the first year of the war. Even as late as September 1942, it was difficult to obtain aircraft for partisan missions. The head of Long Range Aviation, General A. E. Golovanov, told Ponomarenko that it was impossible to schedule regular flights to the partisans, since the aircraft were desperately needed for other duties.[116] By 1943, increased production and a greater allocation of aircraft to partisan operations meant that flights to the occupied territories became more customary. By the war's end, over 109,000 sorties had transported 16,000 tons of supplies and 83,000 people across the lines.[117] In fact, partisans became so dependent on aircraft materially and psychologically that the loss of an airfield to German attack invariably led to a catastrophic collapse of morale and combat effectiveness.[118]

Though the radio and aviation links gave the Central Staff an unprecedented capability to direct and support guerrilla operations, there were still limitations to these technologies. Radios broke down, batteries drained (at least one unit relied on a Rube Goldberg–like, human-powered generator when this occurred),[119] and hastily and poorly trained operators forgot or in-

Portrait of partisans from the Bielski Detachment while guarding an airfield. (Credit: USHMM, courtesy of Moshe Kaganovich)

advertently scrambled codes. Aircraft, too, had their deficiencies, as they were often unavailable due to more pressing military demands. Access to partisan airfields, weather conditions, and even the length of darkness also affected the frequency of flights. The need to maintain and secure airfields further reduced partisan mobility. The famed partisan commander and memoirist Petr Vershigora became so frustrated awaiting the arrival of a flight night after cold night at a partisan airfield that he thought the stories told to pass the time should be titled *A Thousand and One Nights Waiting for Grizodubova's Airplanes, or the Partisan Scheherazade.*[120]

More dangerous from the center's perspective was the ability of the partisans to manipulate these links for their own benefit. The partisans had their own interests and goals, especially maintaining their own safety and security, and they proved ready and willing to subvert the partisan administration whenever they deemed it necessary to do so.

In February 1943, fifteen Belorussian and Kalinin partisan units in the Vitebsk region came under a massive German assault. At that time, no single unit or commander had the authority to organize a coordinated defense. In the midst of an increasingly desperate battle for survival, the commander of the "For Soviet Belarus" Partisan Brigade, A. V. Romanov, claimed to have received a radiogram from Ponomarenko ordering him to take charge of all the units in the area and lead a breakout from the closing German ring.[121] Although Romanov evinced surprise that he, a relatively junior officer, would be given command of such a large force, he used this authority to organize and execute the breakout. However, two partisan staff officials from the Belorussian and Kalinin Staffs, P. S. Shelymagin and A. I. Shtrakhov, respectively, declared that Ponomarenko had sent no such instructions and that Romanov had forged the order. They insisted that Shtrakhov take charge of the Kalinin units, and having accomplished his goal, Romanov stepped down from his "command." In an April 1943 report to the Belorussian Staff, he defended his actions by saying that though he now did not actually know the source of the radio order, "even if the order had been fictitious, it served the general cause," for without it, the Germans would have overwhelmed the partisans' uncoordinated defenses.[122]

In his memoirs, published in 1962, Romanov related that the order had originated from one of his scouts, who, at Romanov's urgings, had twice requested via radio that Moscow establish a local centralized leadership at the beginning of the German attack. When no answer came, apparently without Romanov's knowledge, the scout drafted an order, sent it to Moscow, and asked the answering operator to send it back to Romanov, who then claimed to believe that it was a bona fide order.[123] This part of the episode was not included in the brigade commander's April report, either to protect his subordinate or because Romanov invented this seemingly incredible story. In either case, he and his comrades successfully manipulated the partisan staff apparatus (and the other units) by essentially forging an order from the Central Staff, the very institution that was supposed to curb such wild actions. Yet Romanov, who remained an honored partisan after the war, did not suffer any known repercussions.

Partisans also used the parallelism and undefined jurisdiction of subordinate staffs to their advantage, often playing them off each other. Such was the case in the southern Briansk forest region where the Orel and Ukrainian Staffs had been feuding over the control of partisan assets since the 1941–1942 winter, with each side accusing the other of attempting to co-opt its units and arresting its personnel.[124] This conflict came to a head in the winter of 1943 when the staffs fought for control of the 2nd Voroshilov Partisan Brigade, a well-armed and experienced band. That the commanders of the 2nd Voroshilov apparently had their own plots and plans only complicated the situation further.

The dispute began on 16 December 1942, when T. A. Strokach, the Ukrainian Staff chief, requested that Ponomarenko transfer to him the 2nd Voroshilov Partisan Brigade from D. V. Emliutin's OPO, which itself was subordinated to the Orel Obkom. Strokach claimed that the unit was composed primarily of Ukrainians and that the OPO failed to make use of it. According to Central Staff records, the unit only had 94 Ukrainians out of a total complement of 590,[125] but nonetheless, on 4 February 1943, Ponomarenko ordered the Orel Staff to transfer the entire unit to Ukrainian command. On 12 February, both the Ukrainian and Central Staffs ordered Gudzenko to prepare his unit to undertake a long-range partisan raid into Ukraine, always a risky and potentially very costly operation.[126]

The Orel Staff apparently refused to let go of one of its best units. Having fended off other attempts by Strokach since February 1942 to subordinate their units, including Emliutin's entire command at one point, Orel partisan officials evidently believed this order to be another of his ploys. They protested that the Orel Staff had supplied and equipped Gudzenko's unit and that "in this detachment there weren't any Ukrainians, but a lot of other nationalities."[127] On 15 February 1943, Strokach told Ponomarenko that Gudzenko's immediate superior, Emliutin (who, incidentally, was also an NKVD officer like Strokach), was deliberately delaying the transfer of the 2nd Voroshilov to his command, and he requested that Ponomarenko intervene directly.[128]

Despite Ponomarenko's order to transfer the unit to Ukrainian jurisdiction, the 2nd Voroshilov remained in the Briansk forest under the Orel Staff's authority. On 11 April, Gudzenko sent a radiogram to Strokach informing him that he had been unable to undertake the raid that had been ordered in February. According to Gudzenko, when Emliutin and Matveev learned of the 2nd Voroshilov's imminent transfer, they worked together to issue a series of contradictory marching orders "in the interests of the Orel Staff" that sent the band marching "from one place to the other," as Gudzenko described it. These instructions prevented the unit from launching the raid, even though it had supposedly been ready since 20 February.[129]

Gudzenko then proceeded to request aid from the Ukrainians, for his men had exhausted their food reserves preparing for the raid; they were, he reported, unable to resupply because the Germans had seized grain stores and because the underground Party committees were reserving their food stocks for the advancing Red Army. The Orel Staff would not allocate the 2nd Voroshilov any additional provisions, since it had now supposedly come under Ukrainian jurisdiction. Gudzenko warned that if the detachment did not receive additional supplies in ten days, he would "be forced to break all rule of law and independently take measures according to the situation"—in other words, his partisans would plunder whatever food stores they could find.[130] In the end, the 2nd Voroshilov remained in the Briansk forest, where it was annihilated and Gudzenko himself was killed in a massive German antipartisan operation in June 1943.[131]

It would appear that Gudzenko was a mere pawn in the ongoing struggle between the Orel and Ukrainian Staffs. This seemed to be the conclusion reached in a Central Staff investigation of the incident. The authors of the report prepared after the investigation determined that Matveev, taking advantage of the temporary dissolution of the Central Staff, "delayed the departure of the detachment by explaining that supposedly [Red Army Chief of Staff] Marshal of the Soviet Union A. M. Vasil'evskii had given a task to Gudzenko's detachment to operate in the Briansk forest."[132] If this report was accurate, then Matveev, like Romanov, evidently forged or falsely intimated the sanction of a higher official to justify his own actions.

The misadventures of the 2nd Voroshilov illuminate several important dynamics of the relationship among partisans, subordinate staffs, and the Central Staff. In the face of determined resistance, the Central Staff could not always prevail over subordinate staffs if the latter were willing to employ subterfuge. It is also interesting to note that despite the NKVD affiliation shared by Strokach, Emliutin, and Matveev (the latter had been attached to the security organs in Belorussia before becoming Orel Obkom first secretary), their local interests superseded their corporate ties. Most striking is Gudzenko's role in this affair. Although he acknowledged receiving the order from Strokach to launch the raid, he obeyed the instructions sent by Matveev and Emliutin. He also took the opportunity to cover his tracks with Strokach by criticizing Emliutin's passivity, suggesting that he, Gudzenko, really wanted to go on the raid. In his description to Strokach of his unit's activities, Gudzenko never mentioned Vasil'evskii's supposed intervention. Perhaps the Orel officials invoked his name and Gudzenko forgot to record it, or perhaps the commander was genuinely confused by the receipt of contradictory orders. But it is quite possible that Gudzenko used the Orel-Ukrainian feud as a cover for pursuing his own objectives. Obeying the Orel Staff meant staying in the relatively safe haven of the Briansk forest as opposed to conducting a highly dangerous raid across the open Ukrainian steppes, an undertaking at which many other partisans had balked. Thus, far from being a victim of circumstance, Gudzenko may very well have used the competition over jurisdictions to follow the orders that best suited his interests.

The center was determined to control the partisan movement, and compared to the situation in 1941 and 1942, it largely succeeded. However, this power was certainly not absolute. Difficulties in securing accurate and reliable information and communications, disputes between subordinate agencies, and the willingness of underlings to use these deficiencies for their own purposes all combined to undermine the center's authority. Though neither commanders nor regional staff officials could afford to be perceived as disobeying Moscow, they were not going to follow orders blindly if they thought those instructions put them at substantially increased risk. For their part, regional organizations were not above placing their own interests over other regional or even national objectives as they competed with one another for control over partisan units, much like regions struggled for industrial resources and contracts from the center. Thus, the power in center-periphery relations in the partisan movement was hardly unidirectional, as central and regional officials and partisans all sought to achieve their respective visions of order and stability in the occupied territories.

THE PARTY AND THE PARTISANS

Even with the establishment of the Central Staff, other agencies continued to participate in the partisan war. The security organs through the NKVD's Fourth Administration and its "special sections" attached to units, as well as the counterespionage organization SMERSH (whose name was the abbreviation for the term *Death to Spies!*), all played important roles in the movement. The Red Army still employed its own special reconnaissance detachments and helped coordinate partisan operations with those of army units. The Party, especially through its local organs, maintained the most prominent position. In theory, the partisan bands were subordinated to the local underground district and regional committees, which were to provide ideological guidance, oversee partisan actions, and link the guerrillas to both the people and the partisan staffs. These responsibilities generally followed those of prewar Party organizations. As Stephen Kotkin observed, the Party typically provided ideological rather than technical or practical expertise, to ensure that all actions were guided by *partiinost'* (party-mindedness).[133] Nevertheless, ideological guidance often involved actual oversight, or, as others might see it, the Party interfered and meddled in affairs it knew nothing about. The Party's role created a tension in Soviet society that was never resolved until the end of the Soviet Union itself—the tension between sustaining and implementing a Communist worldview and still achieving real material goals. In the war years, at least at the front and in the Soviet rear area, ideology (here defined as a systematized set of political beliefs) frequently took a back seat to the demands of industrial and national mobilization. Although the Party facilitated the national mobilization drive, other organizations, most notably the State Defense Committee, superceded its ruling functions.[134] In the partisan war, however, ideology and Party oversight were central to the leadership's efforts to control the insurgency and to make clear to the populace and the partisan alike that Soviet power and the Soviet system still prevailed in the occupied territories.

However, more often than not, it was the partisans who dominated the local Party apparatus. The weakness of the underground Party organizations relative to the partisans meant that the power relationships were often reversed. Moreover, some officials in the Soviet rear area as well as some partisans, especially those with army or NKVD backgrounds, resented what they believed was the Party's amateurish interference in military and security affairs. Not surprisingly, then, the role of local Party organizations became a subject of intense negotiation between the partisans and Soviet authorities. At the same time, the Party's status as the keeper and interpreter of the state ideology meant that it could not be ignored. Moreover, as supposedly neutral civilian organizations, local Party organs were sometimes able to resolve disputes among the fractious partisans.

Many Party organizations did not survive the transition to an underground existence, although where they continued to function, they could still exert some power over the incipient partisan groups.[135] More commonly, however, underground Party members abandoned their duties and fled to the safety of the Soviet rear area or were arrested by occupation forces, often when they broke elementary rules of conspiracy.[136] In Leningrad Oblast, for example, only eight of the twenty-six underground raikoms organized in the fall of 1941 were still functioning six months later.[137] By May 1943, attrition among Leningrad raikom secretaries was so great that the Leningrad Obkom asked the Central Committee to confirm new secretarial appointments for the underground organizations and partisan detachments.[138] No underground committees were established in the western Ukrainian oblasts, and in many eastern regions, such as in Dniepropetrovsk, the committees formed by local cadres remained inactive.[139]

Therefore, in most districts, local organs had to be rebuilt, often from scratch. Raikom officials who had escaped to the partisan camps might reconstitute a new committee there.[140] Party organizations in the partisan detachments often provided the nucleus for these new bodies. Sometimes, local partisan leaders themselves supervised Party cadres.[141] In one Belorussian district, for example, the local partisan commander, a senior lieutenant of the border guards, organized a raikom and appointed himself a member. The raikom's bureau, which controlled all other Party organs in the district, was situated in the brigade.[142] In the Orel, Smolensk, and Sumy regions, underground raikoms were openly attached to the detachments, which gave them protection from the enemy. However, these close bonds meant that when the units left their districts, so, too, did the district committees, thus disabling local Communist networks.[143] Moreover, the independence of these Party organs was severely compromised by such arrangements.

The almost wholesale destruction or disappearance of its apparatus in Ukraine essentially meant that the Party had to be reintroduced into the republic. The major raiding complexes reestablished regional and district committees in the areas they settled. The political authority of the complex commanders was cemented by their appointments as plenipotentiaries of the underground Ukrainian Central Committee. Some, such as Fedorov and Begma, were important Party officials even before the war.[144] Hence, Fedorov, the former first secretary of the Chernihiv Obkom, became the first secretary of the reborn underground Volhynia Obkom when his complex moved into the region in 1943, and Begma became head of the reconstituted Rivne Obkom when his unit relocated there. Small organizing teams were parachuted into regions where partisans had not yet penetrated, such as Zhytomyr, where they developed local bands and created underground committees.[145] Because the local Ukrainian organs had, in Moscow's eyes, disgraced themselves, their remnants were basically ignored as the new Party structure was reconstituted by the partisan "carpetbaggers" from outside the regions. After the war, the Ukrainian Party was further recomposed by Red Army veterans and partisans, and the local prewar cadres who remained in occupied territory were largely purged.[146]

In areas where some semblance of an independent underground Party remained, a complex struggle for power emerged between the local Party and partisan leaders. Local Party organizations were concerned about their physical and institutional survival, and they also attempted to exert authority over territories and personnel they believed came under their jurisdiction. The partisans, by contrast—even those who were Communist officials—sought to maximize their autonomy from any kind of oversight, especially when they believed the Party organs were meddling in military affairs. However, they also relied on the same outside Party organs to provide them material and political support. It fell to the Central Staff to find the balance between ideological oversight and operational freedom.

On occasion, partisans attempted to institutionalize their informal domi-nance over the civilian Party organizations. In the fall of 1942, the United Par-tisan Detachments, through its political department and brigade political de-partments, had essentially usurped the functions of the civilian committees, including selecting new raikom secretaries and admitting new members to the Party.[147] Although the OPO defended its actions as an effort to end the duality and parallelism of the partisan and civilian organs, thereby enabling the latter to work more effectively,[148] Ponomarenko would have none of it. He declared that "several comrades had an incorrect understanding of the [raikoms'] role, consequently the party raikoms were removed from the lead-ership of the partisan movement and even from the leadership of the political work inside the detachments." On the contrary, raikoms were supposed to provide the movement's political leadership.[149] Ponomarenko reestablished the primacy of the civilian Party organs, while the brigade political depart-ments apparently soldiered on with drastically reduced functions.[150]

Although he sought to prevent partisan leaders from using their units' internal Party organizations to establish independent fiefdoms, Ponomarenko generally balked at allowing local Party cadres to intervene in the guerrillas' operational affairs. When, in January 1943, the Vitebsk Obkom secretary, I. A. Stulov, complained to Ponomarenko about the "incorrect, and in several cases, anti-Party conduct" of several partisan commanders and commis-sars who ignored his orders, refused to submit reports, and sought instruc-tions from the Belorussian Staff, the partisan chief was not moved.[151] He informed Stulov that although the Party officials had primacy in political affairs in their areas, they did not have the right to interfere in operational matters unless they were acting on higher instructions.[152] Moreover, the fact that the Vitebsk Obkom was not located in occupied territory evidently an-noyed Ponomarenko, for he told Stulov that if the partisans "turned to the Belorussian Staff and the Central Committee—there is nothing to be done about it."[153] In other words, if the obkom was not willing to risk going under-ground, then it had little right to complain when the partisans, who faced constant dangers behind the lines, ignored it. In this instance, Ponomarenko defined further the boundaries between political and military spheres; though he was a staunch defender of a civilianized movement and for Party oversight of it, he maintained that partisan commanders, in general, had to have op-erational control so long as they worked within the official framework. The underlying problem that was never really resolved, however, was how to de-termine which actions were political and which were military, distinctions that are almost always blurred in a guerrilla war.

Yet it would be a mistake to view the relationship between local Party organs and the partisans as one of constant antagonism. Many partisan leaders were themselves local Party officials. Their current views toward the local committees were colored, however, by the threat the former represented to their autonomy and not due to ideological differences (although, of course, there may well have been more powerful political or personal motivations at work for some). More critically, for all the conflicts over jurisdictions, Party organizations and partisan units needed each other to survive. Local Party organs depended on the partisans for their physical existence and for the re-establishment of Soviet power in the liberated zones.[154] The partisans needed Party organs to arbitrate disputes and especially to give them legitimacy in Moscow's eyes. At the August 1942 conference, the commander of the 1st Voroshilov Detachment, Red Army lieutenant G. F. Pokrovskii, sharply criticized the local organs of Soviet power, which, he argued, should have been subordinated to the partisans, for the Party cadres interfered in his operations and challenged his authority. "Let them go deep underground," Pokrovskii said to Ponomarenko and the other assembled partisans. "They can help us in their own way, and when things get difficult we'll help them, but they shouldn't stick their noses where they don't belong."[155]

The other partisans quickly contradicted Pokrovskii. On the contrary, they assured Ponomarenko, local Party organs helped the partisans. M. P. Romashin, a commander—and former local district Party secretary—declared that "neutral" organizations, such as Party organs, were necessary to regulate relations among the partisans. According to Romashin, the absence of local Party organs would "permit anarchy" and enable "every commander to do just what he pleased." In response to an interjection from an unidentified partisan that local Party officials "got in the way," Romashin retorted, "Party and soviet organizations prevent disorder. We go to them, we say we need to have supplies, they order a detail, and they do not allow unauthorized [procurements]."[156] Red Army commander Gudzenko declared, "Pokrovskii misunderstands the role of the party organizations," which, he continued, had been very helpful in providing his detachment with boots, clothing, and overcoats. Gudzenko admitted that some Party officials did not understand that they were supposed to aid the partisans and not dictate to them, but he nevertheless argued that they were essential to the success of the movement.[157] It is worth noting, however, that this was the same Gudzenko who would later threaten to plunder food stores collected by local Party organizations if he did not receive immediate aid.

Although these statements may have been for the benefit of Ponomarenko, who, after all, was a high-ranking Party official, it is also quite clear that partisans believed that neutral people, "who did not have their own detachments," were needed to arbitrate relations both among the units and between the partisans and the surrounding civilian population.[158] In the occupied territories, local Party organs were often the only organizations available to resolve disputes over supply procurements and the demarcation of unit jurisdictions. Other reports show that even though Party organs usually favored Party-dominated units (Red Army okruzhentsy, in particular, perceived this bias), they also could coordinate partisan activities and ensure a relatively equitable distribution of supplies.[159] In the partisans' violent world, where arguments between detachments could easily lead to bloodshed, such purportedly neutral institutions were invaluable. But as will be seen in the next chapter, the ability of local Party organs to negotiate conflicts was limited, for they were fully capable of taking sides in the guerrillas' squabbles.

The Central Staff never managed to resolve the tension between the need for operational independence and political reliability. Nonetheless, Soviet authorities made clear that whatever the specifics of the Party-partisan relationship, the Party had to continue to exist in the occupied territories as the sole source of political authority, even if directly under the auspices of major partisan units, as occurred in the western Ukrainian regions. Even there, the new partisan commanders turned regional Party bosses had been appointed by the Ukrainian Central Committee.

The partisans, too, had an interest in maintaining local Party organizations. Local Party organs helped obtain supplies and mediate conflicts, and the partisans realized that ties with these organs contributed to their credibility with the Central Staff and proved that they continued to uphold Soviet political norms. Hence, the OPO did not abolish local Party organs but sought to control their personnel, thus maintaining a fiction of continued local independence while upholding the Party's physical structure. The Party remained a symbol of the Soviet Union itself. Even if partisans ignored the Party's explicit ideological message, their protection of its apparatus demonstrated allegiance to it and became physical proof of their Soviet patriotism. The show of loyalty to this all-Union institution was especially critical given the deep suspicions that Soviet authorities had concerning the increasingly non–politically affiliated composition of the movement.

At the same time, the Soviet leadership displayed remarkable ability in creating a partisan administration from scratch that addressed the multiple demands of waging a guerrilla war. In less than a year, Soviet leaders established a functional staff network to oversee, coordinate, and direct the rapidly growing partisan movement. The partisan staff system was based on both existing institutions and organizational schemes used by other Soviet bureaucracies developed in the 1920s and 1930s. Yet the partisan administration faced many of the same problems besetting peacetime Soviet bureaucracy, such as overlapping jurisdictions, competing agencies, interagency and intrastaff rivalries, and regional competition. To some extent, the running of the Central Staff was more reminiscent of Stalinist industrial politics than of a military command. Yet for all its deficiencies, the Central Staff network did provide crucial direction for and support of the partisans. As the experiences of both officials and partisans attest, the absence of a centralized partisan agency in 1941 and later, in the spring of 1943, led to confusion and anarchy and hindered operations against the enemy.

Even as the state attempted to impose administrative—and therefore political—order and control over the movement, the partisans were far from being passive appendages. On the contrary, they actively pursued their own interests and occasionally were the tail that wagged Moscow's dog. When necessary, they circumvented, deceived, and used state agencies to achieve their goals. In exploiting interagency competition, the lack of reliable and accurate communications, blurred jurisdictions, and regional rivalries, the partisans often manipulated authorities while appearing to follow instructions.

Nevertheless, the partisans generally recognized that centralized control and intervention were necessary, if only to provide a semblance of order and stability in their relations with other partisans. Without outside supervision, the partisans' ability to strike at vital enemy targets was severely compromised. Just as important, without outside oversight and mediation, conflicts between partisan units could occur. Local Party organs especially benefited from this realization and were often regarded as mediators between competing groups, even though they, too, were sometimes prejudiced against one band or another. For both partisans and state authorities, the regime's management of the vast partisan effort, as haphazard as it was, was a vital administrative and military achievement and an indication to many contemporaries of the Soviet system's viability, even if its all-too-many flaws were masked by the war's victorious conclusion.

4

PEOPLE'S AVENGERS OR *PARTIZANSHCHINA*? THE MAKING OF PARTISAN IDENTITIES, 1941–1942

From the first weeks of the war, the partisan movement served as a propaganda instrument to inspire the Soviet population, on either side of the lines, to resist the enemy. Partisans became among the most celebrated heroes in the central press, especially since there was little news from the front to celebrate in 1941 and 1942.[1] Their stories reminded citizens in Soviet-held territory that the war still raged behind enemy lines. The partisans became a symbol of popular resistance and support for the Soviet system and thus were a key component in the regime's campaign to win legitimacy from the public at large.

These stories also served as guides of behavior for the partisans themselves, indicating the parameters of acceptable actions and values, especially as wider segments of the population joined the bands beginning in the spring of 1942. But even Party-affiliated partisans and other "reliable" veterans were subjected to this official vision of the Red partisan. In 1941 and the first part of 1942, this didactic function was less useful due to the difficulties in distributing information to the occupied territories via newspapers and the radio. By the second half of 1942, however, the increased distribution of newspapers in the occupied territories and the growing number of radios expanded the partisans' exposure to Soviet media. State radio's special broadcasts to the occupied territories beginning in June 1942 were particularly important in this regard.[2]

Stories about partisans were part of the regime's effort to ascribe an official "partisan identity" on the movement and its participants. In this context, the word *identity* refers to a specific set of values, beliefs, and codes of behavior to which individuals and discrete groups adhered or claimed to adhere. In Soviet terms, such identities would theoretically correspond with practices and behaviors that fell within state-sanctioned parameters. From the beginning of Soviet power, the state not only ascribed identities based on class, nationality, and gender but also sought to make social reality conform to its a priori categories.[3] This practice continued into World War II as Soviet mass media and actual policy established the parameters of officially acceptable partisan behaviors and values. State authorities hoped to capitalize on the partisans' romantic image to help attract popular support for the regime and the state-sponsored resistance, but they also had to ensure the partisans remained politically and militarily reliable. Foremost among officials' concerns was the prevention of behaviors they labeled with the term *partizanshchina*, which, as described earlier, Bolshevik authorities had defined as disobedience, lack of political consciousness, possessing unorthodox or even hostile ideology, and pursuing the interests of one's self or one's group over those of the state. In contrast, the model Soviet partisan was not only heroic and dashing but also disciplined and dedicated to defeating the enemy regardless of cost. Most important, the official partisan embodied the popular determination to destroy the enemy and save the *rodina*, or motherland, a term that could refer to a variety of places, including the entire Soviet Union, a native republic, a region, a district, or even one's hometown. Failure to follow these prescriptions could mark a partisan as anti-Soviet, a label that carried grave consequences. Thus, the regime's efforts to project an identity onto the partisans were part of the larger struggle to control the movement and ensure its reliability.

To help establish this official identity, Soviet officials actively sought out persons who would best represent the center's public vision of the partisan as a loyal citizen and a man or woman of the people. For example, Belorussian Party official G. B. Eidinov, on assignment behind enemy lines, reported to Ponomarenko in early June 1942 that in the 1st Belorussian Partisan Brigade commander, M. F. Shmyrev, "we have a strong partisan leader, a man of exceptional intelligence and wonderful personal qualities" who had the respect and love of partisans and civilians alike. Eidinov concluded, "I would say that [he] is a Belorussian folk [*narodnyi*] hero."[4] A short time later, several stories about Shmyrev, using his code name, Bat'ka Minai, appeared in the Soviet press.[5]

Yet the identities imposed on the partisans by the state often conflicted with the partisans' own definitions of themselves and their world. Identities are not formed a priori but are informed by the experiences of everyday life.[6] Although the centrality of the regime in daily life (even separated by the battle lines) meant that the partisans could not ignore official ascriptions, their own experiences were, for the moment, more immediate and powerful. From the first days of the war, the partisans began to develop their own "partisan ethos," which was informed by their lives in peacetime, by the collective memory of past irregular fighters, and by their own experiences as partisans. Almost all partisans adopted at least some aspects of the partisan ethos. In addition, partisans who were affiliated with the Party or the Red Army or who were closely linked to their locality all had their own definitions of what constituted the true Soviet partisan. The struggle over partisan identity was thus fought not only between partisans and state authorities but also among and within the partisan bands. The multiple definitions that emerged during 1941 and 1942 prevailed in the partisans' ranks throughout the war, even as these were later challenged by new recruits as the movement expanded.

As Donald Reid has pointed out, conflicts over identities and representations "are not sterile arguments fought in drawing rooms" (or in today's equivalent, the academic conference) but have real meaning and implications for historical actors in that they "both suggest and limit the possibilities for action, and for describing and analyzing that action."[7] Official and partisan-constructed identities were lenses through which state officials and partisans ordered and explained the realities of combat and everyday life. In the context of the guerrilla war, these identities were crucial in determining who belonged to the Soviet community and what their status was in it.

Partisans defined themselves—and were defined by the state—as possessing unique qualities that distinguished their war from that of the soldiers at the front and the civilians in the rear areas. These interrelated attempts by state authorities to impose an identity on the partisans and the latter's efforts to construct their own demonstrate the ways in which both discourse and practice contributed to efforts to control the partisans or, conversely, to preserve their autonomy. Soviet authorities and the partisans employed common themes and images to define the partisans and the partisan war. These included ethnonational and regional patriotism, the organic connections linking the partisans to the land and people, the desire for revenge, and the representation of the partisan as the idealized Soviet citizen. In addition, attributes associated with the Party and Red Army influenced this identity. Partisans, however, often interpreted these themes quite differently than the propagandists had intended. What enabled these differences to emerge were the ambiguities of both official discourse and the partisans' situation behind enemy lines. When seen through the prisms of their own social backgrounds and war experiences, the partisans could justify a wholly different set of behaviors and attitudes that could be defined either as strictly Soviet or possibly as partizanshchina. Partisans generally synthesized these values, attempting to establish autonomy from state authorities even as they worked to convince officials that they were loyal citizens, and they used these same authorities to protect themselves from other partisan bands. Indeed, the partisans were quite fragmented by competing regional and ethnonational rivalries, corporate allegiances, and other factors. These differences in turn hindered the development of a unified partisan identity, which had important consequences for interpartisan and partisan-state relations.

THE PARTISAN ETHOS

The Soviet partisans were the heirs to a long line of irregular warriors in Russian history, the most recent examples of which were the Red partisans from the Civil War. They were surrounded by the rich historical mythology of the Cossacks' "utopian" military communities and the rough egalitarianism of peasant uprisings, which, in popular culture and memory, envisioned freedom from outside authority and control, social justice, and deliverance from noble oppression.[8] Civil War partisans possessed an earthy, crude, egalitarian, and romantic persona, quite similar to that of their American mythological counterparts, the cowboys.[9] Their exploits lived on in the popular imagination, kept alive by literary and cinematic epics based on the lives of Vasilii Chapaev, Sergei Lazo, N. A. Shchors, and other heroes. Chapaev had a particularly strong romantic appeal, and both partisans and officials, including Ponomarenko, referred to incidents in the 1934 film about him (rather than his actual life) when dealing with real-life situations.[10] During the war, Soviet propagandists kept this mythology alive by referring to the deeds of tsarist guerrillas, such as Denis Davydov, the hero of 1812, and the more recent Civil War Red partisans. These guerrilla forebears were heralded for their imposition of discipline and the struggle to suppress any manifestations of anarchism, even if the reality was often quite different.[11]

Contemporary partisans were also moved by the romantic persona of these historical figures, particularly the Civil War partisans, although it is impossible to know how many of those who took to the woods actually were motivated by the desire, as one observer put it, "to copy the Civil War."[12] In any case, they did hope to live up to this dashing, charismatic image. Partisan memoirist Petr Vershigora worried that he did not fit the proper partisan profile:

In the partisans it is necessary to fight with style, chiefly with gaiety and lightheartedness. With my dull and downcast expression and doleful voice, I did not present the picture of a partisan. Without daring in the eyes, it is possible to go on [dangerous missions] only under compulsion. Volunteers, romantics, and even random people went to the partisans, but first, above all, they had their own style.[13]

The challenge faced by Vershigora and others was how to convey that style, embodied in the partisan ethos, without becoming labeled a practitioner of partizanshchina.

It was against partizanshchina that Soviet propagandists developed their definition of what the partisan and the partisan movement should be. Likewise, almost all partisans adhered to at least some partizanshchina-type behaviors, while simultaneously trying to keep them hidden from the view of authorities or even other partisans for fear of raising suspicions. The challenge the partisans faced was to present themselves as loyal and reliable Soviets while retaining the freedom of action and defining attributes that gave meaning to their lives as partisans. Because the word *partizanshchina* was a pejorative and because almost all partisans subscribed to at least some of the associated behaviors in one form or another, I will instead use the value-neutral term *partisan ethos* to describe these beliefs and values.

At the core of the partisan ethos was freedom, which had several connotations. As one partisan stated in 1941:

Maybe I stayed behind here in the forest on purpose when the Red Army retreated. I'm crazy about partisaning it . . . about freedom without any buts! What d'you mean this one or that one's a commander? The commander's the one the men follow into battle. A partisan's like a forest animal, like a wolf. They get together in a pack when an enemy's got to be fought and when the fight's over each one's his own boss again![14]

Above all, freedom meant an escape from the mental, social, and legal limitations imposed by official Soviet social categories. Physical separation from the Soviet mainland enhanced the opportunities for citizens to live mentally "outside the boundaries of Soviet culture" and the chance to decide their own fates.[15] In the Stalinist context, this meant, in addition to freedom from political oppression, freedom from restrictions on travel and material consumption and from the imposition of hierarchy and discipline.

In the prewar years, public images of plenty contrasted sharply with realities of shortages. Followers of the partisan ethos in turn pursued the so-called good life, which a contemporary observer described as "the free life with arms in one's hands and without government oppression, abundance of home-brewed alcohol, accessible women, [and] opportunities for plunder."[16] Commander A. F. Fedorov criticized such partisans as "fellows who thirsted for 'autonomy.' Reckless adventure, a desperate raid—and then eat, drink and be merry. That was their idea of the partisan life."[17]

This wild, masculinized world offered few of the refinements and none of the rules that constituted the Soviet ideal of modern, urbanized civilization. Living a good life required a plentiful supply of food and other material items. S. A. Kovpak's partisans, who were among the most acclaimed in the Soviet media, did not rebel when they were subjected to stricter discipline. They nearly mutinied, however, when told that their consumption of jam was to be rationed, which they believed was "an infringement on their 'partisan' rights." Kovpak declared the outburst to be a manifestation of partizanshchina.[18] When supplies were needed, partisans imbued with the partisan ethos (and even those who were not) preyed on the peasants to obtain provisions, often stealing valuables such as jewels, watches, furs, and clothing from the defenseless civilians. Rape and murder commonly accompanied these crimes. Thus, one partisan who wanted to clothe his "camp wife" stole goods from a family and killed the father, who he alleged was "an alien element to Soviet power," thus trying to legitimate a murder.[19] Such actions gave credence to German claims that the partisans were nothing more than bandits, especially since the line between plundering and official procurement expeditions was often fuzzy or nonexistent to the peasants. Similar ambiguities existed throughout occupied Europe, wherever resistance movements operated.[20] Though peasants may have envied the freedom and wild life of the fictional and mythologized bandits portrayed in popular memory, the real-life partisans threatened their survival, especially in the harsh conditions of war. Thus, an underground Soviet official stated that inhabitants in one Belorussian district "[did] not consider the "Starik" Brigade to be a partisan unit that defends citizens from the German occupiers, but are themselves robbers."[21]

Alcohol often fueled partisan notions of freedom. As one inebriated partisan told his commander, "You know, all partisans drink home-brew," thereby directly linking the consumption of alcohol and the accompanying lack of discipline to the partisan ethos.[22] Wild drinking sometimes led to violence, as in the extreme case of a commander and a commissar who shot their own partisans, including an officer, a doctor, and their chief of staff.[23] Alcohol could also significantly impair combat operations. One detachment drank itself into a stupor after liberating a distillery and awoke to find itself in the midst of a German raid.[24] In another case, a company on its way to blow up a bridge discovered a vodka warehouse, which led its usually abstemious commander "to go on a binge." The mission to destroy the bridge failed, and the company commander was executed.[25] The partisan ethos might justify these "excesses" as integral to the partisans' freedom, but Soviet authorities and other partisans condemned them as destroying order and discipline.

Freedom of movement was vital to the partisan ethos. Mobility enabled partisans to join units more suitable to their tastes or even to organize their own.[26] One partisan, not finding life in his detachment to his liking, convinced others to join him in forming a new unit by allegedly promising them, in the words of his former commander, "a good life, close to their families, and for [Red Army] officers, command posts."[27] Another left his unit, as one observer put it, "to lead such a life that pleased him."[28] Freedom of movement represented a return to the myth of the free steppe and to the mobility enjoyed by citizens before the introduction of the internal passport system in 1932.[29] Hence, the definition of freedom according to the partisan ethos rejected Stalinism's physical confinements, just as the first Cossacks had rebelled against the constraints of serfdom.

Populism and spontaneity comprised the final aspect of the partisan ethos. In Soviet parlance, the word *spontaneity* was a pejorative, equated with action based on emotion and feeling, without conscious thought directed at achieving a clear political objective. Spontaneity was therefore antithetical to proper, reasoned, calculated political consciousness and, relatedly, to Moscow's intention to control the insurgency for specific military and political objectives. Though state authorities asserted that they led the movement, some partisans claimed that "the value of the partisan movement . . . lies just in that it's a movement of the people arising spontaneously and suddenly out of indignation at the atrocities committed by the invaders."[30] However accurate this statement was and no matter how closely it resembled official representations of the movement in the mass media, which, in fact, emphasized the theme of spontaneous, popular revenge,[31] authorities could not condone the state's playing a secondary role in this presentation. The appearance of such contradictions reveals the fundamental tension between official representation and actual policy.

The values contained in the partisan ethos composed a social vision incompatible with the structured, ordered, hierarchical partisan movement that Soviet authorities attempted to establish, even in 1941 and 1942. From the leadership's perspective, the idea of independent, undisciplined individuals gathering together to attack a target, enjoying their spoils, and then dispersing clearly made little military sense. But in this war for national survival, the partisan ethos also meant abandoning the service of any higher purpose than one's personal happiness and desires.[32] Yet even though Soviet authorities and propagandists often referred to "freedom" (*svoboda*), this freedom "was not for strolling in the forest," as Fedorov put it, even if partisans lived like "free citizens in the occupied territories."[33] Not only were these behaviors anathema to official social and political values, they also had to be suppressed if a militarily effective and politically reliable guerrilla force was to develop. For this to happen, the center and its agents had to impose subordination, order, and discipline.

Almost all Soviet partisans embraced at least some aspects of the partisan ethos, but they had to refrain from or suppress any behaviors that challenged Moscow's authority, even if only implicitly. The partisan ethos's emphasis on freedom, even when it was couched apolitically (at least in the archival record), contrasted sharply with Stalinist norms of political control and subordination, social hierarchy, status, and duty. Thus, bad behavior even in otherwise obedient units could be politicized, in the context of the partisan war, as defiance to the center, whether or not the partisans intended it as such. Conversely, bad behavior—murder, for example—could be legitimated as political retribution, as described earlier. As a form of self-defense, partisans usually disguised, suppressed, or condemned the appearance of the partisan ethos within their units in their reports to Moscow, especially as their connections to the mainland became stronger from mid-1942 onward. But the suppression did not mean that the partisan ethos was excised from the movement; on the contrary, elements of it coexisted, sometimes quite comfortably, with official and other partisan identities.

THEY DEFEND THE MOTHERLAND(S)

Both officials and partisans incorporated nationality and national identity as critical elements of their respective partisan identities. In Soviet usage, the concept of nationality encompassed a variety of factors, including regional and ethnonational allegiances, as well as identification with the rodina and the explicitly politically defined Union. The way in which officials and partisans defined the partisans' relationship to the Soviet Union and the other peoples that comprised it had important implications for the unity of the movement and its power to mobilize popular support for itself and the regime.

The partisans' relationship with the motherland, defined in political and geographic terms, formed a critical part of their official identity and their self-identity. A term used ubiquitously by both Soviet propagandists and partisans, *rodina* had immense emotional and political significance. It was usually defined as "motherland," but the precise meaning of the term was, as noted previously, vague enough to refer to the entire Soviet Union, a republic, a region, or a home district. Nor did the term necessarily have any political connotations, other than one's native land. When used without a defining adjective, as was often the case, it could refer to almost any place the speaker could claim to be home.[34] As defenders of the rodina, partisans were portrayed as supreme patriots. At the same time, it was not always clear just what rodina individual partisans might be defending. Were they protecting the Soviet Union, their republic, their region, or even their native village?

This ambiguity stemmed from the complexities of Soviet nationality policy in the interwar period, which simultaneously attempted to articulate national identities for individual peoples while constructing a multinational socialist union. Far from being a "breaker of nations," the Soviet Union constructed nations and nationalities as part of its own national project. Thus, individuals, in theory, would emerge with at least two national identities: their ethnonational identity conforming to their republics and their identity as Soviet citizens. By the end of the 1930s, these sometimes contradictory goals of constructing ethnonational and Soviet identities had led to the creation of an "affirmative-action empire" that promoted the cultures and identities of previously subjected nations. This empire nonetheless was held together at its Russian core by a Russocentrist "national Bolshevism," which employed Russian symbols and heritage to promote a Marxist-Leninist state.[35] The resulting tensions produced by the confluence of these sometimes conflicting policies became strikingly evident in World War II and especially in the occupied territories.

Ethnonational and regional identifications were possibly enhanced, albeit unwittingly, by the state's initial determination to organize partisan detachments on a strictly local basis, per the instructions of 29 June and 18 July 1941, without any centralized direction. This approach created the impression—and the reality—that the partisan movement actually comprised hundreds of local movements lacking any kind of national coordination.

There were relatively few expressions of pure Soviet identity either in the national media or by the partisans themselves. One group that the state targeted directly was young people. Radio Moscow, in its broadcasts to the occupied territories, included a special section for youth. These broadcasts celebrated Soviet achievements since the Revolution, especially its holidays and festivals, and focused on promises for a bright future.[36] They also called on youth to defend the Soviet land and its people and particularly to help their Red Army comrades at the front.[37] The state hoped that young people, with their lack of familiarity with either pre-Soviet or foreign frames of reference, would thereby more strongly identify with the all-Union Soviet regime.

More commonly, state propaganda emphasized the dual nature of Soviet identity, which combined loyalty to the Union with allegiance to one's republic or region. Some stories and broadcasts limited themselves only to references to the "Soviet people," "Soviet partisans," the "Soviet land," and the "Soviet motherland,"[38] but more often, the media linked the Soviet community to the partisans' love for their native republics and regions. Thus, in a March 1942 story about the partisan war in Leningrad Oblast, *Pravda* claimed that the German goal was "to break the free spirit, to break the Soviet will of collective farmers, to frighten, to intimidate them." However, the story emphasized, this effort failed, for the Leningrad people continued "to live a Soviet life" and remained true in "their thoughts and feelings with [their] native, beloved Leningrad."[39]

State expressions of Soviet patriotism were usually set within the context of the "friendship of peoples" formula, in which all nations of the USSR were depicted as one in their love of the motherland and hatred of the enemy. One September 1942 radio broadcast, celebrating the awarding of nine partisans with the title Hero of the Soviet Union, stated, "Among the new heroes, among those awarded medals and orders are Russians, Ukrainians, Belorussians. The peoples of the Soviet Union are united in their efforts so that the enemy will be destroyed."[40] An article in *Izvestiia* proclaimed, "The Soviet Union is not a mechanical union of heterogeneous peoples and territories. All the republics, and the people in them, which form it, are united in their variety like leaves on the branches of a mighty tree." As such, citizens allegedly fought for the homelands of others: Russians for Ukraine, Latvians for Moscow, Bashkirs for the Don. To flush out this picture of unity, it was noted that standing above Belorussia's green forests, Ukraine's golden fields, Georgia's vineyards, and the Urals' hills was the Kremlin—"the heart and brain of our country, the Soviet rodina."[41] One radio broadcast reminded partisans why they were fighting: "Patriotism begins from the most ordinary [things]: from the tree next to the house, from the lane running down the river with the smell of antonovka apples or the steppe fields. The war helps every Soviet person understand the beauty of his native place."[42]

The broadcast then took its listeners on an audio tour of the Soviet Union, ending at the Kremlin with its "ancient towers, the glory of Rus' and the red stars of the future." Although Russia was privileged in this portrayal, the people of the Soviet Union, "190 million strong," were called on to defend the entire country.[43] Such was the organic unity of the friendship of peoples—or so, at least, propagandists hoped to convince their audience. The intensification of an ethnonationalist discourse in the Soviet media meant not only the growing use of Russian national symbols and figures but also the promotion of those of other nationalities.

The promotion of organic unity meant that non-Russian nationalities were also accorded important roles in the Soviet war effort. Ukrainians, Belorussians, Caucasians, and others heard and read about their own exploits. Allusions to specific national histories and cultures were employed, such as references to the Ukrainian poet Taras Shevchenko and to the feats of Belorussian and Ukrainian partisans during the Civil War.[44] The beauties and virtues of the individual republics were frequently extolled, along with the bravery and resiliency of their inhabitants and how they prospered and developed under Soviet rule.[45] One radio broadcast, for example, reminded Caucasians to stand fast to their own national, martial traditions and to fight shoulder to shoulder with Russians, Ukrainians, and all other Soviet nationalities.[46]

More commonly, however, propagandists conflated Russian and Soviet images and symbols, which simultaneously fueled Russian pride, and encouraged Russians to see themselves as embodying the greater Soviet whole.[47] One broadcast invoked the legacy of the 1812 partisan hero Denis Davydov, reminding the partisans about the skill and bravery of Russian (*russkie*) soldiers. It ended with a declaration that "the Soviet people remember the experience of their forebears and strongly beat the Germans, throwing them off the Soviet land."[48] Even the Orthodox Church was brought into the act. As part of the state-sanctioned resurgence of religion during the war, messages from Metropolitan (later Patriarch) Sergii and other church hierarchs called on partisans to fight the invaders and to free the Soviet land, again linking an institution with deep Russian roots to the rest of the Union.[49] In this vein, the partisans not only were fighting for the promise of the Revolution as heralded in the broadcasts to youth but also were presumably engaged in a sacred and holy battle to save the Third Rome.

As these articles and broadcasts made clear, however, it was historical *Russian* symbols that came to represent the whole of the Soviet Union. Likewise, Russians were depicted as the "first among equals" or the "big brother" of the other Soviet nationalities.[50] This hierarchy was further cemented by stories such as the one in which a young Latvian woman related that she had been with the partisans for over a year. During this time, she had learned Russian, and "in associating with Russian comrades [she] grew politically" and ultimately became a candidate member of the Party.[51] She thus simultaneously confirmed Russia's status as the most advanced nation in the Soviet state and the primacy of the Party—and therefore the Soviet order—while still according Latvia a place in that order, even if it was distinctly secondary. Of course, this and other expressions of loyalty to the Russian-dominated friendship of peoples notion belied the reality of bitter antagonisms that especially affected the Baltic states and other territories annexed in 1939 and 1940.[52]

Partisans less commonly identified themselves in purely Soviet terms. These expressions were manifest particularly in unit names that celebrated places or concepts, such as "For the Soviet Motherland" Partisan Detachment, the "Bolshevik" Partisan Brigade, the "October" Partisan Brigade, and the "Chekist" Partisan Brigade; leaders such as Stalin, Molotov, Frunze, Voroshilov, and Anastas Mikoian; and even such popular heroes as Valerii Chkalov, the late great Soviet flier.[53] Some fought, in the words of one partisan, "to be an honorable Soviet citizen."[54] Women especially linked their identity as Communists and citizens to their participation in the movement.[55] Others found more deadly ways to identify themselves as Soviet. One partisan waxed poetic in his diary about the glories of Russia and the Russian soul and the invincibility of the Russian people. He nevertheless was very proud of his affiliation with the Komsomol and, later, his acceptance as a candidate member of the Party. And when he participated in the execution of three captured policemen, he left a note on their bodies reading, "'Shot for betraying the Rodina' [signed] Soviet saboteurs,"[56] thus highlighting his identification at that moment with the Soviet state.

These and other references to Soviet identity, however, paled in comparison to partisans' public identification with their republics and regions. Leningrad partisans claimed that local peasants regarded them as "patriots of their Russian country who ably defend [the peasants] from the yoke of German slavery."[57] In a letter home, one partisan proudly declared, "Mama and Papa, I know from the history of the whole world, that the Russian people never have been and never will be defeated."[58] Even when separated from their native lands, citizens spoke of their desire to fight for them. Belorussian Nadezhda Medvedeva, then located in the Siberian city of Omsk, wrote a letter to a high-ranking official, describing her love of Belorussia and asking that she be sent there as a partisan: "I love her, [my] native Belorussia, without effusiveness, without high-sounding phrases, I love her fields, forests, her sky-larks."[59]

When combined with hatred for the invaders, this ethnonationalism was a potent mobilizing force. The Belorussian partisans of the "Flame" Partisan Detachment read in their unit-produced journal in late 1943 that they had to "broaden and strengthen their ties with the population" and to help them whenever possible, particularly since the "people's avengers" were the best sons and daughters of the Belorussian people themselves.[60] Graphic stories of German atrocities against Belorussians, especially women and children, drove this point home.[61] One partisan in a Belorussian brigade complained about his unit's inactivity, stating, "I cannot sit here any longer doing nothing, I am Belorussian, and we must defend Belorussia, and not sit."[62]

Partisan ethnonational patriotism and pride had its ugly side—ethnonational prejudice. The Soviet-German war unleashed a series of cataclysmic ethnic conflicts among all the populations of the borderlands area encompassing parts of the Baltic states, Belorussia, Ukraine, Poland, and Romania. Indeed, Alfred Rieber has characterized the ethnic struggles that occurred in the occupied territories as part of a series of civil wars whose roots extended back well before the formation of the Soviet Union but which both Soviet and Nazi policies exacerbated. The German genocide against the Jews was only one part of this terrible story, as Belorussians, Balts, and especially Ukrainians and Poles fought to control historically ethnically diverse territories.[63] When the smoke cleared at the end of the war throughout much of what was now western Belorussia and Ukraine, the Jewish and Polish populations were but a memory, the former wiped out by the Germans and their indigenous helpers and the latter driven out with additional costs of tens of thousands dead, most killed by Ukrainian separatists. The native German population was also swept away.

Ethnic prejudice and violence manifested themselves within the movement in various ways and contributed to the shaping of partisan identities. Moreover, these ethnic conflicts revealed the fragility of the Soviet friendship of peoples and the potentially divisive nature of Soviet nationality policy. Although it certainly would be an exaggeration to refer to the ethnic discord *within* the partisan movement as rising to the level of civil war, partisans often defined themselves against the ethnic "other."

Partisans defined themselves against those nationalities that they believed were weak, cowardly, or treasonous. Jews in particular were a favorite target of the Slavic partisans. One partisan wrote home, after describing German atrocities against the Jews, that "the courageous Russian people are brave and hardy compared to the Jewish people, and do not fall alive into the hands of fascism but go to the forest to the partisan detachments."[64] In areas where Soviet rule was particularly hated, most notably in the areas annexed in 1939 and 1940, Nazi-inspired and indigenous anti-Semitism identified the Jews as Communists, a sentiment that may have influenced the partisans in these areas as well.[65] Conversely (and as occurred in World War I), Jews were also sometimes accused of spying and working for the Germans. Thus, partisans reported that defeatist Kievan Jews had announced the collapse of the Soviet Union following the German capture of the city in September 1941.[66] Rumors circulated in Belorussia that the Germans had trained Jews to infiltrate partisan units and assassinate officers.[67] That the Germans were known to be systematically killing Jews as early as the late summer of 1941 did nothing to alleviate the partisans' suspicions, since they reasoned that a spy would identify himself or herself as a Jew in order to gain the partisans' trust.[68] Even the leadership espoused a distinct anti-Semitism. Ponomarenko wrote to Stalin in July 1941 that peasants were ready to engage in partisan warfare but that Jews were "seized with an animal fear of Hitler and instead of fighting, are fleeing."[69] Given such widespread beliefs, from the top down, it is not surprising that partisans reported to Moscow that "anti-Semitism [in the movement] is quite developed."[70] As a result, Jews had much to fear from the partisans, including outright murder should they venture into the forest, as one underground Soviet official noted.[71]

Even the Slavic partisans were occasionally divided by ethnicity. Ukrainians, in particular, bore the stigma of being collaborators.[72] According to an escaped Soviet POW of unknown nationality, the Germans related better to the Ukrainians, declaring that "the Ukrainians are our people," whereas Russians and Belorussians were identified as "Communists and they keep them in crueler conditions."[73] Rumors circulated that the Germans used Ukrainians, like Jews, to infiltrate detachments in order to destroy them from within.[74] Ukrainians, for their part, reacted angrily to these aspersions. One protested, "It cannot be that all Ukrainians are traitors. There are even Russian traitors and anyone else you wish."[75] Russians also accused Belorussians of not doing their fair share and of being untrustworthy.[76] These negative expressions of ethnonationalist feelings were potentially highly divisive in a multinational state, especially since the Nazis tried to exploit ethnonational tensions in their propaganda.[77] Along with the more positive expressions of ethnonationalism, they also reflected the use of ethnicity by the regime and the area's inhabitants as a powerful—perhaps even the most powerful—

determinant of one's political status, a development that had intensified since the late 1930s.[78] As will be discussed later, the fear of political fragmentation along ethnic lines led Soviet authorities to prioritize political stability at the expense of human lives.

The continued emphasis on all-Union national themes in the public presentation of the partisan war contrasted sharply with the partisans' predominantly ethnonational and regional visions. Though the authorities recognized and indeed encouraged these allegiances to a certain extent, they also had to depict the partisan struggle as part of a larger national war effort. It was critical for public consumption to show citizens in the mainland that the partisans, who theoretically could choose not to fight, were so devoted to the Soviet Union that they would fight and die for it, just as much as for their ethnonational republics and regions.

But this presentation of the partisan war was not only for propaganda purposes. It was also a vision that state authorities had for the movement, a vision that transcended the partisans' ethnonational and personal motivations and connected them to the larger Soviet community. Some Party members and Red Army okruzhentsy, by virtue of belonging to national institutions, may have conceptualized the partisan war in these terms, but it is evident that many partisans, including Communists and former soldiers, saw the trees of ethnonational and regional struggles rather than the forest of the national war. Therefore, from the state's perspective, the partisans' horizons had to broaden to include the whole of the Soviet Union, lest the movement disintegrate into—or rather remain made up of—small groups of uncoordinated factions. For this goal to be achieved, the state had to project an identity on the movement that united the partisans in a common cause.

THE PEOPLE'S AVENGERS

Perhaps the most distinctive feature of official and self-constructed partisan identities was the partisans' dual roles as witnesses to and avengers of enemy atrocities. Unlike Red Army soldiers, who generally observed only the aftermath of these crimes, and the civilians, who "passively" suffered them, the partisans both watched and acted. They kept Moscow informed about crimes in the occupied territories and executed "Soviet justice" against the perpetrators, if sometimes indirectly. But as was the case with other elements of the partisan war, the official and self-ascribed role of people's avenger enabled partisans simultaneously to act according to official definitions and to embrace elements of the partisan ethos. By fighting, they at once protected civilian homes *and* put them at risk, often deliberately, of German reprisals. Civilians, caught in the middle, usually were the losers.

The tension of this relationship was exacerbated by growing civilian participation in the movement beginning in the spring of 1942. In many areas, rising numbers of partisans were locals who fought to protect their homes and families. Soviet media recognized and encouraged this development. One typical article noted a partisan band with elderly, women, and children in its ranks that fought German troops for five hours: "They fought for their native village, which the Hitlerites had seized."[79] Interestingly, the larger Soviet community was rarely mentioned in such stories.

Although the media presented local patriotism as a virtue, many leaders in the movement believed it to be an obstacle to organizing a national partisan struggle. Local fighters, one partisan related to Ponomarenko, wanted to stay in their districts and "not be ordered to transfer to another district."[80] Localism constrained the partisans' mobility, one of the most important assets they had. In one unit, five men deserted when their detachment left their area, saying they wanted to protect their homes. The commissar accepted their action with true Leninist philosophy, recording in his diary, "Let them go, better fewer but better." Later, he noted that it was understandable that they would want to stay close to their families and not face the constant hardships and dangers of the forest.[81] Other partisans and officials were not so sympathetic. The chief of staff of Belorussia's Borisov zone, noting the frequency with which locally recruited partisans deserted, declared, "Practical experience shows that detachments from the central regions are best of all, not [those] organized from the local population."[82] To ward off charges of partizanshchina and peasant anarchism, local units asserted that their thorough knowledge of the territory was a critical component of their military and political success.[83] They also tended to regard units sent from the mainland or those that had relocated from other areas as interlopers in their home territory.[84]

An important part of fighting on their home territory was the partisans' relationship to their native environment. Soviet prewar discourse had declared that all Soviets were at home wherever they were in the Union. One popular 1930s song proclaimed that a citizen could "walk and feel he's the owner of his own unbounded motherland."[85] Soviet propagandists deemed the land itself, whether defined as the socialist or ethnic motherland, to be a natural ally. In the partisan context, this assertion was consistent with popular prerevolutionary depictions of Cossacks, bandits, and partisans finding refuge in the forest and indeed being at home and free in nature.[86]

Both officials and partisans invoked the aid of the Soviet native land in wartime. In Belorussia, *Pravda* observed, the soil itself seemed partial to partisan dugouts, as there were so many that it was "as if they were flung on the ground."[87] *Krasnaia zvezda* also asserted, in December 1941, that "in winter like summer, it is possible to take refuge from the enemy in the forest. Frost does not frighten our partisans. The partisans now have well equipped dugouts," which, especially in the 1941–1942 winter when the bitter conditions were causing units to disintegrate, was certainly more a reflection of wishful thinking than reality.[88] One radio broadcast noted that "forest-swamp country demands from fighters much physical training, efficiency, [and] initiative. But the difficult natural conditions, as confirmed by life itself, do not frighten Soviet troops."[89]

As welcoming as the land was to Soviets, it was portrayed as rejecting foreign invaders. One broadcast claimed, "The forest is a partisan kingdom. In the forest, the Hitlerites get stuck and are destroyed. Not for nothing are the Germans afraid of the forest."[90] *Krasnaia zvezda* asserted that the Belorussian land "burned under the legs of the fascists."[91] The invaders were not even safe in the airspace above the rodina, as a radio broadcast to the occupied territories made clear by describing the shooting down of a German aircraft by rifle fire. The commentator noted that such things could "only happen in Russia," concluding, "Yes, the Russian land inhospitably meets the flying fascist invaders. The land repulses the fascists."[92]

Despite the realities of their often miserable living conditions, the partisans, too, portrayed themselves as having a special relationship with their native land. In so doing, they linked themselves to the heroic warriors of Russian folklore. A partisan in the Grishin regiment claimed in his diary, "The partisan is master [*khoziain*] of the Russian land, even though it is temporarily occupied by the enemy." A song from the same regiment proclaimed:

Beyond the river, as in a fairy tale, in the dark copse
Where the gray fog floats
There, untamed by fascist power
Live the dashing *Grishintsy.*[93]

In contrast, the forest was a tomb for the Germans. M. M. Baibekov wrote to his mother that although the Germans were afraid to go into the forest, the forest gave him health and strength, "since you know how good the air is in the forest."[94] Another recalled that the Germans believed that partisans lurked behind every tree, whereas for the partisans, the forest was a place filled with cheerful camaraderie.[95] Partisans in the "Flame" Detachment imagined the fear the forest inspired in the Germans in a unit song about two enemy troops who met their deaths:

The forest road is full of malice.
Here bones remain!
Hurry, go back!
The partisans follow everybody.[96]

Such claims did indeed accurately depict German perceptions of the forests and swamps and the threat posed by the partisans in these domains. General Franz Halder claimed in his memoirs that "the Russian was able to move about in these impenetrable forests and treacherous swamps with the certain instinct and sense of security of an animal," a statement that revealed the Germans' racially inspired fear and awe of their enemy. Even as early as 1941, German soldiers felt a special fear when approaching Soviet forests, which one soldier described as "dreadful because in them lie hidden terrors."[97]

In the occupied territories, civilians had far more reason than the Germans to feel terrorized. Partisans were eyewitnesses to the pillaging, raping, and killing committed by the occupiers, a role highlighted by the Soviet press. One article described the effects witnessing such events had on a group of partisans who had temporarily returned to the mainland: "In people who have arrived from the partisan detachments, there is something special, distinguishing them from others. A special expression of the face, a special look, their eyes have seen much, things we have not seen. In these people there is a surprising calm, forming from the maximum effort of will and infinite hatred."[98] This was not literary flourish. Even in 1941 and early 1942, partisan reports detailed the mass murder of Soviet citizens (including the reported murder of 30,000 Jews at Dniepropetrovsk) and the looting, burning, and raping carried out in towns and villages.[99]

Officials and ordinary citizens alike demanded revenge for these actions.[100] Indeed, the desire for revenge was deep and primal, a visceral emotion felt both at the national and the personal level. In the partisan war, Soviet propagandists declared that the usual laws of war did not apply. Posters emphasized revenge as a primary theme, such as the 1941 poster captioned "The enemy shall not escape the people's revenge!" which depicted armed civilians led by a grimly determined elderly couple. In the backdrop was the motivation for their revenge: a burning village and a hanged man. Articles in the central newspapers and in films such as *She Defends the Motherland* invoked the desire for revenge as the primary reason why people became partisans.[101] One radio broadcast quoted a student at an antifascist conference of youth as saying, "It is not possible for a person and fascist to co-exist. It is us or them."[102] Another radio broadcast to the partisan detachments in August 1942 proclaimed:

> Not for nothing do the Soviet people call the partisans the people's avengers. The people's avengers—people of selfless courage and bravery, who destroy the enemy for his wild atrocities against defenseless Soviet women, children and the elderly, for burning down our villages, towns and cities, for ruthless tortures, which the Germans subject on our captured soldiers and officers. Blood for blood—such is the iron law of the people's avengers.[103]

Another story further tied the desire for revenge with the fate of the Soviet Union itself:

> Yes, every worker, collective farmer, teacher, attacking the lair of the enemy in the dead of the fall night, has his own score to pay with the Germans. They seek revenge of the fascist scoundrels for the burning down of homes, for the murder of mothers and wives. They seek revenge for their motherland, for the plunder of cities and villages, for the bitter tears of mothers, for the trampling of the fields. The combat detachment is bonded with the blood of Soviet people going to the forest to seek revenge of the enemy. And this detachment will not lay down its arms until that time when the last fascist soldier is swept from the Soviet land.[104]

Thus, the partisans were responsible not only for defending and avenging their native villages and people but for the entire Soviet land and its citizens as well.[105] The official recognition in public discourse that partisans were driven by personal desires and local and ethnonational patriotism became part of an effort to link the personal war with the all-Union national struggle.

This language also followed on prewar official concerns about the purity and cleanliness of Soviet society and the threat posed by internal enemies, who were depicted as "rodents," "scum," "vermin," and "filth."[106]

As actual witnesses to and victims of German atrocities, the partisans required little official encouragement to internalize the appellation "people's avengers." They were profoundly affected by what they saw, as one partisan wrote her husband:

> When I saw the film *Aleksandr Nevskii*, where it showed the German troops throwing children into the fire, I did not believe it. I did not know that there were such cannibals. Now I see with my own eyes how these cannibals destroy our people regardless of nation. I have observed many instances of the annihilation of whole villages together with [their] inhabitants.[107]

Thus, what Soviet citizens in the 1930s may have believed to be exaggerated depictions of the enemy suddenly acquired the power of personal truth in wartime as they actually experienced the reality of these images and themes. Seen in this light, what other previous and seemingly false or hyperbolic official claims might also have been true after all?

The desire for revenge was symbolized in unit names that included words and phrases such as "Revenge" (*Mstitel* and *Nekrome* in Russian and Yiddish, respectively), "Death to the German Occupiers" (*Smert' Nemetskim Okkupantam*), and "Death to Fascism" (*Smert' Fashizmu*). Revenge and patriotism were often intertwined; in a letter home, one partisan stated that he wanted to perform "his holy duty as a Soviet citizen" to kill Germans.[108] Z. A. Bogatyr' recalled the cries of one partisan in the midst of a fight: "Take this, you snakes, [this is] for Kovalev, this is for Gutorov, this is for Burovikhin!" Another related that his unit swore an oath over the grave of a comrade to avenge his death.[109] Jews, in particular, fought to avenge the deaths of their loved ones. Faye Schulman, whose family was murdered by the Germans earlier in the war, wrote, "I resolved to volunteer for active combat operations, to fight for my people—for Jewish dignity and honour—and for an end to the Nazi killing machine.[110] In a report to authorities, a Ukrainian partisan described finding a group of Jewish men hiding in a forest who wanted weapons because "they burned with desire for revenge" for the killing of their families.[111]

As the people's avengers, partisans saw themselves as the judge, jury, and executioners of popular justice, standing outside the rules of regular warfare.

"The Enemy shall not escape the people's revenge!" 1941. (Credit: Hoover Institution Archives, Poster Collection, RU/SU2217)

After protesting the rough handling he received, a captured German officer was told by a partisan, "You want justice? You want fair play and decency? When you burn thousands of villages and bury children and old people alive in mass graves—then you don't think of justice, do you?"[112] In some cases, the partisans handed over German prisoners, Soviet helpers, and nationalist opponents to the proper state authorities, but more commonly, they summarily killed their prisoners.[113] Occasionally, the partisans convened a unit or peasant tribunal, which was invariably followed by execution, and in certain instances, these practices continued even after liberation.[114] These killings sometimes occurred for the pragmatic—though no less cruel and horrendous—reason that the partisans lacked the facilities to hold prisoners,[115] yet there can be little doubt that revenge was a primary motivation. As one partisan wrote in a letter, their function was "to annihilate traitors to the rodina, spies, police, police units, county [administrations], German garrisons."[116]

The urge to destroy the enemy forces was such that no trace of them was to be allowed on Soviet soil. Thus, Commander N. Z. Koliada, leader of Smolensk's "Batia" Partisan Complex (one of the most important in the region through the fall of 1942), informed officials that when a Soviet woman impregnated by a German rapist came to him, he determined that "in order that there be no German heritage among us, I was forced to depart from Soviet law" and allow her to have an abortion.[117] Koliada's sentiments were in keeping with the popular discourse that celebrated the joy in killing mass numbers of Germans, as expressed in poems and articles by such famous writers and journalists as Ilya Ehrenburg, Konstantin Simonov, and Aleksei Surkov.[118] In the context of this most brutal of wars, it was easy for the language of purity to slide into that of racialized killing.

The partisans' official identity and self-identity as avengers separated them from their Red Army counterparts, who were formally bound by the rules of warfare, even if they also frequently violated them.[119] Koliada told newspaper reporters in July 1942 that "now our enemy knows from this one word—'partisans'—which already seizes them with trepidation. They are not afraid of the Red Army or of anybody [else], but they're afraid of the partisans because the partisans don't take prisoners, they simply annihilate them."[120] Koliada's words echoed official depictions of the partisans as purveyors of popular justice, but they also fit into the partisan ethos of living outside the bounds of society and legality.

In taking up the mantle of defenders of the people, partisans claimed to be the saviors of humanity itself. Fedorov reinforced this point in his memoirs, stating, "The partisan, it goes without saying, went into battle not to enrich or feed or clothe himself. He was a warrior in the people's cause, a people's avenger."[121] Rank-and-file partisan Schulman echoed these sentiments in her memoir: "A partisan soldier is not a killer. A partisan fights for peace and justice."[122] Some went to the forest not only to defend their fellow citizens but also "to beat the hated enemy at every step for all of humanity," as one partisan told his sister. Another declared grimly in a letter to family and friends, "Here the people see the 'liberators,' because this war decides the life not only of Soviet power, but even the life of all of humanity on the globe."[123]

Despite the partisans' self-identification as the people's avengers, their actual relationship with civilians was fraught with ambiguities. Partisans portrayed the movement as a demonstration of the people's outrage against enemy invasion and their love for the rodina.[124] They constantly referred to their bond with the people and were proud to report that local civilians would refer to them as "ours" (*nashi, svoi*).[125]

The credibility of partisans as the people's avengers was complicated, however, by the nature of their war and the consequences of their operations — the almost inevitable and vicious retribution the enemy visited on civilians as punishment for the partisans' own actions. The leadership in the war's first year showed very little concern for the fate of the people in the occupied territories, despite occasional references to Stalin's supposed desire to protect them. Rather, newspaper stories heroized partisans who fought for the cause, all the while knowing that their operations would lead to the deaths of their own loved ones, including children.[126] The message to the partisans was clear: conduct your operations without any regard to the losses suffered by the Germans and use German reprisals as an opportunity to recruit more partisans. Nor were partisans told via the press or through direct orders that they should make saving civilian lives part of their operations, until the spring of 1943 when it became state policy to protect human and material resources.[127]

The partisans' actual attitudes toward safeguarding civilians varied, however, revealing the tension many felt between fulfilling their duty to the state and their responsibility to protect their fellow and defenseless citizens and loved ones. The most callous and cynical among them followed the leadership in regarding the populace in purely instrumental terms. They ignored or even encouraged German retribution against civilians, with the justification that the killing of the innocent would only fuel popular outrage against the occupiers and thereby ultimately contribute to a stronger movement.[128] Indeed,

The village of Toropets, near Velikie Luki, is burned in reprisal for partisan operations. (Credit: USHMM, courtesy of Ralf Rossmeissl)

one partisan, well aware of the propaganda value of German atrocities, asked Ponomarenko to send a film crew to the occupied territories to record "the staggering picture: fire-ravaged remains, shootings, cremated corpses."[129]

Others were much more sympathetic to the civilians' plight. One partisan recalled how their mere presence in their villages exposed civilians to mortal danger: "We were armed, and could defend ourselves. But what could [the villagers] do? For giving a loaf of bread to a partisan they were shot. I might stay the night and go away, but if someone informed on them that I had spent the night in that hut, they would all be shot."[130]

Despite these known dangers, many partisans believed that protecting civilians contradicted what they perceived to be their primary mission: the destruction of German infrastructure and communications lines. For one thing, partisan operations required mobility. Hence, even as late as the summer of 1943, when Soviet policy directed that civilians ought to be protected, Commander S. A. Kovpak told the survivors of the Galician Jewish ghetto of Skalat that, due to military necessity, his partisan forces, then embarked on a raid to the Carpathians, could only accept in their ranks those who could endure the rigors of the raid. The remaining Jews were settled in nearby villages and were supplied rations but otherwise left without guard.[131] District

Party secretary turned partisan commander M. I. Duka proclaimed in an interview with officials after his area's liberation: "To take a district—this is a big deal, but to tie oneself to the population as it happened in the southern districts of Orel Oblast—that is incorrect. If [a district] is already taken, then you have to hold it, you have to try to keep it. A pure partisan war and its tactics must not tie [the partisans'] fate to the population."[132] Other commanders protested that the added strain of having to protect civilians, especially relatives, when under attack or when the forest was blockaded and its inhabitants were starving also undermined partisan morale and reduced their combat effectiveness.[133] Thus, to be a partisan required ignoring German retribution and accepting heavy civilian losses.

The primacy of military necessity and the political advantage gained by publicizing enemy atrocities was contested by an opposing vision of the partisan war, which saw it as part of a larger political and perhaps even humanitarian struggle. To some partisans, the saving of civilians became the movement's raison d'être. One commander was confronted by his partisans who wanted to keep a large number of civilians out of the detachment because they could not possibly care for them, for they lacked supplies and would lose their mobility (as one said, "We're here to fight the Huns, and not to nurse children"). He responded, "Only bastards can talk like that. I am ashamed of you! I see you do not understand the duties of partisans. To protect people who are being persecuted by the fascists is our most important task. To save lives is to fight the enemy."[134] For some units, such as the Jewish Bielski Detachment, saving lives (in this case, specifically Jewish lives) became their self-assigned mission. Although many in the unit wanted to avenge Jewish deaths, Tuvia Bielski told them, "Don't rush to fight and die. So few of us are left, we have to save lives. To save a Jew is more important than to kill Germans." Bielski knew that his policy of avoiding offensive combat to preserve lives had to be hidden from Soviet authorities, lest they think his detachment was not participating sufficiently in the war.[135]

For local partisans, the desire to protect their homes and loved ones was an especially urgent matter. But if state authorities believed that this aim took precedence over others, trouble could ensue. When partisans in one Vitebsk brigade labeled local "self-defense" groups as "greens" because the latter allegedly insisted that their sole mission was to protect their villages from the Germans, the implied threat was ominous indeed: the designation referred to the rebellious peasant movement during the Civil War that was suppressed by the Red Army at the cost of tens of thousands of lives and the deportation of a hundred thousand more.[136] It was, in essence, a direct accusation of partizanshchina. The head of the Central Staff's political section requested an investigation as to whether these self-defense groups were actually fighting the Germans and if they were conducting any political work.[137] Understandably, the locals bitterly resented—and no doubt feared—this label, given its connotations of peasant anarchism. Soviet officials threatened to destroy formations whose actions did not meet their disciplinary, military, or political standards. One plenipotentiary warned several Belorussian detachments, which he accused of "plundering and banditry," that if they did not change their ways, he would "officially declare them to be 'green bands' and take measures to destroy them."[138] In fact, local partisans occasionally negotiated informal truces with nearby German garrisons, ensuring quiet for the enemy while safeguarding their families' homes. The center often responded to such occurrences—or suspected occurrences—by introducing "foreign" detachments with no ties to the area to attack the enemy, thus provoking a reprisal against the neighboring civilians. This in turn would induce the survivors to join the partisans and seek revenge against the occupiers.[139]

Others, more pragmatically if less empathetically, regarded civilian vulnerability as a political matter. When the 5th Leningrad Partisan Brigade came under heavy pressure from a German force in the fall of 1943, the brigade's commanders decided to defend the local inhabitants rather than abandon them to their fates, as standard guerrilla tactics required. One officer described this decision as "a question of principle: what impression would this make on the population. Therefore, [we] decided to fight and to fight in such a manner as to transform every village into a fortress of the partisan struggle and leave only when it was impossible to stay any longer."[140] For these partisans, the political and perhaps even the humanitarian dimensions of the war took on greater importance than pure military considerations. They also placed partisans in the position of "protectors of the people," a role usually played in Soviet discourse by Stalin himself.[141] Thus, in this guise, the partisans became Stalin's surrogates in the occupied territories.

Official and partisan declarations that the partisans were the people's avengers raised significant tensions and questions about the nature of the movement. Officials depicted partisans as the embodiments of outrage against the enemy, of the desire for revenge, and of popular justice. This concept could also conform to Stalinist values regarding annihilating enemies and paternalistically protecting the people. As such, the concept of people's avengers was a powerful tool for mobilization and political legitimacy. However, the partisan ethos, too, contained notions of popular justice, echoing popular stories and songs about the rebel Cossacks Stenka Razin and Emelian Puga-

Stalin's surrogate? Partisan as people's protector. (Credit: Minaeva Collection)

chev.[142] Acts of popular justice and revenge, when conducted without state approval, were quite problematic to a leadership that demanded legal order and discipline. Nor did motivations of revenge and the fulfillment of popular justice necessarily translate into a willingness to fight and die for the Soviet system. Such contradictions between official expectations and partisan desires could lead to real problems when authorities issued orders calling for partisans to leave their localities or to pursue national goals over local interests, including the sacrificing of civilians who might well be close relatives and friends.

The partisans' self-identity as the people's avengers also contradicted certain realities, particularly their deep suspicions toward civilians in general. Especially in 1941 and early 1942 but continuing in some degree up to liberation, partisans always felt surrounded by spies, collaborators, and enemy sympathizers. Moreover, their own propensity for plundering and banditry alienated and threatened the peasants. Even regulated procurement operations, with their implicit threat and sometimes explicit use of force, must have reminded the peasants of collectivization and forced state procurements, especially since many partisans were former local Communists and officials. After the first year of occupation, by which time the people in the occupied territories had experienced the true nature of Germany's policies, the gap between the peasants' negative feelings toward the partisans and the latter's heroic self-representation narrowed, for most peasants came to see the partisans as the lesser of two evils. Nevertheless, in general, neither ever fully trusted the other. And of course, the regime remained deeply suspicious of both partisans and civilians in the occupied territories. Although the war effort may have appeared to unite the nation, the same differences and suspicions that had marked Soviet society and politics since the Revolution still lurked beneath the surface. Just as the war itself could unify the population, so, too, could it promote divisions.

PARTISANS AS THE "ADVANCED
PEOPLE OF OUR EPOCH"

To state authorities, the partisan ethos was a social and political atavism, a remnant of bygone times when anarchic rebels lived in the steppes and forests. True Soviet partisans were the embodiment of the "New Soviet Person," defined as a cultured, urban, rational, scientific, and collectively minded individual.[143] Part of this official definition hinged on the partisans' supposed extraordinary talents and personal characteristics that enabled them to survive and triumph in the occupied territories. The war was thus a testing ground that allowed the partisans to demonstrate their Soviet attributes of hardiness, collectivism, martial prowess, and mastery of technology. Partisans, too, imbibed this definition, but their understanding of their own extraordinary qualities could lead to behaviors quite different from those officials expected.

As shown earlier, the Soviet media, from the first days of the German invasion, described the conflict as "a great patriotic war" and "a patriotic war of liberation" that involved the entire nation. Integral to this depiction was that the partisans were volunteers, moved to fight because of their love of their native land and a desire to protect their families—all manifestations of a collective, self-sacrificing mentality. This was true even for the representation of the partisans of 1941, many of whom, as activists or as members of the local elite, were hardly ordinary Soviet citizens, and it also may be one reason why Red Army okruzhentsy received so little press: as servicemen, they were obligated to continue fighting, unlike civilians, who had no such legal compulsion.[144] In fact, in both official and private correspondence, Ponomarenko was adamant that the movement consist only of volunteers, opposing the efforts of some partisans who attempted to augment their bands through the conscription of local civilians.[145] In November 1942, he told one such group, "I forbid categorically the mobilization and concentration of the local population in the forest without weapons. The local population must be drawn into the partisan movement by regular explanatory work; to create hidden reserves for the partisan movement in the villages and towns [must be based] on the principle of voluntarism."[146] And in January 1943, he wrote to Stalin:

> The partisan movement is a people's movement; it is constructed on a different basis than the Red Army. Our citizens are compulsorily drafted to serve in the Red Army. The organization of the partisan movement is conducted not on the basis of compulsory mobilization of citizens into the detachments. The people's masses are included in the active partisan struggle not according to orders, but according to the call of the Party, and as the result of much political work, conducted in the rear by underground party organizations and the partisan detachments. Enrollment in the partisan detachments is conducted only among citizens who have voluntarily decided to become partisans.[147]

Thus, the partisans, according to Ponomarenko, were ordinary people, responding to Soviet patriotism. As such, they represented the best the country had to offer.

Soviet propaganda echoed this theme. The media emphasized that partisans were ordinary, peaceful, and peace-loving people, yet descriptions of their exploits revealed them to be quite extraordinary. One article described the partisans as "modest, inconspicuous in peacetime, [but] they became on the field of battle legendary folk warriors [*narodnye bogatyry*], winning their renown with wondrous achievements for the Soviet motherland."[148] Soviet propagandists squared the circle of ordinary people performing superhuman feats by emphasizing that Soviet patriotism, ethnonational traditions of repulsing invaders, hatred for the enemy, and the unity of peoples combined to create an irresistible force. Just as important were the contributions of the Soviet system itself, which had forged these heroic people. *Krasnaia zvezda* stated that "the Soviet people have not only a high moral composition, but also a high intellectual development." The mastering of weapons and combat skills by peaceful civilians enabled them, so the claim went, to best

A young partisan recruit leaves his family, Leningrad Oblast, 1942. (Credit: RGAKFD)

the vaunted and numerically superior Germans and testified to the cultural achievements of the Soviet Union.[149] Thus, a broadcast from Radio Moscow informed the occupied territories that the partisans were "the embodiment of dedication, courage, staunchness, bravery, and fearlessness. The partisans are the very best, most elevated and rewarded standard-bearers that only exist within the advanced person of our epoch!"[150] It was impossible to imagine such "advanced people" descending into the wildness and indiscipline of partizanshchina.

The partisans' self-representations also highlighted their own heroism and unique qualities. Many seem to have been aware of the adulation they received in the Soviet media, garnered from newspaper accounts and broadcasts to the occupied territories, and they internalized these sentiments. In their view, their exceptionalism not only made them the best representatives of the Soviet people but also accorded them special rights and privileges. Fedorov noted that "this conception of the partisans as some kind of legendary giants—essentially a very harmful conception—had been drummed into people by newspaper feature writers . . . The heroes in these stories were so soundlessly brave that it was hard to believe they were real human beings."

However, he went on to say, "I often regretted that we didn't have a writer in our ranks who might have truthfully told how the most ordinary of Soviet men and women were battling in the forests, how heroism was becoming an everyday necessity for them."[151]

The partisans' exceptionalism began with their separation from the greater Soviet community, which was a constant refrain in their reports, memoirs, and oral testimonies. However free many partisans felt from the formal and informal restraints imposed by Soviet institutions, almost all expressed, at one time or another, a profound anxiety at their lack of contact with these same organs. This isolation had real physical and psychological ramifications. Without contact, they could not receive orders, news, military or medical supplies, or mail, nor could they evacuate their families and their wounded. A partisan who evidently had not heard from his family since June 1941 wrote home in October 1942, asking, "Who is dead? Who lives, how are you living, who is in the army, are they alive?"[152] Vershigora contended that in their isolation, if not in their material and military situation, the partisans' behaviors and moral codes resembled those of the heroic inhabitants of besieged Leningrad who refused to submit to the enemy.[153] Some partisans felt that they had become "the orphaned children of the motherland."[154] The partisan poet Platon Vorenko wrote:

The partisan does not seek mercy
He does not call for help.
He does not call a distant friend
Who is a thousand miles away at the front,
Behind the Don and the blue Bug
Relief does not arrive for us.[155]

These feelings of isolation increased substantially when the partisans came under blockade and attack during major antipartisan operations.[156]

The sense of isolation from the rest of the Soviet community could be acute, particularly in the chaotic days of 1941 when the last contact soldiers and civilians alike had with Soviet power was in the midst of its disintegration.[157] Rumors ranging from the alleged captures of Leningrad and Moscow and the collapse of the Soviet government to Stalin's supposed flight to the United States abounded.[158] Commander S. A. Kovpak claimed that losing contact with Moscow in 1941 was "the heaviest of all things that happened to us in the enemy's rear."[159] One partisan explained his excitement when he heard a radio broadcast from Moscow, "Can't you understand, comrades,

that it's over two weeks since I heard anything. Just deaf, dumb and blind.
Not a single communiqué, not a single article about what's happening in the
world."[160] In contrast, contact meant that the Soviet Union still existed and
that they remained connected to and were part of it. A partisan wrote home,
"We don't live badly. Every day we listen to the radio. We know what is happening at the front and in the rear. The rodina has not forgotten us, and we
do not spare our lives for it."[161] Paradoxically, in their vulnerable and isolated
state, the partisans' attachment to the Soviet system may have been strengthened. For many, in contrast to their precarious and dangerous present, the
connection was to a familiar and seemingly more secure past, and in their
desire to keep in contact with it, their Soviet identity may have been indirectly
reinforced.

Isolation also bred pride in their resourcefulness and autonomy in surviving and accomplishing their objectives.[162] One commissar's report to Soviet
officials in August 1942 typified these feelings:

> For all the time of the organization of the partisan detachment, no one
> helped us, we conducted our organization independently. Of course there
> were mistakes, many mistakes, because no one advised us, we didn't
> have communications with anyone, we alone were responsible . . . The
> partisans were inculcated in such a spirit that every partisan is a hero of
> the Patriotic war, so that every one reports how his actions helped the
> Soviet people.[163]

Another partisan wrote Ponomarenko:

> How much heroism, audacity, courage, selflessness, dedication to
> the Rodina the partisan [shows] in battle. How much ingenuity,
> inventiveness [they show]; not only did our partisans gain combat
> hardening, fearlessness, and stubbornness in battle, but also mainly
> they learned splendidly to beat the Hitlerite beasts.[164]

Their apparent martial prowess led some partisans to compare themselves
favorably to the Red Army. In a letter written some twenty years after the war,
a commissar recalled the observation of an officer who allegedly said, "You
never would believe that those are partisans in the trenches. They fight like
real *gvardeitsy*[165] —with trickery, cleverly, calculatingly, bravely, and with en-
viable stubbornness."[166] Of course, this statement, if true, reveals not only the
commissar's appraisal of his men but also the fact that an army officer was

surprised that partisans could engage in the same stand-up fight that regular soldiers faced every day.

Some partisans further claimed that their isolation imposed a greater hardship than fighting en masse at the front as Red Army soldiers did. Vershigora juxtaposed Kovpak's raid to Right Bank Ukraine in the 1942–1943 fall and winter with the Red Army's epic victory at Stalingrad (thus implying, according to some critics, an equivalence of the partisan raid with the six-month battle, which cost over 1 million Soviet casualties).[167] But he also argued that the partisans, lacking a front, rear, and flanks, were totally alone, with only the people as their support.[168] Other partisans put their situation more gloomily, stating that "the partisan has no future, and if you compare his position to soldiers in the Red Army, it isn't worth a thing. Besides the partisan has nowhere to retreat and nowhere to advance."[169] These fears were underscored by the ever-present threat of destruction by the enemy and by the partisans' justified perception, especially in 1941 and 1942, that they were surrounded by a hostile population harboring internal enemies. More positively, some partisans internalized assertions from the Soviet media and from Stalin himself that they constituted a "second front," which not only was a criticism of Allied inaction but also seemed to equate the partisans' effectiveness with the army's.[170]

Partisans also believed that their war required a degree of personal skill and initiative beyond what was needed at the front. To maintain unit cohesion deep in enemy territory, they asserted, more personal discipline was required from them than from their counterparts at the front or in the Soviet rear area[171]—an assertion that echoed official inferences that the partisans were the New Soviet People. According to one partisan, combat missions such as ambushes, sabotage, and small group raids required greater individual initiative, discipline, autonomy, and decisionmaking than needed in the regular army. Commander N. Z. Koliada explained to reporters from *Komsomol'skaia pravda*:

> We consider every partisan to be [the equal] of ten soldiers because one or two partisans independently solve tactical problems. Let's say there are three people. A column is marching. What should the fighters do, attack it or run away? The comrades decide this question themselves. They do not wait for a special decision, they load the machine guns, let the Germans come near to a short distance and fire. For us one partisan equals ten soldiers. Kurasov—the commander of the 4th [Shock] Army—told me this. "We," he told me, "consider each of your

partisans as ten soldiers, because sometimes our soldiers still don't get it, and to compare your fighters with ours is in any case impossible."[172]

Individual responsibility forced the partisan to make critical decisions either on his or her own or with a small group of comrades. This democratization of power and decisionmaking was at odds with the hierarchical and rigid structure of Soviet society, and it suggested the superiority of the partisans over their regular army counterparts. Of course, the nature of combat imposed these responsibilities on all soldiers (which is why many historians argue that the war led to a "spontaneous destalinization").[173] But the small-unit battles the partisans fought exaggerated these characteristics—and, perhaps more importantly, the partisans' perception of them—even more and thereby further undermined official values of hierarchy and the top-down distribution of power.

Their isolation and individualism imbued partisans with a powerful sense of autonomy from other institutions and controls, a sense that manifested itself in a variety of behaviors. It also was evident in the partisans' interpretations of discipline. Claims of autonomy could only go so far, however. Whatever claims of self-sufficiency they made, the partisans increasingly depended on outside support and guidance, and too much stress on autonomy verged on partizanshchina. Consequently, partisans also had to demonstrate their loyalty to the regime as especially patriotic and ardent defenders of the rodina, the people, and the Soviet order. For instance, they reported the restoration of Soviet institutions and laws in their zones of control to the government.[174] Actual motivations for such actions varied from place to place, no doubt ranging from cynicism and opportunism in currying favor with Moscow to a genuine desire to reestablish a beloved social and political order. Whatever the underlying reasons, reestablishing Soviet power demonstrated publicly that the partisans were dedicated to the regime. Newspapers, in turn, reported the reestablishment of Soviet power to the public at large, thus showing that even in the sea of occupation, islands of Soviet power, defended by real patriots, continued the struggle.[175] These reports also "proved" to readers that citizens who saw what the enemy had to offer "chose" the Soviet way, further demonstrating the system's apparent legitimacy.

The partisans' heroic self-identities, with their emphasis on individual prowess and skill, and their suggestion that they were New Soviet People coincided with official representations of the movement. Official portrayals, however, presented these images without following through on their implications. Although partisan initiative was praised, the possibilities of actual autonomy and freedom were never mentioned publicly. But the partisans were real people and not Soviet stereotypes. The internalization of these values and the fluidity of the guerrilla war influenced many to regard themselves as unique people with special interests, rights, and freedoms. The resulting worldviews and behaviors, if taken too far, appeared very similar to those embodied in partizanshchina. Thus, the commissar of the United Partisan Detachments, A. D. Bondarenko, a Hero of the Soviet Union, apparently believed that his status and that of his partisans was such that they could afford to sit out the rest of the war. "We have fought and have enough glory," he was reported to have said in January 1943, even as the German occupation of his territory continued: "Now we can rest."[176] Ironically, the state's efforts to impose a loyal partisan identity on the movement may well have contributed to sentiments that, though not necessarily anti-Soviet, implicitly challenged official notions of hierarchy, obedience, and order.

IN THE VANGUARD ONCE AGAIN: THE PARTY-RECRUITED PARTISAN

Another critical social marker for many partisans was corporate affiliation. Like ethnonational and regional loyalties, corporate affiliations tended to fragment rather than unite the movement. They were particularly evident among two of the dominant groups in 1941 and 1942: Party-recruited partisans and partisans originating from the Red Army. Yet even as both groups contested the definitions of partisanship and what constituted true patriotism, they also distanced themselves from the state and institutions from which they derived their identities.

Soviet policy initially relied on Party members to form the backbone of the insurgency. As such, they were accorded an appropriate treatment in the media. Party and Komsomol members were invariably depicted as resourceful, brave, and staunch in their devotion to the Soviet order. Zoia Kosmodem'ianskaia, the nineteen-year-old Komsomol who was captured, tortured, and executed by the Germans, epitomized this courage and dedication. In describing her and other Komsomol members' lives and deaths, a *Pravda* reporter wrote that they were "patriots of our socialist motherland." One young activist died allegedly saying, "Long live Communism!" and Zoia's supposed last words on the scaffold to the assembled German and Soviet onlookers were, "Good-bye Comrades! Fight, do not be afraid! Stalin is with us! Stalin is coming!"[177] These portrayals inspired many young people to emulate or at least fantasize about emulating Zoia's bravery and resiliency.[178] Adult Communists were also depicted heroically. In the 1942 film *The Raikom Secretary (Secretar' raikoma)*, a review of which was broadcast to the partisans, Kochet, the eponymous raikom secretary, was described as a "bolshevik, the leader of the partisan detachment, a person completely dedicated to his land, his people."[179]

There is much evidence that Party-recruited partisans internalized these portrayals, whether due to state propaganda or their own sense of self. In so doing, they contrasted their heroic selves with their Party comrades who remained in—or had fled to—Soviet territory and with Red Army partisans, whom they accused of being responsible for the defeats of 1941.

Certainly, Party-recruited partisans regarded themselves as the natural leaders of the movement. Fedorov, for example, insisted that it was the Party's role to direct the partisan movement and that only the Party was "capable of rousing the millions of Soviet men and women for a heroic struggle against the invaders."[180] V. D. Lobarev, a partisan commissar in Belorussia, told Central Staff personnel that in the first winter of the war, his detachment was composed primarily of "Communists, Komsomols, and Jewish youth. Many highly qualified Red Army officers, remaining in encirclement, preferred to lie low." He went on to note that it was the "Party leadership, remaining in the occupied territories . . . that developed the partisan struggle in the rear of the enemy."[181] Other Party-recruited partisans believed that their status as the first to enter the partisan ranks made them the movement's elite. Later, when floods of non-Party civilians joined the detachments, Party members declared themselves the movement's "advanced guard."[182]

Acute isolation further fueled their pride. Communist partisans could not help but believe that they had been abandoned, not only by the non-Party civilian population and the retreating Red Army but also by their own apparatus. Shortly after the war, one Communist in Fedorov's complex noted:

> I consider that those who went with us to the forest to the partisan
> detachment, turned out to be the true patriots of the Rodina. Now look
> at the comrades who had the opportunity together with you to take rifle
> in hand and go to the forest, but did not do this. They left the forest,
> [saying] "Better I should leave for the East" if there were appropriate
> reasons.[183]

Other Communists contrasted the flight of others with their own hardiness. Party officials turned partisans P. P. Makarenko, E. N. Prokhorenko, and A. K. Stel'makh reported in March 1942:

> The work in the enemy's rear is a testing of one's own nerves, a testing of dedication to the Party of Lenin-Stalin, and to our people. The difficult situation, which we did not expect, crashed down like snow on our heads. The Red Army retreats, and individual units even flee in panic, throwing away their weapons, tanks, and other vehicles. The local authorities run away. The vaunted German troops move noisily forward. In this situation, we find ourselves in the forest, we believe in our victory, we gather strength, make our plans, and prepare ourselves for the struggle with the fascists. There was no experience of underground work. It was necessary to take in the experience of every individual [historical] period, and in accordance with this, build our work.[184]

Neither their pride in their own achievements nor their alienation from those who had abandoned them had lessened six months later, when Prokhorenko described in his diary his relations with the Vitebsk Obkom, many of whose members were safely ensconced in the Soviet rear area:

> To me it is simply not good to be at the Obkom. Several [obkom members] will curse and reproach me. And this is most insulting. A year underground, a year in the most difficult living conditions, and here not only our mistakes, but even those actions this year which saved our skins, will be treated with contempt.[185]

Prokhorenko's anger at his erstwhile comrades was a variation of the classic resentment of the frontline soldier toward those in the rear. It reflected the feelings among Party-recruited partisans, chosen by the nation's leaders to be the movement's organizers, that they were a special breed, more devoted to the rodina, Party, and Soviet state than other citizens and Communists.

Accompanying the anger, however, was pride in their ability to survive in that harsh and dangerous environment. Prokhorenko and his comrades had to rely on their own initiative and skill to survive. Other Communists echoed these feelings as they realized that they could no longer depend on higher authorities or committee decisions but had to depend on their own judgment.[186]

Moreover, Communists such as Prokhorenko, surrounded by enemies and engaged in a conspiratorial struggle to overthrow brutal oppressors, were struck by the similarity between their situation and that of Lenin and the Bolsheviks before 1917.[187] As one underground raikom secretary in Smolensk Oblast related:

> Sometimes an extraordinarily complicated situation developed. Before, when difficulties arose, we turned to the higher organizations, asked for advice and quickly received instructions. Now we had to undertake decisions independently, to show maximum initiative. In the underground it is not always possible to be advised by the higher Party centers. In this situation, as never before, [we were] helped [by] the knowledge of the history of our Bolshevik Party and the knowledge of the laws of social development. The underground workers often turned to the works of Lenin for advice. In the works of V. I. Lenin we derived strength in the certainty of our victory over the enemy.[188]

Although these Party members presumably did not flee to the woods toting Lenin's collected works, they certainly believed they were following in his footsteps, an assertion given legitimacy by the presence of Old Bolsheviks in the partisans' ranks.[189]

In their eyes, their bravery, dedication, and initiative contrasted sharply with the cowardice, defeatism, and even treachery displayed by Red Army soldiers, especially since prewar Soviet propaganda had touted the army's invincibility; the Stalinist leadership, by definition, was blameless. A Communist asserted:

> What's a guy who came out of encirclement anyway? That means he didn't die in battle. Take him into the partisans in the forest and he won't want to die here either, he'll begin hiding behind somebody else's back. And that goes double for a prisoner of war. Once he was a prisoner, it means he surrendered. No, we don't need that kind. The Party picked and confirmed us.[190]

Party-recruited partisans doubted not only the okruzhentsy's bravery but their loyalties as well. They asked themselves, why had these Red Army "cowards" suddenly become infused with a fighting spirit? The answer to some was obvious: they were German spies.[191]

Even those okruzhentsy considered loyal were still not regarded as real patriots. Some people believed that okruzhentsy fought to expiate their sin of defeat; others considered them mere opportunists. Fedorov was especially scornful toward okruzhentsy who tried to hide from the war by forming attachments with local women:

> Among the "hubbies" [*primaki*] there were specimens who would have been glad to sit out the war behind a woman's skirt, but the Germans would either drive them off to work in Germany or else make them join the police. After turning this over in his mind such a guy would come to the conclusion that, after all, joining the partisans was more advantageous.[192]

Vershigora spoke for many when he asserted that fighting spirit, which seemed particularly absent in okruzhentsy officers, was far more important than technical military knowledge.[193] These allegations impugned not only the soldiers' abilities, courage, and dedication to the country but also their masculinity, which Party-recruited partisans and others now linked to their patriotism. Consequently, okruzhentsy included in civilian units were often marginalized. Officers, in particular, were often forced to serve as common fighters, subordinated to political cadres who had little military knowledge or experience. Such attitudes, as observers noted, ultimately lowered the effectiveness and raised the casualties of the Party-recruited units.[194]

In likening themselves to the Party's founders, the Party-recruited partisans elevated themselves in moral stature above their brethren in the Soviet rear area and claimed to be Lenin's true heirs. They believed that they embodied the Party's heroic, historic past and represented its true values. They also compared themselves positively to the other national institution, the Red Army. In so doing, they portrayed themselves as the country's real saviors. And even as Party-recruited partisans maintained their connection to the Party and the Soviet state, they imbued their heroism with an elitism that distinguished them both from fellow Party members in the Soviet rear area and from other partisans.

SOLDIERS IN THE ENEMY'S REAR AREA:
THE RED ARMY PARTISANS

The second group that dominated the partisan movement in its first years was composed of former Red Army soldiers, primarily okruzhentsy and escaped POWs, and organizing teams sent by the army to form new units. Their identities specifically as Red Army partisans were not shaped by Soviet propaganda. As indicated earlier, they were practically invisible in the Soviet media, which almost always depicted partisans as civilians. Indeed, when historian I. I. Mints prepared a chapter on the partisans for a text on the war, Central Staff political head V. N. Malin told him to remove references to regular soldiers and units participating in the movement, since the partisan war was supposed to be "inflamed" by local leaders.[195] Instead, the bands that were led and dominated by former Red Army troops represented themselves as military professionals, as soldiers behind enemy lines, which was manifested in their unit structure, appearance, discipline, and military expertise.

Red Army partisans formed, in the words of one commissar, "a separate Red Army unit" behind the lines.[196] Officials and partisan commanders equated military organization and discipline with increased combat capability, in contrast to civilian partisans.[197] One commissar, a former Red Army political officer, reminded his unruly partisans that "Soviet power is not obsolete. We reflect the Red Army and we must conduct ourselves in accordance with the behavior of Red Army men."[198] A. V. Romanov, a Red Army political officer and commissar of the "For Soviet Belarus-Rokossovskii" Partisan Brigade, noted that "discipline in the detachments was strengthened parallel to the growth of the partisan movement and its organizational-administrative formation—the creation of regiments and battalions, selections of command staff and others."[199] A few months later, he added that measures had been implemented "to stamp out *partizanshchina*" among the civilian partisans and raise their discipline to that of soldiers.[200] Even civilian Party officials such as Fedorov, who was extremely critical of okruzhentsy in his memoirs, attempted to strengthen civilian discipline by telling their partisans that they, too, were members of the Red Army.[201] Such efforts to introduce military discipline among the partisans could only go so far.

The Red Army partisans' outward appearance reflected their sense of military professionalism and had a powerful effect on civilians. A. F. Kniazev of the 1st Voroshilov Partisan Detachment told Soviet interviewers that "in the detachment the wearing of military uniforms and badges and signs of rank was obligatory, since the detachment was [organized] from servicemen."[202] Colonel V. I. Nichiporovich, commander of the 208th Partisan Regiment, claimed that his unit's appearance caused locals to exclaim hopefully, if mistakenly, "There goes a Budenyi army. Budennyi has made his way from the Avchustovskii forests, these are simply not partisans, but are regular army formations."[203] Such reactions spoke to the popularity of the Red Army, in

Civilian and Red Army partisans in Kovpak's complex drill before undertaking their raid to the Carpathians, April 1943. (Credit: RGAKFD)

which the loved ones of many citizens served; ironically, given the regime's determination to make civilian Party members the public face of the movement, the okruzhentsy seemed to generate more popular support for the partisans than did those from the Party. This response also suggests the comparative popularity of the two national institutions, at least in the occupied territories.

Just as Party-recruited partisans turned away or marginalized military personnel, so, too, did the Red Army partisans discriminate against those who lacked military experience.[204] The inclusion of women in civilian bands was looked down on as inappropriate in a masculine martial community and was deemed an example of civilian decadence and amateurism. The commander of the 2nd Voroshilov Partisan Brigade claimed that "the enemy was afraid of our brigade because it was one of the 'military' brigades. We had no children or women who could hinder our work."[205] Similarly, Kniazev of the 1st Voroshilov derided the neighboring "Death to the German Occupiers" Partisan Detachment for incompetence, due in part to the fact that each fighter allegedly had two or three women accompanying him. Because of this detachment's supposed ineptitude, the Red Army partisans jokingly referred to its members as the "condemned ones" (*smertniki*), a play on the first word of the unit's name, "death" (*smert'*). To Kniazev, there could be no comparison of the two units: "We always accomplished our tasks, and they did not. We simply pitied them."[206] Thus, the Red Army partisans used concepts of masculinity and professionalism to impugn their civilian counterparts with the stigma of partizanshchina. In actuality, however, the percentage of women in the 1st Voroshilov by the end of the war was just slightly below the average in the movement as a whole (8.8 percent versus 9.3 percent).[207]

The former soldiers did, however, share their Party comrades' estrangement from their parent institution. Despite their pride in their military professionalism, they still defined themselves as partisans, with different needs from those of soldiers in regular army formations. Although a very rare occurrence, Red Army partisans might mutiny—and get away with it—if certain minimal standards of living were not met, behavior unimaginable in a regular Red Army formation. The rank-and-file partisans in the 1st Voroshilov, for example, refused to undertake a long and difficult march unless they were given adequate footwear and provisions. And they persuaded their officers to support their cause. Although officials, including the unit's former commander, ordered the detachment to obey orders, the partisans remained adamant. Their demands were finally met, and the 1st Voroshilov resumed operations, apparently without suffering any consequences for its rebellious action.[208]

Red Army partisans particularly resented the regular army officers with no knowledge of guerrilla warfare who were sometimes sent to command them. The commissar of the "Twenty-fourth Anniversary of the Red Army" Independent Partisan Regiment, a former Red Army political officer, complained that such officers "tried to turn the partisan detachment into a regular Red Army unit" by applying frontline discipline and employing conventional tactics.[209] Leningrad partisans told Soviet officials as late as 1943 that they would reject any conventional army officers sent to command them.[210] Regular officers reciprocated these feelings; one of them, caught behind enemy lines, resisted joining the partisans because he was not "trained in the partisan method": "Partisan warfare is from the last century," he claimed.[211]

By representing themselves as military professionals, Red Army partisans attempted to erase their image as the incompetents and defeatists responsible for the catastrophes of 1941. Rather, they portrayed themselves as the self-appointed military experts who, alone in the movement, were capable of inflicting any damage on the enemy. Hence, they reversed the Party-recruited partisans' image of them. The civilian partisans were now the bumbling amateurs, whereas the military professionals were the true patriots.

But like their Party comrades, they also developed a distinct sense of themselves as partisans. Though they retained the outward forms of military affiliation, they, too, asserted that as partisans, they were different from soldiers serving at the front and deserved special rights and privileges. Red Army partisans also espoused autonomy from the central state agencies, even as they spoke of their contributions to the national war effort.

The dispute between Party-recruited and Red Army partisans was rooted in deeper antagonisms than corporate rivalries. The former's emphasis on spirit, patriotism, and consciousness and the latter's concentration on military professionalism and technical knowledge echoed earlier conflicts about the primacy of "Red versus Expert" that had occurred after the Revolution itself. This debate reemerged in the war at the national level, but by the fall of 1942, the experts (in the guise of the army) had clearly gained the upper hand, as signaled by signs as diverse as Aleksandr Korneichuk's Stalin-inspired play *The Front* and the increased professionalization and institutional independence of the Red Army, marked by the appearance of officer epaulettes and gold braid and the abolition of the post of political commissar.[212] To some extent, in the partisan movement, as in the Red Army, this dichotomy had essentially been a false one, for many of the younger experts and officers were also Party members and had good relations with their commissars. Conversely, many commissars also had military training.[213] Nevertheless, that this conflict arose in the partisan movement, as well as in the overall war effort, shows how much the perception of a divide between ideological commitment and technical knowledge persisted in the Soviet Union. This divide also affected partisan operations.

IDENTITY POLITICS, PARTISAN STYLE

Behind enemy lines, partisans clashed with each other over how the movement and its participants should be defined. The most visible conflict occurred among Party-recruited partisans, okruzhentsy, and the most extreme adherents of the partisan ethos. Local, regional, ethnonational, and Soviet patriotism further influenced partisan identities and actions. The intrusion of the Soviet state through its media and the partisan staffs and other institutions also affected these battles, as did divisions among the state officials themselves. What was at stake were very real issues concerning authority, discipline, freedom, unit culture, and the overall meaning and purpose of the movement.

Those accused of engaging in partizanshchina faced a bleak future. Individuals might be executed, and whole units faced dissolution, incorporation into other units, or even physical destruction. One Red Army detachment commander reported that another group of partisans "declared directly that [it] did not recognize the partisans or the Germans" but instead would operate in its own interests. The detachment was suppressed by the more powerful Red Army band, which disarmed it, shot several of its members, incorporated others, and drove the rest away.[214]

Conflicts between the hierarchically oriented Party and Red Army partisans and those accused of adhering to partizanshchina were particularly dangerous to unit cohesion, as the fate of the Sergei Detachment in Vitebsk Oblast illustrates. The detachment was formed in the spring of 1942 when several small groups of local civilians and okruzhentsy merged. The partisans selected their commanders at a general meeting.[215] Soon after its formation, the Sergei Detachment was incorporated into the "For Soviet Belarus–Rokossovskii" Partisan Brigade, a unit composed of several formerly independent formations welded together by a "team of special appointment" sent by the Twenty-ninth Army. The new commanders attempted to impose regular military discipline, but they met strong resistance from the Sergei partisans, whom the brigade's commissar, A. V. Romanov,[216] accused of being infected with "democratism." In August 1942, Romanov reported to the Central Staff and the Belorussian Central Committee that the Sergei partisans "[did] not have any operational and ideological leadership, [were] sliding toward Makhnoism, [and] corruption, [were] corroded with false democracy, electing and criticizing [their] commanders. Sometimes things came to schisms and anti-Soviet remarks were uttered [such as] 'beat the Communists and commissars.'"[217]

When Romanov insisted that the partisans obey military discipline, several detachment commanders opposed him, arguing that the "partisans were not an army, that many were not trained and therefore front line discipline should not be established here." The commissar of the Sergei Detachment, Kozlovskii, objected to the brigade's plans to militarize the detachment, stating, "It is madness to create a military complex in the deep rear. It'll never amount to anything." Shortly after this incident, Kozlovskii was killed when a gun "accidentally" discharged while its owner, a woman partisan, was allegedly cleaning it. Despite demands from the other partisans that she be punished or at least be banished from the unit, Romanov protected her, saying she was a good fighter.[218] Kozlovskii's death may have been accidental, or it may have been a calculated murder, using notions of female incompetence to hide an assassination by the brigade command. Indeed, after this incident, the male Sergei partisans demanded that all women be removed from the unit, a demand that Romanov ignored.[219]

Whether Kozlovskii was murdered or not, his untimely end worsened the already hostile relations between the Sergei Detachment and the brigade command. In late September or early October 1942, after a surprise raid by a local police unit that left five partisans dead, the Sergei partisans, allegedly backed by their officers, mutinied against the brigade commanders. Romanov later reported to Soviet officials that the Sergei Detachment became a "formless, armed mass" that conducted an "armed demonstration of resistance." The other detachments remained loyal to the brigade's commanders and suppressed the dissidents. Six partisans, including the detachment commander, were shot. The detachment was disbanded, and its personnel were dispersed throughout the brigade.[220] All outward signs of partizanshchina and its espousers had been eliminated or neutralized.

Corporate rivalries within a unit could result in that group's dissolution, as occurred in one detachment operating in Mogilev Oblast. The initial formation was founded by the raikom secretary N. P. Pokrovskii in the summer of 1941. In early 1942, the okruzhenets colonel V. I. Nichiporovich joined the detachment with a number of other officers.[221] Pokrovskii and the other partisans decided that since Nichiporovich was a senior officer, he should command, with Pokrovskii serving as his commissar. After assuming leadership and renaming the detachment the 208th Partisan Regiment, after his last regular army command,[222] Nichiporovich soon began feuding with his commissar, ostensibly because he did not think Pokrovskii a capable fighter. Nichiporovich began attacking Pokrovskii at Party meetings and talking behind his back, impugning his performance. According to Pokrovskii, Nichiporovich told the partisans: "Pokrovskii is not a military man, but a raikom secretary, and how can a raikom secretary fight? And if they receive any kind of misfortune, it's all because of Pokrovskii. [Nichiporovich] created a tale that a raikom secretary is not a military man, and it would be better to have a military man [as commissar]."[223] Nichiporovich himself referred to Pokrovskii as a "big coward" who ran away as soon as any shooting started.[224] After a meeting in which the colonel's friends, mostly okruzhentsy, accused Pokrovskii of drinking and voted that he should be removed from his post, the commissar had had enough. He told Nichiporovich that he was leaving the detachment with any partisans who would go with him. Nichiporovich then spent the night telling the others that they should not leave with Pokrovskii, as he was not a soldier and they would all be killed. The next day, sixty-four "old partisans" from Pokrovskii's original detachment left with him to form a new unit. Nichiporovich then appointed an old crony, Brigade Commissar A. S. Iakovlev, to be the political officer.[225]

The dispute between Nichiporovich and Pokrovskii followed along lines established by the competing partisan representations. Despite Pokrovskii's experience and ability as commander, which enabled his unit to survive through the difficult 1941–1942 winter, he subordinated himself to Nichiporovich's superior military experience. The colonel employed the Red Army partisans' negative attitudes toward the Party-recruited partisans by alleging that Pokrovskii was not a fighter but an inept coward and that remaining under his command was tantamount to a death sentence. This conflict may have been part of a personal grudge Nichiporovich harbored against Pokrovskii or perhaps against the political establishment as a whole due to his being arrested in 1938 as an "enemy of the people."[226] It might also have been fueled by the ongoing corporate struggle between the army and the Party taking place on both sides of the front.

Even Soviet authorities could not overcome the power of partisan identities; indeed, they sometimes succumbed to them as well. In the fall of 1942, Voroshilov, at that time commander-in-chief of the partisan movement, attempted to militarize the partisans by instituting military ranks, organization, pay, and discipline throughout the movement.[227] Ponomarenko opposed this proposal on the grounds that the movement would lose its flexibility, units would lose their internal cohesion, and the partisans would become separated from the local population, evidently leading to the end of a truly genuine all-people's war.[228]

Though it is not clear how many formations actually undertook this reorganization, D. V. Emliutin's OPO apparently did act on it. In the fall of 1942, it ordered the restructuring of all its formations into military-style brigades.[229] Red Army units were little affected by this order, but many civilian detachments were forced to abandon their traditions and their names and accommodate themselves to the cultures of alien units. Numerous local detachments were forced to move to new locations outside their home areas, causing much dissension in the ranks. As a result, as one partisan commissar reported, mistakes were made during the reorganization ("not in our [unit] but in others," he assured debriefers), which resulted in a significant drop in combat capabilities throughout the partisan zone.[230] It is not directly indicated in Central Staff records, but it seems that these results, which justified Ponomarenko's objections, contributed to Voroshilov's removal as supreme partisan commander.[231] Although some Russian historians and contemporaries such as Starinov have argued that the failure to implement Voroshilov's plan was a lost opportunity to raise the insurgency's military effectiveness and professionalism,[232] it is also clear that the powerful emotions associated with unit identities, including "civilian" traditions, could not be extinguished by fiat.

Indeed, identity politics, especially when intermingled with outside corporate and territorial rivalries involving the partisan administration, could paralyze operations in an entire district. Such a situation occurred in Diat'kovo Raion in the Orel region.

Diat'kovo was occupied by the Germans in October 1941. Local Party officials organized a partisan force, which by February 1942 had 129 partisans divided into four groups. In addition, three groups of okruzhentsy, consisting of some 125 partisans, also operated in the area.[233] Eventually, under the prodding of a political officer from the Western Front, a joint civilian-military united staff was formed, with NKVD official N. M. Sentiurin as its head and Lieutenant G. I. Orlov, a Red Army commander and member of the Western Front's political administration, as its chief of reconnaissance.[234]

On 10 February, two representatives from the Orel Obkom, S. G. Turkin and I. V. Dymnikov, arrived to head the movement in the district. Four days later, the partisans literally walked into the town of Diat'kovo itself and proclaimed the reestablishment of Soviet power.[235] Orlov returned to Soviet territory at roughly the same time, where he, along with other Red Army partisans, met with the then commander of the Western Front, Georgi Zhukov. Zhukov, who wanted the partisans to attack German communications lines to support Red Army operations, promoted Orlov to captain and authorized him to organize and subordinate all partisan groups in the Diat'kovo district, including the Party-recruited bands.[236] Zhukov's action provoked a strong response from Matveev and Orel NKVD chief K. F. Firsanov, the heads of Orel's partisan movement. In a letter to Malenkov and Beria in May 1942, Matveev and Firsanov complained that the military had usurped Party authority by sending representatives "with the right to interfere in the detachments' affairs, and even more the right to remove and replace detachment leaders."[237] All cooperation between the Party and the army was ended.

The establishment of subordinate front staffs of the partisan movement in June 1942 further complicated matters, since Diat'kovo Raion lay within the military jurisdiction of the Western Front. Therefore, the military operations of the Diat'kovo partisans were subordinated to the Western Front's partisan staff, headed by Smolensk Obkom first secretary D. M. Popov. All internal Party and organizational matters remained, however, under the purview of the Orel Obkom, thus creating parallel military and political command structures. In August 1942, Popov and the Western Front command created sixteen operational centers behind German lines to unify partisan military and political affairs and to coordinate the operations of all partisan units in their respective districts. Two of Popov's operational centers were located in Orel's Diat'kovo and Kletnia districts. The establishment of these centers thus amounted to a power grab by Smolensk's Popov as he attempted to expand his political jurisdiction to include Orel territory. Command of the Diat'kovo Operational Center was given to Zhukov's protégé, Orlov. Orel officials were furious at this development, contending that the operational centers created a "duality in the leadership in the party organizations, partisan detachments and in the whole partisan movement," meaning that the centers under Popov's control were usurping the powers of the local Orel Party organizations.[238] Thus, by the middle of 1942, a contest for control over Diat'kovo Raion and its partisans was well under way. On one side were Orlov's Red Army partisans, supported by the powerful commander of the Western Front and the partisan front staff (headed by a Smolensk Obkom secretary). They were opposed by the Party-recruited partisans backed by the Briansk Front (later Orel) Staff and by the Orel Obkom. Neither Orlov nor Orel Party officials Turkin and Dymnikov were prepared to subordinate themselves to the other, yet each believed that he had every right to command all the partisans in the district. Thus, the battle lines were drawn.

This division had serious material and military repercussions for the guerrilla war in the district, as the contending factions seemed to have spent as much time harassing each other as they did the Germans. In May 1942, the Diat'kovo Raikom (under Orel control) ordered that no partisan detachment could requisition supplies from civilians without its permission. Despite Orlov's complaints that Party officials refused to provide him with supplies, Party-recruited partisans insisted that he had received plenty from the raikom but nonetheless had systematically pillaged the local population, thereby undermining popular support. They also claimed that he constantly intimidated and threatened the local detachments.[239]

Tensions were heightened by a German antipartisan offensive in June 1942, during which the partisans abandoned Diat'kovo and were swept from the area. Two Orel Party-recruited detachments from outside the district, commanded by M. P. Romashin and M. I. Duka, respectively, encountered Orlov's unit while they were escaping from another German force. Romashin related to Ponomarenko that Orlov apparently allowed the alien Party-recruited partisans to stay in the area, so long as they helped man the defensive perimeter. Orlov then withdrew, however, leaving Romashin and Duka to hold the line against the oncoming Germans. When the civilian partisans later caught up to Orlov, he allegedly threatened to shoot them if they did not subordinate themselves to him, as his men aggressively displayed their automatic weapons.[240] If this account is true, Orlov seems to have been all bluff and bluster, however, for Duka and Romashin remained unscathed and their detachments retained their independence.[241]

Dymnikov, the chair of the Diat'kovo Raion Executive Committee, also complained to Ponomarenko, declaring, "It seems to me that we cannot bring Orlov's unit to order." He pleaded that the Orel partisans in Diat'kovo be transferred from the jurisdiction of Popov's Western Staff to Matveev's Briansk Staff, which would protect the Orel partisans. Dymnikov begged Ponomarenko to "examine and unmask this person."[242]

Dymnikov had also sent telegrams to Stalin and Beria, asking them to bring Orlov under control. Stalin also may have met with Dymnikov at the Kremlin reception in September 1942,[243] for by early September, Dymnikov had orders from Stalin and Voroshilov that all units in Diat'kovo Raion, including the Operations Center, were to be transferred to the Briansk Front Staff.[244] The next month, the Central Staff disbanded the Operations Center, redesignating Orlov's command the Diat'kovo Partisan Brigade.[245] The Red Army partisan leaders were incensed by this decision. Orlov's commissar, E. Kozliuk, protested to Ponomarenko that Orlov's appointment as head of the Operations Center had come from Zhukov himself and that the local detachments had ignored their instructions to subordinate themselves to the Operations Center.[246] In his report on his unit's activities composed after its liberation in October 1943, Orlov blamed the Briansk Staff, led by Orel's Matveev, for disseminating "false information," thereby enabling all local detachments to leave the jurisdiction of the Diat'kovo Center, which caused further "confusion and disorganization."[247]

Even with Orlov's apparent defeat, Dymnikov continued throughout the fall of 1942 to accuse the Red Army partisans of plundering the local inhabitants. Finally, in December, at Ponomarenko's behest, an inquest was held regarding Orlov's activities in Diat'kovo. Fortunately for the accused, the process was conducted by the Western Staff's head of the partisan movement, Orlov's old ally Smolensk Obkom secretary Popov. Although all the witnesses, including Kozliuk, and Orlov's own records affirmed that "individual occurrences of marauding" had taken place in the areas where Orlov's group was stationed, the tribunal ruled that it could not determine whether his partisans were responsible.[248] Orlov was fortunate that the inquest was held under Popov's jurisdiction. Matveev undoubtedly would have supported Dymnikov, given the Red Army officer's feud with the Orel Party-recruited partisans. The inquest also allowed Ponomarenko to appear to satisfy Dymnikov's complaints, while at the same time protecting the commander of a well-armed and experienced unit, who claimed to have close connections with a powerful Red Army general. It also appears to have quieted both Dymnikov and Orlov; in any event, no further documentation has come to light in Central Staff records indicating additional confrontations between the two up to the time of the district's liberation by the Red Army in September 1943.

The story of the partisan movement in Diat'kovo Raion and elsewhere throughout the occupied territories reveals the significance of partisan loyalties and identities in reflecting and shaping relations among the partisans and between the partisans and state authorities. The divisions in the partisan ranks, based on conflicting definitions of what it meant to be a partisan, corporate loyalties, the antagonistic Party-army relationship, the competition between rival subordinate staffs, and regionalism, were exacerbated by the more basic but no less intractable problems of obtaining sufficient food and establishing local authority. Although outside authorities could quell these disputes, they could also fuel them, as local struggles between partisans became embroiled in larger corporate and territorial conflicts. In the case of Diat'kovo, the Central Staff was able to calm the situation, but its intervention resulted in more of a compromise solution rather than a decisive end to the strife.

As the preceding examples indicate, differences in the partisans' identities had significant implications for relations within units. Even though partisans shared common experiences and sentiments and were profoundly affected by ethnonational, regional, and corporate affiliations, these same associations also led to divisions. Competing identities, values, and understandings about the nature and aims of the partisan war inhibited them from finding common ground for resolving disputes or even empowering partisans in their relations with state authorities. Although both partisans and officials spoke of a united *movement*, the plural *movements*, reflecting the social and national divisions embodied within both the insurgency and the greater Soviet society, was perhaps a more accurate term.

In certain broad aspects, the partisans' self-definitions were remarkably similar to those sanctioned by Moscow. Both officials and partisans shared a common terminology and highlighted particular characteristics as being unique to the partisans, including exceptional bravery, skill, patriotism, and initiative. These qualities derived from popular historical and cultural legacies from the tsarist and Soviet past. Yet though partisans and officials used these common terms, they imbued them with different meanings, which could legitimate significantly divergent behaviors. Authorities projected an identity that sanctioned official hierarchies, discipline, and Soviet consciousness. Partisans echoed these definitions to a limited extent, but they also used these exceptional attributes to construct an identity based on autonomy from Soviet norms and constraints—an identity that celebrated their superiority over other citizens and state organizations and marked them as elite members of Soviet institutions. The very vagueness of the term *rodina*, for example, enabled partisans to identify with the regime that employed it so powerfully, even if they were not always fighting for the rodina defined by the state. But by acknowledging and indeed celebrating and sanctifying national and local patriotism, hatred of the enemy, and the desire for revenge, the regime did speak a universal language that established a new and powerful bond with the public and, with it, a new claim for its support. Thus, although officials and partisans spoke a common language, they sometimes understood this language in strikingly different ways. Even within the partisans' ranks, the differences in meaning could be significant, thereby undermining the construction of a common partisan identity. Divisions within the state's own apparatus informed and often intensified these conflicts. It was the ambiguities in this same discourse reflecting real political, ethnic, national, and corporate fractions within Soviet society that enabled multiple voices and interpretations of the partisans' mission to emerge. These conflicts were heightened further as the Soviet leadership attempted to fulfill the policy directives called for in the invocation of the all-people's war as more diverse groups flooded the movement in 1943.

5

THE CRISIS OF PARTISAN IDENTITY, 1943

The dominant partisan identities, established by late 1942, rested on certain key social attributes. The dominant partisans were Slavic, male, and usually connected with a political or military institution. However, by late 1942, two developments threatened the position of the dominant partisans. First, the movement continued to expand dramatically, primarily due to the increasing influx of politically unaffiliated civilians. Second, the government was determined to make the partisan war into a genuine all-people's war, as called for in NKO Order 189. These twin pressures meant not only that the veteran partisans of 1941 and 1942 would be numerically overwhelmed by the new recruits but also that the very character of the movement would change.

In some ways, the officially sanctioned expansion of the partisan movement in 1943 continued an important trend that had become increasingly pronounced in late imperial and Soviet society: the redefinition of the nation to include previously excluded groups so as to broaden the basis of national mobilization. Russian military reformers in the late nineteenth and early twentieth centuries extended the concept of the nation beyond the traditional Slavic core. Soviet policymakers further expanded this concept of nationhood to include women and to promote workers and peasants.[1] Although World War II generally saw these policies continue, there were striking exceptions to them, especially the deportations of ethnonational groups such as the Volga Germans, the Chechens, and the Crimean Tatars. At the beginning of the partisan war, the leadership followed an exclusionary policy, despite the rhetoric of the all-people's war. By the fall of 1942, however, the same leadership sought to make the movement as inclusive as possible in order to make national mobilization a reality, at least in the occupied territories.

A successful inclusive policy reflected in the fulfillment of the all-people's war, the assumption went, would show Soviet citizens, the enemy, and the world that Moscow had won the battle for the hearts and minds of the population in the occupied territories, since the populace could choose between two rival ideologies. The leadership determined that the participation of all social elements was necessary to prove that the entire country was united to save the land, defend the Soviet regime, and destroy the hated enemy. This political goal required that the movement symbolically and physically become a microcosm of the Soviet Union itself to the extent possible, given that the occupation centered principally, if not exclusively, on the three Slavic republics. Consequently, beginning in late 1942, the Central Staff sought to incorporate groups generally not included in the first partisan formations, such as politically unaffiliated civilians, women, non-Slavic nationalities, and even citizens who served the enemy in any capacity. For example, the Ukrainian Staff's Operational Plan for the Development of the Partisan Movement, crafted in the fall of 1942, specifically called for the inclusion of all social elements, including religious groups and the collaborationist auxiliary police.[2] Ponomarenko and other officials also used less formal but no less authoritative instructions to pressure commanders to expand the movement's demographic base.

But just as efforts in the 1930s to include unpopular or subjugated groups in the nation sometimes faced popular resistance (such as the proposal to offer "voting rights" to priests and kulaks in the 1936 Constitution or the promotion of women's emancipation in the 1920s and 1930s),[3] the center's attempts to open the partisan movement met with opposition from veteran partisans. The all-people's war created something of an identity crisis for them, since the Party-recruited and Red Army partisans had prided themselves on their political loyalty and military proficiency, respectively, and, by virtue of the general absence of women and non-Slavic nationals, on their masculinity and Slavic ethnicity. From the veterans' standpoint, the massive influx of untrained, seemingly apathetic peasants, women, non-Slavic (and thus inferior) ethnonationalities, and former traitors threatened to weaken the resistance's military strength, to undermine the veterans' dominance over the movement, and to raise suspicions among Soviet authorities that the partisan ranks were now filled with unreliable elements. The newcomers had their own concerns, most notably to convince veteran partisans and state officials that they were indeed patriotic citizens and brave and worthy fighters. And of course, Moscow's own participation in this process was central. Soviet authorities promoted the full participation of previously excluded groups at the risk of engendering resistance among veteran partisans, undermining the social cohesion of the bands, and therefore ultimately weakening their combat capabilities. Thus, the regime could try to force the veterans to accept the new recruits when its physical control over the partisans remained quite limited, or it could seek a compromise that would include these new groups while allowing for their continued marginalization in the movement. On the one hand, the choice made by the government indicates the limits of its ability and determination to fulfill the objectives of NKO Order 189. On the other hand, it suggests its vision of the proper place and roles of these social groups in wartime Soviet society, as they related to wartime and, later, to postwar elites.

THE EXPANSION OF
THE PARTISAN MOVEMENT IN 1943

The growth of the partisan movement, begun in the spring of 1942, continued into 1943. According to contemporary Central Staff records, there were 102,562 partisans in January 1943. By January 1944, that number had nearly doubled to 181,392, even after taking into account the liberation of most of Ukraine and central Russia, with their large partisan forces.[4] Some areas experienced particularly dramatic growth, such as Belorussia, in which the number of partisans surged from 68,498 in April 1943 to 121,903 by January 1944, not including the nearly 27,000 partisans who had already been liberated.[5]

Growth was no less dramatic at the individual unit level. Hundreds of new detachments were formed in 1943, often around a core of veteran partisans spun off from a "parent" unit or around organizer groups sent from the mainland.[6] Already established units also expanded tremendously. For example, the Zhytomyr Partisan Complex numbered 310 partisans in December 1942; a year later, it counted over 4,300.[7] The 3rd Leningrad Partisan Brigade grew from 288 partisans in January 1943 to 2,760 by the end of November.[8]

This rapid expansion overwhelmed the veteran Party-recruited and Red Army partisans. The new recruits were primarily local inhabitants and former "collaborators" and defectors. The example of the 3rd Leningrad Partisan Brigade is illustrative of this phenomenon: by November 1943, local civilians accounted for 63 percent of the partisans, and former collaborators comprised another 21.8 percent of the unit. Not surprisingly, with its increase in numbers came a decrease in experience: by December 1943, only 11 percent of its partisans had been with the unit since 1941 and 1942; 23.8 percent had enlisted between January and June 1943; and 65.2 percent had taken up arms

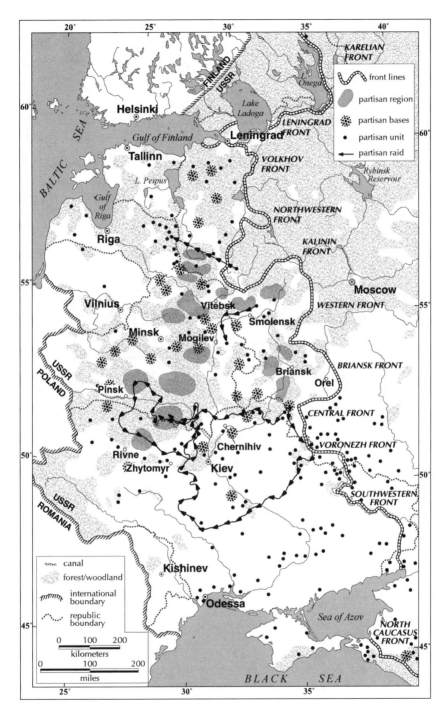

Disposition of partisan bases and operations, summer 1943. (Credit: Dick Gilbreath)

between July and December, meaning that over two-thirds of the unit had less than six months of experience in partisan warfare.[9] In the Zhytomyr Complex, assuming that none of the 310 partisans in late 1942 became casualties (a most unlikely proposition), then by January 1944, these veterans of 1941 and 1942 accounted for only 7 percent of the unit.[10] Such explosive demographic changes could only lower the bands' overall military efficiency and undermine unit cohesiveness, especially since so many new recruits came from socially and politically "unreliable" elements.

The recruits of 1943 joined the partisans for a variety of reasons. First, the victories at Stalingrad and especially at Kursk later on made it clear not only that the Wehrmacht was contained but also that Germany was going to lose the war. Joining the partisans now no longer seemed like a quixotic adventure but rather an act that would contribute to a faster conclusion to the war. Or, for the cynics and opportunists, now was a good time—and perhaps even the last time—for those who had sat out the war to demonstrate their loyalty to Soviet power, lest they have to answer for their behavior when it returned.

Second, as the Soviet partisan movement became more powerful, the Germans' ability to exert control over the occupied population correspondingly shrank. As their forces weakened, the Germans and their allies withdrew their security forces to the larger towns, thereby conceding more influence over population points to the partisans. This expanded the partisans' recruitment base and made it easier for civilians to join the partisans either voluntarily or through indirect pressure. For the partisans, success begat success, whereas for the Germans, the downward spiral of their collapsing authority accelerated.[11]

Third, just as Germany's fortunes on the battlefield declined, German labor-recruiting practices became more draconian. Throughout Europe, occupied civilians were subjected to drafts sending them to labor in the Reich. The results of this conscription were similar, whether in France, the Netherlands, or Greece: the affected populace—primarily young men—fled to the hills and woods, where many eventually joined existing partisan bands or formed their own units. The occupied Soviet Union was no exception in regard to this phenomenon.[12]

Veteran partisans doubted the courage and commitment of their new charges. Kovpak, for one, valued the sergeants who joined the partisans in 1941 more highly than the majors who joined in 1943 because the former demonstrated a much stronger fighting spirit.[13] When encountering peasants who shamefacedly admitted that they had given food to the Germans because they had no choice, partisan recruiters told them they could join the resistance to redeem their mistake.[14] A partisan doctor scornfully recorded in his memoirs that the civilian recruits of 1943 sometimes tried to obtain medical releases indicating they were too old or sick to fight, including one "grandfather" who turned out to be a spry twenty-seven-year-old.[15] Particular contempt was reserved for late-enlisting Communists who had tried to sit out the war. One commander noted, "It is just very unfortunate that prominent party members joined us only when the Red Army took over Cherepashnytsi. These people were here all the time but now come to us and say that they did a lot."[16] The marginalized status of the new recruits often continued after liberation. When the 208th Partisan Regiment was disbanded after meeting with the Red Army in 1944, its partisans were divided into three groups: the leadership became engaged in political work; other veterans helped with economic reconstruction; and the third group, consisting of the newly recruited members of the "local population, [former] police and traitors," were sent to the army.[17]

Many commanders and commissars encouraged local inhabitants to take up arms, but others tried to stem the onrushing flood of new recruits. Commanders complained to state authorities that though they wanted to accept the newcomers, they did not have sufficient arms or supplies to equip them.[18] Left unspoken were their concerns about the effect these inexperienced latecomers would have on overall military effectiveness, unit cohesion, and political reliability.

Attempts to limit the influx of partisans were directly criticized by Ponomarenko and other top officials, such as Komsomol first secretary N. A. Mikhailov, who argued that such restrictions violated NKO Order 189 and played directly into the Germans' hands. In April 1942, Mikhailov wrote to Stalin, Central Committee secretary G. M. Malenkov, and the information bureau chief, A. S. Shcherbakov, that Komsomol secretaries and commanders were not fulfilling orders to "broaden" the movement but were "frequently rejecting inhabitants from the local population in their attempts to join the partisan detachments."[19] He recommended that if a commander was unable to accept new people or form additional detachments, he should nevertheless remain in contact with the aspiring partisans "so that the struggle with the enemy be conducted not only with the strength of the partisan detachment, but carried out in broad and many-sided forms."[20] Responding to similar efforts to restrict enlistment in Smolensk Oblast, Ponomarenko informed Smolensk Obkom secretary and partisan head D. M. Popov in February 1943 that

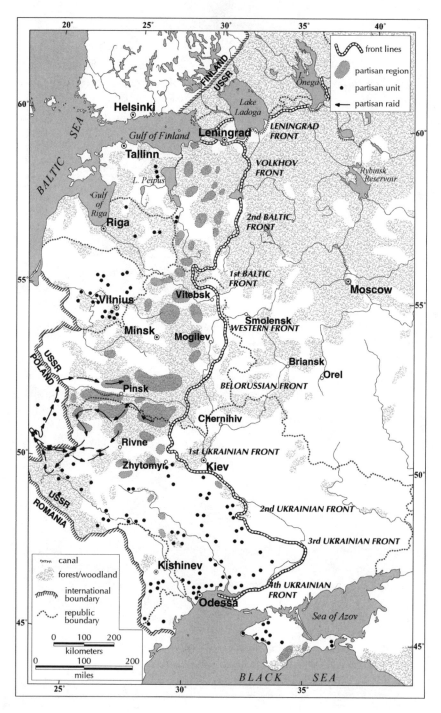

Disposition of partisan bases and operations, winter 1943–1944. (Credit: Dick Gilbreath)

there are several comrades who have the incorrect impression that if there are no weapons available, this means that a person cannot be used in the struggle with the enemy. This understanding is wrong. Every person who opposes the Germans and desires to fight them must be used and drawn into active struggle with the occupiers. The naked refusal of acceptance into the detachment, this is a bad affair, and depending on the local conditions, when the people are in a desperate situation, this can repel people from the partisans.[21]

In July 1943, he further instructed all partisan staffs that because the people "looked to the partisans as their hope, rescuing them from German atrocities," commanders could not use the excuse of insufficient weapons to prevent them "from accepting into operational or newly formed detachments local inhabitants who demand that they be admitted to the partisans." To do otherwise would place these citizens at the Germans' disposal.[22]

What effect Ponomarenko's orders had is difficult to tell. As the movement grew, officials and commanders agreed that integrating the new recruits was an essential task, since the extended time the new partisans had spent under German authority had undermined their capacity for effective resistance. Sitnikov, a member of the Leningrad Staff, stated at a November 1943 conference of partisans and Komsomol officials that it was necessary "to change these youths, who for more than two years have been with the Germans, into real partisans."[23] Speaking at the same conference, the head of the Komsomol in Belorussia, K. T. Mazurov, was much more scathing: a new partisan, he said, "goes to the detachment, and he does not attempt to participate in combat life, on the contrary, he finds any excuse to avoid it, because he has a stomach ache, there are no weapons, he does not try to obtain a weapon himself. Such people exist."[24] Although Sitnikov and Mazerov were ostensibly referring to youth, their sentiments reflected the feelings of many officials and partisans regarding their new comrades regardless of age.

Although new recruits did join the movement, they were often relegated to second-class status, unless they had a special skill or rank. Given their experience, veteran partisans retained or gained leadership positions, thus enabling them to continue to dominate unit life and culture. The subordination of the partisans of 1943 was, in part, a natural consequence of the relationship between green newcomers and combat veterans. However, in the highly politicized context of the Soviet partisan war, state officials and veteran partisans interpreted the tardiness of the new partisans' arrival as a lack of will to fight the invader; they were seen as individuals whose opportunism prevailed over their patriotism. In this way, the Stalinist practice of judging and ranking citizens based on their active commitment to the national cause and the Party continued in the detachments. Even though all citizens were now explicitly encouraged to join the movement, the nature of Soviet inclusiveness made it clear that these latecomers were not the equal of the veteran partisans, just as earlier inclusionary policies for women, national minorities, or peasants did not foster real equality. That the new recruits were mostly peasants (the quintessential second-class citizen in Stalin's Soviet Union), outright traitors, and soldiers and Party cadres who had stayed out of harm's way, thereby violating their oaths, only strengthened this conviction.[25] Thus, in March 1944, a Central Committee decree stated that only Red Army partisans who joined the movement less than three months after their units had been destroyed or captured were eligible for the full veterans' allowance.[26] As the Red Army went over to the strategic offensive in 1943, partisan and state security officials prepared to sort out those they considered to truly have "a clean conscience" from those they deemed did not.

CAMP WIVES AND AMAZONS: WOMEN IN THE PARTISAN MOVEMENT

Soviet policy toward women before the war was designed to make them full-fledged citizens of the state by enabling them to enter male-dominated economic and political spheres. Although these policies were generally emancipatory in their effects and were often touted by Soviet media as one of the legitimating aspects of Soviet rule, the leadership was nevertheless more committed to expanding its political base and labor reserve than to women's emancipation for its own sake. These priorities became strikingly evident when emancipation clashed with other, more pressing state objectives—for instance, when state authorities failed to support the equal treatment of women by male workers on the factory shop floor or when abortion rights were repealed in 1936 in the face of a looming demographic crisis.[27] In a similar vein, the partisan leadership was determined to promote female participation to prove that the partisans comprised an all-people's movement. This policy, however, flew in the face of male intransigence. Men often saw female participation as subverting the movement's military power. The limited effort by the state authorities to overcome this opposition reveals the extent to which the regime was actually committed to female emancipation. As in other areas, inclusion in the insurgency did not mean equality.

At the beginning of the war, women probably accounted for no more than 5 percent of all partisans, and many bands likely never reached that percentage. By the end of the war, women totaled approximately 9.3 percent of the whole movement, according to contemporary sources.[28] This increase was due to the combination of more women seeking admission into the bands and increased pressure from Moscow.[29] But even as their numbers grew, women remained socially marginalized in the units. They invariably occupied traditional positions (as nurses or cooks, for example), which were certainly critical for the unit's functioning and survival but were accorded little respect and status.[30] The exception to this was their employment as couriers, spies, and agitators, which took advantage of the occupiers' leniency toward traveling women, especially if they were accompanied by children.[31] Women who wanted to participate directly in combat, however, were generally frowned on. Commanders refused to allow women to go on combat missions or even to provide them with weapons and training, claiming that since there were not enough arms for men, they certainly were not going to give them to women.[32] Rank-and-file partisans often refused to go on missions with women, since they deemed them incapable of performing "masculine" tasks such as riding horses or planting mines. In any case, it was argued, domestic work in the camps should be the women's primary or even sole concern.[33]

Although sexual relations were forbidden in some units and even punishable by death,[34] male sexual exploitation imposed more hardship on women. As usually only elite men had sufficient power and material resources to have access to women, male partisans often regarded women as nothing more than highly valued commodities.[35] In N. Z. Koliada's "Batia" Complex, for example, women were known as PPZh's (*pokhodnye partizanskie zheny*, or "camp partisan wives"), a pun on PPSh, a much-coveted and hard-to-obtain submachine gun. The more senior the officer, the more PPZh's he had at his disposal.[36] Women who refused the advances of officers might be raped or even worse. One young woman was executed by her unit's head of the NKVD on the grounds that she was a spy; the real reason for her murder was her refusal to submit to the desires of the security chief.[37] Even if women did become camp wives—willing or not—they also literally had to bear the consequences of these liaisons. Commanders typically blamed women for pregnancies and accused them of burdening the unit and reducing its combat effectiveness.[38] Women were sometimes forced to leave the unit or undergo abortions, which frequently resulted in the death or sterilization of the mother.[39] One pregnant woman was sent to Smolensk by her commissar "husband" on the pretext of going on a reconnaissance mission but really to have an abortion. She was discovered by the Germans and executed.[40] Babies born in the partisan camps rarely survived infancy, and at least one commander ordered that a newborn be left to die.[41]

Women had their own reasons for becoming camp wives, aside from fear or coercion. Few had any combat training, and although women's participation in national defense had been part of public discourse, customary attitudes about women's proper roles in wartime persisted among both men and women.[42] Many women believed that they had little choice but to become camp wives if they were to have any physical and material security, particularly since unarmed and unskilled women were at the bottom of the partisan social hierarchy. Others saw it as a way to achieve the so-called good life, which could mean finding safety in a detachment by "marrying" a high-ranking partisan who could provide material comfort and perhaps even emotional support.[43] The women could also wield power through their camp husbands, particularly since the majority of men who had camp wives were officers.[44] Finally, for some women, just as with men, the partisan camps provided an opportunity "to amuse themselves and find love adventures," as one Komsomolka (female Komsomol member) disparagingly put it.[45] Another summarized the plight of female partisans somewhat more sympathetically: "Many girls, in the rough conditions of partisan life, lose their confidence in life, and hence, frivolously live, and take from life everything; and the commanders, the senior comrades, and heads divert the girls from military activities, instead of [providing] normal support."[46] Regardless of their motivations, camp wives received little respect from the other male and female partisans. They were criticized particularly for their loose behavior, for subverting the authority of their commander husbands, for their corrupting influence within the unit, and for undermining the sanctity of the Soviet family, especially since many husbands had abandoned their legal families.[47] Partizanki (female partisans) especially condemned wives who refused to take up arms or who accepted male assertions that they were unqualified to do so. Some contended that a woman could become romantically attached to a man only if she was his equal as a fighter: only when she had earned prestige and respect on her own could she be regarded as a true and equal companion.[48] As one woman put it, if women truly loved the rodina, hated the enemy, and wanted to serve with honor, then "we must be modest in our everyday life."[49] Thus, to these partizanki, the handling of a woman's "private life" became an indicator of her patriotism.

The treatment of women was part of a powerful masculinized partisan identity that marginalized and objectified women while elevating male status.

Martial prowess, technical skill, and even the pursuit of the good life became the attributes of male partisans, which women, by definition, could
not—or should not—possess. Such attitudes prevented women from becoming fully accepted combatants and paralleled the treatment of female workers
by their male coworkers in the 1920s and 1930s, when the latter denigrated
the former's apparent lack of skill so as to preserve male dominance in the
factory.[50]

The opposition of male partisans to female participation, however,
blocked an important state political objective. Soviet political legitimacy was
based partly on the claim of having emancipated women, which propagandists contrasted with German policies that deprived Soviet women under occupation of all rights and instead subjected them to rape, torture, and death.[51]
Moreover, in the wartime context, the portrayal of the partisan movement as
a manifestation of the people's patriotism, love for the Soviet system, and hatred of the enemy meant that *all* people, including women, had to be counted
in its ranks. By serving in the partisan detachments, Soviet women would
demonstrate that the Soviet system had transformed them and enabled them
to be full, active, and equal members of society. This transformation was
demonstrated in a November 1942 radio broadcast describing how Galia, a
pretty, enchanting teenager whose primary peacetime concern had been the
production of her school play, had adapted to partisan life, where only "bravery and daring were valued." In the detachment, Galia "grew up, matured.
[She] became a scout."[52] Another broadcast noted how two female recruits
had initially found partisan life to be "very hard, but they never said a word
about this to anyone." Instead, they adapted to their new lives. Indeed, one
of the women became one of the best machine gunners in the unit, in her free
time having mastered its "complicated mechanism."[53] War thus completed
the job of tempering Soviet women, which had begun with the Revolution
itself. Vershigora's claim that "people do not generally think of women as soldiers, but the fate of [our] women-soldiers particularly clearly shows our
moral superiority over the enemy"[54] further indicates the character of the
transformation Soviet power had supposedly wrought.

Although the overwhelming majority of articles about the partisans in the
central press focused on men, women were portrayed as participants in their
own right, even before September 1942. They were often depicted in nurturing positions (as nurses and cooks and the like); one January 1942 article described two women, one a local Party instructor, the other a deputy factory
head, as cooking and laundering clothes, "displaying a genuine maternal concern for every partisan."[55] But women were also presented in posters and

"We shall have our revenge! We will annihilate the fascist cannibals!" 1941.
(Credit: Hoover Institution Archives, Poster Collection, RU/SU2164)

newspaper articles as active and armed resisters, protecting their homes and avenging atrocities.[56] The poster captioned "We shall have our revenge! We will annihilate the fascist cannibals!" ("*Otomstim! Unichtozhim fashistskikh liudoedov!*") showed a woman clutching a rifle and swearing revenge over a dead baby, presumably her own child. Women were also portrayed as fighting for the national cause, even at the expense of loved ones, which seemingly contradicted their nurturing image. One such story described "a typical Russian girl" who was determined to remain a partisan scout despite German threats against her family. As the correspondent claimed, such dedication among Soviet women was common: "There are many such girls in the detachments. They share all the burdens of the nomadic partisan life. Together with the men they go into battle, they burn and blow up enemy vehicles, they destroy detachments of the German invaders. They are the best scouts, distinguished snipers, staunch fighters for our general cause."[57]

Women partisans exemplifying the physical toughness and political consciousness usually attributed to men were publicly embodied in the person of Zoia Kosmodem'ianskaia, the eighteen-year-old Komsomolka-partisan who was tortured and executed by the Germans in December 1941 after she attempted to burn down some stables and huts. Her story, accompanied by graphic photos showing her execution by hanging and her mutilated corpse, was published in January 1942 in *Pravda*.[58] Posthumously awarded the title Hero of the Soviet Union, she later became the subject of numerous other articles, stories, poems, and books and a 1944 film. Zoia was always portrayed as withstanding the most vicious German tortures, remaining defiant and dedicated to the Soviet cause until the end.[59]

Indeed, a feminine visage became part of the public face of the partisan movement, especially after 1942. The 1943 film *She Defends the Motherland*, described by Denise Youngblood as "the canonical movie of the war years," tells the story of Praskovia, a young woman who becomes a partisan leader to avenge the deaths of her husband and son and possibly her own rape. She is portrayed as ruthless and determined, even willing to kill her fellow citizens who shirk their duty to fight the Germans. In *Rainbow*, another popular partisan film, based on the novella by Wanda Wasilewska, the heroine is a young partisan mother who also defies the Germans despite the sacrifice of her own child and her own subsequent torture and death. Although these and other women were almost always shown to have a nurturing role as a devoted mother, wife, or daughter, they nevertheless demonstrated a physical toughness and dedication to the Soviet cause that would be the envy of any man.[60]

In these Soviet presentations of female partisans, there was no contradic-

The execution of Zoia Kosmodem'ianskaia. (Credit: Minaeva Collection)

tion between women's nurturing and avenging roles, nor in their patriotism. Rather, the combination of personal motivations and defending the national cause necessitated and justified this seemingly dichotomous behavior. As one radio broadcast to the occupied territories proclaimed, women fulfilled the "sacred duty of all Soviet patriots" and took up arms "for our happy life, for Stalin, for our children, for the liberation of the Soviet people from the Hitler-ite filth."[61] Women, just like men if not more so, were encouraged to see that their personal interests could not be separated from the concerns of the na-tion. Private concerns were not submerged in public ones; rather, the two intertwined. Such propaganda sought to blur, if not erase, the line between state (them) and society (us).[62] Indeed, through this linking of the private and the public, propagandists hoped to convince citizens that defense of the Soviet state was central to one's security and personal happiness.

In contrast to their partisan sisters, women soldiers in the regular armed forces were scarcely mentioned in the national press, although they composed approximately 8 percent of the Red Army in 1943. Only the newspaper for women workers, *Rabotnitsa*, provided any significant coverage.[63] Jeffrey Brooks has argued that appeals to Red Army soldiers to protect and liberate women and children and to protect a feminized motherland, often depicted literally as a woman (such as the imposing figure in the famous 1941 poster captioned *"Rodina-mat' zovet!"* (The Motherland Calls), helped masculinize the image of the Red Army.[64] In turn, the increasingly public portrayal of women partisans was perfectly consistent with this policy: the partisans were supposed to represent the people themselves, and in the occupied territories, the people were often feminized as realistic or allegorical women awaiting liberation by the Red Army.[65] Though it might perhaps be "unnatural" for women to fight on a par with men in the regular military, they could fight as representatives of the people in the guerrilla war.[66] Thus, traditional gender roles were not challenged as much as one might think by women partisans, since their combat activities were only part of the popular uprising and not those of conventional military operations. To male partisans, however, who defined themselves partly by their supposed martial skills, this feminization could only be viewed as demeaning for both them and the movement.

Publicizing or propagandizing women's participation was one thing; actually implementing it was quite another, for state officials had to overcome the prejudices of male partisans who preferred to keep the detachments as masculine preserves or at best to limit female participation to that of camp partisan wives. For instance, in January 1943, district Party officials reported to Smolensk Obkom secretary Popov that, although peasant women were desperately trying to join the partisans in order to avoid forced labor in Germany, they were prevented from joining the units by local commanders. The commanders maintained that women had no training and that the units lacked sufficient supplies to accommodate them.[67]

Komsomol head Mikhailov took the lead in official efforts to broaden women's participation. In May 1943, after gathering information about women partisans and sponsoring women partisan conferences, he submitted a draft order for Ponomarenko's approval. To fulfill NKO Order 189, Mikhailov argued, "all Soviet women falling under the German yoke" should be included in the movement. He feared that "without the mass inclusion of women in the

partisan detachments, it is impossible to broaden greatly the partisan movement, it is impossible to make it genuinely an all-people's [movement]." He
proposed that women be given specific combat training so that they could
participate in "combat operations equally with the men," command mixed
detachments, and form all-women combat groups.[68]

Ponomarenko apparently did not sanction this order, possibly because he
doubted the Central Staff's ability to overcome male partisan resistance or
possibly because he was less committed to the reality of women's equal participation, whatever state propaganda might proclaim. He nevertheless directed individual commanders and officials to allow women, even if unarmed
and untrained, to join the partisans, asserting that they still could perform
such useful tasks as reconnaissance, political work, simple sabotage, and col-
lecting supplies.[69] Some republican and regional Party organizations (including the Ukrainian Komsomol), apparently following Ponomarenko's or Mikhailov's signals, also ordered the broader inclusion of women, instructing that
they should be properly trained and armed.[70] Most women, however, continued to serve in support roles, either in housekeeping functions or as nurses.
In this sense, the partisans continued the social practices of the 1930s, which
generally assigned women to secondary positions in society and depicted
them as caretakers, while reserving the heroic roles for men.[71] Of course, the
line between combatant and noncombatant in the occupied world was fuzzy
when the camp itself could be attacked at any moment and when nurses accompanied fighters on missions, often having to care for them under direct
enemy fire.

Many women seemed satisfied with their support functions in the partisan camp; others did aspire to be full combatants, believing it their right
and duty to literally take up arms. They fully understood the social hierarchy in wartime Soviet society and in the partisan detachments, which accorded the most praise to fighters, saboteurs, and scouts, as well as specialists
such as radio operators.[72] These partizanki evaluated their war experience
in terms of the numbers of Germans they killed, of missions they undertook,
and of women who sacrificed their lives for the rodina in combat.[73] Conversely, women who wanted to but did not fight were frustrated by their enforced passivity, which denied them the opportunity to display heroism and
to contribute to the cause to their fullest ability. These sentiments were expressed at a conference of female partisans, sponsored by the Komsomol in
January 1944. One woman complained that although many partizanki in her
unit were trained as scouts, they were instead employed as nurses, referencing

the hierarchy between the two positions.[74] She noted, "Many girls, desiring truly to fight the enemy, were dissatisfied with their place in the detachment."[75] Another reported that in her brigade, "many girls, with tears in their eyes, begged to go on combat operations, but their commander will not take them."[76] Elena Gordeeva stated that in her detachment, the women argued among themselves to see who would go out on missions, and some even took weapons and went along without permission. She also related that two women, specially trained as scouts in the mainland, had their weapons confiscated on reaching the detachment (after walking over 430 miles through occupied territory). They were sent to the kitchen, where "instead of thanks, they hear curses from the fighters if dinner is a little late or the portions are a little less than usual."[77]

Even as fighters, women still retained domestic responsibilities. Fedorov, who was specifically criticized by Komsomol chief Mikhailov for his cavalier attitude toward women's participation, admitted in his memoirs that "upon returning from an action the men would go off to rest, while the poor girls got down to cooking or washing clothes." He apparently had ordered men to do their share of the housework, but they grumbled so loudly and performed their chores so badly that the women took up this work as well out of pity. Thus, the notorious "double shift" of work and housework that afflicted Soviet women in peacetime continued in the detachments.[78] Mothers or guardians of children still had to care for their young ones, particularly since the other partisans often refused to help. Indeed, some women took their children along on missions because they feared the neglect at camp more than the dangers of operations.[79]

The notion of women in combat also raised questions regarding their femininity. On the one hand, women still faced sexual harassment. *Krasnaia zvezda* recorded the angry exclamation of a young partizanka who, after rallying male partisans fleeing from a battlefield, was kissed in gratitude by a male comrade: "It is unworthy of you to do this. I am also a fighter!" Fictional or not, this sentiment was expressed by actual partizanki when they encountered similar situations.[80] On the other hand, both men and civilian women believed that female fighters had lost their femininity. As one Red Army veteran stated, "I can't imagine myself having a sniper for a wife."[81] Thus, in the eyes of many, partizanki had forfeited their ability to be wives and mothers.

Perhaps as a result of this "lost" femininity, women fighters usually gained the respect of their male colleagues as fellow partisans. As Tatiana Ivanova of the "Batia" Complex stated, "Only when I began to fight did the boys regard me as a real partisan. And when I left the detachment, the boys even said, that girl, she was a real partisan."[82] Faye Schulman recorded in her memoirs that women who went on combat missions were "the heroines of the partisans."[83] To partizanki such as Ivanova and Schulman, to be a real partisan meant to be a full-fledged fighter in the guerrilla war. These reactions also suggest that for most men and women, the true partisan was gendered male, regardless of one's actual sex.

This respect hardly gave women the same authority as men. When Leningrad partizanka Nina Zverova was offered the rare opportunity to command a male platoon, she refused, saying, "The boys will not listen to me." Zverova was later given command of an all-women's platoon, but the male platoons had to be ordered to cooperate with it. The fact that the women's platoons often outperformed the men in combat further offended masculine egos, for the officers used the women's superior performance to shame their men into doing better, an approach also used during World War I and the Civil War.[84] The women partisans no doubt enjoyed this praise, but at the same time, it reinforced stereotypes that women were not supposed to fight as well as men and performed better only because the men were slacking.

Although some officials such as Mikhailov and perhaps, to a lesser extent, Ponomarenko attempted to increase not only the quantity of women in the movement but also the quality of their participation, they generally did not achieve the latter goal. Some all-women's subunits were formed, and a few women became commissars, though none became commanders of mixed detachments or brigades. There is little evidence, however, that the male partisan leaders actually obeyed these instructions to incorporate women as full members, as was indicated by the number and nature of the complaints voiced in the women's Komsomol conference in January 1944.[85] The anomaly of women combatants, even for the leadership, became fully apparent during the liberation of the partisan areas. A partizanka recalled after the war, "We [women] were told to hand in our arms and go find ourselves jobs. We could not somehow understand why we had to hand in arms while the war was still going on and Byelorussia alone had been liberated."[86] That most male partisans were immediately inducted into the Red Army indicates that regardless of their "masculine capabilities," women were still not considered the true equals of men in traditional male spheres. In addition, Soviet authorities granted female Party members leniency during postwar Party verification campaigns if they had not joined a resistance organization during occupation because of family obligations, whereas male Communists were given no such exemption, a further suggestion that they did not consider women to have equal political responsibilities.[87]

The situation of the partizanki represented a continuation of women's multifaceted and sometimes contradictory experiences in the Soviet Union in the 1930s, which had powerful personal and public aspects.[88] The state still spoke the language of emancipation and equality and even pursued some policies to achieve these goals. Calling on women to master the machine gun, for example, was a direct reference to Anka, the iconic machine gunner of the cinematic *Chapaev*, who represented female equality and emancipation on the Civil War battlefield. As Anna Krylova has noted, these achievements should not be dismissed as empty gestures.[89] At the same time, however, the regime as a whole was not willing or able to prioritize emancipation over other concerns, just as the promotion of nurturing roles and the curtailment of reproductive rights prioritized production over emancipation in the 1930s. State authorities encouraged women to participate and fight, just as they encouraged them to work and participate in political life in the 1930s, a call to which many women sincerely and fervently responded.[90] However, in the forest camp as in the factory, the authorities allocated few material or political resources to help women achieve these ends. Male morale and stability took precedence. Moreover, the ambivalence of state officials in regard to promoting women as combatants exposed a contradiction in Soviet gender policy from the 1920s onward, which argued that though women were full and active citizens, their participation in the military was limited to supporting positions such as nurses and clerks or as the mothers of soldiers.[91] There were significant exceptions to these policies in World War II, most notably in the deployment of all-women air force units, yet both officials and male soldiers generally retained traditional gendered attitudes toward women in combat. These sentiments also continued in the partisan formations, despite the advocacy of officials such as Mikhailov. In any case, paying lip service to women's equality in both cases was sufficient to meet the leadership's political needs of altering the official representation of the partisan movement and maximizing the mobilization of the entire population, while not affecting the underlying gender relations in the detachments.

In the camp, as on the shop floor and in the apartment, those women who actually wanted the same opportunities as men faced male opposition rooted in traditional expectations of gender roles, which were increasingly supported by the state. Most men and many women no doubt found comfort in the continuation of peacetime behaviors and roles in wartime, as an element of nor-

mality in an otherwise chaotic world. The changes that did take place could
be rationalized for them as necessities brought on by the war, which would
last only for the duration.

Other women, however, saw the war as a chance to prove that they were
full and equal citizens of the Soviet Union, particularly since they indeed had
made comparatively great strides in public life even in the first two decades
of Soviet rule. Thus, it was critical that they be allowed to fight on equal terms
with men. *Chapaev*'s Anka again served as a cultural role model for many
partizanki, for she accepted the romantic advances of a fellow partisan only
after she had proven herself in battle.[92] As one partizanka veteran recalled,
"We were brought up to believe that 'motherland' and 'we' were the same
thing."[93] In their minds, it was the Soviet system that had made these opportunities possible. It is particularly noteworthy that in their accounts, partizanki, many of whom were Komsomol or Party members, often spoke of their
desire to participate in the resistance as simply a matter of course, something
that any patriotic citizen would do. Ina Konstantinova wrote her mother in
November 1942: "Fateful developments are under way in our territory, and it
is very pleasant for me to acknowledge that I, too, am playing a modest part
in them. I lead a meaningful life, Mom. I won't have to feel ashamed of myself after the war. And I'm having a wonderful youth."[94] Another woman related her feelings as the Germans swept through the country: "My only dream
was to avenge, to die and to have a book written about me. I was ready to
do anything for my homeland."[95] Such talk was not hyperbole: one young
woman whose baby and mother were killed by the Germans in reprisal for
her joining the partisans explained matter-of-factly, "I was in the Komsomol
and could not remain passive."[96] In this sense, the Soviet emancipation project could be seen as a success, since many young women wanted to fight because they believed it was their duty as citizens to do so, just like men.[97]

These partizanki identified their own aspirations to serve with the Soviet
state and generally believed, as an unspoken assumption, that the state supported their efforts, even if they did not fully grasp—or perhaps thought best
not to articulate—that this support was lukewarm at best. They may not have
agreed with all of the state's tenets and were most likely motivated by the
same feelings of ethnonational patriotism, hatred, and desire for revenge as
their male counterparts, yet twenty-five years after the Revolution, these partizanki identified even more strongly with the regime that promised them social and political emancipation. The Soviet system appeared to have their interests at heart, even as they were still treated as second-class citizens in the
movement that was supposed to welcome them.

"THE FRIENDSHIP OF PEOPLES" OR
ENEMY NATIONS? NATIONALITY AND
THE PARTISANS REVISITED

The implementation of the all-people's war doctrine in 1943 also brought changes to the national composition of the partisan movement. The government had not systematically prevented any nationalities from joining the movement, but neither had it sought a broad ethnonational inclusion. Instead, it was left to local officials and individual commanders to set policy. Now, the regime called for the presence of heretofore excluded and suppressed national minorities. Their inclusion was critical to Moscow's contention that the entire Soviet family of nations was united in its patriotism and its desire to repel the invaders. As was the case with the civilian recruits of 1943 and with women, however, these new partisans threatened to subvert the dominant partisan identities that denoted Slavs as the backbone of the popular resistance. Because nationality had joined class as an essential marker of loyalty to the Soviet regime by the late 1930s, the inclusion of ethnonational groups allegedly associated with weakness and cowardice or even with treason also threatened to undermine the perceived loyalty and determination of the partisans as a whole.[98] Nor could government leaders shake themselves of the suspicion that certain ethnonational groups were untrustworthy, particularly those diaspora nations that had members living inside and outside Soviet borders.[99] As can be seen in the treatment of Tatars, Jews, Ukrainians, and Russians in the partisan movement, the complex interplay of these policy strands resulted in multinational participation, while clearly making some nationalities more equal than others.

In the Crimea at the outset of the occupation, Slavic partisans identified Tatars as German sympathizers.[100] Regional officials—particularly the top partisan field leaders, Commander A. V. Mokrousov and Commissar S. V. Martynov—accused the "overwhelming majority" of Tatars of actively collaborating. They further asserted that German-organized Tatar "self-defense" groups had even attacked Russian homes and families.[101] Other claims that 15,000 Tatars had completed training for the Wehrmacht also circulated, eventually reaching Ponomarenko.[102] Some Tatars did collaborate, as did members of all nationalities in the Crimea and throughout the occupied territories. Many Tatars did so, in fact, because of the ill treatment they received from the partisans and especially from Party organizers.[103] However, the regional partisan leaders insisted that this individualized and small-group collaboration tainted the entire Tatar population, while refusing to label the

collective Russian and Ukrainian populations in the Crimea as collaborators.[104] The immediate consequence was that Tatars were rarely included in
the original Crimean detachments. Partisans even launched pogroms against
Tatar villages.[105] These actions generally found a positive response in Moscow,
where references to supposed criminal elements in the Tatar population occasionally surfaced in the Soviet press. These references suggested that the loyalty of the Tatar population as a whole was suspect, thus contributing to the
idea that the Tatars should be excluded from the friendship of peoples.[106]

However, even before the adoption of the all-people's war concept, verbal
and physical attacks against the Tatars subsided. In August 1942 at a meeting
of the Crimean Obkom, regional partisan commander A. V. Mokrousov re-
nounced his earlier accusations that the "overwhelming majority" of Tatars
in the mountain regions were traitors.[107] Three months later, in November
1942, the Crimean Obkom condemned indiscriminate attacks on the Tatar
population. Though it admitted that certain "bourgeois-nationalist kulak and
other hostile, criminal elements" sided with the Germans, the obkom insisted
that the fundamental mass of Tatars opposed the occupiers and "with impa-
tience await the return of Soviet power."[108] In February 1943, V. S. Bulatov,
the first secretary of the Crimean Obkom, reported to Ponomarenko, Malenkov, and Politburo member A. A. Andreev that the obkom had at first mistakenly regarded the Tatars as collaborators but had since corrected itself and
now worked diligently with the Tatar population.[109] Soviet media also eased
their condemnations of the Tatars. Bulatov wrote in *Pravda* in November 1942
that although the Germans had tried to "flirt" with the Tatars to sow dissension along nationalist lines, the Tatars saw through these lies and furthermore
had suffered terribly at the Germans' hands.[110] Later articles referred to the
heroic struggle of the Crimean partisans without any reference to nationality,
although at least one story referred to the courageous exploits and death of
a partisan with the obvious Tatar name of Memet Appazov.[111] And indeed,
Tatars began joining the insurgency in force. By the spring of 1944, they comprised 20 percent of the Crimean partisan movement (630 of 3,110 partisans).[112]

The seeming redemption of the Tatars in the eyes of state authorities only
lasted until the enemy was driven out of the Crimea. Although Tatars were
now included in partisan formations and were no longer publicly associated
with treachery, state officials and Slavic partisans remained deeply suspicious
about their loyalty. One Komsomol organizer noted in February 1943 that
cadres needed to be sent to the Crimea quickly, as the peninsula would soon
be liberated and "the Komsomoltsy have much work, because the remaining

Tatar youth have shown their negative side"; this organizer expressed sentiments common among Communist cadres.[113] Local Party officials and partisan organizers apparently wished to cover up their mishandling of the insurgency and sought scapegoats in the form of the Tatars.[114] Almost immediately
after the Red Army's reconquest of the peninsula in May 1944, the NKVD deported the Tatar population to Central Asia.[115] As the Tatar case indicates,
once the Stalinist leadership suspected the collective nation of treason, there
was little possibility of regaining its trust, regardless of whatever service the
nation's members may have rendered the state.

Although Jews were not classified as traitors, as mentioned earlier, before
September 1942, both partisans and officials looked at them with jaundiced
eyes.[116] Even those few Jews who reached the forests might find the partisans
to be their killers instead of their protectors. When a partisan band murdered
a group of Jewish women who had fled from the Nazis, the local command
rationalized the killing as one of those unfortunate events that happen in wartime and did not pursue the matter.[117] In another example, M. I. D'iachkov,
the commander of the 2nd Belorussian Partisan Brigade, arrested a detachment commander from the 3rd Belorussian Partisan Brigade, A. A. Astreiko,
who before becoming a partisan had been the head of a police unit that
had allegedly shot over 300 Jews. When Party officials in German-occupied
Vitebsk Oblast asked D'iachkov why he had arrested an "honorable person,"
D'iachkov retorted, "He shot Jews, this honorable person." These officials ordered D'iachkov to release Astreiko "in order to develop the partisan movement," leading D'iachkov to wonder "what kind of a partisan movement"
this might be.[118]

NKO Order 189 helped Jews win limited acceptance, even though, as
with the Tatars, state authorities never referred to Jews explicitly as bene-
ficiaries of the policy. Rather, the order's broad-based inclusion of all Soviet
peoples by default applied to Jews as well. Soviet commanders now encouraged the few Jews left in the ghettos in late 1942 and early 1943 to make their
way to the detachments. Partisans were also instructed to give weapons to
bands of unarmed Jews who had sought refuge in the forests.[119] Local partisan staffs now protected Jewish units from anti-Semitic groups (independent
and Soviet) and included them in the movement's increasingly formalized organizational structure.[120] Some Jewish units continued to operate as specifically Jewish formations, such as Tuvia Bielski's detachment and Sholem
Zorin's 106th Detachment; others were incorporated or formed subunits
within "Slavic" formations, such as the Jewish companies that fought with
the Korzh and Saburov partisan complexes.[121]

Jews in the occupied territories felt the effects of this policy change almost immediately. Hersh Smolar, a leader of the Communist underground in
the Minsk ghetto, instantly understood the significance of the order's explicit
inclusiveness, although it did not specify Jews by name.[122] I. Iu. Taits, a doctor
serving with a partisan brigade in Baranovichi, credited "Comrade Stalin's
order that the people must be preserved even if they could not fight" with
saving the Jews. The all-Jewish Bielski Detachment also noticed a thaw in its
relations with Slavic units beginning in the 1942–1943 winter.[123]

Soviet commitment to a multinational state, of which the all-people's war
doctrine was one manifestation, gave Jews and others the language to combat
anti-Semitism. When a Slavic commander threatened Tuvia Bielski by suggesting that his Jewish partisans were nothing but robbers and should be shot,
Bielski allegedly replied, "I am the commander of the Soviet company of partisans named for Marshal Zhukov. We are not robbers. If you are a true Soviet
leader, you should know that it is in the interest of our homeland to fight the
German enemy, together. Our homeland does not differentiate between Jews
and non-Jews, it only separates the loyal, disciplined citizens from harmful, destructive bands."[124] The apolitical Bielski, who before 1939 had been a
Polish citizen, convincingly described his detachment as loyal and Soviet.
Though Bielski thought of himself only as a Jew and sought only to save Jewish lives, his skillful use of the language of Soviet nationality policy masked
his true intent so successfully that the local commander of the Baranovichi
partisan forces referred to him as "a good Bolshevik."[125]

Slavic partisans sympathetic to Jews also utilized the rhetoric of the all-
people's war and the fraternity of peoples. A Belorussian commissar told his
partisans that, as Soviet citizens, they were expected to uphold Soviet law,
and therefore, he forbade the use of anti-Semitic expressions; another commissar asserted that the partisans' charge to save lives included all people
persecuted by the fascists, regardless of ethnicity.[126] Anti-Semitic actions by
Germans, collaborators, and even partisans were increasingly punished, as
the Ukrainian partisan Gopko learned to his misfortune: he was executed for,
among other things, killing five Jews.[127] Kovpak's partisans executed three
villagers for betraying the rodina and participating in the killing of Jews.[128]
Efforts to suppress manifestations of anti-Semitism may have been helped by
Soviet military successes, just as defeats led people to look for scapegoats.[129]
Taits, the Minsk partisan doctor, observed, "When the situation at the front
improved, when we began to advance after Stalingrad, anti-Semitism began
to diminish."[130]

Soviet officials, however, did not condone the construction of a Jewish partisan identity, for both pragmatic and anti-Semitic reasons. Unlike other ethnic groups, whose national exploits were explicitly celebrated in the media, Jews were largely ignored in war coverage. Partisan officials worried that the existence of overtly Jewish units would play into Nazi propaganda, which portrayed the partisan movement as being controlled by Jews, thus aggravating relations between the partisans and the local population.[131] Belorussian partisan officials complained that Jewish units did nothing other than take food from the local population, thus denigrating the value of Jewish participation in the movement.[132] Indeed, local authorities in the republic eventually forced the assimilation of many independent Jewish bands into so-called Slavic units, apparently with the approval of their superiors, on the grounds that in the national republics, only the dominant nationality was allowed to form ethnonational units.[133] Some units tried to get rid of their unwanted Jews by foisting them onto the few remaining Jewish groups or simply by expelling them, leaving them to perish in the forest.[134] Jews were also told to abandon their Jewish identity. Thus, Abba Kovner, a leader of the Jewish resistance in the Vilna ghetto, was told by the commander of a Lithuanian partisan unit "to forget who you are" and subsume himself in the identity of a Soviet Lithuanian partisan. The commander, who was also Jewish, adopted the nom de guerre Iurgis in order to hide his own Jewish origins and make his detachment appear more authentically Lithuanian.[135]

Anti-Semitism remained pervasive throughout the movement. In postwar interviews, Jewish partisans recalled that they were as afraid of their gentile comrades, who threatened to shoot them in the back during battle, as they were of the Germans. Others claimed that the anti-Semitism of Slavic partisans remained as bad as that of the Nazis.[136] Gentile partisans were quick to blame the failings of individual Jewish partisans on the Jews as a whole, while condemning Jews who performed bravely as thinking themselves better than Slavs.[137] Popular anti-Semitic beliefs that Jews were natural cowards abounded, indicated in the backhanded compliment "You really are a courageous fighter and excellent partisan, and you don't resemble a Jew at all."[138] Indeed, the condemnation of Jews as cowards and inept soldiers served to feminize Jews as a group, thereby further marginalizing them. Although Jews who had positions of authority in units, such as doctors, could prevent some anti-Semitic outbursts, lower-ranking Jews still found them prevalent.[139] Moreover, the power of central authorities remained limited, and local commanders continued to exercise their independence by resisting, ignoring, or misunderstanding the vague pronouncements coming from Moscow, which never directly ordered that Jews had to be included in the units or that anti-Semitic actions must cease. As Dov Levin has indicated, the attitudes of individual commanders therefore remained paramount in determining the fate of Jews and Jewish partisans.[140]

Official determination to treat the Jews like any other nonrepublican nationality extended into the state's handling of the Holocaust. Specific atrocities against Jews were rarely mentioned publicly, even though these crimes were meticulously recorded and cataloged. Instead, victims were commonly identified as "peaceful Soviet citizens."[141] The most telling example of this treatment, paradoxically, was the Foreign Ministry's declaration "On the Carrying Out of the Plan by the Hitlerite Powers of the Destruction of the Jewish Population in Europe." Issued on 19 December 1942 and published in central newspapers and broadcast to the occupied territories, this statement directly and explicitly condemned the mass murder of the Jews by noting categorically that Germany and its allies had "a special plan for the universal annihilation of the Jewish population on the occupied territories of Europe." While acknowledging Jewish suffering on Soviet territory, it continued, "the overwhelming majority of victims of these orgies of plunder and murder consist of Russian, Ukrainian, and Belorussian peasants, workers, office workers, and intellectuals. There are many victims among the Lithuanian, Latvian, and Estonian peoples, amongst the Moldavans, and amongst the inhabitants of the Karelo-Finnish Republic." The conclusion was that "all nationalities of the Soviet Union" were united "in their burning love of the motherland" and that German atrocities, far from weakening the unity of the Union, "eliminated prejudices and strengthened the solidarity and mutual aid between the victims of the Hitlerite oppression and racial hatred."[142] Even in a bulletin publicizing their special fate, Soviet Jews were portrayed as just another group of victims among a nation of victims and thus were denied any special status. The logical conclusion to this policy occurred in the Soviet war crimes trials held immediately following the war. Although crimes against the Jews formed a large part of the evidence against the accused, they were portrayed as atrocities directed at peaceful Soviet citizens and not specifically at Jews. Consequently, the victims' identity (or at least the identity for which they were killed) was erased, even though the onlookers and perpetrators alike knew full well why they had been murdered.[143]

Although the change in policy in late 1942 led to the inclusion of surviving Jews in the partisan movement, their participation, like that of women, was limited primarily to providing proof that the Soviet peoples were allied by their love for each other, their commitment to the Soviet system, and their hatred of the invaders. Of course, some officials and many Slavic commanders were motivated by genuine humanitarian feelings, as they witnessed with their own eyes the atrocities committed against fellow human beings. In effect, however, the actions of most Slavic partisans continued to marginalize the Jews in the movement even as they were allowed to join it. Soviet officials used the inclusion of Jews as a way of broadening the ethnonational composition of the partisans, but by and large, they showed almost complete indifference to the unique plight of genocide the Jews faced at the enemy's hands. Instead, the Soviet authorities were extremely sensitive to the prejudices of the many Slavic partisans who would rather not fight alongside the Jews, just as they would rather not fight with women. Soviet partisan policy toward the Jews thus became something of a compromise: Jews could fight in the detachments, but they did so frequently on sufferance and sometimes in fear of their lives from their own side.

The Holocaust was but one example of mass ethnic killing in World War II. Indeed, much of the borderlands region encompassing the Baltic states and present-day western Belarus and Ukraine became a site of widespread, horrendous violence as Balts, Belorussians, Ukrainians, Poles, and indigenous Germans claimed territories in which these groups had intermingled for centuries. Defining oneself as part of a reified ethnic group was relatively new to this section of Europe; more commonly, people defined themselves and others simply as belonging or not belonging to a given community or, put another way, whether they were "ours" or "not ours." Ethnicity and language could comprise these definitions, but who ultimately belonged was generally fluid. Hence, many Ukrainians considered Russians a part of their community—but not Jews.[144] As the Polish memoirist Jerzy Stempowski recalled (perhaps with a little tongue in cheek), "Nationality was not a race, but a choice. A Pole could become a German . . . If a Pole married a Russian, their children would usually become Ukrainian or Lithuanian."[145]

The Soviets and Nazis, those practitioners of modern nationalism, which insisted that nationality was a rigid and concrete category, sought to categorize and define such population groups. They were joined in these efforts by Polish and Ukrainian nationalists, who also claimed these territories. The dismemberment of the Eastern empires after World War I, the Soviet annexation of the eastern Polish territories, and the German invasion of the Soviet Union created the possibility of redrawing the Eastern European national and demographic maps. The brutal and often murderous policies followed by the Soviets and Nazis and by the Polish and Ukrainian nationalists forced individuals to claim an ethnonational identity that until then had rarely been a primary concern.[146]

The Ukrainian-Polish borderlands were perhaps the worst site of this ethnonational violence. The prehistory of this violence extended back at least to the Polish policies in the 1930s to polonize these territories at the expense of the Ukrainian population. However, in March 1943, the Organization of Ukrainian Nationalists and its military wing, the Ukrainian Insurgent Army (UPA),[147] launched a massive campaign against the Polish population in Volhynia and Galicia. Whether these killings should be considered a genocide or an ethnic cleansing is debated among some scholars; regardless of the terminology, estimates of Polish deaths in Volhynia and Galicia combined at the hands of the OUN-UPA range from 50,000 to 85,000, with possibly another 350,000 forced to flee their homes.[148] As the struggle continued, Polish Home Army forces and the OUN-UPA fought their own war for possession of these borderlands.

This war within a war very quickly involved the Germans and Soviets. Soviet partisans, already engaged in their fight with the OUN-UPA, allied temporarily with the Poles (many of whom the Soviets had deported from the region in 1939 and 1940), and they helped organize Polish partisan detachments. Khrushchev, apparently acting on his own, ordered the Ukrainian Staff to develop Polish formations to fight in Poland itself.[149] At the same time, the Soviets dispatched partisan forces to western Belorussia/eastern Poland to secure the Soviet presence there against the claims of Poles and the efforts of the Polish Home Army to regain the territories. The Germans, too, recruited Poles to their police auxiliary units, for many of the Ukrainian policemen had defected to the UPA or, less commonly, to the Soviet partisans.[150]

The Ukrainian separatists were a serious threat to Soviet stability and hegemony, unlike the Crimean Tatars and Jews, neither of which were a threat at all. Yet despite the dangers the separatists posed, Ukrainians as a nation were not singled out as traitors. Rather, the importance of Ukraine to the Union meant that a special effort was made to link Ukraine to the Soviet nation even as the war intensified divisions within the friendship of peoples. Ukrainian separatism was countered by attempting to create a uniquely Ukrainian partisan identity, which would give Ukrainians an elevated place in the movement—an identity that would appeal to particularist Ukrainian sentiments, even as other Ukrainians fought for the republic's independence.

As has been noted earlier, partisans in Ukraine utilized the long-distance raid to establish themselves in the republic, especially in the largely hostile Galician and Volhynian regions. Soviet authorities used the image of the raid to connect the partisans to a mythologized Cossack past, thus giving the partisans a "Ukrainian" pedigree.[151] In some of the most famous raiding units, Ukrainians did not even constitute a majority of the partisans.[152] What mattered, however, was that their actions be defined as Ukrainian. Hence, they were depicted stealthily attacking the Germans and paying homage to the grave of Taras Shevchenko, the great Ukrainian poet, during their marches.[153] Visual references to Ukrainian partisans in wartime documentaries sometimes showed them on horses (even if, in actuality, most raiders moved on foot), thereby linking them symbolically to the Cossacks of yore, a central element of Ukrainian national identity.[154] For that matter, Cossacks were sometimes portrayed as stalwart and skilled practitioners of the partisan craft, even if they were now Sovietized collective farmers and skilled proletarians.[155] Another story linking Cossack mythology with contemporary Soviet exploits focused on one Bogdan Neulovimyi (Bogdan the Elusive), a clear, if unstated, reference to the rehabilitated seventeenth-century Cossack hero Bohdan Khmel'nytskyi. The Soviet Bogdan was so mobile and skilled, like his Cossack forebear, that the Germans could not catch his band: "The warriors of Bogdan the Elusive are ordinary Soviet people who before the war had the most peaceful professions."[156] Kovpak, too, referred to himself as a descendent of the Zaporozhe Cossacks.[157] In fact, almost no newspaper account or public figure could mention the Ukrainian partisan movement in 1943 or after without referring specifically to Kovpak's raid on the Carpathians and other heroic missions.[158] Thus, Soviet propagandists transformed the raids into a specific Ukrainian national achievement, a theme echoed by some partisans, as when M. I. Naumov described his unit's raid into southern Sumy Oblast, which was actually conducted on horseback, as "a triumphant march of the Ukrainian partisans."[159]

The heroization of Ukrainian partisans paralleled the efforts of Ukrainian officials and intellectuals to construct an identity that was at once both Ukrainian and Soviet. Ukrainian heroes such as Bohdan Khmel'nytskyi and Danilo of Halych were Sovietized in that it was now claimed that they defended Ukraine against foreign (non-Russian) invaders while seeking friendship with their Russian brothers.[160] The Ukrainian partisans, defined as both the publicly heralded heirs of the Cossacks and dedicated to the Soviet cause, also became part of the larger project to Sovietize Ukraine.[161] Partisans operating in Ukraine thereby became Ukrainian in form but Soviet in the content of their actions.

In addition to the promotion of a Soviet Ukrainian identity that could challenge the Ukrainian separatists' claims to represent the authentic Ukraine, leading officials, such as Ukrainian first secretary Nikita Khrushchev, hoped to sway those who had enlisted in the separatists' ranks to defect to the Soviets. As Timothy Snyder has pointed out, the separatists and partisans drew from the same manpower pool, and relatively few joined either side for ideological reasons. Initial decisions were often made on the basis of material considerations or which side appeared to be winning or even because of coercion.[162] Khrushchev, for his part, argued that many Ukrainians had been tricked into joining the OUN when they had only intended to fight against the Germans, a position the Ukrainian Party boss maintained through June 1943.[163] However, as the Germans were pushed out of Ukraine from 1943 to 1944, fighting between the partisans and separatists became increasingly merciless, complicating Soviet efforts to recruit separatists. Some partisans attempted ruses to recruit Ukrainians, including one commander who tipped off the local German police that Ukrainian separatists were in his ranks. Fearful that they would be shot, the Ukrainians escaped to the woods, where the partisans planned to incorporate them into their detachments. The ruse failed when Ukrainian separatist bands got to the escapees first and recruited them into *their* units.[164]

Soviet and partisan policies toward the separatists were fraught with mixed messages. Some partisans did accept a few defectors who claimed that they had, indeed, been deceived by the separatists.[165] Others, however, purged their detachments of suspected separatists and conducted summary executions.[166] And though informal contacts with separatists were often critical to negotiating their defection, some partisan leaders, possibly including Kovpak, were removed from their posts because they had established truces with local separatist groups.[167]

After Ukraine was recaptured, partisan units, resurrected destruction battalions, and Red Army and NKVD units engaged with separatist bands in a ruthless guerrilla war that lasted until the early 1950s.[168] But even though this fighting was vicious and bloody, Ukrainians were not deported en masse from Ukraine as the Crimean Tatars and others were from their homelands, nor were they written out of the war as the Jews were. The size of the Ukrainian population, notions of Slavic (and perhaps, at some level, even Christian) brotherhood, and the importance of Ukraine and Ukrainians in the Union all helped Ukrainians avoid the same tragic fate.[169] Moreover, in contrast to their handling of the Tatars and Jews, Soviet authorities made a real effort to include Ukrainians rhetorically and physically in the war effort and in the partisan movement. The Ukrainian partisans symbolically and physically contributed to the construction of a "Soviet Ukraine," which enabled the inclusion of Ukrainians as Soviet patriots in a way not possible—or admissible—for the other two groups. Although the all-people's war had given the Tatars an all-too-brief reprieve and facilitated the saving of many Jewish lives, partisans and officials alike could not accept them as genuine members of the Soviet family of nations as they could the Ukrainians, even if they viewed some Ukrainians as their black sheep.

The conscious broadening of the movement to include disparate nationalities came with considerable tensions. Implicit and explicit policies against "suspect" nationalities such as the Tatars and Jews were reversed, if only temporarily. However, the stigma of collaboration was never removed from the Tatars, leading to their eventual deportation, whereas the Jews continued to face persecution and received scant acknowledgment regarding the fact that the Germans sought their complete annihilation. By contrast, more Ukrainians opposed Soviet power on a far larger scale than the Tatars, not to mention the Jews. Yet the shame of collaboration was attributed publicly to a limited number of "bourgeois nationalists" in the OUN-UPA. The actual repression of the nationalist movement required a brutal counterinsurgent war extending into the early 1950s, which had already led to the deaths of over 91,000 OUN-UPA "bandits" by October 1945, according to contemporary sources;[170] meanwhile, an official counterrepresentation of Soviet Ukraine came to symbolize the "true" Ukrainians. Unlike the Jews and Tatars, who were neither offered nor allowed to construct a viable counterrepresentation to their respectively nonexistent and negative images in the official and popular view, Ukrainians could not be removed from the Soviet family. Instead, they became the poster children of the Soviet nationality project: even though they shared common Soviet traits, they fought the war in a way consistent with their (officially approved) national character, thus becoming the embodiment of the formula "nationalist in form, socialist in content."

Even more telling in this regard was the treatment of Russians who fought for the Germans. Despite the existence of General A. A. Vlasov's so-called Russian Liberation Army (Russkaia Osvoboditel'naia Armiia, or ROA), Russian defectors were rarely, if ever, referred to as "bourgeois nationalists" or as serving in nationalist formations, unlike almost every other ethnonationality.[171] To include Russians as seeking a "national liberation" from Soviet dominance seemed impossible and illogical given the official and popular conflation of the Soviet Union with a Russian past and present, a trend that intensified during the war.[172] As a consequence, Russians who fought for the Germans were simply traitors to the rodina, "kulaks," or "formerly repressed people," but they were not accused of any particular nationalist aspirations. Both the claims that segments of the non-Russian peoples were "bourgeois-nationalists" and the unstated assumption that Russians by definition could not be revealed the fissures and hierarchies that undermined the government's efforts to make the Soviet friendship of peoples a reality. Instead, Russianness was equated de facto with Sovietness. Soviet authorities themselves were not prepared fully to take this last logical step, but the Russian-speaking population by and large did.[173]

But the flip side of all Soviet nationalities (aside from the Russians) having their bourgeois nationalists was the celebration of the contributions of all Soviet peoples to the common victory. This formulation enabled members of each ethnonationality to take pride in its group's achievements while acknowledging its place in the larger Union. Again, with the exception of the Russians, these contributions were portrayed as being more or less equal. To do otherwise risked upsetting the delicate balance on which the Union rested. However, this equality was often expressed in negative terms, in the denial by some of other groups' claims to uniqueness. For example, P. M. Masherov, the commissar of Vileisk Oblast's Rokossovskii Partisan Brigade, complained to Ponomarenko about articles written by Ilya Ehrenburg, the famous Jewish correspondent. One particular story described the brave actions of Russian, Ukrainian, Jewish, Armenian, Georgian, Uzbek, and Kazakh partisans, but the only Belorussians mentioned were children murdered by Germans. Masherov asked rhetorically, "How do the Belarusians (*Belorussy*) revenge their children murdered by the Nazis? Do only 'Russians and Ukrainians, Armenians and Georgians, Jews and Uzbeks' fight against the Germans?" The Belorussians, too, deserved their rightful place in the friendship of peoples as warriors and defenders of their native soil.[174] Similarly, in August 1945, when Itzhak Fefer of the Jewish Anti-Fascist Committee (JAFC) contacted the famous partisan commander V. A. Begma for materials on Jewish partisans for a book the JAFC intended to publish, Begma complained to the propaganda section of the Ukrainian Communist Party. Why should there be a special memoir about Jewish partisans, Begma asked, "when in my complex there were tens of other nationalities?"[175] In reality, the Slavs and especially the Russians received far more official acclaim than any other ethnonational group, but the perception that others received more attention threatened to destabilize the "equality" proclaimed by the friendship of peoples.

The war also welded a new element to the Soviet identity: universal victimhood, in which all Soviet peoples, at least those under occupation, suffered equally at Nazi hands.[176] Under this rubric, to admit that any ethnonationality suffered disproportionately would weaken the bonds binding the Union. The determination of the leadership not to publicize the fate of the

Jews or grant them special treatment in the partisan movement was based as much on the pragmatism of maintaining a stable relationship among all nationalities as on the anti-Semitism of Stalin, Ponomarenko, and others. This extreme sensitivity to the delicate balance of ethnonational relations within the Union and the extreme insensitivity to the feelings and treatment of individual ethnonational groups helped lay the groundwork for postwar nationality policies that privileged some groups while marginalizing and excluding others.

ENEMIES OF THE PEOPLE OR PEOPLE'S AVENGERS? FORMER COLLABORATORS AS PARTISANS

It should be recalled that by July 1942, Ponomarenko had come to believe that the obsessive partisan retribution against police and other collaborators that had so defined operations in the first year of the war was diverting guerrillas from more critical military targets. Furthermore, as state authorities became aware of the movement's political significance, they also recognized that the partisans' war of revenge was undermining Soviet efforts to win the hearts and minds of the population. The rationale behind the all-people's war doctrine meant that all citizens should be included in the movement, including those who had betrayed their country by serving the Germans. Although the notion of vengeance and retribution never disappeared completely from the official and partisan psyche, as shown by the treatment of Ukrainian separatists discussed in the previous section, Soviet authorities increasingly encouraged collaborators to redefect. Such redefections would deprive the Germans of human resources, and they would also demonstrate that the Soviet Union granted everyone the possibility of redemption by atonement through service. Above all, the redefection of collaborators was a political coup allegedly showing that the Soviet state retained—or regained—its legitimacy even among those who had the most reason to feel alienated from it. What was less certain to the redefectors was whether their return to the Soviet side would actually cleanse their guilt in the eyes of Soviet authorities, the same authorities who pressed for their return.

For the veteran partisans, accepting these erstwhile traitors was easily the bitterest—and potentially the most dangerous—pill they had to swallow. Given the nature of Stalinist discourse, with its visceral hatred of enemies, as well as the brutal nature of the guerrilla war, having former foes as new comrades took some adjustment for both veteran partisans and their old enemies.

Moreover, if the veterans were suspicious of these new partisans, how would Soviet authorities regard the reliability of the movement that accepted former traitors into its ranks, even if this was done at the behest of these same officials? The answer to this question illuminates the ambiguities and potential dangers embedded within contradictory Soviet attitudes and policy objectives.

Officials and partisans, at least in their public statements, usually portrayed defectors and collaborators as betraying their country for ideological or opportunistic reasons. Yet they failed—or refused—to take into account what actually motivated the approximately 1 million former Soviet soldiers and civilians to join the Germans as policemen, auxiliary soldiers, and laborers.[177] Some did enlist out of political sympathy with the German cause. Some of the more politically motivated, including Cossacks, Ukrainians, and followers of A. A. Vlasov, hoped that the Germans might allow them some form of political independence if they contributed to the Soviet defeat.[178] Many others served for personal reasons to seek revenge against the agents of the hated Soviet regime. Others joined for what might be considered opportunism, for the possibility of obtaining food and scarce goods. But even this charge must be viewed in the context of life in the occupied territories, where catastrophic shortages caused terrible suffering and often led people to commit acts of dubious morality that they might not otherwise do.[179] Many also hoped that their service with the occupiers would enable them to escape the murderous conditions to which they were subjected in the POW camps, including exposure, neglect, and starvation, all of which led literally to the deaths of millions. They also hoped to spare their families the threat of German retribution. As the wife of one policeman said, "Better to be in the police than be shot by the Germans."[180] And by late 1942 as the changing fortunes of war led to a dwindling flow of recruits, the Germans increased conscription to man their police and labor units.[181]

There were those who served the Germans with few qualms, but for many others, the desire for survival conflicted with their own sense of right and honor. A letter from former POW turned partisan Vasilii Chiliniak to his parents in Kazakhstan, written in December 1942, speaks volumes about the mental and physical anguish these unfortunates faced:

> Then the malicious insults, hunger and want forced me to betray
> the Rodina—I transferred to a detachment of traitors. But I wasn't
> there long, just a little, and I made amends and decided to go where the
> Rodina awaits and calls us. I was there for nearly two months, and then I

ran to the Red Partisans, and now I serve in the Red Partisans, I justify and win back confidence, and I will serve and defend until the last drop of blood.

Dear parents. Do not be offended with me that I was a traitor. My stomach betrayed me for life, but [my] soul, that is [my] heart and head, and all my body did not betray, and never will betray, and I will in the future and now defend and will defend with my heart, head, and all my body.[182]

Certainly, the motives behind the expression of these sentiments might be questioned, given that Chiliniak surely suspected any letter he wrote would be read by security officials. But his remorse seems genuine, as does his attachment for the rodina, although we do not know whether he meant the Soviet Union, Russia, Kazakhstan, or all three simultaneously.

State authorities noted that the offer of redemption through service might encourage more citizens like Chiliniak to side with the Soviets.[183] In November 1942, the Central Staff ordered partisans to actively recruit Soviets in the German service by indicating "the possibility to atone for their guilt through personal participation in the struggle for the liberation of the motherland from the German-fascist invaders."[184] A subsequent directive sent in July 1943 instructed partisans "to propagandize broadly" among defectors "that every transfer (*pereshedshii*) to the partisans has the full possibility to merit the pardon of the Soviet people, [but] that for this he must turn [his] arms against the German invaders."[185]

Even the Soviet media, not usually known for their nuanced treatment of enemies, occasionally portrayed collaborators in a sympathetic light if they realized the error of their ways. One newspaper story in April 1943 described a Russian officer serving in a German auxiliary battalion as having tears in his eyes when he learned of the death of a brave partizanka in battle. Such accounts, rare as they were, suggested that if collaborators retained any humanity, they still could be redeemed to fight for the just cause.[186]

Indeed, partisans, too, realized that collaborators might actually be looking for a way to return to the Soviets, even as the people's avengers sought their destruction. One partisan official noted this wartime Stalinist dilemma, stating that though the partisans "must make short work of the police," they also should give them the opportunity to defect.[187]

Beginning in 1942 and increasing steadily throughout 1943, partisans distributed leaflets to auxiliary formations urging them to redefect to the Soviet side. These leaflets called on the defectors "to atone for their guilt" of oppressing their own people by turning their guns against the Germans and joining the partisans. The leaflets usually warned the potential redefectors that time was running out and that if they did not break from the enemy soon, certain death awaited them.[188] Although this propaganda undoubtedly had some effect on the defectors, the German military catastrophes at Stalingrad and Kursk made it readily apparent to all that the German adventure in the Soviet Union was going to end in disaster. As one midlevel partisan official told Soviet historians soon after liberation, "The [re]defections . . . were of course the result of the resolution by arms, and not our propaganda. [The redefectors] knew the situation."[189] These defeats gave the defectors added incentive to join the Soviets and thus possibly avoid or minimize any subsequent punishment, although they still ran the risk that the partisans might shoot them outright.[190] Consequently, thousands of former Soviet soldiers and police redefected to the Soviets, sometimes in whole units.[191]

Not all efforts to encourage redefection relied exclusively on threats. Partisans and Soviets in German service sometimes exchanged gifts and lighthearted insults along with artillery fire and firefights, suggesting that relations between the two groups were closer than Soviet propaganda would admit. These exchanges sometimes convinced would-be redefectors that they would be well treated and better fed if they joined the partisans.[192] They also once again remind us that for many ordinary citizens, the decision to join one side or the other was often dominated not by ideology or nationalism but by the much more immediate concerns of material well-being and personal security at a time when both were in extremely short supply.

Even in the most congenial circumstances, the partisans generally found the idea of accommodating redefectors most unsettling. In accepting redefectors, the security-conscious partisans had to evaluate the trustworthiness of their new comrades. Vershigora mused: "How to realize, how to understand, how to decipher their souls? How to separate the honorable, energetic, possibly deeply misguided but repentant, from the hostile, treacherous, alien?"[193] Consequently, partisans took strict precautions when admitting redefectors into their ranks. One commissar reported that though some police did redefect to the partisans, "many others are afraid to defect to the partisans, but simultaneously are afraid to remain with the Germans, and not wanting to take up arms against the partisans, attempt to flee to another district and hide."[194] For their part, the redefectors had good reason for their anxieties: sometimes, redefectors were shot simply for refusing to give up their boots to the poorly shod partisans.[195] To cite one other example, a detachment reported in November 1943 that of the fifty-three redefectors who attempted to join the unit, eighteen were shot as "accomplices to fascism."[196] Those who survived the initial contact and interrogations were then usually sent on dangerous missions to prove their newfound loyalty to the Soviet cause.[197]

Despite official pressure to incorporate redefectors in the detachments, the partisan leadership and partisans were understandably very reluctant to serve with people who had been, until recently, trying to kill them. The Central Staff ordered that units and groups of defectors were to be placed in their own bands, after being purged of their hostile elements, and operate independently so as to isolate them from Soviet partisan formations. Loyalty was to be ensured by placing a core group of thoroughly inspected partisans in command.[198] Those who defected as individuals were also treated extremely cautiously and were kept under close observation.[199] Many commanders forbade the redefectors to carry weapons until a sufficient trial period had passed. Nina Zverova reported that her unit had many "Vlasovites" (as defectors were often called) and that "in the beginning I was afraid that they would shoot [us] in the back, but they fought well and tried to get us to have faith in them."[200]

The mutual fear and distrust was exacerbated by the growing numbers of redefectors in units as 1943 progressed. For example, by January 1944, some 3,000 Soviets had redefected to the partisans in Leningrad, and in Belorussia during the same period, over 6,500 indigenous police and auxiliary servicemen switched sides.[201] In some detachments, the redefectors consisted of only a few people and were easily isolated, but in many others, they came to comprise significant percentages, often organized into their own subunits led by their former commanders.[202] In some cases, they made up one-quarter of the partisans in a unit, and in at least one case, two-thirds.[203]

The inclusion of large numbers of former collaborators threatened camaraderie and trust within the units and further undermined the aura of reliability the partisans hoped to convey to the regime. Given the regime's inherent suspicions toward partisans, it was essential for all to portray themselves as reliable, disciplined, and loyal.

This was not an idle concern, since state officials, including partisan staff officers, were highly suspicious of the new recruits. A. I. Briukhanov, an officer attached to the Belorussian Staff, referred to those who had sided with the Germans as "cowardly people" who had forsaken their military oath. Try as he might, he could not understand them: "Every time I saw them I attempted to answer for myself several unhappy and difficult questions. Why did these people succumb to the [German] recruiter? What was the primary stimulus in their decision to enter the enemy's service? How did they find the strength to change their minds and transfer to the partisans, in order to save their lives or to atone for their guilt before the Motherland?"[204] Even though state authorities encouraged and promoted redefection, this policy paradoxically reinforced their belief that the partisans were filled with unreliable elements. Moreover, the redefectors, exposed as they were to fascist ideology, could now infect hitherto loyal partisans, whose own ideological orthodoxy was coming under increasing suspicion.[205] Thus, though the official policy of the Leningrad Staff pushed for the redefection of collaborators, its own staff officers believed "that there were too many POWs and former soldiers of the Russian Liberation Army [in the partisan movement] and that these are unreliable people and it is impossible to trust them."[206] Another ominous indication of this danger was the August 1943 attempt by the head of the Soviet counterespionage service SMERSH, V. S. Abakumov, to gain control over the redefectors. He believed the partisans were not capable of conducting proper investigations. He was rebuffed by Ponomarenko, who retorted that SMERSH had no right to the redefectors because the agency had never provided any assistance to the partisan forces, unlike the NKVD.[207] Ponomarenko seems to have won this round, but this exchange did not bode well for the redefectors after the partisans linked up with Soviet forces. Indeed, when the units were eventually disbanded, all partisans were inspected by SMERSH and other intelligence groups. Those who had defected from the German auxiliary units were customarily sent to "the special organs," a euphemism for the security police or Red Army penal units.[208]

The all-people's representation of the movement was thus a double-edged sword: even though it "proved" that all Soviet citizens supported the regime, the very fact that *all* citizens—including those who had opposed (or were suspected of opposing) the regime in some way—could become partisans indicated to state authorities that the partisan movement as a whole could not be trusted. That the partisans were following official policy and instructions and did not really want the redefectors in their units did not matter.

One senses that the veteran partisans were well aware of the leadership's suspicions toward the movement. In their self-representations as loyal defenders of the regime, Soviet partisans contrasted themselves to the defectors who had betrayed their country. Okruzhentsy were particularly sensitive to the label of collaborator or defector, for early in the war, Soviet officials and Party-recruited partisans had cited their supposedly defeatist attitude as proof that they were guilty of selling out their country and their people. Yet even the Party-recruited partisans had to be careful, as they could be tainted by mere association with the erstwhile traitors. In effect, the all-people's war doctrine, while elevating the insurgency as a symbolic and physical manifestation of the Soviet Union itself, also partially delegitimated it, in the eyes of officials, by calling for the inclusion of people with dubious or suspect pasts, along with suspect ethnonationalities. The combination of potential hero and former traitor created a duality in the state's definition of the partisan, a duality that simultaneously heroized the partisans even as it implicitly categorized them as a substantial risk to state security.

The effort to broaden the partisan movement into a genuinely all-people's movement in 1943 brought to the fore a number of issues facing the regime and the partisans. In attempting to include all social elements in the movement, state authorities sought to prove the legitimacy of the regime through mass participation, an essential political objective in this most total of total wars. They also tried again to impose their definition of what the partisan movement should be on the veteran partisans of 1941 and 1942.

Bolsheviks traditionally used the rhetoric of the social and economic equality of women and national minorities as a way of demonstrating that they were creating a just and equal society.[209] Such rhetoric and policies physically and symbolically broadened the concept of who belonged in the nation, which itself was an important justification for the Revolution of 1917. And even the Stalin Constitution of 1936 suggested that former political and class enemies had an opportunity for rehabilitation. The presence of these groups in the partisan movement was a continuation and validation of these inclusive policies because their participation demonstrated that they supported a state that had greatly improved their status (that is, for women and some ethnonational minorities) since the Revolution. In the partisan war, officials and marginalized citizens thus became allies: the latter wanted to join the partisan movement, and the state wanted to incorporate them to meet critical political goals.

Yet woven through this pattern of inclusion was another visible, if contradictory, strand in the late imperial and especially the Soviet period: the determination to rip out those who would stain and befoul the national fabric.[210] The practices followed by the veteran partisans in particular reflected these exclusionary policies. The veterans believed that the inclusion of mass numbers of peasants, women, Jews, and traitors called into question the political consciousness, the masculinity, and, above all, the ultimate loyalty of the movement as a whole. How would state authorities evaluate a partisan movement that now included the partisans of 1943 (mere opportunists), women (military incompetents), Jews (a particularly cowardly and physically weak ethnic group), Tatars (traitors and Muslims), and out-and-out traitors, even as those same officials pressed the partisans to accept these questionable elements into their ranks? The response of the veteran partisans was to go on marginalizing these groups, relegating them to second-class status at best and continuing to repress them in various ways at worst.

Soviet leaders were willing to pursue the inclusionary policy of all-people's war only so far; they had neither the means nor the inclination to force commanders to make real and significant changes in how their units fought and were organized. The political objective of broadening the movement was fulfilled by highlighting the existence of these newcomers in the movement, but the regime was not willing to risk the partisans' combat effectiveness by destabilizing the detachments more than necessary. Moreover, the leadership's own suspicions and doubts about the reliability and military usefulness of the new recruits further limited its desires to regard these arrivals as full-fledged partisans.

The new partisans saw that in addition to increasing their chances of survival in the occupied territories, participation in the movement offered them an opportunity to prove their worth to the Soviet state or to redeem themselves for past crimes, real or imagined. Simply belonging to a detachment was enough for some, but others wanted to be fully engaged in the fight for reasons of revenge or patriotism or because they felt it was their duty as emancipated Soviet citizens. Their continued marginalization, however, exposed their essentially second-class citizenship in the Soviet Union, while the dominance of Communists and Red Army soldiers was maintained, particularly if they were males and Slavs. This arrangement proved to be a foreshadowing of the social status of these groups in the postwar period.

The implementation of the all-people's war doctrine profoundly affected the partisan movement demographically and politically. With its numbers increasing, the movement did indeed become broader as more marginalized groups gained entrance. However, in the effort to incorporate more diverse elements, the same tensions that shaped social, gender, ethnonational, and political relationships in the peacetime Soviet Union were replicated and intensified in the movement. Moreover, the inclusion of "suspicious elements" reinforced Moscow's distrust of the movement in general. In this way, the same lack of trust that dictated the state's policies toward society at large was also reproduced in the relationship between state officials and the partisans. Thus, the Soviet leadership had achieved its goal of making the partisan movement a microcosm of the Soviet Union in two ways, although not as it had intended. First, many of the same divisions and suspicions that permeated the country as a whole were now replayed behind enemy lines. Second, the movement came to embody the political and social hierarchies that were even then coming to dominate the country: the primacy of the Party and the Red Army led by Slavic men.

6

THE IMAGINED STALINIST COMMUNITY

Soviet partisans used terms such as *state within a state, green city, forest city,* and *partisan republic* to describe their camps and zones.[1] Although these labels masked the daily hardships and primitive conditions of partisan life, they also spoke of the organization, divisions of labor, and social structure necessary to maintain the increasingly complex combat communities.

Partisan units were strained by two related factors: first, the difficulty in upholding unit cohesion among disparate social groups in the midst of almost constant physical danger and material insecurity, and second, the importance of allaying the center's suspicions of the partisans' loyalty and dedication to the cause. These pressures, existing from the first days of war, were magnified by the implementation of the all-people's war policy after September 1942, which increased social tensions within units while renewing the government's concerns about partisan reliability.

The partisans had to establish communities that could manage these social problems and the difficulties of provisioning, maintaining security, and conducting military operations. In their formal organization, their communities replicated features of Soviet society, including the centrality of the omnipotent leader; the reestablishment of Party, Komsomol, and NKVD sections; the celebration of Soviet holidays; and the performance of Soviet social and cultural rituals. Western scholars have generally argued that since the partisans were the "'long arm' of the Soviet state," fully controlled by Moscow, these institutions and practices were imposed from above.[2] Soviet histories claim that even though the Party took the lead in reproducing Soviet institutions in the occupied territories, the partisans joyfully and unequivocally embraced the return of Soviet organizations.[3] But to what extent did the partisans, who were proud of their autonomy and dashing image, conform to the rigors of the Stalinist social order? Just how adaptive was this social order in meeting the challenges posed by a guerrilla war, whose most defining traits included defiance of authority and oppression and the search for freedom?

Certainly, on one level, the desire to avoid being labeled anti-Soviet, as earlier Western studies suggested, was a powerful reason for the partisans to reproduce both institutional and societal norms. However, mechanically re-producing Soviet institutions without sincere feeling for or attachment to them on the part of the command staff and rank-and-file partisans would not help hold a unit together when it was faced with the real pressures caused by deprivation, combat, and uncertainty. Nor would it help balance competing social group and individual interests or enable the partisans to live a relatively secure existence in hostile territory. For the partisan units to hold together as communities, less mechanical and more organic social and cultural attach-ments had to form.

The structures and values of Soviet society as it had developed following the Revolution and especially during the 1930s provided possible solutions to these issues. The Arctic explorers of the 1930s faced similar problems, and they became celebrated official and popular heroes for their ability to perse-vere and live exemplary Soviet lives. Could the partisans, consumed as they were by the need to conform visibly to Soviet community models, also employ the Stalinist social vision to live the freer life of the partisan ethos, to which many of them consciously and unconsciously subscribed?

Although the partisans did replicate certain political, social, and cultural forms because of direct or indirect pressure from Moscow, they also modi-fied these elements of Stalinist society to accommodate their needs. Such had been the case in the 1930s when citizens reinterpreted official values and dis-course to suit their own conditions, even as they internalized some official values while learning to "speak Bolshevik."[4] This process was helped along by the contradictory messages embedded within Stalinist values and prac-tices. Within the partisan units, too, communities emerged that integrated Soviet institutional and social structures with social and cultural features in-fluenced by the partisan ethos and by the circumstances of living in enemy-occupied territory. This is not to say that Soviet social institutions and values were employed only for instrumentalist reasons; rather, partisans re-created and relied on them because they were familiar forms of social organization and because they had already internalized many of these values and world-views in their own fashion in the days and years before the war.

By replicating at least some aspects of Soviet institutions, values, and be-haviors even while adapting them to their specific conditions, the partisans retained their citizenship in the Soviet "imagined community," that is, their sense that they remained a part of Soviet society even though they were physically separated from the mainland.[5] Many partisans wanted to minimize or even sever their connections with this society, but many others who were Soviet patriots or just feared the isolation of being in the enemy's rear area sought to replicate Soviet institutional and behavioral norms. Maintaining physical and cultural ties to the Soviet Union provided a foundation for order, stability, and familiarity in an otherwise anarchic, dangerous, and chaotic environment.

ENGLISH KINGS AND LITTLE STALINS: THE COMMANDER IN THE PARTISAN COMMUNITY

The most important individual affecting unit cohesion was the commander. A poor commander, lacking military and leadership skills, could easily cause inactivity, disharmony, and even his unit's destruction. A good commander maintained internal unity, developed an effective esprit de corps, and accomplished military objectives. To establish themselves as powerful leaders, partisan commanders often replicated a leadership style already familiar to millions of Soviet citizens after more than a decade of Stalinist rule.

Commanders had to answer to both Soviet officials and their own troops. Officials expected partisan commanders to be military leaders and models of Soviet behavior as well. Ponomarenko told commanders that as representatives of Soviet power, they were to be "crystal clean" in their personal habits and in their relations with their partisans and local civilians.[6] They were also to be the very embodiment of Soviet power, combining masculinity with cultural achievement and development. One typical newspaper article described a commander as "broad shouldered, stocky, a 35 year old man. The energy, decisiveness, in this person is inexhaustible. He has tremendous physical strength. It seems that this person was born for the partisan struggle. And what was he before the war? A surgeon, a district surgeon."[7] Partisans had their own criteria that they expected commanders to meet. Commanders had to respect and care for their people, as well as lead them in combat.[8] Those who did not live up to these expectations could face desertion or mutinies. In one instance, some partisans asked a neighboring unit to incorporate their detachment because their commander "did not always live in a friendly manner with the troops." The commanders of the two units, as it turned out, were friends, so nothing came of this "offer."[9] Commanders even had to take into account the possibility of assassination. When commander D. N. Medvedev criticized two neighboring detachment commanders, Shitov and Ivanov, for not instilling discipline and order among their drunken, marauding partisans, Shitov, a former battalion commissar, allegedly replied, "What do you want, that our partisans kill us in our first battle?"[10] They were right to be afraid. The first commander of the 1st Voroshilov Detachment, a Red Army okruzhenets, was assassinated by civilian Party members when the latter believed he favored soldiers over civilians in the unit.[11]

Commanders relied on several methods to meet the demands placed on them by Moscow and their own fighters. In units where the partisan ethos prevailed, commanders might be elected or even chosen by lottery.[12] More commonly, they were appointed by higher authorities, or they used their civilian or military rank or status in Soviet society to dominate their detachments. Thus, prewar status contributed to legitimate wartime authority, so long as partisans recognized the legitimacy of Soviet posts. When their status was insufficient to control their troops, commanders used brute force, including summary executions and assassinations, against unruly elements.[13] However, given the physical isolation of the commander, violence was a means of last resort. Otherwise, surrounded by armed people, he, too, ran the risk of eventually being struck down.

Making use of his charisma and developing a cult of personality were far more effective methods of maintaining authority. Some commanders naturally exuded a powerful masculinity that mesmerized both male and female partisans. Raja Kaplinski, a female partisan in Tuvia Bielski's Jewish detachment, recalled:

> Before I met [Bielski], I thought that a partisan commandant would be a big rough fellow, perhaps with a bushy mustache . . . Instead the man walking toward us was tall, graceful, with a smile that seduced all of us. The warmth and the way he received us was touching . . . [Bielski] was like a magnet that pulled us toward him. I had a feeling that with him I was totally secure, that danger could not reach me, and that around him all will be well . . . This man had something that attracted and conquered people. When he got on the horse with his leather coat and the automatic gun we called him Yehuda HaMacabee.[14]

As Kaplinski's reminiscence indicates, a commander could create a mystique around his person based on romantic images of partisans in popular culture. Before she met Bielski, Kaplinski's notion of an ideal partisan commander resembled the film image of Vasilii Chapaev, the quintessential Civil War partisan hero whose image had been made famous in the wildly popular 1934 film.[15] To the Jewish partisans, Bielski resembled another charismatic resistance leader embedded in Jewish history and cultural mythology.

The deliberate use of costumes and other props helped enhance commanders' images, as suggested by Bielski's automatic, leather coat, and horse.[16] After some commanders were given military ranks in 1943, they sometimes combined their dashing partisan garb with military decorations, tunics, and shoulder boards, thereby creating an image that simultaneously conveyed partisan romanticism and Soviet military hierarchy and discipline. Ukrainian partisan commander S. A. Kovpak, for example, sometimes wore a Cossack cape and hat with his Red Army uniform and medals. Through the skillful use of props, code names, and other devices, a commander could physically establish an aura of power and authority; even a lowly Red Army okruzhenets who became a partisan commander, using the code name Baianist because he played the accordion, managed to convince other partisans that he was a "big man from Moscow."[17]

Some commanders bolstered their cult by becoming inaccessible to their partisans, thereby conveying superiority to their troops.[18] In doing so, they mirrored the behavior that Soviet citizens in the 1930s had come to expect from state and Party officials and from the royalty of pre-Revolutionary days. Ordinary partisans and Soviet officials alike occasionally referred to these commanders as "kings" or "feudal lords." Bielski's partisans even disparagingly dubbed the charismatic and otherwise well-liked leader and his immediate circle the "Romanov Court" because they isolated themselves from the rest of the detachment.[19] In Smolensk Oblast, commander N. Z. Koliada, also known as Batia ("Dad"), made himself inaccessible. He rarely gave orders in person and commanded through subordinates, leading one Red Army political officer to condemn him for conducting himself "in the role of an English king."[20] To another staff officer, the supremely confident commanders exuded the sense that they were "lords of their own domains."[21] A. F. Fedorov, too, used this feudal imagery, pejoratively referring to the camp of a rival commander as a "quiet, prosperous estate."[22] Such behavior also mirrored the antics that Soviet citizens had come to expect from their leaders, especially at the local and regional levels, but they also replicated the social distance that the ruled had come to expect from the rulers before the Revolution.

Joshua Sanborn has shown how the use of family imagery to promote national unity within the military transcended the gap between the late imperial and early Soviet periods.[23] Soviet media built on this foundation in the 1930s, headed by that most tender, concerned, and fatherly patriarch, Stalin.[24] Partisan commanders also utilized this familiar theme, to which their charges responded quite positively. Patriarchal code names such as Dedushka ("Granddad"), Batia, and Diadia ("Uncle") contributed to the commanders' authority as father figures whose units then became their families, bonded by patriotism and camaraderie. One young partisan, Titov, described his unit to Soviet officials as a family: "Why do I call the detachment a family? Yes. It is a united fighting family, a family of friendship, of struggle and love for each other. All for one and one for all." Titov's leader was an "exclusively keen military commander, but during leisure time he is a father." Women, too, had their place in this family: "Our girl-partisans are just as good as qualified cooks in preparing food, but they are not only cooks, but also splendid scouts, seamstresses, they are real amazons. The girls are on equal terms with the men, they bear difficulties equally, are always happy, brave, resolute."[25]

In happy families, even the most aloof fathers maintain some personal ties with their children, and the partisan commanders were no exception to this rule, as they also had to convey their paternal concern. Some commanders gave life to their symbolic roles by giving away their partisans at marriage ceremonies.[26] One partisan in Fedorov's complex noted in his diary the strong mutual feelings the partisans and commander had for one another: "Yes, our commander is actually a real hero, he takes care of the fighters as he would himself. Fedorov is us, we are Fedorov."[27] A story in an illustrated journal produced by the Belorussian "Flame" Detachment in December 1943 also depicted the commander in glowing terms, while noting the mutual relations and obligations he and his partisans owed each other. With winter approaching, the commander knew that the detachment needed new winter quarters and ordered the construction of large and comfortable zemlianki, thus ensuring that in the midst of a cruel winter, the partisans remained warm and sheltered. In describing the huts and bathhouses, with their assorted luxuries including a gramophone, musical instruments, portraits of the national leaders, and plentiful food, the story noted that "all this was done thanks to the large concern the detachment command felt for the fighters. To the concern of the command, we partisans must answer with good discipline, with precision fulfilled by all partisans. This is the duty of every partisan."[28] Whether the commander had actually provided for his partisans so well is unknown; however, the expectation of the nature of the relationship between the commander and the partisans was made explicit.

Commanders who radiated power, confidence, and authority instilled in their troops a sense of security, if not invulnerability. Though some partisans

Partisan commander A. F. Fedorov. (Credit: Minaeva Collection)

saw the movement as a chance to escape from authority and hierarchy, many others were frightened by its apparent anarchy. Still more feared—and with good reason—the omnipresent dangers posed by the enemy. Thus, one can imagine the partisans' relief when they were led by men whose personas connoted calm and certainty in their abilities. I. G. Starinov, an officer attached to the Ukrainian Staff of the Partisan Movement, no doubt spoke for many when he described his impressions of Kovpak, Fedorov, Saburov, and others at a Ukrainian commanders' conference held behind enemy lines in the summer of 1943: "I looked around and noticed the happy faces, the confident movements and voices of the men in officers' and generals' uniforms and shoulder boards. These were not exhausted people who had been harried into the woods and outlands: these were powerful lords of their own domains. In order to present that kind of appearance, you had to have triumphed over every kind of grief and failure."[29] In commanding a community filled with disparate and potentially dissident elements in an extremely dangerous environment, this image of omnipotence was crucial for maintaining order. When the commander increased his own authority by portraying himself as a powerful, semimythical figure, the partisans' own sense of security and power was enhanced. Partisan memoirist Petr Vershigora related that "faith in our commander in war means much, and in the partisan war it really is everything. Only half a year had passed [since Vershigora had been in the occupied territories] and I already felt a little this blind faith in authority."[30] A partisan in the 3rd Leningrad Partisan Brigade told Soviet historians after the war that even in the midst of the most serious attacks, the partisans remained calm because the unit commander, A. V. German, "was with us."[31] For some partisans, the feeling that an all-powerful figure was watching and protecting them no doubt reminded them of more secure prewar days, when Stalin had been portrayed as their protector and when his glory was a reflection of the Soviet Union's in general.[32]

When commanders felt confident in their power, there were few constraints on their authority. Commissars and NKVD cadres were supposed to exercise supervisory functions, but their own relationships to their commanders often precluded this role, as will be discussed. Soviet officials, in the form of the partisan staffs, the Party, and other institutions, were far away, and their knowledge was often limited to what the commanders themselves reported. The lack of institutional constraints enabled commanders to commit a variety of offenses. For instance, they frequently used their power to force female partisans to sleep with them. One partizanka reported that a brigade commander had shouted at her when she refused his advances, "If you will not sleep with me, then I will make you twist like a cow's tail."[33] Another partizanka testified at a Komsomol conference that N. N. Popudrenko, a unit commander and Hero of the Soviet Union, demanded that she live with him. She turned to his superior, Fedorov, for protection, but he replied, "[Popudrenko] is a really good man, you can live with him." Another friend shrugged when she sought his help, saying, "You know Sonia, that this is the partisan life." Popudrenko then threatened to shoot both the partizanka and her friend for allegedly giving secrets to the Germans. He warned, "You see, everything is in my hands. I can shoot you and take you away, and I have the right, but all this will end if you live with me." Despite her refusal, he raped her and forced her to live with him. When she became pregnant, Popudrenko forced her out of the unit. After her infant was killed on the orders of her new commander, she was finally evacuated to the mainland.[34] Soon after this incident, Popudrenko died in a German raid, but it is unlikely that an investigation would have occurred had he lived, and to this day, he remains an honored and respected partisan hero.

Far more serious from the regime's standpoint were the attempts by some commanders to amass power by subordinating other units to themselves or by ruling their districts as their own fiefdoms. Such a situation occurred in Klichev Raion, Mogilev Oblast, in 1942 when Colonel V. I. Nichiporovich tried to subordinate all units in the district. Nichiporovich, who according to one NKVD report "exercised exceptionally great authority over his partisans," ordered all local commanders to subordinate themselves to him, telling one who resisted his efforts, "You are military people, you must subordinate yourselves to those more senior."[35] In the end, this man's detachment and others came under Nichiporovich's domain, either because of the colonel's superior rank or because he refused to aid and support them otherwise.[36] Then, Nichiporovich, in his own words, "formed all Soviet power in Klichev Raion and ordered all to act in accordance with the Constitution of the USSR and my personal instructions. I delimited the rights and instructed the raion committee and raion executive committee how to act."[37] His control was furthered by placing his own men and supporters into key administrative posts, including raikom secretary, chair of the raion executive committee, and head of the raion NKVD.[38] Ponomarenko, no doubt aided by reports such as the one cited here, recognized Nichiporovich's power in a memo to Stalin in July 1942, noting favorably that the Red Army officer was one of the leaders of the partisan movement in the district.[39]

Nichiporovich's reign as overlord of Klichev did not last long, however. His conflation of legal and personal power certainly followed the method of rule practiced by Stalin and his provincial underlings, but like the latter in the 1930s, he was exposed to pressures from above and below. Though no details of his administration have yet been uncovered, Nichiporovich's policies were apparently quite idiosyncratic. According to his own head of the NKVD, Nichiporovich ran affairs "as if people had never seen Soviet power."[40] In a November 1942 interview with Soviet historians, Nichiporovich himself admitted that G. K. Zhukov and N. A. Bulganin, the commander and commissar of the Western Front, "ridiculed me in that I gave instructions to take advantage of my personal leadership, that I appointed the raikom and gave it my personal instructions."[41] Like any other "little Stalin," he also evidently felt threatened by the remaining independent detachments in the area, and he incessantly denounced them. To one plenipotentiary, M. Sarychev, he accused F. I. Pavlovskii, among the first partisans to be named a Hero of the Soviet Union, of "drunkenness and even pillaging the population." He also called his former commissar, the raikom secretary N. P. Pokrovskii, "a big coward" and a drunkard, who "lived with many women, and changed them after less than a month."[42] These accusations, contrary to the established reputations of the people in question, and the colonel's drive for personal power led Central Staff officials to conclude that "his behavior was not stable." He was refused permission to return to the occupied territories after he was evacuated to Moscow in November 1942, ostensibly for rest and consultations on the conduct of the partisan war.[43] After being promoted to the rank of major general and appointed deputy commander of a guard cavalry corps in 1943, he was arrested the same year on charges of anti-Soviet conduct. He was shot in 1945.[44]

Even commanders whose rule was sanctified by Soviet authorities were under constant pressure from both superiors and underlings. Certainly, this was the case with D. V. Emliutin, the commander of the United Partisan Detachments of the Briansk forest. Emliutin had begun his life as a partisan while he was an NKVD junior lieutenant heading an operational group overseen by the Fourth Administration. He succeeded in creating one of the most important partisan regions of the war, encompassing over 4,600 square miles and over 10,000 partisans.[45] Nevertheless, at the August 1942 conference in Moscow, he was criticized by his unit commanders in front of Ponomarenko for his handling of partisan operations and the distribution of supplies.[46] Eight months later, I. S. Gudzenko, the commander of the 2nd Voroshilov Partisan Brigade, sent a radiogram to Ukrainian Staff head T. A. Strokach, accusing Emliutin of not "fulfilling the order of Comrade Stalin" directing the partisans to strike at the Germans. Instead, because of the OPO's "poor leadership," Gudzenko wrote, "the partisan brigades withdrew [into the forest] and conducted a passive defense."[47] Nor did the independently minded guerrillas necessarily obey Emliutin's instructions when they were issued. A plenipotentiary noted in August 1942 that there was "a tendency for individual commanders to live as they pleased."[48] Even the head of the OPO's political department, Andreev, admitted to Ponomarenko in January 1943 that the supposedly subordinate detachments placed their own goals above those specified in the OPO's general operational plan. Thus, the Chapaev Brigade conducted twenty-seven operations in November 1942, but not one of these missions fulfilled or attempted to fulfill any of the tasks the OPO assigned it.[49]

Criticism from below was matched by pressure and surveillance from above. Moscow, not surprisingly, kept a close watch on people such as Emliutin, with their command over thousands of partisans and large territories. As mentioned in Chapter Two, Ponomarenko had chastised Emliutin for damaging relations with the nearby civilian population with his zealous requisitioning of cattle; the partisan chief also criticized the OPO commander for his waste of supplies, his lack of vigilance, and, later, his mishandling of Party affairs.[50] In October 1942, another NKVD official, A. P. Gorshkov, a representative of the Central Staff attached to the Briansk Front, was dispatched to head an operational group within Emliutin's command.[51] Although Gorshkov's duties included more mundane tasks, such as organizing intelligence networks, coordinating and training partisan diversionary actions, and expanding radio communications, he also informed Soviet officials about goings-on in the OPO, concentrating, it seems, on Emliutin's deficiencies as a commander. In January 1943, for example, Gorshkov indicated that Emliutin failed to give sufficient direction to his department heads, improperly used intelligence information, and rarely coordinated the activities of individual formations. Gorshkov further attested that "radioed instructions from higher staffs sit for several days in Comrade Emliutin's pocket and are not executed in good time."[52] Unfavorable reports such as this from Gorshkov and other plenipotentiaries probably contributed to the undermining of official confidence in Emliutin.[53] The Central Staff replaced him with Gorshkov during the massive German sweep directed against the Briansk partisans from May to June 1943 as a prelude to the Kursk operation. The OPO was formally redesignated the Southern Operations Group, which Gorshkov continued to command.[54]

At the same time, removing disobedient commanders was often easier said than done. Central Staff officers rarely had a clear idea of what was happening on the other side of the front, for they depended on the commanders' and commissars' reports for most of their information. As Moscow's arm across the lines was hardly as long or as powerful as it was in peacetime, the removal of a commander could be a lengthy process, as the example of V. S. Pyzhikov illustrates. Pyzhikov (code name Starik), a veteran partisan from the Civil War, was dispatched to Borisov Raion in July 1942 by the Belorussian Central Committee (possibly by Ponomarenko himself) to help organize the partisan movement. Once in Borisov, he represented himself as an intimate of Stalin's, allegedly telling local partisans and officials, according to one observer, that "Stalin said to him, that Ponomarenko was not a bad person, but he was not a suitable leader and that [Stalin] dropped the hint that he, Pyzhikov, will direct the [partisan movement] in Belorussia."[55] Although his actual instructions called for him to form and develop his own unit from locally recruited volunteers, his formation grew primarily from the drafting of civilians and the subordination of other bands. By late summer, he had formed the Chapaev Partisan Division. Ponomarenko was outraged at these developments, and in early October, he ordered Pyzhikov to disband the division, which the latter did only in December. By late January 1943, Ponomarenko had heard so many reports about the delinquencies of Pyzhikov and his partisans, including marauding, drunkenness, shirking of military activity, and feuding with other commanders, that he instructed Belorussian Staff head P. Z. Kalinin to send him all his materials on the miscreant leader. He also appointed his own representatives to investigate the goings-on in the Borisov partisan zone. Although Pyzhikov repeatedly blamed other commanders for these misdeeds, Ponomarenko finally had him evacuated to Moscow, probably in April 1943, some six months after the commander had first been reprimanded.[56]

In amassing their power, authority, and personality cult, partisan commanders were not so much English kings, Romanovs, or feudal lords but rather little Stalins who were the bosses of their detachments. Their behavior replicated that of district and regional Party officials in the 1930s who established personal fiefdoms in their localities, even as partisans also sometimes associated their leaders with the pre-Revolutionary social order. Commanders possessed the same qualities that historian Catriona Kelly observed in local officials—"that impossible combination of patronage and disinterest . . . a mixture of incompatible qualities."[57] And like their peacetime predecessors, they were vulnerable to being purged should their actions and abuses come to the attention of central authorities.

The relationship between the commander and his unit paralleled the relationship between Stalin and the Soviet Union, which itself had deep cultural roots.[58] Many elements of Stalin's cult of personality came into play in the relationship between commanders and partisans, including patriarchy; the family as a metaphor for the unit (and the Soviet Union); the personal ties between the commanding and the commanded, moderated by a certain aloofness; and a down-to-earth, roll-up-your-sleeves-and-get-down-to-it manner that showed little patience for bourgeois niceties. And like Stalin, partisan leaders protected their charges from the encircling enemies in the outside world.[59] Other Soviet notables in the 1930s employed similar cults of personality, including local officials and Arctic heroes Otto Shmidt and Ivan Papanin, who also had to maintain authority while physically separated from Soviet society.[60] That both commanders and partisans reproduced so many of these leader-citizen dynamics within the confines of the partisan war suggests how ingrained this conception of the leader-citizen relationship had become to Soviets and how much it spoke to the conditions of partisan war.[61] Indeed, commanders such as Koliada, Nichiporovich, and Pyzhikov may have internalized the Stalinist method of rule all too well: twenty years after the war, Muromtsev, Koliada's last commissar, reflected that the errant commander's main mistake was that he saw himself as "a clan founder, an organizer of the partisan movement," and "did not understand or want to understand" that the chief organizer of the partisan movement was really the Party.[62] Like Stalin, Koliada had, in his own mind, risen above institutions such as the Party. This seems to have been acceptable to Koliada's partisans, but other commanders and officials felt it threatened their own authority and had to be stopped.

The substitution of the commander for Stalin facilitated two needs: first, it enabled the commander to wield effective power and authority when discipline was needed to hold the unit together, and second, it gave those partisans willing to subordinate themselves a sense of comfort, security, and stability in an otherwise chaotic environment. Stalin's own cult in Soviet-held territory grew during and after the war, especially when the Red Army began its march to ultimate victory in 1943.[63] To these partisans (and to Moscow officials), conditions in the partisan camps required strong leadership, which further validated Stalinist methods of rule. Partisans thus replicated the prewar relationship between ruler and ruled, a dynamic that was given additional meaning and strength in the wartime context.

THE PARTY IN THE PARTISAN COMMUNITY

Certainly, one of the central features of Soviet society was the Communist Party. No Soviet community would be complete without its own Party organization, a fact dramatically demonstrated by the experiences of the ill-fated 1934 *Cheliuskin* voyage and the Papanin ice floe expeditions, in which Party organizations were established even in communities stranded in the Arctic.[64] Not only did the Party form the basis for the partisan movement in 1941, but its cadres also dominated leadership positions at all levels of the movement throughout the war. Each Soviet unit had its commissar and Party organization, whose presence, Western historians have generally asserted, enabled the Party to control the partisans from "top to base," ensuring that the movement "was in a sense the tool of the Party."[65] This interpretation, paradoxically, mirrors those of Soviet historians who argued that indeed the Party controlled and directed all partisan activities.[66] But in the conditions of partisan warfare, what meanings did partisans ascribe to the Party? What role did they see it playing in their community?

According to official Soviet practice, every community required an ideological guide and mentor. In the partisan detachments, as in the Red Army up to October 1942, this position was filled by the commissar. Ideally, the commissar would act as a political adviser to the commander. The model for this relationship was portrayed in the film *Chapaev*, in which the politically educated and cultured commissar Klychkov tempered and trained the well-meaning but politically illiterate Chapaev. In World War II—as in the Civil War—reality did not usually adhere to this template. Nevertheless, the commissar and the unit Party organization remained important features of the Soviet partisan movement.

The commissar's official duties included overseeing the unit's political work and education, maintaining military and political discipline, and reporting on the unit's political and social psychology, particularly that of its command staff. Because Central Staff officials knew many commissars personally through their Party contacts, authorities could verify the reliability and accuracy of the commissar reports, thus giving Moscow a clearer picture of what was really happening in the enemy's rear area. In addition, the commissar countersigned all orders issued by the commander, which gave him not only powers of oversight but also burdens of responsibility.[67]

Ideal commissars cared for their charges' ideological and material needs, ensuring that the partisans were politically aware and had sufficient and appropriate food and clothing. They and other political workers were to lead and educate primarily by example. An article in *Pravda*, "Thanks, Commissar!" informed readers that the commissar "himself went on dangerous operations and threw himself forward, inspiring the others."[68] An essay by Soviet leader Mikhail Kalinin read on a radio broadcast to the occupied territories stated that soldiers—and presumably partisans—"cannot study the Party program and the history of the Bolshevik Party at the front. They experience the Bolshevik tradition in the actions, in the practical work and behavior of the commissars, political workers, and agitators."[69] In wartime, action, not theory, was what counted at the front and behind enemy lines.

The extent to which commissars and other political workers were actually prepared to play the dual roles of political mentor and combat leader varied widely. The more senior commissars had the benefit of experience and a more rigorous political training to guide their actions. As noted earlier, however, there was little in the backgrounds of most raikom secretaries to prepare them for conducting underground and armed resistance. Most were inexperienced at political work and had only rudimentary knowledge of Communist ideology. Army political workers, many of whom became partisan political workers, had even less political training.[70]

The ideological training of political workers declined further as the war continued. In their effort to harness the energies and authority of the most decisive and respected soldiers and possibly to forestall their emergence as an independent source of respect and initiative, Party officials, beginning in August 1941, allowed the recruitment of soldiers for Party membership solely based on their performance in combat.[71] Many partisan units appeared to have adopted the same liberal admissions procedures as regular army units at the front. *Pravda* seemingly endorsed this policy in a February 1942 article, which described the admission of several brave partisans into the Party without once referring to any ideological qualifications or knowledge.[72] V. N. Malin, a top partisan official and later head of the Central Staff's Political Department, argued in the summer of 1942 that the relatively open Red Army recruitment policy should be formally adopted for the partisan movement as well. Until the Central Committee ruled on the matter in 1943, it appears that candidates were often admitted without checking references or even testing their ideological knowledge.

Soviets took advantage of this new laxity to join the Party, especially at the front; by December 1944, over 3 million servicemen at the front were enrolled in the Party, comprising 53 percent of its membership.[73] In the occupied territories, the figures were far less impressive, although the lack of appropriate admissions committees, fear of certain execution if captured by the Germans, and the realization that Communists were expected to undertake the most dangerous assignments might have had as much influence on the more limited admissions as any lack of enthusiasm.[74] Some may have joined out of hopes of advancement either in the unit or after the war, but others identified with the Party's cause, even if that was only to win the war. On hearing the news of his acceptance as a candidate member, one partisan wrote in his diary, "This will remain a great memory in my life: joining the Party in the partisans."[75]

Whatever the motivations of the new members, Soviet officials became increasingly concerned that in the occupied territories, suspicious elements were infiltrating the Party through lax admission standards. In the spring of 1943, Komsomol secretary N. A. Mikhailov reported that partisan Party organs permitted far too many okruzhentsy and former POWs to join the Party and that the head of one such major organization was himself an okruzhenets whose Party membership had not been verified. "Such disorder and careless-

ness towards party organization," Mikhailov warned, "means that it is possible to miss spotting any rascal or provocateur."[76] It was these fears that led
the Central Committee to reimpose peacetime restrictions on the partisans in
1943.[77] Mikhailov's worries further demonstrated that despite their deeds in
the partisan war, Red Army soldiers trapped behind the lines were still regarded as less than trustworthy.

The damage to the Party's ideological quality and perhaps its purity was
already done. The commissar of the 3rd Leningrad Partisan Brigade reported
in July 1943 that the general political preparation of the brigade's political
officers "was extremely low, and therefore the quality of oral propaganda in
the detachments leaves much to be desired."[78] One partisan noted in his diary
that the detachment's political officers only read information reports when
pressured and "never talk with anybody." Of the commissar, he reported, "On
every question he tries to affirm his knowledge and [political] literacy but his
literacy is doubtful."[79]

Lack of formal political training coupled with the experience of living
behind enemy lines may have led to the emergence of decidedly un-Soviet
politics among these Communists. There are indications that some partisan
units helped peasants disband collective farms, no doubt contributing to rumors that the entire collective farm system would be abolished after the war.[80]
In August 1944, Minsk Oblast officials forbade former partisan political agitators from working among the population until they had been "retrained."[81]
In April 1944 at the oblast's Party plenum, Leningrad Staff head Nikitin observed that although underground Party workers showed much resourcefulness and bravery, they required an extensive political education to raise their
"ideological-political and theoretical level."[82] It appears, then, that more often than not, these cadres were not effective enforcers or proselytizers of the
Party's "general line."

Considering the general quality of political workers, it is not surprising
that despite the fact that many commissars fulfilled their responsibilities
quite ably, many others failed to be the instruments of oversight and control
that Moscow had intended. They were often dominated by their commanders.
One Soviet official reported in August 1942 that some of the most famous
commanders (including Chernihiv Obkom secretary Fedorov) believed political work was unimportant and "often do not consider the opinions of their
commissars."[83] The partisan commander Baianist (the accordion player),
perhaps identifying a bit too closely with his code name, proudly told Soviet
historians, in an interview conducted in March 1943, that in his unit, "single
command had developed. Commissar Sokolov several times attempted to dis-

obey orders, considering himself to be equal with me, but every time this affair came to a scandal, he was squeezed and forced to play my tune."[84] In
more amiable relationships, commanders and commissars might cooperate to
thwart Moscow's instructions, as happened with the center's efforts to include
women in the partisan detachments.[85] Likewise, when a commander and
commissar formed a unit together, their primary loyalty often seems to have
been to each other, rather than to Party officials in the Soviet rear area.[86]

It would be inaccurate to say, however, that all commissars were completely ineffective. In candid interviews with Soviet historians, ordinary partisans recalled not only the failures and cowards among the political workers
but also the inspiring commissars who maintained discipline in a chaotic environment, negotiated the peaceful procurement of supplies from the civilian
population, and led their troops in battle.[87] Still others provided valuable reports to the center on their units' morale and political mood, commanders'
activities, and the conditions in the occupied territories, which contributed to
the removal of inept, inactive, and corrupt commanders.

The importance of commissars to the center, if not to the partisans, is
illustrated in Voroshilov's failed effort to remove them in October 1942 at
the same time that the post was abolished in the regular armed forces. The
decision to abolish the post in the Red Army was based on the supposition
that army officers had matured politically to the point where they no longer
needed political oversight, whereas the commissars had gained such enormous military experience that they now composed a much-needed command
reserve.[88] Most historians, however, have interpreted this policy as a sign of
the army's growing prestige and independence at the expense of the Party.[89]
In any case, Voroshilov apparently believed that what was good for the army
was good for the partisans, for on 18 October, he ordered the abolition of the
commissars, renaming them deputy commanders for political affairs.[90]

Not surprisingly, commissars complained bitterly, arguing that the partisans fought under very different conditions than the Red Army soldiers, that
constant attention was required to unmask the German propaganda to which
the partisans and civilians were exposed daily, and that they were needed to
maintain discipline amid the temptations of the partisan life. Furthermore,
this policy would essentially mean a demotion for the local Party officials who
had been so instrumental in organizing and leading the movement from its
earliest days.[91]

Ponomarenko took up many of these same arguments in a letter written
to Stalin on 5 January 1943, approximately six weeks after Voroshilov's re-

moval. He contended that though the partisan commanders were well versed in military affairs, they still were "not sufficiently fortified from the political standpoint" and had "insufficient political vision." Playing on Stalin's distrust of the movement, he further noted that commissars were more trustworthy than commanders, especially since they were known personally to many of the Communists working in the Central Staff. This familiarity enabled staff officials to verify the accuracy of the reports coming from the occupied territories.[92] Despite the dubious nature of these claims (many commanders also had a Party background, and commissars were not necessarily any more reliable in their reports), Stalin affirmed the partisan chief's position and reinstated the commissars. This decision demonstrates that Stalin and Ponomarenko still fundamentally distrusted the movement, at a time when the Red Army's operational autonomy was growing. It also shows that in the leadership's vision, commissars and the need for political oversight remained critical elements in the Soviet social order.

Another fundamental part of any Soviet community was the presence of a Party organization. Just as the Arctic heroes of the 1930s had maintained Party life, so, too, did the partisans. Soviet media stressed the importance of partisan Party organizations in leading the insurgency and took note that in occupied territory, even the most seemingly mundane tasks took on a new significance. Thus, *Krasnaia zvezda* commented, "The partisans understand that the party meeting is an excellent school for Communists for Bolshevik inculcation."[93] Party organizations also supposedly inspired partisans to establish close relations with the people.[94] By publicly affirming the necessity of Party organizations in the movement, Soviet officials attempted to articulate another key aspect of Soviet identity.

As with commissars, the actual value of partisan Party organizations varied. Some Party organizations did conduct agitational work within the unit and with the nearby civilian population and also established behavioral and disciplinary standards for Party members and thus indirectly for the entire unit.[95] Most others, however, were content to adhere to the peacetime routine of holding purposeless meetings and giving uninspired reports. At the subdetachment level (companies, platoons), Party cells often existed only on paper or were absent altogether.[96] Even when a viable organization did exist, Communists often conducted propaganda only within the unit.[97] Thus, Komsomol head Mikhailov reported to Stalin that partisan Party organizations were guilty of "rarely conducting their work beyond the borders of the detachments, and weakly expanding their influence among the broad elements of the population." Ponomarenko himself criticized Party groups that worked with nearby civilians only when the Germans had been cleared from the area.[98]

Far from being sources of state control, commissars and Party organizations could be used by enterprising partisans to mask their goals, while providing a facade of adherence to the Soviet cause. For example, the Bielski Partisan Detachment—or, as its members called it for the benefit of Soviet authorities, the Zhukov Detachment—did have a commissar, who was reluctantly appointed by the unit commander, Tuvia Bielski. To partisan officials, this appointment and Bielski's use of Soviet language at appropriate moments gave the detachment the appearance of a regular Soviet partisan band engaged in actively fighting the Germans. In reality, however, the Bielski Detachment was concerned with one mission: saving as many Jews as possible from the Nazis, even if this meant avoiding combat.[99] In a more menacing example, Voroshilovgrad Party cadre Tkachenko and okruzhenets Vill were accused of setting up a false partisan movement, complete with an underground raikom, at German instigation in order "to paralyze" the local partisan movement. According to trial records, they lured honest patriots to their deaths, before the NKVD unmasked and executed them.[100] Concerns that the Party could indeed be a vehicle for enemy agents to worm their way into Soviet life further reduced the faith officials had in the partisan Party organizations. However, they still relied on these organs to help ensure the partisans' reliability.

For both state authorities and partisans alike, commissars and Party organizations were a fundamental part of Soviet society, whose absence, at least in an institutional sense, was unimaginable. Although the Party had lost much of its ideological content and purpose during the war years, it nonetheless remained a very real force in the lives of Soviet citizens. Soviet leaders used the Party, especially through its mass recruitment of Red Army soldiers, to mobilize the population into a national political organization, synonymous with the Soviet Union itself. In occupied territory, this strategy of mass mobilization posed too many risks to the stability and reliability of the Party. Instead, commissars and partisan Party organizations retained their functions as controllers and watchdogs, whose very existence in the detachments helped to reassure Soviet leaders that the partisans remained loyal to Moscow. Even if the commissars and partisan Party organizations failed to exert the degree of control that the leadership sought, their existence still eased, if not erased, fears about potential outbreaks of partizanshchina.

The Party held several different meanings for the partisans in the detachments. For true believers, it still served as the ideological and political vehicle for engineering the revolutionary transformation of Soviet society and for organizing and leading the popular resistance against the occupiers. For others, the Party retained its importance as a Soviet institution, an organization that one supported simply because that was what one did as a Soviet citizen. Consequently, Party membership became as much a manifestation of one's Soviet identity and patriotism behind the lines as it was at the front. For the more cynically minded, establishing Party organizations and commissars indeed signaled to the central authorities that they were loyal to the Soviet cause, even if the partisans demonstrated the same levels of enthusiasm—or lack thereof—for the mundane aspects of Party life as they did in the prewar years. Moreover, for most of the war, ideological content seemed to matter little; to Moscow, the important thing was that the unit had a visible and functioning organization. As an integral part of Soviet society, the partisans' maintenance of Party organizations served both to legitimate the Soviet order consciously and unconsciously and, paradoxically, to enable the partisans to preserve some autonomy from it in certain cases.

TERROR AND VIGILANCE REVISITED

In his memoirs, M. T. Lukashov reflected on the nature of the partisan world after he had caught two collaborators who had been planning to assassinate the command staff: "The partisan life does not roll along a straight and level road. Every day brought some kind of event—good and bad, happy and sad. We lived under eternal tension."[101]

As noted previously, fear of the outside and of outsiders pervaded the partisan movement. The first units were locally organized and based, and local affiliation and regionalism remained important features of partisan life.[102] Red Army personnel formed detachments often composed of men from the same regiment or division, establishing their own sense of community and security. Partisans frequently measured newcomers by how well they were known or where they claimed to have come from. But who knew what the true loyalties of the populace behind German lines actually were? If concerns regarding loyalty, reliability, and authenticity troubled Soviets in peacetime when people were suspected of disguising their pasts or hiding behind "masks," how might the Soviets view the threat of internal subversion in an actual war, particularly when so many of their erstwhile fellow citizens were openly collaborating with or fighting alongside the enemy?

Just as the Party was—or was supposed to be—an integral part of every Soviet community, so, too, were the security police. It was difficult to imagine Soviet life in the 1930s without the security police, who, depending on the citizen's individual perspective, either defended the nation from internal and external enemies or terrorized a largely innocent population. Consequently, attached to most detachments was an NKVD "special section" (*osobyi otdel*), responsible for maintaining internal security from spies and anti-Soviet elements, developing intelligence networks among the local population, and initiating intelligence operations against the enemy. Special sections also reinforced unit discipline by investigating and punishing cases of rape, plundering, and other criminal violations.[103]

The head of the special section (usually holding the position of deputy commander for intelligence) answered to the NKVD's chain of command and therefore acted as a source of control from the security organs.[104] In April 1943, the Red Army's intelligence service was given the right to appoint its own deputy commanders for intelligence; thus, in 1944 in Leningrad Oblast, of the 124 deputy commanders for intelligence, 110 (88.7 percent) were from the Red Army.[105] However, some commanders formed special sections on their own initiative or selected their own intelligence chiefs, thereby managing to stay outside the NKVD umbrella while conforming to the center's ideal structure. Others subverted this control by refusing to cooperate with the security heads or by replacing them with their own men.[106] Obkom secretary Matveev and NKVD chief Firsanov, the Orel partisan heads, angrily declared that such practices "bring harm to the partisan movement" and only happened because "anti-Soviet elements made their way into the detachments . . . and that individual commanders, instead of curbing these hostile actions, themselves establish incorrect relations with NKVD officials."[107] A Leningrad partisan official, apparently less irked by these ploys than his Orel counterparts, reported, "The territorial NKVD organs and the organs of the Special Section of the Front stand to the side. We ourselves have created partisan brigade special departments, and have selected the workers."[108] Partisan staffs and the NKVD repeatedly informed commanders that only the NKVD administration had the right to appoint and remove intelligence heads, which suggests that commanders frequently ignored these instructions.[109] If local commanders essentially controlled their special sections, this gave the former enormous power, furthering the possibility of becoming little Stalins in their zones. This concern led one officer in Belorussia's Borisov zone to request that the special sections be independent from the commanders and attached to the appropriate staffs and Party organs.[110]

Special section heads were not necessarily certain what their tasks were, or how they ought to fulfill them. Z. T. Gobets, an NKVD official in Mogilev Oblast's 208th Partisan Regiment since April 1942, was appointed to head the unit's special section after the death of its previous commander. In November 1942, he wrote to the head of the special sections of the Western Front, requesting instructions for how to deal with marauding, unmasking enemy agents and police, and confirming and verifying the documents of local partisan officials and plenipotentiaries. He pleaded, "Without instructions and leadership, it is impossible for us to work normally."[111] It seems, then, that special section heads were not always the omnipotent enforcers of the center's will.

But that made them no less necessary as far as many partisans were concerned, particularly since they viewed the outside world as teeming with spies and traitors who could assassinate officers, identify vulnerable family members, or communicate a unit's location to the Germans.[112] Thus, one partisan who emigrated from the Soviet Union after the war blamed her unit's destruction on spies who had informed the Germans that a well-armed group had departed for a mission and left the base weakly defended.[113] Strict precautions were usually taken to ensure that no spies infiltrated their ranks, and unfamiliar outsiders were often turned away from the bands. Even those who had documents, such as Party cards, were not automatically accepted.[114] New recruits also underwent a verification process, as one NKVD officer attached to Fedorov's complex explained: "Recently arriving comrades were not immediately allowed to serve fully in the detachment, they were not allowed to be on guard duty near the dugouts, they were not allowed to guard the pickets on their own. We tried to surround all of the recently arrived comrades with our own experienced people, who could observe their behavior, study their mood, and [hear] their conversations and statements."[115] In addition to these precautions, special sections maintained informants within units.[116] Such measures became more critical to the partisans' security as the movement expanded with new arrivals, even if it no doubt distressed individual partisans.

Many partisans, whatever fears they might have had of the special sections, seem to have regarded them as necessary. In a letter to the mainland in October 1942, one partisan wrote that people who had "during Soviet power conducted themselves quietly and inconspicuously, have now emerged as traitors."[117] The number of alleged spies discovered by the partisans attests to the extent of this fear. The Belorussian Staff reported in July 1943 that although its partisans had "unmasked and shot" 944 "Gestapo agents" since the beginning of 1942, it believed that still more spies had successfully infiltrated the units.[118] One Smolensk detachment reported that within a few months, its special section had "unmasked" some 700 "spies, counter-revolutionaries, and police," including a thirteen-year-old boy and the wife of a political officer.[119] Some partisans and officials even believed that the presence of NKVD specialists would *reduce* the number of summary executions in the detachments. As one local official optimistically reported, they "would be directly occupied with the study of every partisan and with the uncovering of actual spies, which should stop pointless shootings."[120] The mass influx of former collaborators in 1943 added to the tension and insecurity, which was assuaged only by maintaining tight vigilance over these suspect newcomers.[121] Not surprisingly, the imagery of unmasking, so prevalent in the discourse and politics of the 1930s Soviet Union, remained a constant theme in the partisan detachments. Indeed, the prewar culture of denunciations was so endemic in the occupied territories that German security forces, too, were overwhelmed with them, leading one analyst to conclude that "the persistence of denunciation under the German occupation is one of the more remarkable continuities in social behavior between peacetime and wartime Soviet society."[122]

The threat posed by marginalized elements, another pervasive motif of the interwar period, also continued in the detachments. Various rumors circulated that the Germans employed Jews, Tatars, Ukrainians, and women (the latter usually infected with syphilis) to infiltrate and destroy the units from within.[123] One rumor claimed (with no actual basis in fact) that the Germans had established an espionage school in Minsk, which had supposedly trained 13,000 Jewish spies.[124] One possible victim of these rumors was Mikhail Breitman-Petrenko, a Jewish political instructor and a former prisoner of war who allegedly confessed to NKVD officers in the "Uncle Vasia" Partisan Brigade (a unit known for its friendliness to Jews) that he had been forced to become a spy for the Germans under the threat of death. It is impossible to determine the truth of the matter now, but the suspicious partisans shot him.[125] These rumors confirmed the prejudices of male Slavic partisans that these marginalized groups were indeed dangerous to the partisans' security and thus required careful scrutiny. Such views also reinforced veterans' claims that *they* were the patriotic and loyal ones, even if the other partisans were not.

The fate of those partisans caught in the special section's net was usually grim. Some were detained in the unit while authorities in Moscow investigated their claims and backgrounds. Torture was evidently employed, as was suffered by some partisans who were captured by another unit when the commander believed them to be spies.[126] Others were evacuated to the mainland, where they might endure further interrogation, trial, and punishment (either execution or the gulag); occasionally, they were exonerated and sent back to their units.[127] Most, however, apparently were summarily executed on the spot, with or without a cursory trial. Indeed, some executions were so hasty that the NKVD cadres failed to interrogate their prisoners thoroughly, neglecting to get such vital information as assignments or the names of other agents.[128] Some units or organizations, such as D. V. Emliutin's United Partisan Detachments, appeared to require a vote by the detachment to sanction an execution, as sometimes occurred in the 1930s, but how fair, contested, or democratic these votes actually were is anybody's guess.[129] Sometimes, an individual might be spared, as occurred with one female partisan in Fedorov's complex who had lost her boots and other property while on a procurement expedition. Although the command staff wanted to shoot her, it was decided to hold an examination in front of the entire detachment, and in the end, according to the special section head, "no one demanded that she be shot."[130]

Such restraint appears to have been rare. Much more common was the shooting of partisans and civilians alike based on the briefest of investigations. Sometimes, partisans, unaware that they were on a hit list, were executed with a shot in the back while on a mission. A regional partisan official condemned this practice because it "disorganized the work of the detachment, and sowed fear in individual partisans and group commanders, that for the slightest dissatisfaction of the command, they will be killed surreptitiously."[131] Some partisans fell victim to the special sections for personal reasons, as occurred to the unfortunate nineteen-year-old partizanka who refused to sleep with the NKVD section chief and was subsequently shot for "spying."[132] Reports of excesses such as these led Central Staff officials to draft an order in June 1943 instructing commanders to stop "baseless shootings" of partisans and civilians and to rely on more political work to maintain discipline. Territorial partisan staff heads were also told to investigate and "adopt the very strictest measures" against command personnel who used excessive force.[133] Whether or not this order was promulgated, it indicates that the practice was widespread enough to attract Moscow's attention. It also suggests that the fear of the arbitrary use of power by the security organs was prevalent among the partisans—and with good reason.

Recorded criticisms of the special sections and their activities in the archival record are rare, but a few examples do emerge. A disgruntled and certainly demoralized Briansk partisan supposedly charged in the fall of 1942, as the Red Army clung desperately to the banks of the Volga at Stalingrad, that "Soviet power destroyed our life, and they will ravage the partisans more and shoot the innocent . . . We cannot expect victory from the Red Army and from Stalin. The Germans are another thing, they have success."[134] Nor did the special sections command universal respect, as one partisan, not very shrewdly giving vent to his true feelings toward the special sections, called his unit's NKVD chief a "yid." This remark led to his being brought before a partisan court.[135] Other partisans doubted the special sections' ability to root out the real enemies. One partisan in Fedorov's complex was overheard to say, "They are beating us because earlier the organs of the NKVD, the procurators, and the courts worked very badly, they did not see the [internal] enemy, and now they have raised their heads and 90% are against us."[136] The Germans also used popular dissatisfaction with the NKVD in their propaganda, leading one underground Party activist to report, "In our agitation we do not try to defend the NKVD, but really emphasize the repression, the atrocities conducted by the Germans."[137] Thus, for some, the catastrophic defeats of 1941 and 1942 and the emergence of collaborators belied the regime's claims that the repressions of the 1930s were necessary and effective. But it also seemed clear that Stalin's warnings of encirclement by external enemies and of the threat from internal enemies had come to pass.

Conditions in the partisan camps and the occupied territories brought to life the worries of the 1920s and 1930s. Then, concerns about external and internal threats justified militarism and repression at home and encouraged thinking about the outside world as being filled with perils for honest Soviets. Now, the outside world was perceived as being even more dangerous, for the external enemies and their indigenous accomplices had actually materialized and were really trying to kill them. In this atmosphere, as in the 1930s, general attitudes toward the security organs were ambivalent in the detachments. In the 1930s, the NKVD occupied a contradictory position. Soviets feared and dreaded an encounter with the NKVD, but many also believed that it protected the country from the conspiracies of foreign spies and internal enemies, at least until they themselves were swept up.[138] A significant number also viewed the terror as an opportunity to get back at managers and Party officials, the new *verkhnye* ("top people") who were using their power to exploit the poor *nizkie* ("masses").[139] Though there might have been doubts about the reality of internal enemies and foreign spies portrayed by the regime in the 1930s, the partisans' experiences in the occupied territories provided powerful evidence that such types actually existed. The appearance of real collaborators in league with a real foreign enemy gave credibility to earlier Stalinist repressions of enemies and infiltrators and gave new meaning to the Stalinist motifs of internal vigilance and the unmasking of spies. Partisans could now look back on the past events of the 1930s with new insight and understanding, thus bolstering their support for the government. Indeed, in the late 1940s, new fears regarding internal enemies helped to deflect popular criticism of the regime.[140] By giving reality to the myth of internal enemies, the war experience not only legitimated state terror in the past but paved the way for more state terror in the future.

CADRES DECIDE EVERYTHING: THE MAKING OF THE PARTISAN ELITE

Far from the egalitarianism embodied within the partisan ethos, almost all partisan bands were marked by social stratification. An elite emerged, composed of several groups that addressed the political, military, and economic needs of the detachments. The emergence of this elite echoed the formation of a Soviet elite in the 1930s, although the resulting social patterns both replicated and diverged from those of prewar Soviet society.

The unit leadership cores, including military and political officers and NKVD section chiefs, headed the partisan elite. Their wartime elite status usually corresponded to their status in peacetime society, as many officers belonged to the local and regional elite. However, upward mobility was also possible, since ordinary Red Army men and common citizens could become partisan commanders, officers, and specialists in their own right if they had sufficient skill, charisma, and luck.

In most units, ordinary Party and Komsomol members were part of the elite. They composed the leadership reserve and were frequently selected for advanced training and special missions, such as conducting sabotage and agitational-propaganda work among the surrounding population. As befitted an elite, they were also expected to take on the most hazardous assignments and maintain higher standards of discipline, although theory and practice did not always merge.

Trained military specialists *(spetsialisty)*, including saboteurs, scouts, and radio operators, formed a third category.[141] Unit leaders sometimes allocated scarce and valuable weapons, such as submachine guns and other automatics, to particularly brave and skilled fighters, bestowing elite status on them as well.[142] In so-called noncombat formations, such as the Bielski Detachment, armed partisans were an elite below only the command staff. Their weapons enabled them to obtain supplies and goods from the local population that the others could not.[143]

Other specialists who practiced more benign trades critical to the survival of the unit as a community also enjoyed elevated status. Metalworkers, tailors, barbers, shoemakers, leatherworkers, and other artisans were in great demand, for the detachments had to manufacture or repair weapons, clothing, and other equipment.[144] These artisans provided services for their own detachments, and units such as the Bielski Detachment became manufacturing centers in the forest and supplied needed goods to other detachments in return for food, raw materials, and protection.[145] Ponomarenko, always looking for ways to avoid sending supplies to the partisans, noted in a memo to the head of the Belorussian Staff that partisan-manufacturers of homemade weapons were particularly valuable because arms shortages plagued the detachments.[146] Medical personnel were also accorded much respect, including individuals who were otherwise marginalized, such as Jews or women.[147]

Civilian specialists not only raised standards of living and morale in detachments but also became a source of unit pride. Partisan commander Nichiporovich proudly noted that he had established a bakery and a sausage-making plant. Although his sausage maker had to make his products without salt, Nichiporovich complimented this "distinguished specialist" (*krupnyi spetsialist*), stating that the sausage was "pretty good."[148] The commander of a neighboring unit, S. A. Mazur, in turn told Soviet officials that his detachment had constructed a bakery, with good "baker-specialists" (*pekari-spetsialisty*), and boasted, "We make sausage. I have better specialists than even Nichiporovich. We have very good sausage."[149] Civilian specialists provided the essentials of existence and could even be used to demonstrate the superiority of one unit over another. Moreover, as specialists and complex divisions of labor were characteristics of the modern, urban-based society the Bolsheviks were trying to build, units that had specialists were, by implication, living in a Soviet manner.

Because of their perceived worth, the elite received additional food, material allotments, and salaries.[150] In Fedorov's complex, all the officers had warm leather or sheepskin coats, but many rank-and-file partisans had no such winter garments.[151] Most ordinary partisans slept in bare zemlianki on cold dirt floors; one partizanka recalled, "For the two years I was with the partisans I never slept in a bed."[152] Commanders and other high-ranking officers, however, usually had separate quarters, which could be comparatively luxurious. One Crimean detachment commander gleefully noted in his diary that his quarters were "not a dugout but a 'forest palace.' Beds, a table, chairs, bedding, mats—is this really a partisan dugout?"[153] Another in Briansk reported that his hut was "upholstered with parachutes, so civilized."[154] Other scarce luxuries, such as personal weapons, food, and (for male partisans) women, also were "allotted" to the elite. Partisans on special missions away from the main body also had opportunities for trading with or plundering from the civilian population, which gave them additional material resources and social advantages.[155]

Elite status conferred more individual autonomy, especially for saboteurs, scouts, and radio operators. Radio operators used their specialized skill to avoid going on combat and procurement missions and to seek better conditions in other detachments, leaving their former units without any radio contact.[156] Female radioists employed their elevated status as a means to escape the unwanted advances of other partisans, including commanders.[157] Because other partisans did not understand their arcane craft, radio operators could also report whatever information they wished. In an extreme instance, one operator, posing as his commander, sent in false information, which resulted in his receiving a government award.[158] Not surprisingly, commanders complained to Ponomarenko; one commented that "radio operators must be sent who will be fully and completely under the authority of the commander of the detachment."[159]

Saboteurs were also known for their autonomy, based on their skill and the nature of their missions, which demanded that they operate in small groups away from the main unit. One plenipotentiary complained to Moscow: "Groups of diversionists, trained in the Central Staff school, as a general rule, act alone in the detachment, do not include in their ranks the [other] fighters of the detachment, do not take part in scouting or guard duties, and do not train the [other] partisans in sabotage."[160] Other officials echoed this charge.[161] Their autonomy even enabled them occasionally to buck the authority of higher officials. N. N. Plekhanov, a model Komsomol demolitions specialist, refused to obey the commissar of the school to which he was sent after the completion of his first tour in August 1942. The latter wanted to split up Plekhanov's group to give green units the benefit of the more experienced saboteurs. Plekhanov went over the head of the commissar to Belorussian Central Committee secretaries G. B. Eidinov and N. E. Avkhimovich, both of whom supported the rebellious young partisan.[162]

Saboteurs enjoyed another, if ironic, privilege. The celebration of sabotage and the saboteur highlights the ambiguity of Stalinist discourse, especially during the war years. In both Soviet media and among the partisans, the saboteur's skill was compared to that of those most honored members of the Soviet industrial proletariat, the skilled heavy industrial and railroad workers. That countless people were executed or sent to the gulag for the alleged crime of sabotage just a few years earlier was, of course, never mentioned. Now, Soviet citizens were expected to become saboteurs in the service of the state. The author of one article, apparently aware of this implicit but unspoken contradiction, made special note of the fact that partisans had no prior experience conducting sabotage![163] The saboteur helped define the partisan movement and was a certified member of the partisan elite, just as Stakhanovites, the labor elite of the mid-1930s, were celebrated. But the partisan-saboteur was more than just a skilled industrial worker. He or she combined technical skill with the romance and charisma of the bandits, Cossacks, and Red partisans of yore, bringing together the responsibility of consciousness and expertise of modern technology with the dash and excitement of spontaneity. In so doing, the saboteur had come full circle, at least temporarily: no longer an enemy of the people, he or she was now a Stalinist hero.

Of course, the existence of upward mobility and elites required their opposite—downward mobility and a "subaltern" group. Those with little practical knowledge of how to fight or survive in the forest, such as urban dwellers, white-collar workers, and members of the intelligentsia, were often among the most downtrodden, receiving the poorest quality and quantity of food, goods, and respect. In one unit, barbers even shaved them with dull blades, refusing to waste sharp ones on "useless" people.[164]

These supposedly useless people often had had superior standing in pre-war Soviet society and had lived, according to Catriona Kelly, a "rarefied existence."[165] In the partisan camp, they were regarded more as a hindrance than a help. Those with rural survival skills, such as peasants, could find themselves raised in status and privilege over urban rivals, and sometimes, they achieved a social mobility they otherwise would not have had. In the Bielski Detachment, for example, the daughter of an oral surgeon and a dentist married a "simple uneducated youth who had guts and a gun," in order to obtain goods and protection.[166] Stratification in the partisan movement brought the possibility of the urban-rural role reversal that had been sought by the peasant and Cossack utopians.

Partisans reacted in various ways to inequality. Some accepted the continuation of hierarchy. As one veteran recalled after the war, "Those in power had to eat better. There is no equality in any place and there was no equality in the forest either."[167] Others were more disgruntled by the unequal distribution of personal luxuries. One male partisan in the 1st Kursk Partisan Brigade complained, "Why do they forbid me from having a third wife, but the com-

"Our Arithmetic: Problem No. 3: A German train goes from point A to point B. When will the train arrive at point B if the distance between the points is 100 km. and the train's speed is 30 km. per hour? Answer: The train will never arrive at point B because the partisans blew it up." (Credit: Hoover Institution Archives, Poster Collection, RU/SU2514)

mander can?"[168] Central and local officials observed that the scarcity of personal luxuries in the detachments and "the insufficient attention paid to the troops" by commanders and political workers contributed to a lack of unit discipline and poor morale, the looting of the civilian population, and the general corruption within the movement.[169] This corruption and the desire for goods sometimes endangered lives, as occurred when the commanders of one small unit traded six submachine guns for two gold watches and a leather coat. According to local partisan officials, the commander and commissar then "consciously led the unarmed mass to their deaths" when the detachment tried to cross enemy lines.[170]

In the 1930s, the Stalinist slogan "Cadres decide everything" marked the need to develop Soviet experts capable of running an advanced industrial society. In the partisan environment, specialists were required to meet the difficult political, economic, and military demands placed on the detachments. In conditions of shortage, those partisans whose skills were considered essential by unit leaders commanded a greater share of the resources and personal luxuries. The resulting social hierarchies and stratification mirrored the stratification that occurred in prewar Soviet society in four ways. First, in the 1930s, Soviet authorities instituted a rationing and, later, a payment system that rewarded individual performance and skill, and they ordained that certain jobs, affiliations, and even geographic areas were more valuable than others. The partisans adopted both practices.[171] Second, both interwar Soviet society and the partisan units existed in conditions of extreme deprivations. The effect of these material shortages was quite similar: one definition of power in both communities was the ability to acquire scarce goods through specialized skills or access to personal networks, a pattern that intensified on both sides of the front during the war years.[172] Third, despite some pretense of equality in both Soviet and partisan discourse, women, ethnic minorities, and the unskilled found themselves on the lowest rungs of partisan social hierarchy. And fourth, the effects of stratification and competition undermined solidarity among the partisans, just as competing workers' interests and experiences inhibited the formation of a united and politically self-conscious Soviet working class on the shop floor.[173] Thus, though the war created opportunities for many partisans to realize the egalitarianism of the partisan ethos, for many others it legitimated and reinforced the authoritarian and hierarchical Stalinist vision of socialism, which allowed for upward mobility but explicitly rejected egalitarianism. Rather, the postwar years were marked by a heightened desire for material acquisition and social gain.[174]

THE IMPORTANCE OF BEING CULTURED

The partisans' Stalinist social vision was further reflected in their efforts to demonstrate that despite their isolation from the Soviet mainland, they remained true citizens of the Soviet Union. One way to prove their adherence to Soviet norms was to show that, even in the forests and in enemy-occupied territory, they were still cultured Soviet men and women.

"Culture" and "being cultured" (*kul'turnost'*) were essential components of Soviet identity in official peacetime discourse. In both pre-Revolutionary and Soviet society, culture was associated not only with appreciation of the arts but also with proper behavior, politeness, rationality, general learning, and cleanliness. Being cultured meant overcoming the "backwardness" that seemingly always afflicted Russian society. In the Soviet context, culture became synonymous with the creation of the New Soviet Person and was therefore a fundamental part of the official Soviet self-description.[175]

In the discourse of the 1930s, Soviet culture triumphed over its abstract opponents, nature and backwardness. Advice literature, such as *How to Read a Book* and *The Book of Tasty and Nutritious Food*, sought to eradicate cultural illiteracy among the masses.[176] Collectivization purportedly brought civilization to the countryside, and the exploration and development of the Arctic not only supposedly tamed a wild and exotic region but also demonstrated that Soviets (that is, Slavs) could maintain cultural norms and teach them to the native peoples.[177] This discourse evidently had become so ingrained in Soviet consciousness that the partisans, too, in their reports to their superiors and in other self-representations, employed their natural, open-air existence as a backdrop to demonstrate just how cultured—and therefore Soviet—they actually were. In so doing, they would prove beyond any doubt that they were free from any infections of partizanshchina. At the same time, however, the aim of proving oneself a cultured Soviet partisan conflicted with the partisans' desire to represent themselves as dashing and romantic figures. And yet, the pursuit of culture also created the possibility of living certain aspects of the good life featured in the partisan ethos, while maintaining the appearance of being an ideal Soviet citizen.

A cultured Soviet life was ordered, disciplined, and rational, moving to an urban, industrialized rhythm. To establish structure and discipline, commanders commonly imposed daily schedules on their units, denoting just how the typical day was supposed to be spent, as the schedule for I. F. Fedorov's brigade indicates:[178]

0600	reveille
0600–0700	personal hygiene, care of horses
0700–0800	breakfast
0800–0900	cleaning of weapons
0900–1200	military training
1200–1400	personal work
1400–1500	lunch
1600–1800	cultural work
1900–2000	care of horses
2000–2100	dinner
2200–0600	sleep

It is unknown whether Fedorov's partisans followed this routine, but the partisans' day was to be regulated, at least on paper, just as it was on the factory floor or collective farm.

Maintaining good hygiene in the imperial and Soviet eras was also a part of being cultured. In the partisan environment, it was, of course, essential in preventing skin ailments and devastating diseases such as typhus, which easily could decimate an afflicted unit. But good hygiene was also a vital part of some partisans' self-representation to both Soviet authorities and the surrounding population. In an interview immediately following liberation, one commissar proudly related how his partisans maintained their daily personal hygiene: "We washed and shaved. The Germans sometimes portray the partisans as goblins in the woods, but we partisans shaved. If we did not have stones for stropping, then we brought [our razors] to the population, and if we did not have soap for baths, then we used birch twigs. There were baths in the forest and villages. We washed in the baths every week."[179] Another commander reported that German propaganda efforts to convince Soviets that the partisans were "primitive, wild savages" failed because "the population saw the partisans fight the Germans daily and well, and what's more, were dressed better than the Germans and were cleaner."[180] The political benefits of good hygiene to the partisans were clear: cleanliness was akin to Sovietness, as well as being an effective propaganda weapon against the Germans.

During the 1930s, an explicit part of the Stalinist social vision was material prosperity and the acquisition of consumer goods as indicators and rewards of culture and progress, even if the goods to be acquired seemed paltry by Western standards.[181] The partisans also embraced this aspect of Soviet life. Detachments that "lived well" were the envy of others. One partisan exclaimed in his diary during a visit to a neighboring unit, "The 3rd Detachment is the best detachment in the whole brigade. Here all is in perfect order! Here there is a club, a bath, a laundry, a tailor's, a sausage maker and even a home-brew 'factory'!"[182] Emliutin boasted that his partisans in the Briansk partisan region enjoyed electrified dugouts capable of holding up to 300 people and camps equipped with clubs, kitchens, leather factories, and telephones.[183] By claiming to have access to the accoutrements of modern, urban civilization, supported by specialists even in the forest, partisans demonstrated their resourcefulness, their ability to overcome nature, their desire for culture, and their acceptance and idealization of Soviet civilization. These descriptions also stood in sharp contrast to the often miserable living conditions most partisans actually endured, especially for those who could not establish permanent camps in partisan-controlled zones.

What was culture if it did not improve body and mind? Intellectual and physical self-improvements were also essential aspects of the New Soviet Person,[184] and certainly, the partisans were not going to let living in the woods and swamps and fighting the enemy prevent them from accomplishing these goals. In reports, debriefings, and memoirs, partisans cited reading and discussing literary works, including the Tolstoys (Lev seems to have been preferred over Aleksei), Turgenev, the obligatory Pushkin, Shakespeare, Dickens, socialist realist classics such as *How the Steel Was Tempered*, and newspapers sent from the mainland.[185] Wall newspapers and regular newspapers were also published, even though obtaining supplies (ink, type, paper) was often extremely difficult. News relayed from Moscow by radio would usually be printed in newspapers, which would then be distributed throughout the unit and the surrounding territory. Wall newspapers, a particular form of Soviet journalism, reported events and happenings in individual units. One partisan described the special effect of the wall newspaper on new recruits: "The wall newspaper. A modest, ordinary bit of Soviet life. And it immediately became clear—he had come home, to Soviet land."[186] Wall newspapers also gave partisans a chance to tell their own stories, in which they became the heroes of their own narratives.

Partisans also took time for lighthearted amusements, including cards, chess, and volleyball.[187] Drama and music were also favorite pastimes. When Starinov visited V. A. Begma's complex in Rivne, he noted that the camp was filled with partisans playing instruments, leading him to exclaim, "This isn't a formation—it's an orchestra! You're living well, Vasiliy Andreyevich!" Begma replied, "Can't complain, we can't complain. The people need cultural recreation."[188] Partisan acting and musical ensembles did the forest

Partisans listen to a report from a newspaper, 1943. (Credit: Minaeva Collection)

camp circuit, traveling from detachment to detachment, including one particularly popular group that specialized in "partisan jazz."[189] Dances were
also held, and on one special night, A. F. Fedorov taught his men the fox-
trot.[190] Even the occasional movie was shown for a few fortunate units, including *Aleksandr Nevskii*, *The Destruction of the Germans at Moscow*, and
(of course) *Chapaev*.[191] These activities mirrored those of the Soviet Arctic
explorers, who also enjoyed Soviet culture, including volleyball, in the frozen
wastes, further illustrating that the partisans were equal to these most famous
and audacious heroes of the 1930s.[192]

In presenting themselves as cultured, not only did partisans follow the
conventions of Soviet discourse established in the interwar years, they also
justified partaking in culture as a patriotic act. Thus, A. E. Kleshchov, a secretary of the Pinsk underground obkom, told Central Staff officials that despite German efforts to portray the partisans as "wild, uncultured," the partisans as "representatives of our people were able, even in the farthest rear of
the enemy, to construct their daily life properly."[193] In a letter to her brother,
a rank-and-file partisan made the connection between culture and Soviet patriotism even more explicit: "That despite everything, we live in the forest, we
live culturally, joyfully. We have a gramophone: the guys are happy, vigorous.

They go against the Germans happily, with songs, with the words 'For Stalin, For the Motherland, Forward.'"[194] Another claimed that he and his fellows lived so well that even a Frenchman serving with the Germans defected to the Soviets when he "saw in how civilized a manner we lived and worked," thus giving Western European validation to the supremacy of Soviet culture, even in the woods.[195] At the same time, the Stalinist materialist definition of culture enabled elite (and sometimes even rank-and-file) partisans to enjoy the good life as a characteristic of cultured Soviet citizens. What supposedly separated them from partizanshchina was their adherence to Stalinist discipline: their acceptance of authority and hierarchy; their fulfillment of their obligations and duties to the collective; and their maintenance of purity in mind, body, and deed. Indeed, one commander contrasted the undisciplined detachments with better-organized ones, stating that the latter were "most cultured and have the best relations towards the peasants."[196]

Some partisans, however, believed that culture and the intellectualism and urban elitism inherent in it were antithetical to the partisan ethos. The popular appeal of the partisan was not based on culture and discipline but rather on a romantic style that reflected a unique, vibrant, and dashing personality.[197] Some Soviet partisans explicitly rejected the notion that culture belonged in the forest. Thus, Vershigora cited a partisan scout who "knew *Anna Karenina* and other artistic works by heart, but [who] was a poor scout."[198] Crude behavior and swearing, viewed by many as the true marks of a partisan, were so prevalent that this vulgarity became known among them as "partisan chic."[199] Male partisans took particular pride in telling off-color anecdotes around the campfire, although they themselves were shocked when even less modest partizanki told stories, as one male partisan recalled, "that would make your ears burn."[200] Some partisans rejected the importance of shaving and the usual clean-shaven Soviet visage (with allowance for a heavy mustache or a trim goatee), and they joked that they would only shave their beards when the Red Army recaptured specific cities. One song, "The Partisan Beard," celebrated facial hair as a mark of distinction.[201] Even regional commander and NKVD official A. P. Gorshkov disputed the importance of culture in the rough-and-tumble partisan world and rejected the equation of culture with military effectiveness and discipline: "The partisan can curse, he can express himself in ways that show his lack of culture and lack of self-control, but I can declare, with a feeling of complete responsibility, that there was not one case when my orders regarding military activities were not fulfilled or were in any way questioned."[202]

That Soviet partisan views toward culture could embrace those held by

Kleshchov, on the one hand, and Gorshkov, on the other, indicates the flexibility and ambiguity of both the partisans' social vision and Stalinist definitions of culture. Of course, many societies strive toward material acquisition and comfort, but for the Soviet Union, this was an explicit purpose for its existence. Partisans who rejected self-representations of being cultured stayed closer to the romantic partisan ideal, but they couched their patriotism and loyalty in their heartfelt dedication to the rodina and ferocity in combat. Those who referred to themselves as cultured were at odds with important elements of the partisan ethos and maintained that they continued to live a Soviet life under the most adverse conditions. Yet in so doing, they legitimated enjoying the luxuries of the good life while portraying themselves as Soviet patriots. Thus, these partisans could use official notions of culture to embrace elements of the partisan ethos while simultaneously deflecting any accusations of engaging in partizanshchina.

It is also interesting to note that the records are remarkably silent about religion in the partisan units. The regime had suppressed religious practice, with varying degrees of intensity, throughout its history. However, the war years saw a resurrection of religion sanctioned by the state, as the Soviet regime sought to mobilize the population and to counteract German efforts to use religious sentiments to win hearts and minds. Senior members of the Orthodox Church, including Metropolitan—later Patriarch—Sergii, spoke to the occupied territories on Gosradio, calling on Soviet citizens to "help God" by helping the partisans to free the Soviet land.[203] Officials also instructed partisans to reach out to religious communities and leaders to join the national resistance.[204] However, the partisans said little about religion in their own reports or in postwar interviews and memoirs. It is possible that they feared that such activities would eventually be punished by Soviet authorities and that this information went unreported as a consequence. It is also possible that most partisans simply did not practice religion, either because of a lack of clergy or simply out of a lack of belief. It is important to remember that many of the partisans were quite young, and having been raised in a Soviet environment, they tended to be indifferent or hostile to religion.[205] There may be no atheists in foxholes, but there is little available evidence to suggest that there was strong religious belief in the partisan camps.

Sports, musical performances, telling stories around the campfire, and other unit happenings, whether cultured or not, were also critical to the creation of a viable and functioning community. These events helped the partisans bond with each other and the unit. One member of a partisan musical troupe recalled, "The poems and songs were probably bad, but they were sung to melodies long familiar to all, therefore they were successful since all new songs were topical, and touched everyone, exciting feelings and thoughts."[206] These songs boosted morale and strengthened the partisans' identity with their cause. Even tales told around the campfire not only provided psychological benefits but also enabled veterans to give impromptu lectures and tips to wide-eyed newcomers and familiarize them with partisan life and unit traditions.[207]

Culture in the partisan movement thus had multiple meanings. On one level, culture could be acquired or rejected, depending on the idiom the individual partisan wanted to follow. On another level, adherence to Soviet cultural norms, in the broadest meaning, could instill a stronger sense of discipline and self-control in the detachments. On a deeper level, culture served as a means to connect the partisans with the larger Soviet community on the other side of the front. Some hoped to show that by upholding Soviet culture, they remained true citizens reproducing the Soviet community under the most extreme conditions. Being cultured and living well was more than self-improvement: it was a patriotic act that heightened one's feelings toward Soviet society at large and gave significance to what otherwise would be mundane actions. At the same time, establishing a "Soviet" cultural regime, whether as a ruse or sincerely, did allow, conveniently, for an alternative form of the fabled good life, while seeming to curb the most wild and extreme aspects of the partisan ethos. In this sphere, at least, partisans seeking to fulfill the apparently contradictory aims of living the partisan ethos *and* proving their loyalty to the Soviet cause could literally have their cake and eat it, too.

CELEBRATIONS BEHIND ENEMY LINES

A fundamental part of Soviet culture as it developed in the 1930s was the celebration of holidays and the marking of significant historical and yearly events, which were used to promote a stronger sense of identity with the Soviet state.[208] It was these public rituals that provided the partisans with their greatest opportunities to identify with their units, the movement, and the regime itself. Partisans celebrated two types of holidays: those associated with their unit and national holidays linked to the Soviet state.

Important events in a unit's life included the anniversary of its founding, the swearing of a partisan oath, and the awarding of medals and orders. Partisans proudly traced their unit's origins and its subsequent achievements in unit journals, histories, chronicles, and oral tales.[209] Unit anniversaries celebrated the community's continued survival, noted its past accomplishments, and were usually marked by triumphal meetings, concerts, and dramatic performances.[210] Even units with questionable pasts celebrated their anniversaries. The "For Soviet Belarus" Partisan Brigade traced its origins, in part, to the Sergei Partisan Detachment, which had eventually mutinied against the brigade command and was subsequently disbanded. Nevertheless, the brigade celebrated the Sergei Detachment's founding, with the approval of A. V. Romanov, a main target of the mutiny, because the detachment had been a "pioneer of the partisan movement in the Dretun'-Idritsi-Bokrovichi territory."[211] These celebrations reinforced the unit's identity and its own particular traditions, especially among the detachment's newer members.[212]

These symbolic events in a unit's history often coincided with national holidays. Many units used national holidays as the appropriate occasions to announce the reestablishment of Soviet power in their district, to receive or unveil unit banners, and to take partisan oaths, making such a day a "double holiday" by linking communal and national commemorations and thereby imbuing it with even greater significance.[213] For example, Red Army units, such as Smolensk Oblast's "Twenty-fourth Anniversary of the Red Army" Partisan Regiment, composed primarily of okruzhentsy, were formally established on that highly symbolic day.[214]

Prewar holiday rituals were often reproduced at these times. Just as Soviet workers in the 1930s engaged in socialist competitions and endeavored to break production records to celebrate important national holidays, so, too, did the partisans compete, but their competitions involved attempting to kill the largest number of Germans or derailing the most trains.[215] The winners of these competitions might receive better rations or the honor of guarding the detachment banner.[216] To Soviet officials and many partisan political officers, it was of the utmost importance that the traditional Soviet holiday rituals of attending meetings, talks, reports, and parades and listening to Stalin's holiday radio address were observed, when possible.[217] Just as in peacetime, partisans dressed in their holiday finery to mark whatever occasion they were celebrating, although the conditions of partisan life limited their sartorial splendor.[218] As one partisan recalled, the parade for one Red Army Day celebration was marred because "in truth the [parade] did not look entirely seemly, because everyone was in threadbare clothes, in bast-shoes, in rags, but nevertheless everyone was cheerful."[219]

In peacetime, Soviets had used official holidays and celebrations for their own agendas, particularly for relaxing, partying, and blowing off steam.[220] The partisans continued this practice. One Leningrad partisan remarked that the only evening her detachment relaxed was on New Year's night in 1944. She and her comrades built a bonfire, "fixed our hair and danced to the tune of a captured harmonica."[221] Whenever possible, holidays were marked with increased rations, a wider variety of food, and perhaps even the distilling of home-brew alcohol if the partisans were especially fortunate. In fact, these events often became excuses for excessive eating and drinking, another chance to live the good life of the partisan ethos while ostensibly fulfilling their patriotic duty.[222] Thus, a commissar in Koliada's complex told historians about his unit's celebration of the October Revolution. Although he mentioned in passing the fashioning of a red flag from a kerchief, he spent much more time describing the partisans' efforts to distill moonshine, ending with the assertion, "No one was drunk, but no one was bored either."[223] Such markings of national holidays clearly show the primacy of personal over official political goals, but they also helped build a sense of community through mutual enjoyment and celebration, which in turn was vital to maintaining unit cohesion. Hence, Romanov of the "For Soviet Belarus" Brigade ordered that a scheduled dance continue even though nearby German troops threatened to attack. As he informed partisan officials, "This was not a romantic decision, but an objective reality of the distinctive piquancy of partisan life and activities."[224]

Not surprisingly, holidays were sites of confrontation between the occupiers and the occupied. Wearing their best clothes on Soviet holidays was a relatively easy and safe form of protest and resistance for civilians.[225] Germans used Soviet holidays to symbolize the victory of the New Order by launching antipartisan operations, spreading anti-Soviet propaganda, and conducting genocide, as occurred on 7 November 1941 when the first *Aktion* ("action," with connotations of anti-Jewish violence) in the Minsk ghetto took place.[226] For their part, partisans marked holidays by conducting sabotage operations or sometimes merely firing what little artillery or rockets they had in the Germans' direction. On May Day 1943, Germans in one Belorussian village used the holiday to conduct meetings and distribute leaflets. Several partisans infiltrated these meetings and distributed their own leaflets, thus subverting the Germans' intentions of using the May Day celebrations to display the dominance of German power.[227]

The celebration of national holidays gave partisans and civilians alike an opportunity to reaffirm their links with the broader Soviet community or, on a more personal level, to reestablish emotional ties with loved ones at the front or in the Soviet rear area. Many partisans felt physically and emotionally cut off, not only from their family and friends on the other side of the lines but also from their past connections to the Soviet Union.[228] For one partisan commander, the celebration of Soviet holidays was an important indication of normality and showed that the partisans continued to live "a full Soviet life."[229] Moreover, by celebrating unit and national holidays jointly, partisans linked their own local community to the broader national one, in the process strengthening, even if inadvertently, their relationship to the larger society and state.

The celebration of Soviet holidays reveals additional ambiguities. Partisans did celebrate holidays according to standard Soviet practices. These rituals, for many citizens, had lost their ability to inspire or perhaps were even rejected in peacetime, but their performance in occupied territory gave them new meaning and significance; rather than just being empty acts, they became significant forms of resistance and patriotism and implicitly lent fresh legitimacy to the Soviet regime in the hearts and minds of its celebrating citizens. Holidays also gave partisans a chance to get some relaxation from the omnipresent tension and enjoy increased rations, alcohol, dances, and other entertainments.[230] As in the broader understanding of culture, celebrating holidays gave partisans a chance to fulfill their civic obligations and at the same time reaffirm their identities as Soviet citizens and to live the good life, embodying simultaneously both Sovietness and the partisan ethos.

It would seem that a significant tension existed within the partisan movement between dueling visions of living the free and good life, on the one hand, and the precepts of Stalinist society that emerged in the 1930s, on the other. The demand for efficient military organization and the need to allay the suspicions of state authorities helped to establish the Stalinist vision as the dominant one in the partisan movement. Important elements of Stalinism, such as the feeling of security derived from an omnipotent leader, the presence of the Party, and the fear of internal and external enemies, also resonated in the partisan world. Rather than only creating an opportunity for freedom, the war, at least in the occupied territories, also confirmed, for many, essential aspects of the Stalinist worldview and the necessity of Stalinist solutions for particular problems. Given the regime's negative appraisal of the partisan ethos, it had to be suppressed either voluntarily or by force or at least be masked behind officially sanctioned behaviors. Of course, in keeping with this concern, other partisans adhered to Stalinist norms in a purely instrumental way and saw their adherence as a necessity to prevent repression by the state; still others chose to accept some aspects of Stalinism while rejecting others.

The ambiguities present in the Stalinist vision, however, gave partisans some room to pursue particular aspects of the partisan ethos while enabling them to live "Soviet" lives. Social stratification created haves and have-nots, but it also allowed for the upward mobility of some who would have been on the bottom in Stalinist society. The Stalinist materialist definition of culture enabled partisans to live the good life even as they claimed that they were loyal citizens upholding Soviet civilization.

The social dynamics of the partisan community helped engender the personal bonds so necessary for the community's survival and ability to function.[231] Though many elements of Stalinist social practice were quite divisive in their facilitation of political and social stratification, other features, such as commander paternalism, the maintenance of culture and unit "cultural" life, and celebrating holidays, all in an atmosphere of danger, provided venues for forging and strengthening personal bonds within the unit. Even marginalized groups could find partial belonging and acceptance by participating in shared activities and events, so long as the dominant partisans allowed them to do so, and the marginalized suppressed their own counteridentities.

The life-or-death struggle of the war gave the Stalinist vision of society a new power and legitimacy, just as the war gave new legitimacy to the Soviet political and economic system as a whole. The wartime threat transformed banal or even negative features of Stalinism into virtues to be celebrated or at least supported because they were necessary for physical security and because they identified the enactors of Soviet culture as "ours." Although many features of Stalinist society reemerged due, in part, to partisan efforts to satisfy Moscow, their appropriateness to the objective conditions of the partisan war and life in the occupied territories added to their overall legitimacy. The values and societal norms associated with Stalinism, rightly or wrongly, became connected with the values and behaviors that made victory possible. This association was probably even more intense for those partisans desperately seeking to maintain their ties with the unoccupied Soviet Union. Far from discarding or undermining the Stalinist social vision, the war helped to cement many of its attributes to Soviet society.

CONCLUSION:
LIBERATION AND LEGACY

The Red Army's advance through the occupied territories in 1943 and 1944 brought an end to the partisan war, but it did not end the partisans' relationship with the state or their own identities as partisans. For that matter, Soviet authorities did not regard the liberation of the partisan territories as the end of the movement in either a literal or a figurative sense. Some units were ordered to move west ahead of the retreating Germans to the western territories annexed in 1939 and 1940 in order to reinforce the relatively moribund resistance movements there. Approximately ninety detachments, consisting of 20,000 partisans, were dispatched to Poland to combat the Germans and promote Soviet interests, and others groups raided as far away as Slovakia.[1] Many of the partisans in these units were unhappy that their liberation had been delayed. As one recalled, "I had had enough, and most of our men felt the same way. We didn't express our feelings openly, but we could feel in each other the same thought—that we had done our share."[2]

Some units were dispatched farther into Eastern Europe, where they continued to operate until the end of the war, but closer to home, the partisans still had important roles to play in the state's dramatic representation of the war. The critical factor was to ensure that formerly autonomous partisans did not ruin the performance by speaking unauthorized lines.

Two problems arose, both centering on the question of state control and partisan autonomy. First and most immediate was the physical reintegration of the largely independent partisans into the more disciplined and constrained Soviet world. This process was partly facilitated by the partisans' own continuation of peacetime Soviet practices, but their interpretations of Soviet values, behaviors, and institutions could be quite unorthodox. Moreover, their highly prized autonomy certainly did not fit with the stricter regulations of the Red Army. Soviet officials, already suspicious of the guerrillas' reliability, were keenly aware of this deviance. Given these attitudes and behaviors, the reabsorption of the partisans into the greater Soviet community would be difficult at best.

A second concern formed around the tension between official and veteran postwar representations, histories, and memories of the movement. State efforts to promote the partisans as heroic representatives of the Soviet people valorized the former resistance fighters but only so long as their stories reflected the official myth of the war.[3] How would partisan veterans—or, for that matter, all veterans and civilian participants—react when told that their public memories would have to conform to Moscow's dictates?

The problems generated by the "repatriation" of partisans were a microcosm of much larger tensions as millions of Red Army veterans, former POWs, and civilians in the occupied territories were reintegrated into Soviet society. Even ordinary civilians in the Soviet rear area, who had not directly encountered the enemy, had to readjust to peacetime normalcy after the tumult of the war years. For officials, the answer to these problems was relatively simple: reestablish and maintain control over the population and its discourse. Partisan veterans faced the more difficult emotional and psychological challenge of maintaining their identification with a regime that attempted to delegitimate their own wartime experiences and sacrifices.

WHEN VANYA COMES MARCHING HOME: REINTEGRATING THE PARTISANS

The liberation of the occupied territories and the reintegration of the partisans into the Soviet community posed difficult challenges for the regime. What should be done with the hundreds of thousands of armed men and women who had spent the war in enemy-held territory, exposed to different ideologies, and had engaged in a more or less autonomous resistance (albeit one supported by the state) against a totalitarian occupying power? How would the state distinguish those cadres who had proven leadership skills and demonstrated their loyalty to the regime from those whose service was motivated by fear or opportunism or, even worse, those who masked anti-Soviet thoughts and actions under an appearance of loyalty and patriotism?

For their part, the partisans awaited the impending arrival of the Red Army with a mixture of joy, anxiety about last-gasp German attacks, and confusion.[4] For those whose pasts may not have been crystal clean, these feelings were certainly accompanied by dread as they wondered (and, again, with good reason) what their fate would be in Soviet hands. Nevertheless, for most

partisans, the initial contact with the advancing troops was marked by spontaneous celebrations filled with, in the words of one partisan, "great happiness."[5] The reactions of the partisans from the 1st Voroshilov were typical:
they were so happy to see the troops that "every partisan tried to help the Red
Army men in some way: pulling stuck cars, dragging wagons by hand, and
even carrying the soldiers' ammunition."[6]

Amid the joy of liberation was also a trace of sadness. A. P. Gorshkov, the
last commander of the Briansk forest partisans, recalled the reactions of his
fighters when they heard the news that the Red Army had cleared the area of
German troops:

> I gave the order: such and such comrades go to Orel with me, others
> can go home. And here, suddenly, they began to cry. Not only the young
> ones cried, but even those older ones up to 60 years. "Why are you
> crying? Aren't you going to your homes?" They [had been] a collective,
> and when they left, they felt some sort of emptiness, they suddenly were
> struck with horror at being alone. And it would seem that there should
> be elation: they were returning home. The collective had been so
> cemented in two years, that all felt amazingly strong feelings for it.[7]

The emptiness and sadness experienced by so many as their units were disbanded indicated the powerful bonds that had been forged within the community and showed how much the partisan experience had shaped their lives.

Before their demobilization as partisans, the guerrillas often participated
in officially organized celebrations, usually occurring in the district or regional capital, which simultaneously acknowledged their achievements, began the process of postwar mythologizing, and signaled the formal return of
Soviet power.[8]

The celebration marking the liberation of Minsk was one of the most
elaborate. It was organized by the Operations Department of the Belorussian
Staff, although partisan commanders also had some input. One of the stick-
ing points for the commanders was the poor state of the partisans' clothes.
They wanted the Belorussian Staff to provide proper holiday apparel for the
partisans, whose appearance, they felt, would otherwise spoil "the impression
of the triumphant march of the partisans." One staff officer replied that the
Belorussian Staff simply could not provide new uniforms. In any case, he argued, the partisans should march in the same garb they had worn when they
had fought the enemy: "Since the parade will be filmed, it is very important
for history that the partisans look natural in their appearance and not so

dressed up and dandified."⁹ Perhaps aware, too, of the importance of myth-making and the romantic image they would present, the partisans accepted this explanation.

Amid banners and before a tribune, the parade took place on 16 July 1944 in an atmosphere that reminded one observer of prewar celebrations. To another, Minsk resembled "one tremendous partisan camp." Thousands of fully armed partisans from over thirty units marched in columns past the tribune, on which stood Ponomarenko, 3rd Belorussian Front commander I. D. Cherniakhovskii, Central Staff political head and Belorussian Central Committee secretary Malin, Belorussian Staff chief Kalinin, Minsk Obkom secretary V. I. Kozlov, and other official representatives. Partisan Hersh Smolar described it: "None of us had ever seen a parade like this before. Brigade after brigade, men in part-civilian and part-military clothing, carrying the most diverse kind of weapons, some of them 'hand-made' with partisan inventiveness." After the parade, officials, partisans, Minsk civilians, and soldiers gave speeches. In his speech, Ponomarenko noted the heroism of the Belorussian people, the great friendship of Soviet peoples, and the 150,000 Minsk citizens who died under Nazi occupation. He neglected to mention, however, the wholesale destruction of Minsk's Jewish community, which accounted for between 90,000 and 100,000 of the victims there.¹⁰ The celebration indicated that the partisans had truly returned home to the Soviet community. Even as the troops marched, symbolically concluding their war, Soviet authorities continued to shape the movement's image and consequently its official history and memory.

Following their demobilization from their bands, partisans were generally reassigned in accordance with a Central Staff decree from November 1943.¹¹ For most male partisans, liberation did not mean the end of fighting. Party members and many partisan officers, roughly between 10 percent and 15 percent of the demobilized personnel, were assigned to leading posts in the local government and Party administrations. The overwhelming majority of partisans, between 85 percent and 90 percent, were sent to the army, a transition made more difficult by the harsher discipline of the regular military formations.¹² As of 31 August 1944, some 92,000 former partisans were counted in the ranks of the Red Army.¹³

As John Armstrong has noted, the partisan war served as "a testing ground for new leadership personnel."¹⁴ The returning partisans did fill, at least initially, the leadership vacuum throughout liberated lands, often heading district and regional state and Party offices, including raikoms and obkoms.¹⁵ Of the 1,072 Party and Soviet officials in Minsk Oblast in the summer of 1944, over 60 percent (646) were former partisans.[16] In Vinnytsia, former partisans dominated the administration until 1947, but in Ukraine overall, even as late as 1955, approximately 75 percent of regional secretaries and most Central Committee members were guerrilla veterans.[17]

Women also joined reconstruction efforts if their political rank was high enough. Most, however, were simply told to return to civilian life and take up their customary roles. One resistance fighter participated in a partisan parade in Leningrad. On arrival, she and her comrades were told to hand in their weapons. "We turned them over," she recalled, "but we had a very strange, unfamiliar feeling."[18] Another veteran partizanka remembered, "We were told to hand in our weapons and go find ourselves jobs. We could not understand why we had to hand in arms while the war was still going on and Byelorussia alone had been liberated."[19] Partisan commander V. Z. Korzh told his daughters, both of whom had fought in a regular Red Army cavalry unit, "There was a war and you served in it. Now forget about it. I have two pretty daughters . . . You must both study and you must marry."[20] But finding husbands might have been a problem, for the war's demographic impact on the male population was catastrophic and caused a significant gender imbalance, with 13 million more women than men in the Soviet population.[21] Moreover, women who had served in the partisans or the army had another prejudice to overcome. For years after the war, women veterans were customarily confronted by strangers who wanted to know how they earned their medals, insinuating that they received them for granting sexual favors.[22] The respect and autonomy that women had earned as fighters were also coming to an end.

The Soviet press celebrated the partisan leaders now involved in postwar reconstruction, calling them "splendid people" who would rebuild the country just as they resisted the occupiers. In keeping with this tone, one partisan veteran was reported to have reassured the workers of a wrecked machine tractor station (MTS), "I give you [my] word as a partisan, our MTS will be the best in the oblast."[23] An article stated that the same "sharp political vision [and] excellent tempering in combat" meant that the former partisans could overcome any obstacle. Yet the skills and deeds that defined them as partisans, such as sabotage, were remarkably different from those required as rebuilders. This same article reported the criticism by a former commander (now a raikom secretary) of one of his subordinates who had been an expert saboteur during the war but had now failed in an assigned reconstruction task. In what had to be the final reversal of the saboteur as enemy/saboteur as hero theme, the commander exclaimed, "38 enemy trains derailed, and you cannot construct 15 huts!"[24] As this story perhaps unintentionally revealed, derailing trains was relatively simple compared to the complexities of managing reconstruction after such a destructive war. One also wonders whether the irony of having partisans rebuild what they themselves had often destroyed was perceived by these participants and observers.

The regime also relied on selected partisans to replenish the ranks of the security organs and to combat the numerous bandit gangs, so-called false partisans, and Polish and Ukrainian separatist formations that emerged behind Soviet lines in the wake of the Red Army. Central Staff deputy chief General S. S. Bel'chenko sent three groups to the occupied territories in late 1943 to select former members of the security organs and other qualified partisans to serve in the NKVD and police units.[25] Sometimes, whole units (minus their "doubtful elements") were assigned to the NKVD after liberation, such as the 1st and 2nd Voroshilov Detachments, which became the nucleus of the Orel NKVD.[26] As Belorussia was retaken, Bel'chenko was appointed to command partisan, NKVD-NKGB, and Red Army forces against some 300 anti-Soviet and Polish guerrilla groups in the republic, and the last overall commander of the Briansk forest partisans, A. P. Gorshkov, became the chief of the First Department of the Main Directorate for the Struggle against Banditry (GUBB NKVD), the primary agency responsible for the destruction of Ukrainian separatist bands.[27] Gorshkov was joined by many Ukrainian partisans who continued their ongoing war with the separatists, either remaining in their units or as members of reconstituted NKVD squads.[28] The movement, in one manner, had come full circle: just as the NKVD played a leading role in the insurgency's earliest stages, now, at the war's end, the former partisans became a critical part of the security organs' counterinsurgency campaign.

For other partisans, the return of Soviet power had a more ominous note, especially for those who had joined the insurgency late in the war or had murky or ambiguous pasts. As mentioned earlier, the leadership's distrust of the movement, though it had moderated, had never disappeared. With the integration of the partisans back into Soviet society, the regime became consumed with the need to identify the truly loyal Soviet citizens and those they deemed to be collaborators, traitors, and opportunists or even those who were simply apathetic, lest these elements infiltrate and corrupt the community.[29] Ideological unorthodoxy was also a major concern. In contrast to the partisans' earlier preservation of some autonomy from the state, there was little they could do now to escape Moscow's control.

As early as January 1942, with the liberation of the first territories under enemy occupation, Soviet authorities filtered out those citizens suspected of having collaborated with the enemy or violated their military oaths.[30] In April 1943, the security organ SMERSH was established to uncover spies by investigating former POWs, okruzhentsy, and others suspected of anti-Soviet activity who might penetrate Soviet territory.[31] In late September 1943, Ponomarenko ordered all subordinate staffs, working in conjunction with local Party and NKVD organs, to identify and collect information on every partisan in their jurisdictions. Included in the list of questions each partisan had to answer were queries about how and from where the partisan had joined his or her detachment and if he or she had been a German prisoner.[32] Another decree, issued in November 1943, ordered that recent recruits and partisans, about whom no information existed, were to be interrogated by security officials, whereas redefectors were automatically transferred to the jurisdiction of the special organs.[33] These instructions were soon followed by another command to the subordinate staffs to investigate missing weapons. Local officials were warned that this task "has much state significance and the person in charge who shows a lax attitude towards its fulfillment, will be brought to account . . . as for an official crime."[34]

Redefectors and other suspicious types were dispatched to the NKVD or to the punishment battalions of the Red Army. But even those who survived the initial filtration process could not be certain that they were safe. After liberation came a rigorous campaign to purge Party and Komsomol ranks of members who could not prove that they had acted properly under occupation. Reasons for dismissal included staying behind enemy lines without permission, failing to take up arms against the occupier (or even joining a unit late in the war), and destroying a Party card. By 1946, perhaps some 10 percent of Komsomols who had been in occupied territory had been purged from the youth organization.[35] In some areas, such as Vinnytsia, purges removed 80 percent of Communists from the Party, with the majority of the expulsions taking place after April 1946 when the Ukrainian Central Committee set stricter standards for retaining Party membership.[36] It is also possible that the weakening of A. A. Zhdanov's power at the beginning of 1948 was, in part, related to his support of veteran partisans.[37] Overall, between 1945 and 1947, 29.2 percent of all expulsions from the Party were caused by remaining behind in the occupied territories, the second most common reason after corruption.[38] The leadership's increasing concern that suspicious and doubtful people had entered the Party's ranks, reflected in these purges, was part of the general feeling of suspicion and fear, at least in elite circles, that emerged most visibly in the postwar purging of the Leningrad Party apparatus after Zhdanov's death in 1948 (the "Leningrad Affair") and the attacks on intellectuals and Jews manifested in the "anticosmopolitan campaign" and the "Doctors' Plot."[39]

The fate of those caught in the filtration net was especially tragic, particularly after the hardships they had already endured for their country. The example of one such unfortunate, T. M. Glukhovchenko, is illustrative. He had been ordered to Radomyshl' Raion in Zhytomyr Oblast by Zhytomyr Complex commander S. F. Malikov to reestablish Soviet power there. Glukhovchenko destroyed his Party card, no doubt because he realized that if the Germans found it, it would mean his death. Soviet authorities arrested him for this act in 1944 and condemned him to forced labor under armed guard at the NKVD's Special Camp 240 in Stalino Oblast. Working alongside others accused of collaboration, including former police and village elders, Glukhovchenko complained in a letter to his former commander about the harsh treatment and insults he received from his jailers. Outraged that Glukhovchenko and other former resisters were now called traitors to the Motherland by the camp commandant, Malikov in turn wrote to the Ukrainian NKVD and Central Committee. Although his letter sparked an investigation, resulting in the removal of the camp commandant and the improvement of the conditions for the former partisans and officers, they still remained prisoners.[40]

The liberation of the partisan zones finally cemented Moscow's physical control over the movement. Once the partisans came into contact with the concrete manifestations of the regime's power, they had little room to oppose or manipulate it. The fortunate few who had moved into local administration or security work, consisting mainly of the partisan command, now had an opportunity to apply the management and leadership skills they had acquired as partisans and to solidify their position as members of the elite. Their wartime experience had forged within them both a sense of their own autonomy and an understanding of the need for Soviet institutions to maintain harmony and get things done, following the same principles that had seemed to work so well during the war.[41] As for the regime, its simultaneous purging of suspicious elements and employment of partisans in the security services indicated that its ambivalent feelings toward the movement and what it represented persisted. This ambivalence would continue even as the partisans became a cornerstone of the official Soviet mythology of the war.

MEMORY AND ITS DISCONTENTS

The end of the war did not mean the end of the partisans' service to their country, nor did it end their complex relationship with state authorities. The movement became a critical part of the Soviet Union's official myth of the war that the regime used as a source of its own legitimacy. The partisans—or, rather, a sanitized version of them—became mythic heroes but only at the cost of the suppression of many of their actual experiences and memories. Although veterans gloried in the state's promotion of them as heroes, some were also angered at its distorted portrayal of their war experiences. These veterans contested the state's efforts to control the representation of *their* accounts, while otherwise accommodating themselves to the official war myth. An unequal struggle emerged between these partisan veterans and government officials for discursive control over the movement's history and legacy. Consequently, the partisans' struggle for autonomy within the framework of a Soviet identity continued well into the postwar years.

Even before the war had ended, Soviet officials realized the importance of mythologizing the partisan movement. Plans for partisan unit histories were set in motion. The Commission on the History of the Great Patriotic War interviewed major commanders and rank-and-file partisans alike almost immediately after they returned to Soviet lines, and Ponomarenko instructed that "partisan relics" be collected for use in future museums.[42]

However, the initial construction of the postwar myth of the conflict downplayed the role of the army and people in securing the Soviet victory. Rather, it was Stalin, with the help of the Party, who received all the credit. According to this myth, Stalin's military genius defeated the Germans; the Soviet people and even the Red Army were relegated to supporting roles.[43] Projects depicting popular participation in the war effort, such as a volume based on the interviews conducted by the Commission on the History of the Great Patriotic War, were shut down. Even Victory Day was demoted from a state holiday to an ordinary working day.[44]

Paradoxically, the late Stalin era saw the publication of some of the most candid partisan war memoirs until the glasnost era, including Vershigora's *People with a Clean Conscience* (1946) and G. M. Lin'kov's *War in the Enemy's Rear* (1947). The latter exposed, among other things, the animosity between Party members and Red Army soldiers, the fragmentation of the resistance movement, and the use of force (including killing) against unruly commanders.[45]

Vershigora wrote self-consciously from the perspective of an "experienced person" (his term), that is, someone whose personal experiences gave

him the best vantage point from which to write about events.[46] He argued that
the people who had lived through the war had "reflect[ed] a lot. The defenders of the fatherland have the moral right to share with contemporaries these
thoughts . . . Besides the direct conscious use and aesthetic satisfaction, they
could play a significant role in the formulation of the history of the Great
Patriotic War."[47] His position implied that the history of the movement and,
indeed, the war in general belonged to those who participated in it, not to the
official historians and mythmakers.

Despite Vershigora's popularity with the public, his version of the partisan war came under attack from several quarters, including partisan and
army veterans, and from Ponomarenko himself. Red Army veterans criticized
his assessment of several officers who had been cut off behind enemy lines
as cowards and incompetents. Others contended that the relationship Vershigora depicted between Kovpak and his commissar, Rudnev, did not conform to the standard commander-commissar relationship first established in
that canon of socialist realist literature, the Civil War novel *Chapaev*, and
they complained that Kovpak was portrayed as a country bumpkin. And
Ponomarenko, who was regarded by many partisan veterans (and by himself
as well) as the final authority on partisan history, asserted that Vershigora
drew a false picture of the partisan movement when he heroized figures who
were so-called doubtful elements, that is, speculators, opportunists, and former
enemies of the people. Such persons, Ponomarenko argued, were not true Soviet partisans or patriots.[48]

These critics were less concerned about the overall veracity of Vershigora's account than they were about his undermining the official discourse
about the partisan war as subscribed to by various constituents. According
to Ponomarenko, the works of Vershigora and other "experienced people"
"propagandized a petty-bourgeois partisan anarchism, disseminated damaging political views towards the Soviet Army and its officers, Party cadres, and
[made] slanderous fabrications about the Red Army."[49]

Accusations such as these had a decisive effect in the postwar Stalinist
Soviet Union. Vershigora's publication success was the exception rather than
the rule, although he, too, found some of his work suppressed when, in one
piece, his characterization of Ukrainian separatists as "well-organized" and
"staunch" ran afoul of the censors and other partisan veterans.[50] Most partisan veterans who attempted to publish their memoirs found their works suppressed or heavily sanitized. Thus, I. Vergasov's *In the Tavrii Hills* (1949) was
pulled from bookstores and libraries because, according to Party officials, it
contained favorable references to "compromised people" who were later shot

as traitors and because it "did not give an objective illumination of the partisan movement from the Party's point of view."[51] Likewise, partisan commander Dmitrii Medvedev's firsthand accounts were criticized, censored, and suppressed until after Stalin's death for supposedly glorifying Ukrainian nationalists, failing to put the Ukrainian partisan struggle into a larger Soviet context, and relying on the testimony of suspect persons who did not really resist the Germans.[52]

Even famous and powerful conformist writers were compelled to adhere to strict ideological demands, as illustrated in the controversy surrounding Aleksandr Fadeev's 1945 novel *The Young Guard*. While he was head of the Writers Union, Fadeev researched the real-life exploits of a youth resistance group, and his book portrayed its members as young enthusiasts acting without much ideological or practical leadership from Communist authorities. The novel was initially greeted with official acclaim and won a Stalin Prize in 1946. Within two years, however, Fadeev came under sharp criticism in the journal *Culture and Life* and in *Pravda* for failing to depict the Communist Party as the inspiration and leader of the resistance movement. He was forced to rewrite the novel, elevating the Party to the role designated for it in the official discourse.[53]

As part of the de-Stalinization campaign that began soon after Stalin's death in 1953, a major reappraisal of the Great Patriotic War took place. The exclusive Stalinist war myth was replaced by a more inclusive version that conformed to Nikita Khrushchev's reform efforts to mobilize the masses while maintaining complete Party control.[54] The new and improved war myth attempted to reconcile these two aims by heralding the exploits not only of the Communist Party but also of the army and the people. This new war myth—or master narrative, as Nina Tumarkin has called it—remained remarkably consistent from Khrushchev to glasnost, with Stalin's role being the only major variable.[55]

The partisans reemerged as central figures in this new myth of the war. According to the official partisan myth, the Soviet people, under the wise and brave leadership of the Communist Party, engaged in collective acts of resistance against the occupiers. Only members of bourgeois nationalist groups, former kulaks, and the other usual enemies of the people collaborated with the occupation forces. The Party's postwar political legitimacy rested on this leadership role, but at the same time, ordinary Soviet citizens were given key parts to play. Thus, a 1968 memoir by the former head of the Belorussian Staff of the Partisan Movement, P. Z. Kalinin, duly noted the participation of all Soviet social groups and *most* nationalities in order to respond to claims that the partisan forces were composed only of Red Army soldiers.[56]

It might seem, in the context of Khrushchev's de-Stalinization policies, that the legacy of the Soviet partisans would be similar to that of other European resistance movements, as mythic sources for reforming and reshaping the postwar world and specifically as a leading moral force for de-Stalinization. In Europe, the myth of the resistance was that of political, social, and moral reconstruction. The reformist and revolutionary elements in the European resistance opposed not only Nazism, fascism, and collaboration but also much of the entire prewar social and political order. These resisters hoped that their activities would help sweep away the old inequities and hierarchies of European life and lead to a new and egalitarian political, economic, and social community. That they failed to meet many of these objectives, especially in Western Europe, did not diminish the aura surrounding the resistance fighters.[57] In fact, it gave the resisters the even more enduring and romantic dash of fighting for a lost cause.

Just as important as the concrete goals and objectives of the resistance was its symbolic value to European society. The resistance proved that there remained in Europe men and women from all political currents who had the moral courage to oppose dictatorship and defend collective and individual human rights and dignity. The resistance showed that Europe was capable of renewing itself, of arising out of the ashes of war and political oppression with its moral values intact and strengthened. This legacy further contributed to the mystique of the resistance.[58]

In marked contrast, stability and the popular desire to keep the status quo antebellum (that is, after the Molotov-Ribbentrop Pact and before Operation Barbarossa) became the public legacy of the Soviet partisan movement. Unlike the conquered nations of Nazi-occupied Europe, the Soviet regime remained undefeated and continued to wage a military campaign that ultimately crushed Nazi Germany. The partisans fought, so the official myth went, for the retention of the Soviet system with all that this entailed, including the leading position of the Communist Party and the maintenance of the collective farms. The partisans were thus depicted as a political and social rock in the occupied territories that the Nazi tide could engulf but not erode or destroy. Even during the de-Stalinization campaigns of the late 1950s and early 1960s, when Khrushchev attempted to overhaul the Stalinist system, no attempt was made to portray the partisans as representing an anti-Stalinist but still pro-Soviet political alternative. Perhaps this was not surprising, given the risks to the regime's stability such a depiction would have entailed, but neither was there any attempt to provide a more nuanced and complicated account of the partisan struggle.

Instead, the myth of the all-people's war was a vital element in the glue that held the people to the state-constructed narrative. According to the myth, the partisans, united by their hatred for the enemy and their love for the Soviet rodina and ably organized and led by the Communist Party, symbolized the organic class and national unity of the Soviet Union and the effectiveness of the Soviet system. Unity, patriotism, obedience, love of country and people, hatred for enemies—these were the official moral legacies of the partisan movement. This formulation still excluded all those whose stories did not fit the grand narrative, including punished peoples such as Tatars, Chechens, Volga Germans, and even Jews, as well as prisoners of war, members of the punishment battalions, and, of course, collaborators of any stripe.[59] As a result, millions of participants both at the front and in the rear area found their experiences depicted only in artificial, heroized, and mythologized terms, distorting or obliterating their actual experiences. Those who could not be integrated into the official myth were excluded from the new myth and thus also from history.

The lifting of the most overt forms of Stalinist repression and the inclusion of "ordinary people" in the master narrative did open the floodgates for a new wave of memoirs on the war in general and the partisan war in particular. Vershigora's experienced people believed that they were now going to get their say. Such was the tone enunciated by I. D. Vetrov, an organizer of the partisan movement in Pinsk Oblast. Vetrov told a gathering of historians at the Belorussian Academy of Sciences in 1958 that the Stalinist historiography of the partisan war distorted the real truth of the war by failing to include the experiences of individuals engaged in the national struggle.[60] He advised the assembled historians to "write history as our Party demands," which he defined as describing and recognizing the deeds of the actual participants.[61]

In fact, state publishers did recognize the importance of personal stories in creating meaning in the war myth. As the introduction to a collection of partisan memoirs published in 1965 stated: "We will, with special respect and expectation go through these collections, read and get used to the restrained lines of the partisan stories and say to our children: 'Read these pages, think about them—these pages are about the great struggle for the motherland, for the happiness of humanity.'"[62] As a contemporary Western scholar observed: "The theme of a daring band of dedicated young men living robustly in the open air, fighting against terrible odds, and wreaking vengeance on the blackest villains has attracted young people from the days of Robin Hood to the Wild West. Add to this recipe the ingredients of a detective thriller, and an ideal vehicle for indoctrination is at hand."[63]

The use of the war myth for didactic purposes, to tell the story of the Party's and People's heroic struggle, meant that the personal was once again to be subordinated to the master narrative. To Vershigora, Vetrov, and other so-called experienced people, however, the writing of history ideally would be a collaborative effort by historians and participants to establish the one truth about a particular event. The question remained: how was the truth to be found when memories differed from the master narrative? The answer for the veterans was not to be a happy one.

In the mid-1960s, the Institute of the History of the Party attached to the Belorussian Central Committee undertook a massive, three-volume history of the Belorussian underground and partisan movement. The work, conducted by professional historians, relied extensively on archival materials and included extraordinary detail regarding the activities of Belorussian resistance groups. Although some veterans participated in its making, others felt shut out and believed that the scholarly work failed to depict the reality of their war. One resistance veteran, R. N. Machul'skii, a secretary of the underground Minsk Obkom, was so incensed that he sent a letter in 1974 to the first secretary of the Belorussian Communist Party, P. M. Masherov, himself a partisan veteran.

Machul'skii wrote that the partisan war struck a deep emotional chord for the Belorussian people and that he and other veterans were overjoyed that such "scholarly capital work" was being done. He nevertheless criticized those historians who had not been partisans and had not relied on the personal reminiscences of partisan veterans: "I don't want to hide [the fact] that many veterans, including myself, supposed out of sincere expectations that for the writing of such a serious collection . . . scholars would, for explanation, turn to our notes, memoirs, use direct knowledge of the practicalities of the patriotic struggle in the enemy's rear. But alas! This did not happen. Several [historians] decided to rely on the archives and their knowledge."[64] Machul'skii asserted further that many veterans had "spent some time in the archives, and in their memories in order to reflect truthfully on their activities in their description of the history of events."[65] Because the veterans were informed by both direct personal experience and archival knowledge, they were indispensable sources for the truth. In contrast, the historians' archival knowledge of the partisan movement was really a false knowledge: the events and organizations that were supposedly neatly laid out in archival documents did not correspond to the chaos of partisan reality.[66]

If getting history wrong because of honest mistakes was not bad enough, Machul'skii argued, the conscious "falsification" of history was even worse. Thus, he accused historians depicting a German punitive operation against partisans in Vitebsk Oblast of relying on one version of events. Other versions that contradicted the first story were ignored.[67] An outraged Machul'skii wrote, "What is this? Is this a cunning hand or a swindle?" He came to the conclusion that the historians "in several cases consciously misrepresented the facts," sometimes due to personal animosities and feuds.[68]

Machul'skii's anger stemmed from what he believed was the historical establishment's exclusion of him and other veterans. For these veterans, the partisan war experience was *their* war experience; hence, the privilege of telling the story of the partisan war was theirs. Professional historians, outsiders with only book knowledge of these events, were distorting it. For Machul'skii and other veterans, experienced people all, history belonged to those who participated in it, not those who wrote it. Only those who experienced it could know the real truth. Implicit in this argument was that the official historians, tied to the Party's narrative, could only get History wrong.

Even when veterans wrote their own memoirs, they found it difficult to meet the requirements of Soviet censors who demanded that their experiences conform to the narrative of the war myth. Such was the case for A. V. Romanov, the former embattled commissar and commander of the "For Soviet Belarus" Partisan Brigade who, in the late 1960s, evidently attempted to revise his already published memoir, *In the Unconquered Land*, which first appeared in 1962. The editors at the Belarus publishing house rejected Romanov's revisions to the original memoir. Apparently, he failed to place his experiences in a broader historical context while focusing excessively on his own personal tragedies and losses. Furthermore, he did not discuss sufficiently the activities of other underground Party organizations or other partisan units, and he was accused of misrepresenting the command-control apparatus of the partisan movement in Belorussia. Romanov interpreted these criticisms as instructions to change his story to fit the master narrative and to include in it events and phenomena regardless of whether he had experienced them or not.[69]

Archival records suggest that Romanov was a stubborn and abrasive commander, and his written reply to the Belarus editors (a copy of which he sent to Ponomarenko) indicates that neither age nor peacetime had mellowed him. Romanov stated that his memoirs were about *him* and that he could not write about units or organizations of which he had no direct knowledge or experience. If the editors wanted more information about other units, he retorted, let the commanders of those units write their own memoirs. Moreover, he rejected the idea that his memoirs should conform to any artificial narrative, as memoirs were supposed to be based on personal experiences.[70] At the same time, he contended that his personal experiences were shared by the nation: his own losses represented the "tragedy of millions of others" and were therefore relevant to the fight against fascism. Interestingly enough, he defended his characterization of command-and-control structures by citing the then authoritative, six-volume official history of the war.[71]

Romanov then expanded his critique of the Soviet construction of history. He told the editors that "history . . . is composed from folklore, the dissemination of commonplace tales,"[72] thus implying that history, at least in the hands of Soviet historians, did not represent actual truth. These historians were "attempting to kill not only the story of the popular struggle, but primarily, the stories of those who led the participants of this struggle, those who fulfilled the instructions of the Party."[73] When historians changed the facts, he declared, "[they] show[ed] their true selves."[74] Romanov rejected the idea that his personal experiences should conform to any artificial narrative, saying that memoirs were supposed to be based on the experiences of the participants. Evidently, he refused to make the changes necessary for publication, for his revised memoir does not seem to have been published.

Romanov's ordeal in the Soviet publishing world was hardly unique. Even major literary figures were subjected to this deadening censorship and conformity. In 1966, Soviet censors decided not to publish a collection of letters edited by Konstantin Simonov, the doyen of Soviet war novelists, on the grounds that the personalized and individualized material did not take into account the war's big picture. The work also implicitly raised questions about the complicity of the Soviet regime in the disasters of 1941, thereby complicating the Brezhnevite rehabilitation of Stalin.[75]

Similar incidents happened in other venues of commemoration and remembrance. To take one example, the Khrushchev and Brezhnev years saw the opening of scores of museums dedicated to the Great Patriotic War. Visitors at these sites could experience the "relics" of the partisan war, such as weapons, (deactivated) explosives, printing presses, radios, leaflets, uniforms, medals, and banners. However, when a veteran partizanka took a blouse and underclothes made out of parachute silk to one museum, the museum workers, she recalled, "just chuckled, 'Whatever for? Who needs it? What's so heroic about it?'"[76] This small example is telling. Only the "heroic" — that is, items that directly glorified the military victory and the master narrative — was to be remembered: the truly personal and thus the heartfelt objects were discarded as irrelevant to the myth and master narrative. By extension, this meant that the experiences of ordinary people were essentially irrelevant as well. This story also suggests that the gendered hierarchy that prevailed in the movement during wartime continued in the construction of the movement's postwar mythology, as women's roles were carefully tailored to fit the master narrative.

Romanov, the other veterans discussed here, and writers such as Simonov and Grossman were infuriated by the willingness of professional historians to discard their memories in the search for examples that conformed to the war myth. Indeed, the process of distortion and omission in war memoirs contributed to a historical literature that Mark von Hagen has aptly described as "remarkably void of specific context, and of any genuine sense of human agency." Only in fiction, art, and film could the human element and the nuances and paradoxes of the war be investigated, albeit in a limited way.[77]

Of course, when writing their memoirs, veterans suppressed an astonishing number of incidents that contradicted the Party line or, as Catherine Merridale noted, any personal remembrances that were particularly harrowing or that revealed the guilt, panic, filth, stench, and boredom of war.[78] Yet though the veterans, willingly or not, accepted the suppression or creative retelling of many events, the distortion or falsification by others of their own histories that were not so politically sensitive deeply pained them. Perhaps if the historians had been pursuing their own individual research or agendas or if multiple interpretations were permitted, the veterans would not have been so devastated. But these works of official history were fundamental to the construction of the war myth's master narrative, which itself was the crucial legitimating myth of the Communist Party and the postwar Soviet state. When these veterans criticized the historians' treatment of history, they implicitly criticized the regime's depiction of the war and its failure to be true to its own principles. When the truth was ignored or distorted, as one veteran wrote to Ponomarenko in 1974, it was a betrayal of the official slogan, "Nothing is forgotten, no one is forgotten."[79] To recognize that the war myth distorted or falsified their own experiences was to recognize that the government was distorting and falsifying them as well. It is important to remember that Vershigora, Vetrov, Machul'skii, and Romanov were all loyal Party members who had sacrificed much for Soviet victory. If they felt betrayed, then how would non-Party war veterans feel? The result was that even in the discursive realm, the partisans had lost their battle for autonomy even as they were identified and celebrated as key participants in the Soviet Union's victory in the Great Patriotic War. This treatment, of course, was applied to all the participants in the war. They were war heroes, to be sure, but not of the war in which they had actually fought.

What made the regime's suppression and falsification of the war so disheartening to these and other veterans was that so many of them had come to identify so closely with the regime. Although most partisans had sought autonomy from the regime, they also remained, consciously or unconsciously, largely within a Soviet ideological mind-set. Their experiences in the war encouraged them to internalize or at least tacitly accept many of the regime's basic principles, including its ever-present stress on vigilance and its hierarchical, repressive, disciplined, and highly structured version of socialism. What the partisans seemed to want was some autonomy within this political and social order. After the fighting was over, their inability to tell their own story underscored the extent to which the state rejected this possibility, even as it relaxed the most oppressive aspects of Stalinist rule after Stalin's death. This, then, was the gratitude that the veterans received for the enormous sacrifices they made during those terrible years.

MEANINGS OF A PARTISAN WAR

Soviet war mythology affirmed the friendship of peoples and the union of state and society under the leadership of the Party, which defined the basis of the regime's legitimacy. This mythology is quite different from Vasilii Grossman's story of House 6/I, described at the beginning of this book, which metaphorically depicted some of the tensions and conflicts that permeated wartime Soviet society, including the partisan movement. Grossman's soldiers and the partisans ostensibly fought for many of the same reasons: patriotism, freedom, protection of the motherland, hatred of the invaders and avenging of their victims, defense of the Soviet system, and also its opposite, the reform and even rejection of the Soviet system. The divisions emerged in the definitions. What did it mean to be a patriot in the context of the war between Nazi Germany and Stalin's Soviet Union? What did freedom mean? Whose and what motherland was being protected? What Soviet values were to be preserved, and which were to be rejected? Did the fighting and ultimate victory confirm the necessity of the Stalinist social vision, or did it prove the efficacy of autonomous and more egalitarian ideals—albeit within a strictly limited gendered and ethnonational framework—evoked by the followers of the partisan ethos? These queries, taken together, lead to a set of larger and even more complicated questions. What was the meaning of the war to Soviet citizens? How did the war affect the way they understood the Stalinist regime? To address these questions, I will return to the three themes introduced at the beginning of this book: the tension between state control and popular autonomy, the centrality of identities for understanding the war experience, and defining who belonged in the partisan movement.

Soviet leaders, even Ponomarenko, never lost their inherent distrust of the partisans, although the nature of that suspicion changed as the war progressed. Thus, control of the partisans was always the state's primary objective. At first, the mechanism for control relied on limiting the movement to the politically affiliated, a strategy that was unworkable for both demographic and pragmatic reasons. The establishment of a full-fledged partisan administration proved to be a much more successful approach, especially in coordinating and directing partisan operations. The Central Staff was further augmented by other organizations, most notably the Party and the NKVD, whose local organs, often attached to the bands, also provided oversight. Finally, state propaganda attempted to establish discursive control over the movement, thereby defining legitimate and illegitimate partisan behaviors.

The partisan administration not only enhanced state control over the partisans; its relative success also reinforced the legitimacy of the system. The ability of this and other wartime administrations to control the partisans, direct the economy, survive brutal sieges, and defeat an advanced enemy supposedly demonstrated the worth of the prewar system, as Stalin himself observed in a speech in February 1946.[80] And if the system had succeeded in wartime, would it not be even more successful in the less demanding work of peacetime? The answer, of course, was no, largely because, as Martin Malia pointed out, the "system was essentially a political-military mode of social organization" that was "operating in its natural element" in wartime.[81] As Elena Zubkova has observed, it was much easier to point to the real achievement of liberating cities and towns than "to confer a credible concreteness on the idea of building Communism."[82] Thus, the war validated the system, but the system's seeming success in wartime obscured its waste, inefficiency, and inability to manage the complexities of a peacetime economy, in which human and material sacrifices as experienced in war could not be justified.

The conditions of partisan life, with its isolation, need for self-reliance, and small group actions demanding individual initiative, meant that partisans greatly valued their group and individual autonomy. Because they were so vulnerable to both the Germans and the more powerful "friendly" units, they were highly sensitive to threats and took whatever actions they deemed necessary for survival. This in turn meant that partisans at times ignored, circumvented, or even actively disobeyed Soviet authorities. Such behaviors, however, were not uncommon among ordinary citizens, economic managers, and Communist officials, even in the 1930s. Thus, the partisans relied on many of the same strategies for dealing with authorities that they had used in the years preceding the war. At the same time, partisans also realized that these very authorities were needed to prevent disorder in the occupied territories, especially among rival partisan groups. The Central Staff, the Party, and even the NKVD each had important functions that protected the partisans against myriad dangers and enemies, even if the partisans had their own complaints about these institutions. They were even willing to call for help from the regime to suppress rival bands, quite similar to the earlier struggles waged by artists and intellectuals who requested state support to stamp out their opponents. Not only did the partisans follow this familiar pattern but, in asking for state intervention, they also granted Soviet institutions legitimacy in their roles as providers of order and stability.

The formation of partisan identities indicated the ways in which the regime and its citizens both shared common assumptions about the war and differed in how they understood the meaning of certain terms. The state defined identities for two reasons: to portray the partisan war to the Soviet public and to delineate the boundaries of acceptable and unacceptable values and behaviors. The partisans brought to this process their own a priori assumptions about partisan warfare, but even more critically, their experiences behind the lines and their social backgrounds shaped their conceptions of what a partisan ought to be and how a partisan war ought to be fought. The point at which state values and objectives intersected with the partisans' experiences and self-representation was where mutually accepted partisan identities were formed. On this common ground were located public and private emotions and motivations. As Lisa Kirschenbaum has argued, "private values," those of "native place (rodina), home, and family emerged as key constituents of Soviet patriotism."[83] Jeffrey Brooks noted that the media themes that had real meaning for Soviet citizens included honor, patriotism, citizenship, obligation, motivation, and courage. As Brooks put it, "The opening of the public sphere to the emotions and experience of a wider public was part of the national resurgence that brought victory."[84] In short, personal feelings and emotions became recognized as part of the greater war effort. Certainly, for the partisans, the convergence of state and personal motivations and goals bonded them more closely to the regime. Even the state's use of eth-nonational patriotism, within the larger formula of the friendship of peoples, accorded most groups their own special place in the partisan movement and thus further tied the partisans' interests with those of the state.

But the identities formed by the partisans also revealed very real frac-tures in Soviet society and between the government and its citizens. Party-recruited, Red Army, and local partisans articulated general sentiments about the need to adhere to Soviet norms or to the desire to defend the motherland, but what those norms actually were or which motherland was to be defended remained points of contention beneath the surface of supposed agreement. These conflicts were exacerbated by the ambiguity of Soviet discourse, which seemed to endorse contradictory beliefs and practices, allowing the partisans to pursue the good life of the partisan ethos while maintaining the cover of living as cultured Soviet citizens. At the time, the line dividing an officially acceptable partisan identity from partizanshchina was razor thin or even hopelessly blurred, as the complexities surrounding the partisans' role as people's avengers illustrate. In addition, the narrowness of the partisan iden-tities established by Party and Red Army partisans in 1941 and 1942 inhibited the formation of a uniform and inclusive partisan identity. Ethnonational, re-gional, and gender divisions exacerbated tensions further, indicating larger rifts within Soviet society. Soviets may have been bound together by the de-sire to win the war, but the diverse motivations and loyalties that impelled them to fight also tended to fragment them.

Nowhere can these tensions be seen more readily than in an examination of who "belonged" in the movement. Despite rhetoric to the contrary that defined the war as a national all-people's war, Soviet officials at the beginning of the conflict defined membership in the movement as including only the politically active, the local elites, and members of the security services. This was almost a knee-jerk reaction to the dangers posed by invasion and re-flected Moscow's suspicions of its own population, for state authorities be-lieved that in this national emergency, only those with a stake in the system would actually defend it. As the military crisis deepened and as politically unaffiliated civilians and Red Army soldiers joined the movement beginning in 1942, the government realized the political and military advantages to be gained by reformulating policy to encourage all citizens to join the partisans. Thus, Soviet policy in both word and deed truly worked toward a national mobilization, eventually including even those who had earlier betrayed their country. By demonstrating that the citizens in the occupied territories—who were theoretically out of Moscow's reach—voted with their feet and joined the

partisan movement, government leaders could point to the popular legitimacy of the system. The contradictory responses of not trusting the population while simultaneously seeking to mobilize and include it in a national effort have their precedents, for example, in the process of drafting the Stalinist
Constitution of 1936 and the subsequent election campaign for the Supreme
Soviet. Yet the reaching out to former collaborators and suspect nationalities
did signal that the Soviet polity was being reorganized on a more inclusive
basis, at least temporarily. After the liberation and victory, the processes of
filtration, purging, and deportation continued, not to end until Stalin's death.

More limitations to the inclusiveness of the all-people's war doctrine are
evident when the issue is examined from the partisans' perspective. Whatever differences the veteran partisans of 1941 and 1942 had among themselves,
they were slight when compared to the problems many of these individuals
had with the partisans of 1943. The veteran partisans felt these latecomers
were little more than opportunists who had not shown proper patriotism or
staunchness. Beyond that, their ranks also included suspect national minorities who were labeled as either cowards or traitors, and women represented a
further undermining of the movement's military role. Although partisan officials forced the veteran partisans to accept the newcomers into their units,
these individuals were still marginalized. For the Soviet leadership, what was
important was that all citizens participated in the movement, not that they
had equal standing. Thus, the separation of partisan society into unequal
parts roughly replicated prewar social structures: Communists, Red Army
officers, and military and civilian specialists, most of whom were Slavs and
men, composed the upper strata, what might be referred to as the *verkhnye*.
Unskilled and politically unaffiliated men, almost all women, most non-
Slavic national minorities, and all former collaborators comprised the more
numerous lower strata, the *nizkie*. This division of society, with gradations of
power and privilege in each group, also reflected the structure of postwar
Soviet society. That society, though generally more inclusive than its 1930s
predecessor, nonetheless marginalized several particular groups, including
lower-skilled workers and peasants, in whose name the country supposedly
existed. Others, especially suspect nationalities such as Jews, and those accused of actual collaboration with the enemy, such as the Crimean Tatars and
Chechens, were symbolically and even physically excluded from the postwar
Soviet Union. Yet as long as there was a perception that upward mobility and
material improvement were still possible, even the nizkie acquiesced to the
Soviet project.

The story of the partisan movement points to ways that the war may have simultaneously helped to legitimate the Soviet state while also undermining it. Scholars in the past generally agreed that victory enhanced Soviet legitimacy, but until recently, there has been little rigorous examination of this issue.[85] Since the mid-1990s, however, the war and its effects have come under increased scrutiny, with historians debating whether the conflict reinforced the dictatorship or gave rise to de-Stalinization.[86] Much of this debate rests on the extent to which the war experience transformed Soviet citizens either into free-thinking and critical individuals or into a hardened, brutalized population, willing to accept discipline and violence in order to "get things done." A second, related question emerges as well: did the war represent a break with the past, or did it reinforce already existing social values and behaviors?

Certainly, many contemporaries, including veterans, writers such as Grossman, and foreign observers, recalled the war years as a time of relative freedom.[87] For them, the war, with all its horrors, was a liberating experience, enabling Soviets to undergo personal de-Stalinizations in which they came to believe that whether the war was won or lost depended on their own actions.[88] With this evidence in mind, Gennadi Bordiugov argued that people began to think for themselves in the war, to take responsibility for their decisions and their lives.[89] E. S. Seniavskaia, in her social-psychological study of the "front generation," concluded that the crucible of war forged a new Soviet man who was "inclined to take risks, capable of making independent decisions in extreme situations, courageous and decisive"—quite the antithesis of the Stalinist *homo sovieticus* of the 1930s. It was precisely these people, she claimed, who would take the lead for reform during the Khrushchevian "thaw." Thus, the front generation was not only the "generation of victors" but also the "generation of the Twentieth [Party] Congress."[90] The behaviors and values embodied in the partisan ethos were perhaps the most radical expressions of this drive for autonomy. Even partisans who strongly identified with and believed in the regime and its corporate institutions developed and maintained a powerful sense of autonomy and independence from Soviet authorities. But did this desire for autonomy constitute a major change in the relationship between Soviet citizens and the regime?

As George Mosse and Omer Bartov contended in their respective studies of German soldiers in World Wars I and II, the experience of war often lends itself not to liberal democratic beliefs that respect political freedom and the value of human life but rather to their opposite.[91] According to Red Army veteran Lev Kopelev, war led to an acceptance of brutality and the idea that whatever contributed to victory was good, no matter what the action or cost.[92] Other recent studies on the Soviet wartime and postwar experiences have

supported these observations. Elena Zubkova asserted that the war did facilitate the development of a more independent, enterprising, and critical citizenry, yet she also noted that Stalinist notions of threat and danger remained
prominent in postwar years and that Stalin himself was sincerely popular
among veterans.[93]

Most notably, Amir Weiner, in his wartime and postwar study of the Vinnytsia region, rejected the notion of de-Stalinization emerging from the war,
contending that the war experience taught the soldiers who would later become the Party cadres and the transmission belts linking regime and society
that what mattered was order and discipline and that violence and brutality
were part of everyday life.[94] For Weiner, the war was both a culmination of
the Bolshevik Revolution and the final cleansing of anti-Soviet elements. The
drive for purity, which Weiner saw as a defining element of the Revolution,
continued through the war experience, categorizing certain ethnic groups,
most notably Jews, as "irredeemable" and needing to be "excised" from Soviet society. At the same time, Weiner also argued that the war created a decisive break with the past and "forever divided Soviet history into two distinct
phases."[95] He allowed that the war did reinforce some aspects of prewar Soviet life, namely, the endurance of the Communist Party, the continuation of
the social-economic order, and the necessity of purges. But he believed the
changes that resulted, including the possibility that class enemies could be
redeemed while whole ethnic groups were purged and deported and the re-
placement of all other founding and legitimating myths by the Great Patriotic
War, signified the massive transformations that the war had wrought.

Evidence from the present study supports his conclusion that the war did
little to enhance liberal democratic values. But even though Weiner's argument that the war created massive transformations on the Soviet body politic
is compelling, it is also crucial to note the powerful continuities that persisted
from the 1930s into the wartime period and beyond. In the partisans' environment, the war affirmed many of the basic tenets of prewar Stalinist ideology,
with its emphasis on internal and external threats, the dangers of capitalist
encirclement, the need for vigilance and order, the subsequent use of terror to
keep order, and the importance of a powerful and paternal overlord to protect
the community. Even the cult of specialists, the efforts to live in a "modern
cultured" style in the forest, and the celebration of Soviet institutions and
holidays reinforced the Stalinist vision of society. In some cases, prewar practices were consciously incorporated, if only to convince outsiders that the partisans remained loyal Soviets. At times, however, prewar practices seem to
have been unconsciously adopted, indicating the extent to which citizens had

internalized Stalinist norms even if they strongly disliked important elements of the regime, including Stalin himself. Indeed, what mattered was not formal knowledge of Soviet Marxism, of which the partisans were either ignorant or even quite unorthodox in terms of their interpretations, but rather the partisans' internalization and tacit approval of the regime's core values. This internalization contributed to partisans' bonding their interests with or believing in the Soviet state.

Many of these sentiments continued into the postwar era. Interviews of Soviet émigrés conducted in the late 1940s and 1950s indicated that although many ostensibly abhorred the Soviet regime, decrying the arbitrary power and abuses of the secret police, they nonetheless expressed pride in Soviet accomplishments and believed in the necessity of a powerful state, including the existence of a strong, if constrained, secret police, a paternalistic leader and welfare state, and centralized planning. They accepted the legitimacy of a socially stratified society in which "he who works best eats best," so long as opportunities for upward mobility existed.[96] These values were quite similar to those emerging before the war and were later championed by the partisans. And even in the mass protests that arose in the 1950s and 1960s, popular demands often centered on the regime's "betrayal" of its own ideological values as protestors looked to Moscow to solve the problems seemingly caused by corrupt local officials, rather than seeking to overthrow or even radically reform the Communist state itself.[97] Seen from this angle, the war had indeed justified the Soviet system as realized by Stalin.

But even though many prewar values and behaviors persisted into the war years and beyond, the wartime autonomy experienced by partisans, soldiers, and civilians also remained and became embedded in postwar generations. The same postwar studies and surveys that indicated Soviets had come to accept much of the Stalinist social and political order also revealed that these citizens wanted more autonomy in their daily lives.[98] These sentiments were transmitted to and echoed by the young specialists of the Brezhnev generation, who saw the basic social and political system as legitimate even as they condemned the regime's inefficiency, the lack of personal choice and autonomy, and the constraints on professional satisfaction and advancement.[99] Thus, Soviet citizens were willing to accept the social and political order that they associated with victory, but they also hoped that the autonomy they had exercised to help bring this about would continue after the war was over. A significant contradiction therefore developed in Soviet society: its citizens accepted the hierarchal and structured political and social order, yet they also wanted more choice and freedom in their personal and professional spheres, which threatened to undermine the foundations of the Soviet order.

For most citizens, this desire for personal autonomy did not necessarily translate into a quest for political freedom. As one veteran recalled in the 1990s, at a time when Russians were experiencing their greatest political liberty in modern history, "there is a colossal difference between that time and now. We knew our motherland, we knew Stalin, we knew where we were going."[100] There certainly were political implications associated with the drive for autonomy, but this desire seemed to have found its most generalized expression in the voices of young professionals in the 1970s and 1980s who accepted the political status quo while demanding the professional and personal autonomy to fulfill objectives in their careers and personal lives.[101] A contributing factor to the political collapse of the 1980s was the Communist regime's inability to deal with these contradictions in the face of worsening economic and social crises.

The Soviet war experience, of which the partisan movement formed one part, thus generally strengthened values and behaviors that were developing before the war, while facilitating the desire for more autonomy and personal —as opposed to political—freedom. The realities of wartime gave renewed credence to the Stalinist creed and way of doing things. But even as the war pointed to the efficacy of Stalinist values and actions, it also gave soldiers, civilians, and partisans a new sense of their own worth and ability to solve problems. As a result, many citizens internalized a complex set of values that at once contradicted and affirmed many aspects of the Stalinist system, including a new appreciation for the Soviet state and for Stalinism, whose harsh vision and brutality had indeed found its natural home in war.

NOTES

The following acronyms are used throughout the Notes section:

GARF   Gosudarstvennyi arkhiv Rossiiskii Federatsii (State Archive of the Russian Federation, Moscow)

IIAN ORF   Institut istorii akademiia nauk otdel rukopisnykh fondov (Institute of History of the Academy of Sciences, Department of Manuscript Collections, Moscow)

IVMV   *Istoriia vtoroi mirovoi voiny, 1939–1945,* ed. A. A. Grechko and D. F. Ustinov (Moscow: Voenizdat, 1975)

IVOVSS   *Istoriia Velikoi Otechestvennoi voiny Sovetskogo soiuza, 1941–1945,* ed. P. N. Pospelov (Moscow: Voenizdat, 1961–1965)

RGASPI   Rossiiskii gosudarstvennyi arkhiv sotsial'no-politicheskoi istorii (Russian State Archive of Social-Political History, Moscow)

TsDAHOU   Tsentral'nyi derzhavnyi arkhiv hromads'kykh ob'iednan Ukrainy (Central State Archives of Civic Organizations of Ukraine, Kiev)

TsKhDMO   Tsentral'nyi khraneniia dokumentov molodezhnykh organizatsii (Central Repository of Documents of Youth Organizations, Moscow)

TsMVS   Tsentral'nyi muzei Vooruzhennykh Sil (Central Museum of the Armed Forces, Moscow)

USHMM   U.S. Holocaust Memorial Museum

YVA   Yad Vashem Archive

In addition, the following Russian archival abbreviations are used: f. = fond (in English, fond or collection); raz. = razdelenie (division); op. = opis (inventory); d. = delo (file); l. = list (page); ll. = listy (pages); T. or t. (tom) = volume; and Kn. = book.

INTRODUCTION

1. Vasily Grossman, *Life and Fate,* trans. Robert Chandler (New York: Harper & Row, 1987), 419.

2. Ibid., 424–429.

3. John Erickson, *The Road to Stalingrad: Stalin's War with Germany*, vol. 1 (New Haven, Conn.: Yale University Press, 1999), 241.

4. Among the innumerable Soviet histories of the partisan movement, some of the more useful sources are: N. I. Makarov, ed., *Partiinoe podpol'e: Deiatel'nost podpolnykh partiinykh organov i organizatsii na Okkupirovannoi Sovetskii territorii v gody Velikoi Otechestvennoi voiny* (Moscow: Politizdat, 1983); V. E. Bystrov, ed., *Sovetskie partizany: Iz istorii partizanskogo dvizheniia v gody Velikoi Otechestvennoi voiny* (Moscow: Politizdat, 1961); V. N. Andrianov, ed., *Voina v tylu vraga: O nekotorykh problemakh istorii sovetskogo partizanskogo dvizheniia v gody Velikoi Otechestvennoi voiny* (Moscow: Politizdat, 1974); Iu. P. Petrov, *Partizanskoe dvizhenie v Leningradskoi oblasti, 1941–1944* (Leningrad: Lenizdat, 1973); P. K. Ponomarenko, *Vsenarodnaia bor'ba v tylu nemetsko-fashistkikh zakhvatchikov, 1941–1944* (Moscow: Nauka, 1986); A. S. Zalesskii, *V partizanskikh kraiakh i zonakh: Patrioticheskii podvig Sovetskogo krestianstva v tylu vraga, 1941–1944* (Moscow: Sotsial'no-Ekonomicheskoi literatury, 1962), and the relevant sections of the two multivolume histories of the war entitled *Istoriia Velikoi Otechestvennoi voiny Sovetskogo soiuza, 1941–1945* (Moscow: Voenizdat, 1961–1965), and *Istoriia Vtoroi Mirovoi voiny, 1939–1945* (Moscow: Voenizdat, 1973–1982).

5. Restrictions on what could be written about the partisans remained on paper at the former Central Party Archive up to the fall of 1991. When I first opened the directory of materials on the partisan movement, I was confronted with a list of sixteen forbidden subjects, including information on "nationalist" formations, "amoral" partisan behavior, the execution of civilians by partisans, the destruction of enemy hospitals and medical trains by the partisans, disputes between partisan commanders, and hostile relations between partisans and civilians, to name just a few.

6. See, for example, V. A. Zolotarev, ed., *Partizanskoe dvizhenie: Po opytu Velikoi Otechestvennoi voiny, 1941–1945 gg.* (Moscow: Kuchkovo Pole, 2001); Aleksei Popov, *NKVD i partizanskoe dvizhenie: Fakty i dokumenty* (Moscow: OLMA-PRESS, 2003), and *Diversanty Stalina: Deiatelnost' organov Gosbezopasnosti na okkupirovannoi sovetskoi territorii v gody Velikoi Otechestvennoi voiny* (Moscow: Iauza, Eksmo, 2004); B. T. Shumilin, ed., *Istoriia partizanskogo dvizhennia v Rossiiskoi Federatsii v gody Velikoi Otechestvennoi voiny, 1941–1945* (Moscow: Atlantida, 2004); V. I. Boiarskii, *Partizany i armiia: Istoriia uteriannykh vozmozhnostei* (Minsk: Kharvest, 2003).

7. John Armstrong, ed., *The Soviet Partisans in World War II* (Madison: University of Wisconsin Press, 1964), esp. 3–71. This view is also found in Alexander Dallin, *German Rule in Russia: A Study of Occupation Policies*, 2nd ed. (Boulder, Colo.: Westview Press, 1981); Matthew Cooper, *The Phantom War: The German Struggle against the Soviet Partisans, 1941–1944* (London: MacDonald & James, 1979); Brooks McClure, "Russia's Hidden Army," in Franklin Mark Osanka, ed., *Modern Guerrilla Warfare: Fighting Communist Guerrilla Movements, 1941–1961* (New York: Free Press, 1962), 80–99. See also C. Aubrey Dixon and Otto Heilbrunn, *Communist Guerrilla Warfare* (London: George Allen, 1954); Edgar Howell, *The Soviet Partisan Movement, 1941–1944* (Washington, D.C.: Department of the Army, 1956); Alexander Pro-

nin, "Guerrilla Warfare in the German-Occupied Soviet Territories, 1941–1944" (Ph.D. diss., Georgetown University, 1965). For an attempted synthesis of Western and Soviet arguments about the partisan movement, see Leonid Grenkevich, *The Soviet Partisan Movement, 1941–1944*, edited and with a foreword by David M. Glantz (London and Portland, Ore.: Frank Cass, 1999).

    8. John Armstrong, "Introduction," in Armstrong, *The Soviet Partisans*, 40.

    9. Some examples include Truman Anderson, "Incident at Baranivka: German Reprisals and the Soviet Partisan Movement in Ukraine, October–December 1941," *Journal of Modern History* 71, 3 (September 1999): 585–623; Martin Dean, *Collaboration in the Holocaust: Crimes of the Local Police in Belorussia and Ukraine, 1941–1944* (New York: St. Martin's Press, 2000); Alexander Hill, *The War behind the Eastern Front: The Soviet Partisan Movement in North-West Russia, 1941–1944* (New York: Frank Cass, 2005).

    10. See, for example, Jeffrey Burds, "*Agentura:* Soviet Informants Networks in Galicia, 1944–1948," *Eastern European Politics and Societies* 11, 1 (Winter 1997): 89–130, and "Gender and Policing in Soviet West Ukraine, 1944–1948," *Cahiers du Monde Russe* 42, 2–4 (April–December 2001): 279–320; Alfred Rieber, "Civil Wars in the Soviet Union," *Kritika* 4, 2 (Winter 2003): 129–162; Timothy Snyder, *The Reconstruction of Nations: Poland, Ukraine, Lithuania, Belarus, 1569–1999* (New Haven, Conn.: Yale University Press, 2003).

    11. Note that this definition does not include commando or reconnaissance/intelligence units that went behind German lines only for short periods of time.

    12. See, for example, Sarah Davies, *Popular Opinion in Stalin's Russia: Terror, Propaganda and Dissent, 1934–1941* (Cambridge: Cambridge University Press, 1997), 183–187; see also the political jokes recorded in Richard Stites and James von Geldern, eds., *Mass Culture in Soviet Russia: Tales, Poems, Songs, Movies, Plays, and Folklore, 1917–1953* (Bloomington: Indiana University Press, 1995), 212–213, 284–285, 328–330.

    13. Konstantin Simonov, *Days and Nights*, trans. Joseph Barnes (New York: Simon and Schuster, 1945), 65.

    14. There is a vast literature on the European resistance. The following is but a small selection: Istvan Deak, Jan T. Gross, and Tony Judt, eds., *The Politics of Retribution: World War II and Its Aftermath* (Princeton, N.J.: Princeton University Press, 2000); Milovan Djilas, *Wartime*, trans. Michael B. Petrovich (New York: Harcourt Brace Jovanovich, 1977); International Conference on the History of the Resistance Movements, *European Resistance Movements, 1939–1945: First International Conference on the History of the Resistance Movements Held at Liege-Bruxelles-Breedonk, 14–17 September 1958* (London: Pergamon, 1960); International Conference on the History of the Resistance Movements, *European Resistance Movements, 1939–1945: Second International Conference on the History of the Resistance Movements, Milan, 1960* (London: Pergamon, 1964); M. R. D. Foot, *Resistance: An Analysis of European Resistance to Nazism* (London: Eyre Methuen, 1979); Jan T. Gross, *Polish Society under German Occupation: The Generalgouvernment, 1939–1944* (Princeton, N.J.: Princeton University Press, 1979); Stephen Hawes and Ralph White, *Resistance in*

Europe, 1939–1945 (London: Allen Lane, 1975); Jorgen Haestrup, *European Resistance Movements, 1939–1945* (Westport, Conn.: Meckler Publishing, 1981); John Louis Hondros, *Occupation and Resistance: The Greek Agony, 1941–1944* (New York: Pella Publishing, 1983); Tony Judt, ed., *Resistance and Revolution in Mediterranean Europe, 1939–1948* (London: Routledge, 1989); H. R. Kedward, *In Search of the Maquis: Rural Resistance in Southern France, 1942–1944* (Oxford: Clarendon Press, 1993), and *Resistance in Vichy France* (Oxford: Oxford University Press, 1978); Roderick Kedward and Roger Austin, eds., *Vichy France and the Resistance: Culture and Ideology* (London: Croom Helm, 1985); Keith Macksey, *The Partisans of Europe in World War II* (London: Hart-David, MacGibbon, 1975); Mark Mazower, *Inside Hitler's Greece: The Experience of Occupation, 1941–1944* (New Haven, Conn.: Yale University Press, 1993); Henri Michel, *The Shadow War: Resistance in Europe, 1939–1945* (London: Andre Deutsch, 1972); Bob Moore, ed., *Resistance in Western Europe* (Oxford: Berg Publishers, 2000); Werner Rings, *Life with the Enemy: Collaboration and Resistance in Hitler's Europe* (London: Weidenfeld and Nicolson, 1982); John Sweets, *Choices in Vichy France: The French under Nazi Occupation* (Oxford: Oxford University Press, 1986), and *The Politics of Resistance in France (1940–1944): A History of the Mouvements Unis de la Résistance* (DeKalb: Northern Illinois University Press, 1976); Tzvetan Todorov, *A French Tragedy: Scenes of Civil War, Summer 1944*, trans. Mary Byrd Kelly (Hanover, N.H.: University Press of New England, 1996).

15. Sarah Farmer, "The Communist Resistance in the Haute-Vienne," *French Historical Studies* 14, 1 (1985): 89–116.

16. Alexander Werth, *Russia at War, 1941–1945* (New York: Avon, 1964), 651. Italics in the original.

CHAPTER ONE. PUTTING THE PEOPLE INTO "ALL-PEOPLE'S WAR," 1941–1942

1. *Pravda*, 3 July 1941, p. 1. Translated in Joseph Stalin, *The Great Patriotic War of the Soviet Union* (New York: International Publishers, 1945), 15.

2. Ibid.

3. RGASPI, f. 625, op. 1, d. 61, l. 490.

4. V. I. Boiarskii, *Partizany i armiia: Istoriia uteriannykh vozmozhnostei* (Minsk: Kharvest, 2003), 16–26.

5. For an overview of the Cossack myth in the nineteenth century, see Judith Deutsch Kornblatt, *The Myth of the Cossack Hero in Russian Literature* (Madison: University of Wisconsin Press, 1992), 3–20. See also Jeffrey Brooks, *When Russia Learned to Read: Literacy and Popular Literature, 1861–1917* (Princeton, N.J.: Princeton University Press, 1985), 166–213, for a discussion of the image of the bandit in *lubok* literature. See also Richard Stites, *Russian Popular Culture: Entertainment and Society since 1900* (Cambridge: Cambridge University Press, 1992), 13, 17–18, 31.

6. John Erickson, *The Road to Stalingrad: Stalin's War with Germany*, vol. 1 (New Haven, Conn.: Yale University Press, 1999), 241.

7. Orlando Figes, *A People's Tragedy: The Russian Revolution, 1891–1924* (New York: Penguin, 1996), 657–658; Peter Kenez, *Civil War in South Russia, 1919–1920: The Defeat of the Whites* (Berkeley and Los Angeles: University of California Press, 1977), 161–163; Mark von Hagen, *Soldiers in the Proletarian Dictatorship: The Red Army and the Soviet Socialist State, 1917–1930* (Ithaca, N.Y.: Cornell University Press, 1990), 52–55.

8. Boiarskii, *Partizany*, 41–44.

9. Leonid Grenkevich, *The Soviet Partisan Movement, 1941–1944* (London: Frank Cass, 1999), 56.

10. Figes, *A People's Tragedy*, 657–658; Kenez, *Civil War in South Russia*, 161–163; Von Hagen, *Soldiers in the Proletarian Dictatorship*, 52–53.

11. Grenkevich, *The Soviet Partisan Movement*, 52.

12. Ibid., 54–56; Von Hagen, *Soldiers in the Proletarian Dictatorship*, 52–55; Dmitrii Fedotoff White, *The Growth of the Red Army* (Westport, Conn.: Hyperion Press, 1981), 64–65; Figes, *A People's Tragedy*, 583; Kenez, *Civil War in South Russia*, 13–15.

13. Stites, *Russian Popular Culture*, 45.

14. For one example of partisans in popular literature, see Vsevolod Ivanov, "Armored Train 14–69," in Carl Proffer, Ellendea Proffer, Ronald Meyer, and Mary Ann Szporluk, eds., *Russian Literature of the 1920s: An Anthology* (Ann Arbor, Mich.: Ardis, 1987), 151–214.

15. Isaac Babel, *Red Cavalry* (New York: W. W. Norton, 2003); Dmitry Furmanov, *Chapayev* (Moscow: Progress Publishers, 1955); Kornblatt, *The Myth of the Cossack Hero*, 107–125, 165–168; Stites, *Russian Popular Culture*, 44–46; Katerina Clark, *The Soviet Novel: History as Ritual* (Chicago: University of Chicago Press, 1981), 84–88.

16. Mark von Hagen, "The *Levée en Masse* from Russian Empire to the Soviet Union, 1874–1938," in Daniel Moran and Arthur Waldron, eds., *The People in Arms: Military Myth and National Mobilization since the French Revolution* (Cambridge: Cambridge University Press, 2003), 181–182.

17. See, for example, S. S. Kamenev, "Byt' na-cheku," *Sputnik agitatora* 13 (July 1927): 41–48; B. Verkhovskii, *Metodika izucheniia trudiashchegosia naseleniia polosy voennykh deistvii: Posobie dlia kruzhkov samooborony Osoaviakhimi* (Minsk, 1930), 38–40; Colonel I. G. Starinov, *Over the Abyss: My Life in Soviet Special Operations*, trans. Robert Suggs (New York: Ivy Books, 1995), 39. For more on Osoaviakhim, see William Odom, *The Soviet Volunteers: Modernization and Bureaucracy in a Mass Public Organization* (Princeton, N.J.: Princeton University Press, 1973), and Kenneth Slepyan, "The Limits of Mobilization: Party, State and the 1927 Civil Defence Campaign," *Europe-Asia Studies* 45, 5 (1993): 851–868.

18. Boiarskii, *Partizany*, 26.

19. Erickson, *The Road to Stalingrad*, 27–28, 243; *IVOVSS*, 6:272; Starinov, *Over the Abyss*, 51.

20. IIAN ORF, f. 2, raz. 2, op. 4, d. 37, l. 1.

21. Starinov, *Over the Abyss*, 34–41.

22. Erickson, *The Road to Stalingrad*, 27–28, 240–241; Starinov, *Over the Abyss*,

63–65. For more on the expansion, rearmament, and war planning of the Red Army in the 1930s, see Roger R. Reese, *Stalin's Reluctant Soldiers: A Social History of the Red Army* (Lawrence: University Press of Kansas, 1996); Lennart Samuelson, *Plans for Stalin's War Machine: Tukhachevskii and Military-Economic Planning* (New York: St. Martin's Press, 2000); Jacques Sapir, "The Economics of War in the Soviet Union during World War II," in Ian Kershaw and Moshe Lewin, eds., *Stalinism and Nazism: Dictatorships in Comparison* (Cambridge: Cambridge University Press, 1997), 209–216; David M. Glantz and Jonathan House, *When Titans Clashed: How the Red Army Stopped Hitler* (Lawrence: University Press of Kansas, 1995), 6–13; Richard Overy, *Russia's War: Blood upon the Snow* (New York: TV Books, 1997), 79–80.

23. Cited in B. T. Shumilin, ed., *Istoriia partizanskogo dvizheniia v Rossiiskoi Federatsii v gody Velikoi Otechestvennoi voiny, 1941–1945* (Moscow: Atlantida, 2001), 15–16.

24. Cited in Seweryn Bialer, ed., *Stalin and His Generals: Soviet Military Memoirs of World War II* (Boulder, Colo.: Westview Press, 1984), 71.

25. Cited in Robert Conquest, *The Great Terror* (Oxford: Oxford University Press, 1990), 206; Starinov, *Over the Abyss*, 151–152.

26. See Jeffrey Burds, "The Soviet War against 'Fifth Columnists': The Case of Chechnya, 1940–1945," paper presented at the Watson Institute for International Studies, Brown University, 1 February 2005.

27. Starinov estimates that of the 9,000 trained partisan cadres, only 90 survived. However, this figure grossly exaggerates Red Army/NKVD purge mortality rates; Starinov, *Over the Abyss*, 56. See also Aleksei Popov, *Diversanty Stalina: Deiatel'nost' organov Gosbezopastnosti na okkupirovannoi Sovetskoi territorii v gody Velikoi Otechestvennoi voiny* (Moscow: Iauza, Eksmo, 2004), 51–53.

28. I. Tarankanova, "Iz istorii Komissii po delam byvshikh druzhnikov 1905 g., Krasnogvardeitsev i krasnykh partisan (1930–1935 gg.)," manuscript, 15.

29. Conquest, *The Great Terror*, 289; *IVOVSS*, 6:272.

30. IIAN ORF, f. 2, raz. 2, op. 6, d. 11, l. 2; P. K. Ponomarenko, *Vsenarodnaia bor'ba v tylu nemetsko-fashistkikh zakhvatchikov* (Moscow: Nauka, 1986), 30.

31. For an extended discussion of Soviet modernity, see David Hoffmann, *Stalinist Values: The Cultural Norms of Soviet Modernity, 1917–1941* (Ithaca, N.Y.: Cornell University Press, 2003).

32. Jay Leyda, *Kino: A History of the Russian and Soviet Film* (Princeton, N.J.: Princeton University Press, 1983), 314.

33. RGASPI, f. 69, op. 1, d. 28, l. 66; IIAN ORF, f. 2, raz. 2, op. 19, d. 25, l. 7.

34. John Haynes, *New Soviet Man: Gender and Masculinity in Stalinist Soviet Cinema* (Manchester, UK, and New York: Manchester University Press, 2003), 164.

35. Ibid., 163; Marc Ferro, *Cinema and History*, trans. Naomi Greene (Detroit: Wayne State University Press, 1988), 61.

36. Ferro, *Cinema and History*, 66–67.

37. Dmitrii Volkogonov, *Stalin: Triumph and Tragedy*, ed. and trans. Harold Shukman (Rocklin, Calif.: Prima Publishing, 1992), 403–411.

38. *Pravda*, 15 July 1941.

39. *Pravda*, 11 July 1941, p. 3. For other examples of collective farmers' responses, see *Pravda*, 22 July 1941, p. 2, 8 August 1941, p. 2, 26 January 1942, p. 2, 27 January 1942, p. 2; *Krasnaia zvezda*, 16 July 1941, p. 2, 16 September 1941, p. 2, 20 September 1941, p. 4, 3 March 1942, p. 3, 26 March, 1942, p. 3.

40. *Krasnaia zvezda*, 1 November 1941, p. 2.

41. *Pravda*, 6 September 1941, p. 1. See also *Pravda*, 5 August 1941, p. 1, 8 August 1941, p. 2, 23 November 1941, p. 2.

42. *Pravda*, 29 March 1942, p. 3.

43. *Pravda*, 7 August 1941, p. 3.

44. *Krasnaia zvezda*, 18 February 1942, p. 2.

45. Boiarskii, *Partizany*, 176.

46. *Izvestiia TsK KPSS* 6 (1991): 218–220. The document is reproduced in full.

47. *Izvestiia TsK KPSS* 7 (1990): 217–218. The document is cited in full.

48. Ibid.

49. Ibid., italics added.

50. S. V. Stepashin and V. Iampol'skii, eds., *Organy Gosudarstvennoi Bezopasnosti SSSR v Velikoi Otechestvennoi voine: Sbornik dokumentov*, T. 2, Kn. 1, *Nachalo: 22 Iunia–31 Avgusta, 1941 goda* (Moscow: Izdatel'svo Rus', 2002), 375, 417.

51. Alexander Werth, *Russia at War, 1941–1945* (New York: Avon Books, 1964), 168; Overy, *Russia's War*, 205.

52. A. F. Fedorov, *Podpol'nyi obkom deistvuet* (Kiev: Politizdat Ukrainy, 1986), 21–22; IIAN ORF, f. 2, raz. 2, op. 4, d. 47, l. 3; op. 6, d. 14, ll. 1–3; d. 9, ll. 4–9; op. 2, d. 25a, ll. 5–7; RGASPI, f. 69, op. 1, d. 28, ll. 56, 62; d. 1067, l. 198.

53. John Armstrong, "Introduction," in Armstrong, ed., *The Soviet Partisans in World War II* (Madison: University of Wisconsin Press, 1964), 46–47. Another Moscow detachment reported that of its 177 partisans, 69 were members or candidate members of the Party and 24 were Komsomols; K. I. Bukov ed., *Kliatvu vernosti sderzhali: Partizanskoe Podmoskov'e v dokumentakh i materialiakh* (Moscow: Moskovskii rabochii, 1982), 67.

54. V. A. Zolotarev, ed., *Partizanskoe dvizhenie: Po opytu Velikoi Otechestvennoi voiny, 1941–1945 gg.* (Moscow: Kuchkovo Pole, 2001), 36.

55. *IVMV*, 4:56; N. P. Galitskaia and Ia. P. Valuev, eds., *Partizanskaia bor'ba s Nemetsko-fashistskimi okkupantami na territorii Smolenshchiny, 1941–1943* (Smolensk: Smolenskoe knizhnoe izdatel'stvo, 1962), 22; Howell, *The Soviet Partisan Movement*, 46; F. I. Il'in and P. T. Tron'ko, eds., *Kievshchina v gody Velikoi Otechestvennoi voiny* (Kiev: Kievskoe oblastnoe khizhnoe-gazetnoe izdatel'stvo, 1963), 103–104; T. I. Arkhipova, ed., *Kurskaia oblast' v period Velikoi Otechestvennoi voiny Sovetskogo soiuza 1941–1945 gg.: Sbornik dokumentov i materialov*, T. 1 (Kursk: Kurskoe knizhnoe izdatel'stvo, 1960), 38–39, 77.

56. Galitskaia and Valuev, *Partizanskaia bor'ba*, 23; R. R. Kruchok, ed., *Vsenarodnoe partizanskoe dvizhenie v Belorussii v gody Velikoi Otechestvennoi voiny: Dokumenty i materialy T. 1* (Minsk: Belarus', 1967), 132–135; T. Lesniak, "Nekotorye voprosy organizatsii i vedeniia partizanskoi bor'by v pervye mesiatsy voiny," *Voenno-istoricheskii zhurnal* 9 (1963): 34.

57. IIAN ORF, f. 2, raz. 2, op. 19, d. 25, l. 5.

58. *Izvestiia KPSS* 9 (1990): 198; Mikhail Orlov, "Brigada Osobogo Naznach-eniia," in A. P. Kovalenko, ed., *Spetszadanie: Voina v tylu vraga (Sbornik)* (Moscow: Izd. MOF "Pobeda 1945 god," 1994), 6–19; Popov, *Diversanty Stalina*, 78–83; Boiar-skii, *Partizany*, 141–145.

59. IIAN ORF, f. 2, raz. 2, op. 6, d. 11, l. 4.

60. Zolotarev, *Partizanskoe dvizhenie*, 138–139. The following breakdown gives a rough idea how the partisans fared by region and by republic. In September 1941, there were 7,200 partisans operating in Belorussia but only 4,518 by January. In Leningrad in 1941, there were between 14,000 and 18,000 partisans but only 1,965 at the beginning of 1942. Ukraine also suffered devastating losses, with over 27,000 partisans reported in September but only 5,000 by January 1942.

61. Popov, *Diversanty Stalina*, 67; John Armstrong and Kurt DeWitt, "Organization and Control of the Partisan Movement," in Armstrong, *The Soviet Partisans*, 85–86. By June 1942, Moscow registered the existence of only 12,000 partisans throughout the whole of Ukraine (almost all of whom had found refuge in the southern reaches of the vast and dense Briansk forest), a reduction of more than 20,000 from 1941; RGASPI, f. 69, op. 1, d. 24, l. 11. Another Central Staff report, composed in March 1943, stated that there were only 3,300 Ukrainian partisans by June 1942; RGASPI, f. 69, op. 1, d. 563, l. 95.

62. See, for example, the articles in *Pravda*, 25 July 1941, p. 2, 2 August 1941, p. 2, 6 September 1941, p. 1, 26 January 1942, p. 2.

63. IIAN ORF, f. 2, raz. 2, op. 9/2, d. 57, l. 1.

64. Fedorov, *Podpol'nyi obkom deistvuet*, 22.

65. Boiarskii, *Partizany*, 191.

66. IIAN ORF, f. 2, raz. 2, op. 6, d. 11, l. 2; Ponomarenko, *Vsenarodnaia bor'ba*, 30. Not until late 1941 or early 1942 did a revised basic partisan field manual appear, *Sputnik partizana*; Werth, *Russia at War*, 649–650.

67. USHMM, 1996.A.169, reel 39 (YVA M-37/1256 – TsDAHOU, f. 62, op. 9, d. 2, l. 5).

68. USHMM, 1996.A.169, reel 1 (YVA M-37/81 – TsDAHOU, f. 1, op. 22, d. 663, ll. 1–2). See also L. G. Dovzhinets and I. Ia. Makukhin, eds., *Sumskaia oblast v period Velikoi Otechestvennoi voiny, 1941–1945: Sbornik dokumentov i materialov (izdanie vtoroe, dopolnenie)* (Kiev, 1988), 8; P. I. Kurbatova, *Smolenskaia partiinaia organizatsiia v gody Velikoi Otechestvennoi voiny* (Smolensk: Smolenskoe kn. Izdatel'stvo, 1958), 4.

69. T. H. Rigby, *Communist Party Membership in the USSR, 1917–1969* (Princeton, N.J.: Princeton University Press, 1968), 251; *IVOVSS*, 2:54.

70. Rigby, *Communist Party Membership*, 233–235.

71. In 1941, western Belorussia accounted for 46 percent of the total Belorussian population but only 21.3 percent of the Belorussian Communists; V. N. Andrianov, ed., *Voina v tylu vraga: O nekotorykh problemakh istorii sovetskogo partizanskogo dvizheniia v gody Velikoi Otechestvennoi voiny* (Moscow: Politizdat, 1974), 26. For more on the impact of the annexations in 1939 and 1940, see Dov Levin, *Fighting Back:*

Lithuanian Jewry's Armed Resistance to the Nazis, 1941–1945, translated from the Hebrew by Moshe Kohn and Dina Cohen (New York and London: Holmes & Meier, 1985), 21–24; Nicholas Vakar, *Belorussia: The Making of a Nation* (Cambridge: Cambridge University Press, 1956), 155–172; Jan T. Gross, *Revolution from Abroad: The Soviet Conquest of Poland's Western Ukraine and Western Belorussia* (Princeton, N.J.: Princeton University Press, 1988).

72. Rigby, *Communist Party Membership*, 230.

73. Fedorov, *Podpol'nyi obkom deistvuet*, 11.

74. IIAN ORF, f. 2, raz. 2, op. 6, d. 27, l. 1; USHMM, 1996.A.196, reel 39 (YVA M-37/1257—TsDAHOU, f. 62, op. 9, d. 3, l. 5).

75. USHMM, 1996.A.169, reel 1 (YVA M-37/70—TsDAHOU, f. 1, op. 22, d. 588, l. 1).

76. Fedorov, *Podpol'nyi obkom deistvuet*, 13.

77. IIAN ORF, f. 2, raz. 2, op. 6, d. 11, l. 3; John Barber and Mark Harrison, *The Soviet Home Front: A Social and Economic History of the USSR in World War II* (London: Longman Group, 1991), 65; Ponomarenko, *Vsenarodnaia bor'ba*, 79; N. I. Makarov, ed., *Partiinoe podpol'e: Deiatel'nost podpolnykh partiinykh organov i organizatsii na Okkupirovannoi Sovetskii territorii v gody Velikoi Otechestvennoi voiny* (Moscow: Politizdat, 1983), 57. The shortage of portable radios was so severe that in October 1941, even General G. K. Zhukov, Stalin's chief military troubleshooter, did not have his own mobile radio; Albert Seaton, *Stalin as Military Commander* (New York: Praeger Publishers, 1976), 127.

78. RGASPI, f. 17, op. 88, d. 481, l. 59.

79. IIAN ORF, f. 2, raz. 2, op. 3, d. 2, l. 2; RGASPI, f. 69, op. 1, d. 25.

80. Stepashin and Iampol'skii, *Organy Gosudarstvennoi Bezopasnosti SSSR*, T. 2, Kn. 1, 409.

81. Boiarskii, *Partizany*, 80–81.

82. IIAN ORF, f. 2, raz. 2, op. 6, d. 11, l.1. In Sumy Oblast, the destruction battalions had at their disposal a mere 73 machine guns, 255 rifles, and 100 grenades for 6,000 members; Dovzhinets and Makukhin, *Sumskaia oblast*, 42–43.

83. RGASPI, f. 69, op. 1, d. 206, ll. 53, 90; d. 1067, ll. 63–68.

84. RGASPI, f. 69, op. 1, d. 215, l. 5; see also Alexander Hill, *The War behind the Eastern Front: The Soviet Partisan Movement in North-West Russia, 1941–1945* (New York: Frank Cass, 2005), 47.

85. TsKhDMO, f. 1, op. 53, d. 11a, l. 61.

86. IIAN ORF, f. 2, raz. 2, op. 4, d. 53, l. 2; RGASPI, f. 69, op. 1, d. 1067, ll. 43, 172; Alexander Dallin, *German Rule in Russia: A Study of Occupation Policies*, 2nd ed. (Boulder, Colo.: Westview Press, 1981), 65, 214; Martin Dean, *Collaboration in the Holocaust: Crimes of the Local Police in Belorussia and Ukraine, 1941–1944* (New York: St. Martin's Press, 2000), 13, 31; Vakar, *Belorussia*, 172; Kruchok, *Vsenarodnoe partizanskoe dvizhenie v Belorussii*, 1:78; *Izvestiia TsK KPSS* 7 (1990): 217; Fedorov, *Podpol'nyi obkom deistvuet*, 12–13. For European examples of this behavior, see H. R. Kedward, *Resistance in Vichy France: A Study of Ideas and Motivations—The Southern Zone, 1940–1942* (Oxford: Oxford University Press, 1978), 218, 229–230; Werner

Rings, *Life with the Enemy: Collaboration and Resistance in Hitler's Europe* (London: Weidenfeld and Nicolson, 1982), 60–62, 73–85; Stephen Hawes, "The Individual and the Resistance Community in France," in Stephen Hawes and Ralph White, *Resistance in Europe, 1939–1945* (London: Allen Lane, 1975), 124–125.

87. Alexander Hill, "The Partisan War in North-West Russia, 1941–1944: A Reexamination," *Journal of Strategic Studies* 24, 3 (September 2002): 39–40; RGASPI, f. 69, op. 1, d. 576, l. 20.

88. Hill, *The War behind the Eastern Front*, 60–61.

89. Ben Shepard, *War in the Wild East: The German Army and Soviet Partisans* (Cambridge, Mass.: Harvard University Press, 2004), 64.

90. See the articles by Hannes Heer, Theo Schulte, Manfred Messerschmidt, and Bernd Boll and Hans Safrian in Hannes Heer and Klaus Naumann, eds., *War of Extermination: The German Military in World War II, 1941–1944* (New York: Berghahn Books, 2000); see also Stephen G. Fritz, *Frontsoldaten: The German Soldier in World War II* (Lexington: University Press of Kentucky, 1995, 58–59, 195–200.

91. Dean, *Collaboration in the Holocaust*, 33–34; Matthew Cooper, *The Phantom War: The German Struggle against the Soviet Partisans, 1941–1944* (London: MacDonald & James, 1979), 83–84, 97–98; Shepard, *War in the Wild East*, 84–85; see also Horst Boog, ed., *Germany and the Second World War*, vol. 4, *The Attack on the Soviet Union* (Oxford: Oxford University Press, 1996), 1217–1219; Omer Bartov, *Hitler's Army: Soldiers, Nazis and War in the Third Reich* (New York: Oxford University Press, 1991), 92.

92. Raul Hilberg, *The Destruction of the European Jews* (New York: Holmes and Meier, 1985), 111–125; Timothy Mulligan, "Reckoning the Cost of 'People's War': The German Experience in the Central USSR," *Russian History/Histoire Russe* 9, 1 (1982): 30; see also Yitzhak Arad, Shmuel Krakowski, and Shmuel Spector, eds., *The Einsatzgruppen Reports* (New York: Holocaust Library, 1989).

93. RGASPI, f. 17, op. 88, d. 480, ll. 77–78; a published version of this document is in Kruchok, *Vsenarodnoe partizanskoe dvizhenie v Belorussii*, 92.

94. RGASPI, f. 69, op. 1, d. 1065, l. 32; d. 1072, ll. 6–8, 29–41.

95. USHMM, RG 22.005M, reel 3 (RGASPI, f. 69, op. 1, d. 347, ll. 25–27).

96. RGASPI, f. 69, op. 1, d. 65, l. 22. These figures do not agree with those produced by postwar Soviet secondary sources, which give much larger numbers. Thus, *Istoriia Velikoi Otechestvennoi voiny Sovetskogo souiza*, T. 2, states that there were over 36,000 partisans operating in Ukraine in the spring of 1942, although the contemporary Central Staff sources I examined state there were only 12,100 partisans there in July 1942. Likewise, *IVOVSS*, T. 3, claims that over 120,000 partisans were active in the occupied Soviet Union in January 1943, whereas Central Staff contemporary sources cite 110,000. The biggest discrepancy lies at the end of 1943, when *IVOVSS* claims a partisan force of over 250,000 partisans, whereas contemporary Central Staff records state there were little more than 181,000 partisans. Regardless of which figures are used, their veracity must be taken with a grain of salt, given the fluidity of partisan war and the difficulty in obtaining any kind of accurate information. The point re-

mains, however, that the partisan movement grew substantially during the period under discussion. See *IVOVSS*, 2:350, and *IVOVSS*, 3:447, 461.

97. RGASPI, f. 69, op. 1, d. 28, l. 37; IIAN ORF, f. 2, raz. 2, op. 2, d. 25a, l. 25.

98. Grenkevich, *The Soviet Partisan Movement*, 201.

99. Christian Streit, "Partisans—Resistance—Prisoners of War," *Soviet Union/Union Sovietique* 18, 1–3 (1991): 267.

100. For example, okruzhentsy composed 28 percent of all partisans in Leningrad, 30 percent in Vitebsk and Mogilev Oblasts, 50 percent in Kalinin Oblast, and between 40 percent and 60 percent in the Orel and Smolensk regions; V. A. Perezhogin, "Iz okruzheniia i plena—v partizany," *Otechestvennaia istoriia* 3 (2000): 29; Grenkevich, *The Soviet Partisan Movement*, 128.

101. Christian Streit, "Soviet Prisoners of War in the Hands of the Wehrmacht," and Theo J. Schulte, "Korück 582," both in Heer and Naumann, 81–91 and 317–320; for prisoners' accounts of this treatment, see Marius Broekmeyer, *Stalin, the Russians, and Their War*, trans. Rosalind Buck (Madison: University of Wisconsin Press, 2004), 145–151.

102. Shepard, *War in the Wild East*, 103–104.

103. A. V. Romanov, *Na zemle nepokorennoi* (Minsk: Belarus', 1962), 138; Dean, *Collaboration in the Holocaust*, 39, 55.

104. IIAN ORF, f. 2, raz. 2, op. 4, d. 125, l. 6; op. 6, d. 12, ll. 47, 48. See also Chapter Four.

105. P. P. Vershigora, *Liudi s chistoi sovest'iu* (Moscow: Moskovskii rabochii, 1946), 49.

106. Ibid., 68.

107. RGASPI, f. 69, op. 1, d. 28, l. 166.

108. Shumilin, *Istoriia partizanskogo dvizheniia v Rossiiskoi Federatsii*, 131.

109. Boog, *Germany and the Second World War*, 1141–1172; Bartov, *Hitler's Army*, 72–80.

110. Karel C. Berkhoff, *Harvest of Despair: Life and Death in Ukraine under Nazi Rule* (Cambridge, Mass.: Belknap Press of Harvard University Press, 2004), 140.

111. Cited in Evgennii Zhirnov, "Na okkupirovannykh territoriiakh," *Kommersant vlast'*, part 2, no. 30 (31 July 2001).

112. Hill, *The War behind the Eastern Front*, 52.

113. Cited in M. I. Koval, "The Nazi Genocide of the Jews and the Ukrainian Population," in Zvi Gitelman, ed., *Bitter Legacy: Confronting the Holocaust in the USSR* (Bloomington: Indiana University Press, 1997), 53. See also Boog, *Germany and the Second World War*, 1189–1244; Dallin, *German Rule in Russia*, 215; Hiroaki Kuromiya, *Freedom and Terror in the Donbas: A Ukrainian-Russian Borderland, 1870s–1990s* (Cambridge: Cambridge University Press, 1998), 251–295; Amir Weiner, *Making Sense of War: The Second World War and the Fate of the Bolshevik Revolution* (Princeton, N.J.: Princeton University Press, 2001), 277–287. For Soviet partisan observations of German occupation policies, see, for example, RGASPI, f. 69, op. 1, d. 164, ll. 31–32; USHMM, RG 22.005M, reel 1 (RGASPI, f. 69, op. 9, d. 14, ll. 26,

30; f. 17, op. 88, d. 134, ll. 13–17; d. 135, ll. 12–13), reel 3 (RGASPI, f. 69, op. 1, d. 741, ll. 39–41).

114. Hill, *The War behind the Eastern Front*, 58–59; Berkhoff, *Harvest of Despair*, 239–252.

115. Truman Anderson, "Incident at Baranivka: German Reprisals and the Soviet Partisan Movement in Ukraine, October–December 1941," *Journal of Modern History* 71, 3 (September 1999): 607–609.

116. USHMM, 1996.A.169, reel 33 (YVA M-37/412—TsDAHOU, f. 62, op. 1, d. 129, ll. 1–6).

117. IIAN ORF, f. 2, raz. 2, op. 2, d. 25a, l. 110.

118. Cited in Berkhoff, *Harvest of Despair*, 224.

119. For a more detailed discussion, see Chapter 2.

120. IIAN ORF, f. 2, raz. 2, op. 9/5, d. 11, l. 12.

121. Hill, *The War behind the Eastern Front*, 145–146.

122. Dean, *Collaboration in the Holocaust*, 146.

123. Stepashin and Iampol'skii, *Organy Gosudarstvennoi Bezopasnosti*, T. 2, Kn. 2, 375–376.

124. *Krasnaia zvezda*, 16–18, 22, and 27 January 1942, and 1, 11–15, and 18–21 February 1942.

125. See Chapter Three.

126. M. M. Kir'ian, A. S. Galitsan, and N. G. Andronikov, eds., *Velikaia Otechestvennaia voina, 1941–1945: Slovar'-spravochnik*, 374–375; Werner G. Hahn, *Postwar Soviet Politics: The Fall of Zhdanov and the Defeat of Moderation, 1946–1953* (Ithaca, N.Y.: Cornell University Press, 1982), 55.

127. Ponomarenko had a bitter rivalry with Khrushchev. In recollections relayed to noted Soviet historian G. A. Kumanev in the 1970s, Ponomarenko sharply criticized Khrushchev's political and personal conduct during and after the war, including when he headed the Soviet Union; see G. A. Kumanev, "Otvety P. K. Ponomarenko na voprosy G. A. Kumanev 2 noiabria 1978 g." *Otechestvennaia istoriia* 6 (1998): 133–134, 148–149.

128. Aleksei Popov, *15 Vstrech s generalom KGB Bel'chenko* (Moscow: OLMA-PRESS, 2002), 165.

129. Starinov, *Over the Abyss*, 297. Bel'chenko attributed Starinov's criticisms, in part, to anger that Ponomarenko never accorded Starinov proper credit for his role in helping to develop the partisan movement, as well as to Starinov's close working relationship with Ponomarenko's rival, Khrushchev; Popov, *15 Vstrech*, 171–172.

130. Memo to Stalin excerpted in *Izvestiia TsK KPSS* 11 (1990): 189.

131. See, for example, Ponomarenko's article "Razgoraetsiia plamia partizanskoi voiny v Belorussii," in *Pravda*, 22 July 1941, p. 2.

132. USHMM, RG 22.005M, reel 1 (RGASPI, f. 17, op. 88, d. 480, ll. 153–160); Memo to Stalin excerpted in *Izvestiia TsK KPSS* 8 (1990): 209–211; Memo to Stalin in *Izvestiia TsK KPSS* 11 (1990): 189.

133. RGASPI, f. 69, op. 1, d. 69, l. 53; Starinov, *Over the Abyss*, 199.

134. RGASPI, f. 69, op. 1, d. 24, ll. 12–13.

135. For a perceptive rendering of the Soviet mood in the summer of 1942, see Werth, *Russia at War*, 384–401.

136. The first apparent use of this formulation occurred in the 1200 broadcast on 12 July 1942; GARF, f. 6903, op. 20, d. 3, l. 479; d. 4, l. 13 (1 August 1942).

137. Andrianov, *Voina v tylu vraga*, 56; Ponomarenko, *Vsenarodnaia bor'ba*, 90. The conference participants included D. V. Emliutin (commander of the United Partisan Detachments of the Briansk forest), G. F. Pokrovskii (commander of the 1st Voroshilov Partisan Detachment), I. S. Gudzenko (commander of the 2nd Voroshilov Partisan Detachment), M. I. Duka (commander of the Briansk City Partisan Detachment), M. P. Romashin (commander of the Briansk Rural Partisan Detachment), I. S. Voropaev (commander of the "Death to Fascism" Partisan Detachment), M. I. Senchenkov (commander of the Stalin Partisan Detachment), V. I. Koshelev (commander of the Chapaev Partisan Detachment), A. N. Saburov (commander of the "Twenty-fourth Anniversary of the Red Army" Partisan Detachment), S. A. Kovpak (commander of the Putivl' Partisan Detachment), I. V. Dymnikov (chair of the district executive committee of the Diat'kovo liberated district), E. S. Kozlov (commander of the Bozhenko Partisan Detachment), M. F. Shmyrev (commander of the 1st Belorussian Partisan Brigade), I. S. Shurman (detachment commissar in the K. S. Zaslonov Partisan Brigade), and A. P. Matveev (first secretary of the Orel Obkom and head of the Briansk Staff of the Partisan Movement). Several other commanders, including A. F. Fedorov and V. I. Kozlov, were also invited to the conference but were unable to attend.

138. RGASPI, f. 69, op. 1, d. 28, l. 14.

139. RGASPI, f. 69, op. 1, d. 28, ll. 83, 143, 145.

140. RGASPI, f. 69, op. 1, d. 28, l. 33.

141. RGASPI, f. 69, op. 1, d. 28, ll. 33, 83, 143, 145.

142. RGASPI, f. 625, op. 1, d. 61, l. 540.

143. RGASPI, f. 689, op. 1, d. 1067, l. 179.

144. IIAN ORF, f. 2, raz. 2, op. 6, d. 14, ll. 12–13. Stalin's attention to details, many of them trivial, was noted by many observers; Volkogonov, *Stalin*, 419–420.

145. Cited in V. A. Perezhogin, "Partizany no prieme u I. V. Stalina," *Otechestvennaia istoriia* 3 (1999): 188.

146. RGASPI, f. 69, op. 1, d. 1067, l. 179.

147. RGASPI, f. 625, op. 1, d. 61, l. 544; Overy, *Russia's War*, 209.

148. RGASPI, f. 69, op. 1, d. 1, ll. 1–16; Starinov, *Over the Abyss*, 296–297.

149. Overy, *Russia's War*, 209–210; Glantz and House, *When Titans Clashed*, 129; Erickson, *The Road to Stalingrad*, 371–372. See also Bernd Bonwetsch, "Stalin, the Red Army, and the Great Patriotic War," in Ian Kershaw and Moshe Lewin, eds., *Stalinism and Nazism: Dictatorships in Comparison* (Cambridge: Cambridge University Press, 1997), 185–207.

150. A. I. Briukhanov, *V shtabe partizanskogo dvizheniia* (Minsk: Belarus', 1980), 31.

151. RGASPI, f. 69, op. 1, d. 3, ll. 12–17.

152. RGASPI, f. 69, op. 1, d. 13.

153. RGASPI, f. 69, op. 1, d. 3, ll. 14–17.

154. Boiarskii, *Partizany*, 165–166.

155. RGASPI, f. 69, op. 1, d. 3, l. 14.

156. RGASPI, f. 69, op. 1, d. 3, l. 14.

157. *IVMV*, 5:288.

158. *Krasnaia zvezda*, 29 September 1942, p. 1.

159. *Pravda*, 14 November 1942, p. 1.

160. Twelve personnel lists from ten detachments and brigades were examined, as well as more general figures produced by the detachments and various partisan staffs. The following units were examined (including date compiled): "Uncle Aleksei" Partisan Brigade, August 1942; 3rd Belorussian Partisan Brigade, Vitebsk, Belorussia, September 1942; Pinsk Partisan Complex, Pinsk, Belorussia, January 1943; I. F. Fedorov Partisan Detachment, Sumy, Ukraine, June 1942; Ivanov Partisan Detachment, Sumy, Ukraine, June 1942; 1st and 2nd Battalions (later the 1st and 2nd Brigades), "Batia" Complex, Smolensk, Russia, March 1942; 1st Kursk Partisan Brigade, Russia, 1943; Kravtsov Partisan Brigade, 25 percent sample, Orel, Russia, September 1943; 1st Voroshilov Partisan Detachment, Orel, Russia, September 1943.

161. RGASPI, f. 69, op. 1, d. 65, l. 22. These figures were compiled by officials in the Operations Department of the Central Staff of the Partisan Movement in February 1944, and they differ dramatically from the scope of the numbers cited in Soviet secondary sources. Central Staff records often did not include units operating under NKVD or Red Army command, nor would they include formations that had not, for whatever reason, registered with partisan staff authorities; see Grenkevich, *The Soviet Partisan Movement*, 231. However, the general trends between the contemporary Central Staff figures and those in published Soviet sources are the same.

162. RGASPI, f. 69, op. 1, d. 29, ll. 24, 36; I. P. Kondranov and A. A. Stepanova, eds., *Krym v period Velikoi Otechestvennoi voiny, 1941–1945* (Simferopol': Tavriia, 1973), 322.

163. RGASPI, f. 69, op. 1, d. 1067, ll. 51, 57.

164. RGASPI, f. 69, op. 1, d. 29, l. 20.

165. Figures derived from *Partizanskoe dvizhenie*, 138–139.

166. Ponomarenko claims that Party members suffered 40 percent higher casualties than non-Party partisans; Ponomarenko, *Vsenarodnaia bor'ba*, 130.

167. See Conclusion.

168. Makarov, *Partiinoe podpol'e*, 132, Ponomarenko, *Vsenarodnaia bor'ba*, 128–129; Earl Ziemke's estimates, based on German intelligence reports, put the percentage at a much lower 5 percent; see Ziemke, "Composition and Morale of the Partisan Movement," in Armstrong, *The Soviet Partisans*, 145.

169. Ponomarenko, *Vsenarodnaia bor'ba*, 128, Ziemke, "Composition and Morale," in Armstrong., *The Soviet Partisans*, 145.

170. See, for example, the Zhytomyr Partisan Complex for 1943–1944, USHMM, 1996.A.169, reel 36 (YVA M-37/820—TsDAHOU, f. 67, op. 1, d. 1, ll.17, 53, 107, 141); the Leningrad region from November 1942 to April 1943, RGASPI, f. 69, op. 1, d. 479, l. 167; d. 480, ll. 112–113, 126–127, 131–132; the Kovpak, Saburov, and Fedorov Complexes in November 1942, RGASPI, f. 69, op. 1, d. 583, ll. 72–73.

171. Ponomarenko, *Vsenarodnaia bor'ba*, 30.

172. Figures cited in Perezogin, "Iz okruzheniia i plene—v partizany," taken originally from RGASPI, f. 69, op. 8, d. 27, l. 31.

173. In a few units, the percentages of Red Army soldiers remained the same despite dramatic growth. See, for example, the Zhytomyr Partisan Complex, which grew from 310 partisans in January 1943 to 4,300 by January 1944, whereas the percentage of Red Army partisans remained at slightly over 80 percent; USHMM, 1996.A.169, reel 36 (YVA M-37/820—TsDAHOU, f. 67, op. 1, d. 1, ll. 17, 53, 107, 147).

174. IIAN ORF, f. 2, raz. 2, op. 22, d. 1, ll. 21–46, 171–177.

175. RGASPI, f. 69, op. 1, d. 1068, ll. 104–105.

176. RGASPI, f. 69, op. 1, d. 29, l. 42.

177. See Chapter Five.

178. V. E. Bystrov, ed., *Sovetskie partizany: Iz istoriia partizanskogo dvizheniia v gody Velikoi Otechestvenno voiny* (Moscow: Politizdat, 1961), 237; *IVOVSS*, 6:256; *IVMV*, 8:156; Ponomarenko, *Vsenarodnaia bor'ba*, 129; Ziemke, "Composition and Morale," in Armstrong, *The Soviet Partisans*, 141–151.

179. V. M. Koval'chuk and A. R. Dzeniskevich, eds., *V tylu vraga: Bor'ba partisan i podpol'shchikov na okkupirovannoi territorii Leningradskoi oblast' 1943: Sbornik dokumentov* (hereafter cited as *V tylu vraga: Leningrad, 1943*) (Leningrad: Lenizdat, 1983), 351; RGASPI, f. 69, op. 1, d. 480, ll. 131–132. The decrease in okruzhentsy no doubt reflects losses in combat, but the splitting off of one of the brigade's detachments to form the 10th Leningrad Partisan Brigade in the fall of 1943 may also account for the reduction of okruzhentsy.

180. Koval'chuk and Dzeniskevich, *V tylu vraga: Leningrad, 1943*, 350. Alexander Hill pointed out that many of the partisans identified as "local" in personnel lists may have been local to the oblast but not necessarily to the districts in which the units were operating; Hill, *The War behind the Eastern Front*, 127.

181. RGASPI, f. 69, op. 8, d. 525; d. 685; d. 871, ll. 3–37, 112–119; d. 497; d. 682; IIAN ORF, f. 2, op. 22, d. 1, ll. 21–46; d. 171–177; Koval'chuk and Dzeniskevich, *V tylu vraga: Leningrad, 1943*, 351.

182. RGASPI, f. 69, op. 8, d. 27, cited in *Velikaia Otechestvennaia: Partizanskoe dvizhenie*, 481.

183. The 5 percent figure is taken from a report on partisan activity in the Karelo-Finnish Republic in January 1942, whereas in Stalingrad, women comprised only 2.4 percent of all partisans when they were initially mobilized; RGASPI, f. 69, op. 1, d. 1066, ll. 18–19; Stepashin and Iampol'skii, *Organy Gosudarstvennoi Bezopasnosti*, T. 3, Kn. 1, *Krushenie 'blitskriga', 1 Ianvia–30 Iunia, 1942 goda* (Moscow: Izdatel'svo Rus', 2002), 77.

184. RGASPI, f. 69, op. 1, d. 1062, l. 5; IIAN ORF, f. 2, raz. 2, op. 2, d. 25a, ll. 31, 114–115; op. 6, d. 54, l. 3.

185. RGASPI, f. 69, op. 8, d. 27, cited in *Velikaia Otechestvennaia: Partizanskoe dvizhenie*, 481. This figure, though not high, is considerably greater than the 2 to 3 percent usually cited in Western works. See, for example, Ziemke, "Composition and Morale," in Armstrong, *The Soviet Partisans*, 147.

186. Ponomarenko, *Vsenarodnaia bor'ba*, 128. Hence, it is conceivable that Ukrainian partisan commanders may have doubted that women could endure the long, rapid marches required in this type of partisan war; IIAN ORF, f. 2, raz. 2, op. 6, d. 20, l. 3.

187. See, for example, the figures from the 2nd, 3rd, and 5th Leningrad Partisan Brigades in April 1943; RGASPI, f. 69, op. 1, d. 480, ll. 131–132.

188. For example, in the Kravtsov Partisan Brigade, operating in Orel at the time of its liberation in September 1943, women partisans equaled 19.5 percent of the detachment's strength; RGASPI, f. 69, op. 8, d. 685, ll. 1–39.

189. In the "Uncle Aleksei" Partisan Brigade as of December 1942, of the 182 women, 37.4 percent were less than 20 years old (compared to 33 percent of the men), 47.3 percent were between 21 and 25 years old (24 percent of men), 4.9 percent were between 26 and 30 years old (14.5 percent of men), and 10.4 percent were over 30 (29 percent of men), whereas in the 1st Voroshilov as of September 1943, 71 percent of the women were 25 years old or younger, compared to 40 percent of the men; RGASPI, f. 69, op. 8, d. 525, d. 682.

190. In a sample of five units (the 1st Voroshilov, the "Uncle Aleksei" Brigade, the 2nd Belorussian Brigade, the Ivanov Detachment, and the I. F. Fedorov Detachment), between 41 percent and 71 percent of the women had political affiliations, compared to 23 percent to 49 percent of the men. In all cases, a higher percentage of women belonged to the Party or Komsomol than men; see RGASPI, f. 69, op. 8, d. 495, d. 682; d. 871, ll. 3–37, 112–119; d. 525.

191. RGASPI, f. 69, op. 8, d. 682.

192. V. M. Koval'chuk and A. R. Dzeniskevich, eds., *V tylu vraga: Bor'ba partisan i podpol'shchikov na okkupirovannoi territorii Leningradskoi oblast' 1944: Sbornik dokumentov* (hereafter cited as *V tylu vraga: Leningrad, 1944*) (Leningrad: Lenizdat, 1985), 274–275.

193. Ponomarenko, *Vsenarodnaia bor'ba*, 128.

194. See the composition of the 4th Detachment of the "Uncle Aleksei" Partisan Brigade, the 2nd Belorussian Partisan Brigade, and the 3rd Belorussian Brigade; RGASPI, f. 69, op. 1, d. 179; op. 8, d. 495; d. 497. In each unit, respectively, 63 percent, 71 percent, and 81 percent of the partisans were Belorussian; 32 percent, 23 percent, and 13 percent were Russian; 2 percent, 2 percent, and 4 percent were Ukrainian; and 3 percent, 3 percent, and 2 percent were of other nationalities.

195. Gross, *Revolution from Abroad*, 4. According to figures reported by the Belorussian Staff in April 1944, 700 Poles fought in the Belorussian partisan force. V. A. Zolotarev and A. S. Emelin, eds., *Russkii arkhiv: Velikaia Otechestvennaia: SSSR i Polsha: 1941–1945: K istorii voennogo soiuza: Dokymenty i materialy* (Moscow: Terra, 1994), 104.

196. RGASPI, f. 69, op. 8, d. 560.

197. Dallin, *German Rule in Russia*, 65; John A. Armstrong, *Ukrainian Nationalism*, 3rd ed. (Englewood, Colo.: Ukrainian Academic Press, 1990), 95, 102–104.

198. RGASPI, f. 69, op. 1, d. 28, ll. 82, 89–90.

199. These figures are taken from Reuben Ainsztein, citing an article in *Pravda*

Ukrainy, 26 May 1967. See Reuben Ainsztein, *Jewish Resistance in Nazi Occupied Eastern Europe* (London: Elek Books, 1974), 382–383.

200. In A. N. Saburov's complex in May 1943, of 3,331 partisans, 1,119 (34 percent) were Ukrainian;, 974 (28.2 percent) were Russian; 716 (21.3 percent) were Belorussian; and the remaining 522 (15.7 percent) were of other nationalities; Z. A. Bogatyr': *V tylu vraga: Boeviia deiatel'nost' soedineniia partizanskikh otriadov pod komandovaniem Geroia Sovetskogo Soiuza A. N. Saburova* (Moscow: Sotsekgiz, 1963), 318.

201. RGASPI, f. 69, op. 8, d. 871, ll. 3–37.

202. Ponomarenko, *Vsenarodnaia bor'ba*, 128.

203. Armstrong, "Introduction," in Armstrong, *The Soviet Partisans*, 44.

204. This disparity is even more striking if one considers that at the time of this tally, the eastern regions of Gomel and Mogilev, both containing substantial partisan forces, had already been liberated and thus were not included in these figures; RGASPI, f. 69, op. 1, d. 65, ll. 156–160.

205. See Chapters Two and Five.

206. IIAN ORF, f. 2, raz. 2, op. 6, d. 12, l. 35.

207. For example, G. S. Amirov, a Red Army politruk from Kazakhstan, became the commissar of the "Twenty-fourth Anniversary of the Red Army" Independent Partisan Regiment operating in Smolensk Oblast; see Amirov, *Nepokorennaia zemlia* (Alma Ata, Kazakhstan, USSR: Kazakhstan, 1975).

208. Kenneth Slepyan, "The Soviet Partisan Movement and the Holocaust," *Holocaust and Genocide Studies* 14, 1 (Spring 2000): 6.

209. Leonid Smilovitsky, "Righteous Gentiles, the Partisans, and Jewish Survival in Belorussia, 1941–1944," *Holocaust and Genocide Studies* 11, 3 (Winter 1997): 317; Lester Eckman and Chaim Lazar, *The Jewish Resistance: The History of Jewish Partisans in Lithuania and White Russia during the Nazi Occupation, 1940–1945* (New York: Shengold, 1977), 84–85; Yitzhak Arad, "Jewish Family Camps in the Forests— An Original Means of Rescue," in Michael Marrus, ed., *The Nazi Holocaust: Historical Articles on the Destruction of the European Jews*, vol. 7, *Jewish Resistance to the Holocaust* (Westport, Conn.: Meckler, 1989), 222.

210. Dov Levin estimates that 81 percent of Lithuanian Jews who tried to reach the partisans did not survive the war; Levin, *Fighting Back*, 176.

211. This transformation will be discussed in more detail in Chapter Five.

212. Ainzstein, *Jewish Resistance*, 309–310, 331, 367, 382–383. Jews composed approximately 10 percent of Korzh's Pinsk Partisan Complex, RGASPI, f. 69, op. 8, d. 560; RGASPI, f. 69, op. 1, d. 562, l. 19.

213. Weiner, *Making Sense of War*, 218.

214. Ainzstein, *Jewish Resistance*, 394; Yitzhak Arad, "The Holocaust of Soviet Jewry in the Occupied Territories of the USSR," *Yad Vashem Studies*, vol. 21 (Jerusalem: Yad Vashem, 1991), 41. After the liberation of Minsk, Hersh Smolar asked the head of the Belorussian Staff's cadres department how many Jews had served in Belorussian detachments. He was told, apparently with a straight face, that the staff kept no statistics on nationality; Smolar, *The Minsk Ghetto: Soviet Jewish Partisans against the Nazis* (New York: Holocaust Library, 1989), 150.

215. RGASPI, f. 69, op. 1, d. 65, l. 11.
216. Bystrov, *Sovetskie partizany*, 604–605.

CHAPTER TWO. BREAD AND BULLETS:
THE CONDITIONS OF PARTISAN SURVIVAL

1. The literature on these policies is far too extensive and well known to warrant extended discussion here. For an extremely helpful historiographical survey and bibliography, see Rolf-Dieter Müller and Gerd R. Ueberschär, *Hitler's War in the East, 1941–1945: A Critical Assessment* (Providence, R.I.: Berghahn Books, 1997), 284–341.
2. See, for example, the collection of essays in Hannes Heer and Klaus Naumann, eds., *War of Extermination: The German Military in World War II, 1941–1944* (New York: Berghahn Books, 2000).
3. Matthew Cooper, *The Phantom War: The German Struggle against the Soviet Partisans, 1941–1944* (London: MacDonald & James, 1979), 44–45, 144; Ben Shepard, *War in the Wild East: The German Army and Soviet Partisans* (Cambridge, Mass.: Harvard University Press, 2004), 48–51; John Armstrong, "Introduction," in John Armstrong, ed., *The Soviet Partisans in World War II* (Madison: University of Wisconsin Press, 1964), 37–38, Theo J. Schulte, "Korück 582," in Heer and Naumann, *War of Extermination*, 315–317; see also Truman Anderson, "Incident at Baranivka: German Reprisals and the Soviet Partisan Movement in Ukraine, October–December 1941," *Journal of Modern History* 71, 3 (September 1999): 585–623.
4. Ben Shepard, "The Continuum of Brutality: *Wehrmacht* Security Division in Central Russia, 1942," *German History* 21, 1 (2003): 60n34.
5. Martin Dean, *Collaboration in the Holocaust: Crimes of the Local Police in Belorussia and Ukraine, 1941–1944* (New York: St. Martin's Press, 2000), 60.
6. Cooper estimated that occasionally the Germans may have had up to 900,000 men at their disposal for rear-area security, but this figure includes supply and construction troops as well as members from the Reich Labor Service whose military worth was dubious at best; Cooper, *The Phantom War*, 145–146. John Armstrong put the effective number of occupation forces at between 200,000 and 250,000 in 1943 and 1944, of whom half were German. This total, however, is probably too low; Armstrong, "Introduction," in Armstrong, *The Soviet Partisans*, 37–38.
7. Shepard, *War in the Wild East*, 76–77, 97–98.
8. Cooper, *The Phantom War*, 64–65; Armstrong, "Introduction," in Armstrong, *The Soviet Partisans*, 18. Decreased German firepower also occurred at the front where the Ostheer underwent a significant "demodernization"; see Omer Bartov, *Hitler's Army: Soldiers, Nazis and War in the Third Reich* (New York: Oxford University Press, 1991), 12–28.
9. See, for example, John Horne and Alan Kramer, "German 'Atrocities' and Franco-German Opinion, 1914: The Evidence of German Soldiers' Diaries," *Journal of Modern History* 66, 1 (March 1994): 1–33; Shepard, *War in the Wild East*, 41–45.
10. Dean, *Collaboration in the Holocaust*, 119–147. For an examination of an

alternative approach to partisan warfare, see Shepard, "The Continuum of Brutality,"
49–81.

11. Cooper, *The Phantom War*, 125–142; Theo J. Schulte, *The German Army and
Nazi Policies in Occupied Russia* (New York: Berg Publishers, 1989), 145–147.

12. Shepard, "The Continuum of Brutality," 76–77.

13. Another attempt to infiltrate a partisan camp by an auxiliary formation pre-
tending to be a Soviet partisan detachment failed when the faux partisans' "commissar" defected and told the Soviets about the upcoming attack; RGASPI, f. 69, op. 1,
d. 748, ll. 36, 129–130.

14. Cooper, *The Phantom War*, 150–161; Armstrong, "Introduction," in Armstrong, *The Soviet Partisans*, 28–31; Shepard, *War in the Wild East*, 122–124; Colin
Heaton, *German Anti-partisan Warfare in Europe, 1939–1945* (Atglen, Pa.: Schiffer
Military History, 2001), 143–155; P. Z. Kalinin, *Partizanskaia respublika* (Minsk: Belarus', 1968), 99.

15. IIAN ORF, f. 2, raz. 2, op. 6, d. 35, l. 10; d. 12, l. 13; RGASPI, f. 69, op. 1, d. 212,
l. 14; David M. Glantz and Jonathan House, *When Titans Clashed: How the Red Army
Stopped Hitler* (Lawrence: University Press of Kansas, 1995), 157.

16. See, for example, RGASPI, f. 69, op. 1, d. 165, ll. 58–77; d. 214, ll. 1–2; d. 1067,
ll. 111–112; d. 1080, ll. 4–11; TsMVS, f. 4/36.415, ll. 11–12; USHMM, RG 22.005M, roll 1
(RGASPI, f. 17, op. 88, d. 134, ll. 18–19); Faye Schulman, *A Partisan's Memoir: Woman
of the Holocaust* (Toronto: Second Story Press, 1995), 179–189.

17. RGASPI, f. 69, op. 1, d. 1082, ll. 6–7.

18. Muromtsev later admitted that referring to Grishin's actions as "desertion"
and "treachery" was perhaps too strong; RGASPI, f. 625, op. 1, d. 61, ll. 763–767.

19. RGASPI, f. 69, op. 1, d. 164, l. 154.

20. IIAN ORF, f. 2, raz. 2, op. 6, d. 12, l. 20; RGASPI, f. 69, op. 1, d. 748, l. 132.

21. RGASPI, f. 69, op. 1, d. 748, l. 132; for excerpts of other letters reflecting the
partisans' mood, see ll. 130–133.

22. RGASPI, f. 69, op. 1, d. 214, ll. 1–2, 16–17; IIAN ORF, f. 2, raz. 2, op. 6, d. 20,
l. 1; Earl Ziemke, "Composition and Morale of the Partisan Movement," in Armstrong,
The Soviet Partisans, 173–175.

23. IIAN ORF, f. 2, raz. 2, op. 9/2, d. 30, l. 15.

24. RGASPI, f. 69, op. 1, d. 1080, l. 47; see also d. 214, l. 16; d. 748, l. 52.

25. IIAN ORF, f. 2, raz. 2, op. 6, d. 20, l. 1; G. F. Krivosheev, ed., *Rossiia i SSSR v
voinakh XX veka: Statisticheskoe issledovanie* (Moscow: OLMA-PRESS, 2001), 452.

26. For a detailed discussion of the debates and practices surrounding German
pacification efforts, see Horst Boog, ed., *Germany and the Second World War*, vol. 4,
The Attack on the Soviet Union (Oxford: Oxford University Press, 1998), 1189–1225;
Anderson, "Incident at Baranivka," 593–596, Bartov, *Hitler's Army*, 89–94; Cooper,
The Phantom War, 37–57, 77–107; Alexander Dallin, *German Rule in Russia: A Study
of Occupation Policies*, 2nd ed. (Boulder, Colo.: Westview Press, 1981), 74–76, 209–213;
Schulte, *The German Army*, passim; Shepard, *War in the Wild East*, passim. For a
comparison of Nazi pacification policies in occupied Greece, see Mark Mazower, *Inside
Hitler's Greece: The Experience of Occupation, 1941–1944* (New Haven, Conn.: Yale

University Press, 1993), 191–200, and for a general overview, see Heaton, *German Antipartisan Warfare.*

27. Cited in Kazimiera J. Cottam, ed. and trans., *Defending Leningrad: Women behind Enemy Lines* (Nepean, Ontario: New Military Publishing, 1998), 58.

28. RGASPI, f. 69, op. 1, d. 14, l. 25.

29. Leo Heiman, "Organized Looting: The Basis of Partisan Warfare," *Military Review* 45, 2 (February 1965): 66; A. S. Zalesskii, *V partizanskikh kraiakh i zonakh: Patrioticheskii podvig Sovetskogo krestianstva v tylu vraga, 1941–1944* (Moscow: Sotsial'no-Ekonomicheskoi literatury, 1962), 207; William Moskoff, *The Bread of Affliction: The Food Supply in the USSR during World War II* (Cambridge: Cambridge University Press, 1990), 29, 42, 44–49.

30. Zalesskii, *V partizanskikh kraiakh i zonakh,* 270.

31. Moskoff, *The Bread of Affliction,* 211.

32. RGASPI, f. 69, op. 1, d. 81, l. 137.

33. RGASPI, f. 69, op. 1, d. 1084, ll. 42, 65; IIAN ORF, f. 2, raz. 2, op. 4, d. 25, l. 9; Moskoff, *The Bread of Affliction,* 128. Of course, soldiers often did not receive this standard ration.

34. RGASPI, f. 69, op. 1, d. 286, l. 42. Some partisans claimed in memoirs, however, that they and others rarely suffered from gastrointestinal maladies; A. A. Tumanian, "Lesnoi gospital'," in N. P. Sudoplatov and A. A. Tumanian, *Zapiski partizanskikh vrachei: O podvigakh medrabotnikov v tylu vraga v gody Velikoi Otechestvennoi voiny* (Tula, USSR: Prioskoe knizhnoe izdatel'stvo, 1989), 226.

35. IIAN ORF, f. 2, raz. 2, op. 6, d. 15, l. 10.

36. RGASPI, f. 69, op. 1, d. 748, l. 47; d. 753, l. 31; d. 474, l. 35.

37. Cited in Cottam, *Defending Leningrad,* 78. The wearing of German uniforms sometimes caused confusion. When D. N. Medvedev, a commander in Ukraine, saw some of S. A. Kovpak's men in German uniforms, he initially believed that he was surrounded on three sides by German units; USHMM, 1996.A.169 (YVA M-37/1177–TsDAHOU, f. 166, op. 2, d. 378, l. 7).

38. RGASPI, f. 69, op. 1, d. 1068, l. 70; f. 625, d. 28, l. 75.

39. RGASPI, f. 69, op. 1, d. 24, ll. 152–154.

40. RGASPI, f. 69, op. 1, d. 29, l. 145; f. 625, op. 1, d. 28, l. 32; TsKhDMO, f. 1, op. 53, d. 252, l. 25; P. P. Vershigora, *Liudi s chistoi sovest'iu* (Moscow: Moskovskii rabochii, 1946), 202.

41. RGASPI, f. 69, op. 1, d. 1062, l. 8.

42. TsKhDMO, f. 1, op. 53, d. 252, ll. 24–25. Some enterprising partizanki fashioned brassieres out of parachute silk; see Svetlana Aleksievich, *War's Unwomanly Face* (Moscow: Progress Publishers, 1988), 60.

43. Ziemke, "Composition and Morale," in Armstrong, *The Soviet Partisans,* 160–161.

44. IIAN ORF, f. 2, raz. 2, op. 6, d. 35, l. 10.

45. RGASPI, f. 625, op. 1, d. 28, l. 9.

46. TsKhDMO, f. 1, op. 53, d. 252, l. 24.

47. Ziemke, "Composition and Morale," in Armstrong, *The Soviet Partisans,* 162.

48. Schulman, *A Partisan's Memoir*, 165–173.

49. *Krasnaia zvezda*, 13 November 1941, p. 4.

50. Cited in Aleksievich, *War's Unwomanly Face*, 217.

51. A. F. Fyodorov, *The Underground Committee Carries On*, trans. L. Stolitsky (Moscow: Foreign Language Publishing House, 1952), 422.

52. RGASPI, f. 69, op. 1, d. 164, ll. 151–152.

53. RGASPI, f. 69, op. 1, d. 28, l. 86; d. 215, l. 15; see l. 46 for a complete listing of medical cases reported by the Diat'kovo brigade's medical department from April 1942 to September 1943.

54. IIAN ORF, f. 2, raz. 2, op. 9/4, d. 7, l. 12. See also Tumanian, "Lesnoi gospital'," in Sudoplatov and Tumanian, *Zapiski partizanskikh vrachei*, 214.

55. IIAN ORF, f. 2, raz. 2, op. 4, d. 117, l. 7.

56. Schulman, *A Partisan's Memoir*, 107–108.

57. Nahum Kohn and Howard Roiter, *A Voice from the Forest* (New York: Holocaust Books, 1980), 118.

58. RGASPI, f. 69, op. 1, d. 180.

59. Kohn and Roiter, *A Voice from the Forest*, 118.

60. N. P. Sudoplatov, "Poka my zhila," in Sudoplatov and Tumanian, *Zapiski partizanskikh vrachei*, 118–121.

61. IIAN ORF, f. 2, raz. 2, op. 4, d. 117, l. 7. The field hospital for the "Batia" Complex in Smolensk Oblast reported that between 1 July and 27 October 1942, of the 477 partisans treated, 221 were evacuated to the rear, 94 were prescribed rest or sent to other hospitals, 146 returned to their units, and 16 died in hospital; RGASPI, f. 69, op. 1, d. 1401, ll. 2–42.

62. Sudoplatov, "Poka my zhila," 132–134; Tumanian, "Lesnoi gospital'," in Sudoplatov and Tumanian, *Zapiski partizanskikh vrachei*, 247–248.

63. RGASPI, f. 69, op. 1, d. 65, l. 223; d. 81, l. 108; d. 212, ll. 71–72; d. 213, ll. 9–13.

64. Schulman, *A Partisan's Memoir*, 167.

65. RGASPI, f. 69, op. 1, d. 1084, l. 51.

66. RGASPI, f. 69, op. 1, d. 1082, l. 24.

67. See the descriptions of daily life in Elena Osokina, *Our Daily Bread: Socialist Distribution and the Art of Survival in Stalin's Russia, 1927–1941*, trans. Kate Transchel and Greta Bucher (Armonk, N.Y.: M. E. Sharpe, 2001). See also Sheila Fitzpatrick, *Everyday Stalinism: Ordinary Life in Extraordinary Times—Soviet Russia in the 1930s* (Oxford: Oxford University Press, 1999), 42–50, 54–62; David Hoffmann, *Peasant Metropolis: Social Identities in Moscow, 1929–1941* (Ithaca, N.Y.: Cornell University Press, 1994), 127–157; Stephen Kotkin, *Magnetic Mountain: Stalinism as Civilization* (Berkeley: University of California Press, 1995), 239–279.

68. V. I. Boiarskii, *Partizany i armiia: Istoriia uteriannykh vozmozhnostei* (Minsk: Kharvest, 2003), 132.

69. RGASPI, f. 69, op. 1, d. 1084, l. 66.

70. Heiman, "Organized Looting," 62.

71. IIAN ORF, f. 2, raz. 2, op. 6, d. 12, l. 7; Heiman, "Organized Looting," 65.

72. IIAN ORF, f. 2, raz. 2, op. 2, d. 25a, l. 115.

73. RGASPI, f. 69, op. 1, d. 1108, ll. 6, 7.

74. RGASPI, f. 69, op. 1, d. 1108, l. 7; see also d. 747, l. 49.

75. IIAN ORF, f. 2, raz. 2, op. 6, d. 27, l. 16; Heiman, "Organized Looting," 67.

76. USHMM, 1996.A.169, roll 37 (YVA M-37/1140—TsDAHOU, f. 166, op. 2, d. 32, l. 5).

77. Amir Weiner, *Making Sense of War: The Second World War and the Fate of the Bolshevik Revolution* (Princeton, N.J.: Princeton University Press, 2001), 74.

78. IIAN ORF, f. 2, raz. 2, op. 4, d. 75, ll. 3–4; op. 6, d. 27, l. 16.

79. RGASPI, f. 69, op. 1, d. 159, l. 22; see also d. 475, l. 69; IIAN ORF, f. 2, raz. 2, op. 2, d. 25a, l. 50.

80. See, for example, Sarah Farmer, "The Communist Resistance in the Haute-Vienne," *French Historical Studies* 14, 1 (1985): 98; Mazower, *Inside Hitler's Greece*, 124–129.

81. IIAN ORF, f. 2, raz. 2, op. 4, d. 75, l. 3; d. 125, l. 3; RGASPI, f. 69, op. 1, d. 585, l. 19.

82. IIAN ORF, f. 2, raz. 2, op. 2, d. 25a, l. 89.

83. IIAN ORF, f. 2, raz. 2, op. 22, d. 4, l. 6.

84. V. T. Shumilin, ed., *Istoriia partizanskogo dvizheniia v Rossiiskoi Federatsii v gody Velikoi Otechestvennoi voiny, 1941–1945* (Moscow: Atlantida, 2001), 134; USHMM, 1996.A.169, reel 1 (YVA M-37/70—TsDAHOU, f. 1, op. 22, d. 588, l. 2). See also the case of Zoia Kosmodem'ianskaia, the famous Soviet partisan heroine. According to Soviet legend, she was one of the many young Komsomols sent behind the lines in December 1941 to destroy German infrastructure. However, she was caught by the Germans while attempting to burn a stable housing German troops and was tortured and hanged. In actuality, her mission meant destruction of the houses and barns of Soviet citizens. According to recent research, it was the local citizenry who turned her over to the Germans, an element left out of the mythology of her Soviet martyrdom; E. S. Seniavskaia, *Frontovoe Pokolenie: Istoriko-psikhologichesskoe issledovanie* (Moscow: Institut rossiiskoi istorii, RAN, 1995), 140–142. See Rosalinde Sartorti's discussion of the mythology surrounding Kosmodem'ianskaia in "On the Making of Heroes, Heroines, and Saints," in Richard Stites, ed., *Culture and Entertainment in Wartime Russia* (Bloomington: Indiana University Press, 1995), 182–190.

85. RGASPI, f. 69, op. 1, d. 19, l. 34.

86. Timothy Mulligan, *The Politics of Illusion and Empire: German Occupation Policy in the Soviet Union, 1942–1943* (New York: Praeger, 1988), 95–96.

87. RGASPI, f. 69, op. 1, d. 180, l. 44.

88. RGASPI, f. 69, op. 1, d. 471, l. 35.

89. RGASPI, f. 69, op. 1, d. 287, ll. 8–9.

90. RGASPI, f. 69, op. 1, d. 1097, l. 6.

91. One *pud* equals approximately 36 pounds.

92. RGASPI, f. 69, op. 1, d. 28, ll. 75–76.

93. A few days later, Stalin heard about Emliutin's cows and also wondered what the United Partisan Detachments was doing with such a large herd. Emliutin told the

vozhd that he had taken them only from the Germans and police, although they had originally belonged to the peasants, and that he had already returned "a significant part"; IIAN ORF, f. 2, raz. 2, op. 6, d. 14, l. 13; V. A. Perezhogin, "Partizany na prieme u I. V. Stalina," *Otechestvennaia istoriia* 3 (1999): 189.

94. RGASPI, f. 69, op. 1, d. 19, l. 34.

95. RGASPI, f. 69, op. 1, d. 1062, l. 17.

96. See Moshe Lewin, "'Taking Grain': Soviet Policies of Agricultural Procurement before the War," in Lewin, *The Making of the Soviet System: Essays in the Social History of Interwar Russia* (New York: Pantheon Books, 1985), 142–177.

97. Zalesskii, *V partizanskikh kraiakh i zonakh*, 213.

98. *Pravda*, 10 March 1943, p. 1.

99. *Pravda*, 1 May 1943, p. 1.

100. RGASPI, f. 69, op. 1, d. 1098, ll. 3–5, 14–18; TsKhDMO, f. 1, op. 53, d. 4, ll. 35–36.

101. GARF, f. 6903, op. 20, d. 14, ll. 273–274 (6 June 1943); d. 15, ll. 106–109 (28 August 1943); d. 15, ll. 128–129 (29 August 1943).

102. In the context of the multiple and interrelated wars fought in the German-occupied territories (the German-Soviet war, the partisan war, and the ethnonational "civil" wars), the definition of *collaborator* requires some discussion. When seen through the eyes of a purely national struggle, those Soviets who sided with the Axis, particularly without compulsion, were clearly collaborators in the usual value-laden meaning of the term. However, when viewed from the prism of nationality politics or from the experience of the repressions of the preceding decades, the term is much more problematic. Should those who lost their families in collectivization, the ensuing famine, or the purges be viewed as traitors if they welcomed and aided the forces they thought were overthrowing what was already known to be a murderous regime? As Jan T. Gross observed, "Collaboration—its logic, its appeal or self-justification, its social base—emerges in each country precisely at the intersection between the occupier's intent and the occupied's perception about the range of options at their disposal." Jeffrey Jones also noted that contemporary Soviets often implicitly distinguished between those who fully collaborated with the Nazi regime and those whose behaviors were "collaborationist," meaning that their actions, such as continuing to teach in a German-controlled school, enabled the occupation regime to function, even if they did not support the occupation itself. Since this study focuses on the war experience of the partisans, however, I will continue to use *collaborator* to identify indigenous people who served the Axis in some capacity, including those who were forced to do so in order to survive, such as former POWs who joined the occupation police often under threat of starvation. In so doing, I do not intend to make moral judgments regarding their participation; immoral and illegal actions that they might have performed in German service are another matter; Jan T. Gross, "Themes for a Social History of War Experience and Collaboration," in Jan T. Gross, Tony Judt, and Istvan Deak, eds., *The Politics of World War II and Its Aftermath* (Princeton, N.J.: Princeton University Press, 2000), 15–35, esp. 26–27; and Jeffrey Jones, "'Every Family Has Its Freaks: Perceptions

of Collaboration in Occupied Soviet Russia, 1943–1948," *Slavic Review* 64, 4 (Winter 2005): 754. See also Gross, *Polish Society under German Occupation: The General-gouvernment, 1939–1944* (Princeton, N.J.: Princeton University Press, 1979), 117–144, and Werner Rings, *Life with the Enemy: Collaboration and Resistance in Hitler's Germany, 1939–1945*, trans. Maxwell Brown John (London: Weidenfeld and Nicolson, 1982), as well as the forum on collaboration in Poland and the Soviet Union during World War II (which included Jones's article): Klaus-Peter Friedrich, "Collaboration in a 'Land without a Quisling': Patterns of Cooperation with the Nazi Occupation Regime in Poland during World War II," John Connelly, "Why the Poles Collaborated So Little—and Why That Is No Reason for Nationalist Hubris," Tanja Penter, "Collaboration on Trial: New Source Material on Soviet Postwar Trials against Collaborators," and Martin Dean, "Where Did All the Collaborators Go," *Slavic Review* 64, 4 (Winter 2005): 711–798.

103. USHMM, RG 22.005M, reel 3 (RGASPI, f. 69, op. 1, d. 450, ll. 2, 7); IIAN ORF, f. 2, raz. 2, op. 6, d. 12, l. 27.

104. USHMM, RG 22.005M, reel 3 (RGASPI, f. 69, op. 1, d. 347, ll. 26, 54).

105. USHMM, 1996.A.169, reel 33 (YVA M-37/459—TsDAHOU, f. 62, op. 1, d. 4, l. 18).

106. RGASPI, f. 69, op. 1, d. 1067, l. 182; Leningrad example cited in Alexander Hill, *The War behind the Eastern Front: The Soviet Partisan Movement in North-West Russia, 1941–1944* (New York: Frank Cass, 2005), 164.

107. TsMVS, f. 4/36.415, l. 5.

108. *Izvestiia*, 26 June 1942, p. 2; *Krasnaia zvezda*, 16 September 1941, p. 2, 2 November 1941, p. 4, 16 November 1941, p. 4; *Pravda*, 23 November 1941, p. 2, 15 December 1941, p. 1, 28 January 1942, p. 2.

109. RGASPI, f. 69, op. 1, d. 206, l. 96; d. 283, l. 2; d. 576, l. 14; d. 1094, l. 2; f. 625, op. 1, d. 10, ll. 10–11; d. 61, l. 91; IIAN ORF, f. 2, raz. 2, op. 4, d. 13, l. 11.

110. RGASPI, f. 69, op. 1, d. 1072, l. 25; A. F. Fedorov, *Podpol'nyi obkom deistvuet* (Kiev: Politizdat Ukrainy, 1986), 69–70.

111. Cited in Timothy Mulligan, "Reckoning the Cost of People's War: The German Experience in the Central USSR," *Russian History/Histoire Russe* 9, 1 (1982): 33.

112. Hill, *The War behind the Eastern Front*, 146.

113. TsKhDMO, f. 1, op. 53, d. 252, l. 6.

114. RGASPI, f. 69, op. 1, d. 28, l. 49.

115. *Balalaika, Balalaika / Netu kury, netu iaku / Netu masla, netu shpik / Politsai—ne chelovek*; cited in Shumilin, *Istoriia partizanskogo dvizheniia*, 149.

116. RGASPI, f. 69, op. 1, d. 283, l. 7.

117. IIAN ORF, f. 2, raz. 2, op. 2, d. 25a, l. 31.

118. Document reproduced in Armstrong, *The Soviet Partisans*, 751–752.

119. IIAN ORF, f. 2, raz. 2, op. 6, d. 12, l. 25.

120. RGASPI, f. 625, op. 1, d. 28, l. 45.

121. RGASPI, f. 69, op. 1, d. 196, l. 21.

122. M. T. Lukashov, *Po tylam vraga* (Kiev: Politizdat Ukrainy, 1974), 112–124.

123. P. P. Vershigora, *Liudi s chistoi sovest'iu* (Moscow: Moskovskii rabochii, 1946), 334.

124. Aleksei Popov, *15 Vstrech s generalom KGB Bel'chenko* (Moscow: OLMA-PRESS, 2002), 207–208.

125. IIAN ORF, f. 2, raz. 2, op. 6, d. 12, l. 25.

126. *Krasnaia zvezda*, 1 November 1941, p. 2.

127. See Chapter Five.

128. Timothy Snyder, "The Causes of Ukrainian-Polish Ethnic Cleansing," *Past and Present* 179 (May 2003): 208–211.

129. USHMM, RG 22.005M, reel 2 (RGASPI, f. 69, op. 1, d. 1074, ll. 46–47); reel 3 (RGASPI, f. 69, op. 1, d. 713, l. 8); IIAN ORF, f. 2, raz. 2, op. 3, d. 18, ll. 1–3; RGASPI, f. 69, op. 1, d. 1080, l. 24; R. R. Kruchok, ed., *Vsenarodnoe partizanskoe dvizhenie v Belorussii v gody Belikoi Otechestvennoi voiny*, T. 1 (Minsk: Belarus', 1967),142–143, 146.

130. See Daniel Romanovsky, "Soviet Jews under Nazi Occupation in Northeastern Belarus and Western Russia," in Zvi Gitelman, ed., *Bitter Legacy: Confronting the Holocaust in the USSR* (Bloomington: Indiana University Press, 1997), 239–250; Weiner, *Making Sense of War*, 269–297.

131. Armstrong, *The Soviet Partisans*, 40.

132. See Chapter Three.

133. P. K. Ponomarenko, *Vsenarodnaia bor'ba v tylu nemetsko-fashistkikh zakhvatchikov* (Moscow: Nauka, 1986), 144.

134. IIAN ORF, f. 2. raz. 2, op. 4, d. 125, l. 3.

135. Vershigora, *Liudi s chistoi sovest'iu*, 199–200.

136. Leonid Grenkevich, *The Soviet Partisan Movement, 1941–1944: A Critical Historiographical Analysis*, edited and with a foreword by David M. Glantz (London: Frank Cass, 1999), 242; Shepard, *War in the Wild East*, 205.

137. Kohn and Roiter, *A Voice from the Forest*, 118.

138. Iu. V. Petrov, *Partizanskoe dvizhenie v Leningradskoi Oblasti, 1941–1944* (Leningrad: Lenizdat, 1973), 163–164.

139. Ponomarenko, *Vsenarodnaia bor'ba*, 125–126; V. E. Bystrov, ed., *Sovetskie partizany: Iz istorii Partizanskogo dvizheniia v gody velikoi Otechestvennoi voiny* (Moscow: Politizdat, 1961), 358; M. M. Kir'ian, A. S. Galitsan, and N. G. Andronikov, eds., *Velikaia Otechestvennaia voina, 1941–1945: Slovar'-spravochnik* (Moscow: Politizdat, 1988), 350–351; Shumilin, *Istoriia partizanskogo dvizheniia*, 178; RGASPI, f. 69, op. 1, d. 470, ll. 34–35.

140. RGASPI, f. 69, op. 1, d. 24, l. 14; d. 579, l. 88; d. 1112, l. 83; f. 625, op. 1, d. 61, l. 558; Vershigora, *Liudi s chistoi sovest'iu*, 229.

141. See Chapter Three.

142. USHMM, RG 22.005M, reel 2 (RGASPI, f. 69, op. 1, d. 1079, l. 29).

143. Vershigora, *Liudi s chistoi sovest'iu*, 216.

144. RGASPI, f. 69, op, 1, d. 82, ll. 178, 185–186; d. 94, ll. 8–11, 15, 40–42; d. 15, ll. 1–4.

145. For example, see the song about a partisan scout written by a friend, "Petia . . . da . . . da . . . da," in the journal of the "Flame" Partisan Detachment; TsMVS, f. 4/338347, ll. 75–77; see also Vershigora, *Liudi s chistoi sovest'iu*, 217–222.

146. TsKhDMO, f. 1, op. 53, d. 14, ll. 114–115; see also Kohn and Roiter, *A Voice from the Forest*, 131–176, 188–215; Report by Deputy Representative of the Central Staff to the Briansk Front, Gorshkov, reproduced in Alekei Popov, *NKVD i partizanskoe dvizhenie: Fakty i dokumenty* (Moscow: OLMA-PRESS, 2003), 339–340.

147. Popov, *15 Vstrech*, 229.

148. RGASPI, f. 69, op. 1, d. 1093, l. 5; IIAN ORF, f. 2, raz. 2, op. 6, d. 12, l. 14; V. N. Andrianov, ed., *Voina v tylu vraga: O nekotorykh problemakh istorii sovetskogo partizanskogo dvizheniia v gody Velikoi Otechestvennoi voiny* (Moscow: Politizdat, 1974), 148, 196; Cooper, *The Phantom War*, 133–134.

149. *Krasnaia zvezda*, 9 April 1943, p. 4.

150. Dean, *Collaboration in the Holocaust*, 134–135.

151. RGASPI, f. 69, op. 1, d. 4, ll. 79–82; d. 1080, ll. 14–15; d. 1094, ll. 4–5.

152. M. Rudakov, "Rol' voennykh sovetov frontov i armii v rukovodstve boevymi deistviiami partizan v gody Velikoi Otechetsvennoi voiny," *Voenno-istoricheskii zhurnal* 7 (1962): 12.

153. Boiarskii, *Partizany*, 238–240.

154. *IVOVSS*, 4:487.

155. Ralph Mavrogordato and Earl Ziemke, "The Polotsk Lowland," in Armstrong, *The Soviet Partisans*, 545–547. See also A. I. Briukhanov's account, in A. I. Briukhanov, *V shtabe partizanskogo dvizheniia* (Minsk: Belarus, 1980), 198–203.

156. Cited in Heaton, *German Anti-partisan Warfare*, 210.

157. IIAN ORF, f. 2, raz. 2, op. 4, d. 13, l. 7.

158. Cited in Boiarskii, *Partizany*, 184.

159. RGASPI, f. 69, op. 1, d. 28, l. 68.

160. RGASPI, f. 69, op. 1, d. 286, ll. 44–48.

161. V. A. Perezhogin, "Partizany u priema Stalina," *Otechestvennaia istoriia* 3 (1999): 189.

162. RGASPI, f. 69, op.1, d. 467, l. 18. These figures do not include desertion. Given the nature of partisan warfare, the total of 98 partisans missing in action also seems quite low.

163. RGASPI, f. 69, op. 8, d. 27, ll. 3–93, cited in V. A. Zolotarev and A. S. Emelin, eds., *Russkii arkhiv: Velikai Otechestvennaia: Partizankoe dvizhenie v gody Velikoi Otechestvennoi voiny 1941–1945 gg.: Dokumenty i materialy*, vol. 9 (Moscow: Terra, 1999), 485–486.

164. RGASPI, f. 69, op. 1, d. 29, l. 22.

165. *Izvestiia TsK KPSS*, 11 (1990): 189–190.

166. RGASPI, f. 69, op. 1, d. 4, ll. 28–30; d. 29, l. 40; d. 62, ll. 1–21; d. 159, ll. 57–58; TsKhDMO, f. 1, op. 53, d. 4, l. 20; Colonel I. G. Starinov, *Over the Abyss: My Life in Soviet Special Operations*, trans. Robert Suggs (New York: Ivy Books, 1995), 201–366; I. Buianov, "Deiatel'nost Tsentral'nogo Shtaba partizanskogo dvizheniia po obepecheniiu partizan vooruzheniem," *Voenno-istoricheskii zhurnal*, 5 (1975): 119.

167. Figures cited in V. A. Zolotarev, ed., *Partizanskoe dvizhenie: Po opytu Veli-koi Otechestvennoi voiny, 1941–1945 gg.* (Moscow: Kuchkovo Pole, 2001), 191.
168. IIAN ORF, f. 2, raz. 2, op. 6, d. 12, l. 10.
169. RGASPI, f. 69, op. 1, d. 1096, l. 25.
170. RGASPI, f. 69, op. 1, d. 1060, ll. 8–9.
171. RGASPI, f. 69, op. 1, d. 473, l. 24.
172. RGASPI, f. 69, op. 1, d. 28, l. 41.
173. IIAN ORF, f. 2, raz. 2, op. 4, d. 125, l. 7; RGASPI, f. 69, op. 1, d, 212, l. 11; d. 473, l. 13; d. 1067, l. 250, Fedorov, *Podpol'nyi obkom deistvuet*, 485; Kohn and Roiter, *A Voice from the Forest*, 109–114, Starinov, *Over the Abyss*, 322; Popov, *15 Vstrech*, 165–166. For German countermeasures, see Cooper, *The Phantom War*, 130–131; Schulte, *The German Army*, 129; Grenkevich, *The Soviet Partisan Movement*, 240–241, Heaton, *German Anti-partisan Warfare*, 147–148. For an account of a reprisal patrol from a German perspective, see Guy Sajer, *The Forgotten Soldier*, trans. Lily Emmet (New York: Harper & Row, 1967), 295–302.
174. RGASPI, f. 69, op. 1, d. 473, l. 6.
175. Cited in Vershigora, *Liudi s chistoi sovest'iu*, 157. Partisans sometimes used advanced chemical and magnetic mines flown in from the Soviet mainland but more often employed unsophisticated devices made of TNT or the material from unexploded bombs, shells, or batteries; Starinov, *Over the Abyss*, 350–351.
176. IIAN ORF, f. 2, raz. 2, op. 4, d. 125, l. 7; RGASPI, f. 69, op. 1, d, 212, l. 11.
177. IIAN ORF, f. 2, raz. 2, op. 6, d. 12, l. 11; TsKhDMO, f. 1, op. 53, d. 4, l. 21.
178. RGASPI, f. 625, op. 1, d. 28, l. 39.
179. Of the 170 qualified demolitions experts in Fedorov's complex, 80 percent were either youth or *komsomoltsy*; TsKhDMO, f. 1, op. 6, d. 257, l. 154. For more on the connection between sabotage and youth/Komsomol, see TsKhDMO, f. 1, op. 53, d. 4, ll. 20–23; RGASPI, f. 69, op. 1, d. 212, l. 9; TsMVS, f. 4/38347, l. 33.
180. RGASPI, f. 69, op. 1, d. 212, l. 10; IIAN ORF, f. 2, raz. 2, op. 4, d. 125, l. 7. Actually, a count of the 252 partisans awarded the title Hero of the Soviet Union reveals that only 34 (13.5 percent) were given to saboteurs. Unit commanders easily composed the largest percentage, at approximately 45 percent; Zolotarev, *Partizanskoe dvizhenie*, 397–410.
181. RGASPI, f. 69, op. 1, d. 4, l. 173.
182. See, for example, *Izvestiia*, 19 August 1942, p. 4, 22 November 1942, p. 2; *Pravda*, 2 April 1943, p. 2, 12 December 1943, p. 3, 2 February 1944, p. 2, 16 March 1944, p. 2; GARF, f. 6903, op. 20, d. 1, ll. 164–167 (5 June 1942), d. 2, ll. 223–226 (20 June 1942), d. 2, ll. 38–351 (25 June 1942), d. ll. 69–70 (2 August 1942), d. 4, ll. 539–540 (13 August 1942), d. 9, l. 291 (11 November 1942), d. 15, l. 67 (21 August 1943); E. Vilen-skii, *Syn Belorussii* Moscow: Molodaia gvardiia, 1943); Vadim Lukashevich, *Makar Goncharov: Sviazist-partizan* (Moscow, 1945).
183. *Izvestiia*, 11 August 1942, p. 2.
184. RGASPI, f. 69, op. 1, d. 159, ll. 57–58.
185. TsKhDMO, f. 1, op. 6, d. 299, l. 68.
186. Ponomarenko, *Vsenarodnaia bor'ba*, 234.

187. RGASPI, f. 69, op. 1, d. 10, ll. 80–81; d. 25, ll. 128–132.

188. RGASPI, f. 69, op. 1, d. 148, ll. 17–25; Grenkevich, *The Soviet Partisan Movement*, 244–245.

189. Edgar Howell, *The Soviet Partisan Movement, 1941–1944* (Washington, D.C.: Department of the Army, 1956), 206; *IVMV*, 7:307–308.

190. RGASPI, f. 69, op. 1, d. 148, l. 25; Boiarskii, *Partizany*, 226.

191. Starinov, *Over the Abyss*, 324–326.

192. Boiarskii, *Partizany*, 227.

193. Stephen G. Fritz, *Frontsoldaten: The German Soldier in World War II* (Lexington: University Press of Kentucky, 1995), 141, 143–144; Dean, *Collaboration in the Holocaust*, 137.

194. RGASPI, f. 69, op. 1, d. 65, ll. 15–16.

195. Boiarskii, *Partizany*, 227.

196. For more discussion of the June 1944 operation, see Grenkevich, *The Soviet Partisan Movement*, 257–262; *IVOVSS*, 4:168.

197. Contemporary Central Staff records indicate that on 15 August 1942, there were 7,571 partisans in Ukraine, approximately 8.1 percent of all partisans at that time; RGASPI, f. 69, op. 1, d. 19, l. 54.

198. IIAN ORF, f. 2, raz. 2, op. 6, d. 14, l. 13. Kovpak's description of this meeting in his memoirs portrays Stalin as suggesting that Kovpak undertake the raid and that the partisan commander should "think about it"; S. A. Kovpak, *Ot Putivlia do Karpat* (Leningrad: Gos-izdat Detskoi Literaturny, 1945), 89–90.

199. A. A. Grechko and D. F. Ustinov, eds., *Istoriia Vtoroi Mirovoi voiny, 1939–1945*, T. 5 (Moscow: Voenizdat, 1975), 292.

200. RGASPI, f. 69, op. 1, d. 550, ll. 61–62; d. 551, ll. 86–93; d. 555, ll. 30–53; USHMM, 1996.A.169, reel 36 (YVA M-37/775—TsDAHOU, f. 66, op. 1, d. 1, ll. 11, 15; Ponomarenko, *Vsenarodnaia bor'ba*, 119–121; John Armstrong and Earle Ziemke, "Organization and Control of the Partisan Movement," in Armstrong, *The Soviet Partisans*, 114–116; L. G. Dovzhinets and I. Ia. Makukhin, eds., *Sumskaia oblast' v period Velikoi Otechestvennoi voiny, 1941–1945* (Kiev: Nauk. dumka, 1988), 140–141; Z. A. Bogatyr', *V tylu vraga: Boeviia deiatel'nost' soedineniia partizanskikh otriadov pod komandovaniem geroi Sovetskogo soiuza A. N. Saburova* (Moscow: Sotsekgiz, 1963), 151.

201. RGASPI, f. 69, op. 1, d. 563, l. 100.

202. Kovpak, *Ot Putivlia do Karpat*, 94.

203. Shumilin, *Istoriia Partisankogo dvizheniia*, 218.

204. USHMM, 1996.A.169, reel 35 (YVA M-37/714—TsDAHOU, f. 65, op. 1, d. 1, ll. 2, 5). See also RGASPI, f. 69, op. 1, d. 563, ll. 97, 101.

205. N. I. Makarov, ed., *Partiinoe podpol'e: Deiatel'nost podpolnykh partiinykh organov i organizatsii na Okkupirovannoi Sovetskii territorii v gody Velikoi Otechestvennoi voiny* (Moscow: Politizdat, 1983), 80–81, 327–328.

206. John Armstrong, *Ukrainian Nationalism*, 3rd ed. (Englewood, Colo.: Ukrainian Academic Press, 1990), 105–110; Weiner, *Making Sense of War*, 177–179; RGASPI, f.

69, op. 1, d. 582; d. 747, l. 165; USHMM, 1996.A.169, reel 1 (YVA M-37/14—TsDAHOU, f. 1, op. 22, d. 75, ll. 1–7, 12–19; reel 33 (YVA M-37/424—TsDAHOU, f. 62, op. 1, d. 21, l. 49).

207. RGASPI, f. 625, op. 1, d. 61, l. 671.

208. Vershigora, *Liudi s chistoi sovest'iu*, 135–136.

209. Excerpt from Rudnev's diary, cited in Dovzhinets and Makukhin, *Sumskaia oblast v period Velikoi Otechestvennoi voiny*, 169.

210. Vershigora, *Liudi s chistoi sovest'iu*, 45. The American translator of Starinov's memoirs, based on uncredited evidence—"a communication . . . from a Soviet source of the highest reliability"—claims that Rudnev was assassinated by Pavel Sudoplatov for allegedly having a too comfortable relationship with Ukrainian nationalists. Without corroborating information or identification of the source, it is impossible to verify, and thus, it is hard to give credence to this claim; Starinov, *Over the Abyss*, 339–340.

211. USHMM, 1996.A.169, reel 36 (YVA M-37/776—TsDAHOU, f. 66, op. 1, d. 3, ll. 4–5; Armstrong, *The Soviet Partisans*, 26–27.

212. USHMM, 1996.A.169, reel 36 (YVA M-37/775—TsDAHOU, f. 66, op. 1, d. 1, ll. 6–7); Bogatyr', *V tylu vraga*, 132–133. See also Chapter Seven.

213. Vershigora, *Liudi s chistoi sovest'iu*, 229.

214. RGASPI, f. 625, op. 1, d. 61, l. 558.

215. Kovpak, *Ot Putivlia do Karpat*, 89.

216. RGASPI, f. 625, op. 1, d. 61, ll. 663, 665–666, 677.

217. Vershigora, *Liudi s chistoi sovest'iu*, 223–224.

218. For comparison for the first half of 1943, Belorussian partisans (who comprised the majority of partisans) were the subject of 100 Sovinformburo reports, with 87 in 1942; there were 54 stories about Russian units in the first half of 1943 but 337 in 1942; RGASPI, f. 69, op. 1, d. 1064, l. 144.

219. The article was read on Gosradio broadcast to the occupied territories; GARF, f. 6903, op. 20, d. 11, ll. 232–234 (25 December 1942).

CHAPTER THREE. BUREAUCRATS AND GUERRILLAS: THE SOVIET SEARCH FOR ORDER AND CONTROL IN THE OCCUPIED TERRITORIES

1. Jørgen Haestrup, *European Resistance Movements, 1939–1945: A Complete History* (Westport, Conn.: Meckler Publishing, 1981), 147.

2. Moshe Lewin, "Bureaucracy and the Stalinist State," in Ian Kershaw and Moshe Lewin, eds., *Stalinism and Nazism: Dictatorships in Comparison* (Cambridge: Cambridge University Press, 1997), 53–74. For a discussion of the ideology of planning (and that of the First Five Year Plan in particular), see Martin Malia, *The Soviet Tragedy: A History of Socialism in Russia* (New York: Free Press, 1994), 184–190.

3. This was most notable regarding food supply; see William Moskoff, *The*

Bread of Affliction: The Food Supply in the USSR during World War II (Cambridge: Cambridge University Press, 1990). See also John Barber and Mark Harrison, *The Soviet Home Front: A Social and Economic History of the USSR in World War II* (London: Longman Group, 1991).

4. John Armstrong and Kurt DeWitt, "Organization and Control of the Partisan Movement," in John Armstrong, ed., *The Soviet Partisans in World War II* (Madison: University of Wisconsin Press, 1964), 134. See also Jan Gross's discussion of the Soviet annexation of what became the western Ukrainian and Belorussian districts, in which he argued that the Soviet regime's institutional chaos was a deliberate part of totalitarian policy meant to deprive individuals of the ability to plan and act; Jan T. Gross, *Revolution from Above: The Soviet Conquest of Western Ukraine and Western Belorussia* (Princeton, N.J.: Princeton University Press, 1988), 69–70.

5. John Armstrong, "Introduction," in Armstrong, *The Soviet Partisans*, 52–53.

6. IIAN ORF, f. 2, raz. 2, op. 6, d. 12, l. 21.

7. Haestrup contended that the experiments of the 1930s gave the Soviets an advantage over other countries in preparing for partisan war; Haestrup, *European Resistance Movements*, 149.

8. V. E. Bystrov, ed., *Sovetskie partizany: Iz istorii Partizanskogo dvizheniia v gody Velikoi Otechestvennoi voiny* (Moscow: Politizdat, 1961), 440–441.

9. RGASPI, f. 69, op. 1, d. 1067, l. 1.

10. John Erickson, *The Road to Stalingrad: Stalin's War with Germany* (New Haven, Conn.: Yale University Press, 1975), 243; Armstrong and DeWitt, "Organization and Control," in Armstrong, *The Soviet Partisans*, 75–76.

11. V. I. Boiarskii, *Partizany i armiia: Istoriia uteriannykh vozmozhnostei* (Minsk: Kharvest, 2003), 179.

12. P. K. Ponomarenko, *Vsenarodnaia bor'ba v tylu nemetsko-fashistkikh zakhvatchikov, 1941–1944* (Moscow: Nauka, 1986), 53; V. N. Andrianov, ed., *Voina v tylu vraga: O nekotorykh problemakh istorii sovetskogo partizanskogo dvizheniia v gody Velikoi Otechestvennoi voiny* (Moscow: Politizdat, 1974), 46; *IVMV*, 4:352.

13. N. I. Makarov, ed., *Partiinoe podpol'e: Deiatel'nost podpolnykh partiinykh organov i organizatsii na Okkupirovannoi Sovetskii territorii v gody Velikoi Otechestvennoi voiny* (Moscow: Politizdat, 1983), 57, 63, 90.

14. Ponomarenko, *Vsenarodnaia bor'ba*, 29; Iu. V. Petrov, *Partizanskoe dvizhenie v Leningradskoi oblasti, 1941–1944* (Leningrad: Lenizdat, 1973), 146. Edgar Howell stated the date is 10 July 1941, but this is not confirmed by Soviet sources; Howell, *The Soviet Partisan Movement, 1941–1944* (Washington, D.C.: Department of the Army, 1956), 47; Armstrong and Dewitt, "Organization and Control," in Armstrong, *The Soviet Partisans*, 82.

15. The operational group of the Southwestern Front was created on 1 November 1941, and the Northwestern Front established its own operational group later that month. See M. Rudakov, "Rol' voennykh sovetov frontov i armii v rukovodstve boevymi deistviiami partisan v gody Velikoi Otechestvennoi voiny," *Voenno-istoricheskii zhurnal* 7 (1962): 5–6; *IVOVSS*, 6:271.

16. Boiarskii, *Partizany*, 136–140.

17. USHMM, 1996.A.169 (YVA M-37/1259—TsDAHOU, f. 62, op. 9, d. 6, l. 35); Ponomarenko, *Vsenarodnaia bor'ba*, 29.

18. Cited in Armstrong, *The Soviet Partisans*, 661–662.

19. See Chapter One.

20. Boiarskii, *Partizany*, 82.

21. *Izvestiia KPSS*, 9 (1990): 198; Aleksei Popov, *NKVD i partizanskoe dvizhenie: Materialy i dokumenty* (Moscow: OLMA-PRESS, 2003), 53–61; Pavel and Anatolii Sudoplatov, with Jerrold L. Schecter and Leona Schecter, *Special Tasks: The Memoirs of an Unwanted Witness—A Soviet Spymaster* (Boston: Little, Brown, 1994), 126–127; V. A. Zolotarev, ed., *Partizanskoe dvizhenie: Po opytu Velikoi Otechestvennoi voiny, 1941–1945 gg.* (Moscow: Kuchkovo Pole, 2001), 39.

22. USHMM, 1996.A.169, reel 39 (YVA M-37/1255—TsDAHOU, f. 62, op. 1, d. 1, l. 4).

23. USHMM, 1996.A.169, reel 39 (YVA M-37/1255—TsDAHOU, f. 62, op 1, d. 1, l. 4).

24. USHMM, 1996.A.169, reel 39 (YVA M-37/1255—TsDAHOU, f. 62, op. 1, d. 1, l. 13).

25. USHMM, 1996.A.169, reel 39 (YVA M-37/1259—TsDAHOU, f. 62, op. 9, d. 6, ll. 37–38).

26. RGASPI, f. 69, op. 1, d. 1076, ll. 10–16.

27. T. Lesniak, "Nekotorye voprosy organizatsii i vedeniia partizanskoi bor'by v pervye mesiatsy voiny," *Voenno-istoricheskii zhurnal* 9 (1963): 35.

28. IIAN ORF, f. 2, raz. 2, op. 6, d. 9, l. 9; RGASPI, f. 69, op. 1, d. 470, l. 9.

29. A. I. Briukhanov, *V shtabe partizanskogo dvizheniia* (Minsk: Belarus', 1980), 175; RGASPI, f. 69, op. 1, d. 206, ll. 119–121; IIAN ORF, f. 2, raz. 2, op. 6, d. 11, l. 12.

30. B. T. Shumilin, ed., *Istoriia partizanskogo dvizheniia v Rossiiskoi Federatsii v gody Velikoi Otechestvennoi voiny, 1941–1945* (Moscow: Atlantida, 2001), 158–159.

31. IIAN ORF, f. 2, raz. 2, op. 6, d. 9, l. 9; d. 14, l. 2; RGASPI, f. 69, op. 1, d. 28, l. 96.

32. GARF, f. 8355, op. 1, d. 213, ll. 55–56.

33. USHMM, 1996.A.169, reel 39 (YVA M-37/1259—TsDAHOU, f. 62, op. 9, d. 6, l. 36).

34. IIAN ORF, f. 2, raz. 2, op. 6, d. 15, l. 8.

35. RGASPI, f. 17, op. 43, d. 1435, l. 29.

36. Petrov, *Partizanskoe dvizhenie*, 27–29; Andrianov, *Voina v tylu vraga*, 19; Alexander Hill, "The Partisan War in Northwest Russia, 1941–1944: A Re-examination," *Journal of Strategic Studies* 25, 3 (September 2002): 39–42.

37. Alexander Hill, *The War behind the Eastern Front: The Soviet Partisan Movement in North-West Russia* (New York: Frank Cass, 2005), 75–76.

38. Petrov, *Partizanskoe dvizhenie*, 12; Andrianov, *Voina v tylu vraga*, 36.

39. RGASPI, f. 69, op. 1, d. 458, l. 76.

40. Petrov, *Partizanskoe dvizhenie*, 234; Bystrov, *Sovetskie partizany*, 28. Hill argued for a total of 4,000 partisans in December 1941; Alexander Hill, "The Soviet Partisan Movement in North-West Russia: A Re-Examination," *Journal of Strate-*

gic Studies 25, 3 (September 2002): 46. A report from the Northwestern Front's head of partisan operations stated that there were fewer than 3,000 partisans, but the front's operational jurisdiction did not cover the entire region; RGASPI, f. 69, op. 1, d. 470, l. 19.

41. P. K. Ponomarenko, "Bor'ba Sovetskogo naroda v tylu vraga," *Voenno-isotricheskii zhurnal* 4 (1965): 34; General I. V. Boldin, "Sorok-piat' dnei v tylu vraga," *Voenno-istoricheskii zhurnal* 4 (1961): 81.

42. RGASPI, f. 69, op. 1, d. 18, ll. 2–4; *Izvestiia KPSS* 10 (1990): 21; Ponomarenko, *Vsenarodnaia bor'ba*, 73.

43. Ponomarenko, *Vsenarodnaia bor'ba*, 72–73; Colonel I. G. Starinov, *Over the Abyss: My Life in Soviet Special Operations*, trans. Robert Suggs (New York: Ivy Books, 1995), 243–245. The initial decision to form the Central Staff in December 1941 has led some Western historians to assert that the organization was actually operating by the 1941–1942 winter. See John Erickson, *The Soviet High Command* (Boulder, Colo.: Westview Press, 1984), 629, and Capt. N. Galay, "The Partisan Forces," in B. H. Liddell Hart, ed., *The Red Army* (New York: Harcourt Brace, 1956), 162.

In his memoirs, Ponomarenko did not mention Starinov at all in his depiction of the events leading up to the formation of the Central Staff. For his part, Starinov, in his memoirs, essentially accused Ponomarenko of stealing his ideas for the Central Staff. Not surprisingly, the two men engaged in a bitter feud after the war, continuing at least into the 1960s.

44. Ponomarenko, *Vsenarodnaia bor'ba*, 74; I. N. Artem'ev, *V efire partizany* (Moscow: Voenizdat, 1971), 22; the draft plan for an all-Union partisan staff, whose language and concepts closely resemble Ponomarenko's, is located in TsKhDMO, f. 1, op. 53, d. 10, ll. 94–101.

45. Cited in G. A. Kumanev, "Otvety P. K. Ponomarenko na voprosy G. A. Kumanev 2 noiabria 1978 g.," *Otechestvennaia istoriia* 6 (1998): 142.

46. Aleksei Popov, *Diversanty Stalina: Deiatel'nost' organov Gosbezopastnosnosti na okkupirovannoi Sovetskoi territorii v gody Velikoi Otechestvennoi voiny* (Moscow: Iauza, Eksmo, 2004), 88; Shumilin, *Istoriia partizanskogo dvizheniia*, 28.

47. Ponomarenko, "Bor'ba Sovetskogo naroda, 34; Popov, *Diversanty Stalina*, 62; Alfred J. Rieber, "Civil Wars in the Soviet Union," *Kritika* 4, 2 (Winter 2003): 152.

48. Richard Overy, *Russia's War: Blood upon the Snow* (New York: TV Books, 1997), 155–156.

49. Ponomarenko, *Vsenarodnaia bor'ba*, 75; Starinov, *Over the Abyss*, 259.

50. Ponomarenko, *Vsenarodnaia bor'ba*, 75.

51. Dmitri Volkogonov, *Stalin: Triumph and Tragedy*, ed. and trans. Harold Shukman (Rocklin, Calif.: Prima Publishing, 1992), 432.

52. Shumilin, *Istoriia partizanskogo dvizheniia*, 29.

53. Cited in Kumanev, "Otvety P. K. Ponomarenko," 143.

54. RGASPI, f. 644, op. 1, d. 36, ll. 235–236.

55. Petrov, *Partizanskoe dvizhenie*, 12; Andrianov, *Voina v tylu vraga*, 36.

56. John McCannon, *Red Arctic: Polar Exploration and the Myth of the North*

in Soviet Russia, 1932–1939 (Oxford: Oxford University Press, 1998), esp. chaps. two and six.

57. In its original configuration, the Central Staff had eight departments (*otdely*): operations, information and intelligence, communications, cadres, material and technical assistance, codes, administrative, and finance. These departments were mirrored in the staffs of the partisan movement attached to the fronts. In late September 1942, the Central Staff was reorganized into four administrations (*upravlenie*)— operations, information-intelligence, political, and supply—and seven departments— communications, sabotage, personnel, finance, "secret," codes, and administrative-economic. On 26 November 1942, the GKO ordered another reorganization of the Central Staff. The administrations were converted back into departments, and the sabotage and supply departments were merged. An administrative housekeeping section (*administrativno-khoziaistvennaia chast'*) was also added. The Central Staff retained this structure until its final disbandment in January 1944. RGASPI, f. 69, op. 1, d. 1, ll. 4–13, 29, 71; d. 4, l. 85; V. A. Tsar'kov, "Bez zatish'ia i pereryva: Iz opyta politicheskoi raboty Tsentral'nogo shtaba partizanskogo dvizheniia," *Voenno-istoricheskii zhurnal* 11 (1988): 40.

58. RGASPI, f. 69, op. 1, d. 1, l. 4, 32–33.

59. RGASPI, f. 69, op. 1. d. 1., ll. 33–35; d. 4, l. 86. Partisan staffs even organized concerts and films in the occupied territories; see P. Z. Kalinin, *Partizanskaia respublike respublika* (Minsk: Belarus', 1968), 285.

60. RGASPI, f. 69, op. 4, d. 3359, l. 4; op. 1, d. 67, ll. 39–41; d. 300, l. 75; d. 4, ll. 107–111; d. 1067, l. 172.

61. RGASPI, f. 69, op. 1, d. 10, ll. 34–35; d. 14, l. 25; d. 24, l. 152; d. 83, l. 21; d. 1062, l. 17.

62. T. Lesniak, "Sovershenstvovanie rukovodstva partizanskim dvizheniem," *Voenno-istoricheskii zhurnal* 7 (1967): 25; Ponomarenko, *Vsenarodnaia bor'ba*, 75.

63. By 1945, both Sergienko and Bel'chenko were lieutenant generals in SMERSH, the counterespionage agency; Michael Parrish, *The Lesser Terror: Soviet State Security, 1939–1953* (Westport, Conn.: Praeger, 1996), 332.

64. RGASPI, f. 69, op. 1, d. 24, ll. 137–140; d. 10, l. 74; Briukhanov, *V shtabe partizanskogo dvizheniia*, 14; Starinov, *Over the Abyss*, 290–293, 298–299.

65. RGASPI, f. 644, op. 1, d. 55, l. 55. Ponomarenko remained the Central Staff's chief of staff.

66. Volkogonov, *Stalin*, 453–454; Armstrong, *The Soviet Partisans*, 75.

67. Briukhanov, *V shtabe partizanskogo dvizheniia*, 32; Starinov, *Over the Abyss*, 298–299.

68. Cited in Shumilin, *Istoriia partizanskogo dvizheniia*, 34.

69. Alexander Pronin, "Guerrilla Warfare in the German-Occupied Soviet Territories, 1941–1944" (Ph.D. diss., Georgetown University, 1965), 71; Armstrong and DeWitt, "Organization and Control," in Armstrong, *The Soviet Partisans*, 103.

70. These issues will be covered in detail in Chapter Four.

71. RGASPI, f. 644, op. 1, d. 69, l. 24.

72. Starinov, *Over the Abyss*, 302; N. Ia. Komerov, *GKO postanulet . . . : Dokumenty, vospominaniia, komentarii* (Moscow: Voenizdat, 1990), 27; *IVMV*, 5:290.

73. The dates on which the subordinate staffs were created are as follows: the territorial Ukrainian and Leningrad Staffs and the frontal Briansk, Western, Kalinin, and Karelo-Finnish Staffs on 30 May 1942; the Southern Staff on August 30, 1942; the territorial Belorussian Staff on 9 September 1942; the territorial Estonian, Lithuanian, and Latvian Staffs on 3 and 26 November 1942 and 8 January 1943, respectively; the Crimean Staff in July 1943; and the Voronezh Staff in October 1942; Ponomarenko, *Vsenarodnaia bor'ba*, 75.

74. Bystrov, *Sovetskie partizany*, 604–605; Ponomarenko, *Vsenarodnaia bor'ba*, 75–76. The subordinate staffs were: Ukrainian: T. A. Strokach, NKVD; Belorussian: P. Z. Kalinin, Belorussian Central Committee secretary; Karelian-Finnish: S. Ia. Vershinin, NKVD; Lithuanian: A. Iu. Snechkus, Lithuanian Central Committee first secretary; Latvian: A. K. Sprogis, Army-GRU; Estonian: N. G. Karottam, Estonian Central Committee first secretary; Leningrad: M. N. Nikitin, Leningrad Obkom; Kalinin: S. S. Bel'chenko, NKVD, who was succeeded by I. I. Ryzhikov, Belorussian Central Committee; Smolensk (Western Front): D. V. Popov, Smolensk Obkom first secretary; Orel (Briansk Front): A. P. Matveev, Orel Obkom first secretary; Voronezh Front: L A. M. Nekrasov, Voronezh Obkom first secretary; Southern Front: P. I. Seleznev, Krasnodar Kraikom first secretary; Stavropol: M. A. Suslov, Stavropol Obkom first secretary; Crimea: V. S. Bulatov, Crimean Obkom first secretary. As occurred in standard Soviet practice, the Russian Republic did not have its own republican partisan staff, whereas the Moldavan Staff operated as a department of the Ukrainian Staff. Of the fifteen territorial staffs, eleven were led by Party officials, and four were headed by security-intelligence cadres.

75. RGASPI, f. 69, op. 1, d. 24, ll. 137–140; Ponomarenko, *Vsenarodnaia bor'ba*, 76; Andrianov, *Voina v tylu vraga*, 111.

76. Andrianov, *Voina v tylu vraga*, 53; Briukhanov, *V shtabe partizanskogo dvizheniia*, 33.

77. IIAN ORF, f. 2, raz. 2, op. 4, d. 125, ll. 3–4; RGASPI, f. 69, op. 1, d. 4, ll. 1–3; d. 81, ll. 100–101; Andrianov, *Voina v tylu vraga*, 113; Rudakov, "Rol' voennykh sovetov frontov i armii," 7.

78. RGASPI, f. 69, op. 1, d. 10, ll. 53, 69.

79. RGASPI, f. 644, op. 1, d. 96, l. 4.

80. *IVMV*, 7:300.

81. Briukhanov, *V shtabe partizanskogo dvizheniia*, 66; Starinov, *Over the Abyss*, 317.

82. Briukhanov, *V shtabe partizanskogo dvizheniia*, 34.

83. RGASPI, f. 69, op. 1, d. 1093, l. 10.

84. RGASPI, f. 625, op. 1, d. 10, l. 3.

85. See the example of General K. K. Rokossovskii's questioning of the success of a partisan operation against a key bridge over the Desna River; IIAN ORF, f. 2, raz. 2, op. 6, d. 14, ll. 14–17; Ponomarenko, *Vsenarodnaia bor'ba*, 207–208.

86. RGASPI, f. 644, op. 1, d. 63, l. 32.

87. Armstrong and DeWitt, "Organization and Control," in Armstrong, *The Soviet Partisans*, 110–111; RGASPI, f. 69, op. 1, d. 563, ll. 93–95.

88. Boiarskii, *Partizany*, 189.

89. RGASPI, f. 69, op. 1, d. 11, ll. 2–4.

90. TsKhDMO, f. 1, op. 53, d. 7, ll. 199–200; M. Amsaliamov and V. Andrianov, "Organizatsiia partizanskikh sil i fronty rukovodstva ikh boevoi deiatel'nostiiu v Otechestvennoi voine," *Voenno-istoricheskii zhurnal* 9 (1966): 18–26; Briukhanov, *V shtabe partizanskogo dvizheniia*, 208–209; Boiarskii, *Partizany*, 187.

91. Rieber, "Civil Wars in the Soviet Union," 152; Briukhanov, *V shtabe partizanskogo dvizheniia*, 33.

92. RGASPI, f. 69, op. 1, d. 1080, ll. 14–115.

93. IIAN ORF, f. 2, raz. 2, op. 4, d. 125, l. 15.

94. RGASPI, f. 69, op. 1, d. 458, ll. 76–80.

95. RGASPI, f. 69, op. 1, d. 4, l. 86; d. 550, l. 28.

96. See James Harris, *The Great Urals: Regionalism and the Evolution of the Soviet System* (Ithaca, N.Y.: Cornell University Press, 1999); David Shearer, *Industry, State, and Society in Stalin's Russia, 1926–1934* (Ithaca, N.Y.: Cornell University Press, 1996), 25–133.

97. IIAN ORF, f. 2, raz. 2, op. 6, d. 11, l. 12.

98. RGASPI, f. 69, op. 1, d. 24, ll. 211–213. Unfortunately, no archival record has been found indicating how or why Stalin made this decision.

99. RGASPI, f. 69, op. 1, d. 213, l. 102.

100. RGASPI, f. 69, op. 1, d. 1062, l. 64; see also f. 625, op. 1, d. 10, l. 34.

101. Artem'ev, *V efire partizany*, 16.

102. TsKhDMO, f. 1, op. 53, d. 4, l. 44.

103. Briukhanov, *V shtabe partizanskogo dvizheniia*, 14.

104. Ibid., 110.

105. The Surazh Gates existed from April to September 1942. During that time, personnel and supplies traveled relatively unhindered through the front lines. Up to 25,000 recruits for the Red Army, mobilized by the partisans, were sent through, and specialists, plenipotentiaries, and scarce weapons and explosives went to the occupied territories; see Kalinin, *Partizanskaia respublika*, 105–115; M. M. Kir'ian, A. S. Galitsan, and N. G. Andronikov, eds., *Velikaia Otechestvennaia voina, 1941–1945: Slovar'-spravochnik* (Moscow: Politizdat, 1988), 439; Leonid Grenkevich, *The Soviet Partisan Movement, 1941–1944: A Critical Historiographical Analysis*, edited and with a foreword by David M. Glantz (London: Frank Cass, 1999), 85, 151, 178, 200.

106. RGASPI, f. 69, op. 1, d. 206, l. 15.

107. USHMM 1996.A.169, reel 39 (YVA M-37/1259—TsDAHOU, f. 62, op. 9, d. 6, l. 39). See also USHMM, 1996.A.169, reel 39 (YVA M-37/1256—TsDAHOU, f. 62, op. 9, d. 2, l. 28).

108. Popov, *Diversanty Stalina*, 42; Boiarskii, *Partizany*, 45.

109. RGASPI, f. 69, op. 1, d. 4, l. 30. Of these 3,000, almost 25 percent did not

survive the war; see Colonel General A. G. Pavlov, "Voennaia razvedka SSSR 1941–1945 gg.," *Novaia i noveishaia istoriia* 2 (1995): 39.

110. The "Sever" (North) and "radiostantsiei partizanskikh otriadov" (radio station of the partisan detachments, or RPO) were the primary models supplied to the partisans. Only the RPO was powerful enough to reach Soviet lines from the westernmost territories of Belorussia and Ukraine; Artem'ev, *V efire partizany,* 60–61; Pavlov, "Voennaia razvedka SSSR 1941–1945 gg.," 29.

111. *IVOVSS,* 2:487; Andrianov, *Voina v tylu vraga,* 125.

112. RGASPI, f. 69, op. 1, d. 19, ll. 54, 98; d. 25, ll. 5, 81, 123, 158–159, 163.

113. Zolotarev, *Partizanskoe dvizhenie,* 64–65.

114. Shumilin, *Istoriia partizanskogo dvizheniia,* 42.

115. RGASPI, f. 69, op. 1, d. 81, l.108.

116. RGASPI, f. 69, op. 1, d. 81, l. 39.

117. Grenkevich, *The Soviet Partisan Movement,* 196.

118. RGASPI, f. 69, op. 1, d. 212, ll. 71–73. For a detailed discussion of airpower and the partisans, see Gerhard Weinberg, "The Role of Airpower in the Formation and Control of Partisan Units," in Armstrong, *The Soviet Partisans,* 361–385.

119. IIAN ORF, f. 2, raz. 2, op. 6, d. 43, l. 4.

120. P. P. Vershigora, *Liudi s chistoi sovest'iu* (Moscow: Moskovskii rabochii, 1946), 179. V. S. Grizodubova, a famous woman flier from the 1930s, commanded an air unit that came to specialize in transport flights to and from the occupied territories; see Kazimiera J. Cottam, "Grizodubova, Valentina Stepanova," in Reina Pennington, ed., *Amazons to Fighter Pilots: A Biographical Dictionary of Military Women,* vol. 1 (Westport, Conn.: Greenwood Press, 2003), 186–188.

121. It is important to note that radio contact was often through telegram, not voice contact.

122. RGASPI, f. 69, op. 1, d. 1080, ll. 4–9.

123. A. V. Romanov, *Na zemle nepokorennoi* (Minsk: Belarus', 1962), 226–255.

124. IIAN ORF, f. 2, raz. 2, op. 6, d. 11, l. 13; RGASPI, f. 69, op. 1, d. 585, l. 3. It is interesting to note that both Firsanov and Strokach, the Ukrainian partisan leader, were from the NKVD, which might have encouraged a corporate alliance. However, Firsanov seems to have been in the political security branch (given his involvement in executing political prisoners in 1941 and his later appointment in SMERSH), whereas Strokach was a member of the border guards. The two branches were involved in feuds within the NKVD; see Parrish, *The Lesser Terror,* 69–70; Armstrong, "Introduction," in Armstrong, *The Soviet Partisans,* 50–51.

125. RGASPI, f. 69, op. 1, d. 562, l. 19.

126. RGASPI, f. 69, op. 1, d. 562, l. 20; d. 10, l. 19; d. 82, l. 51.

127. IIAN ORF, f. 2, raz. 2, op. 6, d. 11, l. 13.

128. RGASPI, f. 69, op. 1, d. 550, l. 94.

129. RGASPI, f. 69, op. 1, d. 82, ll. 52–53.

130. RGASPI, f. 69, op. 1, d. 82, ll. 53–54.

131. IIAN ORF, f. 2, raz. 2, op. 6, d. 20, l. 1.

132. RGASPI, f. 69, op. 1. d. 82, l. 51. It was not stated why the Red Army's chief

of staff should have taken an interest in a 600-man partisan detachment. The report included a radiogram message from Vasil'evskii dated "April 1942" ordering Matveev, Emliutin, and Gudzenko to transfer the 2nd Voroshilov to Ukrainian command. Scrawled across the radiogram was a handwritten "Not Sent."

133. Stephen Kotkin, *Magnetic Mountain: Stalinism as Civilization* (Berkeley: University of California Press, 1995), 293–298.

134. Barber and Harrison, *The Soviet Home Front*, 46–48, 108–112.

135. M. A. Il'in and V. S. Papin, eds., *Stranitsy narodnogo podviga: Kalininskaia oblast' v gody Velikoi Otechestvennoi voiny* (Moscow: Moskovskii rabochii, 1974), 82–83.

136. Makarov, *Partiinoe podpol'e*, 93; see also Chapter One.

137. Petrov, *Partizanskoe dvizhenie*, 174.

138. Ibid., 287.

139. USHMM, 1996.A.169, reel 33 (YVA M-37/459 — TsDAHOU, f. 62, op. 4, d. 18, ll. 2–4).

140. RGASPI, f. 69, op. 1, d. 1067, l. 199.

141. Kalinin, *Partizanskaia respublike respublika*, 274–276.

142. IIAN ORF, f. 2, raz. 2, op. 4, d. 130, l. 4.

143. RGASPI, f. 69, op. 1, d. 576, l. 60; TsKhDMO, f. 1, op. 53, d. 10, ll. 153–154.

144. Tsar'kov, "Bez zatish'ia i pereryva," 42; *IVOVSS*, 3:448.

145. USHMM, 1996.A.169, reel 36 (YVA M-37/781 — TsDAHOU, f. 66, op. 1, d. 18, l. 5), reel 33 (YVA M-37/456 — TsDAHOU, f. 62, op. 4, d. 12, l. 9).

146. Makarov, *Partiinoe podpol'e*, 80–81; Tsar'kov, "Bez zatish'ia i pereryva," 42. Both Begma and Fedorov retained their positions well into the postwar period, thus indicating that partisans remained dominant in these regions' politics. In Vinnytsia Oblast, however, many partisans themselves were purged over the course of several years. For a more detailed discussion of the personnel developments in the Vinnytsia and Ukrainian organizations, see Amir Weiner, *Making Sense of War: The Second World War and the Fate of the Bolshevik Revolution* (Princeton, N.J.: Princeton University Press, 2001), 70–126.

147. RGASPI, f. 69, op. 1, d. 1093, ll. 2–4.

148. RGASPI, f. 69, op. 1, d. 1084, l. 37.

149. RGASPI, f. 69, op. 1, d. 1112, l. 82.

150. IIAN ORF, f. 2, raz. 2, op. 6, d. 15, l. 13.

151. RGASPI, f. 69, op. 1, d. 1062, ll. 38–39.

152. RGASPI, f. 69, op. 1, d. 1112, l. 93.

153. Ibid.

154. IIAN ORF, f. 2, raz. 2, op. 2. d. 25a, ll. 108–109; RGASPI, f. 69, op. 1, d. 19, l. 22; op. 4, d. 3429, ll. 6–7.

155. RGASPI, f. 69, op. 1, d. 28, l. 35.

156. RGASPI, f. 69, op. 1, d. 28, l. 42.

157. RGASPI, f. 69, op. 1, d. 28, ll. 135–137.

158. IIAN ORF, f. 2, raz. 2, op. 4, d. 25, l. 13.

159. RGASPI, f. 69, op. 1, d. 1067, l. 112; d. 159, l. 25.

CHAPTER FOUR. PEOPLE'S AVENGERS
OR *PARTIZANSHCHINA*?

1. E. S. Seniavskaia concluded that more fictionalized accounts and essays were published in 1941 and 1942 when the Red Army was retreating as compared to 1943 and later when Soviet forces were advancing and more factual material was reported; Seniavskaia, *Frontovoe Pokolenie: Istoriko-psikhologichesskoe issledovanie* (Moscow: Institut rossiiskoi istorii, RAN, 1995), 59.

2. Sovnarkom authorized Gosradio to commence regularly scheduled broadcasts to the occupied territories and the partisans on 22 May 1942, a week before the establishment of the Central Staff. Broadcasts began early the following month; see James von Geldern, "Radio Moscow: The Voice from the Center," in Richard Stites, ed., *Culture and Entertainment in Wartime Russia* (Bloomington: Indiana University Press, 1995), 61n58. Many of the transcripts of these broadcasts are located at the GARF, f. 6903, op. 20, d. 1–20.

3. Sheila Fitzpatrick, "Ascribing Class: The Construction of Social Identity in Soviet Russia," *Journal of Modern History* 65, 4 (1993): 745–770.

4. RGASPI, f. 69, op. 1, d. 286, l. 4.

5. See, for example, *Izvestiia*, 26 June 1942; GARF, f. 6903, op. 20, d. 4, ll. 69–73 (2 August 1942). Sometimes, officials guessed wrong in their choice of heroes. Smolensk commander N. Z. Koliada, code-named Batia, was accorded celebrity status in the summer of 1942—before it was discovered that his unit operated in a manner that embodied the worst forms of partizanshchina. Koliada was then quietly removed from command.

6. Donald Reid, *Paris Sewers and Sewermen: Representations and Realities* (Cambridge, Mass.: Harvard University Press, 1991), 5.

7. Ibid., 87.

8. Judith Deutsch Kornblatt, *The Cossack Hero in Russian Literature: A Study in Cultural Mythology* (Madison: University of Wisconsin Press, 1992); Paul Avrich, *Russian Rebels: 1600–1800* (New York: W. W. Norton, 1972), 59–61, 256–273; Jeffrey Brooks, *When Russia Learned to Read: Literacy and Popular Literature, 1861–1917* (Princeton, N.J.: Princeton University Press, 1985), esp. 166–213; Hiroaki Kuromiya, *Freedom and Terror in the Donbas: A Ukrainian-Russian Borderland, 1870s–1990s* (Cambridge: Cambridge University Press, 1998), 35–40; Richard Stites, *Revolutionary Dreams: Utopian Visions and Experimental Life in the Russian Revolution* (Oxford: Oxford University Press, 1989), 14–19. For a general discussion of social banditry in popular culture, including its Russian variants, see Eric Hobsbawm, *Bandits* (New York: Penguin Books, 1985).

9. Richard Stites, *Russian Popular Culture: Entertainment and Society since 1900* (Cambridge: Cambridge University Press, 1992), 45.

10. RGASPI, f. 69, op. 1, d. 28, l. 66; IIAN ORF, f. 2, raz. 2, op. 19, d. 25, l. 7.

11. See, for example, the account of the exploits of Nikolai Shchors, GARF, f. 6903, op. 20, d. 8, l. 341 (15 November 1942); see also d. 5, ll. 62–63 (3 September 1942);

d. 9, ll. 106–107 (19 November 1942); d. 9, ll. 363–364 (28 November 1942); d. 9, ll. 409–411 (30 November 1942).

12. IIAN ORF, f. 2, raz. 2, op. 6, d. 12, l. 47.

13. P. P. Vershigora, *Liudi s chistoi sovest'iu* (Moscow: Moskovskii rabochii, 1946), 43.

14. Cited in A. F. Fyodorov, *The Underground Committee Carries On*, trans. L. Stolitsky (Moscow: Foreign Language Publishing House, 1952), 263.

15. Jochen Hellbeck, "Fashioning the Stalinist Soul: The Diary of Stepan Podlubnyi," *Jahrbucher für Geschichte Osteuropas* 44, 3 (1996): 353; Kuromiya, *Freedom and Terror in the Donbas*, 275.

16. N. Galay, "The Partisan Forces," in B. H. Liddell Hart, ed., *The Red Army* (New York: Harcourt Brace, 1956), 167. Although the statement indicates a male-centric view, women could and did partake actively in this good life as well.

17. Fyodorov, *The Underground Committee*, 196.

18. Vershigora, *Liudi s chistoi sovest'iu*, 97–98.

19. RGASPI, f. 69, op. 1, d. 1067, l. 188.

20. See Mark Mazower, *Inside Hitler's Greece: The Experience of Occupation, 1941–1944* (New Haven, Conn.: Yale University Press, 1993), 123–129; Roderick Kedward, "The Maquis and the Culture of the Outlaw," in Roderick Kedward and Roger Austin, eds., *Vichy France and the Resistance: Culture and Ideology* (London: Croom Helm, 1985), 240–241, 248.

21. RGASPI, f. 625, op. 1, d. 61, l. 172.

22. IIAN, f. 2, raz. 2, op. 4, d. 23, l. 10.

23. RGASPI, f. 69, op. 1, d. 748, ll. 80–81.

24. RGASPI, f. 69, op. 1, d. 28, l. 69; d. 1067, l. 239.

25. Vershigora, *Liudi s chistoi sovest'iu*, 291–292.

26. RGASPI, f. 69, op. 1, d. 164, ll. 21–122; d. 1081, l. 46.

27. RGASPI, f. 69, op. 1, d. 164, ll. 221–222.

28. Z. A. Bogatyr', *V tylu vraga: Boeviia deiatel'nost' soedineniia partizanskikh otriadov pod komandovaniem geroi Sovetskogo soiuza A. N. Saburova* (Moscow: Sotsekgiz, 1963), 62.

29. Stephen Kotkin, *Magnetic Mountain: Stalinism as a Civilization* (Berkeley and Los Angeles: University of California Press, 1995), 94–103; Kuromiya, *Freedom and Terror*, 186–187.

30. Cited in Fyodorov, *The Underground Committee*, 354.

31. See the discussion on revenge later in the chapter.

32. Vershigora, *Liudi s chistoi sovest'iu*, 98.

33. A. F. Fedorov, *Podpol'nyi obkom deistvuet* (Kiev: Politizdat Ukrainy, 1986), 245.

34. Lisa A. Kirschenbaum, "'Our City, Our Hearths, Our Families': Local Loyalties and Private Life in Soviet World War II Propaganda," *Slavic Review* 59, 4 (Winter 2000): 825; see the discussion of the ambiguity of "motherland" in the 1943 debate over *History of the Kazaksh S.S.R.* Lowell Tillet, *The Great Friendship: Soviet Histo-*

rians and Non-Russian Nationalities (Chapel Hill: University of North Carolina Press, 1969), 73–74.

35. See Terry Martin, *The Affirmative Action Empire: Nations and Nationalism in the Soviet Union, 1932–1939* (Ithaca, N.Y.: Cornell University Press, 2001); David Brandenberger, *National Bolshevism: Stalinist Mass Culture and the Formation of Modern Russian National Identity, 1931–1956* (Cambridge, Mass.: Harvard University Press, 2002). See also Yuri Slezkine, "The USSR as a Communal Apartment, or, How a Socialist State Promoted Ethnic Particularism," *Slavic Review* 53, 2 (1994): 414–442.

36. GARF, f. 6903, op. 20, d. 8, ll. 37–38 (3 November 1942); ll. 136–139 (6 November 1942); ll. 149–153 (8 November 1942); d. 9, ll. 217–219 (22 November 1942); d. 10, l. 144 (7 December 1942).

37. GARF, f. 6903, op. 20, d. 8, l. 345 (15 November 1942); d. 9, l. 323 (27 November 1942); d. 11, l. 178 (19 December 1942); ll. 175–179 (22 December 1942).

38. See, for example, GARF, f. 6903, op. 20, d. 4, l. 552 (13 August 1942); d. 7, ll. 53–54 (3 October 1942); d. 14, l. 137 (10 June 1943), ll. 327–328 (23 June 1943); *Krasnaia zvezda*, 3 March 1942, 3.

39. *Pravda*, 16 March 1942, 1.

40. GARF, f. 6903, op. 20, d. 5, l. 34 (2 September 1942).

41. *Izvestiia*, 15 October 1942, p. 2.

42. GARF, f. 6903, op. 20, d. 2, l. 491 (30 June 1942). Such use of idyllic hometown imagery to motivate national patriotic feelings was not limited to the Soviet Union. American wartime songs, such as "I'll Be Seeing You" and "This Is Worth Fighting For," illustrate this point.

43. GARF, f. 6903, op. 20, d. 2, ll. 491–494 (30 June 1942).

44. GARF, f. 6903, op. 20, d. 1, l. 382 (10 June 1942); d. 4, ll. 438–441 (10 August 1942); d. 5, ll. 62–67 (3 September 1942); d. 8, ll. 247–248 (12 November 1942); d. 9, ll. 363–364 (28 November 1942); d. 14, ll. 371–374 (26 June 1943).

45. For a small sample, see *Izvestiia*, 26 June 1942, p. 2, 23 August 1942, p. 2, 8 July 1943, p. 3; *Krasnaia zvezda*, 22 August 1941, p. 4, 13 April 1943, p. 3, 31 December 1943, p. 3; *Pravda*, 25 July 1941, p. 2, 23 November 1942, p. 2, 7 April 1943, p. 2.

46. GARF, f. 6903, op. 20, d. 9, ll. 46–48 (17 November 1942).

47. For a slightly different take on the question of conflation and its effects, see Brandenberger, *National Bolshevism*, 226–234.

48. GARF, f. 6903, op. 20, d. 7, l. 355 (14 October 1942).

49. GARF, f. 6903, op. 20, d. 12, l. 265 (15 January 1943); d. 14, l. 369 (26 June 1943). For a broader discussion of Soviet-church relations during the war, see Steven Merritt Miner, *Stalin's Holy War: Religion, Nationalism and Alliance Politics, 1941–1945* (Chapel Hill: University of North Carolina Press, 2003).

50. GARF, f. 6903, op. 20, d. 1, l. 105 (3 June 1942).

51. GARF, f. 6903, op. 20, d. 5, l. 107 (4 September 1942).

52. In fact, the Baltic states contributed, at best, only 10,000 people to the partisan movement, whereas it is estimated that in Lithuania alone, over 100,000 participated in anti-Soviet resistance; see V. A. Zolotarev, ed., *Partizanskoe dvizhenie: Po opytu Velikoi Otechestvennoi voiny, 1941–1945 gg.* (Moscow: Kuchkovo Pole, 2001),

272; Alfred J. Rieber, "Civil Wars in the Soviet Union," *Kritika* 4, 2 (Winter 2003): 158–159.

53. One must be cautious about reading too much significance into these names. The Bielski detachment, organized by Jews from eastern Poland (or western Belorussia), was first officially called the Zhukov Detachment and later the Kalinin Detachment. Most of its members, including its leaders, had no particular allegiance to the Soviet Union, however.

54. IIAN ORF, f. 2, raz. 2, op. 4, d. 125, l. 6.

55. See Chapter Five.

56. TsKhDMO, f. 1, op. 53, d. 88, ll. 59, 83, 93, 109, 114.

57. RGASPI, f. 69, op. 1, d. 474, l. 13.

58. RGASPI, f. 625, op. 1, d. 28, l. 77.

59. RGASPI, f. 625, op. 1, d. 28, l. 12. It is not known whether Medvedeva's request was granted.

60. TsMVS, f. 4/38347, l. 30.

61. TsMVS, f. 4/38347, ll. 36–42, 44–46.

62. RGASPI, f. 625, op. 1, d. 61, l. 145.

63. Rieber, "Civil Wars in the Soviet Union"; for other treatments, see also Kate Brown, *A Biography of No Place: From Ethnic Borderland to Soviet Heartland* (Cambridge, Mass.: Harvard University Press, 2004), and Timothy Snyder, *The Reconstruction of Nations: Poland, Ukraine, Lithuania, Belarus, 1569–1999* (New Haven, Conn.: Yale University Press, 2003).

64. RGASPI, f. 625, op. 1, d. 28, l. 37.

65. Shalom Cholawsky, *The Jews of Bielorussia during World War II* (Amsterdam: Harwood Academic Publishers, 1998), 12–14; Dov Levin, *Fighting Back: Lithuanian Jewry's Armed Resistance to the Nazis, 1941–1945*, translated from the Hebrew by Moshe Kohn and Dina Cohen (New York and London: Holmes and Meier, 1985), 21–25; Andrew Ezergailis, *The Holocaust in Latvia, 1941–1944: The Missing Center* (Riga and Washington, D.C.: Historical Institute of Latvia and the U.S. Holocaust Memorial Museum, 1998), 70–72, 84–94; Jan Gross, "The Jewish Community in the Soviet-Annexed Territories on the Eve of the Holocaust," in Lucjan Dobroszycki and Jeffrey Gurock, eds., *The Holocaust in the Soviet Union: Studies and Sources on the Destruction of the Jews in the Nazi-Occupied Territories of the USSR, 1941–1945* (Armonk, N.Y.: M. E. Sharpe, 1993), 155–171. The linking of Jews and Communists was especially unfortunate for Jews, as it enabled nationalist groups in the occupied territories to connect their military-political struggle for independence with the Nazi genocide; see Amir Weiner, *Making Sense of War: The Second World War and the Fate of the Bolshevik Revolution* (Princeton, N.J.: Princeton University Press, 2001), 240–246, 258–269.

66. USHMM, 1996.A.169, reel 3 (YVA M-37/1565—TsDAHOU, f. 62, op. 8, d. 61, l. 8); for World War I accusations, see Joshua A. Sanborn, *Drafting the Russian Nation: Military Conscription, Total War, and Mass Politics, 1905–1925* (DeKalb: Northern Illinois University Press, 2003), 121–122.

67. RGASPI, f. 69, op. 1, d. 1067, l. 169.

68. See the account of V. A. Andreyev, cited in Jack Nusan Porter, ed., *Jewish Partisans: A Documentary of Jewish Resistance in the Soviet Union during World War II*, vol. 1 (New York: University Press of America, 1982), 107–111.

69. Cited in *Izvestiia KPSS* 7 (1990): 211.

70. RGASPI, f. 69, op. 1, d. 1067, l. 242.

71. Evgenii Zhirnov, ed., "Na okkupirovannykh territoriiakh," *Kommersant vlast'*, part 3, no. 31 (7 August 2001).

72. RGASPI, f. 69, op. 1, d. 164, ll. 37–38, 173, d. 475, l. 106; f. 625, op. 1, d. 10, ll. 10–11; TsKhDMO, f. 1, op. 53, d. 88, ll. 99, 101.

73. IIAN ORF, f. 2, raz. 2, op. 19, d. 8, l. 12.

74. RGASPI, f. 69, op. 1, d. 61, l. 167.

75. IIAN ORF, f. 2, raz. 2, op. 4, d. 25, l. 5.

76. RGASPI, f. 69, op., 1, d. 28, l. 166.

77. See, for example, IIAN ORF, f. 2, raz. 2, op. 9/2, d. 30, l. 11; RGASPI, f. 69, op. 1, d. 550, l. 30; d. 748, l. 80; USHMM RG 22.005M, reel 3 (RGASPI, f. 69, op. 1, d. 741, ll. 39–41).

78. See Martin, *Affirmative Action Empire*, and Weiner, *Making Sense of War*.

79. *Krasnaia zvezda*, 5 November 1942, p. 2.

80. RGASPI, f. 625, op. 1, d. 10, l. 35.

81. RGASPI, f. 69, op. 1, d. 164, ll. 147, 149.

82. RGASPI, f. 625, op. 1, d. 61, 82.

83. RGASPI, f. 625, op. 1, d. 9, l. 178; d. 10, l. 37.

84. N. P. Sudoplatov, "Poka my zhila," in N. P. Sudoplatov and A. A. Tumanian, *Zapiski partizanskikh vrachei: O podvigakh medrabotnikov v tylu vraga v gody Velikoi Otechestvennoi voiny* (Tula, USSR: Prioskoe knizhnoe izdatel'stvo, 1989), 28.

85. "Song of the Motherland," cited in Richard Stites and James von Geldern, eds., *Mass Culture in Soviet Russia: Tales, Poems, Songs, Movies, Plays, and Folklore, 1917–1953* (Bloomington: Indiana University Press, 1995), 271–272. For discussions of prewar man-nature discourse, see Katerina Clark, *The Soviet Novel: History as Ritual* (Chicago: University of Chicago Press, 1981), 101–105; Karen Petrone, *Life Has Become More Joyous, Comrades: Celebrations in the Time of Stalin* (Bloomington: Indiana University Press, 2000), 53–56.

86. Brooks, *When Russia Learned to Read*, 189.

87. *Pravda*, 20 December 1942, p. 2.

88. *Krasnaia zvezda*, 26 December 1941, p. 3.

89. GARF, f. 6903, op. 20, d. 1, ll. 192–195 (6 June 1942).

90. GARF, f. 6903, op. 20, d. 4, l. 72 (2 August 1942). See also *Izvestiia*, 18 August 1942, p. 4.

91. *Krasnaia zvezda*, 22 August 1941, p. 4.

92. GARF, f. 6903, op. 20, d. 1, l. 8 (1 June 1942).

93. TsKhDMO, f. 1, op. 6, d. 309, ll. 67, 146.

94. RGASPI, f. 625, op. 1, d. 28, l. 7.

95. IIAN ORF, f. 2, raz. 2, op. 9/2, d. 57, l. 5.

96. TsMVS, f. 4/38347, l. 73.

97. Cited in Stephen G. Fritz, *Frontsoldaten: The German Soldier in World War II* (Lexington: University Press of Kentucky, 1995), 125–126.

98. *Izvestiia*, 26 September 1942, p. 2.

99. RGASPI, f. 69, op. 1, d. 576, l. 28; USHMM, RG 22.005M, reel 1 (RGASPI, f. 17, op. 88, d. 480, l. 156); reel 2 (RGASPI, f. 69, op. 1, d. 1074, l. 2); reel 3 (RGASPI, f. 69, op. 1, d. 347, l. 27; d. 713, ll. 7–8). For discussions on German atrocities during the first year of the war, see Hannes Heer, "The Killing Fields: The Wehrmacht and the Holocaust in Belorussia, 1941–1942," and "The Logic of Extermination: The Wehrmacht and the Anti-Partisan War," both in Hannes Heer and Klaus Naumann, *War of Extermination: The German Military in World War II, 1941–1944* (New York: Berghahn Books, 2000), 55–79, 92–126.

100. Argyrios Pisiotis, "Images of Hate in the Art of War," in Stites, *Culture and Entertainment in Wartime Russia*, 150–152.

101. *Krasnaia zvezda*, 1 November 1941. For a discussion of *She Defends the Motherland*, one of the signature films of the war years, see Denise Youngblood, "A War Remembered: Soviet Films of the Great Patriotic War," *American Historical Review* 106, 3 (June 2001): 841–844; see also Peter Kenez, "Black and White: The War on Film," in Stites, *Culture and Entertainment in Wartime Russia*, 167–169.

102. GARF, f. 6903, op. 20, d. 9, ll. 55–59 (17 November 1942); see also d. 3, l. 29 (1 July 1942).

103. GARF, f. 6903, op. 20, d. 4, l. 541 (13 August 1942).

104. *Krasnaia zvezda*, 15 November 1941, p. 4.

105. See also *Krasnaia zvezda*, 7 August 1941, p. 1, 22 August 1941, p. 4, 1 November 1941, p. 2; *Izvestiia*, 26 June 1942, p. 2.

106. Jeffrey Brooks, *Thank You, Comrade Stalin! Soviet Public Culture from Revolution to Cold War* (Princeton, N.J.: Princeton University Press, 2000), 128, 131–135. For a discussion on the importance of purity in Soviet ideology and policy, see Amir Weiner, "Nature, Nurture, and Memory in a Socialist Utopia: Delineating the Soviet Socio-ethnic Body in the Age of Socialism," *American Historical Review* 104, 4 (October 1999): 1114–1155.

107. RGASPI, f. 625, op. 1, d. 28, l. 95. For a general discussion of the effect of *Aleksandr Nevskii* on prewar audiences, see Brandenberger, *National Bolshevism*, 101–104.

108. RGASPI, f. 625, op. 1, d. 28, l. 39.

109. Bogatyr', *V tylu vraga*, 237; IIAN ORF, f. 2, raz. 2, op. 6, d. 12, l. 15.

110. Faye Schulman, *A Partisan's Memoir: Woman of the Holocaust* (Toronto: Second Story Press, 1995). 100.

111. USHMM, RG 22.005M, reel 3 (RGASPI, f. 69, op. 1, d. 746, l. 220). See also Mordechai Altshuler, "Jewish Warfare and the Participation of Jews in Combat in the Soviet Union as Reflected in Soviet and Western Historiography," in Zvi Gitelman, ed., *Bitter Legacy: Confronting the Holocaust in the USSR* (Bloomington: Indiana University Press, 1997), 151–166.

112. Cited in Nahun Kohn and Howard Roiter, *A Voice from the Forest* (New York: Holocaust Library, 1980), 173.

113. See, for example, the documents cited in John Armstrong, ed., *The Soviet*

Partisans in World War II (Madison: University of Wisconsin Press, 1964), 734. The deputy chief of the Central Staff, NKVD general S. S. Bel'chenko, told Russian historian Aleksei Popov that 23,128 German officers and soldiers were captured by the partisans (undoubtedly an exaggerated figure) and that a significant number of them were of interest to Red Army intelligence and were sent back to the mainland. He was silent about the fates of the rest; Aleksei Popov, *15 Vstrech s generalom KGB Bel'chenko* (Moscow: OLMA-PRESS, 2002), 229.

114. Weiner, *Making Sense of War*, 171–182.

115. Aleksei Popov, *Diversanty Stalina: Deiatelnost' organov Gosbezopasnosti na okkupirovannoi Sovetskoi territorii v gody Velikoi Otechestvennoi voiny* (Moscow: Iausa, Eksmo, 2004), 205.

116. RGASPI, f. 625, op. 1, d. 28, l. 87.

117. TsKhDMO, f. 1, op. 53, d. 252, l. 38.

118. Alexander Werth, *Russia at War, 1941–1945* (New York: Avon, 1964), 387–388, 391, 870–874; Horst Boog, ed., *Germany and the Second World War*, vol. 4, *The Attack on the Soviet Union* (Oxford: Oxford University Press, 1998), 912–918; Pisiotis, "Images of Hate," 141–156.

119. Boog, ed., *Germany and the Second World War*, 913–919. See also Antony Beevor, *Stalingrad: The Fateful Siege: 1942–1943* (New York: Viking, 1998), 60–61, 363, 386.

120. TsKhDMO, f. 1, op. 53, d. 252, l. 6.

121. Fedorov, *Podpol'nyi obkom deistvuet*, 406. Translation in Fyodorov, *The Underground Committee*, 425.

122. Schulman, *A Partisan's Memoir*, 177.

123. RGASPI, f. 625, op. 1, d. 28, ll. 37, 70.

124. RGASPI, f. 1, op. 1, d. 164, l. 57; d. 473, l. 41; d. 1096, l. 23.

125. IIAN ORF, f. 2, raz. 2, op. 6, d. 15, l. 9; d. 12, ll. 8, 28; RGASPI, f. 69, op. 1, d. 159, l. 22.

126. *Izvestiia*, 17 July 1942, p. 2; *Krasnaia zvezda*, 5 November 1942, p. 2, 8 July 1943, p. 3; *Pravda*, 9 January 1942, p. 3, 26 August 1942, p. 2, 23 November 1942, p. 2.

127. In October 1942, the Central Staff forbade the publication of information that could lead to harsher repression in the occupied territories; RGASPI, f. 69, op. 1, d. 28, l. d, IIII, l. 22.

128. IIAN ORF, f. 2, raz. 2, op. 6, d. 9, l. 21; G. M. Lin'kov: *Voina v tylu vraga* (Moscow: Gos. izdatelst'vo khudozhestvennoi literatury, 1951), 92. Matthew Cooper argued that not only were the partisans indifferent to civilian casualties, they even welcomed attacks against civilians, since the partisans "were not fighting to preserve, but to destroy the old form of society, and, in its place, help create a new one"; Cooper: *The Phantom War: The German Struggle against the Soviet Partisans, 1941–1944* (London: MacDonald & James, 1979), 8.

129. RGASPI, f. 625, op. 1, d. 10, l. 37.

130. Cited in Svetlana Aleksievich, *War's Unwomanly Face* (Moscow: Progress Publishers, 1988), 200–201.

131. Vershigora, *Liudi s chistoi sovest'iu*, 498, 501–503; Reuben Ainzstein, *Jewish Resistance in Occupied Eastern Europe* (London: Elek Books, 1974), 382–383.

132. IIAN ORF, f. 2, raz. 2, op. 6, d. 9, l. 22.

133. IIAN ORF, f. 2, raz. 2, op. 6, d. 11, l. 11.

134. Cited in Ainzstein, *Jewish Resistance*, 355. The civilians in question were Jews, but the nature of the partisans' complaints, which were put pragmatically, suggests that anti-Semitism was not a decisive factor in *this* instance, although it probably contributed to the partisans' sentiments.

135. Cited in Nechama Tec, *Defiance: The Bielski Partisans* (Oxford: Oxford University Press, 1993), 82.

136. Orlando Figes, *A People's Tragedy: The Russian Revolution, 1891–1924* (New York: Penguin, 1996), 751–758, 768–769.

137. RGASPI, f. 69, op. 1, d. 142, ll. 47–48.

138. RGASPI, f. 69, op. 1, d. 1067, l. 172.

139. V. I. Boiarskii, *Partizany i armiia: Istoriia uteriannykh vozmozhnostei* (Minsk: Kharvest, 2003), 233.

140. RGASPI, f. 69, op. 1, d. 474, l. 19.

141. Brooks, *Thank You, Comrade Stalin*, 179.

142. Kornblatt, *The Cossack Hero*, 103–104.

143. David Hoffmann, *Stalinist Values: The Cultural Norms of Soviet Modernity, 1917–1941* (Ithaca, N.Y.: Cornell University Press, 2003), 45–56.

144. V. A. Perezhogin, "Iz okruzheniia i plena—v partizany," *Otechestvennaia istoriia* 3 (2000): 27.

145. RGASPI, f. 69, op. 1, d. 142, l. 37; d. 286, l. 87; d. 1110, ll. 45–47.

146. RGASPI, f. 625, op. 1, d. 61, l. 41.

147. RGASPI, f. 69, op. 1, d. 25, l. 1.

148. *Pravda*, 18 August 1941, p. 2.

149. *Krasnaia zvezda*, 16 May 1942, p. 2. See also the transcript of the 12 June 1942 Radio Moscow broadcast to the occupied territories, in GARF, f. 6903, op. 20, d. 1, ll. 441–444. Soviet propagandists claimed that, in contrast to the usual Western image, the Germans were numerically superior but technologically inferior to the Soviets.

150. GARF, f. 6903, op. 20, d. 8, l. 154 (8 November 1942).

151. Fyodorov, *The Underground Committee*, 509. Fedorov omitted the reference to "Soviet men and women," instead calling them "the most ordinary people"; Fedorov, *Podpol'nyi obkom deistvuet*, 480.

152. RGASPI, f. 625, op. 1, d. 28, l. 13. Even Ponomarenko apparently lost track of his mother; he was informed by a subordinate in March 1943 that she had been evacuated to Krasnodar; RGASPI, f. 625, op. 1, d. 10, ll. 2–4.

153. Vershigora, *Liudi s chistoi sovest'iu*, 197.

154. IIAN ORF, f. 2, raz. 2, op. 4, d. 25, l. 13.

155. Cited by Vershigora, *Liudi s chistoi sovest'iu*, 235; translation in Weiner, *Making Sense of War*, 76.

156. See the excerpts from partisan letters in RGASPI, f. 69, op. 1, d. 748, ll. 131–134.

157. Alexander Hill, *The War behind the Eastern Front: The Soviet Partisan Movement in North-West Russia, 1941–1944* (New York: Frank Cass, 2005), 60–61.

158. IIAN ORF, f. 2, raz. 2, op. 19, d. 8, l. 9; RGASPI, f. 69, op. 1, d. 576, l. 20.

159. S. A. Kovpak, *Ot Putivlia do Karpat* (Leningrad: Gos-izdat detskoi litera-tury, 1945), 84.

160. Cited in Fyodorov, *The Underground Committee*, 131.

161. RGASPI, f. 625, op. 1, d. 28, l. 27.

162. Bogatyr', *V tylu vraga*, 112; see also Weiner, *Making Sense of War*, 75–77.

163. RGASPI, f. 69, op. 1, d. 283, l. 7.

164. RGASPI, f. 625, op. 1, d. 10, l. 37.

165. Soldiers in the elite guards units.

166. RGASPI, f. 625, op. 1, d. 61, l. 751.

167. RGASPI, f. 625, op. 1, d. 61, l. 585.

168. Vershigora, *Liudi s chistoi sovest'iu*, 234–235; see also Weiner, *Making Sense of War*, 75–76.

169. Fedorov, *Podpol'nyi obkom deistvuet*, 324.

170. RGASPI, f. 69, op. 1, d. 1067, ll. 179, 180; f. 625, op. 1, d. 61, l. 544; Ver-shigora, *Liudi s chistoi sovest'iu*, 241.

171. Vershigora, *Liudi s christoi sovest'iu*, 48, 57, 96–97; Weiner, *Making Sense of War*, 74.

172. TsKhDMO, f. 1, op. 53, d. 252, l. 16.

173. See, for example, Nina Tumarkin, *The Living and the Dead: The Rise and Fall of the Cult of World War II in Russia* (New York: Basic Books, 1994), 64–66.

174. IIAN ORF, f. 2, raz. 2, op. 4, d. 75, ll. 3–4; op. 6, d. 27, l. 16; N. I. Makarov, ed., *Partiinoe podpol'e: Deiatel'nost podpolnykh partiinykh organov i organizatsii na Okkupirovannoi Sovetskii territorii v gody Velikoi Otechestvennoi voiny* (Moscow: Poli-tizdat, 1983), 318; A. S. Zalesskii, *V partizanskikh kraiakh i zonakh: Patriotiches-kii podvig Sovetskogo krestianstva v tylu vraga, 1941–1944 g.* (Moscow: Sotsial'no-Ekonomicheskoi literatury, 1962), 79.

175. See, for example, *Pravda*, 9 January 1942, p. 3, 1 March 1942, p. 2, 19 April 1942, p. 4, 2 July 1942, p. 2; *Krasnaia zvezda*, 27 November 1942, p. 4.

176. RGASPI, f. 69, op. 1, d. 1093, l. 5.

177. *Pravda*, 17 February 1942, p. 1.

178. Ludmilla Alexeyeva and Paul Goldberg, *The Thaw Generation: Coming of Age in the Post-Stalin Era* (Boston: Little, Brown, 1990), 20–21.

179. GARF, f. 6903, op. 20, d. 10, l. 70 (3 December 1942).

180. Fyodorov, *The Underground Committee*, 239, 340.

181. RGASPI, f. 69, op. 1, d. 10–67, l. 227.

182. Bogatyr', *V tylu vraga*, 201.

183. IIAN ORF, f. 2, raz. 2, op. 9/2, d. 57, l. 1.

184. RGASPI, f. 69, op. 1. d. 1067, ll. 55–56.

185. RGASPI, f. 69, op. 1, d. 164, l. 157. See also the thoughts of F. I. Federen'ko, a Crimean partisan commander, on his feelings of abandonment by the Crimean Obkom in *Istoriia partizanskogo dvizheniia v Rossiiskoi Federatsii v gody Velikoi Otechestvennoi voiny* (Moscow: Atlantida, 2001), 22.

186. Fedorov, *Podpol'nyi obkom deisvuet*, 235.

187. RGASPI, f. 69, op. 1, d. 1067, ll. 55–56.

188. Cited in P. I. Kurbatova, *Smolenskaia partiinaia organizatsiia v gody Velikoi Otechestvennoi voiny* (Smolensk: Smolenskoe knizhnoe izdatel'stvo, 1958), 33–34.

189. T. A. Kliatskii, ed., *Partizanskie byli* (Moscow: Politizdat, 1965), 23, 206.

190. Cited in Fyodorov, *The Underground Committee*, 237.

191. IIAN ORF, f. 2, raz. 2, op. 19, d. 12, ll. 3–4; Leningrad Obkom KPSS, ed., *Leningrad v Velikoi Otechestvennoi voine Sovetskogo Soiuza: Sbornik dokumentov i materialov, T. 2: Iiunia 1943–mart 1944* (Leningrad: Lenizdat, 1947), 300.

192. Cited in Fyodorov, *The Underground Committee*, 422.

193. Vershigora, *Liudi s chistoi sovest'iu*, 235–236, 412.

194. RGASPI, f. 69, op. 1, d. 1076, ll. 14–15; d. 1094, l. 6.

195. RGASPI, f. 69, op. 1, d. 1111, l. 7.

196. RGASPI, f. 69, op. 1, d. 283, ll. 2, 3.

197. RGASPI, f. 69, op. 1, d. 28, l. 72; d. 1076, l. 10.

198. IIAN ORF, f. 2, raz. 2, op. 4, d. 117, l. 8.

199. RGASPI, f. 69, op. 1, d. 1080, l. 25.

200. RGASPI, f. 69, op. 1, d. 1080, l. 39.

201. Fedorov, *Podpol'nyi obkom deistvuet*, 245–246.

202. IIAN ORF, f. 2, raz. 2, op. 6, d. 12, l. 10.

203. IIAN ORF, f. 2, raz. 2, op. 4, d. 23, ll. 7, 10. See also RGASPI, f. 69, op. 1, d. 550, l. 50.

204. RGASPI, f. 69, op. 1, d. 1067, l. 171.

205. IIAN ORF, f. 2, raz. 2, op. 6, d. 20, l. 3.

206. IIAN ORF, f. 2, raz. 2, op. 6, d. 12, ll. 6, 10, 18–19. Other partisan officials asserted that, in fact, the "Death to the German Occupiers" was a very good "civilian" detachment, yet it is still clear in the minds of these officials that a hierarchy of partisan military effectiveness existed, in which the civilian detachments came out second best; RGASPI, f. 69, op. 1, d. 28, l. 72.

207. RGASPI, f. 69, op. 8, d. 682.

208. IIAN ORF, f. 2, raz. 2, op. 6, d. 15, l. 17.

209. RGASPI, f. 69, op. 1, d. 283, l. 9.

210. RGASPI, f. 69, op. 1, d. 474, l. 26.

211. Cited in A. V. Romanov, *Na zemle nepokorennoi* (Minsk: Belarus', 1962), 138.

212. *The Front* proclaimed the superiority of professionally trained military technocrats over the revolutionary spirit of old Civil War "warhorses." The Red Army's independence was indicated by the return of epaulettes to officers and the abolition of political commissars in October 1942.

213. Timothy Colton, *Commissars, Commanders, and Civilian Authority: The Structure of Soviet Military Politics* (Cambridge: Cambridge University Press, 1979), 87–88, 107, 109, 112, 167.

214. RGASPI, f. 69, op. 1, d. 283, l. 9. It is possible that the commander invented this story to justify taking over another unit, but in any case, he spoke a language that Moscow understood clearly.

215. RGASPI, f. 69, op. 1, d. 1077, l. 12.

216. Romanov himself was an okruzhenets who joined a detachment of the Twenty-ninth Army after escaping from a German concentration camp; Romanov, *Na zemle nepokorennoi*, 52.

217. RGASPI, f. 69, op. 1, d. 1080, l. 17.

218. RGASPI, f. 69, op. 1, d. 1080, ll.18–19.

219. RGASPI, f. 69, op. 1, d. 1080, l. 19.

220. RGASPI, f. 69, op. 1, d. 1080, ll. 31–32. In his memoirs, Romanov described the hostility as emanating from a small group of disgruntled partisans, led by a commander and section leader who had become traitors and had entered German service; Romanov, *Na zemle nepokorennoi*, 194–196.

221. Nichiporovich later claimed, without corroboration from other witnesses, that he had organized the detachment; IIAN ORF, f. 2, raz. 2, op. 4, d. 23, ll. 3–4.

222. The 208th Rifle Division.

223. IIAN ORF, f. 2, raz. 2, op. 4, d. 47, l. 11.

224. IIAN ORF, f. 2, raz. 2, op. 6, d. 23, l. 12.

225. Several documents from a variety of sources discuss the dispute between Nichiporovich and Pokrovskii, and all agree remarkably on the parameters of the conflict; RGASPI, f. 69, op. 1, d. 1067, l. 212, op. 4, d. 3009, ll. 5–7; IIAN ORF, f. 2, raz. 2, op. 4, d. 47, ll. 10–11.

226. John Erickson, *The Road to Stalingrad: Stalin's War with Germany*, vol. 1 (New Haven, Conn.: Yale University Press, 1975), 138. For more on Nichiporovich's conduct and fate, see Chapter Six.

227. Colonel I. G. Starinov, *Over the Abyss: My Life in Soviet Special Operations*, trans. Robert Suggs (New York: Ivy Books, 1995), 299–300.

228. Ibid., 299; A. I. Briukhanov, *V shtabe partizanskogo dvizheniia* (Minsk: Belarus', 1980), 37–38; P. K. Ponomarenko, *Vsenarodnaia bor'ba v tylu nemetsko-fashistkikh zakhvatchikov, 1941–1944* (Moscow: Nauka, 1986), 146–149.

229. RGASPI, f. 69, op. 1, d. 1084, l. 41; IIAN ORF, f. 2, raz. 2, op. 6, d. 12, l. 13.

230. RGASPI, f. 69, op. 1, d. 1084, l. 100; IIAN ORF, f. 2, raz. 2, op. 6, d. 12, ll. 13–14; d. 15, l. 12.

231. RGASPI, f. 644, op. 1, d. 69, l. 214; Briukhanov, *V shtabe partizanskogo dvizheniia*, 81; Starinov, *Over the Abyss*, 302.

232. Shumilin, *Istoriia partizanskogo dvizheniia*, 34; Boiarskii, *Partizany*, 108–109, Starinov, *Over the Abyss*, 300, 365–366.

233. RGASPI, f. 69, op. 1, d. 206, ll. 90–91.

234. RGASPI, f. 69, op. 1, d. 215, ll. 3–5.

235. RGASPI, f. 69, op. 1, d. 215, l. 6. No Germans were garrisoned in the town.

236. RGASPI, f. 69, op. 1, d. 206, l. 121; d. 215, ll. 7–8; Shumilin, *Istoriia partizanskogo dvizheniia*, 160–161. At the August 1942 Conference, Dymnikov asserted that Orlov had managed to contact friends attached to the Western Front, who then summoned him to front headquarters. However, in an earlier report on Orlov's behavior, Orel Obkom secretary Matveev stated that Orlov had gone to the Western Front "without permission"; RGASPI, f. 69, op. 1, d. 28, l. 52; d. 206, l. 121. Orlov himself was silent on the matter, merely indicating that Zhukov later gave him command of the

new partisan formations sent to Diat'kovo Raion. One of Orlov's partisans told Soviet historians in an interview that Orlov was sanctioned to subordinate the other detachments in late August 1942, but other sources do not corroborate this statement; IIAN ORF, f. 2, raz. 2, op. 6, d. 43, l. 7.

237. RGASPI, f. 69, op. 1, d. 206, l. 122.

238. RGASPI, f. 69, op. 1, d. 213, l. 100.

239. RGASPI, f. 69, op. 1, d. 215, ll. 10–11; op. 4, d. 3429, ll. 6–7.

240. In a report on Orlov's activities, Dymnikov asserted that Orlov's detachment had over 200 submachine guns for 450 partisans, well above the average ratio for automatic weapons in a partisan detachment; RGASPI, f. 69, op. 4, d. 3429, l. 7.

241. RGASPI, f. 69, op. 1, d. 28, ll. 41–42.

242. RGASPI, f. 69, op. 1, d. 28, ll. 52–53.

243. RGASPI, f. 69, op. 1, d. 28, l. 53. See Chapter One.

244. RGASPI, f. 69, op. 1, d. 300, l. 52.

245. RGASPI, f. 69, op. 1, d. 4, ll. 107–108.

246. RGASPI, f. 69, op. 1, d. 300, l. 52.

247. RGASPI, f. 69, op. 1, d. 215, l. 14.

248. RGASPI, f. 69, op. 1, d. 94, l. 300; d. 215, ll. 10–13, 15.

CHAPTER FIVE. THE CRISIS OF
PARTISAN IDENTITY, 1943

1. For a discussion of military reforms as a means to redefine the nation, see Joshua A. Sanborn, *Drafting the Russian Nation: Military Conscription, Total War, and Mass Politics, 1905–1925* (DeKalb: Northern Illinois University Press, 2003). See also Mark von Hagen, "The *Levée en Masse* from Russian Empire to Soviet Union, 1874–1938," in Daniel Moran and Arthur Waldron, eds., *The People in Arms: Military Myth and National Mobilization since the French Revolution* (Cambridge: Cambridge University Press, 2003), 159–188.

2. RGASPI, f. 69, op. 1, d. 551, ll. 86–93.

3. J. Arch Getty, "State and Society under Stalin: Constitutions and Elections in the 1930s," *Slavic Review* 50, 1 (Spring 1991): 26–27; Sarah Davies, *Popular Opinion in Stalin's Russia: Terror, Propaganda and Dissent, 1934–1941* (Cambridge: Cambridge University Press, 1997), 60–61, 105–106.

4. RGASPI, f. 69, op. 1. d. 65, l. 22.

5. RGASPI, f. 69, op. 1, d. 65, ll. 158–159. Other regions also experienced significant gains. From May 1943 to January 1944 in the Leningrad region, the partisan movement grew from 2,876 to 25,062; in Kalinin Oblast, the movement grew from 3,751 partisans in April 1943 to 7,291 in January 1944, notwithstanding the liberation of fourteen detachments during that time; in Smolensk, the number of new recruits almost doubled, from 7,500 in April 1943 to 13,500 in September when the region was liberated. Even the Baltic republics experienced remarkable growth, at least in proportional terms: between May 1943 and January 1944, the number of partisans in-

creased in Latvia from 240 to 812, in Lithuania from 168 to 1,500, and in Estonia from 21 to 205; Iu. V. Petrov, *Partizanskoe dvizhenie v Leningradskoi oblasti, 1941–1944* (Leningrad: Lenizdat, 1973), 314–321; RGASPI, f. 69, op. 1, d. 65, ll. 60–61, 186, 193.

6. For example, the number of detachments in Belorussia rose from 522 in April 1943 to 723 by January 1944, and in Leningrad, the number of detachments for the same period expanded from 64 to 182. In many other areas, such as the Smolensk, Kalinin, and Orel regions, the overall number of detachments remained the same or even fell as the number of partisans grew, due to the consolidation of many independent formations or the liberation of their operational areas; RGASPI, f. 69, op. 1, d. 65, ll. 60–61, 158–159, 186, 193, 215.

7. USHMM, 1996.A.169 (YVA M-37/820—TsDAHOU, f. 67, op. 1, d. 1, l. 137).

8. V. M. Koval'chuk and A. R. Dzeniskevich, eds., *V tylu vraga: Bor'ba partizan i podpol'shchikov na okkupirovannoi territorii Leningradskoi oblasti, 1943 g.: Sbornik dokumentov* (hereafter cited as *V tylu vraga: Leningrad, 1943 g.*) (Leningrad: Lenizdat, 1983), 76–77, 351.

9. Ibid., 352.

10. USHMM, 1996.A.169, roll 36 (YVA M-37/820—TsDAHOU, f. 67, op. 1, d. 1, l. 137).

11. Martin Dean, *Collaboration in the Holocaust: Crimes of the Local Police in Belorussia and Ukraine, 1941–1944* (New York: St. Martin's Press, 2000), 133–137.

12. Karel Cornelis Berkhoff, *Harvest of Despair: Life and Death in Ukraine under Nazi Rule* (Cambridge, Mass.: Belknap Press of Harvard University Press, 2004), 259–274; Dean, *Collaboration in the Holocaust*, 113–118; Alexander Hill, *The War behind the Eastern Front: The Soviet Partisan Movement in North-West Russia, 1941–1944* (New York: Frank Cass, 2005), 150–151.

13. P. P. Vershigora, *Liudi s chistoi sovest'iu* (Moscow: Moskovskii rabochii, 1946), 235–236.

14. Z. A. Bogatyr', *V tylu vraga: Boeviia deiatel'nost' soedineniia partizanskikh otriadov pod komandovaniem geroi Sovetskogo soiuza A. N. Saburova* (Moscow: Sotsekgiz, 1963), 165.

15. A. A. Tumanian, "Lesnoi gospital'," in N. P. Sudoplatov and A. A. Tumanian, *Zapiski partizanskikh vrachei: O podvigakh medrabotnikov v tylu vraga v gody Velikoi Otechestvennoi voiny* (Tula, USSR: Prioskoe knizhnoe izdatel'stvo, 1989), 259.

16. Cited in Amir Weiner, *Making Sense of War: The Second World War and the Fate of the Bolshevik Revolution* (Princeton, N.J.: Princeton University Press, 2001), 90.

17. TsKhDMO, f. 2, op. 4, d. 252, l. 20.

18. See, for example, USHMM 1996.A.169, roll 36 (YVA M-37/853).

19. RGASPI, f. 69, op. 1, d. 1060, l. 1.

20. RGASPI, f. 69, op. 1, d. 1060, l. 2.

21. RGASPI, f. 69, op. 1, d. 1062, l. 18.

22. RGASPI, f. 69, op. 1, d. 15, l. 9.

23. TsKhDMO, f. 1, op. 53, d. 4, l. 30.

24. TsKhDMO, f. 1, op. 53, d. 4, l. 27.

25. RGASPI, f. 69, op. 1, d. 1096, l. 23; TsKhDMO, f. 1, op. 53, d. 4, ll. 27, 33.

26. Weiner, *Making Sense of War*, 79.

27. Diane Koenker, "Men against Women on the Shop Floor in Early Soviet Russia: Gender and Class in the Socialist Workplace," *American Historical Review* 100, 5 (December 1995): 1438–1464; Wendy Z. Goldman, *Women, the State and Revolution: Soviet Family Policy and Social Life, 1917–1936* (Cambridge: Cambridge University Press, 1993), 288–295, 331–336; Choi Chatterjee, *Celebrating Women: Gender, Festival Culture, and Bolshevik Ideology, 1910–1935* (Pittsburgh, Pa.: University of Pittsburgh Press, 2002), 135–158. See also Elizabeth A. Wood, *The Baba and the Comrade: Gender and Politics in Revolutionary Russia* (Bloomington: Indiana University Press, 1997).

28. See Chapter One.

29. See Chapter Two.

30. RGASPI, f. 69, op. 1, d. 1073, l. 20; TsKhDMO, f. 1, op. 53, d. 14, l. 22.

31. RGASPI, f. 69, op. 1, d. 1065, ll. 9, 21. One woman courier would rub salt on her infant's skin to redden his appearance and raise his temperature. German sentries believed the child had typhus and let her pass. Others would wrap leaflets around their babies, and one pregnant woman smuggled a mine under her clothes, "next to the beating heart of her baby." See Svetlana Aleksievich, *War's Unwomanly Face* (Moscow: Progress Publishers, 1988), 39, 45. By contrast, the occupiers sometimes were particularly suspicious of women and children *because* of their presumed innocence; Omer Bartov, *Hitler's Army: Soldiers, Nazis and War in the Third Reich* (Oxford: Oxford University Press, 1992), 93–94. For a discussion of the use of women in intelligence roles in the postwar conflict between Soviet forces and Ukrainian nationalists, see Jeffrey Burds, "Gender and Policing in Soviet West Ukraine, 1944–1948," *Cahiers du Monde Russe* 42, 2–4 (April-December 2001): 279–320.

32. RGASPI, f. 625, op. 1, d. 28, l. 56; TsKhDMO, f. 1, op. 53, d. 13, ll. 51–52; IIAN ORF, f. 2, raz. 2, op. 9/5, d. 11, ll. 20–21.

33. IIAN ORF, f. 2, raz. 2, op. 4, d. 75, ll. 8–9; RGASPI, f. 69, op. 1, d. 29, l. 37; TsKhDMO, f. 1, op. 53, d. 14, ll. 65, 190.

34. Faye Schulman, *A Partisan's Memoir: Woman of the Holocaust* (Toronto: Second Story Press, 1995). 146.

35. TsKhDMO, f. 1, op. 53, d. 14, l. 239.

36. RGASPI, f. 69, op. 1, d. 1082, l. 3.

37. Aleksei Popov, *Diversanty Stalina: Deiatel'nost' organov Gosbezopasnoti na okkupirovannoi sovetskoi territorii v gody Velikoi Otechestvennoi voiny* (Moscow: Iauza, Eksmo, 2004), 205.

38. "Selected Soviet Sources on the World War II Partisan Movement," in John Armstrong, *The Soviet Partisans in World War II* (Madison: University of Wisconsin Press, 1964), 737.

39. RGASPI, f. 69, op. 1, d. 1084, l. 54; Nechama Tec, *Defiance: The Bielski Partisans* (Oxford: Oxford University Press, 1993), 67.

40. RGASPI, f. 69, op. 1, d. 1082, l. 3.

41. IIAN ORF, f. 2, raz. 2, op 9/2, d. 53, l. 25; TsKhDMO, f. 1, op. 53, d. 14, l. 212.

42. Susanne Conze and Beate Fiesler, "Soviet Women as Comrades-in-Arms: A Blind Spot in the History of the War," in Robert W. Thurston and Bernd Bonwetsch, eds., *The People's War: Responses to World War II in the Soviet Union* (Urbana: University of Illinois Press, 2000), 214–218.

43. This fact was noted by K. T. Mazurov, the head of the Belorussian Komsomol; TsKhDMO, f. 1, op. 53, d. 4, l. 25.

44. RGASPI, f. 625, op. 1, d. 28, ll. 85, 125; TsKhDMO, f. 1, op. 53, d. 14, ll. 13–14, 16, 56, 225; "Selected Soviet Sources," in Armstrong, *The Soviet Partisans*, 753; Tec, *Defiance*, 156–164.

45. TsKhDMO, f. 1, op. 53, d. 14, l. 20; also l. 165.

46. TsKhDMO, f. 1, op. 53, d. 14, ll. 86–87.

47. IIAN ORF, f. 2, raz. 2, op. 2, d. 25a, l. 99; TsKhDMO, f. 1, op. 53, d. 14, ll. 17, 87, 165, 236; V. M. Koval'chuk and A. R. Dzeniskevich, eds., *V tylu vraga: Bor'ba partizan i podpl'shchikov na okkupirovannoi territorii Leningradskoi oblasti, 1944: Sbornik dokumentov* (Leningrad: Lenizdat, 1985), 59; "Selected Soviet Sources," in Armstrong, *The Soviet Partisans*, 753. For his part, Ponomarenko condemned commanders who had "incorrect" relations with the women in their command and instructed them that their behavior had to be "crystal clean" because they were representatives of Soviet power; RGASPI, f. 69, op. 1, d. 1112, ll. 84–85; TsMVS, f.4/42973, l. 3.

48. TsKhDMO, f. 1, op. 53, d. 14, ll. 17, 77, 233.

49. TsKhDMO, f. 1, op. 53, d. 14, l. 87.

50. Koenker, "Men against Women," 1451–1457; Chatterjee, *Celebrating Women*, 123–128.

51. See, for example, GARF, f. 6903, op. 20, d. 3, ll. 498–499 (12 July 1942); d. 4, l. 107 (3 August 1942); *Izvestiia*, 8 March 1944, p. 1. See also the poster by N. Vatolina, "Fascism—the worst enemy of women," depicting an outraged modern Soviet woman pointing at burning buildings, and dead mothers and children; see N. I. Baburina, ed., *Russia 20th Century: History of the Country in Posters* (Moscow: Panorama, 1993), 132.

52. GARF, f. 6903, op. 20, d. 9, l. 83 (18 November 1942).

53. GARF, f. 6903, op. 20, d. 11, l. 110 (7 January 1943).

54. Vershigora, *Liudi s chistoi sovest'iu*, 349.

55. *Pravda*, 27 January 1942, p. 2.

56. *Krasnaia zvezda*, 1 August 1941, p. 3; *Krasnaia zvezda*, 23 November 1941.

57. *Krasnaia zvezda*, 27 November 1941, p. 4.

58. *Pravda*, 27 January 1942, p. 2; 17 February 1942, p. 1.

59. See, for example, GARF, f. 6903, op. 20, d. 7, l. 266 (11 October 1942); d. 12, ll. 122–125 (7 January 1943). See also Rosalinde Sartorti, "On the Making of Heroes, Heroines, and Saints," in Richard Stites, ed., *Culture and Entertainment in Wartime Russia* (Bloomington: Indiana University Press, 1995), 182–191.

60. Denise J. Youngblood, "A War Remembered: Soviet Films of the Great Patriotic War," *American Historical Review* 106, 3 (June 2001): 841–844; See also Peter Kenez, "Black and White: The War on Film," in Stites, *Culture and Entertainment*,

167–169; John Haynes, *New Soviet Man: Gender and Masculinity in Stalinist Soviet Cinema* (Manchester, UK, and New York: Manchester University Press, 2003), 165–166. For more depictions of Soviet women partisans, see *Pravda*, 8 March 1943, p. 3; *Krasnaia zvezda*, 16 October 1942, p. 3, 5 November 1942, p. 2.

61. GARF, f. 6903, op. 20, d. 4, l. 331 (8 July 1942).

62. See also Lisa A. Kirschenbaum, "'Our City, Our Hearths, Our Families': Local Loyalties and Private Life in Soviet World War II Propaganda," *Slavic Review* 59, 4 (Winter 2000): 831; Richard Stites, "Soviet Russian Wartime Culture: Freedom and Control, Spontaneity and Consciousness," in Thurston and Bonwetsch, *The People's War*, 174–176.

63. Conze and Fiesler, "Soviet Women," 212, 219–224.

64. Jeffrey Brooks, *Thank You, Comrade Stalin! Soviet Public Culture from Revolution to Cold War* (Princeton, N.J.: Princeton University Press, 2000), 179.

65. See, for example, the depiction of a mother protecting her child from a bloody bayonet in V. Koretskii's "Voin Krasnoi Armii, Spasi!" in Baburina, *Russia 20th Century*, 133; and Viktor Ivanov's and Olga Burova, "Vsiia nadezhda na tebiia, Krasnoi Voin!" in Peter Paret, Beth Irwin Lewis, and Paul Paret, eds., *Persuasive Images: Posters of War and Revolution from the Hoover Institution Archives* (Princeton, N.J.: Princeton University Press, 1992), 163 (poster 229).

66. Conze and Fiesler, "Soviet Women," 219–224.

67. RGASPI, f. 69, op. 1, d. 1062, l. 5.

68. RGASPI, f. 69, op. 1, d. 1060, ll. 16–19. For an earlier draft proposal, see TsKhDMO, f. 1, op. 53, d. 13, ll. 2–4.

69. RGASPI, f. 69, op. 1, d. 1062, ll. 17–18.

70. RGASPI, f. 625, op. 1, d. 28, l. 219.

71. Karen Petrone, *Life Has Become More Joyous, Comrades: Celebrations in the Time of Stalin* (Bloomington: Indiana University Press, 2000), 71–75.

72. RGASPI, f. 625, op. 1, d. 28, l. 125; IIAN ORF, f. 2, raz. 2, op. 9/5, d. 11, l. 21.

73. IIAN ORF, f. 2, raz. 2, op. 3, d. 18, l. 2; op. 4, d. 75, l. 8.

74. RGASPI, f. 69, op. 1, d. 474, l. 21; d. 1067, l. 79; IIAN ORF, f. 2, raz. 2, op. 3, d. 2, l. 3; TsMVS, f. 4/36415, l. 7; Conze and Fiesler, "Soviet Women," 212.

75. TsKhDMO, f. 1, op. 53, d. 14, l. 59.

76. TsKhDMO, f. 1, op. 53, d. 13, l. 51.

77. TsKhDMO, f. 1, op. 53, d. 14, ll. 224–225.

78. A. F. Fedorov, *Podpol'nyi obkom deistvuet* (Kiev: Politizdat Ukrainy, 1986), 390–391; Schulman, *A Partisan's Memoir*, 119. See also the song composed by partisans in one detachment, celebrating the achievements of their women comrades; USHMM, 1996.A.169, roll 38 (YVA M-37/1903—TsDAHOU, f. 69, op. 1, d. 42, l. 6). For Mikhailov's comments, see RGASPI, f. 69, op. 1, d. 1060, l. 5.

79. Thus, one woman literally carried her four-year-old daughter on missions before she was finally airlifted to safety; Aleksievich, *War's Unwomanly Face*, 217. See also Faye Schulman's account of caring for an "adopted" eight-year-old girl in her unit; Schulman, *A Partisan's Memoir*, 127–136. Young children, in fact, were signifi-

cant risks, since their playing or crying could alert the enemy to the partisans' position, especially if the unit was trying to evade patrols; Tumanian, "Lesnoi gospital'," 206–207.

80. *Krasnaia zvezda*, 8 July 1943, p. 3; IIAN ORF, f. 2, raz. 2, op. 3, d. 15, ll. 16–17.

81. Cited in Aleksievich, *War's Unwomanly Face*, 64; Conze and Fiesler, "Soviet Women," 224.

82. IIAN ORF, f. 2, raz. 2, op. 2, d. 25a, ll. 87–88.

83. Schulman, *A Partisan's Memoir*, 140.

84. IIAN ORF, f. 2, raz. 2, op. 3, d. 15, ll. 9–10; Wood, *The Baba and the Comrade*, 52, 57; Sanborn, *Drafting the Russian Nation*, 151–152.

85. TsKhDMO, f. 1, op. 53, d. 14, ll. 11–254; see also RGASPI, f. 625, op. 1, d. 28, l. 219.

86. Cited in Aleksievich, *War's Unwomanly Face*, 45.

87. Weiner, *Making Sense of War*, 85, 108.

88. For a discussion of the personal/public dichotomy in women's autobiographies, see Anne E. Gorsuch, "Women's Autobiographical Narratives: Soviet Presentations of Self," *Kritika* 2, 4 (Fall 2001): 835–847.

89. Anna Krylova, "Stalinist Identity from the Viewpoint of Gender: Rearing a Generation of Professionally Violent Women-Fighters in 1930s Stalinist Russia," *Gender and History* 16, 3 (November 2004): 626–653.

90. Barbara Alpern Engel and Anastasia Posadskaya-Vandbeck, eds., *A Revolution of Their Own: Voices of Women in Soviet History* (Boulder, Colo.: Westview Press, 1998), 220–221.

91. Sanborn, *Drafting the Russian Nation*, 155–159; Wood, *The Baba and the Comrade*, 57–59.

92. Marc Ferro, *Cinema and History* (Detroit: Wayne State University Press), 63–64.

93. Cited in Aleksievich, *War's Unwomanly Face*, 45.

94. Cited in Kazimiera J. Cottam, ed. and trans., *Defending Leningrad: Women behind Enemy Lines* (Nepean, Ontario: New Military Publishing, 1998), 60.

95. Cited in Aleksievich, *War's Unwomanly Face*, 39.

96. Ibid., 40. See also IIAN ORF, f. 2, raz. 2, op. 3, d. 18, ll. 2–3.

97. Krylova, "Stalinist Identity," 629.

98. For an extended discussion of this process, see Terry Martin, *The Affirmative Action Empire: Nations and Nationalism in the Soviet Union, 1923–1939* (Ithaca, N.Y.: Cornell University Press, 2001), esp. 311–343; Weiner, *Making Sense of War*, 139–146; Hiroaki Kuromiya, *Freedom and Terror in the Donbas: A Ukrainian-Russian Borderland, 1870s–1990s* (Cambridge: Cambridge University Press, 1998), 195–196, 231–236.

99. Martin, *The Affirmative Action Empire*, 460–461.

100. I. P. Kondranov and A. A. Stepanova, eds., *Krym v period Velikoi Otechestvennoi voiny, 1941–1945: Sbornik dokumentov i materialov* (Simferpol': Tavriia, 1973), 218. See also the reports filed by partisans cited in full in Evgenii Zhirnov, ed., "Na okkupirovannykh territoriiakh," *Kommersant vlast'*, part 1 (24 June 2001).

101. USHMM, RG 22.005M, reel 3 (RGASPI, f. 69, op. 1, d. 741, l. 39); IIAN ORF,

f. 2, raz. 2, op. 4, d. 117, l. 5; Aleksandr Nekrich, *The Punished Peoples* (New York: W. W. Norton, 1978), 26.

102. Nekrich, *The Punished Peoples*, 26. Many of these so-called volunteers had been forced into service and, moreover, were not Tatars at all but from the Caucasus, Central Asia, and the Volga region.

103. Alexander Statiev, "The Nature of Anti-Soviet Armed Resistance, 1942–1944: The North Caucasus, the Kalmyk Autonomous Republic, and the Crimea," *Kritika* 6, 2 (Spring 2005): 307.

104. Nekrich, *The Punished People*, 32–34.

105. RGASPI, f. 69, op. 1, d. 1062, ll. 50–51; Nekrich, *The Punished People*, 28–29.

106. See, for example, *Krasnaia zvezda*, 30 April 1942, p. 2; GARF, f. 6903, op. 20, d. 1, l. 44; see also Alfred J. Rieber, "Civil Wars in the Soviet Union," *Kritika* 4, 2 (Winter 2003): 148–149.

107. Nekrich, *The Punished People*, 31.

108. RGASPI, f. 69, op. 1, d. 1062, ll. 50–52.

109. RGASPI, f. 69, op. 1, d. 1062, l. 45.

110. *Pravda*, 1 November 1942, p. 2.

111. *Izvestiia*, 4 December 1943, p. 3. See also *Krasnaia zvezda*, 25 May 1943, p. 3; *Pravda*, 26 December 1943, p. 3.

112. Statiev, "The Nature of Anti-Soviet Armed Resistance," 313.

113. TsKhDMO, f. 1, op. 53, d. 10, l. 144. The actual liberation of the Crimea began in April 1944.

114. Statiev, "The Nature of Anti-Soviet Armed Resistance," 314.

115. Norman Naimark, *Fires of Hatred: Ethnic Cleansing in Twentieth-Century Europe* (Cambridge, Mass.: Harvard University Press, 2001), 99–104; Vera Tolz, "New Information about the Deportation of Ethnic Groups in the USSR during World War 2," in John Garrard and Carol Garrard, eds., *World War 2 and the Soviet People: Selected Papers from the Fourth World Congress for Soviet and East European Studies, Harrogate, 1990* (New York: St. Martin's Press, 1993), 163–168; Rieber, "Civil Wars in the Soviet Union," 160.

116. Kenneth Slepyan, "The Soviet Partisan Movement and the Holocaust," *Holocaust and Genocide Studies* 14, 1 (Spring 2000): 6.

117. Hersh Smolar, *The Minsk Ghetto: Soviet Jewish Partisans against the Nazis* (New York: Holocaust Library, 1989), 127–128.

118. RGASPI, f. 69, op. 1, d. 1067, ll. 183–184.

119. USHMM, RG 22.005M, roll 3 (RGASPI, f. 69, op. 1, d. 746, l. 220).

120. Tec, *Defiance*, 94–95; Smolar, *The Minsk Ghetto*, 122–123; Reuben Ainzstein, *Jewish Resistance in Occupied Eastern Europe* (London: Elek Books, 1974), 310; Shmuel Spector, "The Jews of Volhynia and Their Reaction to Extermination," in Michael Marrus, ed., *The Nazi Holocaust: Historical Articles on the Destruction of the European Jews*, vol. 7, *Jewish Resistance to the Holocaust* (Westport, Conn.: Meckler, 1989), 213–216.

121. Ainzstein, *Jewish Resistance*, 394; Yitzhak Arad, "The Holocaust of So-

viet Jewry in the Occupied Territories of the USSR," *Yad Vashem Studies*, vol. 21 (Jerusalem: Yad Vashem, 1991), 41. After the liberation of Minsk, Hersh Smolar asked the head of the Belorussian Staff's cadres department how many Jews had served in Belorussian detachments. He was told, apparently with a straight face, that the staff kept no statistics on nationality; Smolar, *The Minsk Ghetto*, 150.

122. USHMM 1996.A.169, roll 4 (YVA M-41/260—Belorussian National Archive, f. 4, op. 33a, d. 662, l. 24).

123. IIAN ORF, f. 2, raz. 2, op. 4, d. 117, l. 5; Tec, *Defiance*, 109. Because Taits did not give a specific date in his reference to "Stalin's order," it is possible that he was referring to Stalin's order on May Day 1943, which, among other things, called on the partisans to protect the civilian population. Regardless of the order to which Taits referred, the general line of Soviet policy was understood.

124. Cited in Tec, *Defiance*, 97.

125. Cited in ibid., 105, 109.

126. IIAN ORF, f. 2, raz. 2, op. 4, d. 117, l. 8; Ainzstein, *Jewish Resistance*, 355.

127. USHMM, 1996.A.169 roll 38 (YVA M-37/886—TsDAHOU, f. 69, op. 1, d. 9, ll. 2–3); Weiner, *Making Sense of War*, 211.

128. USHMM, 1996.A.169, roll 35 (YVA M-37/656—TsDAHOU, f. 63, op. 1, d. 219, l. 5.

129. The attitudes of the Moscow population during the mass panic of October 1941 are a case in point; see Mikhail M. Gorinov, "Muscovites' Moods, 22 June 1941 to May 1942," in Thurston and Bonwetsch, *The People's War*, 123, 126.

130. IIAN ORF, f. 2, raz. 2, op. 4, d. 117, l. 8.

131. USHMM, 1996.A.169, roll 4 (YVA M-41/250—Belorussian National Archive, f. 3500, op. 2, d. 44, l. 1).

132. Smolar, *The Minsk Ghetto*, 128.

133. Dov Levin, *Fighting Back: Lithuanian Jewry's Armed Resistance to the Nazis, 1941–1945*, translated from the Hebrew by Moshe Kohn and Dina Cohen (New York and London: Holmes & Meier, 1985), 184, 204.

134. Smolar, *The Minsk Ghetto*, 129–130; Schulman, *A Partisan's Memoir*, 185–187.

135. *The Partisans of Vilna* (produced by Aviva Kempner, 1986); see also Schulman, *A Partisan's Memoir*, 102.

136. *Partisans of Vilna*; Levin, *Fighting Back*, 208; Schulman, *A Partisan's Memoir*, 142.

137. Schulman, *A Partisan's Memoir*, 105–106.

138. Cited in Levin, *Fighting Back*, 206.

139. IIAN ORF, f. 2, raz. 2, op. 4, d. 117, l. 8.

140. Levin, *Fighting Back*, 206.

141. In another article about the killing grounds at Babyi Yar, where over 33,000 Jews were killed, Jews were mentioned only once among the list of national victims; *Krasnaia zvezda*, 20 November 1943.

142. GARF f. 6903, op. 20, d. 11, l. 77 (19 December 1942).

143. Alexander Victor Prusin, "'Fascist Criminals to the Gallows! The Holocaust

and Soviet War Crimes Trials, December 1945–February 1946," *Holocaust and Genocide Studies* 17, 1 (Spring 2003): 1–30.

144. Berkhoff, *Harvest of Despair*, 207.

145. Cited in Kate Brown, *A Biography of No Place: From Ethnic Borderland to Soviet Heartland* (Cambridge, Mass.: Harvard University Press, 2004), 39–40.

146. See ibid., 192–225; Timothy Snyder, *The Reconstruction of Nations: Poland, Ukraine, Lithuania, Belarus, 1569–1999* (New Haven, Conn.: Yale University Press, 2003), 156–163.

147. The OUN was divided into two rival factions, the OUN-B, under Stepan Bandera, and the OUN-M, led by Andrei Mel'nyk. The UPA, once an independent organization, gradually came under the control of OUN-B; see John Armstrong, *Ukrainian Nationalism*, 3rd ed. (Englewood, Colo.: Ukrainian Academic Press, 1990).

148. Snyder, *The Reconstruction of Nations*, 170, 176; Alexander V. Prusin, "Revolution and Ethnic Cleansing in Western Ukraine: The OUN-UPA Assault against Polish Settlements in Volhynia and Eastern Galicia, 1943–1944," in Steven Béla Várdy, T. Hunt Tooley, and Agnes Huszár Várdy, eds., *Ethnic Cleansing in Twentieth-Century Europe* (Boulder, Colo.: Social Science Monographs, 2003), 534.

149. Colonel I. G. Starinov, *Over the Abyss: My Life in Soviet Special Operations*, trans. Robert Suggs (New York: Ivy Books, 1995), 363–364.

150. Snyder, *The Reconstruction of Nations*, 172–173.

151. See Serhy Yekelchyk, "Stalinist Patriotism as Imperial Discourse: Reconciling the Ukrainian and Russian 'Heroic Pasts,' 1939–1945," *Kritika* 3, 1 (Winter 2002): 51–80; Andrew Wilson, *The Ukrainians: Unexpected Nation*, 2nd ed. (New Haven, Conn.: Yale University Press, 2002), 143.

152. See Chapter One.

153. *Izvestiia*, 24 June 1943, p. 2.

154. The review of the film *Narodnye mstiteli* specifically identified horse-mounted partisans as Ukrainians; *Izvestiia*, 18 August 1943, p. 4. See also Kovpak's description of an accountant transformed into a romantic cavalryman, including his noting the man's "Cossack forelock"; S. A. Kovpak, *Ot Putivlia do Karpat* (Leningrad: Gos-izdat Detskoi Literaturny, 1945), 110. Judith Kornblatt observed that the Cossack forelock is part of the traditional Cossack image; Kornblatt, *The Cossack Hero in Russian Literature: A Study in Cultural Mythology* (Madison: University of Wisconsin Press, 1992), 15.

155. *Izvestiia*, 30 October 1942, p. 2.

156. *Krasnaia zvezda*, 17 June 1943.

157. Kovpak, *Ot Putivlia do Karpat*, 3.

158. See, for example, *Izvestiia*, 18 June 1944, p. 3, 9 August 1944, p. 1; *Pravda*, 16 August 1944, p. 1; N. S. Khrushchev, 15 February 1944, as cited in Vershigora, *Liudi s chistoi sovest'iu* (Moscow: Pravda, 1986), 744–746.

159. USHMM, 1996.A.169, reel 36 (YVA M-37/775—TsDAHOU, f. 66, op. 1, d. 1, l. 18); Kovpak, *Ot Putivlia do Karpat*, 101; R. Sidel'skii, *Bor'ba sovetskikh partizan protiv fashistskikh zakhvatchikov* (Moscow: Gosizdat, 1944), 23–24. Interestingly, the

Germans also appealed to Cossack heritage and traditions in *their* efforts to recruit the legendary horsemen; see Rieber, "Civil Wars in the Soviet Union," 153–154; Samuel J. Newland, *Cossacks in the German Army, 1941–1945* (Portland, Ore.: Frank Cass, 1991), 122–123, 127–137.

160. Yekelchyk, "Stalinist Patriotism," 58–73.

161. Weiner, *Making Sense of War*, 331–336.

162. Timothy Snyder, "The Causes of Ukrainian-Polish Ethnic Cleansing, 1943," *Past and Present* 179 (May 2003): 216, 218.

163. USHHM, 1996.A.169, reel 34 (YVA M-37/574—TsDAHOU, f. 63, op. 1, d. 4, l. 9).

164. Snyder, "Causes," 217.

165. USHMM, 1996.A.169, reel 1 (YVA M-37/14—TsDAHOU, f. 1, op. 122, d. 75, ll. 3–4).

166. IIAN ORF, f. 2, raz. 2, op. 9/5, d. 2, l. 15.

167. Kovpak was officially removed from command after the costly Carpathian raid out of respect to his age, health, and dedicated service to the rodina and was replaced by Vershigora. His popular commissar, Rudnev, died in the raid, but it has been alleged by some that he was executed by the NKVD—possibly by his radio operator—also because of his supposedly unorthodox relations with the separatists; see the editor's commentary in Starinov, *Over the Abyss*, 339–340.

168. Weiner, *Making Sense of War*, 162–269, Kuromiya, *Freedom and Terror in the Donbas*, 278–283; Rieber, "Civil Wars in the Soviet Union," 159–160; Jeffrey Burds, "*Agentura*: Soviet Informants Networks in Galicia, 1944–1948," *Eastern European Politics and Societies* 11, 1 (Winter 1997): 89–130, and "The Early Cold War in Soviet West Ukraine, 1944–1948," *Carl Beck Papers in Russian and East European Studies*, 1505 (January 2001).

169. For more detailed discussions of the handling of nationalists, see Weiner, *Making Sense of War*, esp. 239–297, and Kuromiya, *Freedom and Terror in the Donbas*, 275–291. Alexander Statiev suggests that the prejudices of Christian Caucasians such as the NKVD's Vsevolod Merkulov may have contributed to the deportation of Muslim Caucasians; Statiev, "The Nature of Anti-Soviet Armed Resistance," 317. For discussions of Soviet deportations in general, see Naimark, *Fires of Hatred*, 85–107; Tolz, "New Information," 161–179; Nekrich, *The Punished Peoples*, 13–85.

170. Burds, "*Agentura*," 97.

171. RGASPI, f. 69, op. 1, d. 14, l. 40; IIAN ORF, f. 2, raz. 2, op. 4, d. 25, l. 5. This discourse continued in postwar Soviet historiography. In one respected work, for example, the section on the partisans' struggle with "bourgeois-nationalist" groups discusses the treacherous behavior of almost every Soviet nationality, except the Russians; see V. N. Andrianov, ed., *Voina v tylu vraga: O nekotorykh problemakh istorii sovetskogo partizanskogo dvizheniia v gody Velikoi Otechestvennoi voiny* (Moscow: Politizdat, 1974), 395–446. For a discussion of the ROA, see Catherine Andreyev, *Vlasov and the Russian Liberation Movement: Soviet Reality and Emigré Theory* (Cambridge: Cambridge University Press, 1987).

172. For a discussion of this phenomenon, see David Brandenberger, *National*

Bolshevism: Stalinist Mass Culture and the Formation of Modern Russian Identity (Cambridge, Mass.: Harvard University Press, 2002), esp. 115–180.

173. Ibid., 226–234.

174. RGASPI, f. 625, op. 1, d. 61, ll.5–7.

175. USHMM, 1996.A.169, reel 32 (YVA M-37/192—TsDAHOU, f. 1, op. 23, d. 1576, l. 3).

176. For the role of victimhood in establishing political legitimacy, see Omer Bartov, "Defining Enemies: Making Victims—Germans, Jews, and the Holocaust," *American Historical Review* 102, 3 (June 1998): 771–816. For the importance of victimhood in the Soviet commemoration of World War II, see Nina Tumarkin, *The Living and the Dead: The Rise and Fall of the Cult of World War II in Russia* (New York: Basic Books, 1994), esp. 125–157.

177. Richard Overy, *Russia's War: Blood upon the Snow* (New York: TV Books, 1997), 162.

178. Newland, *Cossacks in the German Army*, 93–96; Andreyev, *Vlasov*, esp. 89–164.

179. Alexander Dallin, "The Kaminsky Brigade: A Case Study of Soviet Disaffection," in Alexander Rabinowitch and Janet Rabinowitch, eds., *Revolution and Politics in Russia: Essays in Memory of B. I. Nicolaevsky* (Bloomington: Indiana University Press, 1972), 255. See also Daniel Romanovsky, "Soviet Jews under Nazi Occupation in Northeastern Belarus and Western Russia," in Zvi Gitelman, ed., *Bitter Legacy: Confronting the Holocaust in the USSR* (Bloomington and Indianapolis: Indiana University Press, 1997), 248–250.

180. IIAN ORF, f. 2, raz. 2, op. 2, d. 25a, ll. 23–24.

181. Dean, *Collaboration in the Holocaust*, 60, 66; Overy, *Russia's War*, 161–162; Robert W. Thurston, "Cauldrons of Loyalty and Betrayal: Soviet Soldiers' Behavior, 1941 and 1945," in Thurston and Bonwetsch, *The People's War*, 242–243.

182. RGASPI, f. 625, op. 1, d. 28, l. 33.

183. RGASPI, f. 69, op. 1, d. 142, l. 79.

184. RGASPI, f. 69, op. 1, d. 14, l. 41.

185. RGASPI, f. 69, op. 1, d. 15, l. 11.

186. *Krasnaia zvezda*, 22 April 1943, p. 3.

187. IIAN ORF, f. 2, raz. 2, op. 4, d. 37, l. 5.

188. See, for example, RGASPI, f. 69, op. 1, d. 165, ll. 108–111; f. 625, op. 1, d. 44, l. 238; TsKhDMO, f. 1, op. 53, d. 10, ll. 234–235. See also the collection of translated leaflets in "Selected Soviet Sources," in Armstrong, *The Soviet Partisans*, 710–722.

189. IIAN ORF, f. 2, raz. 2, op. 6, d. 15, l. 14.

190. RGASPI, f. 69, op. 1, d. 1102, l. 67.

191. See, for example, Alexander Dallin and Ralph S. Mavrogordato, "Rodionov: A Case Study in Wartime Redefection," *American Slavic and East European Review* 18 (1959): 25–33.

192. IIAN ORF, f. 2, raz. 2, op. 6, d. 12, l. 31.

193. Vershigora, *Liudi s chistoi sovest'iu*, 215.

194. RGASPI, f. 69, op. 1, d. 1067, l. 201.

195. IIAN ORF, f. 2, raz. 2, op. 6, d. 20, l. 3.
196. RGASPI, f. 69, op. 1, d. 159, l. 30.
197. IIAN ORF, f. 2, raz. 2, op. 4, d. 23, l. 18; d. 75, l. 4; RGASPI, f. 69, op. 1, d. 159, l. 59.
198. RGASPI, f. 69, op. 1, d. 14, ll. 40–42; IIAN ORF, f. 2, raz. 2, op. 4, d. 75, l. 4.
199. RGASPI, f. 69, op. 1, d. 14, l. 41.
200. IIAN ORF, f. 2, raz. 2, op. 3, d. 15, l. 18; TsMVS, f. 4/69036. Auxiliary formations were almost always referred to as part of the Russian Liberation Army (ROA), or as Vlasovites, after their "commander" General A. A. Vlasov, even though this army existed in name only until the last months of the war. For more on Vlasov and the Russian Liberation Movement, see Alexander Dallin, *German Rule in Russia: A Study in Occupation Policies*, 2nd ed. (Boulder, Colo.: Westview Press, 1981), 613–659; George Fischer, *Soviet Opposition to Stalin: A Case Study in World War II* (Cambridge, Mass.: Harvard University Press, 1952); Andreyev, *Vlasov*, passim.
201. RGASPI, f. 69, op. 1, d. 65, ll. 60, 148. By January 1944, the total strength of the partisan movement was 20,662; RGASPI, f. 69, op. 1, d. 65, ll. 60–61.
202. IIAN ORF, f. 2, raz. 2, op. 4, d. 75, l. 4.
203. RGASPI, f. 69, op. 1, d. 159, ll. 14, 29, 56; op. 8, d. 685, ll. 1–9; Tumanian, "Lesnoi gospital'," 260.
204. A. I. Briukhanov, *V shtabe partizanskogo dvizheniia* (Minsk: Belarus', 1980), 155.
205. See Chapter Six.
206. RGASPI, f. 69, op. 1, d. 474, l. 19.
207. Aleksei Popov, *NKVD i partizanskoe dvizhenie: Dokumenty i materialy* (Moscow: OLMA-PRESS, 2003), 150–151, 283–286.
208. RGASPI, f. 69, op. 1, d. 10, l. 127.
209. See, for example, Richard Stites, *The Women's Liberation Movement in Russia: Feminism, Nihilism and Bolshevism, 1860–1930* (Princeton, N.J.: Princeton University Press, 1978), 317–345. Gregory Massell, *The Surrogate Proletariat: Moslem Women and Revolutionary Strategies in Soviet Central Asia, 1919–1929* (Princeton, N.J.: Princeton University Press, 1974); Yuri Slezkine, *Arctic Mirrors: Russia and the Small Peoples of the North* (Ithaca, N.Y.: Cornell University Press, 1994), esp.131–183.
210. Weiner, *Making Sense of War*, 21–39.

CHAPTER SIX. THE IMAGINED STALINIST COMMUNITY

1. *The Partisans of Vilna* (produced by Aviva Kempner, 1986); RGASPI, f. 625, op. 1, d. 28, l. 35; IIAN ORF, f. 2, raz. 2, op. 9/2, d. 53, l. 8; Nahum Kohn and Howard Roiter, *A Voice from the Forest* (New York: Holocaust Library, 1980), 99; B. T. Shumilin, ed., *Istoriia partizanskogo dvizheniia v Rossiiskoi Federatsii v gody Velikoi Otechestvennoi voiny* (Moscow: Atlantida, 2001), 174.
2. These arguments are most strongly articulated in C. Aubrey Dixon and Otto

Heilbrunn, *Communist Guerrilla Warfare* (London: George Allen, 1954). The following works, less strident in tone, make the same point: Edgar Howell, *The Soviet Partisan Movement, 1941–1944* (Washington, D.C.: Department of the Army, 1956), 4; John Armstrong, ed., *The Soviet Partisans in World War II* (Madison: University Press of Wisconsin, 1964), and Alexander Dallin, *German Rule in Russia: A Study in Occupation Policies*, 2nd ed. (Boulder, Colo.: Westview Press, 1981).

   3. See, for example, V. E. Bystrov, ed., *Sovetskie partizany: Iz istorii Partizanskogo dvizheniia v gody Velikoi Otechestvennoi voiny* (Moscow: Politizdat, 1961), 106–108, 159–162, 467, and A. S. Zalesskii, *V partizanskikh kraiakh i zonakh: Patrioticheskii podvig Sovetskogo krestianstva v tylu vraga, 1941–1944* (Moscow: Sotsial'no-Ekonomicheskoi literatury, 1962), 70–83, 281–297. A recent post-Soviet synthesis of these views is offered by Leonid Grenkevich, *The Soviet Partisan Movement: A Critical Historiographical Analysis*, edited and with a foreword by David M. Glantz (London: Frank Cass, 1999).

   4. Stephen Kotkin, *Magnetic Mountain: Stalinism as a Civilization* (Berkeley and Los Angeles: University of California Press, 1995), 198–237. For opposing views on the ability of Soviet citizens to escape the official Soviet worldview, see Jochen Hellbeck, "Fashioning the Stalinist Soul: The Diary of Stepan Podlubnyi," *Jahrbucher für Geschichte Osteuropas* 44, 3 (1996): 344–373, and Anna Krylova, "The Tenacious Liberal Subject in Soviet Studies," *Kritika* 1, 1 (Winter 2000): 119–146.

   5. Benedict Anderson, *Imagined Communities: Reflections on the Origins and Spread of Nationalism*, rev. ed. (London: Verso, 1991).

   6. RGASPI, f. 69, op. 1, d. 1112, l. 85; TsMVS, f. 4/42973, ll. 2–3.

   7. *Pravda*, 20 December, 1942, p. 2.

   8. TsMVS, f. 4/37544; RGASPI, f. 69, op. 1, d. 164, l. 151.

   9. IIAN ORF, f. 2, raz. 2, op. 6, d. 14, l. 14.

   10. USHMM, 1996.A.169 (YVA M-37/1177—TsDAHOU, f. 166, op. 2, d. 378, l. 7).

   11. IIAN ORF, f. 2, raz. 2, op. 6, d. 12, l. 48.

   12. A. F. Fedorov, *Podpol'nyi obkom deistvuet* (Kiev: Politizdat Ukrainy, 1986), 245.

   13. RGASPI, f. 69, op. 1, d. 286, l. 96; d. 1080, ll. 31–32; G. M. Linkov, *Voina v tylu vraga* (Moscow: Gosudarstvennoe Izdatel'stvo-khudozhestvennoi literatury, 1951), 400–402; Nechama Tec, *Defiance: The Bielski Partisans* (Oxford: Oxford University Press, 1993), 179–183, 199–200.

   14. Cited in Tec, *Defiance*, 4.

   15. The cinematic image differed significantly from Furmanov's description of "an ordinary looking man, thin, of middle height, apparently not very strong, and with slender, almost feminine hands." His partisans, however, had "sunburnt, stern-looking masculine faces"; Dmitry Furmanov, *Chapayev* (Moscow: Progress Publishers, 1955) 62–63.

   16. Fedorov, *Podpol'nyi obkom*, 479.

   17. IIAN ORF, f. 2, raz. 2, op. 2, d. 25a, l. 117.

   18. IIAN ORF, f. 2, raz. 2, op. 2., d. 25a, l. 103.

   19. Tec, *Defiance*, 140.

20. RGASPI, f. 69, op. 1, d. 67, l. 39.

21. Colonel I. G. Starinov, *Over the Abyss: My Life in Soviet Special Operations*, trans. Robert Suggs (New York: Ivy Books, 1995), 334.

22. Fedorov, *Podpol'nyi obkom*, 226.

23. Joshua A. Sanborn, *Drafting the Russian Nation: Military Conscription, Total War, and Mass Politics, 1905–1925* (DeKalb: Northern Illinois University Press, 2003), 103–110.

24. Katerina Clark, *The Soviet Novel: History as Ritual* (Chicago: University of Chicago Press, 1981), 114–135; Jeffrey Brooks, *Thank You, Comrade Stalin! Soviet Public Culture from the Revolution to Cold War* (Princeton, N.J.: Princeton University Press, 2000), 69–70.

25. RGASPI, f. 69, op. 1. d. 1072, ll. 19–20.

26. A. S. Zalesskii, *V partizanskikh kraiakh i zonakh*, 332.

27. IIAN ORF, f. 2, raz. 2, op. 9/2, d. 30, l. 13.

28. TsMVS, f. 4/38347, l. 56.

29. Starinov, *Over the Abyss*, 334.

30. P. P.Vershigora, *Liudi s chistoi sovest'iu* (Moscow: Moskovskii rabochii, 1946), 299.

31. IIAN ORF, f. 2, raz. 2, op. 3, d. 18, l. 2. After his death in battle, German's name was officially attached to the brigade's designation.

32. For example, Kovpak's partisans, known throughout the movement as Kovpaktsky, were fiercely proud that their commander was twice named Hero of the Soviet Union; his achievements gave meaning, significance, and prestige to their own; Vershigora, *Liudi s chistoi sovest'iu*, 198.

33. RGASPI, f. 1, op. 1, d. 748, ll. 82–83.

34. TsKhDMO, f. 1, op. 53, d. 14, ll. 211–212. See also RGASPI, f. 69, op. 1, d. 1110, l. 15, and reports from the Komsomol women's conference (TsKhDMO, f. 1, op. 53, d. 14) for other incidents.

35. IIAN ORF, f. 2, raz. 2, op. 4, d. 252, l. 5. See also IIAN ORF, f. 2, raz. 2, op. 4, d. 23, l. 10; d. 25, l. 2; RGASPI, f. 69, op. 1, d. 164, l. 33; op. 4, d. 3359, l. 4; IIAN ORF, f. 2, raz. 2, op. 4; S. V. Stepashin and I. P. Iampol'skii, eds., *Organy gosudarstvennoi bezopasnosti SSSR v Velikoi Otechestvennoi voine: Sbornik i dokumentov*, T.3, Kn. 2, *Ot oborony k nastupleneiiu, 1 Iulia–31 Dekabria 1942 goda* (Moscow: Izdatel'stvo 'Rus', 2002), 59.

36. IIAN ORF, f. 2, raz. 2, op. 4, d. 23, l. 11; d. 25, l. 3; d. 252, l. 5.

37. IIAN ORF, f. 2, raz. 2, op. 4, d. 23, l. 11.

38. Ibid.

39. RGASPI, f. 69, op. 1, d. 19, ll. 20–22.

40. IIAN ORF, f. 2, raz. 2, op. 4, d. 25, l. 72.

41. IIAN ORF, f. 2, raz. 2, op. 4, d. 23, l. 11.

42. RGASPI, f. 69, op. 1, d. 1067, l. 171; IIAN ORF, f. 2, raz. 2, op. 4, d. 23, l. 12. Nichiporovich later testified to Sarychev's "psychotic" behavior when the unit was attacked by the Germans; IIAN ORF, f. 2, raz. 2, op. 4, d. 23, l. 14.

43. RGASPI, f. 69, op. 4, d. 3359, l. 4.

44. Stepashin and Iampol'skii, *Organy gosudarstvennoi bezopasnosti SSSR v Velikoi Otechestvennoi voine*, T. 3, Kn. 2, 59.

45. Aleksei Popov, *Diversanty Stalina: Deiatel'nost organov Gosbeszopasnosti na okkupirovannoi sovetskoi territorii v gody Velikoi Otechestvennoi voiny* (Moscow: Iauza, Eksmo, 2004), 66.

46. RGASPI, f. 69, op. 1, d. 28, ll. 42, 65–66, 75–76, 93, 140–141.

47. RGASPI, f. 69, op. 1, d. 82, l. 52. One should remember, however, that Gudzenko was probably covering up, at least in part, his apparent disobedience in refusing to go on a raid into Ukraine; see Chapter Three.

48. RGASPI, f. 69, op. 1, d. 550, l. 48.

49. RGASPI, f. 69, op. 1, d. 1084, l. 74. Such criticisms and ignoring of instructions were hardly unique to Emliutin: K. S. Zaslonov, one of the more celebrated commanders in Belorussia, reported to the Vitebsk Obkom in September 1942 that Boiko, the commander of United Staffs in the Orsha region of Vitebsk, sat "in the deep forest" and did nothing to activate the partisans under his command. Zaslonov asserted that he made these criticisms not "to gain a position" but because his one year of experience behind enemy lines gave him "the right to make practical, Bolshevik observations"; see RGASPI, f. 69, op. 1, d. 164, l. 227.

50. RGASPI, f. 69, op. 1, d. 28, ll. 65–70.

51. RGASPI, f. 69, op. 1, d. 1076, l. 22.

52. RGASPI, f. 69, op. 1, d. 212, l. 13.

53. RGASPI, f. 69, op. 1, d. 1093, ll. 5–6.

54. RGASPI, f. 69, op. 1, d. 65, l. 220; d. 212, l. 63–65. A report prepared by the Operations Department of the Central Staff in February 1944 noted that the German attack "clearly revealed the incapacity of the United Staffs of the partisan detachments under the command of Comrade Emliutin to lead the partisan detachments of the Briansk forests"; RGASPI, f. 69, op. 1, d. 65, l. 220. Emliutin continued to serve as a representative of the Central Staff, for which he performed "special tasks"; RGASPI, f. 69, op. 1, d. 82, l. 117.

55. RGASPI, f. 625, op. 1, d. 61, ll. 194, 203–206.

56. The materials collected as "The Affair of the Commander of the Starik Partisan Brigade" are in Ponomarenko's personal collection; RGASPI, f. 625, op. 1, d. 61, ll. 32–218.

57. Catriona Kelly, *Refining Russia: Advice Literature, Polite Culture, and Gender from Catherine to Yeltsin* (Oxford: Oxford University Press, 2001), 238.

58. For discussions on the "cult" of the leader in pre-Revolutionary and Soviet society, see Richard Wortman, *Scenarios of Power: Myth and Ceremony in Russian Monarchy* (Princeton, N.J.: Princeton University Press, 1995); Nina Tumarkin, *Lenin Lives: The Lenin Cult in Soviet Russia* (Cambridge, Mass.: Harvard University Press, 1983); Graeme Gill, *The Origins of the Stalinist Political System* (Cambridge: Cambridge University Press, 1990).

59. For a detailed discussion of the leader cult in Stalin's Russia, see Clark, *The Soviet Novel*, 122–129, 142–149; Brooks, *Thank You, Comrade Stalin*, 59–77, 83–105.

60. Karen Petrone, *Life Has Become More Joyous, Comrades: Celebrations in the*

Time of Stalin (Bloomington: Indiana University Press, 2000), 65–71; John McCannon, *Red Arctic: Polar Exploration and the Myth of the North in Soviet Russia, 1932–1939* (Oxford: Oxford University Press, 1998), 129–131, 133.

61. Clark, *The Soviet Novel*, 129; Sarah Davies, *Popular Opinion in Stalin's Russia: Terror, Propaganda and Dissent, 1934–1941* (Cambridge: Cambridge University Press, 1997), 155–167; Sheila Fitzpatrick, *Everyday Stalinism: Ordinary Life in Extraordinary Times—Soviet Russia in the 1930s* (Oxford: Oxford University Press, 1999), 24, 31.

62. RGASPI, f. 625, op. 1, d. 61, l. 757.

63. John Barber, "The Image of Stalin in Soviet Propaganda and Public Opinion in World War 2," in John Garrard and Carol Garrard, eds., *World War 2 and the Soviet People: Selected Papers from the Fourth World Congress for Soviet and East European Studies, Harrogate, 1990* (New York: St. Martin's Press, 1993), 38–49; Elena Zubkova, *Russia after the War: Hopes, Illusions, and Disappointments, 1945–1957* trans. Hugh Ragsdale (Armonk, N.Y.: M. E. Sharpe, 1998), 77; Brooks, *Thank You, Comrade Stalin*, 205.

64. For discussions on how the Arctic heroes lived on the ice and on the ensuing creation of the Arctic mythology, see McCannon, *Red Arctic*, chaps. three to five, and Petrone, *Life Has Become More Joyous*, 46–84.

65. Dixon and Heilbrunn, *Communist Guerrilla Warfare*, 67; John Armstrong and Kurt DeWitt, "Organization and Control of the Partisan Movement," in Armstrong, *The Soviet Partisans*, 128, 130.

66. A. A. Grechko and D. F. Ustinov, eds., *Istoriia Vtoroi Mirovoi voiny, 1939–1945*, t.9 (Moscow: Voenizdat, 1978), 222; Bystrov, *Sovetskie partizany*, 161.

67. This summary of duties, taken from the 16 July 1941 order reinstating commissars in the Red Army, also seems to have applied to the partisan forces; V. N. Malin and V. P. Petrovksii, eds., *KPSS o Vooruzhenikh Silakh Sovetskogo Soiuza: Sbornik dokumentov, 1917–1958* (Moscow: Politizdat, 1958), 358–361. See also Ponomarenko's evaluation of the role of the commissar in his 5 January 1943 memo to Stalin, RGASPI, f. 69, op. 1, d. 25, ll. 1–4.

68. *Pravda*, 26 January 1942, p. 2.

69. GARF, f. 6903, op. 20, d. 4, l. 148 (4 August 1942).

70. In 1940, the only readings required for army political personnel were *The History of the Communist Party—Short Course*; the *Red Army Man's Political Textbook*; Lenin's "State and Revolution" and "Imperialism"; and Stalin's report to the 18th Party Congress. Considering this low level of political education, coupled with an extremely fluid political environment, the last responsibilities that most partisan commissars were prepared to fulfill were those of political watchdog and ideological mentor; Stephen White, *Political Culture and Soviet Politics* (New York: St. Martin's Press, 1979), 397–398. See also Roger R. Reese, *Stalin's Reluctant Soldiers: A Social History of the Red Army, 1925–1941* (Lawrence: University Press of Kansas, 1996), 92–95.

71. T. H. Rigby, *Communist Party Membership in the USSR, 1917–1967* (Princeton, N.J.: Princeton University Press, 1968), 237–238, 251.

72. *Pravda*, 20 February 1942, p. 3. See also *Krasnaia zvezda*, 26 March 1942, p. 3.

73. Rigby, *Communist Party Membership*, 241, 251–252.

74. Zubkova, *Russia after the War*, 79; N. I. Makarov, ed., *Partiinoe podpol'e: Deiatel'nost podpolnykh partiinykh organov i organizatsii na Okkupirovannoi Sovetskii territorii v gody Velikoi Otechestvennoi voiny* (Moscow: Politizdat, 1983), 128, 130. According to this source, only 6,000 citizens joined the Party in Moscow, Leningrad, Orel, Smolensk, Kalinin, and Kursk Oblasts combined during their periods of occupation, which appears to be a low figure.

75. TsKhDMO, f. 1, op. 53, d. 88, l. 114.

76. RGASPI, f. 69, op. 1, d. 1093, l. 4.

77. RGASPI, f. 69, op. 1, d. 1091, ll. 20–21; Iu. V. Petrov, *Partizanskoe dvizhenie v Leningradskoi oblasti, 1941–1944 gg.* (Leningrad: Lenizdat, 1973), 350; Makarov, *Partiinoe podpol'e*, 128, 130.

78. V. M. Koval'chuk and A. R. Dzeniskevich, eds., *V tylu vraga: Bor'ba partizan i podpol'shchikov na okkupirovannoi territorii Leningradskoi Oblasti 1943 g.: Sbornik dokumentov* (Leningrad: Lenizdat, 1983), 120.

79. IIAN ORF, f. 2, raz. 2, op. 9/2, d. 30, l. 10.

80. Soviet historians argue that this decision was intended to secure socialist property from German pillaging by distributing it among the peasants. Western historians speculate, however, that such actions were either manifestations of opposition to the Stalinist system or possibly a ruse to trick peasants into thinking the regime would abolish the collective farms for good at the end of the war; see Zalesskii, *V partizanskikh kraiakh i zonakh*, 122, 128; Alexander Dallin, Ralph Mavrogordato, and Wilhelm Moll, "Partisan Psychological Warfare and Popular Attitudes," in Armstrong, *The Soviet Partisans*, 313–315. For rumors regarding the dissolution of the *kolkhozy*, see RGASPI, f. 69, op. 1, d. 1060, l. 3.

81. RGASPI, f. 17, op. 88, d. 272, l. 15.

82. *V tylu vraga: Leningrad, 1944*, 303.

83. RGASPI, f. 69, op. 1, d. 550, l. 51.

84. IIAN ORF, f. 2, raz. 2, op. 2, d. 25a, l. 119.

85. TsKhDMO, f. 1, op. 53, d. 14, ll. 232–233.

86. RGASPI, f, 69, op. 4, d. 3009, ll. 5–7.

87. IIAN ORF, f. 2, raz. 2, op. 2, d. 43, l. 8; op. 4, d. 117, l. 8; RGASPI, f. 69, op. 1, d. 164, l. 151.

88. See the editorial printed in *Krasnaia zvezda*, 11 October 1942, p. 1.

89. John Erickson, *The Road to Stalingrad: Stalin's War with Germany* (New Haven, Conn.: Yale University Press, 1975), 372; Richard Overy, *Russia's War: Blood upon the Snow* (New York: TV Books, 1997), 230–231.

90. RGASPI, f. 69, op. 1, d. 4, l. 117.

91. RGASPI, f. 69, op. 1, d. 1067, l. 228; d. 1084, ll. 37–38.

92. RGASPI, f. 69, op. 1, d. 25, ll. 1–4.

93. *Krasnaia zvezda*, 26 March 1942, p. 3.

94. See, for example, *Pravda*, 29 March 1942, p. 3, 31 July 1942, p. 2, 16 April 1944, p. 1; *Krasnaia zvezda*, 3 March 1942, p. 3.

95. RGASPI, f. 69, op. 1, d. 473, l. 24; see also "Selected Soviet Sources on the World War II Partisan Movement," in Armstrong, *The Soviet Partisans*, 703–704.

96. RGASPI, f. 69, op. 1, d. 1068, ll. 106–107; d. 1082, ll. 18–19; d. 1084, l. 88.

97. IIAN ORF, f. 2, raz. 2, op. 3, d. 15, l. 19; RGASPI, f. 69, op. 1, d. 1067, l. 245.

98. RGASPI, f. 69, op. 1, d. 1060, l. 3; d. 1062, l. 17.

99. Tec, *Defiance*, 43, 74, 81, 112.

100. USHMM, 1996.A.169, reel 1 (YVA M-37/160—TsDAHOU, f. 1, op. 23, d. 683, ll. 3–16).

101. M. T. Lukashov, *Po tylam vraga* (Kiev Politizdat Ukrainy, 1974), 216.

102. IIAN ORF, f. 2, raz. 2, op. 6, d. 12, ll. 13–14.

103. RGASPI, f. 69, op. 1, d. 29, l. 29; f. 625, op. 1, d. 61, l. 179.

104. Armstrong, *The Soviet Partisans*, 130–132, Aleksei Popov, *NKVD i partizan-skoe dvizhenie: Fakty i dokumenty.* (Moscow: OLMA-PRESS, 2003), 141.

105. RGASPI, f. 69, op. 1, d. 3, l. 30; Koval'chuk and Dzeniskevich, *V tylu vraga*, 352.

106. Popov, *NKVD i partizanskoe dvizhenie*, 141.

107. Stepashin and Iampol'skii, *Organy gosudarstvennoi bezopasnosti SSSR v Velikoi Otechestvennoi voine*, T. 3, Kn. 2, 519.

108. RGASPI, f. 69, op. 1, d. 470, ll. 45–46; d. 283, l. 3; IIAN ORF, f. 2, raz. 2, op. 4, d. 23, l. 11.

109. Popov, *NKVD i partizanskoe dvizhenie*, 141.

110. RGASPI, f. 625, op. 1, d. 61, l. 179.

111. RGASPI, f. 69, op. 1, d. 1112, l. 59. The letter was forwarded to the NKVD's deputy head of cadres, Svinelupov.

112. IIAN ORF, f. 2, raz. 2, op. 9/2, d. 53, l. 19; Martin Dean, *Collaboration in the Holocaust: Crimes of the Local Police in Belorussia and Ukraine, 1941–1944* (New York: St. Martin's Press, 2000), 128, 134.

113. Faye Schulman, *A Partisan's Memoir: Woman of the Holocaust* (Toronto: Second Story Press, 1995), 157.

114. IIAN ORF, f. 2, raz. 2, op. 6, d. 11, l. 4; RGASPI, f. 69, op. 1, d. 296, l. 75; Fedorov, *Podpol'nyi obkom*, 217; A. V. Romanov, *Na zemle nepokorennoi* (Minsk: Belarus', 1962), 51.

115. IIAN ORF, f. 2, raz. 2, op. 9/2, d. 53, l. 15.

116. RGASPI, f. 69, op. 1, d. 196, l. 76.

117. RGASPI, f. 625, op. 1, d. 28, l. 87.

118. USHMM, RG 22.005M, reel 2 (RGASPI, f. 69, op. 9, d. 14, ll. 74–76).

119. RGASPI, f. 69, op. 1, d. 283, l. 7. In a rare gesture of mercy, the boy's life was spared. The political officer's wife was not so fortunate.

120. RGASPI, f. 69, op. 1, d. 1081, l. 46.

121. IIAN ORF, f. 2, raz. 2, op. 9/2, d. 53, ll. 15, 19.

122. Nicholas Terry, "Enforcing German Rule in Russia, 1941–1944: Policing the Occupation," in Gerard Oram, ed., *Conflict and Legality: Policing Mid-Twentieth Century Europe* (London: Francis Boutle Publishers, 2003), 130.

123. RGASPI, f. 69, op. 1, d. 1067, l. 169; f. 625, op. 1, d. 44, ll. 103–108; IIAN ORF, f. 2, raz. 2, op. 4, d. 117, l. 8; Schulman, *A Partisan's Memoir*, p. 146. These fears paralleled the German belief that the Soviets also used syphilitic women as spies and vectors of biological warfare; see Omer Bartov, *The Eastern Front, 1941–1945: Ger-*

man Troops and the Barbarization of Warfare (New York: St. Martin's Press, 1986), 126–129.

124. RGASPI, f. 69, op. 1, d. 1067, l. 169. The obsession that Jews were particularly prone to spying was noticeable during World War I as well; Sanborn, *Drafting the Russian Nation*, 121. For an examination of this and other rumors, see Evgennii Zhirnov, ed., "Na okkupirovannykh territoriiakh," *Kommersant vlast'*, part 3, no. 31 (7 August 2001).

125. RGASPI f. 625, op. 1, d. 44, ll. 108–114; USHMM, RG 22.005M, reel 2 (RGASPI, f. 69, op. 1, d. 1092, ll. 62–68). Jews also executed other Jews whom they believed to be spies; Jack Kagan and Dov Cohen, *Surviving the Holocaust with the Russian Jewish Partisans* (London: Valentine Mitchell, 1998), 69–70.

126. Popov, *Diversanty Stalina*, 205.

127. RGASPI, f. 69, op. 1, d. 762, ll. 4, 29, 40–41, 55, 60, 76–77, 109–110, 166, 168; USHMM, RG 22.005M, reel 3 (RGASPI, f. 69, op. 1, d. 747, l. 56; d. 749, l. 6); 1996.A.169, roll 1 (YVA M-37/160—TsDAHOU, f. 1, op. 23, d. 683, ll. 3–16).

128. Popov, *Diversanty Stalina*, 205.

129. RGASPI, f. 69, op. 1, d. 28, l. 77.

130. IIAN ORF, f. 2, raz. 2, op. 9/2, d. 30, l. 10.

131. RGASPI, f. 69, op. 1, d. 1108, l. 14; IIAN ORF, f. 2, raz. 2, op. 2, d. 25a, l. 43; Schulman, *A Partisan's Memoir*, 109.

132. See Chapter Five.

133. RGASPI, f. 69, op. 1, d. 1108, ll. 15–16.

134. RGASPI, f. 69, op. 1, d. 1084, l. 51.

135. RGASPI, f. 69, op. 1, d. 750, l. 137.

136. IIAN ORF, f. 2, raz. 2, op. 9/2, d. 30, l. 12.

137. Cited in Zhirnov, "Na okkupirovannykh territoriiakh," *Kommersant vlast'*, part 2, no. 30 (31 July 2001).

138. See the discussions in Robert Thurston, *Life and Terror in Stalin's Russia, 1934–1941* (New Haven, Conn.: Yale University Press, 1996), 137–163; Fitzpatrick, *Everyday Stalinism*, 209–217; Gabor Rittersporn, "The Omnipresent Conspiracy: On Soviet Imagery of Politics and Social Relations in the 1930s," in J. Arch Getty and Roberta T. Manning, eds., *Stalinist Terror: New Perspectives* (Cambridge: Cambridge University Press, 1993), 99–115.

139. Davies, *Popular Opinion in Stalin's Russia*, 124–144; Hiroaki Kuromiya, *Freedom and Terror in the Donbas: A Ukrainian-Russian Borderland, 1870s–1990s* (Cambridge: Cambridge University Press, 1998), 181–184; Kotkin, *Magnetic Mountain*, 341–348.

140. Zubkova, *Russia after the War*, 85–86.

141. See, for example, RGASPI, f. 69, op. 1, d. 28, l. 65.

142. IIAN ORF, f. 2, raz. 2, op. 6, d. 12, l. 12.

143. Tec, *Defiance*, 81, 137, 141.

144. Thus, in all of Fedorov's unit in the winter of 1942, there were only seven spades, five hatchets, and one crowbar. He also related that the partisans obtained their flatware in a "fiery battle" with the Germans; Fedorov, *Podpol'nyi obkom*, 389–390.

145. Tec, *Defiance*, 109, 151, 180.

146. RGASPI, f. 69, op. 1, d. 83, l. 21.

147. RGASPI, f. 69, op. 1, d. 37; op. 1, d. 1067, l. 79; IIAN ORF, f. 2, raz. 2, op. 4, d. 117, ll. 7–8; Schulman, *A Partisan's Memoir*, 113.

148. IIAN ORF, f. 2, raz. 2, op. 4, d. 23, ll. 8, 13.

149. IIAN ORF, f. 2, raz. 2, op. 4, d. 25, l. 9.

150. Radio operators, for example, received between 375 and 500 rubles per month, based on the operator's rank. In contrast, rank-and-file partisans could expect a base pay of 250 rubles, and Heroes of the Soviet Union received 500 rubles per month. Commanders and commissars received between 750 and 1,800 rubles per month, depending on the size of the unit; RGASPI, f. 69, op. 1, d. 2, l. 18; d. 10. l. 85; d. 25, ll. 82–89, 121–122, 154–157.

151. Fedorov, *Podpol'nyi obkom*, 387.

152. Schulman, *A Partisan's Memoir*, 166.

153. TsMVS, f. 4/69036, l. 10.

154. IIAN ORF, f. 2, raz. 2, op. 6, d. 14, l. 14.

155. Increased contact with the population also had its downside; saboteurs and scouts apparently had higher rates of infectious diseases such as typhus; A. A. Tumanian, "Lesnoi gospital'," in N. P. Sudoplatov and A. A. Tumanian, *Zapiski partizanskikh vrachei: O podvigakh medrabotnikov v tylu vraga v gody Velikoi Otechestvennoi voiny* (Tula, USSR: Prioskoe knizhnoe izdatel'stvo, 1989), 228.

156. RGASPI, f. 69, op. 1, d. 28, ll. 36, 139.

157. TsKhDMO, f. 1, op. 53, d. 10, l. 254.

158. RGASPI, f. 69, op. 1, d. 28, l. 36.

159. Ibid.

160. RGASPI, f. 69, op. 1, d. 1060, l. 8.

161. RGASPI, f. 69, op. 1, d. 29, l. 37.

162. TsKhDMO, f. 1, op. 53, d. 88, ll. 91–92.

163. *Pravda*, 2 April 1943.

164. Tec, *Defiance*, 148–150.

165. Kelly, *Refining Russia*, 240–241.

166. Tec, *Defiance*, 136–137, 160–161.

167. Cited in ibid., 141.

168. RGASPI, f. 69, op. 1, d. 1082, l. 24.

169. RGASPI, f. 69, op. 1, d. 1108, l. 7.

170. RGASPI, f. 625, op. 1, d. 61, ll. 160–161.

171. Alec Nove, *An Economic History of the USSR* (New York: Penguin Books, 1982), 209–210; see also Moshe Lewin, "Social Relations Inside Industry during the Prewar Five-Year Plans," in Lewin, *The Making of the Soviet System: Essays in the Social History of Interwar Russia* (New York: Pantheon Books, 1985), 241–257; Kotkin, *Magnetic Mountain*, 242–256; Elena Osokina, *Our Daily Bread: Socialist Distribution and the Art of Survival in Stalin's Russia,1927–1941*, trans. Kate Transchel and Greta Bucher (Armonk, N.Y.: M. E. Sharpe, 2001), 82–101.

172. William Moskoff, *The Bread of Affliction: Food Supply in the USSR During*

World War II (Cambridge: Cambridge University Press, 1990), 148–140, 178–180; John Barber and Mark Harrison, *The Soviet Home Front, 1941–1945: A Social and Economic History of the USSR in World War II* (London: Longman Publishing Group, 1991), 79–82, 94–112; Fitzpatrick, *Everyday Stalinism*, 62–66, 95–106.

173. David Hoffmann, *Peasant Metropolis: Social Identities in Moscow, 1929–1941* (Ithaca, N.Y.: Cornell University Press, 1994), 125; Hiroaki Kuromiya, "The Crisis of Proletarian Identity in the Soviet Factory, 1928–1929," *Slavic Review* 44, 2 (Summer 1985): 280–297.

174. For a discussion of postwar social stratification and materialism, see Vera Dunham, *In Stalin's Time: Middleclass Values in Soviet Fiction* (Cambridge: Cambridge University Press, 1976).

175. See, for example, Lewis Siegelbaum's discussion of the role of Stakhanovites in creating a "cultured" working class, in *Stakhanovism and the Politics of Productivity in the USSR, 1935–1941* (Cambridge, Cambridge University Press, 1988), esp. 210–246; David Hoffmann, *Stalinist Values: The Cultural Norms of Soviet Modernity* (Ithaca, N.Y.: Cornell University Press, 2003), esp. 15–56.

176. Kelly, *Refining Russia*, 230–311.

177. Lynne Viola, *Peasant Rebels: Collectivization and the Culture of Peasant Resistance* (Oxford: Oxford University Press, 1996), 13–44; Clark, *The Soviet Novel*, 101–103; Yuri Slezkine, *Arctic Mirrors: Russia and the Small Peoples of the North* (Ithaca, N.Y.: Cornell University Press, 1994), 219–263; McCannon, *Red Arctic*, passim, esp. chaps. four and five.

178. USHMM, 1996.A.169, reel 36 (YVA M-37/853). I. F. Fedorov is not to be confused with A. F. Fedorov.

179. IIAN ORF, f. 2, raz. 2, op. 4, d. 75, l. 6.

180. RGASPI, f. 69, op. 1, d. 29, l. 151.

181. See, for example, the discussion of the New Year's holiday and fir trees in Petrone, *Life Has Become More Joyous*, 85–109; Kelly, *Refining Russia*, 284–289.

182. TsMVS, 4/69036, l. 6.

183. RGASPI, f. 69, op. 1, d. 28, l. 58; IIAN ORF, f. 2, raz. 2, op. 6, d. 35, l. 10.

184. Kelly, *Refining Russia*, 279.

185. IIAN ORF, f. 2, raz. 2, op. 2, d. 25a, l. 25; Fedorov, *Podpol'nyi obkom deistvuet*, 420; Vershigora, *Liudi s chistoi sovest'iu*, 58; R. R. Kruchok, ed., *Vsenarodnoe partizanskoe dvizhenie v Belorussii v gody Velikoi Otechestvennoi voiny: Dokumenty i materialy*, t. 1 (Minsk: Belarus', 1967), 146.

186. Fedorov, *Podpol'ny obkom deistvuet*, 408. See also T. A. Kliatskii, ed., *Partizanskie byli* (Moscow: Politizdat, 1965), for memoirs on the adventures of partisan newspaper publishing.

187. IIAN ORF, f. 2, raz. 2, op. 9/2, d. 30, ll. 5, 10.

188. Starinov, *Over the Abyss*, 340.

189. IIAN ORF, f. 2, raz. 2, op. 6, d. 12, l. 13; RGASPI, f. 69, op. 1, d. 1084, l. 24; Makarov, *Partiinoe podpol'e*, 283; Zalesskii, *V partizanskikh kraiakh i zonakh*, 305.

190. IIAN ORF, f. 2, raz. 2, op. 9/2, d. 57, ll. 4, 7.

191. Shumilin, *Istoriia partizanskogo dvizheniia*, 151.

192. Petrone, *Life Has Become More Joyous*, 65–70; McCannon, *Red Arctic*, 65–66, 77, 90.

193. RGASPI, f. 69, op. 1, d. 29, l. 151.

194. RGASPI, f. 625, op. 1, d. 28, l. 56.

195. IIAN ORF, f. 2, raz. 2, op. 4, d. 25, l. 7.

196. IIAN ORF, f. 2, raz. 2, op. 4, d. 23, l. 12.

197. Indeed, the significant tension in Vershigora's memoirs reflects his attempt to reconcile claims of partisan discipline and consciousness with the desire to portray the partisans as free-spirited romantics. This conflict was embodied within his own person, as suggested by his discussion of partisan literary circles and rejection of shaving on the same page (58). Critics, including Soviet censors, charged that he failed to square this particular circle; see RGASPI, f. 625, op. 1, d. 61, ll. 581–587, 1065–1070.

198. Vershigora, *Liudi s chistoi sovest'iu*, 394.

199. TsKhDMO, f. 1, op. 53, d. 14, l. 24.

200. IIAN ORF, f. 2, raz. 2, op. 9/2, d. 57, l. 5.

201. Vershigora, *Liudi s chistoi sovest'iu*, 58. For a recording of "The Partisan Beard" (*Partizanskaia boroda*), see *Partizanskie pesni*, Bomba Music, 2000.

202. IIAN ORF, f. 2, raz. 2, op. 4, d. 15, l. 10.

203. GARF, f. 6903, op. 20, d. 12, l. 265 (15 January 1943); see also d. 8, l. 179 (9 November 1942); d. 14, ll. 367–369 (26 June 1943).

204. RGASPI, f. 69, op. 1, d. 550, l. 90; TsKhDMO, op. 53, d. 11a, l. 6; d. 9, l. 9.

205. See also Stephen Merrit Miner, *Stalin's Holy War: Religion, Nationalism, and Alliance Politics, 1941–1945* (Chapel Hill: University of North Carolina Press, 2003), esp. 1–202; on the ambiguity of popular piety in Ukraine, see Karel Berkhoff, *Harvest of Despair: Life and Death in Ukraine under Nazi Rule* (Cambridge, Mass.: Belknap Press of Harvard University Press, 2004), 238–252.

206. Cited in *Istoriia partizanskogo dvizheniia*, 149.

207. Shumilin, *Istoriia partizanskogo dvizheniia*, 148.

208. Petrone, *Life Has Become More Joyous*, passim.

209. IIAN ORF, f. 2, raz. 2, op. 2, d. 25a, l. 92; RGASPI, f. 69, op. 1, d. 1084, l. 96; A. F. Fyodorov, *The Underground Committee Carries On*, trans. L. Stolitsky (Moscow: Foreign Languages Publishing House, 1952), 486; V. M. Koval'chuk and A. R. Dzeniskevich, eds., *V tylu vraga: Bor'ba partizan i podpol'shchikov na okkupirovannoi territorii Leningradskoi oblast', 1944: Sbornik dokumentov* (Leningrad: Lenizdat, 1985), 21. See also the self-published journal produced by the "Flame" Partisan Detachment; TsMVS, f. 4/38347. Some units returned to experimental dramatic forms such as "living newspapers," popular during the Civil War and NEP, to convey this information; IIAN ORF, f. 2, raz. 2, op. 9/2, d. 57, l. 14.

210. IIAN ORF, f. 2, raz. 2, op. 6, d. 12, l. 15.

211. RGASPI, f. 69, op. 1, d. 1080, l. 2. In his memoirs, Romanov treated the Sergei partisans, particularly their late, eponymous leader, with reverence.

212. IIAN ORF, f. 2, raz. 2, op. 6, d. 12, l. 13; RGASPI, f. 69, op. 1, d. 467, l. 75; d. 470, l. 47; d. 474, l. 22.

213. IIAN ORF, f. 2, raz. 2, op. d. 25a, ll. 108–109.

214. RGASPI, f. 69, op. 1, d. 283, l. 3.

215. IIAN ORF, f. 2, raz. 2, op. 6, d. 12, l. 12.; RGASPI, f. 69, op. 1, d. 1068, l. 1; d. 1084, ll. 23–24.

216. IIAN ORF, f. 2, raz. 2, op. 6, d. 12, l. 14.

217. IIAN ORF, f. 2, raz. 2, op. 6, d. 12, ll. 6, 8, 12, 14, 48; RGASPI, f. 69, op. 1, d. 29, ll. 20, 27; d. 475, l. 115; d. 1067, l. 71; d. 1068, l. 1; d. 1080, l. 40; d. 1084, ll. 23–32; d. 1091, l. 1; TsMVS, f.4/36.415, l. 17.

218. RGASPI, f. 69, op. 1, d. 475, l. 115; d. 1067, l. 71.

219. IIAN ORF, f. 2, raz. 2, op. 6, d. 12, l. 6; op. 9/2, d. 57, l. 7.

220. Petrone, *Life Has Become More Joyous*, 19–20.

221. IIAN ORF, f. 2, raz. 2, op. 3, d. 15, l. 19.

222. RGASPI, f. 69, op. 1, d. 474, ll. 12–13; d. 1080, l. 39.

223. IIAN ORF, f. 2, raz. 2, op. 2, d. 25a, l. 19.

224. RGASPI, f. 69, op. 1, d. 1080, l. 41. There was always the possibility of violence within the unit during holidays, another customary happening of the prewar period, made all the more dangerous by the behavior of drunken, belligerent, heavily armed men; RGASPI, f. 69, op. 1, d. 1080, l. 39.

225. Zalesskii, *V partizanskikh kraiakh i zonakh*, 311.

226. IIAN ORF, f. 2, raz. 2, op. 4, d. 117, l. 5; Hersh Smolar, *The Minsk Ghetto: Soviet Jewish Partisans against the Nazis* (New York: Holocaust Library, 1989), 40.

227. RGASPI, f. 69, op. 1, d. 29, l. 119.

228. Fyodorov, *The Underground Committee*, 131; Kliatskii, *Partizanskie byli*, 188.

229. RGASPI, f. 69, op. 1, d. 1067, l. 71.

230. RGASPI, f. 69, op. 1. d. 474, ll. 12–13; d. 1080, ll. 41; Makarov, *Partiinoe podpol'e*, 283; Zalesskii, *V partizanskikh kraiakh i zonakh*, 305.

231. For the importance of personal bonds in the performance of combat units, see S. L. A. Marshall, *Men against Fire* (New York: William Morrow, 1947), 138–156, and J. Glenn Gray, *The Warriors: Reflections on Men in Battle* (New York: Harcourt Brace, 1959), 39–51.

CONCLUSION: LIBERATION AND LEGACY

1. V. A. Zolotarev and A. S. Emelin, eds., *Russkii arkhiv: Velikaia Otechestvennaia: SSSR i Polsha: 1941–1945 — K istorii voennogo soiuza: Dokymenty i materialy* (Moscow: Terra, 1994), 104; John Armstrong, "Introduction," in John Armstrong, ed., *The Soviet Partisans in World War II* (Madison: University of Wisconsin Press, 1964), 58–64.

2. Nahum Kohn and Howard Roiter, *A Voice from the Forest* (New York: Holocaust Books, 1980), 214.

3. I borrow this term from George Mosse's discussion "Myth of the War Experience"; see his *Fallen Soldiers: Reshaping the Memory of the World Wars* (Oxford: Oxford University Press, 1990), 7–11. For other discussions of the postwar Soviet my-

thology surrounding the war, see Nina Tumarkin, *The Living and the Dead: The Rise and Fall of the Cult of World War II in Russia* (New York: Basic Books, 1994), and Amir Weiner, "The Making of a Dominant Myth: The Second World War and the Construction of Political Identities within the Soviet Polity," *Russian Review* 55, 2 (October 1996): 638–660.

4. IIAN ORF, f. 2, raz. 2, op. 3, d. 15, l. 16. See also the fears of the Bielski partisans in Nechama Tec, *Defiance: The Bielski Partisans* (Oxford: Oxford University Press, 1993), 196.

5. IIAN ORF, f. 2, raz. 2, op. 3, d. 15, l. 16; op. 6, d. 15, l. 10; V. M. Koval'chuk and A. R. Dzeniskevich, eds., *V tylu vraga: Bor'ba partizan i podpol'shchikov na okkupirovannoi territorii Leningradskoi Oblasti 1944 g.: Sbornik dokumentov* (Leningrad: Lenizdat, 1985), 148–149. For an official description of these reunions, see *Pravda*, 9 July 1944, p. 3.

6. IIAN ORF, f. 2, raz. 2, op. 6, d. 12, l. 22.

7. IIAN ORF, f. 2, raz. 2, op. 6, d. 15, l. 10.

8. See, for example, the press coverage of the triumphant partisan celebration in Orel: *Izvestiia*, 21 September 1943, p. 3; *Krasnaia zvezda*, 21 September 1943, p. 4; *Pravda*, 22 September 1943, p. 3.

9. A. I. Briukhanov, *V shtabe partizanskogo dvizheniia* (Minsk: Belarus', 1980), 228.

10. Hersh Smolar, *The Minsk Ghetto: Soviet Jewish Partisans against the Nazis* (New York: Holocaust Library, 1989), 151; Briukhanov, *V shtabe partizanskogo dvizheniia*, 230; P. Z. Kalinin, *Partizanskaia respublika* (Minsk: Belarus', 1968), 363–365; *Izvestiia*, 18 July 1944; Leni Yahil, *The Holocaust: The Fate of European Jewry* (Oxford: Oxford University Press, 1990), 269–270.

11. RGASPI, f. 69, op. 1, d. 10, ll. 127–128.

12. Thus, in Smolensk Oblast, of the 15,180 partisans who crossed Soviet lines during the region's liberation, 13,553 (89.3 percent) were reassigned to the Red Army, 130 (0.8 percent) were sent to hospitals, and 1,497 (9.9 percent) were assigned to government and Party agencies; RGASPI, f. 69, op. 1, d. 65, l. 207. In Orel, of the 12,766 partisans present during the liberation of the oblast, 10,872 (85.2 percent) were sent to the Red Army, and 1,894 (14.8 percent) remained in the Soviet rear area to conduct political and administrative work; RGASPI, f. 69, op. 1, d. 65, l. 233. Neither the Orel nor Smolensk figures make any reference to those partisans who were taken into custody by the security organs. They were probably included among those reassigned to the Red Army. See also Armstrong, "Introduction," in Armstrong, *The Soviet Partisans*, 65. In his history of the war, Alexander Werth states that 20 percent of the partisans later drafted by the Red Army were deemed medically unfit for military service. Although this is a believable figure, Werth gives no attribution for it; see Werth, *Russia at War, 1941–1945* (New York: Avon Books, 1964), 663.

13. V. A. Zolotarev, ed., *Partizanskoe dvizhenie: Po opytu Velikoi Otechestvennoi voiny, 1941–1945 gg.* (Moscow: Kuchkovo Pole, 2001), 272, citing GARF, f. 4, op. 33, d. 692, l. 33.

14. Armstrong, "Introduction," in Armstrong, *The Soviet Partisans*, 65.

15. Ibid., 66–67; Kees Boeterbloem, *Life and Death under Stalin: Kalinin Province, 1945–1953* (Montreal and Kingston, Canada: McGill-Queen's University Press, 1999), 63; Werth, *Russia at War*, 634.

16. RGASPI, f. 17, op. 88, d. 272, l. 3.

17. Amir Weiner, *Making Sense of War: The Second World War and the Fate of the Bolshevik Revolution* (Princeton, N.J.: Princeton University Press, 2001), 70–71.

18. IIAN ORF, f. 2, raz. 2, op. 3, d. 15, l. 17.

19. Cited in Svetlana Aleksievich, *War's Unwomanly Face* (Moscow: Progress Publishers, 1988), 45. See also IIAN ORF, f. 2, raz. 2, op. 3, d. 15, l. 18.

20. Cited in Aleksievich, *War's Unwomanly Face*, 122.

21. By 1959, only two-thirds of the women who had reached the age of twenty between 1929 and 1939 were married; John Barber and Mark Harrison, *The Soviet Home Front, 1941–1945: A Social and Economic History of the USSR in World War II* (London: Longman Group, 1991), 207.

22. Aleksievich, *War's Unwomanly Face*, 8, 71.

23. *Izvestiia*, 18 June 1944, p. 3.

24. *Izvestiia*, 22 March 1944, p. 3. See also *Izvestiia*, 12 June 1944, p. 3, 7 July 1944, p. 2; *Pravda*, 4 July 1944, p. 3, 6 August 1944, p. 3.

25. Aleksei Popov, *15 Vstrech s generalom KGB Bel'chenko* (Moscow: OLMA-PRESS, 2002), 262.

26. IIAN ORF, f. 2, raz. 2, op. 6, d. 12, l. 23; d. 20, l. 2. The redefectors from the 1st and 2nd Voroshilov were transferred to the Red Army, where they presumably served in the penal battalions.

27. Popov, *15 Vstrech*, 262–263, 268–271; Jeffrey Burds, "Gender and Policing in Soviet West Ukraine, 1944–1948," *Cahiers du Monde Russe* 42, 2–4 (April-December 2001): 282.

28. Weiner, *Making Sense of War*, 178–179. See also A. F. Fedorov's recommendation to Khrushchev that two or three partisan formations be left intact after liberation to fight the nationalists in western Ukraine; USHMM, 1996.A.169, reel 1 (YVA M-37/14—TsDAHOU, f. 1, op. 22, d. 75, l. 19); reel 39 (YVA M-37/1314—TsDAHOU, f. 100, op. 1, d. 2, l. 2). For more on the war between the Soviets and Ukrainian separatists, see Burds, "Gender and Policing," and "*Agentura*: Soviet Informants' Networks in Galicia, 1944–1948," *Eastern European Politics and Societies* 11, 1 (Winter 1997): 89–130.

29. Such cases were still being investigated well into the 1950s at least; RGASPI, f. 17, op. 122, d. 99, ll. 44–52; f. 625, op. 1, d. 44, ll. 7–8; TsKhDMO, f. 1, op. 53, d. 23, ll. 15, 18.

30. TsKhDMO, f. 1, op. 53, d. 10, ll. 26–27.

31. RGASPI, f. 644, op. 1, d. 108, ll. 153–157.

32. RGASPI, f. 69, op. 1, d. 10, ll. 95–97.

33. RGASPI, f. 69, op. 1, d. 10, ll. 127–128.

34. RGASPI, f. 69, op. 1, d. 10, ll. 136–139.

35. This estimate is derived from reports by Komsomol committees in Belorussia,

Briansk, and Kalinin. By 1946, the Belorussian Komsomol had purged approximately 8.8 percent of its members, and in Smolensk, approximately 9.8 percent were excluded. In the Crimea, around 21 percent of the Komsomols were kicked out, but this number includes Tatars, who were collectively punished as a disloyal nation; see TsKhDMO, f. 1, op. 6, d. 309, l. 152; d. 229, l. 157; d. 322, l. 51.

36. Weiner, *Making Sense of War*, 99–101. More local research needs to be done to see how representative Vinnytsia was for all of the occupied Soviet territories.

37. John Armstrong, *The Politics of Totalitarianism: The Communist Party of the Soviet Union from 1934 to the Present* (New York: Random House, 1961), 177.

38. Elena Zubkova, *Russia after the War: Hopes, Illusions, and Disappointments, 1945–1957*, trans. Hugh Ragsdale (Armonk, N.Y.: M. E. Sharpe, 1998), 79.

39. For a discussion of the political conflicts of the late Stalin years, see Werner G. Hahn, *Postwar Soviet Politics: The Fall of Zhdanov and the Defeat of Moderation* (Ithaca, N.Y.: Cornell University Press, 1982). See also E. S. Seniavskaia, *Frontovoe Pokolenie: Istoriko-psikhologichesskoe issledovanie* (Moscow: Institut rossiiskoi istorii, RAN, 1995), 93.

40. USHMM, 1996.A.169, reel 1 (YVA M-37/181 — TsDAHOU, f. 1, op. 23, d. 1364, ll. 1–3).

41. Weiner, *Making Sense of War*, 314–315.

42. Briukhanov, *V shtabe partizanskogo dvizheniia*, 163. For more on the history of the commission, see Matthew Gallagher, *The Soviet History of World War II: Myths, Memories and Realities* (New York: Frederick A. Praeger, 1963), 79–82.

43. Gallagher, *The Soviet History of World War II*, 3.

44. Ibid., 79–82; Tumarkin, *The Living and the Dead*, 104.

45. G. M. Lin'kov, *Voina v tylu vraga* (Moscow: Sovetskii pisatel', 1947).

46. RGASPI, f. 625, op. 1, d. 61, l. 1057.

47. Cited in Weiner, "The Making Sense of a Dominant Myth," 652.

48. RGASPI, f. 625, op. 1, d. 61, ll. 536, 537, 1058–1062, 1067.

49. RGASPI, f. 625, op. 1, d. 61, l. 1056.

50. RGASPI, f. 17, op. 125, d. 631, ll. 1–4.

51. RGASPI, f. 625, op. 1, d. 61, ll. 573, 578. The memoir was subsequently published, in 1969.

52. RGASPI, f. 17, op. 125, d. 651, ll. 3, 4; Weiner, "The Making of a Dominant Myth," 650–651; Armstrong, *The Soviet Partisans*, 67–68. Medvedev died in 1954.

53. Gallagher, *The Soviet History of World War II*, 59, Katerina Clark, *The Soviet Novel: History as Ritual* (Chicago: University of Chicago Press, 1981), 160–162.

54. Gallagher, *The Soviet History of World War II*, 133–146.

55. Tumarkin, *The Living and the Dead*, 134, dates the master narrative as beginning with Brezhnev.

56. Kalinin, *Partizanskaia respublika*, 367–368. Jews were not included in Kalinin's list; see the discussion later in this section.

57. See, for example, James D. Wilkinson, *The Intellectual Resistance in Europe* (Cambridge, Mass.: Harvard University Press, 1981). Of course, other resistance move-

ments, such as the Home Army in Poland and the Chetniks in Serbia, and more conservative branches in Western Europe, fought German occupation but hoped to preserve much of the prewar order.

58. For a history of the resistance—and its accompanying collaborationist—mythology in France, see Alan Morris, *Collaboration and Resistance Reviewed: Writers and the Mode Rétro in France* (Providence, R.I.: Berg Publishers, 1992), and Henry Rousso, *The Vichy Syndrome: History and Memory in France since 1944*, trans. Arthur Goldhammer (Cambridge, Mass.: Harvard University Press, 1991).

59. Aleksandr Nekrich, *The Punished Peoples* (New York: W. W. Norton, 1978), 32–35, 167–179; Catherine Merridale, *Night of Stone: Death and Memory in Twentieth-Century Russia* (New York: Viking Press, 2000), 227–228.

60. RGASPI, f. 625, op. 1, d. 61, l. 969.

61. RGASPI, f. 625, op. 1, d. 61, l. 971.

62. T. A. Kliatskii, ed., *Partizanskie byli* (Moscow: Politizdat, 1965), 6.

63. Armstrong, "Introduction," in Armstrong, *The Soviet Partisans*, 69.

64. RGASPI, f. 625, op. 1, d. 10, l. 68.

65. Ibid.

66. RGASPI, f. 625, op. 1, d. 10, ll. 70–71.

67. RGASPI, f. 625, op. 1, d. 10, ll. 73–74.

68. Malchul'skii believed that one falsification was a historian's revenge against him because he had written to the Belorussian Central Committee denigrating the historian's role in the creation of the Minsk underground obkom; RGASPI, f. 625, op. 1. d. 10, l. 75.

69. RGASPI, f. 625, op. 1, d. 61, ll. 771–807. The editor's criticisms are derived from Romanov's reply to them; unfortunately, the original letter from Belarus was not included in this file.

70. RGASPI, f. 625, op. 1, d. 61, l. 776.

71. RGASPI, f. 625, op. 1, d. 61, ll. 773–776, 786–787.

72. RGASPI, f. 625, op. 1, d. 61, l. 776.

73. Ibid.

74. RGASPI, f. 625, op. 1, d. 61, l. 804.

75. David Ruffley, *Children of Victory: Young Specialists and the Evolution of Soviet Society* (New York: Praeger Publishers, 2003), 62–64. Ruffley's account is derived from an article by Iurii Burtin, "Vlast' protiv literatury (60-e gody)," *Voprosy literatury* 2 (1994): 223–306. For other examples of censorship in the 1960s, see Tumarkin, *The Living and the Dead*, 133–135.

76. Cited in Aleksievich, *War's Unwomanly Face*, 60.

77. Mark von Hagen, "From 'the Great Fatherland War' to the Second World War: New Perspectives and Future Prospects," in Ian Kershaw and Moshe Lewin, eds., *Stalinism and Nazism: Dictatorships in Comparison* (Cambridge: Cambridge University Press, 1997), 238. See also Tumarkin, *The Living and the Dead*, 138–141, 146–150.

78. Merridale, *Night of Stone*, 213.

79. The letter writer requested the former partisan chief's help in obtaining an award for which he had been nominated. The veteran twice used the slogan in his letter, and he told Ponomarenko that previously, modesty had prevented him from pursuing his award. However, the principle at stake was too important: "In [this] country, this idea of ours, must be respected: nothing is forgotten, no one is forgotten"; RGASPI, f. 625, op. 1, d. 10, ll. 12–14.

80. Cited in Robert Daniels, ed., *A Documentary History of Communism in Russia from Lenin to Gorbachev* (Hanover, N.H.: University Press of New England, 1993), 233–235.

81. Martin Malia, *The Soviet Tragedy: A History of Socialism in Russia, 1917–1991* (New York: Free Press, 1994), 289. For a discussion of the militarization of the prewar Soviet economy, see David R. Stone, *Hammer and Rifle: The Militarization of the Soviet Union, 1926–1933* (Lawrence: University Press of Kansas, 2000).

82. Zubkova, *Russia after the War*, 141.

83. Lisa A. Kirschenbaum, "'Our City, Our Hearths, Our Families': Local Loyalties and Private Life in Soviet World War II Propaganda," *Slavic Review* 59, 4 (Winter 2000): 828. See also Richard Stites, "Soviet Wartime Culture: Freedom and Control, Spontaneity and Consciousness," in Robert Thurston and Bernd Bonwetsch, eds., *The People's War: Responses to World War II in the Soviet Union* (Urbana: University of Illinois Press, 2000), 171–184.

84. Brooks, *Thank You, Comrade Stalin*, 193.

85. Lewis Siegelbaum, Review of Amir Weiner's *Making Sense of War*, in *Slavic Review* 60, 4 (Winter 2001): 865.

86. For a general survey of the literature, see Amir Weiner, "Saving Private Ivan: From What, Why and How," *Kritika* 1, 2 (Spring 2000): 305–336.

87. For the latter, see Werth, *Russia at War*, 384–401, 844–859.

88. Marius Broekmeyer, *Stalin, the Russians, and Their War, 1941–1945*, trans. Rosalind Buck (Madison: University of Wisconsin Press, 2004), 211–213; Merridale, *Night of Stone*, 212, 214; Tumarkin, *The Living and the Dead*, 66–67.

89. Gennadi Bordiugov, "The Popular Mood in the Unoccupied Soviet Union: Continuity and Change during the War," in Thurston and Bonwetsch, *The People's War*, 54–70.

90. E. S. Seniavskaia: *Frontovoe Pokolenie: Istoriko-psikhologichesskoe issledovanie* (Moscow: Institut rossiiskoi istorii, RAN, 1995), 158, 161–162.

91. Mosse, *Fallen Soldiers*, 159–181; Omer Bartov, *Hitler's Army: Soldiers, Nazis, and War in the Third Reich* (Oxford: Oxford University Press, 1992).

92. Merridale, *Night of Stone*, 220.

93. Zubkova, *Russia after the War*, 16–17, 77, 88.

94. Weiner, *Making Sense*, 50–52.

95. Ibid., 7.

96. See Raymond A. Bauer, Alex Inkeles, and Clyde Kluckhohn, *How the Soviet System Works* (New York: Vintage Books, 1960), esp. 111–143.

97. See Vladimir A. Kozlov, *Mass Uprisings in the USSR: Protest and Rebellion*

in the Post-Stalin Years, ed. and trans. Elaine McClarnand MacKinnon (Armonk, N.Y.: M. E. Sharpe, 2002).

    98. Bauer, Inkeles, and Kluckhohn, *How the Soviet System Works,* 111–143.

    99. Ruffley, *Children of Victory,* 5, 25–43.

    100. Cited in Merridale, *Night of Stone,* 214.

    101. See Ruffley, *Children of Victory,* 85–174.

BIBLIOGRAPHY

ARCHIVES

Gosudarstvennyi arkhiv Rossiiskii Federatsii (GARF)
(State Archive of the Russian Federation, Moscow)

f. 6903, Gosradio (State Radio)
f. 8355, Osoaviakhim (Society of Friends of Defense and Aviation-Chemical Construction)

Institut istorii akademiia nauk otdel rukopisnykh fondov
(Institute of History of the Academy of Sciences,
Department of Manuscript Collections, Moscow)

f. 2, raz. 2, Records of the Commission on the History of the Great Patriotic War—The
Partisan Movement

*Rossiiskii gosudarstvennyi arkhiv
kinofotodokumentov (RGAKFD)*
(Russian State Archive of Film and Photography,
Khimki, Russia)

Photographs of the partisan movement

*Rossiiskii gosudarstvennyi arkhiv sotsialno-
politicheskoi istorii (RGASPI)*
(Russian State Archive of Social-Political History,
Moscow)

f. 17, the Central Committee
f. 69, the Central Staff of the Partisan Movement
f. 625, personal collection of P. K. Ponomarenko
f. 644, State Defense Committee

Tsentral'nyi khraneniia dokumentov molodezhnykh organizatsii (TsKhDMO—now integrated with RGASPI)
(Central Repository of
Documents of Youth Organizations, Moscow)

f. 1, Record of the Central Committee of the Communist Youth League

Tsentral'nyi muzei Vooruzhennykh Sil (TsMVS)
(Central Museum of the Armed Forces, Moscow)

f. 4, documents and objects of the Soviet Partisan Movement

U.S. Holocaust Memorial Museum (USHMM),
Washington, D.C.

Record Group 22, Records from Soviet-era archives (includes national and local archives from Belarus, Russia, and Ukraine)
1996.A.169, Records from the Yad Vashem Archive (with material from Soviet-era archives, including national and local archives from Belarus, Russia, and Ukraine)

NEWSPAPERS

Izvestiia
Krasnaia zvezda
Pravda

JOURNALS

American Historical Review
American Slavic and East European Review
Cahiers du Monde Russe
Eastern European Politics and Societies
Europe-Asia Studies
French Historical Studies
Gender and History
Holocaust and Genocide Studies
Izvestiia Tsk KPSS
Jahrbucher für Geschichte Osteuropas
Journal of Modern History
Kommersant vlast
Kritika: Explorations in Eurasian History

BIBLIOGRAPHY 377

Military Review
Novaia i noveishaia istoriia
Otechestvennaia istoriia
Russian History/Histoire Russe
Russian Review
Slavic Review
Soviet Union/Union Sovietique
Sputnik agitatora
Voenno-istoricheskii zhurnal
Yad Vashem Studies
Yale Review

BOOKS AND ARTICLES

Ainzstein, Reuben. *Jewish Resistance in Occupied Eastern Europe*. London: Elek Books, 1974.

Aleksievich, Svetlana. *War's Unwomanly Face*. Moscow: Progress Publishers, 1988.

Alexeyeva, Ludmilla, and Paul Goldberg. *The Thaw Generation: Coming of Age in the Post-Stalin Era*. Boston: Little, Brown, 1990.

Allilyueva, Svetlana. *Twenty Letters to a Friend*. Trans. Priscilla John McMillan. New York: Harper & Row, 1967.

Altshuler, Mordechai. "Jewish Warfare and the Participation of Jews in Combat in the Soviet Union as Reflected in Soviet and Western Historiography." In *Bitter Legacy: Confronting the Holocaust in the USSR*, ed. Zvi Gitelman, 151–166. Bloomington: Indiana University Press, 1997.

Amirov, G. S. *Nepokorennaia zemlia*. Alma Ata, Kazakhstan, USSR: Kazakhstan, 1975.

Amsaliamov, M., and V. Andrianov. "Organizatsiia partizanskikh sil i fronty rukovodstva ikh boevoi deiatel'nostiiu v Otechestvennoi voine." *Voenno-istoricheskii zhurnal* 9 (1966): 18–26.

Anderson, Benedict. *Imagined Communities: Reflections on the Origins and Spread of Nationalism*. Rev. ed. London: Verso, 1991.

Anderson, Truman. "Incident at Baranivka: German Reprisals and the Soviet Partisan Movement in Ukraine, October–December 1941." *Journal of Modern History* 71, 3 (September 1999): 585–623.

Andreyev, Catherine. *Vlasov and the Russian Liberation Movement: Soviet Reality and Emigré Theory*. Cambridge: Cambridge University Press, 1987.

Andrianov, V. N., ed. *Voina v tylu vraga: O nekotorykh problemakh istorii sovetskogo partizanskogo dvizheniia v gody Velikoi Otechestvennoi voiny*. Moscow: Politizdat, 1974.

Arad, Yitzhak. "The Holocaust of Soviet Jewry in the Occupied Territories of the USSR." *Yad Vashem Studies* 21 (1991): 1–47.

——. "Jewish Family Camps in the Forests—An Original Means of Rescue." In *The Nazi Holocaust: Historical Articles on the Destruction of the European Jews.* Vol. 7, *Jewish Resistance to the Holocaust,* ed. Michael Marrus, 219–239. Westport, Conn.: Meckler, 1989.

Arad, Yitzhak, Shmuel Krakowski, and Shmuel Spector, comps. and eds. *The Einsatzgruppen Reports.* New York: Holocaust Library, 1989.

Arkhipova, T. I., ed. *Kurskaia oblast' v period Velikoi Otechestvennoi voiny Sovetskogo soiuza 1941–1945 gg.: Sbornik dokumentov i materialov,* vol. 1. Kursk: Kurskoe knizhnoe izdatel'stvo, 1960.

Armstrong, John. *The Politics of Totalitarianism: The Communist Party of the Soviet Union from 1934 to the Present.* New York: Random House, 1961.

——, ed. *The Soviet Partisans in World War II.* Madison: University of Wisconsin Press, 1964.

——. *Ukrainian Nationalism.* 3rd ed. Englewood, Colo.: Ukrainian Academic Press, 1990.

Armstrong, John, and Kurt Dewitt. "Organization and Control of the Partisan Movement." In *The Soviet Partisans in World II,* ed. John Armstrong, 73–140. Madison: University of Wisconsin Press, 1964.

Artem'ev, N. *V efire partizany.* Moscow: Voenizdat, 1971.

Avrich, Paul. *Russian Rebels: 1600–1800.* New York: W. W. Norton, 1972.

Babel, Isaac. *Red Cavalry.* New York: W. W. Norton, 2003.

Baburina, N., ed. *Russia 20th Century: History of the Country in Posters.* Moscow: Panorama, 1993.

Barber, John. "The Image of Stalin in Soviet Propaganda and Public Opinion in World War 2." In *World War 2 and the Soviet People: Selected Papers from the Fourth World Congress for Soviet and East European Studies, Harrogate, 1990,* ed. Carol Garrard and John Garrard, 38–49. New York: St. Martin's Press, 1993.

Barber, John, and Mark Harrison. *The Soviet Home Front: A Social and Economic History of the USSR in World War II.* London: Longman Group, 1991.

Bartov, Omer. "Defining Enemies, Making Victims: Germans, Jews, and the Holocaust." *American Historical Review* 102, 3 (June 1998): 771–816.

——. *The Eastern Front, 1941–1945: German Troops and the Barbarization of Warfare.* New York: St. Martin's Press, 1986.

——. *Hitler's Army: Soldiers, Nazis and War in the Third Reich.* New York: Oxford University Press, 1991.

Bauer, Raymond, A., Alex Inkeles, and Clyde Kluckhohn. *How the Soviet System Works.* New York: Vintage Books, 1960.

Beevor, Antony. *Stalingrad: The Fateful Siege, 1942–1943.* New York: Viking, 1998.

Berkhoff, Karel C. *Harvest of Despair: Life and Death in Ukraine under Nazi Rule.* Cambridge, Mass.: Belknap Press of Harvard University Press, 2004.

Bialer, Seweryn, ed. *Stalin and His Generals: Soviet Military Memoirs of World War II.* Boulder, Colo.: Westview Press, 1984.

Boeterbloem, Kees. *Life and Death under Stalin: Kalinin Province, 1945–1953.* Montreal and Kingston, Canada: McGill-Queen's University Press, 1999.

Bogatyr', Z. A. *V tylu vraga: Boeviia deiatel'nost' soedineniia partizanskikh otriadov pod komandovaniem geroi Sovetskogo soiuza A. N. Saburova.* Moscow: Sotsekgiz, 1963.

Boiarskii, V. I. *Partizany i armiia: Istoriia uteriannykh vozmozhnostei* (Minsk: Kharvest, 2003).

Boldin, General I. V. "Sorok-piat' dnei v tylu vraga." *Voenno-istoricheskii zhurnal* 4 (1961): 64–82.

Boll, Bernd, and Hans Safrian. "On the Way to Stalingrad: The 6th Army in 1941–1942." In *War of Extermination: The German Military in World War II, 1941–1944,* ed. Hannes Heer and Klaus Naumann, 237–271. New York: Berghahn Books, 2000.

Bonnell, Victoria. *Iconography of Power: Soviet Political Posters under Lenin and Stalin.* Berkeley and Los Angeles: University of California Press, 1997.

Bonwetsch, Bernd. "Stalin, the Red Army, and the 'Great Patriotic War.'" In *Stalinism and Nazism: Dictatorships in Comparison,* ed. Ian Kershaw and Moshe Lewin, 185–207. Cambridge: Cambridge University Press, 1997.

———. "War as a 'Breathing Space': Soviet Intellectuals and the 'Great Patriotic War.'" In *The People's War: Responses to World War II in the Soviet Union,* ed. Robert W. Thurston and Bernd Bonwetsch, 137–153. Urbana: University of Illinois Press, 2000.

Boog, Horst, ed. *Germany and the Second World War.* Vol. 4, *The Attack on the Soviet Union.* Oxford: Oxford University Press, 1998.

Bordiugov, Gennadi. "The Popular Mood in the Unoccupied Soviet Union: Continuity and Change during the War." In *The People's War: Responses to World War II in the Soviet Union,* ed. Robert W. Thurston and Bernd Bonwetsch, 54–70. Urbana: University of Illinois Press, 2000.

Brandenberger, David. *National Bolshevism: Stalinist Mass Culture and the Formation of Modern Russian Identity.* Cambridge, Mass.: Harvard University Press, 2002.

Briukhanov, A. I. *V shtabe partizanskogo dvizheniia.* Minsk: Belarus', 1980.

Broekmeyer, Marius. *Stalin, the Russians, and Their War.* Trans. Rosalind Buck. Madison: University of Wisconsin Press, 2004.

Brooks, Jeffrey. *Thank You, Comrade Stalin! Soviet Public Culture from Revolution to Cold War.* Princeton, N.J.: Princeton University Press, 2000.

———. *When Russia Learned to Read: Literacy and Popular Literature, 1861–1917.* Princeton, N.J.: Princeton University Press, 1985.

Brown, Kate. *A Biography of No Place: From Ethnic Borderland to Soviet Heartland.* Cambridge, Mass.: Harvard University Press, 2004.

Buianov, I. "Deiatel'nost Tsentral'nogo Shtaba partizanskogo dvizheniia po obespecheniiu partizan vooruzheniem." *Voenno-istoricheskii zhurnal* 5 (1975): 118–122.

Bukov, K. I., ed. *Kliatvu vernosti sderzhali: Partizanskoe Podmoskov'e v dokumentakh i materialiakh.* Moscow: Moskovskii rabochii, 1982.

Burds, Jeffrey. "*Agentura:* Soviet Informants Networks in Galicia, 1944–1948." *Eastern European Politics and Societies* 11, 1 (Winter 1997): 89–130.

———. "Gender and Policing in Soviet West Ukraine, 1944–1948." *Cahiers du Monde Russe* 42, 2–4 (April–December 2001): 279–320.

Bystrov, V. E., ed. *Sovetskie partizany: Iz istorii partizanskogo dvizheniia v gody Velikoi Otechestvennoi voiny.* Moscow: Politizdat, 1961.

Chatterjee, Choi. *Celebrating Women: Gender, Festival Culture, and Bolshevik Ideology, 1910–1939.* Pittsburgh, Pa.: University of Pittsburgh Press, 2002.

Cherniavsky, Michael. "Corporal Hitler, General Winter and the Russian Peasant." *Yale Review* 51 (June 1962): 547–558.

Cholawsky, Shalom. *The Jews of Bielorussia during World War II.* Amsterdam: Harwood Academic Publishers, 1998.

Clark, Katerina. *The Soviet Novel: History as Ritual.* Chicago: University of Chicago Press, 1981.

Colton, Timothy. *Commissars, Commanders, and Civilian Authority: The Structure of Soviet Military Politics.* Cambridge: Cambridge University Press, 1979.

Conquest, Robert. *The Great Terror.* Oxford: Oxford University Press, 1990.

Conze, Susanne, and Beate Fiesler. "Soviet Women as Comrades-in-Arms: A Blind Spot in the History of the War." In *The People's War: Responses to World War II in the Soviet Union,* ed. Robert W. Thurston and Bernd Bonwetsch, 211–234. Urbana: University of Illinois Press, 2000.

Cooper, Matthew. *The Phantom War: The German Struggle against the Soviet Partisans, 1941–1944.* London: MacDonald & James, 1979.

Cottam, Kazimiera J., ed. and trans. *Defending Leningrad: Women behind Enemy Lines.* Nepean, Ontario: New Military Publishing, 1998.

Dallin, Alexander. *German Rule in Russia: A Study of Occupation Policies.* 2nd ed. Boulder, Colo.: Westview Press, 1981.

———. "The Kaminsky Brigade: A Case Study of Soviet Disaffection." In *Revolution and Politics in Russia: Essays in Memory of B. I. Nicolaevsky,* ed. Alexander and Janet Rabinowitch, 243–280. Bloomington: Indiana University Press, 1972.

Dallin, Alexander, and Ralph S. Mavrogordato. "Rodionov: A Case Study in Wartime Redefection." *American Slavic and East European Review* 18 (1959): 25–33.

Dallin, Alexander, Ralph Mavrogordato, and Wilhelm Moll. "Partisan Psychological Warfare and Popular Attitudes." In *The Soviet Partisans in World War II,* ed. John Armstrong, 197–337. Madison: University of Wisconsin Press, 1964.

Daniels, Robert V., ed. *A Documentary History of Communism of Russia from Lenin to Gorbachev.* Hanover, N.H.: University Press of New England, 1993.

Davies, R. W. *Soviet History in the Gorbachev Revolution.* Bloomington: Indiana University Press, 1989.

Davies, Sarah. *Popular Opinion in Stalin's Russia: Terror, Propaganda and Dissent, 1934–1941.* Cambridge: Cambridge University Press, 1997.

Deak, Istvan, Jan T. Gross, and Tony Judt, eds. *The Politics of Retribution: World War II and Its Aftermath.* Princeton, N.J.: Princeton University Press, 2000.

Dean, Martin. *Collaboration in the Holocaust: Crimes of the Local Police in Belorussia and Ukraine, 1941–1944.* New York: St. Martin's Press, 2000.

Dewitt, Kurt. "The Partisans in Soviet Intelligence." In *The Soviet Partisans in World War II*, ed. John Armstrong, 338–360. Madison: University of Wisconsin Press, 1964.

Dixon, C. Aubrey, and Otto Heilbrunn. *Communist Guerilla Warfare*. London: George Allen, 1954.

Djilas, Milovan. *Wartime*. Trans. Michael B. Petrovich. New York: Harcourt Brace Jovanovich, 1977.

Dobrosyzcki, Lucjan, and Jeffrey Gurock. *The Holocaust in the Soviet Union: Studies and Sources on the Destruction of the Jews in the Nazi-Occupied Territories of the USSR, 1941–1945*. Armonk, N.Y.: M. E. Sharpe, 1993.

Dovzhinets, L. G., and I. Ia. Makukhin, eds. *Sumskaia oblast' v period Velikoi Otechestvennoi voiny, 1941–1945*. Kiev: Nauk. dumka, 1988.

Dower, John. *War without Mercy: Race and Power in the Pacific War*. New York: Pantheon Press, 1986.

Dunham, Vera. *In Stalin's Time: Middleclass Values in Soviet Fiction*. Cambridge: Cambridge University Press, 1976.

Eckman, Lester, and Chaim Lazar. *The Jewish Resistance: The History of Jewish Partisans in Lithuania and White Russia during the Nazi Occupation, 1940–1945*. New York: Shengold, 1977.

Ellis, Frank. "The Army and Party in Conflict: Soldiers and Commissars in the Prose of Vasily Grossman." In *World War 2 and the Soviet People: Selected Papers from the Fourth World Congress for Soviet and East European Studies, Harrogate, 1990*, ed. Carol Garrard and John Garrard, 180–201. New York: St. Martin's Press, 1993.

Engel, Barbara Alpern, and Anastasia Posadskaya-Vandbeck, eds. *A Revolution of Their Own: Voices of Women in Soviet History*. Boulder, Colo.: Westview Press, 1998.

Erickson, John. *The Road to Berlin*. Vol. 2 of *Stalin's War with Germany*. New Haven, Conn.: Yale University Press, 1983.

———. *The Road to Stalingrad*. Vol. 1 of *Stalin's War with Germany*. New Haven, Conn.: Yale University Press, 1975.

———. *The Soviet High Command*. Boulder, Colo.: Westview Press, 1984.

———. "Soviet Women at War." In *World War 2 and the Soviet People: Selected Papers from the Fourth World Congress for Soviet and East European Studies, Harrogate, 1990*, ed. Carol Garrard and John Garrard, 50–76. New York: St. Martin's Press, 1993.

Ezergailis, Andrew. *The Holocaust in Latvia, 1941–1944: The Missing Center*. Riga and Washington, D.C.: Historical Institute of Latvia and U.S. Holocaust Memorial Museum, 1998.

Farmer, Sarah. "The Communist Resistance in the Haute-Vienne." *French Historical Studies* 14, 1 (1985): 89–116.

Fedorov, A. F. *Podpol'nyi obkom deistvuet*. Kiev: Politizdat Ukrainy, 1986.

Fedotoff White, Dmitrii. *The Growth of the Red Army*. Westport, Conn.: Hyperion Press, 1981.

Ferro, Marc. *Cinema and History*. Trans. Naomi Greene. Detroit: Wayne State University Press, 1988.

Figes, Orlando. *A People's Tragedy: The Russian Revolution, 1891–1924*. New York: Penguin, 1996.

Fischer, George. *Soviet Opposition to Stalin*. Cambridge, Mass.: Harvard University Press, 1952.

Fitzpatrick, Sheila. "Ascribing Class: The Construction of Social Identity in Soviet Russia." *Journal of Modern History* 65, 4 (December 1993): 745–770.

———, ed. *Cultural Revolution in Russia, 1928–1931*. Bloomington: Indiana University Press, 1978.

———. *Everyday Stalinism: Ordinary Life in Extraordinary Times: Soviet Russia in the 1930s*. Oxford: Oxford University Press, 1999.

———. "The Legacy of the Civil War." In *Party, State, and Society in the Russian Civil War*, ed. Diane P. Koenker, William G. Rosenberg, and Ronald Grigor Suny, 385–398. Bloomington: Indiana University Press, 1989.

———. *Stalin's Peasants: Resistance and Survival in the Russian Village under Collectivization*. Oxford: Oxford University Press, 1994.

Foot, M. R. D. *Resistance: An Analysis of European Resistance to Nazism*. London: Eyre Methuen, 1979.

Fritz, Stephen G. *Frontsoldaten: The German Soldier in World War II*. Lexington: University Press of Kentucky, 1995.

Furmanov, Dmitry. *Chapayev*. Moscow: Progress Publishers, 1955.

Fyodorov, A. F. *The Underground Committee Carries On*. Trans. L. Stolitsky. Moscow: Foreign Language Publishing House, 1952.

Galay, Captain N. "The Partisan Forces." In *The Red Army*, ed. B. H. Liddell Hart, 153–171. New York: Harcourt Brace, 1956.

Gallagher, Matthew. *The Soviet History of World War II: Myths, Memories and Realities*. New York: Frederick A. Praeger, 1963.

Garrard, Carol, and John Garrard, eds. *World War 2 and the Soviet People: Selected Papers from the Fourth World Congress for Soviet and East European Studies, Harrogate, 1990*. New York: St. Martin's Press, 1993.

Getty, J. Arch. "State and Society under Stalin: Constitutions and Elections in the 1930s." *Slavic Review* 50, 1 (Spring 1991): 18–35.

Getty, J. Arch, and Roberta T. Manning, eds. *Stalinist Terror: New Perspectives*. Cambridge: Cambridge University Press, 1993.

Gill, Graeme. *The Origins of the Stalinist Political System*. Cambridge: Cambridge University Press, 1990.

Gitelman, Zvi, ed. *Bitter Legacy: Confronting the Holocaust in the USSR*. Bloomington: Indiana University Press, 1997.

Glantz, David M., and Jonathan House. *When Titans Clashed: How the Red Army Stopped Hitler*. Lawrence: University Press of Kansas, 1995.

Goldman, Wendy Z. *Women, the State and Revolution: Soviet Family Policy and Social Life, 1917–1936*. Cambridge: Cambridge University Press, 1993.

Gorinov, Mikhail M. "Muscovites' Moods, 22 June 1941 to May 1942." In *The People's*

War: Responses to World War II in the Soviet Union, ed. Robert W. Thurston and Bernd Bonwetsch, 108–134. Urbana: University of Illinois Press, 2000.

Gorsuch, Anne E. "Women's Autobiographical Narratives: Soviet Presentations of Self." *Kritika* 2, 4 (Fall 2001): 835–847.

Gray, J. Glenn. *The Warriors: Reflections on Men in Battle.* New York: Harcourt Brace, 1959.

Grechko, A. A., and D. F. Ustinov, eds. *Istoriia Vtoroi Mirovoi voiny, 1939–1945,* 12 vols. Moscow: Voenizdat, 1973–1982.

Grenkevich, Leonid. *The Soviet Partisan Movement, 1941–1944: A Critical Historiographical Analysis.* Edited and with a foreword by David M. Glantz. London: Frank Cass, 1999.

Gross, Jan T. "The Jewish Community in the Soviet-Annexed Territories on the Eve of the Holocaust." In *The Holocaust in the Soviet Union: Studies and Sources on the Destruction of the Jews in the Nazi-Occupied Territories of the USSR, 1941–1945,* ed. Lucjan Dobrosyzcki and Jeffrey Gurock, 155–171. Armonk, N.Y.: M. E. Sharpe, 1993.

———. *Polish Society under German Occupation: The Generalgouvernment, 1939–1944.* Princeton, N.J.: Princeton University Press, 1979.

———. *Revolution from Abroad: The Soviet Conquest of Poland's Western Ukraine and Western Belorussia.* Princeton, N.J.: Princeton University Press, 1988.

———. "Themes for a Social History of War Experience and Collaboration." In *The Politics of World War II and Its Aftermath,* ed. Jan T. Gross, Tony Judt, and Istvan Deak, 15–25. Princeton, N.J.: Princeton University Press, 2000.

Grossman, Vasily. *Life and Fate.* Trans. Robert Chandler. New York: Harper Row Publishers, 1987.

Haestrup, Jørgen. *European Resistance Movements, 1939–1945.* Westport, Conn.: Meckler Publishing, 1981.

Hahn, Werner G. *Postwar Soviet Politics: The Fall of Zhdanov and the Defeat of Moderation, 1946–1953.* Ithaca, N.Y.: Cornell University Press, 1982.

Harris, James. *The Great Urals: Regionalism and the Evolution of the Soviet System.* Ithaca, N.Y.: Cornell University Press, 1999.

Harrison, Mark. "The Soviet Union: The Defeated Victor." In *The Economics of World War II: Six Great Powers in Comparison,* ed. Mark Harrison, 268–301. Cambridge: Cambridge University Press, 1998.

Hawes, Stephen. "The Individual and the Resistance Community in France." In *Resistance in Europe, 1939–1945,* ed. Stephen Hawes and Ralph White, 117–134. London: Allen Lane, 1975.

Hawes, Stephen, and Ralph White. *Resistance in Europe, 1939–1945.* London: Allen Lane, 1975.

Haynes, John. *New Soviet Man: Gender and Masculinity in Stalinist Soviet Cinema.* Manchester, UK, and New York: Manchester University Press, 2003.

Heaton, Colin. *German Anti-partisan Warfare in Europe, 1939–1945.* Atglen, Pa.: Schiffer Military History, 2001.

Heer, Hannes. "The Killing Fields: The Wehrmacht and the Holocaust in Belorussia,

1941–1942." In *War of Extermination: The German Military in World War II, 1941–1944*, ed. Hannes Heer and Klaus Naumann, 55–79. New York: Berghahn Books, 2000.

———. "The Logic of Extermination: The Wehrmacht and the Anti-partisan War." In *War of Extermination: The German Military in World War II, 1941–1944*, ed. Hannes Heer and Klaus Naumann, 92–126. New York: Berghahn Books, 2000.

Heer, Hannes, and Klaus Naumann, eds. *War of Extermination: The German Military in World War II*. New York: Berghahn Books, 2000.

Heilbrunn, Otto. *Partisan Warfare*. New York: Frederick A. Praeger, 1967.

Heiman, Leo. "Organized Looting: The Basis of Partisan Warfare." *Military Review* 45, 2 (February 1965): 61–68.

Hellbeck, Jochen. "Fashioning the Stalinist Soul: The Diary of Stepan Podlubnyi." *Jahrbucher für Geschichte Osteuropas* 44, 3 (1996): 344–373.

Hilberg, Raul. *The Destruction of the European Jews*. New York: Holmes & Meier, 1985.

Hill, Alexander. "The Partisan War in North-West Russia, 1941–1944: A Re-examination." *Journal of Strategic Studies* 24, 3 (September 2002): 37–55.

———. *The War behind the Eastern Front: The Soviet Partisan Movement in North-West Russia, 1941–1944*. New York: Frank Cass, 2005.

Hirsch, Francine. "Race without the Practice of Racial Politics." *Slavic Review* 61, 1 (Spring 2002): 30–44.

Hobsbawm, Eric. *Bandits*. New York: Penguin Books, 1985.

Hoffmann, David L. *Peasant Metropolis: Social Identities in Moscow, 1929–1941*. Ithaca, N.Y.: Cornell University Press, 1994.

———. *Stalinist Values: The Cultural Norms of Soviet Modernity, 1917–1941*. Ithaca, N.Y.: Cornell University Press, 2003.

Holquist, Peter. "To Count, to Extract, and to Exterminate: Population Statistics and Population Politics in Late Imperial and Soviet Russia." In *A State of Nations: Empire and Nation-Making in the Age of Lenin and Stalin*, ed. Ronald Grigor Suny and Terry Martin, 111–144. Oxford: Oxford University Press, 2001.

Hondros, John Louis. *Occupation and Resistance: The Greek Agony, 1941–1944*. New York: Pella Publishing, 1983.

Horne, John, and Alan Kramer. "German 'Atrocities' and Franco-German Opinion, 1914: The Evidence of German Soldiers' Diaries." *Journal of Modern History* 66, 1 (March 1994): 1–33.

Howell, Edgar. *The Soviet Partisan Movement, 1941–1944*. Washington, D.C.: Department of the Army, 1956.

Il'in, F. I., and P. T. Tron'ko, eds. *Kievshchina v gody Velikoi Otechestvennoi voiny*. Kiev: Kievskoe oblastnoe khizhnoe-gazetnoe izdatel'stvo, 1963.

Il'in, M. A., and V. S. Papin, eds. *Stranitsy narodnogo podviga: Kalininskaia oblast' v gody Velikoi Otechestvennoi voiny*. Moscow: Moskovskii rabochii, 1974.

International Conference on the History of the Resistance Movements. *European Resistance Movements, 1939–1945: First International Conference on the History of the Resistance Movements Held at Liege-Bruxelles-Breedonk, 14–17 September 1958.* London: Pergamon, 1960.

———. *European Resistance Movements, 1939–1945: Second International Conference on the History of the Resistance Movements, Milan 1960.* London: Pergamon, 1964.

Jones, Jeffrey. "'Every Family Has Its Freak': Perceptions of Collaboration in Occupied Soviet Russia, 1943–1948." *Slavic Review* 64, 4 (Winter 2005): 747–770.

Judt, Tony, ed. *Resistance and Revolution in Mediterranean Europe, 1939–1948.* London: Routledge, 1989.

Kagan, Jack, and Dov Cohen. *Surviving the Holocaust with the Russian Jewish Partisans.* London: Valentine Mitchell, 1998.

Kalinin, P. Z. *Partizanskaia respublika.* Minsk: Belarus', 1968.

Kamenev, S. S. "Byt' na-cheku." *Sputnik agitatora* 13 (July 1927): 41–48.

Kedward, H. R. *In Search of the Maquis: Rural Resistance in Southern France, 1942–1944.* Oxford: Clarendon Press, 1993.

———. *Resistance in Vichy France.* Oxford: Oxford University Press, 1978.

Kedward, Roderick. "The Maquis and the Culture of the Outlaw." In *Vichy France and the Resistance: Culture and Ideology,* ed. Roderick Kedward and Roger Austin, 232–251. London: Croom Helm, 1985.

Kedward, Roderick, and Roger Austin, eds. *Vichy France and the Resistance: Culture and Ideology.* London: Croom Helm, 1985.

Kelly, Catriona. *Refining Russia: Advice Literature, Polite Culture, and Gender from Catherine to Yeltsin.* Oxford: Oxford University Press, 2001.

Kenez, Peter. "Black and White: The War on Film." In *Culture and Entertainment in Wartime Russia,* ed. Richard Stites, 157–175. Bloomington: Indiana University Press, 1995.

———. *Civil War in South Russia, 1919–1920: The Defeat of the Whites.* Berkeley and Los Angeles: University of California Press, 1977.

Kershaw, Ian, and Moshe Lewin, eds. *Stalinism and Nazism: Dictatorships in Comparison.* Cambridge: Cambridge University Press, 1997.

Khrushchev, Nikita. *Khrushchev Remembers.* Trans. and ed. Strobe Talbott. Boston: Little, Brown, 1970.

Kir'ian, M. M., A. S. Galitsan, and N. G. Andronikov, eds. *Velikaia Otechestvennaia voina, 1941–1945: Slovar'-spravochnik.* Moscow: Politizdat, 1988.

Kirschenbaum, Lisa A. "'Our City, Our Hearths, Our Families': Local Loyalties and Private Life in Soviet World War II Propaganda." *Slavic Review* 59, 4 (Winter 2000): 825–847.

Kliatskii, T. I., ed. *Partizanskie byli.* Moscow: Politizdat, 1965.

Knight, Amy. *Beria, Stalin's First Lieutenant.* Princeton, N.J.: Princeton University Press, 1993.

Koenker, Diane. "Men against Women on the Shop Floor in Early Soviet Russia: Gender and Class in the Socialist Workplace." *American Historical Review* 100, 5 (December 1995): 1438–1464.

Kohn, Nahun, and Howard Roiter. *A Voice from the Forest*. New York: Holocaust Library, 1980.

Komerov, N. Ia, ed. *GKO postanulet . . . : Dokumenty, vospominaniia, komentarii.* Moscow: Voenizdat, 1990.

Kondranov, I. P., and A. A. Stepanova, eds. *Krym v period Velikoi Otechestvennoi voiny, 1941–1945: Sbornik dokumentov i materialov.* Simferpol': Tavriia, 1973.

Kornblatt, Judith Deutsch. *The Myth of the Cossack Hero in Russian Literature.* Madison: University of Wisconsin Press, 1992.

Kotkin, Stephen. *Magnetic Mountain: Stalinism as Civilization.* Berkeley and Los Angeles: University of California Press, 1995.

Koval, M. I. "The Nazi Genocide of the Jews and the Ukrainian Population." In *Bitter Legacy: Confronting the Holocaust in the USSR*, ed. Zvi Gitelman, 51–60. Bloomington: Indiana University Press, 1997.

Koval'chuk, V. M., and A. R. Dzeniskevich, eds. *V tylu vraga: Bor'ba partizan i podpol'shchikov na okkupirovannoi territorii Leningradskoi oblasti, 1942 g.: Sbornik dokumentov.* Leningrad: Lenizdat, 1981.

———. *V tylu vraga: Bor'ba partizan i podpol'shchikov na okkupirovannoi territorii Leningradskoi oblasti, 1943 g.: Sbornik dokumentov.* Leningrad: Lenizdat, 1983.

———. *V tylu vraga: Bor'ba partizan i podpol'shchikov na okkupirovannoi territorii Leningradskoi oblasti, 1944 g.: Sbornik dokumentov.* Leningrad: Lenizdat, 1985.

Kovpak, S. A. *Ot Putivlia do Karpat.* Leningrad: Gos-izdat Detskoi literaturny, 1945.

Kozlov, Vladimir A. *Mass Uprisings in the USSR: Protest and Rebellion in the Post-Stalin Years.* Ed. and trans. Elaine McClarnand MacKinnon. Armonk, N.Y.: M. E. Sharpe, 2002.

Krivosheev, G. F., ed. *Rossiia i SSSR v voinakh XX veka: Statisticheskoe issledovanie.* Moscow: OLMA-PRESS, 2001.

Kruchok, R. R., ed. *Vsenarodnoe partizanskoe dvizhenie v Belorussii v gody Velikoi Otechestvennoi voiny (iiun'-uuku' 1944): Dokumenty i materialy,* 3 vols. Minsk: Belarus', 1967–1981.

Krylova, Anna. "Stalinist Identity from the Viewpoint of Gender: Rearing a Generation of Professionally Violent Women-Fighters in 1930s Stalinist Russia." *Gender and History* 16, 3 (November 2004): 626–653.

———. "The Tenacious Liberal Subject in Soviet Studies." *Kritika* 1, 1 (Winter 2000): 119–146.

Kumanev, G. A. "Otvety P. K. Ponomarenko na voprosy G. A. Kumanev 2 noiabria 1978 g." *Otechestvennaia istoriia* 6 (1998): 133–149.

Kurbatova, P. I. *Smolenskaia partiinaia organizatsiia v gody Velikoi Otechestvennoi voiny.* Smolensk: Smolenskoe knizhnoe izdatel'stvo, 1958.

Kuromiya, Hiroaki. "The Crisis of Proletarian Identity in the Soviet Factory, 1928–1929." *Slavic Review* 44, 2 (Summer 1985): 280–297.

———. *Freedom and Terror in the Donbas: A Ukrainian-Russian Borderland, 1870s–1990s.* Cambridge: Cambridge University Press, 1998.

———. "Stalinist Terror in the Donbas: A Note." In *Stalinist Terror: New Perspectives,* ed. J. Arch Getty and Roberta T. Manning, 215–222. Cambridge: Cambridge University Press, 1993.

Leningrad Obkom KPSS, ed. *Leningrad v Velikoi Otechestvennoi voine Sovetskogo Soiuza: Sbornik dokumentov i materialov*, vol. 2, *Iiunia 1943–mart 1944*. Leningrad: Lenizdat, 1947.

Lesniak, T. "Nekotorye voprosy organizatsii i vedeniia partizanskoi bor'by v pervye mesiatsy voiny." *Voenno-istoricheskii zhurnal* 9 (1963): 30–39.

——. "Sovershenstvovanie rukovodstva partizanskim dvizheniem." *Voenno-istoricheskii zhurnal* 7 (1967): 24–31.

Levin, Dov. *Fighting Back: Lithuanian Jewry's Armed Resistance to the Nazis, 1941–1945*. Translated from the Hebrew by Moshe Kohn and Dina Cohen. New York and London: Holmes & Meier, 1985.

Lewin, Moshe. "Bureaucracy and the Stalinist State." In *Stalinism and Nazism: Dictatorships in Comparison*, ed. Ian Kershaw and Moshe Lewin, 53–74. Cambridge: Cambridge University Press, 1997.

——. *The Making of the Soviet System: Essays in the Social History of Interwar Russia*. New York: Pantheon Books, 1985.

Leyda, Jay. *Kino: A History of the Russian and Soviet Film*. Princeton, N.J.: Princeton University Press, 1983.

Lieberman, Sanford. "Crisis Management in the USSR: The Wartime System of Administration and Control." In *The Impact of World War II on the Soviet Union*, ed. Susan Linz, 59–76. Totowa, N.J.: Rowman & Allanheld, 1985.

Lin'kov, G. M. *Voina v tylu vraga*. Moscow: Sovetskii pisatel', 1947; repr. Moscow: Gos. izdatelst'vo khudozhestvennoi literatury, 1951.

Linz, Susan, ed. *The Impact of World War II on the Soviet Union*. Totowa, N.J.: Rowman & Allanheld, 1985.

Lukashevich, Vadim. *Makar Goncharov: Sviazist-partizan*. Moscow, 1945.

Lukashov, M. T. *Po tylam vraga*. Kiev: Politizdat Ukrainy, 1974.

Macksey, Keith. *The Partisans of Europe in World War II*. London: Hart-David, Mac-Gibbon, 1975.

Makarov, N. I., ed. *Partiinoe podpol'e: Deiatel'nost podpolnykh partiinykh organov i organizatsii na Okkupirovannoi Sovetskii territorii v gody Velikoi Otechestvennoi voiny*. Moscow: Politizdat, 1983.

Malia, Martin. *The Soviet Tragedy: A History of Socialism in Russia*. New York: Free Press, 1994.

Malin, V. N., and V. P. Petrovskii, eds. *KPSS o Vooruzhenikh Silakh Sovetskogo Soiuza: Sbornik dokumentov, 1917–1958*. Moscow: Politizdat, 1958.

Manning, Roberta T. "The Great Purges in a Rural District: Belyi Raion Revisited." In *Stalinist Terror: New Perspectives*, ed. J. Arch Getty and Roberta T. Manning, 168–197. Cambridge: Cambridge University Press, 1993.

Marshall, S. L. A. *Men against Fire*. New York: William Morrow, 1947.

Martin, Terry. *The Affirmative Action Empire: Empire, Nations and Nationalism in the Soviet Union, 1923–1939*. Ithaca, N.Y.: Cornell University Press, 2002.

Massell, Gregory. *The Surrogate Proletariat: Moslem Women and Revolutionary Strategies in Soviet Central Asia, 1919–1929.* Princeton, N.J.: Princeton University Press, 1974.

Mazower, Mark. *Inside Hitler's Greece: The Experience of Occupation, 1941–1944.* New Haven, Conn.: Yale University Press, 1993.

McCannon, John. *Red Arctic: Polar Exploration and the Myth of the North in Soviet Russia, 1932–1939.* Oxford: Oxford University Press, 1998.

McClure, Brooks. "Russia's Hidden Army." In *Modern Guerrilla Warfare: Fighting Communist Guerrilla Movements, 1941–1961,* ed. Franklin Mark Osanka, 80–99. New York: Free Press, 1962.

Merridale, Catherine. *Night of Stone: Death and Memory in Twentieth-Century Russia.* New York: Viking, 2000.

Messerschmidt, Manfred. "Forward Defense: The 'Memorandum of the Generals' for the Nuremberg Court." In *War of Extermination: The German Military in World War II, 1941–1944,* ed. Hannes Heer and Klaus Naumann, 381–399. New York: Berghahn Books, 2000.

Michel, Henri. *The Shadow War: Resistance in Europe, 1939–1945.* London: Andre Deutsch, 1972.

Miner, Steven Merritt. *Stalin's Holy War: Religion, Nationalism, and Alliance Politics, 1941–1945.* Chapel Hill: University of North Carolina Press, 2003.

Moore, Bob, ed. *Resistance in Western Europe.* Oxford: Berg Publishers, 2000.

Morris, Alan. *Collaboration and Resistance Reviewed: Writers and the Mode Rètro in France.* Providence, R.I.: Berg Publishers, 1992.

Moskoff, William. *The Bread of Affliction: The Food Supply in the USSR during World War II.* Cambridge: Cambridge University Press, 1990.

Mosse, George. *Fallen Soldiers: Reshaping the Memory of the World Wars.* Oxford: Oxford University Press, 1990.

Müller, Rolf-Dieter, and Gerd R. Ueberschär. *Hitler's War in the East, 1941–1945: A Critical Assessment.* Providence, R.I.: Berghahn Books, 1997.

Mulligan, Timothy. *The Politics of Illusion and Empire: German Occupation Policy in the Soviet Union, 1942–1943.* New York: Praeger, 1988.

———. "Reckoning the Cost of People's War: The German Experience in the Central USSR." *Russian History/Histoire Russe* 9, 1 (1982): 27–48.

Naimark, Norman. *Fires of Hatred: Ethnic Cleansing in Twentieth-Century Europe.* Cambridge, Mass.: Harvard University Press, 2001.

Nekrich, Aleksandr. *The Punished Peoples.* New York: W. W. Norton, 1978.

Newland, Samuel J. *Cossacks in the German Army, 1941–1945.* London: Frank Cass, 1991.

Nove, Alec. *An Economic History of the USSR.* New York: Penguin Books, 1982.

Odom, William. *The Soviet Volunteers: Modernization and Bureaucracy in a Mass Public Organization.* Princeton, N.J.: Princeton University Press, 1973.

Orlov, Mikhail. "Brigada Osobogo Naznacheniia." In *Spetszadanie: Voina v tylu vraga (Sbornik),* ed. A. P. Kovalenko. Moscow: Izd. MOF "Pobeda 1945 god," 1994.

Osanka, Franklin Mark. *Modern Guerrilla Warfare: Fighting Communist Guerrilla Movements, 1941–1961.* New York: Free Press, 1962.

Osokina, Elena. *Our Daily Bread: Socialist Distribution and the Art of Survival in Stalin's Russia, 1927–1941.* Trans. Kate Transchel and Greta Bucher. Armonk, N.Y.: M. E. Sharpe, 2001.

Overy, Richard. *Russia's War: Blood upon the Snow.* New York: TV Books, 1997.

Paret, Peter, Beth Irwin Lewis, and Paul Paret, eds. *Persuasive Images: Posters of War and Revolution from the Hoover Institution Archives.* Princeton, N.J.: Princeton University Press, 1992.

Parrish, Michael. *The Lesser Terror: Soviet State Security, 1939–1953.* Westport, Conn.: Praeger, 1996.

Pavlov, A. G. "Voennaia razvedka SSSR 1941–1945 gg." *Novaia i noveishaia istoriia* 2 (1995): 26–40.

Pennington, Reina, ed. *Amazons to Fighter Pilots: A Biographical Dictionary of Military Women,* vol. 1. Westport, Conn.: Greenwood Press, 2003.

Perezhogin, V. A. "Iz okruzheniia i plena—v partizany." *Otechestvennaia istoriia* 3 (2000): 25–33.

———. "Partizany na prieme u I. V. Stalina." *Otechestvennaia istoriia* 3 (1999): 186–192.

Peris, Daniel. *Storming the Heavens: The Soviet League of the Militant Godless.* Ithaca, N.Y.: Cornell University Press, 1998.

Petrone, Karen. *Life Has Become More Joyous, Comrades: Celebrations in the Time of Stalin.* Bloomington: Indiana University Press, 2000.

Petrov, Iu. P. *Partizanskoe dvizhenie v Leningradskoi oblasti, 1941–1944.* Leningrad: Lenizdat, 1973.

Pisiotis, Argyrios K. "Images of Hate in the Art of War." In *Culture and Entertainment in Wartime Russia,* ed. Richard Stites, 141–156. Bloomington: Indiana University Press, 1995.

Pomerantz, Jack, and Lyric Wallwork Winik. *Run East: Flight from the Holocaust.* Urbana: University of Illinois Press, 1997.

Ponomarenko, P. K. "Bor'ba sovetskogo naroda v tylu vraga." *Voenno-istoricheskii zhurnal* 4 (1965): 26–36.

———. *Vsenarodnaia bor'ba v tylu nemetsko-fashistkikh zakhvatchikov, 1941–1944.* Moscow: Nauka, 1986.

Popov, Aleksei. *Diversanty Stalina: Deiatelnost' organov Gosbezopasnosti na okkupirovannoi sovetskoi territorii v gody Velikoi Otechestvennoi voiny.* Moscow: Iauza, Eksmo, 2004.

———. *15 Vstrech s generalom KGB Bel'chenko.* Moscow: OLMA-PRESS, 2002.

———. *NKVD i partizanskoe dvizhenie: Fakty i dokumenty.* Moscow: OLMA-PRESS, 2003.

Porter, Jack Nusan, ed. *Jewish Partisans: A Documentary of Jewish Resistance in the Soviet Union during World War II,* vol. 1. New York: University Press of America, 1982.

Pospelov, P. N., ed. *Istoriia Velikoi Otechestvennoi voiny Sovetskogo soiuza 1941–1945,* 6 vols. Moscow: Voenizdat, 1960–1965.

Proffer Carl, Ellendea Proffer, Ronald Meyer, and Mary Ann Szporluk, eds. *Russian Literature of the 1920s: An Anthology.* Ann Arbor, Mich.: Ardis, 1987.

Prusin, Alexander Victor. "'Fascist Criminals to the Gallows! The Holocaust and Soviet War Crimes Trials, December 1945–February 1946." *Holocaust and Genocide Studies* 17, 1 (Spring 2003):1–30.

——. "Revolution and Ethnic Cleansing in Western Ukraine: The OUN-UPA Assault against Polish Settlements in Volhynia and Eastern Galicia, 1943–1944." In *Ethnic Cleansing in Twentieth-Century Europe*, ed. Steven Béla Várdy, T. Hunt Tooley, and Agnes Huszár Várdy, 517–535. Boulder, Colo.: Social Science Monographs, 2003.

Reese, Roger R. *Stalin's Reluctant Soldiers: A Social History of the Red Army.* Lawrence: University Press of Kansas, 1996.

Reid, Donald. *Paris Sewers and Sewermen: Representations and Realities.* Cambridge, Mass.: Harvard University Press, 1991.

Rieber, Alfred J. "Civil Wars in the Soviet Union." *Kritika* 4, 2 (Winter 2003): 129–162.

Rigby, T. H. *Communist Party Membership in the USSR, 1917–1967.* Princeton, N.J.: Princeton University Press, 1968.

——. "A Conceptual Approach to Authority, Power, and Policy in the Soviet Union." In *Authority, Power and Policy in the USSR: Essays Dedicated to Leonard Schapiro*, ed. T. H. Rigby, Archie Brown, and Peter Reddaway, 9–31. London: Macmillan Press, 1980.

Rings, Werner. *Life with the Enemy: Collaboration and Resistance in Hitler's Europe.* London: Weidenfeld and Nicolson, 1982.

Rittersporn, Gabor. "The Omnipresent Conspiracy: On Soviet Imagery of Politics and Social Relations in the 1930s." In *Stalinist Terror: New Perspectives*, ed. J. Arch Getty and Roberta T. Manning, 99–115. Cambridge: Cambridge University Press, 1993.

Romanov, A. V. *Na zemle nepokorennoi.* Minsk: Belarus', 1962.

Romanovsky, Daniel. "Soviet Jews under Nazi Occupation in Northeastern Belarus and Western Russia." In *Bitter Legacy: Confronting the Holocaust in the USSR*, ed. Zvi Gitelman, 230–252. Bloomington: Indiana University Press, 1997.

Rousso, Henry. *The Vichy Syndrome: History and Memory in France since 1944.* Trans. Arthur Goldhammer. Cambridge, Mass.: Harvard University Press, 1991.

Rudakov, M. "Rol' voennykh sovetov frontov i armii v rukovodstve boevymi deistviiami partisan v gody Velikoi Otechestvennoi voiny." *Voenno-istoricheskii zhurnal* 7 (1962): 3–14.

Ruffley, David. *Children of Victory: Young Specialists and the Evolution of Soviet Society.* New York: Praeger Publishers, 2003.

Sajer, Guy. *The Forgotten Soldier.* Trans. Lily Emmet. New York: Harper & Row, 1967.

Samuelson, Lennart. *Plans for Stalin's War Machine: Tukhachevskii and Military-Economic Planning.* New York: St. Martin's Press, 2000.

Sanborn, Joshua A. *Drafting the Russian Nation: Military Conscription, Total War, and Mass Politics, 1905–1925.* DeKalb: Northern Illinois University Press, 2003.

Sapir, Jacques. "The Economics of War in the Soviet Union during World War II." In *Stalinism and Nazism: Dictatorships in Comparison*, ed. Ian Kershaw and Moshe Lewin, 208–236. Cambridge: Cambridge University Press, 1997.

Sartorti, Rosalinde. "On the Making of Heroes, Heroines, and Saints." In *Culture and*

Entertainment in Wartime Russia, ed. Richard Stites, 176–193. Bloomington: Indiana University Press, 1995.

Schulman, Faye. *A Partisan's Memoir: Woman of the Holocaust.* Toronto: Second Story Press, 1995.

Schulte, Theo J. *The German Army and Nazi Policies in Occupied Russia.* New York: Berg Publishers, 1989.

———. "Korück 582." In *War of Extermination: The German Military in World War II, 1941–1944,* ed. Hannes Heer and Klaus Naumann, 314. New York: Berghahn Books, 2000.

Seaton, Albert. *Stalin as Military Commander.* New York: Praeger Publishers, 1976.

Seniavskaia, E. S. *Frontovoe Pokolenie: Istoriko-psikhologichesskoe issledovanie.* Moscow: Institut rossiiskoi istorii, RAN, 1995.

Shearer, David. *Industry, State, and Society in Stalin's Russia, 1926–1934.* Ithaca, N.Y.: Cornell University Press, 1996.

Shepard, Ben. "The Continuum of Brutality: *Wehrmacht* Security Division in Central Russia, 1942." *German History* 21, 1 (2003): 49–81.

———. *War in the Wild East: The German Army and Soviet Partisans.* Cambridge, Mass.: Harvard University Press, 2004.

Shumilin, B. T., ed. *Istoriia partizanskogo dvizhenia v Rossiiskoi Federatsii v gody Velikoi Otechestvennoi voiny, 1941–1945.* Moscow: Atlantida, 2004.

Sidel'skii, R. *Bor'ba sovetskikh partizan protiv fashistskikh zakhvatchikov.* Moscow: Gosizdat, 1944.

Siegelbaum, Lewis. Review of Amir Weiner, "Making Sense of War: The Second World War and the Fate of the Bolshevik Revolution." *Slavic Review* 60, 4 (Winter 2001): 865–866.

———. *Stakhanovism and the Politics of Productivity in the USSR, 1935–1941.* Cambridge: Cambridge University Press, 1988.

Simonov, Konstantin. *Days and Nights.* Trans. Joseph Barnes. New York: Simon and Schuster, 1945.

Slepyan, Kenneth. "The Limits of Mobilization: Party, State and the 1927 Civil Defence Campaign." *Europe-Asia Studies* 45, 5 (1993): 851–868.

———. "The Soviet Partisan Movement and the Holocaust." *Holocaust and Genocide Studies* 14, 1 (Spring 2000): 1–27.

Slezkine, Yuri. *Arctic Mirrors: Russia and the Small Peoples of the North.* Ithaca, N.Y.: Cornell University Press, 1994.

———. "The USSR as a Communal Apartment, or How a Socialist State Promoted Ethnic Particularism." *Slavic Review* 53, 2 (Summer 1994): 414–452.

Smilovitsky, Leonid. "Righteous Gentiles, the Partisans, and Jewish Survival in Belorussia, 1941–1944." *Holocaust and Genocide Studies* 11, 3 (Winter 1997): 301–329.

Smirnov, I. F., and V. I. Fefelov. *Orlovskaia oblast' v gody Velikoi Otechestvennoi voiny, 1941–1945: Sbornik dokumentov i materialov.* Orel, USSR: Orlovskoe knizhnoe izdatel'stvo, 1960.

Smolar, Hersh. *The Minsk Ghetto: Soviet Jewish Partisans against the Nazis.* New York: Holocaust Library, 1989.

Smolensk Obkom KPSS, ed. *Partizanskaia bor'ba s Nemetsko-fashistskimi okkupan-tami na territorii Smolenshchiny, 1941–1943.* Smolensk: Smolenskoe knizhnoe izdatel'stvo.

Snyder, Timothy. "The Causes of Ukrainian-Polish Ethnic Cleansing." *Past and Present* 179 (May 2003): 197–234.

———. *The Reconstruction of Nations: Poland, Ukraine, Lithuania, Belarus, 1569–1999.* New Haven, Conn.: Yale University Press, 2003.

Spector, Shmuel. "The Jews of Volhynia and Their Reaction to Extermination." In *The Nazi Holocaust: Historical Articles on the Destruction of the European Jews.* Vol. 7, *Jewish Resistance to the Holocaust,* ed. Michael Marrus, 191–218. Westport, Conn.: Meckler, 1989.

Stalin, Joseph. *The Great Patriotic War of the Soviet Union.* New York: International Publishers, 1945.

Starinov, Colonel I. G. *Over the Abyss: My Life in Soviet Special Operations.* Trans. Robert Suggs. New York: Ivy Books, 1995.

Statiev, Alexander. "The Nature of Anti-Soviet Armed Resistance, 1942–1944: The North Caucasus, the Kalmyk Autonomous Republic, and the Crimea." *Kritika* 6, 2 (Spring 2005): 285–318.

Stepashin, S. V., and I. P. Iampol'skii, eds. *Organy gosudarstvennoi bezopasnosti SSSR v velikoi otechestvennoi voine: Sbornik dokumentov,* vols. 1–6. Moscow: Izdatel'stvo Rus', 1997–2003.

Stites, Richard, ed. *Culture and Entertainment in Wartime Russia.* Bloomington: Indiana University Press, 1995.

———. *Revolutionary Dreams: Utopian Visions and Experimental Life in the Russian Revolution.* Oxford: Oxford University Press, 1989.

———. *Russian Popular Culture: Entertainment and Society since 1900.* Cambridge: Cambridge University Press, 1994.

———. "Soviet Wartime Culture: Freedom and Control, Spontaneity and Consciousness." In *The People's War: Responses to World War II in the Soviet Union,* ed. Robert W. Thurston and Bernd Bonwetsch, 171–184. Urbana: University of Illinois Press, 2000.

———. *The Women's Liberation Movement in Russia: Feminism, Nihilism and Bolshevism, 1860–1930.* Princeton, N.J.: Princeton University Press, 1978.

Stites, Richard, and James von Geldern, eds. *Mass Culture in Soviet Russia: Tales, Poems, Songs, Movies, Plays, and Folklore, 1917–1953.* Bloomington: Indiana University Press, 1995.

Stone, David R. *Hammer and Rifle: The Militarization of the Soviet Union.* Lawrence: University Press of Kansas, 2000.

Streit, Christian. "Partisans-Resistance-Prisoners of War." *Soviet Union/Union Sovietique* 18, 1–3 (1991): 260–276.

———. "Soviet Prisoners of War in the Hands of the Wehrmacht." In *War of Extermination: The German Military in World War II, 1941–1944,* ed. Hannes Heer and Klaus Naumann, 80–91. New York: Berghahn Books, 2000.

Sudoplatov, N. P., and A. A. Tumanian. *Zapiski partizanskikh vrachei: O podvigakh medrabotnikov v tylu vraga v gody Velikoi Otechestvennoi voiny.* Tula, USSR: Prioskoe knizhnoe izdatel'stvo, 1989.

Sudoplatov, Pavel, and Anatolii Sudoplatov (with Jerrold L. Schecter and Leona Schecter). *Special Tasks: The Memoirs of an Unwanted Witness—A Soviet Spymaster.* Boston: Little, Brown, 1994.

Suny, Ronald Grigor, and Terry Martin, eds. *A State of Nations: Empire and Nation-Making in the Age of Lenin and Stalin.* Oxford: Oxford University Press, 2001.

Sweets, John. *Choices in Vichy France: The French under Nazi Occupation.* Oxford: Oxford University Press, 1986.

——. *The Politics of Resistance in France (1940–1944): A History of the Mouvements Unis de la Résistance.* DeKalb: Northern Illinois University Press, 1976.

Tec, Nechama. *Defiance: The Bielski Partisans.* Oxford: Oxford University Press, 1993.

Terry, Nicholas. "Enforcing German Rule in Russia, 1941–1944: Policing the Occupation." In *Conflict and Legality: Policing Mid-Twentieth Century Europe,* ed. Gerard Oram, 121–148. London: Francis Boutle Publishers, 2003.

Thurston, Robert. "Cauldrons of Loyalty and Betrayal: Soviet Soldiers' Behavior, 1941 and 1945." In *The People's War: Responses to World War II in the Soviet Union,* ed. Robert W. Thurston and Bernd Bonwetsch, 235–257. Urbana: University of Illinois Press, 2000.

——. *Life and Terror in Stalin's Russia, 1934–1941.* New Haven, Conn.: Yale University Press, 1996.

——. "The Stakhanovite Movement: Background to the Great Terror in the Factories, 1935–1938." In *Stalinist Terror: New Perspectives,* ed. J. Arch Getty and Roberta T. Manning, 142–160. Cambridge: Cambridge University Press, 1993.

Thurston, Robert W., and Bernd Bonwetsch, eds. In *The People's War: Responses to World War II in the Soviet Union.* Urbana: University of Illinois Press, 2000.

Tillet, Lowell. *The Great Friendship: Soviet Historians and Non-Russian Nationalities.* Chapel Hill: University of North Carolina Press, 1969.

Todorov, Tzvetan. *A French Tragedy: Scenes of Civil War, Summer 1944.* Trans. Mary Byrd Kelly. Hanover, N.H.: University Press of New England, 1996.

Tolz, Vera. "New Information about the Deportation of Ethnic Groups in the USSR during World War 2." In *World War 2 and the Soviet People: Selected Papers from the Fourth World Congress for Soviet and East European Studies, Harrogate, 1990,* ed. Carol Garrard and John Garrard, 161–179. New York: St. Martin's Press, 1993.

Tsar'kov, V. A. "Bez zatish'ia i pereryva: Iz opyta politicheskoi raboty Tsentral'nogo shtaba partizanskogo dvizheniia." *Voenno-istoricheskii zhurnal* 11 (1988): 40–46.

Tumarkin, Nina. "The Invasion and War as Myth and Reality." *Soviet Union/Union Sovietique* 18, 1–3 (1991): 277–296.

——. *Lenin Lives: The Lenin Cult in Soviet Russia.* Cambridge, Mass.: Harvard University Press, 1983.

——. *The Living and the Dead: The Rise and Fall of the Cult of the War.* New York: Basic Books, 1994.

Vakar, Nicholas. *Belorussia: The Making of a Nation.* Cambridge, Mass.: Harvard
    University Press, 1956.
Verkhovskii, B. *Metodika izucheniia trudiashchegosia naseleniia polosy voennykh
    deistvii: Posobie dlia kruzhkov samooborony Osoaviakhimi.* Minsk, 1930.
Vershigora, P. P. *Liudi s chistoi sovest'iu.* Moscow: Moskovskii rabochii, 1946; repr.
    Moscow: Pravda, 1989.
Vilenskii, E. *Syn Belorussii.* Moscow: Molodaia gvardiia, 1943.
Viola, Lynne. "The Aesthetic of Stalinist Planning and the World of the Special Vil-
    lages." *Kritika* 4, 1 (Winter 2003): 101–128.
——. *Peasant Rebels under Stalin: Collectivization and the Culture of Peasant Re-
    sistance.* Oxford: Oxford University Press, 1996.
Volkogonov, Dmitri. *Stalin: Triumph and Tragedy.* Ed. and trans. Harold Shukman.
    Rocklin, Calif.: Prima Publishing, 1992.
Von Geldern, James. "Radio Moscow: The Voice from the Center." In *Culture and En-
    tertainment in Wartime Russia,* ed. Richard Stites, 44–61. Bloomington: Indiana
    University Press, 1995.
Von Hagen, Mark. "From 'the Great Fatherland War' to the Second World War: New
    Perspectives and Future Prospects." In *Stalinism and Nazism: Dictatorships in
    Comparison,* ed. Ian Kershaw and Moshe Lewin, 285–310. Cambridge: Cam-
    bridge University Press, 1997.
——. "The *Levée en Masse* from Russian Empire to the Soviet Union, 1874–1938."
    In *The People in Arms: Military Myth and National Mobilization since the French
    Revolution,* ed. Daniel Moran and Arthur Waldron, 159–188. Cambridge: Cam-
    bridge University Press, 2003.
——. *Soldiers in the Proletarian Dictatorship: The Red Army and the Soviet Social-
    ist State, 1917–1930.* Ithaca, N.Y.: Cornell University Press, 1990.
——. "Soviet Soldiers and Officers on the Eve of the German Invasion: Towards a
    Description of Social Psychology and Political Attitudes." *Soviet Union/Union
    Sovietique* 18, 1–3 (1991): 79–101.
War Documentation Staff, comp. *The Soviet Partisan Movement in World War II:
    Summary and Conclusion (Unclassified Title)—Project "Alexander."* Maxwell Air
    Force Base, Ala.: Human Resources Research Institute, 1954.
Weinberg, Gerhard. "Airpower in Partisan Warfare." In *The Soviet Partisans in World
    War II,* ed. John Armstrong, 361–388. Madison: University of Wisconsin Press,
    1964.
Weiner, Amir. "The Making of a Dominant Myth: The Second World War and the Con-
    struction of Political Identities within the Soviet Polity." *Russian Review* 55, 2
    (October 1996): 638–660.
——. *Making Sense of War: The Second World War and the Fate of the Bolshevik
    Revolution.* Princeton, N.J.: Princeton University Press, 2001.
——. "Saving Private Ivan: From What, Why and How." *Kritika* 1, 2 (Spring 2000):
    305–336.
Werth, Alexander. *Russia at War, 1941–1945.* New York: Avon, 1964.

White, Stephen. *Political Culture and Soviet Politics.* New York: St. Martin's Press, 1979.

Wilkinson, James D. *The Intellectual Resistance in Europe.* Cambridge, Mass.: Harvard University Press, 1981.

Wilson, Andrew. *The Ukrainians: Unexpected Nation.* 2nd ed. New Haven, Conn.: Yale University Press, 2002.

Wood, Elizabeth A. *The Baba and the Comrade: Gender and Politics in Revolutionary Russia.* Bloomington: Indiana University Press, 1997.

Wortman, Richard. *Scenarios of Power: Myth and Ceremony in Russian Monarchy.* Princeton, N.J.: Princeton University Press, 1995.

Yahil, Leni. *The Holocaust: The Fate of European Jewry.* Oxford: Oxford University Press, 1990.

Yekelchyk, Serhy. "Stalinist Patriotism as Imperial Discourse: Reconciling the Ukrainian and Russian 'Heroic Pasts,' 1939–1945." *Kritika* 3, 1 (Winter 2002): 51–80.

Youngblood, Denise. "A War Remembered: Soviet Films of the Great Patriotic War." *American Historical Review* 106, 3 (June 2001): 839–857.

Zalesskii, A. S. *V partizanskikh kraiakh i zonakh: Patrioticheskii podvig Sovetskogo krestianstva v tylu vraga, 1941–1944.* Moscow: Sotsial'no-Ekonomicheskoi literatury, 1962.

Zhirnov, Evgenii, ed. "Na okkupirovannykh territoriiakh." *Kommersant vlast'*, part 1, no. 29 (24 June 2001), part 2, no. 30 (31 July 2001), part 3, no. 31 (7 August 2001).

Ziemke, Earl. "Composition and Morale of the Partisan Movement." In *The Soviet Partisans in World War*, ed. John Armstrong, 141–196. Madison: University of Wisconsin Press, 1964.

Zolotarev, V. A., ed. *Partizanskoe dvizhenie: Po opytu Velikoi Otechestvennoi voiny, 1941–1945 gg.* Moscow: Kuchkovo Pole, 2001.

Zolotarev, V. A., and A. S. Emelin, eds. *Russkii arkhiv: Velikaia Otechestvennaia: Partizanskoe dvizhenie v gody Velikoi Otechestvennoi voiny 1941–1945 gg.: Dokumenty i materially*, vol. 20 (9). Moscow: Terra, 1999.

———. *Russkii arkhiv: Velikaia Otechestvennaia: SSSR i Polsha: 1941–1945: K istorii voennogo soiuza: Dokymenty i materially.* Moscow: Terra, 1994.

Zubkova, Elena. *Russia after the War: Hopes, Illusions, and Disappointments, 1945–1957.* Trans. Hugh Ragsdale. Armonk, N.Y.: M. E. Sharpe, 1998.

UNPUBLISHED ARTICLES, DISSERTATIONS, AND PAPERS

Altman, Ilya. "The NKVD and the Holocaust." Paper presented at the U.S. Holocaust Memorial Museum, June 1998.

Brody, Richard J. "All for the Front! Party Authority, Popular Values and the Soviet Civilian Experience of World War II." Ph.D. diss., University of Michigan, 1994.

Burds, Jeffrey. "The Soviet War against 'Fifth Columnists': The Case of Chechnya,

1940–1945." Paper presented at the Watson Institute for International Studies, Brown University, February 2005.

Pronin, Alexander. "Guerrilla Warfare in the German-Occupied Soviet Territories, 1941–1944." Ph.D. diss., Georgetown University, 1965.

Tarankanova, Irina. "Iz istorii Komissii po delam byvshikh druzhnikov 1905 g., Krasnogvardeitsev i krasnykh partisan (1930–1935 gg.)." Paper.

DOCUMENTARIES AND RECORDINGS

"The Partisan Beard" (Partizanskaia boroda). Music by L. Bakalov, words by M. Lapirov. In *Partizanskie pesni,* Bomba Music, 2000.

The Partisans of Vilna. Documentary film produced by Aviva Kempner, directed by Josh Waletzky. Distributed by the National Center for Jewish Film, 1986.

Russia's War: Blood upon the Snow. Documentary series produced and directed by Tengiz Semenov and Victor Lisakovitch. IBP Films Distribution, 1997.

INDEX

399